DATE DUE

OC 14 '97			

921 Young, Hugo

The IRON LADY

The Iron Lady

THE
IRON LADY
A Biography of
Margaret Thatcher

by Hugo Young

Farrar Straus Giroux

New York

Copyright © 1989 by Hugo Young
All rights reserved
First published in 1989 by Macmillan London Limited
under the title *One of Us*
Printed in the United States of America
First American edition, 1989

Library of Congress Cataloging-in-Publication Data
Young, Hugo.
The Iron Lady : a biography of Margaret Thatcher / Hugo Young. —
1st American ed.
Bibliography: p.
Includes index.
1. Thatcher, Margaret.   2. Prime ministers—Great Britain—
Biography   3. Great Britain—Politics and government—1979–
I. Title.
DA591.T47Y68   1989   941.085'8'092—dc20   89-11875

PICTURE ACKNOWLEDGMENTS
Section I: Camera Press, pages 2 above, 4 below, 6 above. The *Daily
Telegraph*, page 6 below left. Popperfoto, pages 3, 4 above, 5, 7 above.
Press Association, page 8. Sally Soames, page 1. Topham Picture
Library, pages 2 below, 6 below right. *Section II*: Camera Press, pages
3 above, 4 below. Hulton Picture Company (Keystone Collection),
pages 2 below, 5 above. *Illustrated London News*, page 7 above right.
Popperfoto, pages 1, 3 below. Press Association, pages 5 below, 7 above
left and below, 8. Sally Soames, pages 2 above, 4 above, 6. *Section III*:
Associated Press, page 7. Camera Press, pages 4 below, 5 above left,
below right (photo Norman Parkinson). The *Daily Telegraph*, page 8
(photo David Mansell). Hulton Picture Company (Keystone
Collection), page 4 above. Popperfoto, pages 2 below, 3 below. Press
Association, pages 1 above, 3 above, 5 above right. Sally Soames, page 2
above. Topham Picture Library, pages 1 below, 5 below left, 6.

To my parents,
Gerard and Diana Young,
with love and gratitude

Contents

Part Three: One of Us
1983–1987

Preface

MARGARET THATCHER is the most famous British leader since Winston Churchill. As well as being the only prime minister this century whose name has become synonymous with a political philosophy – 'Thatcherism' has no antecedents – she is the object of a singular personal fascination all round the world. This began early, at the unexpected hands of the Soviet Union. In 1976, the Russians designated her the Iron Lady after two speeches she made, announcing with a ferocity that long pre-dated the presidency of Ronald Reagan her militant hostility to the Communist empire and all its works. It was arguably the finest favour any foreigner, certainly any Russian, ever did her. It established her importance, less than a year into her leadership of the Conservative Party. It expunged such images of feebleness as might cling to a female politician. It gave her a global identity in which she has revelled, carrying her reputation before her as a warrior who never surrenders, and a negotiator who will use every feminine craft to get her way in a male-dominated world.

Iron Lady conveys, however, an incomplete impression. It is the most favoured self-image, but it does its subject both more and less justice than she deserves. It exaggerates her metallic consistency, while giving a one-dimensional picture of her personality. It entirely obscures her evolution from one sort of politician into another, and tends to efface the complexity, even the deviousness, which have been crucial to the survival of a remarkable political leader. I hope my book will enable an American audience to understand rather more completely a woman who has captured a place in their own iconography mainly on the basis of resonant sound-bites, copious photo-opportunities and her own un-abashed admiration for the American way of life.

At the root of her story lies a question. It explains the arrangement of this book. 'Is he one of us?' became the emblematic question of the Thatcher years. Posed by Mrs Thatcher herself, it defined the test which politicians and other public officials aspiring to her favour were required

to pass. It epitomised in a single phrase how she saw her mission. This
was to gather a cadre of like-minded people who would, with her, change
the face of the Conservative Party and launch the recovery of Britain.
But the phrase concealed the phrase-maker's own past. Throughout her
early years, she was one of 'them': that is, a typically opportunistic
exponent of traditional Conservatism. Margaret Thatcher's personal
odyssey carried her from this conventional position (covered here by
Part One), through a series of mighty struggles with the old order (Part
Two), towards a full flowering as the personification of all that is conveyed by that first, subversive, question (Part Three).

As well as journeying round the Iron Lady, therefore, my book chronicles an historic campaign. On the one hand, it is an account of how
one woman and her band of partisans succeeded, from a narrow faith,
in taking over the broad church of British Conservatism. On the other,
it examines her claim, after three election victories, to be 'one of us' in
a different sense: supremely so, as leader of a nation transformed into
her own image. Lurking within that claim is the sense, more prevalent
in the world than within Britain itself, that she has supplanted Britannia
as the legendary embodiment of her country.

The book is the result of a privileged existence. I began to write a
political column two years after Mrs Thatcher became leader of the
Conservative Party, and have enjoyed that way of life, first on the *Sunday
Times* and now on the *Guardian*, ever since. It has given me both a
reason and an opportunity to pay close attention to the life and work of
the prime minister for the best part of twelve years. My main way of
doing this, apart from witnessing and reporting on many of her public
activities, has been through regular conversations with a large number
of the politicians, civil servants and other advisers who have worked
closely with her at all stages in her political career. It is the fruit of these
conversations, usually noted at the time, which forms a main part of the
source material for this book, and is the basis for such claim as it might
make to illuminate the historical record.

The names of a fair number of these witnesses appear in the text,
whether as participants or informants, or both. But I should like to
acknowledge their help more comprehensively. First, Mrs Thatcher
herself. Although I sought no assistance from her in writing the book,
I have interviewed her and conversed with her a number of times over
the years. Additionally, her staff have been unfailingly responsive to my
factual inquiries.

Others, however, have necessarily been more available. For help rendered, often many times, usually but not invariably over lunch, I thank

the following Conservative politicians, whom I feel obliged to list, quite misleadingly, in alphabetical order: Kenneth Baker, John Biffen, Rhodes Boyson, Leon Brittan, Peter Carrington, Alan Clark, Kenneth Clarke, Edward du Cann, Norman Fowler, Ian Gilmour, Ian Gow, Grey Gowrie, John Gummer, Michael Havers, Barney Hayhoe, Edward Heath, Michael Heseltine, Geoffrey Howe, David Howell, Douglas Hurd, Patrick Jenkin, Keith Joseph, Nigel Lawson, John MacGregor, Patrick Mayhew, Cecil Parkinson, Christopher Patten, Jim Prior, Francis Pym, Malcolm Rifkind, Richard Ryder, the late Christopher Soames, Norman St John Stevas, Norman Tebbit, Christopher Tugendhat, William Waldegrave, Peter Walker, William Whitelaw, Janet Young and George Younger.

Civil servants are a more delicate matter. In London, unlike Washington, a certain irregularity attaches to contacts between journalists and civil servants – and the more so with Mrs Thatcher riding high. Few journalists would gamble the careers of their acquaintances in Whitehall against the consequences of being named in a book like this. So there I draw a veil. But some may surely be permitted to come out from behind it. Nobody can hope to get close to Mrs Thatcher without getting even closer to Bernard Ingham, probably the most effective prime ministerial press secretary in the short history of that office. I also feel safe enough in thanking some distinguished former officials for intermittently giving me the benefit of their wisdom, particularly Robert Armstrong, Ian Bancroft, John Hunt, Patrick Nairne, Anthony Parsons, William Pile and Douglas Wass.

Outside the world of career Conservatives and officials, there is a growing diaspora of people with some entitlement to call themselves past or present 'Thatcher advisers'. Their true relationship to the prime minister is decidedly variable. But there are some who are or have been deeply involved with her, and who have been at different times generous with their insights. In this category I would especially thank Tim Bell, Brian Griffiths, John Hoskyns, Alistair McAlpine, Adam Ridley, Alfred Sherman, Norman Strauss and Alan Walters. Beyond them again stands a more anonymous band of men and women, eddying through the half-world between business and politics, whose wisps of intelligence are often recorded somewhere here.

I have a number of professional and private debts. Cathy McNeil did valuable research for me in the early stages. After I had begun, Anne Sloman, my regular producer on BBC Radio Four, commissioned a documentary series, *The Thatcher Phenomenon*, which stimulated me to get on with this book. I owe a lot to her perceptions. My agent and friend, Anne McDermid, supplied much warm encouragement. At my

British publishers, Macmillan, I am particularly indebted to Philippa Harrison, for her support, to Adam Sisman, to Tom Weldon, my editor, to Angela Martin, and to Juliet Brightmore, for her ingenious picture research. In that regard, I also benefited from the generosity of Sally Soames, who let me trawl through the collection of her own unpublished, and unrivalled, political photographs. And Dominic Young was a supremely efficient systems manager, without whom the text would not have emerged from the word processor.

Above all, I want to thank my wife, Helen Mason, for generously enduring a longer haul than either of us expected.

London, May 1989   Hugo Young

Part One

One of Them
1925–1979

1

The Alderman's Daughter

MARGARET THATCHER WAS born to be a politician. Her lineage and formation allowed of few other possibilities. Politics infused the atmosphere in which she was reared. The political life, with its parallel attractions of service and of power, was the only life set before her as a model superior to that of shopkeeping. In this respect her origins accorded closely with those of the majority of Conservative leaders. A political family handed down the tradition of political commitment from one generation to the next. Unlike some of those predecessors, and also some of her contemporaries, she may never have imagined that she was born to rule. She certainly did not do so when she was young. When she attained her crowning eminence, it was an important part of her stock-in-trade to cultivate national astonishment that she should ever have got there. But her father laid out the path of duty just as clearly as any grandee who placed his sons on the road to Parliament.

She was born on 13 October 1925 in Grantham, Lincolnshire. Grantham was, as it remains today, the epitome of middle England: a place that prides itself on the ordinariness of its daily life, the unexciting decency of its people and the slowness of their responses to change in the outside world. Grantham has that quiet complacency which has always made middle England a comfortable yet sometimes a frustrating place to live. It has probably always been like that, but certainly has been for the last half century. The civic environment in which Margaret grew up is well conveyed by the *Grantham Journal*, writing shortly before the outbreak of the Second World War. Critical voices had evidently been raised about the boredom of life in the town. There were suggestions that it lacked 'the excitement and amenities of other ultra-modern places and was just content to jog along in an imperturbable way'. The *Journal* counselled against such impatience. Grantham should not ape the speed and noise of 'fashionable' towns. It was quite modern and progressive enough, and should above all preserve its 'priceless atmosphere of peace and contentment'.

Bestriding the politics of this cosy little place was, by then, a tall, pious white-haired man, Alderman Alfred Roberts, of whom Margaret was the younger daughter. On the day she entered 10 Downing Street as prime minister, in May 1979, she asserted that there was an unbroken link between what she learned from him and what she now believed, between the values of the Roberts household and the message that carried her to victory. 'I owe almost everything to my father,' she said. And this was not a ritual nod to sentiment. Six years later, when time might be held to have modified such obligations, her gratitude was undiminished. Asked by a television interviewer what she owed to him, she said: 'Integrity. He taught me that you first sort out what you believe in. You then apply it. You don't compromise on things that matter.'[1]

Alfred Roberts was a paragon among political parents, an influence acknowledged with repeated and explicit reverence by his daughter throughout years when other political leaders might have been pleased to see their present achievements obliterate their past.

In Margaret's adult mind, Alfred was as prominent as her mother was obscure. Numerous interviews after she became famous managed to exclude all references to Beatrice Roberts. There was an almost obsessive reluctance to refer to her. Whenever a question was asked about Beatrice, the interviewee tended to take the conversation straight back to Alfred. If she was alluded to at all, it was under the patronising designation of 'rather a Martha'. Beatrice was a practical, downtrodden housewife who played remarkably little part in the development of her younger daughter: a fact duly made manifest by her exclusion from Margaret's biographical entry in *Who's Who*. There Margaret always appeared as the daughter of Alfred Roberts and no other. Rather like her sister Muriel, who trained as a physiotherapist and never featured importantly in Margaret's life again, Beatrice fell victim to a life which established very early in its course that most of the people who mattered were men.

There is scarcely an aspect of Alfred that has failed to find its way into the politics of his daughter. Rarely in the history of political leadership could one find an example of such extravagant filial tribute.

Alfred was a self-made man. The son of a Northamptonshire shoemaker, he left school at thirteen and went into the grocery business. But he was ambitious. After moving to Grantham and getting married, he had saved enough to buy a grocery shop of his own at the crossroads of the A1 and the road to Nottingham. His two daughters were born above the shop. It is from this place, and the upright patriarch who presided over it, that many lessons were learned which touched the governance of Britain fifty years later.

This was not an easy time for shopkeepers. In the early 1930s, as the young Margaret was acquiring the beginnings of an awareness of the world around her, few such businesses prospered. As one historian has written, 'It was certainly not a heroic time, and there was much gloom overhanging it, particularly in the distressed areas.'[2]

While Grantham, as a small town rather than an industrial city, could not be categorised as distressed, nor was it flourishing. Careful husbandry was necessary to ensure that a business survived. This Alfred had little difficulty in providing. He was by nature a cautious, thrifty fellow, who had inherited an unquestioning admiration for certain Victorian values: hard work, self-help, rigorous budgeting and a firm belief in the immorality of extravagance. Margaret often testified later to the inextinguishable merit of having served in a shop, as she sometimes did, and having watched the meticulous reckoning of income and expenditure. The experience was a model for the management of economies small and large. 'Some say I preach merely the homilies of housekeeping or the parables of the parlour,' prime minister Thatcher told the Lord Mayor's Banquet in November 1982. 'But I do not repent. Those parables would have saved many a financier from failure and many a country from crisis.' The more often these simplicities were ridiculed, the more insistently did she tend to repeat them.

Alfred, formally ill-educated himself, had a Victorian passion for education, which was the key, he thought, to a full and useful life. Margaret later called him 'the best-read man I ever knew'. Self-made, he was also self-taught, a tireless user of the local library, and determined that his younger daughter, the one who showed real academic promise, should have every educational opportunity which he had been denied. From an early age there were therefore piano lessons, compulsory library visits and an elementary school not close to the shop but at the smarter end of town where the teaching was better and the child's peer group would be properly motivated. Margaret was a bright child, still remembered by her contemporaries at that young age for her bulging satchel and earnest questioning in class. The questioning went on at home. Alfred's own didactic tendencies never waned. He was determined to equip Margaret with every precept and perception about life that he had ever learned, most particularly where these concerned money. Later, she described with awe his Micawberish lessons in the practice of saving, to which end every penny piece she came by as a child had to be devoted.

The spiritual dimension through which this commitment to self-help was filtered was entirely of a piece. Alfred and Beatrice Roberts were both dedicated Methodists, and Margaret spent every Sunday of her childhood years trekking to and from the Methodist church in the centre of Grantham. Like many other buildings associated with her youth, including both her schools, the Finkin Street Methodist Church still stands; Grantham, of all the towns in England, has been one of the least touched by the developer's hammer. A square, imposing room, with space for a thousand worshippers, this place of worship was later replaced in Margaret's spiritual preferences by an irregular association with the Church of England. The world of chapel was left behind.[3] But Finkin Street was close to the centre of the child's life, the fount of the unfailing seriousness that surrounded her. Visited at least twice every Sunday, it symbolised how little time she had for joy. On Sundays every kind of pleasure was banned, even a Sunday newspaper. The church was also where recitals were attended and concerts given. It was where Alfred himself preached, and the centre from which he set out, in his maturer years, to deliver the Methodist message to the villages around the town.

It was, perhaps especially, the place where Margaret first worked out her own connection between the religious and the practical life, a connection which emphasised the latter rather more than the former. 'We were Methodists, and Methodist means method,' she primly told an earlier biographer.[4]

Order, precision and attention to detail are the hallmarks of this kind of piety, along with a methodical approach to the differences between right and wrong. 'There were certain things you just didn't do, and that was that,' she added. 'Duty was very, very strongly ingrained into us. Duties to the church, duties to your neighbour and conscientiousness were continually emphasised.'

This household, then, was meritorious. It exhibited many social virtues, struggled constantly to adhere to creditable values, and its children were instructed with unimpeachable devotion. It was not, however, poor. The Roberts children had few possessions, and were indulged in fewer fripperies. They had no bicycles, and visits to the cinema or theatre were a rarity. But this was the result not of poverty so much as thrift carried to the point of parsimony. In later years, Margaret made much of the material sparseness of her upbringing. She used to cite as evidence for the grinding poverty of her origins the lack of both a lavatory and running hot water in the house until after the war. Although this was the norm in her part of Grantham, it cannot have been due, in the Roberts' case, to a straightforward lack of money. Before war began, Alfred's shop had prospered sufficiently for him to buy another on the other side of town. He was a small businessman on the way up. Choice not necessity led him to make his family take baths in an unplumbed tub for the first twenty years of Margaret's life: the muscular meanness of a man who positively frowned on the smallest form of self-indulgence.

Although no one can question that he pulled himself up from the humblest origins by hard work and driving determination, Margaret's own life did not follow the same pattern. She was reared in spartan circumstances as much because of Alfred's belief in self-denial as because he started poor. The Roberts she knew belonged to the rising petty bourgeoisie not the beleaguered working class. In the mid-1930s, according to a historian,[5] 75 per cent of all families were officially designated as working-class, earning £4 weekly or less. As the owner of two shops, Alfred was already among the 20 per cent who could call themselves, if they chose, middle-class.

But these moral qualities, growing out of this self-imposed penury, were not the whole of Alfred's legacy to the future political leader. A significant part of his formidable energy was devoted not to his business but to public life. Even before Margaret first went to school, he was a local councillor, nominated by the Chamber of Trade. His political life, which he conducted with great intensity across the narrow field of one town and its problems, awakened appetites in his daughter which made it the reverse of surprising that she should eventually have sought national office.

She did not, however, inherit her party affiliation. Alfred was first elected councillor as an Independent and never, actually, as a Conservative. His earliest-known intellectual attachment was to the programme of the Lloyd George Liberals. Other biographers of his daughter,[6] in fact, record it as the opinion of Grantham's Conservative Party agent in the post-war years that Alfred, whom he knew well, was at heart a right-wing Labour man. What stopped him doing anything about this was probably the strength of the local Co-operative Party, which controlled Labour in Grantham and was, of course, particularly hostile to private shopkeepers in competition with the Co-op's own chain of stores.

But this, in a sense, is nitpicking. The more important truth is that formal affiliations mattered little in local politics. The Independents in Grantham usually voted on the Conservative side. At the 1935 General Election, Alfred Roberts was one of the signatories of the nomination papers of the Conservative candidate, Sir Victor War-render. This was the election when Margaret did her first political work, aged ten, running canvass lists and messages between polling stations and party headquarters. Most of Alfred's utterances reveal a Conservative at heart. The moral code of the thrifty, God-fearing property-owner, preached in a score of Methodist halls, was imported into his political life by his stern tenure for many years of the Council finance committee. 'There is in public spending, like all things, a limit,' he said in 1937, regretfully announcing a sevenpence increase in the rates. He also had, at a time when many of the British intelligentsia were flirting with alien creeds and new loyalties, a plain man's fierce patriotism. 'I would sooner be a bootblack in England', he told his presidential dinner of the Grantham Rotarians in the same year, 'than a leading citizen in a good many of the other leading countries in the world today, because I know I can get tolerance and justice from my fellow men.'

The *Grantham Journal*'s account of this dinner is accompanied by a photograph, which opens another window on the world of Alfred Roberts. There he stands, in full white tie and tails, a well-scrubbed, confident-looking man. Beatrice, shy and dour-faced, is by his side. With them is Lord Brownlow, the main guest at the dinner. The Brownlow family was the local nobility, its seat a few miles north of Grantham at Belton House. But Brownlow was more than a lofty spectator of Grantham's affairs. He was almost as devoted a municipal servant as Roberts himself. He did his time as mayor, like Alfred himself did in 1945. The landowner and the grocer did much political business together. While they may not have been intimates, and certainly were not equals, the Brownlow link was another of Alfred's legacies that Margaret was later able to exploit, through the son of Alfred's friend. Over forty years on, as the chatelaine of 10 Downing Street, she often drew visitors' attention to the silver pieces with which she had covered many of the bare surfaces in the public rooms. 'Lord Brownlow has lent them to us,' she would casually say. The family connection, usually unspoken, had been sealed with the loan of some of the family treasure.

In politics, Alfred was a moralist capable of standing out stubbornly against fashion. One of his most urgent injunctions to his children, Margaret often recalled with pride, was never to hold an opinion merely because other people held it. Wisdom was never right just because it was conventional. Over the relaxation of sabbatarian laws, Alfred lived out his own teaching. He had resisted all incursions into the traditional Sabbath, finally acquiescing with great reluctance in the Sunday opening of cinemas. During the war, pressure mounted to permit games to be played in Grantham's parks on Sundays, not least for the benefit of munitions workers who needed a break. The council voted by 11–10 for games to be allowed, but only over the protesting oratory of Roberts, who had now become an alderman.

'I work as many hours and as hard as any munitions worker,' the shopkeeper declared in 1942. 'I have to work every Sunday, and I've only had two days off from business since August 1939.' He said he would certainly rather see people playing bowls in the park than 'tearing along the road to Skegness', but he would prefer still more to see neither happening. But cinemas were a different matter; cinema-goers caused no offence to people who chose not to go.

The argument neatly brought together the casuist and the moralising elder that lurked in Alfred's character. Many people in Grantham, he said, liked to rest peacefully in parks on a Sunday, uninterrupted by raucousness. Besides, Sunday was the day for acquiring 'a spiritual outlook'. Countries which had given up Sabbath observance and Christian worship had become thoroughly decadent. He cited France, which was 'corrupt from top to bottom', and Germany.

In November 1945, Alfred became mayor of Grantham. For a small-town politician, it was the climax, though by no means the end, of an unremunerated career devoted daily to the public good. Within his world it was as high as he could get, and it happened at a time when, with the war just over, municipal leadership was especially necessary. In his inaugural speech, the new mayor showed once again that he knew where he stood, this time on the subject of war. He seemed to see it as an inescapable therapy in this vale of tears. 'Again and again in our human life, we learn that without the shedding of blood there is no remission,' he gloomily reflected. But he also knew the proper priorities, which were little different from those of every high-spending local government leader determined to rebuild his town – as a munitions centre, Grantham had been a target for German bombs. Alfred called for a massive programme of expenditure to improve roads, public transport, health and child welfare services, and to 'build houses by the thousand'. It was, said the *Grantham Journal*, one of the best mayoral speeches for years, 'modest, brilliantly delivered and full of promise'.

In his smaller territory, Alfred Roberts emerges as almost as committed a municipal activist as Herbert Morrison, who bestrode the London County Council between the wars. There was more than a touch of Morrisonian idealism in his mayoral address. It was a time when few people seriously challenged the necessity for public action to ameliorate the condition of cities and their people; and it would never have occurred to Alfred that the business of local government was to scale itself down or reduce its own importance, the position which Margaret in later life came to espouse as a matter of faith. He may not have been a Conservative, but insofar as he was allied with Conservative ideals, this placed him firmly among the Tory reformers rather than those romantics who still imagined that Britain could somehow revert to the minimalist State of the pre-war years.

Upon an observant and ambitious adolescent, this towering local leader could not but have a powerful impact. He brought Margaret up in his own image. In a different time and different circumstances, she came to have a different opinion about the value of municipal expenditure and the role of the State as the upholder of the common weal. But as regards public duty, and the satisfaction to be gained from being a public person, Margaret's father was the model whose example she was drawn early to follow. His shopkeeping business was secondary: the necessary source of a living, and the origin of many a moral and economic lesson, but essentially a base for public work. Alfred exhibited no ideological belief in the superiority of the wealth-producing or commercial way of life, as against a lifetime spent supervising the expenditure of public money. Quite the contrary. Public spending, properly directed, seems to have been in his eyes the acme of public morality.

Most valued of all areas of public spending was education. Alfred was deeply involved here too. His daughters were sent to Kesteven & Grantham Girls School of which, inevitably, he was already a governor. Later, just as predictably, he became chairman of the governors: another exercise in local commitment by this compulsively active man.

At school, Margaret fulfilled all that he expected of her. As a grant-aided grammar school, Kesteven normally required parents to pay half the fees, but Margaret secured a county scholarship. She was not particularly brilliant, but she was very hard-working, and her contemporaries remember her as a model pupil of demure habits and tediously impeccable behaviour. She never put a foot wrong, in the classroom or on the hockey field. Every term from autumn 1936 to summer 1943, her school reports read with an uncritical consistency that even the most doting parents might get a little tired of. In December 1936, she had 'very definite ability and her cheeriness makes her a very pleasant member of her form'. Two years later, 'she is keenly interested in all she does and her conduct is very satisfactory.' By July 1940 she had 'the makings of a real student', which in the sixth form she confirmed with her 'intelligence and determination'. Logic and diligence, the two of them identifying her as a natural head girl, were the intellectual qualities most frequently attributed to her by her teachers. 'Margaret is ambitious and deserves to do well' was the verdict in her final report.

Those were the days when English secondary education still left some room for variety. In the lower sixth, instead of devoting themselves exclusively to two subjects, as their own children would often do, the pupils of the war years continued to escape the fiercest specialisation. Margaret started Latin and continued with English and geography, as well as the sciences to which she was by then more fully committed: chemistry, biology, zoology. The choice of science, and most specifically chemistry, did not spring from an overwhelming natural preference, more from the fact that some choice had to be made and the accident that the chemistry teacher at Kesteven was especially inspiring. It was not a choice which always pleased Mrs Thatcher. To Tricia Murray she recounted her memory that science had been 'the coming thing', but also recalled her adolescent disappointment on realising too late that what she really wanted to be was a lawyer. Accompanying her father to court (he was, naturally, a Justice of the Peace), she conceived a fascination with the law which, alas, could not now be satisfied. Chemistry she had picked, and a chemist she would have to stay until she qualified.

If school had an impact on Margaret's political formation it was, with one exception, at a subconscious level. Kesteven was a completely orthodox girls' grammar school, and such institutions had few of the perquisites and none of the history of other places more precisely designed for the preparation of public men. The public schools existed in substantial part for this purpose, and it was from public schools that the ruling class not only of the Conservative Party, but of the Labour Party as well, was then substantially drawn. Girls' schools were keen enough on academic success, and Kesteven had its share of this with a thin but steady stream of pupils passing on to Oxford and Cambridge. But they did not expect to go into politics or the civil service. For the most part, girls simply didn't. Besides, for Margaret there was the abiding problem of money. She has always said that she knew from an early age that she would have to get a job and keep herself; and this excluded politics, an ill-paid, expensive activity which the Conservative Party was still, in the 1940s, encouraging its aspirant performers to pay to enter, even to the extent of making part-purchase of their seats sometimes a condition of selection as a candidate.

So there was no serious thought of professional politics lurking yet in the young girl's mind. But she did exhibit one political talent. The school had a debating club in which Margaret shone. She had a good deal of practice in argument at her father's knee – it seems to have been the main didactic tool of that intensely didactic man. Although reputedly quiet in class, she debated with more self-confidence than any of her contemporaries. They did not think her brilliant, but she was unrelenting. Visiting speakers would always receive a question from Margaret Roberts: slow and careful questions, so they say, in a voice still tinged with the Lincolnshire accent which the elocutionists later buried, but clear and ringing all the same. In debate, determined and unselfconscious, she was hard to beat.

This, then, was Alfred Roberts' girl. She came from a contented but pretty joyless home. Father and daughter were happy in their earnestness. 'I don't think she has much of a sense of humour, I don't think her father had and I certainly don't think her mother had,' recalled her friend and contemporary Margaret Wickstead.[7] 'They were all very serious-minded, and they worked too hard. Life was a serious matter to be lived conscientiously.'

They were full of the sense of public duty, of which Alfred, however, was the sole and dominant exponent. Their household experienced the pervading sense of poverty, if not the painful fact of it. What Margaret would frequently describe in later years as the disadvantaged background from which she sprang would in fact have been more accurately described as a home of aggressive thrift. Alfred was not rich, but neither was he poor. And more important than his financial state was his role as the moral arbiter who in her eyes could do no wrong – a view she never changed. Few scions of the nobility, however high their destiny in the Conservative Party, have been able to say the same.

2

Into the Network

OXFORD IN 1943 was a university in the middle of a war. Sun-drenched quadrangles and lazy days on the river formed a smaller part of the undergraduate experience than fire-watching and the clatter of marching troops. Many of the young men who should have been there were either fighting or dead. Colleges were temporarily merged, as the army or the civil service commandeered their buildings. The science faculties, in particular, were dominated by the demands of war work. Laboratories were taken over for every kind of vital intellectual undertaking. Oxford was the home of intensive work on radar, on penicillin, on nitrogen mustard gas, on hydrocarbon research and much else besides. Any thrusting seventeen-year-old intent on going up to Oxford to read chemistry had to contend with the knowledge that this would not be the place of their dreams, and that undergraduates would inevitably take second place to thrilling but totally secret activities crucial to the defeat of Germany.

This did not deter Margaret Roberts, although she nearly failed to get there. Her offer of a place at Somerville came only at the last minute. She had had to mug up Latin, and had failed to reach Somerville's priority list for entrance. Only when someone dropped out was she hoisted off the waiting list and offered the chance to fulfil the ambition of many self-taught parents: to send their child to the peak of the educational system which they themselves had been obliged to quit in the foothills. 'Yes, I think my father did try to realise his ambitions in me,' she told Tricia Murray. He also managed to put together the money to send her, since she was not awarded a scholarship.

Although Alfred had given her almost all she had in the way of standards and ambition, one thing he had been unable to supply was the experience of freedom from his influence. Before she went up to Oxford, Margaret had hardly spent a single night away from home. Dreary Grantham and the priggish solemnities of its Methodist chapel set the limits of her social experience. The biggest event in her life had been a week's excursion to London, to see the Changing of the Guard and *The Desert Song*, an occasion so unusual that as late as 1978 she could say of it: 'I was so excited and thrilled by it that I've never forgotten that week.' It was a fleeting dabble in what looked from Grantham like a glamorous world, the bright lights shining even in wartime: just like an equally ephemeral flirtation with the theatre itself. 'At one stage I really would have liked to have been an actress,' she told Tricia Murray. But these were the briefest of escapes from Alfred's purposeful impositions. Recalling them later, Margaret revealed the more puritanical state of mind that has been her truest impulse before and since. 'No one I know of', she rather dismally said in 1978, 'has a glamorous life. I don't think it exists.'

Wartime Oxford was by no means glamorous, but it marked a first ambition completed. It was also not Grantham, which made it both an alarming and an exciting place for an untravelled, unsophisticated head girl from a small town in Lincolnshire. Not for her the camaraderie of the swells who, if they had not gone to war, had come up from Eton, Marlborough and the other forcing grounds of young Conservatism determined to enjoy themselves. Although she had a friend or two from Grantham, she didn't mind admitting she was homesick. Two driving preoccupations, one far more enduring than the other, rescued her from this embarrassed misery, and now began to fashion the adult who later became famous. Just as, after considering her early life as Alfred's adored creation, one is obliged to revise the common belief that her entry to Oxford was remarkable, so, on examining her life at Oxford, one sees it as the beginning of a lifetime's dedication to Conservative politics that led her in due course to 10 Downing Street.

Margaret's first preoccupation was with her work. It was a time when hard work was both obligatory and fashionable. No shades of *Brideshead* here. Lectures and labs were in heavy demand. According to Sidney Bailey, a contemporary of Miss Roberts, who has taught chemistry at Oxford ever since he graduated, the fear of being sent down for poor work or failed exams was more pressing then than it has been since. Margaret, predictably, never ran any risk of that. She is remembered, by Bailey and many others who dredge their recollection for any sightings of a then pretty unmemorable girl, as a hard-working, efficient, well-organised performer in the labs, though not as a particularly brilliant practitioner of academic chemistry.

The chemistry was important. It formed a part of her mind. As it happened, two formidable scholar–teachers converged on Somerville during her time, and they recall a limited talent. Janet Vaughan, who became principal in 1945, supplies the more caustic verdict: 'She was a perfectly adequate chemist. I mean nobody thought anything of her. She was a perfectly good second-class chemist, a beta chemist.'[1] Professor Dorothy Hodgkin, who taught her and later won a Nobel Prize, has a rather warmer memory: 'I came to rate her as good. One could always rely on her producing a sensible, well-read essay.'[2] She was good enough, at any rate, to be invited by Professor Hodgkin to work as her research assistant during her fourth year at Oxford, pursuing investigations the professor had begun into the structure of a new antibiotic, Gramicidin S. (It turned out to be an excessively ambitious quest, which was completed only thirty years later by another hand.)

Dorothy Hodgkin is probably the most eminent woman Margaret Thatcher has ever had dealings with. As a politician she was to be noticeably wary of letting competent women anywhere near her. But she was fortunate to chance upon such a distinguished teacher, although there are few signs of her recognising as much in the numerous interviews she gave to the biographers who clustered round when she looked as though she might become prime minister. Professor Hodgkin, for her part, while not an admirer of her pupil's political work, acknowledges the importance of the scientific formation. Margaret Thatcher is the only prime minister in British history whose formal education was devoted to the physical sciences. What, according to the Nobel Laureate, does the study of chemistry do to a person's mind? 'I think it should interest you in the problems of finding out as much as you can about the way we work, the way matter is put together. And it should give you an interest in using the results.'

This blueprint for the practical mind, a marriage between speculative and empirical habits, is one which as a politician Mrs Thatcher consistently made much of. She retained a genuine interest in science, which Dorothy Hodgkin concedes. It equipped her, says the professor, to take serious decisions on scientific matters and 'to see what scientists are doing'. In the politician, her lack of any outstanding scientific talent was less significant than her rare capacity to understand the scientific mind at all. Margaret Thatcher, both as Education Secretary in 1970 and as prime minister from 1979, lost no opportunity to exploit it, even when the credential seemed a little far-fetched. In December 1984, for example, when she visited Washington to consult with President Ronald Reagan over his commitment to the Strategic Defense Initiative, or Star Wars, she reputedly told the president in a moment of exasperation: 'But I'm a chemist. I *know* it won't work.'

Science, however, was not the most important thing she did at Oxford. It filled her daytime hours and supplied her with a decent second-class degree. It also made her employable in the way she had always determined to be, making her own living away from home. But it did not transform her life or open up her true vocation. As an influence on her impressionable mind it took a poor second place to the Conservative Party. The discovery of Conservatism was what ensured that Oxford would not be a trivial or transient experience in her life.

In the year she went to university and immediately joined the Conservative Association, OUCA, the Conservative Party nationally existed in the limbo created by the wartime coalition. If one called oneself a convinced Conservative in 1943, it was not altogether clear what one was claiming to believe in. The war and its conduct dominated everything, Conservatism and the party that upheld it being submerged in the necessities, and for some the unvarnished pleasures, of running a highly centralised government machine. This had been going on for some time. A perceptive historian of the period, Paul Addison, quotes a letter written by a Conservative backbencher, Lord William Scott, to the chief whip in October 1942: 'Throughout the country, the Conservative Party has become a cheap joke: the press and the BBC treat us with the contempt that we have earned and deserve. . . . You must agree with the fact that as an effective body of opinion either in the House or in the country, the Conservative Party has ceased to exist.'[3]

Presiding over this was a leader who cared only intermittently about the dire condition Scott diagnosed – and Scott was not alone. Winston Churchill, never a reliable party man, was thought by some not to be a Conservative at all. As Addison nicely puts it, he 'regarded the party system as the essential base of his role in history as a world leader, but he resented the claims it made on his time'. He did not care deeply about the political formulae of the period as long as they secured his position as national leader. The formula that worked was one which kept Clement Attlee and the leadership of the Labour Party inside the Government. That this, with its emphasis on planning and controls and the direction of industry, should enrage some of the Tory rank and file did not matter to Churchill. Already by 1943, indeed, he was contemplating an extension of the coalition into the post-war era.

There was, nevertheless, a debate beginning about what the party ought to stand for when the dust settled. Categories later to be labelled down the years as moderates and extremists, progressives and reactionaries, libertarians and corporatists, wets and drys, were discernible as the war wound towards what turned out to be its close. Even Conservatives wanted something to believe in; the question was what?

The coalition had created its own counterforce, which consisted of backbenchers on the right of the party who yearned for a return to the Conservatism they understood. They were particularly horrified by the industrial planning which had been deemed essential for the war effort. State direction of industry was anathema to people who had last been elected in the wholly different world of 1935. By 1943, with the transformation of the war itself into one which the Allies looked as though they would win, the inhibitions against political debate were slipping away. Many Conservative politicians were convinced that the controls over business would be carried on in peacetime unless they mounted a defence of the principles of laissez-faire and industrial freedom which they had always understood their party to uphold.

Propounded by a substantial army of backbenchers from the backwoods, this view also had important support in the cabinet from Lord Beaverbrook, along with his faithful ally in the struggle for Churchill's mind, Brendan Bracken. Free enterprise, the abolition of controls, the minimisation of social reform and, of course, the breakup of the coalition, was the programme this group was mobilising to defend well before the war ended.

They were not, however, the only dynamic element at work on Conservative thought and action. And here we catch the earliest glimpse of characters who were, all unknowing, to be a presence many years later in the public life of Margaret Thatcher: the first appearance on the scene of persons who came to embody the continuity between that Churchillian world and the Thatcherite world which was to be fashioned four decades later in the century.

In the year Margaret Roberts went up to Oxford, the unremarkable daughter of a Grantham grocer, the young Quintin Hogg left the army. Along with another young officer, Peter Thorneycroft, Hogg had decided to return to politics to save the Conservative Party from the reactionaries he perceived to be driving it into oblivion. A researcher into this period of Conservative politics has described their motives. With other MPs such as Lord Hinchingbrooke, each had 'on the basis of impressions gained from discussions with the troops, independently reached the conclusion that it was politically necessary for the Conservative Party to change its public image'. Or, as Quintin Hogg put it more pithily in the House of Commons in March 1943: 'If you do not give the people social reform, they are going to give you social revolution.'[4]

The Tory Reform Committee, as this group of thirty-six MPs constituted itself, set up a counterblast to the Beaverbrookites. It strongly backed the Beveridge Plan for social security, and voiced support for a paternalist, interventionist government. It appeared to reject the entire trend of Conservatism since the First World War, deriding the old order in the strongest terms. Addison quotes Lord Hinchingbrooke:

> True Conservative opinion is horrified at the damage done to this country since the last war by 'individualist' businessmen, financiers and speculators ranging freely in a laissez-faire economy and creeping unnoticed into the fold of Conservatism to insult the party with their vote at elections, to cast a slur over responsible government through influence exerted in Parliament, and to injure the character of our people. It would wish nothing better than that these men should collect their baggage and depart.

The reformers pressed their radicalism hard. During the passage of the 1944 Education Act, Hogg led them into the anti-Government lobby on two decidedly modernist amendments, first to raise the school-leaving age to sixteen by 1951, and second to legislate for equal pay for women teachers. Both were defeated, yet they signalled how far the war had driven some younger Conservatives towards a philosophy of social justice which had been barely contemplated by any faction in the party a decade earlier. Hogg, indeed, was even ahead of R. A. Butler and Harold Macmillan, who were themselves to become the greatest exponents of post-Churchillian, New Deal Conservatism.

Macmillan thought the Conservatives would lose the election, and he was not wrong. Chips Channon's diary has him saying that 'the Conservatives will be lucky to retain a hundred seats'. It wasn't quite as bad as that, but the election was a watershed for the modern Conservative Party. And it meant, among other things, that any young person then embarking on Conservative politics would be present at the start of the remaking of their party: even, in some minor ways, be able perhaps to contribute to the direction it took.

Margaret Roberts' decision to join the Conservative Association immediately she arrived at Oxford does not appear to have been a calculated political act. She told Tricia Murray: 'What particularly interested me was the opportunity of meeting an enormous amount of people from vastly different backgrounds.' It is plain enough, however, that it would not have occurred to her to seize this opportunity in any other club, which she easily could have done. Although her father was not an out-and-out Conservative, neither does he appear to have been remotely drawn to the Labour Party. The turmoil of ideas in the thirties, which drove so many young people to make romantic expeditions to the Spanish Civil War and to flirt, however briefly, with communism, passed by the grocer's shop, and probably the whole of Grantham. Margaret was crucially too young to have been caught up, even out of curiosity, in the rise of fascism and the leftist response to it. For her father, although he was not an entirely insular character, the expansion of horizons owed more to the Rotary International and the Methodist Church than to any adventurous political awakening.

For her first two university years, OUCA was little more than the social club she had expected it to be. The gathering argument inside the party had not yet reached far outside the Commons, and was hardly articulated at all at a university still deprived by the war of a lot of its natural undergraduates. Margaret did voluntary work in military canteens, and began to learn how to make public speeches by touring under OUCA's aegis round Oxfordshire villages as a member of political brains-trusts.

The 1945 election was the small beginning of her visible career in politics, the formative event which launched her on the road. We have two glimpses of her, in Oxford and Grantham. In Oxford, she canvassed for Quintin Hogg who fought the city seat against Frank Pakenham, another durable piece of the furniture of later-twentieth-century British life. To Margaret herself, this was her baptism. 'The first real election meeting I ever went to was in the town hall where Quintin was speaking,' she later recalled.[5] But during the long campaign she was also to be seen in Grantham.

In 1942, Grantham had lifted itself briefly out of its customary anonymity by staging the first wartime by-election in which the coalition candidate had been defeated. Such a defeat, the *Manchester Guardian* said at the time, had come to be regarded as being about as probable as 'the suspension of the law of gravitation'. The winner, however, had been not a socialist but an arms manufacturer, Denis Kendall, standing as an Independent. In 1945 he remained the upholder of the anti-Tory vote, and Alfred Roberts' daughter made her first appearance in the *Grantham Journal*, which reported her campaigning against him. The *Journal* noted that she had 'her father's gift for oratory' and accorded her a role she may not have been altogether pleased with. 'The presence of a young woman of the age of 19,' it said, 'with such decided convictions, has been no small factor in influencing the women's votes in the division, if that were necessary.'

Tantalisingly, we do not learn what these convictions were. Yet for the prime minister who later never ceased to proclaim that she was a 'conviction politician', it is a matter of some interest to plot the doctrinal evolution. As one who, in her prime, came to stand for such pronounced and definite ideas, which she readily depicted as eternal verities, how committed was she originally to the notions that made her famous, and even gave to her name the status of a philosophy? What has been the mix, at different times, between pragmatic opportunism, on the one hand, and ideological consistency on the other? These are questions which will crop up many times in this story.

In 1945, the answer is in fact pretty clear. No aspiring young Conservative, especially one without family connections, could afford to place themselves anywhere other than in the reformers' camp. To the Hoggites, the party had allowed itself to become completely out of touch with the electorate, and especially with the poor bloody infantry who had gone to war. It fought the election on a platform that harked back too clearly to the past, under a leader who, for all his unchallengeable greatness as the victor over Hitler, had forgotten what the voters really wanted. When Churchill said, in one of the notorious blunders of British electoral history, that the introduction of socialism into Britain 'would require some form of Gestapo', he badly mistook the mood of a country that had come to see the merits of strong government, and could envisage no other means of securing the jobs, homes and welfare it desperately craved.

Although the official Tory manifesto was relatively innocuous, on this central point about state planning it gave much scope for the rightists in the party who wished above all to make an abrasive attack on the control of industry. At the heart of the propaganda on this point, moreover, were the ideas propounded in a book that had swept both Britain and America the year before, *The Road to Serfdom*, by an Austrian refugee at the London School of Economics, Professor Friedrich von Hayek. Hayek's work, which argued that all forms of socialism and economic planning ended inescapably in tyranny, played an important part, according to Dr Addison, in amplifying the message of the anti-reformers in the Tory Party and hence in securing the Labour landslide at the election.

Margaret Roberts was among the thousands of people who devoured Hayek's book in 1945. This has not always been apparent. When, in 1974, she was recovering from the defeat of Edward Heath's government and beginning to equip herself with a group of teachers and thinkers who would help her to discover an alternative to the corporatist philosophy just demolished at the polls, she was supplied with reading lists that included the works of F. A. von Hayek. One of her familiars, arguably her chief intellectual provider, was Alfred Sherman; and it was certainly Sherman's impression at the time that she had not read Hayek before then. When I once tackled her on the point, she said that she had read *The Road to Serfdom* at Oxford, although she conceded that it was only in the 1970s that she grappled with some of Hayek's other work, notably *The Constitution of Liberty*.[6]

The important point is, however, that Hayek's apocalyptic vision of a 'statist' world made only a limited impression on the politics of the time, including politics at Oxford. What he argued was anathema to the very people in the Conservative Party who, after the 1945 débâcle, Oxford University Conservatism was most closely drawn to. Oxford shared the sense that the party stood in need of renovation, and that this was not to be sought by a return to some halcyon age when the war had not happened and socialism could be pretended not to exist. The most energetic forces in the national party after 1945 began groping for a synthesis that would align Conservatism with the observable social facts and aspirations of post-war Britain.

Harold Macmillan, along with R. A. Butler, was at the forefront of this tendency, allying himself with the Hoggs and Thorneycrofts of the Reform Committee. These people were not in any way socialists. In 1945 Quintin Hogg published *The Left was Never Right*, and two years later his trenchant *Case for Conservatism*. But, as Macmillan observed in his memoirs,[7] the Conservative Party was moribund, and still dominated by MPs who thought that they merely had to sit around waiting for the electoral pendulum to swing back to them. Such people, moreover, were 'strongly represented in the safe seats and still in the full vigour of their incapacity'. What the party needed,

Macmillan thought, was an updated policy programme. 'We had to convince the great post-war electorate that we accepted the need for full employment and the welfare state; that we accepted equally the need for central planning and even, in times of scarcity, physical controls.' The position he identified was one 'between the old liberalism and the new socialism'.

Simultaneously with this evolving debate at national level, the OUCA was endeavouring to reorganise itself; and the leading figure in this enterprise was Margaret Roberts. She was now beginning her third year at Oxford and, following the path of several other women, had risen up the ladder of office. She had also rubbed shoulders, as Oxford political activists have always been privileged to do, with the great men of the party. She was now well experienced in the social skills required for these encounters. By the autumn of 1945 she was the OUCA general agent, with the presidency a certainty if she stayed for long enough. And it is from this period that her earliest coherent political statement survives. OUCA set up a policy sub-committee of three with a brief to restate its purpose and re-examine its organisation. Among the signatories of the sub-committee's report, the name of M. Roberts appears as the first author.

As a statement of philosophy, the report is in many ways a callow piece of work. It seeks to trace the roots of Conservatism, finding them in a deep scepticism about all claims of pure reason to settle the affairs of men. 'The Conservative', say the authors, 'denies that reason can give a necessarily correct answer to the dilemmas of society, an absolutely valid solution to the problem of state structure and everyday behaviour, and is inevitably sceptical of man's ability to produce by logic alone a statement of either the ideal state or the future course of events.'

A larger proportion of pretentious flannel finds its way through the Roberts typewriter than would have been permitted by her mature embodiment, as in the observation that 'a purely scientific judgment, such as that Copernican astronomy is preferable to Ptolemaic, depends ultimately on Occam's Razor.' But many of the principles which the document laboriously works its way through are statements of the obvious that certainly found their echo in later decades. Thus: 'Concrete particulars are a better basis than general ideas'; or 'Industrial enterprise is the mainspring of all progress'; or 'The rate of change in Conservatism corresponds to evolution rather than revolution.'

But there is no doubt which wing of post-war Conservatism Miss Roberts and her colleagues were joining. Their analysis resounds with the urgent need for change. The 1945 election result, they said, had far more radical implications than most of the party yet appreciated. 'A reorientation of Conservatism will be necessary if the party is to avoid annihilation.' Defeat should not be thought of solely as a normal swing of the pendulum that would swing back – the very phrase echoed Macmillan's. Further, although policy had to be distinctively Conservative, criticism of the Labour Government, which was carrying out a mandate, should be 'helpful and not factious'.

These were the voices of young Conservatives highly conscious of the need to position themselves in the new mainstream of post-war thought. No trace of nineteenth-century liberalism is to be found anywhere in their thinking. Although Hayek may have been all the rage in some quarters, he is missing from this manifesto. Having picked out its philosophy, it goes on to prescribe a ferocious organisational programme. Here the later Margaret Thatcher is more accurately prefigured in the no-nonsense vigour of the actions Margaret Roberts urges on her membership.

She had already begun to make a mark in the national party. As a delegate to the Federation of Conservative and Unionist Associations in March 1946, she spoke for Oxford's impatience with old-guard attitudes at Central Office. She personally moved a resolution demanding that reiterated promises of a party which would encourage 'more working-class officers' should be implemented forthwith. The Oxford view was that the party had much to learn from the zeal of the socialists and their presentation of policy. Nor, in expressing it, was Miss Roberts in any way the object of either political or sexist comment. There was nothing odd about being a female among these political tyros. Almost one-third of the Federation delegates were women, who, according to the *Evening Standard*, had entirely acceptable, down-to-earth attitudes and ran 'rather to tweeds and bare heads – they are not formidable-looking bluestockings'. This description plainly encompassed Margaret Roberts. 'I remember her as rather a brown girl,' recalled one contemporary, Rachel Kinchin-Smith. 'She had an attractive brown head of hair, was quiet, nicely dressed and very pleasant to be with, but definitely other than the way one sees her today.'[8]

Quite apart from this kind of blooding, the new president had now met all the leading Conservatives who worked the student circuit. In the year before she reached the top, Harold Macmillan, Peter Thorneycroft, Oliver Stanley, Walter Elliott, Geoffrey Lloyd, Hugh Molson and Oliver Lyttelton were among the eminent men who dined with the OUCA officers and spoke to OUCA meetings. The speakers' lists revealed a heavy bias towards the men with a future. The Beaverbrook faction, with its yearning for 'free' economics and an urgent reduction of government, held little interest for these ambitious undergraduates.

Margaret's presidential term was quite a triumph. Her university political career has often been represented in retrospect as either eccentric or obscure, or both. Janet Vaughan, her academic overseer at Somerville, remembered it with acidulous scorn forty years later. Margaret Roberts had made an impression on her, she said, for only one reason. 'She was to me extremely interesting because she was a Conservative. The young at that time, especially at Somerville, were all pretty left-wing. She wasn't an interesting person, except as a Conservative.' It was for this alone, it seems, that Margaret was permitted to grace the Principal's soirées. 'If I had interesting, amusing people staying with me, I would never have thought of asking Margaret Roberts – except as a Conservative.'[9]

Yet Conservative views were not, in truth, all that rare, and the efforts of Miss Roberts and her colleagues to revive OUCA paid off in the autumn of 1946 when, under her presidency, membership rose well past one thousand. The university proved itself to be by no means a hotbed of socialism. On 21 March 1946, the Oxford Union defeated by 615 votes to 397 a motion which stated that the Conservative Party offered no constructive alternative.

Margaret made no contribution to that debate. Two more decades would pass before women ceased to be excluded from the Union. To that extent, she could not look back on her Oxford career as one in which she had trodden the well-worn path towards cabinet office walked by most of her predecessors in high Conservative politics. Debating skills honed in the Union, and election to successive offices within it, had been among the early accoutrements of Macmillan, for example, and gave the necessary veneer of polish to the meritocratic Edward Heath.

It was unfortunate for a woman that she could never say the same. But in all other respects, Margaret's career in Oxford politics, which she pursued with exceptional diligence, equipped her with the record and the contacts of any other denizen of that most powerful enclave. She entered and, for her brief span, dominated a world that was assumed to lead to a political career if such were desired. The people she ran into, as is the way in the confined circle of British political society, were often to reappear later in her life. Although she seems to have made little impact on their memory at the time, their names were fixed quite firmly and systematically in hers.

In her term as president of OUCA, the man elected treasurer of the Union was one A. N. Wedgwood-Benn – 'nominally a socialist', reported the OUCA news digest, 'but his views, which he holds with great sincerity, seem eminently liberal.' Elected secretary of the Union at the same time was Sir Edward Boyle, who was also following Margaret up the OUCA ladder. The first man to speak for her was a young Scottish peer, Lord Dunglass, who gave an address on the reconstruction of Europe.

With each of these men she later enjoyed a special relationship. It was, in a sense, a singular version of that familiar Oxford phenomenon, the old-boy network, which is replicated in countless varieties in the adult lives of so many of those whose youth was touched by it.

Wedgwood-Benn was only a name; they do not appear even to have met at Oxford. But much later they were locked in a combat which defined the politics of the age in which they both reached their peak: she as leader of the Conservative Party, he as the leader of that faction in the Labour Party which drew particular strength from her success, citing it as proof of the virtue of immoderate political convictions – and which also, by its disruptive activities in the Labour Party, played a decisive part in ensuring the absence of an effective opposition to the Thatcher Government. Benn, as he became known, was Margaret Thatcher's symbiotic opposite. In the early 1980s especially, they needed each other, thrived on each other's passionate ideological hostility, and in this way proved that natural enmity can sometimes do as much for a politician as the friendship of a lifetime.

Edward Boyle was no less of a presence later on, again more as a source of abrasion than comradeship. He it was whom Mrs Thatcher succeeded on the threshold of the job that first made her a national figure, when he left his post as shadow secretary for Education in 1968 to enter academic life. A brilliant and humane intellectual, Boyle had earlier resigned from government over Suez. When restored to front-bench life by Edward Heath, he pursued a notably unaggressive form of opposition to the Labour Government's policy on comprehensive schools. His refusal to resist this policy by every means, which displeased both the party and its leader, paved the way for Margaret Thatcher, with her more aggressive approach, to consolidate her position in the shadow cabinet.

As for Lord Dunglass, his presence on Margaret Roberts' list of speakers anticipated a still more elevated relationship. Lord Dunglass became the Earl of Home: then Sir Alec Douglas-Home, prime minister: then Lord Home, Foreign Secretary and Mrs Thatcher's cabinet colleague in the Heath Government.

Questioned in 1985, Home appeared to have no memory of the young OUCA president for whom he had spoken on European reconstruction, nor of the thrusting politician who was the joint parliamentary secretary at the Ministry of Pensions and National Insurance in his own Government in 1963. It was on sitting at Heath's cabinet table, he recalled, that he first noticed her. 'I came back one day and said to my wife, "You know, she's got the brains of all of us put together, and so we'd better look out." '[10]

Between Lord Dunglass and Quintin Hogg there was a nice symmetry. Hogg supplied Margaret's first remembered and active political experience. Dunglass was an early jewel in her presidential crown. As Lord Hailsham and Lord Home in their later years they re-entered her life as, in one case, a full-time, and in the other a retired but unfailingly loyal, supporter in government. Thus did Oxford prepare in classic style the aspirant politician, and infuse itself, as it has for so many generations, through all the adult life of a British prime minister.

3

Finchley Decides

MARGARET THATCHER WAS born a northerner but became a southerner, the quintessence of a Home Counties politician. Oxford was the agency through which this evolution occurred, and the choices she made on leaving Oxford permanently defined the sort of politician she would become. These choices involved her in little agonising and no conscious shift of habit or outlook. Wherever she was born, she was now acquiring the classless, unplaceable, homogenised mind and manners which are typical of suburban southern England.

True northerners might not grant Grantham status as a northern town. More accurately it is part of the north Midlands. But from London it looks a long way away, and in spirit it could hardly be further from the metropolitan excitements of the capital. Since leaving Grantham, Mrs Thatcher has never had much time for it. Not for her, save in one respect, the sentimental attachment to birthplace and roots often exhibited by upwardly mobile Labour politicians. After leaving home, she rarely returned there. Her attitude became one of ambivalence verging on faintly haughty hostility. When she got into Parliament she went there even less frequently. Grantham was the place she had worked to get away from. Only when she became party leader was it restored to favour as the town that made her, the equivalent of the log cabin from which every mythic American president has stumbled triumphantly into the White House.

The exception to this pattern, the shining light within an otherwise oddly jaundiced memory, was, of course, her father. Grantham may have disappeared over her horizons, but Alfred did not. He keeps reappearing, as stern guide and comforting presence, throughout her political career, right up to his death in 1969, only months before his daughter finally reached the cabinet. Alfred's encouragement, and the model he represented, stood constantly before the tyro politician as she launched herself without delay on local Conservative Associations – never more so than in 1952, when he was unceremoniously sacked as an alderman by the controlling Labour group in Grantham. This episode sharpened Margaret's detestation of socialists, just as it confirmed her distaste for her home town. More than three decades later, and well into her second term as prime minister, the memory of it was still enough to make her shed tears before a somewhat startled nation during a television interview. 'Such a tragedy,' she gulped, unable to contain herself.[1]

There was never any question of returning north after Oxford. On the other hand, Margaret had never had any doubt that she would have to earn a living, and a chemistry degree was unlikely to lead to a job wholly consistent with her consuming passion for politics. In the post-war years, an association with productive industry rather than the professions was a less valued mark of Conservative eligibility than it became some decades later. Nor was industrial work particularly easy to run in harness with the ceaseless demands of political activism. Nonetheless, a research chemist is what she first became, at a firm called British Xylonite Plastics, in Manningtree, Essex, which produced the plastic for spectacle frames and other household goods. Later she took a job in the research department of J. Lyons, in Hammersmith, London, testing the quality of cake-fillings and ice-cream.

These two jobs, lasting barely three years in all, constitute the totality of Margaret Thatcher's first-hand contact with the world of commerce and industry. They were not particularly auspicious; contemporaries have recalled, for example, the frequent embarrassment she experienced in trying to make contact with the men on the shop floor. They compare variably with the experience in the same field of the other prime ministers of her time, who also spent much of their period in office struggling to bring about Britain's economic recovery and, in the process, being obliged frequently to tell the business world how to do its job. The Thatcher experience with plastic macs and swiss-roll fillings was, on the face of it, a less instructive preparation than Harold Macmillan underwent as a publisher, Harold Wilson as a consultant on East–West trade or Edward Heath as an embryonic merchant banker. On the other hand, it took her, however briefly, closer to the coalface than either a landowner like Alec Douglas-Home or the tax-clerk James Callaghan. In any case, prime minister Thatcher never tried to make political capital out of these fugitive involvements. They were incidental to her political ambition and she has never pretended otherwise. They made her a living, while she devoted most of her psychic energy to the greater and more glamorous task.

This had been made easier, in any case, by changes in the rules of the Conservative Party designed precisely to encourage the likes of Margaret Roberts to strive for eminence within it. Alongside the ferment of policy debate precipitated by the Labour landslide of 1945, major alterations were taking place in the terms and conditions of employment that confronted any aspiring member of Parliament.

The first of these was effected by the Labour Government itself. Concerned about the lack of private means of almost all its large influx of MPs, in 1946 it raised MPs' pay from £600 to £1,000 a year. For once in her life, Margaret had cause to show some tacit gratitude to an act inspired by egalitarian socialism. 'From that moment on,' she later told Tricia Murray, 'it became possible to think in terms of a political career.'

But this was not only due to Labour's reform. The Conservative Party, too, was changing. Its chairman, Lord Woolton, was determined to end the practice, still observable in the 1940s, of putting safe seats up for sale to the highest respectable bidder. To this end, the 1948 party conference in Llandudno voted that no Conservative candidate should be permitted to pay more than £25 into the local party fund. Although the effect of this on the overall social composition of the Tory benches took years to make itself felt, the new rules were undoubtedly well framed to assist the ambitions of grocers and their daughters.

These Margaret Roberts began to deploy from the moment she left university. Their first focus was Conservative Essex. Working in Manningtree and living in Colchester, she plunged instantly into the Colchester Conservative Association. As a representative of the Oxford University Graduates Association, she attended the Llandudno party conference where she impressed herself sufficiently on the right people to be offered the chance of a parliamentary candidacy without delay. She knew a man who knew a man who was the Conservative chairman in Dartford, and they happened to sit down together – and lo! this impressive and dedicated young woman became, at twenty-four, the youngest woman to contest the 1950 General Election. The seat was a certain loser, with a 20,000 Labour majority, but this was a classic, if accelerated, version of the new meritocratic Conservatism at work, rewarding the combination of talent, connection and brass neck that has always been a main criterion of party preferment.

Margaret offered, in return, an earnest of her priorities, promptly giving up her plastics job and taking up with Lyons ice-cream, living in Dartford and commuting to Hammersmith. From 1949, when she was nominated, we begin to get first glimpses of Margaret the campaigning politician.

By now the state of the Tory argument had significantly changed. The reformers had won and the party was positioned for the assault on half-a-decade of active socialist government. There were no longer many serious disputes about what Conservatism consisted of. Having been settled in the reformers' favour, with a balancing of emphasis between the state's responsibilities and the need for some decontrol of the economy, they were being replaced by a united campaign against Labour and all its works. At Margaret's adoption meeting in February 1949, the person who may best have caught the anti-socialist tide then running everywhere outside the Labour Party was Alderman Alfred Roberts. Speaking from the platform, he said that although his family had always been Liberal, he now saw no difference between what the Liberals once stood for and what Conservatism now consisted of, not least in its deep suspicion of the links between Labour and the trade unions.

The tenor of Margaret's own first election campaign was defined by robust simplicities, drawn from the dead centre of committed anti-socialist rhetoric. She described the election as a contest between proponents of slavery and proponents of freedom. Labour was the party of class hatred and natural envy on which 'you cannot build a great nation or a brotherhood of man'. Her own belief in freedom was couched in language that was still doing service thirty years later. Labour's proposals, she said, 'looked so reasonable on the surface, but underneath were most pernicious and nibbled into our national life and character'. The welfare state produced people who resembled a caged bird: 'It has social security. It has food and it has warmth, and so on. But what is the good of all that if it has not the freedom to fly out and live its own life?'

Other future images also began to appear at this early moment of her serious political career. She told a ladies' luncheon club audience:

> Don't be scared of the high-flown language of economists and cabinet ministers. Think of politics at our own household level. After all, women live in contact with food supplies, housing shortages and the ever-decreasing opportunities for children, and we must therefore face up to the position, remembering that as more power is taken away from the people, so there is less responsibility for us to assume.[2]

31

Labour held on to power in 1950, and Margaret lost Dartford. She
lost it again the next year, when the Conservatives were returned with
a majority of 17, to begin what proved to be more than a decade of
Tory rule. But she had established her métier and entered a world
which paid her due respect, and which she found entirely congenial.
She had campaigned with thoroughness and verve, quite overcoming
the objections which arose from her being a woman. No one, it seems,
sniped at her for being too clever or too ambitious, as they had done
in Grantham. Nor did her lack of pedigree count against her. She
was at home among the unpretentious bourgeoisie who were the life
and soul of the Conservative Party in north Kent. They were her kind
of people, as they always have been. Besides, as the youngest woman
fighting in both 1950 and 1951, she had got more publicity than a
hundred middle-aged male candidates in other hopeless seats. It
brought her to the attention of Conservative Central Office – an early
example of the particular value she has repeatedly drawn from her
sex as an instrument of politics.

The chemistry degree, meanwhile, remained an oppressively
inadequate qualification for a suitable professional life. Analysing
cake-fillings was no career for an ambitious Conservative politician.
After becoming a candidate, the final assurance that she really was a
politician, Margaret began to read for the Bar, a more respectable
vocation and also one which gave its self-employed practitioners the
necessary freedom to come and go. She had avowed some interest in
the law ever since, as a teenager, she had accompanied the alderman
to court cases in which he sat as a Justice of the Peace alongside the
recorder of Grantham. But it was not to criminal law, the daily
pabulum of the Grantham Quarter Sessions, that she turned in 1950.
When she enrolled as a part-time student at the Council for Legal
Education, the narrow specialism of the patent Bar is what she
envisaged, because it could make use of her scientific training. Later
she switched to tax law; and with her customary zeal she duly passed
her Bar exams in December 1953.

This legal formation was to leave certain marks on her political
career, although they are not of the first importance. She did not
practise for long – no more than five years, off and on – and her
commitment of time was always qualified by the demands of politics.
She had trouble finding chambers that would give her a tenancy, the
essential base from which to work. The fact that this was largely
due to her being a woman – the prejudice was redoubled by her
determination to practise tax law, a male preserve – left oddly few

scars. She showed no residue of antagonism to the oppressively masculine biases observable throughout the Bar, which had diminished only modestly by the time she became prime minister. She is remembered, by those few contemporaries who have any memory at all of someone whose presence among them was so fleeting, as a businesslike, hardworking performer, with a particular talent for research into precedents.[3] As for the permanent impact the law made on her life, it can be divided into the social, the professional and the intellectual.

Socially, the Bar was a place to meet many other aspiring Conservative politicians. Naturally Margaret joined the Society of Conservative Lawyers, becoming in due course the first woman elected to its executive committee. In her passage through various chambers as pupil and hopeful tenant, she collided with several men whose ambition was the same as hers. The Bar has always been, after land and public school, the location of the most influential Conservative network. In one set of chambers, she encountered Michael Havers, whom many years later she appointed Attorney-General. There, also, she came across a war hero by the name of Airey Neave, the man who had led a wartime breakout from Colditz prison in Germany. Neave became a friend for life: not at the time a particularly useful one, since he had few outstanding political qualities, but a friend in the end well chosen. Two decades on, it was Neave, with the officer's capacity to organise and the secret agent's conspiratorial turn of mind, who put these abilities at Margaret Thatcher's service when she launched her campaign for the party leadership.

In terms of its substance, and its effect on the Thatcher mind and outlook, the legal experience was variable. Although superficially the barrister's life is a good grounding for the parliamentarian because it gives practice in public argument, the tax barrister's life is different. It involves little court work and no appearances before a jury. Its appeal for Margaret was more particular. 'I was keenly interested in the financial side of politics,' she once explained, 'so I went into the revenue side of the law.'

Certainly this interest in figuring, combined with a rare capacity to follow the thread of the most intricate financial arguments, grew richly over time and, as she has acknowledged, was much assisted by the conundrums she was obliged to master at the tax Bar. There was a happy meeting of mind and the matter it was best suited to dealing with.

In her later memory, however, the substance of her legal work

33

takes a lower place than the philosophy surrounding it, and the way this fits into the big political picture. The law is part of the romance of freedom, she suggested to a BBC interviewer in August 1974.[4] She liked the law very much, enjoyed going back to the Inns, welcomed the company of lawyers. But its fundamental appeal was 'its importance in a free democracy'. She went on:

> I think people in this country would have called themselves free men long before we had one man, one vote. That was because of the early importance of getting equality before the law. . . . I don't think it is generally realised how much freedom and democracy owes to the rule of law, and I sometimes wonder now if that is one of the things which is changing.

It requires no special training to absorb this belief. Margaret Thatcher was certainly not alone in expressing it, at a time when the country had only recently torn itself apart over the legality or otherwise of the miners' union defying the ordinances of Edward Heath's Government. But one gift a legal training bequeaths to anyone is a refusal to be intimidated by the minutiae of the law or the protocols of lawyers. Without ever being more than a pedestrian lawyer herself, who did not stay long enough at the Bar even to exercise the MP's traditional entitlement to become a Queen's Counsel, Mrs Thatcher was at least immune from such a disadvantage.

To many politicians the law inhabits a world as mysterious as that of medicine, and lawyers share with doctors the status of a kind of priesthood, by turns bitterly resented and excessively respected. Legal detail, although it is what the law-makers are elected to concern themselves with, often baffles them. As prime minister, Mrs Thatcher used the law relentlessly as an instrument of political change. Having been a lawyer, she was at home with the thinking and language this process imposed: the first prime minister of the modern, statute-bound political era who could say as much.

Acquiring this invaluable credential was a turning-point in Margaret's career. It was accompanied, and crucially facilitated, by another: marriage to a man of means.

Denis Thatcher was a better-breeched product of north Kent Conservatism than many others in the party when Margaret Roberts became the candidate at Dartford. They did not meet at a Young Conservatives' dance but, in rarer and more earnest style, on the night of her adoption in 1949. There can be little doubt that to the life and politics of Margaret Thatcher Denis has been the longest-serving, most influential contributor – and she has never forgotten it.

Denis had a family business. He was the grandson of a farmer–entrepreneur who had started making weed-killer and sheep-dip. When the Atlas Preservative Company, as it became, was handed down to Denis from his father, it had expanded into paint and other chemicals, and was making good money for the family. Denis was the managing director and, with a break for the war (Mentioned in Despatches), had worked there since 1934. He is described as being athletic and even handsome at the time. He certainly seems to have been on the lookout for a wife. In the most devoted of the early biographies of Margaret, one of the few works in which Denis has allowed himself to be directly quoted, George Gardiner recreates a scene which is redolent of a certain kind of courtship. One gets the impression that Denis had produced a number of potential spouses for the inspection of his business friends. After going out with Margaret for quite a while, Gardiner reports, he took her to the annual dinner dance of his trade association. It was there that the romance received final approval. Gardiner writes, without a blush: 'Towards the end of the evening, his company chairman leaned over to mutter in his ear, "That's it, Denis – that's the one!"'[5]

This verdict, on which Denis in due course acted, is one which Margaret herself has never had any cause to regret. They always had quite a lot in common: an interest in economics, whether from the political or the business angle, and an abiding belief in the unchallengeable virtues of the Conservative Party. Denis himself was never a politician, although he once stood in the Ratepayers' interest for the Kent County Council. But he was and always has been an utterly dependable upholder of all the things his wife believed in.

Denis's first service to her was as agent of her definitive break with the past. When she married him in December 1951, she broke with her town, her class and her religion. From Grantham and its lower bourgeoisie she was already detached by her years at Oxford. Marriage marked and sealed the distance she had come. Never very fond of her home town, she would now return there even less frequently. By marrying the successful inheritor of a medium-sized family business, she placed herself in the affluent rather than the struggling middle class. She married above herself, he, by conventional standards, below. Nobody who knows them denies that it has been a very happy match, which has flourished on the pressures of her life rather than being at all diminished by them.

But the most jarring rupture marriage brought was with the Methodism of her youth. Denis had been married before, just as the war was starting. When he returned from the fighting, the pair found themselves to be strangers and got divorced. At that time, the strict code of Methodism still did not entirely approve of divorce and remarriage, and Margaret had been reared as a strict Methodist. This does not appear to have caused her to hesitate. Other factors did: this was no instant love-match, and the courtship took two years to mature. But the injunctions of Methodism were set aside. In any case they weren't so stern as to preclude the marriage taking place in the very temple of British Methodism, Wesley's Chapel in City Road, London. Alderman Roberts, doubtless wincing at such a repudiation of the orthodoxies, gave his daughter away. Kent Conservatism was prominently represented among the guests, and from now on, if there was any religious leaning in the Thatcher household, it was towards that more comfortable Tory solace, the Church of England.

These were only the opening contributions Denis made to Margaret's public character. Having married him, she didn't need to earn a living.. This is what enabled her to read for the Bar. 'It was Denis's money that helped me on my way,' she readily admitted when she became famous. When she had children, he could afford a living-in nanny, thus enabling her to work. When she began to practise at the Bar, this wasn't out of any driving economic need. Her real ambition, after all, was for a career that was not at all well rewarded. The career itself is what she wanted, and in one of the earliest of her opinions to have been preserved she wrote about this with fiery prescience. Invited to contribute to a popular newspaper series about women and public life, the young Mrs Thatcher wrote in the *Sunday Graphic* in February 1952 that women should not feel obliged to stay at home. They should have careers. 'In this way, gifts and talents that would otherwise be wasted are developed to the benefit of the community.' She thought it nonsense to say that the family suffered. Women, indeed, should not merely work but strive to reach the top of their profession. Above all should this be true in politics. There should be more women at Westminster – there were then only 17, out of 625 MPs – and they should not be satisfied with the lesser posts. 'Should a woman arise equal to the task, I say let her have an equal chance with the men for the leading Cabinet posts. Why not a woman Chancellor? Or Foreign Secretary?'

In 1952 these trenchant demands were being made by a woman without a job, who was in the early stages of reading for the Bar. It was Denis who afforded her the luxury of making them. He thus fulfilled the role that can sometimes give a woman politician her one big advantage over a male: the financial security she herself has not had to earn. In this respect, the early Margaret Thatcher bore some resemblance to the Conservative landed gentry, the element in the party which she later came most powerfully to despise. She may not have inherited a private income, but she married an alternative to it. Financially she belonged to the leisured classes. This fortunate condition enabled her to pursue a political career with undistracted single-mindedness.

Denis had no political ambition himself. He has always been a prop, never a rival. From the beginning, self-effacement has been his lot. He stuck to his last, as a businessman. 'I've always taken the view that my job comes first,' he told George Gardiner. 'People have often said, "You do so much for Margaret in politics." It's a beautiful theory, but it's not really true. I've had a wife and two kids to keep, and my job comes first.'

Later, the job grew and fructified. With the family business taken over by Castrol in 1965, and then Castrol taken over by Burmah Oil, Denis ascended through the pecking-order of boardrooms from minor local concern to major national company, with the perquisites to match. The original sale, which raised £560,000, made him rich, and the Burmah board gave him a bigger income as well as a Daimler, to which he appended the number-plate DT3. When he retired from Burmah in 1975, the Daimler had become a Rolls-Royce, which he took with him and was still discreetly using ten years later.

By marrying him, Margaret secured a like-minded consort for the post she was eventually to attain. His retirement happily coincided with her own elevation to the party leadership, which made him more available for service on the road – 'always half a step behind', as he would wryly say. As it turned out, he agreed with everything important she stood for, by the time this settled itself into the collection of ideas to which he gave his name – Thatcherism. He believed in them with decidedly fewer qualifications than she did. Publicly, one of his talents was to remain the soul of almost unfailing discretion. Give or take the occasional after-dinner speech to a rugby club – he had been a first-class rugby referee – Denis gave nothing away. But privately he was an influence of positive importance.

He retained during all these years the innocence of the non-politician, the plain man in the Home Counties saloon bar. He gave the prime minister a direct line to every 19th hole in the country. Everything he felt and thought – from staunch hostility to socialists and trade unions, through his no-nonsense approach to business accountancy, to his inextinguishable affection for white South Africa – could be privately expressed without regard for the hesitations deemed prudent by public people. At home he did not shrink from expressing them. Coinciding as they usually did with the raw instincts of his wife, they played their part in the ceaseless struggle between gut instinct and political calculation which became so prominent among the motifs threading themselves through her prime minister-ship. Denis, after all, saw her almost every day, and he was not a shrinking violet.

After their marriage, he might have had his moments of ambivalence about precisely how much he wanted to involve himself as a stage extra in the great drama of British government. Reports would occasionally surface of his eagerness to escape from 10 Downing Street, and he retained a number of business interests. But he remained an affectionate comrade-in-arms. 'When I'm in a state,' his wife told a reporter shortly after becoming prime minister, 'I have no one to turn to except Denis. He puts his arm round me and says, "Darling, you sound just like Harold Wilson." And then I always laugh.'[6]

The caricature which immortalised him as a major satirical character in *Private Eye* was in some respects defective. In showing his love of golf and golf-clubs, and his preference for businessmen over politicians, it was true to life, but the image of a man frightened of his wife or less than loyally affectionate was misleading. The vows they made in Wesley's Chapel were put to the test far more severely than either can have expected, both for better and for worse. But the bond endured. When the values thus conjoined were put in charge of the country, they survived remarkably unimpaired.

Preliminary to this, a seat had to be found and Parliament had to be entered. The ambition was uncluttered and the funds were available, but the search was not easy. The blooding in Dartford counted for little. In this respect, marriage had actually made politics harder to pursue. It was followed by children – twins, Mark and Carol, were born in 1953 – and Margaret's clarion-call for the rights of women hardly spoke for mainstream Conservative opinion. Several local Conservative Associations turned her down. Later she made a virtue of this. The mid-fifties, say Gardiner and other biographers, were designed to be devoted to the rearing of her children. She could manage two commitments, to the law and to family, but not a third, to politics. And it is certainly true that Conservative selection committees at that time had firm views about the proper priorities for a woman with young children.

All the same, the new Mrs Thatcher tried quite hard. Barely a year after giving birth, she was manoeuvring for the nomination at a by-election in Orpington. Short-listed but rejected there, she was too late for consideration in any other seat that met her specifications for the 1955 General Election – it must be winnable and close to home. In 1957, Beckenham and Maidstone both turned her down, the first on explicitly sexist grounds (although the epithet was not then in currency). She also tried but failed to get Oxford.

But all these disappointments proved to be blessings. In 1958, the pick of the bunch fell vacant: Finchley, closest of all to Westminster and with a Conservative majority of 12,000. All parliamentary nominations are more or less of a lottery, and when safe Tory seats present themselves for capture to 200 aspiring candidates, luck plays an inescapable part. Margaret Thatcher was by now a hardened campaigner on the circuit, and evidently put up a very good show. Against a short-list made up of three chips off the old Tory block – officers and gentlemen with a public school and a good war behind them – she emerged the winner on the second ballot.

Still quite young at thirty-two, she was a glamorous arrival in the staid world of a seat that had been held by the same unremarkable man for more than twenty years. The local press was delighted. From it we catch another glimpse of a politician who was by now fully accomplished across the field of party policy, including those areas which she had no personal reason to know anything about. The *Finchley Press* encapsulated her adoption meeting in a single ecstatic sentence:

> Speaking without notes, stabbing home points with expressive hands, Mrs Thatcher launched fluently into a clear-cut appraisal of the Middle East situation, weighed up Russia's propagandist moves with the skill of a housewife measuring the ingredients in

a familiar recipe, pinpointed Nasser as the fly in the mixing bowl, switched swiftly to Britain's domestic problems (showing a keen grasp of wage and trade union issues), then swept her breathless audience into a confident preview of Conservatism's dazzling future.[7]

The Finchley of 1959, which returned Margaret Thatcher to Parliament with a majority of 16,260, was demographically as well as physically congruent with her personality and her politics, and it remained true to character throughout her tenure. When she won it, owner–occupiers were already the largest group; by 1981 they made up 61.7 per cent of the constituency. Finchley was middle-class and upwardly mobile. In 1964, over a third of the adults there were from the managerial, executive and professional echelons. Finchley has had a growing proportion of its children, always far ahead of the national average, educated beyond the minimum school-leaving age, and an impressive number of graduates. When Mrs Thatcher won it, about 20 per cent of the constituency was reckoned to be Jewish. And it is with some of the Jewish virtues that she has often been most closely identified: not the part of Jewish tradition which emphasises caring and compassion, but rather that which elevates self-help, an absence of materialistic guilt, and the community of the self-sufficient.[8]

These links with a particular Jewish outlook, coupled with an intense admiration for men who most successfully manifested it in their lives, were to make themselves felt when Mrs Thatcher's career reached its unexpected peak. But meanwhile Finchley was hers. It epitomised the woman she had become, and the psychic distance by which Grantham had now been left behind.

4

Years of Misrule

THE 1959 ELECTION caught the high tide of consensual post-war Conservatism. Under the leadership of Harold Macmillan, the party had a landslide victory, returning for its third consecutive term with a majority of 100. The manifesto on which this triumph was achieved was notably free of the language of challenge and contained few specific promises. Macmillan himself called it short and simple, and crystallised its message into two justifiably complacent questions. 'Do you want to go ahead on the lines which have brought prosperity at home? Do you want your present leaders to represent you abroad?' These questions aptly epitomised the two notable strands of his leadership since taking over from Anthony Eden in January 1957. He had led the party successfully out of its traumatic crisis over Suez, and had asserted himself with great energy as an international statesman. He also rejoiced in an uncomplicated way at the material advancement the electorate had enjoyed during this Conservative decade. Barely six months after reaching Downing Street, he had coined a phrase with which he was to be for ever associated – at first favourably, though later, when he was sliding, in terms of jubilant derision. 'Let's be frank about it,' he said on 20 July 1957, 'most of our people have never had it so good.' He went on to say that they should not now throw it all away by making excessive wage claims. But the phrase stuck. The truth that lay behind it helped produce the 1959 landslide. And in few places had the people had it better than in the lush political territory of upwardly mobile Finchley.

The time would come when this period of Conservative history was identified as the beginning of British decline, the moment the party began to go badly wrong. When Mrs Thatcher was elected party leader fifteen years later, the origin of everything that she had to set right was invariably traced back, by her zealous supporters, to the Macmillan years. These were damned for their loose fiscal discipline, their reckless quest for growth and full employment, their insufficient

41

hatred of public spending, their historic culpability as the motor of inflation. What Harold Wilson then scorned as the 'candyfloss society' would eventually be stigmatised by the Conservative revisionists of the 1970s in almost similar terms.

But at the time few if any Tory voices were raised in this refrain, not even that of the fiercely opinionated Enoch Powell, who, along with the Chancellor of the Exchequer, Peter Thorneycroft, had resigned from the Treasury in 1958 because of Macmillan's cavalier attitude to a few million extra pounds of public spending. The euphoria of victory, and the common belief that it was an unqualified endorsement of Macmillanite Conservatism, lasted long enough to carry Mr Powell uncomplaining into the Ministry of Health within a year of the election, and ultimately into the cabinet. It was a period, at least until the midpoint of Macmillan's five years, when the economy flourished, and Conservative divisions were mostly confined to the rantings of the imperialist right against his perception that a 'wind of change' was blowing through Africa. Mainstream Tory politics was what every half-ambitious Conservative, young and old, wanted to belong to. And none was more ambitious than the new young MP for Finchley.

She entered a Parliament peopled by several politicians already known to her. Nobody so intensely active in Conservative politics as she was from Oxford onwards fails to acquire a certain familiarity with the great men and the rising stars of the party. They speak at the same by-elections, work the same conferences, sit on the same study-groups and sub-committees. Opportunities to mingle with the leadership are always available to an aspiring MP determined enough to exploit them. All the same, before entering Parliament, Mrs Thatcher belonged to no set of cronies, and had few really close political friends. Women didn't – especially women born in Grantham without a network based on school or family to cling to. Margaret Thatcher was well known to the party professionals at Central Office and retained the acquaintances produced by a decade's work in Home Counties Conservatism. But it was only having reached the House of Commons that she could hope to be treated by her fellow politicians on truly equal terms.

Macmillan, the leader, and R. A. Butler, deputy leader and Home Secretary, were naturally far above her. But already in place were several men whose lives were going to be much affected by collision with hers.

Thus, she remade from afar some acquaintance with Lord Hailsham: the same Quintin Hogg whose candidature for Oxford in the 1945 election had given her her first blooding in active electoral politics. And rather closer, although still pretty grand, was one Edward Heath, an acquaintance from Kent.

They had appeared on the same platforms during the 1950 election, when Heath won Bexley, which was close to Dartford. Indeed, it was to a Heath audience, the Bexley Conservative ladies' luncheon club, that this Kentish neighbour had delivered one of her earliest harangues on the subject of women in politics – even earlier than her article for the *Sunday Graphic*. 'Don't be scared of the high-flown language of economists and cabinet ministers,' she had told Heath's ladies. In view of the opinions of the later Heath on the subject of female politicians, a certain irony attaches to the venue of this early statement of an enduring Thatcher theme. But by 1959 Heath, an older man, had far outdistanced her. He had been high in party councils almost from the start of his parliamentary career, as Churchill's deputy chief whip. Now, after four warmly acclaimed years in the key post of chief whip, he was Minister of Labour and halfway up the cabinet. If he still had anything to do with his platform colleague of a decade earlier, neither has ever acknowledged it. As for their roles in a leadership struggle to the death, these lay indecipherably far into the future. In 1959, such a contest was simply not imaginable.

Another future combatant was more accessible to Margaret Thatcher at that time. This was the MP for Leeds North-East, Sir Keith Joseph, Bt. Joseph too had risen fast, having got into the Commons at a by-election in 1956. Now his foot was on the first rung of the ladder, with a job as parliamentary secretary at the incongruously combined Ministry of Housing, Local Government and Welsh Affairs. Yet he was not out of reach. Far from it. He played a critical part in the earliest parliamentary appearance Margaret Thatcher made, just as he was to be the decisive figure when her career reached its climax. In the years between these episodes, a bond was established, uneven in its intimacy and certainly stronger at the end than at the beginning, but with a roughly coherent symmetry. The Thatcher–Joseph connection became one of the most formative political relationships of modern times.

Among those whose entry to the Commons coincided with hers were several men who must have reckoned their own chances of a glittering Conservative career greater than hers. James Prior was elected for Lowestoft, Peter Tapsell for Nottingham West,

Julian Critchley for Rochester & Chatham, Nicholas Ridley for Cirencester.

But not one of them made their mark as soon as she did, something she owed to luck. Often described later as a lucky prime minister, she was indubitably a lucky backbencher in that she had scarcely arrived at Westminster before coming second in the annual ballot for time to introduce a Private Member's Bill. Most unusually, her maiden speech itself was therefore devoted not to the customary forgettable bromides but to the businesslike introduction of her own measure, the Public Bodies (Admission to Meetings) Bill. Its purpose was to give the press a right of access to the meetings of local councils.

Mrs Thatcher's mode of introducing her measure was early evidence of a well-thought-out political style, heavily dependent on encyclopaedic self-briefing and tireless forensic preparation. She spoke for twenty-seven minutes with barely a reference to notes, pulling out of the air a catalogue of relevant statistics which bore witness to the incontrovertible right of the citizenry to be informed about the vast amounts of money local authorities were spending. It was, in a minor way, a parliamentary *tour de force*, which produced many compliments.

Barbara Castle, the Labour MP for Blackburn, commending the fluency of the proposer, said she would support the Bill despite her party's opposition to it. For the government, the Minister of Housing, Henry Brooke, was quite bowled over. 'No words of mine', he said in giving the Bill a general welcome, 'can be too high praise for the brilliance of the speech with which the Member for Finchley opened the debate.' To wind it up there appeared a voice which showed that there was a bit of a network, albeit an unfashionable one, to which the Thatchers did belong. W. F. Deedes, MP for Ashford, another man of Kent and a friend of Denis Thatcher, sponsored the Bill and praised in particular the 'courage' of the new Member who had introduced it.

Like others, Deedes also belonged to the future. For one thing, his friendship with Denis was immortalised in the *Private Eye* satire, Deedes being the 'Dear Bill' to whom Thatcher's fortnightly commentary on affairs was supposedly addressed. But he also became editor of the *Daily Telegraph*, house newspaper of the Conservative Party, just before Margaret Thatcher was elected party leader, and stayed there until the middle of her second term. In that role, he and his judgments, invariably supportive, were to have an important impact on her fortunes among the party faithful.

But for the moment, in 1960, it was on Keith Joseph that she made the more significant mark. As Henry Brooke's junior, he was the minister deputed to help her take her Bill through the legislative process. Together they worked out amendments to it, in particular one which extended rights of access beyond the press to the public at large.

The Public Bodies (Admission to Meetings) Act 1960 has always presented a puzzle to students of Mrs Thatcher's evolution. Ostensibly a measure directed towards more open government, it accords with no other interest in such matters ever shown by her, in or out of power. It appeared to be motivated by a strong desire to make the press more free: indeed, in its original form it offered nothing to the wider public and gave the press a special privilege. Yet freedom of the press, while never repudiated by Mrs Thatcher, has also never been high among the liberties she fought to defend. Why did this new MP select, out of any number of possible legislative ideas, a measure not obviously close to her heart, as well as one which the Conservative group on the local council in Finchley, sensing that even Tories might want some day to exclude the press, opposed?

The answer is that the choice was not entirely hers, and the motive was not entirely to do with journalism. The Conservative Party committed itself to some such measure in the 1959 election manifesto, and for an MP high in the Private Members' ballot to take it over did the government, and particularly the whips' office, a favour. The reason the party was committed was only secondarily out of any belief in the freedom of the press. A more potent influence was the desire to turn back trade union power. During the newspaper strike of 1958, certain Labour councils had voted to support the strikers by excluding from council meetings reporters who worked for papers being produced with strike-breaking labour. Although the press were from time to time excluded for other reasons by other councils, including some under Conservative control, the strike exposed a loophole in the law through which union power could run free. The parliamentary debate, as the Thatcher Bill was advancing, makes reference to the need for fuller public information, but it is the town hall as proxy union battleground that was the real target of Conservative indignation.

And here is the link with the later Thatcher. Hatred of union power has been a consistent theme in a way that greater openness has not. In a career which has been true to a handful of unchanging shibboleths, as well as exhibiting some crucial irregularities, belief in the virtues of more open government for its own sake has never been much of a feature of the Thatcher rhetoric.

Markers closer to her heart were also put down at this time. As a backbencher she took an early interest in tax. Two themes which could be taken almost word for word from numerous speeches she later made as prime minister began to make a trenchant appearance. Her greatest worry, she told her local party after eighteen months in the House, was the control of public spending. 'It is in fact very much more difficult than I ever thought it would be in theory,' she said. 'We are chasing after the hundreds and the thousands, but tending to let the millions go by. Some time we must alter the system of public accountability and the nation must present its accounts to Parliament as a company does to its shareholders.' Only in this way could tax be reduced. But secondly, the tax system should have a bias in favour of productive industry and against the entirely unmeritorious playing of the stock market. 'It is the speculators in shares that we want to get at,' she told the Commons during the debate on the 1961 budget, 'the person who is making a business of buying and selling shares, not to hold them for their income-producing properties, but to live on the profit which he makes from the transactions.' Although, as a consequence of her financial policies as prime minister, many thousands of people were to get very rich indeed by precisely such methods, it was a feature of budgets during the 1980s that they did the banks and other money-changers few favours. The puritanical moralist of the 1960s did her best to survive into the later era.

The main significance of this period, however, was that it saw the quiet launching of Margaret Thatcher into government. The smooth management of her Bill had proved her qualities as a speaker and a willing compromiser in the party interest. She showed she could play the game. To elevate her above the jostling crowd of ambitious new MPs she also had, once again, the advantage of being a woman.

In her own estimation she owed her first job, in October 1961, to this fact not least. She was offered the post of parliamentary secretary at the Ministry of Pensions, she told George Gardiner, because the vacancy had been created by the departure of another woman, Pat Hornsby-Smith. Even in those days, convention required a certain proportion of women to be admitted to the male preserve of government, and there were not many in the Macmillan Tory Party to choose from. The minister whose junior she became, John Boyd-Carpenter, began by being somewhat scornful. 'I thought quite frankly', he recalled later, 'when Harold Macmillan appointed her that it was just a little bit of a gimmick on his part. Here was a good-looking young woman and he was obviously, I thought, trying to brighten up the image of his government.'[1] As it happened, this particular woman, with her tax background and her relish for the fiddling details of a junior pensions minister's work, was admirably qualified for the job. But being a woman was nonetheless a special help. It set her early on a career which gave her a front-bench seat for the rest of her political life.

Her occupation of the post was of only modest interest. She did nothing memorable in it. How could it be otherwise? In any listing of the least glamorous positions in government, parliamentary secretary to the Ministry of Pensions would be near the top. Mrs Thatcher lived on a daily diet of individual complaints and inquiries about national insurance and national assistance, hundred upon hundred of them to be considered by civil servants and adjudicated by the junior minister. At this class of work she proved to be thoroughly adept, and Boyd-Carpenter soon revised his early judgment. 'I couldn't have been more wrong, because once she got there she very quickly showed a grip on the highly technical matters of social security – and it's an extraordinarily technical, complex subject – and a capacity for hard work which she's shown ever since, and which quite startled the civil servants and certainly startled me.'

A somewhat sourer memory was offered a little earlier than this to other biographers.[2] The permanent secretary at the Ministry of Pensions and National Insurance in 1961 was Sir Eric Bowyer. He evidently disapproved of her appointment to the job. He asked whether as a young mother she would work hard enough. Twenty years on, he also pulled out of the past a recollection that had surely by then become a misleading cliché. 'She would turn up looking as if she had spent the whole morning with the coiffeur and the whole afternoon with the couturier.' However, in the end the civil service had 'got at least as much work from her as anyone else and probably a bit more'.

In these condescending words may lie a clue to the one enduring impact Mrs Thatcher's first government job made on her political life. It offered few opportunities to shine in Parliament, though what she had to do she did capably enough. At the bottom of the totem pole, it brought no publicity either. Margaret Thatcher gained no kind of celebrity as the junior minister of pensions. But she did learn about civil servants, and this was an awakening she never forgot. In a career punctuated by many tempestuous relationships with officials, Pensions is where the seeds of her aggression were sown.

This was not simply a matter of rejecting the social attitudes, often incorrigibly anti-feminist, of the typical Whitehall mandarin, so aptly conveyed by Bowyer's phraseology. These attitudes in the early sixties were at their loftiest. It was still the era when the civil service could make a plausible claim to be running the country. In the plenitude of their self-confidence, which had not yet been broken by economic decline or any perception that the consensus which they embodied might be in error, top civil servants looked upon junior ministers as a very low form of life – and here was one junior minister less prepared than some to overlook the slights.

But the moral she drew was somewhat deeper. Civil servants, it appeared to her, were above all not interested in argument. While concerned to maintain their power and eager to keep the ship of state on an even keel, they were essentially uncreative people. Because the Ministry of Pensions was almost never subject to political crisis or the need for a sudden decision to be made, the remorseless tide of casework could be offset by more discussion of long-term policy than is possible in most departments. The experience gave Mrs Thatcher an insight into a Whitehall trait she found uncongenial under each of the three ministers she served during her three years in the post. 'It was interesting to sit in on the policy meetings', she told George Gardiner in 1975, 'and see how the advice offered by the civil service changed according to the minister. I came to the conclusion that the civil service tend not to put up advice that they think the minister will reject. After a minister has been some time in a department, therefore, you tend to get rather limited advice coming up.'

Later, this perception of Whitehall was dramatically turned on its head. The blind acquiescence that Mrs Thatcher deplored in the 1960s became, once converted into zealous commitment to her own ideas in the 1980s, a positive demand she made on all the mandarins who came in sight of her. But what has been consistent is her irreverence, her refusal to show much awe for the occupants of historic positions: and this was the main residue of her otherwise arid first three years in government.

This aridity, however, was not alien to her temperament. That she could put up with it, indeed enjoy it, not hankering after a post more suited to the conventional high-flyers in the party – something in the

Foreign Office or the Treasury – suggests a politician who at this stage was glad of any job she could pick up. The ceaseless detail suited her practical mind. She was certainly ambitious, and had publicly speculated about a woman becoming Chancellor of the Exchequer. But her humble post, combined with the common instinct that set the sights of any woman in politics cautiously low, left her far from great events.

When Macmillan resigned because of ill-health in September 1963, few people wanted to know the opinion of the junior pensions minister about who should succeed him. Like most junior ministers and almost all MPs, she had neither voice nor vote in the matter. The most that she, like all of them, could hope to exercise was one small fragment of a collective veto against any leader the party establishment decided was the favourite. Mrs Thatcher, backing what looked like the safe horse, seems just to have favoured R. A. Butler. So, at least, she told Gardiner. But since these were the days before any Tory leader was formally elected, a public commitment was not required. A leader evolved out of the miasma, leaving MPs, as sole compensation for their lack of a vote, the opportunity to climb aboard whichever bandwagon was ahead. When Lord Home, the Foreign Secretary, in one of the most shocking modern coups against elective politics, triumphed over Butler and everyone else, Mrs Thatcher raised no objection. She was slightly concerned, as were others, that Home might not get elected to the Commons. But he had quality. 'One knew that Alec was very, very good, and so easy to talk to,' she said.

She would hardly have called him Alec at the time. But under him she served out her apprenticeship. A year later he led the party to narrow defeat. In Finchley Mrs Thatcher was safely home, her majority reduced to a mere 9,000. But, with a majority of four in the Commons, the Labour years of Harold Wilson began.

At the time, the passing of the Tory Government did not seem, to Mrs Thatcher or many other people, like the end of a disaster. It was traumatic to lose power, but the scornful chant denouncing 'thirteen years of Tory misrule' was a slogan exclusive to the Labour Party. Only later did Conservatives begin to purloin such thinking for their own side. That exercise in revisionism was going to be a complicated intellectual process, with many cross-currents of opinion and personality and more than one false start.

Analysis of the Macmillan years was to become the defining intellectual event, the condition precedent, of the redefinition of Conservatism as Thatcherism. But for the moment, in October 1964, to the Member for Finchley office under Macmillan and Home was simply something she had unfortunately lost, until the wheel of fortune once again came round.

5

Heath's Woman

THE 1964 ELECTION was the beginning of the end for Conservatism
of Churchillian pedigree. Those who ran the party for the first two
post-war decades were all, in one way or another, Churchill's protégés.
Home's appointment as party leader was the last gasp of the post-war
generation, and of the system which had perpetuated its power and
influence. When Home lost the election, he had to go, leaving behind
him, as the only permanent legacy of one of the most decent men to
occupy 10 Downing Street, a new system for the formal election of
his successor. All who took part in it were conscious of voting for a
new era.

The candidates for the first elected Tory leadership were Reginald
Maudling, Enoch Powell and Edward Heath. Each of them has been
of some importance in the life of Margaret Thatcher: one as her friend,
another as her intellectual mentor, the third, after years of enforced
and chilly association, as the sworn enemy of all she stood for. She
voted for her future enemy, the man with whom she had shared
platforms in the old days, Edward Heath.

This was not her first instinct. She originally leaned towards
Maudling, her friend and everybody's favourite to win. George Gardiner tells us why this was. Apart from being closer to him than to
the others, 'she greatly respected the judgments which he had made as
Chancellor.' At the time, this was the conventional view of Maudling.
Macmillan had sent him to the Treasury in 1962 with a brief for
growth and expansion which he duly carried through. Quite soon,
with Labour in office, Maudling's prodigality was widely blamed
for the balance-of-payments crisis which kept the new government
permanently in its grip. Later still, when revisionism was sweeping
the Tory Party and the monetarist analysis probed backwards to lay
bare the alleged errors of the past, the Maudling Chancellorship was
held to epitomise the degeneracy over which Macmillan had presided.
But in July 1965 that was not the way it looked, to Margaret Thatcher
or anyone else. On the contrary, Maudling's economic policies were

51

the main commendation for his candidature. Heath was ultimately preferred, both by her and by the party, for having greater manifest toughness than the casual Maudling, and for his more promising ability to match the talents of Harold Wilson. As for Powell, the future mentor, he secured only 15 votes, to Heath's 150 and Maudling's 133. He was a renegade figure, too far outside the mainstream for any ambitious young politician to contemplate supporting him. Margaret Thatcher did not give his candidature a second glance.

Ted Heath's arrival in the Conservative leadership was a beacon of promise to many of his contemporaries, and all younger Conservatives, who saw in him the proof that the age of the meritocracy had dawned. In Britain's class-obsessed society, this was what immediately mattered most about Heath – his humble origins, the tortured vowel-sounds that betrayed them, the proof he embodied that you did not need to be a toff to lead the toffs' party. That was the first and overwhelming excitement. The second was the political image that went with this fracturing of the social mould: the new direction in which Heath would lead the party, the abrasive dynamism which would finally wipe away the prevailing image of Conservatism, whether symbolised by Macmillan's drooping moustache and Edwardian weariness, or Home's confession that he was unable to think about economic policy without the aid of matchsticks. Since both these apparent transformations, the leap down the social scale and the definition of a new brand of Conservatism, insinuated themselves into the personal odyssey of Margaret Thatcher, they repay a little study.

Ostensibly, her background and Heath's were almost identical. And certainly he paved some of the way for her ascent. It would have been more difficult for the Tory Party to contemplate electing the daughter of a Grantham grocer to the leadership in 1975 if it had not elected the eldest son of a Broadstairs carpenter ten years earlier. But the points of difference in their formation are as notable as the similarities and, given the accepted mythology, rather more interesting. Overhanging all of them is the signal fact that, whereas Margaret Thatcher constantly gloried in her origins, Ted Heath spent a lifetime escaping from his own.

Heath was a genuine working-class boy, the son of a man who was proud of it and never aspired to climb the social scale. 'We're a working-class family and no two ways about it,' William Heath, the father, told Ted's biographer, Margaret Laing, in 1972. He was therefore different from Alfred Roberts. The family homes of the two future prime ministers enshrined some of the same values: thrift, cleanliness, a belief in education. But where Heath was reared, neither politics nor social pretensions coloured the domestic scene. According to Laing, William 'vaguely believed he was a Liberal', but did nothing about it. During the First World War he was so poor that he had to beg for coal and potatoes. The aldermanic aura of the Grantham petty bourgeoisie had no counterpart in the upbringing of Edward Heath. In Grantham, Alfred Roberts was rather grand. His life took him into ruling circles. He met politicians and rubbed shoulders with Lord Brownlow, an intimate of the Prince of Wales during the Abdication crisis. Nothing like this was any part of Heath's early years. Even education itself was sometimes a struggle. When Ted got a place at Balliol College, Oxford, he did not originally secure a scholarship – this only came later – and his father was doubtful whether he should go at all. If we are speaking of Conservatives who have triumphed over apparent social adversity, Heath travelled a longer road than his successor.

Oxford, however, did much the same for both of them. Two diligent grammar-school toilers were transmuted into dedicated Conservative politicians, and, strengthened by the indestructible benefits of the Oxford experience, took every chance of fulfilling their high political ambitions. But there was at least one important difference. Heath used his undergraduate years, like many others, to travel, whereas Margaret Thatcher's first journey abroad was on her honeymoon. A crucial ten years before, pre-war not post-war, Heath was drawn towards a Europe then in turmoil, travelling to Germany in 1937 and Spain in 1938 in the middle of the Spanish Civil War. On each journey he witnessed historic events. In Germany it was the Nuremberg Rally. 'I can still recall that rally, every moment of it,' he told Laing. 'What struck me was the hysteria of the whole thing.' In Spain, visiting the Republican forces, he was bombed out of his hotel in Barcelona. As late as the summer of 1939 he was in Poland and Germany, returning home only two days before war was declared.

Heath grew up politically at a time when politics was dominated by foreign affairs, and this imposed its influence on his entire career. An attitude to foreign policy decisively shaped his youthful Conservatism, the origins of which were less specific than Margaret Thatcher's. Although Heath was as clear as she was from an early age that he wanted to become a politician, his allegiance was not quite so predetermined. He grew up at a time when the majority of educated young men experienced many confusions, lured towards Communism by the rise of Hitler and the romantic war against Franco, or towards the rearmament lobby in the Tory Party by the complaisant vacillations of the Baldwin Government. Heath, however, soon made up his mind. He was as repelled by Labour's pacifism as by the appeasing Tory leadership. President of OUCA in 1937, he was elected President of the Oxford Union six months after Munich, having taken a prominent part in the Oxford City by-election of October 1938, supporting Lindsay, the master of Balliol, against the appeasement candidate, who was none other than Quintin Hogg. Truly does Hogg go back, erratically, into the past, penetrating the life of every leading Conservative for the last fifty years.

One consequence of Oxford was identical in both the Heath and the Thatcher cases. The university gave them a reputation in the party and acquainted them with the right people to know. Heath did it by taking OUCA into the anti-appeasement camp, against Neville Chamberlain and the party leadership. This was a bold piece of defiance for a working-class boy, but it earned the approval of future patrons like Harold Macmillan. By the end of his time, according to a Balliol contemporary, Julian Amery, he had become 'the leading Conservative figure in the university'.

This process of recognition had its almost exact parallel a decade later, when Margaret Roberts took a similar part in thrusting OUCA into the post-war era. Each had to overcome difficulties, she because she was a woman and unfashionable to boot, he because he arrived at Oxford as a shy, withdrawn young man without any money. Each triumphantly succeeded.

The man who arrived in the Conservative leadership in 1965, however, was very different from the woman who got there in 1975. Each event was the climax of a different strategy, a fact which profoundly influenced the course each adopted as leader and the fate each underwent as prime minister. It was also, eventually, responsible for nurturing one of the bitterest exhibitions of personal antagonism between two leaders of the same party in the politics of the twentieth century. British political history may be littered with famous personal resentments, between Asquith and Lloyd George, for example, or Macmillan and Butler, or Harold Wilson and George Brown. None lasted so long, at such a peak of unremitting acrimony, as that between Heath and Mrs Thatcher in their later years.

After the fall of Home, Heath became leader as the complete establishment man. His was an updated Conservatism, and his way of expressing it seemed to put him on equal terms with his chief antagonist, Wilson, the *wunderkind* of a modernised Britain. But Heath had got to the top by becoming the perfect mimic of his elders. The brief anti-leadership phase before the war was replaced, from the moment he got into Parliament in 1950, by an unswerving eye for the location of power. Within a year he was taken into the whips' office, within three he was deputy chief whip and quite close to Churchill himself. From 1955 to the 1959 election, as chief whip, he was responsible for steering the party relatively intact through the Suez crisis, as well as for the distribution of large amounts of patronage. Any self-doubt the boy from Broadstairs might have had about his ability to shake off his unfavoured past, and any doubts the party had about his right to be regarded on equal terms with its most famous men, had long since vanished.

When Margaret Thatcher reached the House, Heath was a full member of the ruling circle, frequenting its clubs, dining at its tables, discoursing on the subject it still took more seriously than anything else, international affairs. When he took his part in the removal of Home – a role he has always denied, but one which the Home family never quite forgot – he had equipped himself with a record in office marking him as the man to carry on the middle-way Conservatism of Macmillan, to whom he was devoted, while shaking off some of its more decadent encrustations. He had been briefly Minister of Labour; had led Britain's first, unavailing attempt to join the European Community; had, as President of the Board of Trade, driven his reluctant party to cut through antiquated protectionism and abolish what was known as Resale Price Maintenance. This supposed opening-up of internal free trade by the decontrol of prices, while highly contentious on the shopkeeper wing of the Conservative Party, was a fitting symbol of the world Heath promised for the sixties and seventies: competitive, modernised and much given to the ritual slaughtering of sacred cows.

In this historic process Margaret Thatcher was allotted only a minor role. She had done enough in government to earn her a place in the front-bench shadow team, and Heath moved her rapidly from junior post to junior post: first Pensions, then Housing and Land in October 1965, and thence to the Treasury team six months later. She was promoted to the shadow cabinet in October 1967, with the Power portfolio, although apparently with due apprehensions on Heath's part about what this might portend. Jim Prior was consulted on who should be what he terms the 'statutory woman' in the shadow cabinet. When he recommended Mrs Thatcher, Heath replied, after a long silence, 'Yes, Willie [Whitelaw] agrees that she's much the most able, but he says once she's there we'll never be able to get rid of her.'[1]

A year later, in contentious circumstances, she became shadow minister of Education. This gave her a broad range of training in the work of a succession of domestic departments, and the opportunity to shine occasionally in Parliament against some of the more celebrated Labour ministers, notably the Chancellor of the Exchequer, James Callaghan. But what is more striking about this period is how small and tentative were her contributions to the debate which raged about the future of Conservatism.

This got under way in earnest only in 1966, after the Wilson Government called another election and, in accordance with most predictions, strengthened its hold on power. With a majority of 97, it was clearly in place for a full term. The Conservative Party could afford to devote itself to a serious examination of its past and its future.

In later years, Heath's period as leader of the Opposition has often been remembered as a time mainly devoted to the discovery of ideological purity. Now was the time, it has been said, when the modern Tory Party shook off the chains of quasi-socialist compromise in which Macmillan and Butler had mistakenly shackled it. Those closest to prime minister Thatcher are particularly attached to this version of history. It was integral to the mythology of the late 1970s and beyond. To put it simply: Heath was construed as the leader who had once believed in most of the ideas Mrs Thatcher came to stand for, had led the party of the 1960s towards them, but then reneged on them halfway through his own prime ministership. The image of Heath the Betrayer, so crucial to support for the ragbag of ideas called Thatcherism, was fashioned from memories that began as early as 1966.

There is some truth in this account of events, but less than is often claimed. What, in fact, did Heath stand for? In part, certainly, for a revamped Conservatism that began with an analysis similar to Mrs Thatcher's ten years later. For example, he placed great emphasis on the need to curb trade union power with new laws. *Putting Britain Right Ahead*, the party manifesto for the 1966 election, gave this a central place in a policy designed to reinvigorate the economy by increasing competition. Competition was the Heath watchword, and attacking trade unions became an avowed part of the strategy for increasing it. The 'one-nation' philosophy, the inherited slogan of generations of Tory reformers, was explicitly recommended for revision. According to one progressive thinker of the time, Timothy Raison, the party should develop 'a clear anti-union bias'. The Conservatives' problem, he wrote, was that they had tried to operate a 'largely capitalist economy without a capitalist ideology'. We must now accept, said the heretical Raison, that life was largely about conflict and that 'there *are* two sides in industry'.[2]

Another young theoretician, also quite close to Heath, recommended the philosophy of class war even more starkly. David Howell, then director of the Conservative Political Centre, wrote: 'Strikes do at least indicate that toughness is being shown on the management side in face of unreasonable demands. . . . The absence of strikes may well be evidence of a tacit conspiracy between management and work people to do nothing new and disturbing, to give in to all wage demands swiftly, and in general to preserve a cosy climate of inefficiency.' The conclusion of this analysis, that the party should launch itself bald-headed into anti-union legislation, was accepted without demur by the entire Conservative Party. Indeed, it became for a time the conventional cross-party wisdom, as was shown by Harold Wilson's unavailing attempt to pass an anti-union law of his own in 1969.

Secondly, Heathism anticipated Thatcherism in its desire to reshape the welfare state. Controlling the social service budget, and confining its benefits to people 'in need' was a dream of the Conservative leadership twenty years before Mrs Thatcher, as prime minister, began to put it seriously into action in the mid-1980s. Sir Keith Joseph, whom Heath placed in charge of this area of policy, was developing the concept of 'selectivity' in social provision even before the 1966 election, and the attack on universal provision persisted as a Tory theme throughout the period of opposition, although with no great consistency beyond it.

Thirdly, Heath wanted to give top priority to business and the interests of businessmen. Hand in hand with more competition was to go a great rebirth of the spirit of *laissez-faire*. Technocrats and industrial managers were to be elevated into the new elite. Again this was a new bias similar to that which Mrs Thatcher later asserted. Partly it was a matter of setting business free. To this end, incomes policy was to be completely dismantled. But partly it was a matter of culture. Entrepreneurs, Heath said, were the pacemakers of society:

'They are the people who are blessed with particular skills, with greater imagination, with foresight, with inventiveness and with administrative ability, who can give the lead and who can help us to the fore in world affairs.' This cry, passionately felt if dully put, was taken up in identical terms ten years later.

But in other respects the Heath of the sixties was decidedly not the precursor of the Thatcher of the seventies. For one thing, he continued to believe unashamedly in the power of the state and the need to mobilise it as a key weapon of economic policy. 'Waste' in government spending was an evil to be eradicated, but no serious assault was promised on the state's economic power. On the contrary, in the pursuit of growth the state had to be an active partner. The need for state intervention in the expansion of productive investment was seen as a positive necessity by Howell, as it was by another young journalist–politician, Nigel Lawson.[3]

The strategy enshrined efficiency and growth as twin deities. But it favoured thoroughly corporatist methods of propitiating them. Along with the obsessive determination to carry Britain into the European Economic Community, it sprang from a managerial view of the British problem – which could be cured essentially by institutional change, rather than by a painful philosophical challenge to the status quo which Wilson was establishing.

This points to the pervasive difference between the periods 1966–70 and 1975–9. As perceived by contemporary observers of the earlier period, including many voters, there was little fundamental to choose between Heath and Wilson. Heath's plan to curb union power for a time provided it; but when Wilson succumbed to the same ambition in 1969, even this difference largely dissolved. What Heath offered was seen in large part as a more efficient version of the kind of technocratic state Wilson had long talked about without being able to bring it very conspicuously to birth. Heath in fact recoiled from anything so grand as a philosophy with which to challenge socialism. His interest and aptitude drew him relentlessly towards the detail of policy and away from any broad coherent message that might lie behind it. He thought all problems would fall before the logic and efficiency of the businesslike approach.

Heath was, in short, the opposite of an ideologue. That he should ever have been represented as one he owed principally to a single event – and, even here, later interpretation probably overcoloured the truth of what occurred. In January 1970, the shadow cabinet met for a heavily publicised pre-election weekend at the Selsdon Park

Hotel outside London. As a result of the strident communiqué issued at the end of it, stressing the need for tax cuts, more selectivity in social services and above all a more vigorous approach to law and order, 'Selsdon Man' was born in Labour rhetoric: a hairy, primeval beast threatening to gobble alive all the benefits which socialism had spread around post-war British society. This graphic conceit, invented largely by Wilson himself, was credited with having persuaded him to call a general election that June, an election he thought he was sure to win against such a monster. And certainly, by depicting Heath in this way, Wilson endowed him with more vivid coherence than his pedestrian collected speeches could ever aspire to.

But 'Selsdon Man' did not lose the election. On the contrary, Robert Blake, the historian of the Tory Party, judges that the image 'did the Conservatives more good than harm'.[4] It was in any case a false image. Although central to the picture of Heath's prime ministership as a great betrayal, which the Thatcher years are supposed belatedly to have rectified, it is a significant misrepresentation. It overlooks the extent to which Heath's decade as the Conservative leader was spent in open warfare with the very influences which were eventually to shape the most important elements of his successor's appeal.

Far to the right of Selsdon Man was a classical right by whom Heath was regarded as unsatisfactory from the start. Here there was a yearning for something more recognisable as a Conservative alternative to socialism, a rounded and even fundamentalist philosophy. This school had several prominent spokesmen. Among the earliest was Angus Maude, who was sacked from the shadow cabinet as early as 1966 after expressing his anxiety that the party was becoming a 'meaningless irrelevance'. 'For the Tories simply to talk like technocrats', Maude wrote, 'will get them nowhere.'[5] Economic growth itself was a quite insufficient objective. 'Every political party needs some solid ground of philosophy to stand on – otherwise it is apt to be swept along by the tides of passing fashion and fancy.'

These too were the years when the Monday Club flourished. Its members were not merely imperialist dreamers, though it had been Macmillan's decolonisation policies in Africa which caused it to be founded. They strode confidently into the domestic arena. In one of their pamphlets, John Biggs-Davison MP declared: 'Under the creeping socialism of a generation we have been stripped well-nigh naked of our monetary, military and moral defences. The threat to our kinsfolk and partners overseas is matched by the threat to domestic economy and social order.' To have any impact on this, Biggs-Davison argued, the Conservatives had to shed their own 'degeneracy and materialism' and undertake 'an almost superhuman labour of national rescue and revival'. None of this, it would appear, was the Heath leadership preparing to supply. As another spokesman for the right, Dr Rhodes Boyson, put it, when compared with Labour 'the Conservatives offered no alternative morality of politics.'

These thinkers, Heath's critics and enemies, do not now sound in every respect like early Thatcherites. In both Maude and Boyson there was a fastidious distaste for materialism nowhere to be found in the Conservative Party of the 1980s. Maude called growth 'a sterile cycle of increasing production for increasing consumption of increasingly trivial things'. By the time he had become a member of Mrs Thatcher's cabinet he allowed himself no such expressions of austerity.

In general, however, the resemblances are strong. There is a striking similarity of thought and phrasing between what the anti-Heathites were saying in the late 1960s and what the pro-Thatcherites said in the late 1970s. When Biggs-Davison called for Heath's Government to 'end consensus politics', he was minting the motto that would later epitomise Thatcherism. When Boyson lamented that throughout the Macmillan years 'the country continued to advance step by step to socialism and more government control, more egalitarianism, and to a reduced-choice, heavily taxed economy,' he was voicing the theme, if not the explicit historical reference, of a thousand Thatcher speeches delivered after 1975.

A still more resonant spokesman for proto-Thatcherism was also at work during this period. Enoch Powell, who had left the Macmillan Government in 1958 on a point of principle concerning excessive public expenditure, was the most prominent exponent of precisely the kind of unambiguous alternative to socialism that Heath did not stand for, and never regarded as a serious option. As the exemplar of the difference between Heathism and Thatcherism, the ultimate disproof of the betrayal theory as applied to Heath's record, one could find no more authoritative figure than Powell.

What Powell argued for then was a position that has now become very familiar. But in the later sixties, and certainly for most of Heath's time as prime minister, it was the height of unorthodoxy. His concerns were mainly economic. He was determined to establish the superiority of market forces over state planning and control, whether in housing, the social services or the level of the exchange rate. He believed in competition, as did Heath. But he adamantly resisted the role of the state in encouraging it. Having left Macmillan's Government he became, in Andrew Gamble's words, 'the foremost critic of the new interventionist state the Conservatives developed to help restructure capital and contain wages'.

A good many of Powell's preoccupations, which then seemed to be those of an almost lone fanatic, were to float into the mainstream of the Thatcher age. Inflation, he kept insisting, was not caused by rising wages or prices but by governments printing money. Public spending was the curse of a free society when it was financed by printing or borrowing. Inflation, he added, was an excuse for imposing prices and incomes policies which, besides being ineffective, were another arm of state control. Almost everything, further, depended on the money supply. 'Upon the sound working of the money system,' he wrote in 1969, 'and above all upon the stability and honesty of the currency, depend not only the operations of industry and commerce but . . . the structure of society itself.'[6]

Many of Powell's economic ideas later became commonplace. But to Heath they were mostly anathema. The entire Powellite package of Conservative populism was almost the opposite of what Heath defined as his priorities. Heath believed in state intervention, in the corporatism of the big battalions, in an economy that needed only to be better managed not radically reorganised. Powell despised all these ideas. Heath put entry into the Common Market at the centre of his programme. Powell fought it with every weapon he could find. Heath was an internationalist, Powell a fierce nationalist as well as an anti-American. Heath accepted, without very obviously welcoming, the multi-racial society. Powell chose the immigration issue as the one on which to speak with such unbridled venom that it marked the end of his career as a front-bench Conservative politician. For, despite their differences, he was a member of Heath's shadow cabinet until 1968. Although Heath always disliked him, and was baffled by his insinuating intellect, he broke with the guru of the new right only after a nakedly racist attack on coloured immigrants in April of that year. In his view of the consequences of large-scale immigration for Britain's cities, Powell paraphrased the prophecy of the Sybil in Book VI of Virgil's *Aeneid*. 'As I look ahead,' he said, 'I am filled with foreboding. Like the Roman, I seem to see the River Tiber foaming with much blood.' Heath despatched Powell into the wilderness from which he never returned in person – although he lived to see the arrival into power, by proxy as it were, of many of the ideas he spent his later years self-righteously proclaiming.

But where was his proxy at this time? Her Jewish constituents in Finchley would certainly not have permitted her to utter the slightest sympathy for Powell's racism, even had she been free to do so by voting against the 1968 Race Relations Act. But how did Margaret Thatcher contribute to the first serious contest of her mature political life between different strands of Conservative thinking? Whatever view one takes in retrospect of the 'betrayal' to be discerned in the Heath record, this is an interesting question. Was Mrs Thatcher to be found, as one might expect from her later record, in the Powell camp? Was she seriously committed to the kind of programmatic assault on socialism that Heath could not be persuaded to embark on? And thus to a position that would put her at odds with the mainstream party leadership? Or did she essentially conform to the prevailing wisdom, half-baked though it seemed to many people on the right of the party?

The truth is that she took little part in these great debates. She contributed in no serious way save one to the arguments which her own prime ministership later saw to a different conclusion. The annals of pamphleteering and speech-making between 1965 and 1970 are almost devoid of mention of her name. For she had one thing at least in common with Heath. Her cast of mind was that of a problem-solver. She was happier with particular issues needing particular solutions than with the dangerously unlimited scope of a sophisticated discussion of first principles. As a junior shadow minister of Housing, she sank her teeth into Labour's plan to set up a Land Commission. After the 1966 election, moved to Treasury affairs, she delivered with enormous relish an impressive onslaught against Callaghan's proposal for a selective employment tax. When the Government was driven to introduce a Prices and Incomes Bill, she enjoyed nothing better than fighting every individual order made under it. Moved once more to the Fuel and Power portfolio and promoted to the shadow cabinet, she had to learn about natural gas, nuclear energy and the horror of the Aberfan pit disaster. Later still, handling Transport affairs, she was confronted by intensely practical problems, requiring mastery of many facts and figures, which played to her forensic strength. But the evidence strongly suggests a Heath-like aversion from offering general reflections on the cosmic nature of the political struggle.

The single exception came in 1968. She was invited to deliver the Conservative Political Centre lecture at the party conference. It is a prestigious event in the party year, and she must have made a mark to be invited at all. But it cannot have been as a controversialist or thinker that she was asked, because her record in either of these guises was virtually blank. The lecture constitutes the first comprehensive attempt at an articulate political philosophy which the future prime minister ever publicly essayed.

Read twenty years later, it emerges as a strangely hesitant effort. It was entitled 'What's Wrong with Politics?' The broad answer, Mrs Thatcher felt, lay in too much criticism and too little belief. The lecture contained echoes of several mentors, past and future. She showed a Maudeian scepticism about the merits of economic growth, placing the origins of this obsession in the early 1960s and suggesting that it was an aberration. 'The doctrine found favour at the time and we had a bit of a contest between the parties about the highest possible growth rate. Four per cent, or more? But the result was that for the time being the emphasis in political debate ceased to be about people and became about economics.'

She also emphasised the positive moral virtue that lay behind the Conservatives' hostility to incomes policies. 'There is nothing wrong in principle in people wanting larger incomes. What is wrong is that people should want more without giving anything in return. The condition precedent to high wages and high salaries is hard work. This is a quite different and much more stimulating approach than one of keeping down incomes.'

The evil of consensus politics was another persistent theme, now making its first appearance in the Thatcher vocabulary. The consensus approach, as she then defined it, was inimical to the British constitution. It threatened to break up the system which allowed for interplay between a government and an opposition. Britain had always had a proper opposition. 'We have therefore not suffered the fate of countries which have had a "consensus" or central government without an official opposition.' Any aim for a consensus, she went on, 'could be an attempt to satisfy people holding no particular views about anything'.

If the lecture had a core, however, this lay in its discussion of the role of government. Mrs Thatcher was against excessive government intervention, but in terms that were inoffensive to the views of Heath and the leadership. She was against bureaucratic power. 'What we need now is a far greater degree of personal responsibility and decision, far more independence from government, and a comparative reduction in the role of government.' People must become less dependent on the state, and be free to choose how to spend their money – money it was essential they should be able to accumulate as freely and plentifully as they knew how. An image she very frequently called on in later years was now summoned up: 'The point is that even the Good Samaritan had to have the money to help, otherwise he too would have had to pass on the other side.'

Further, she was much struck by the power the government gained through information, and by the looming threat of computerised files of personal data. She waxed uncommonly eloquent on this theme:

> Consider our relations with government departments. We start as a birth certificate; attract a maternity grant; give rise to a tax allowance and possibly a family allowance; receive a national health number when registered with a doctor; go to one or more schools where educational records are kept; apply for an educational grant; get a job; start paying national insurance and tax; take out a television and a driving licence; buy a house with a mortgage; pay rates; buy a few premium bonds; take out life assurance; purchase some shares; get married; start the whole thing over again; receive pension and become a death certificate and death grant, and the subject of a file in the Estate Duty office! Every one of these incidents will require a form or give rise to some office. The amount of information collected in the various departments must be fabulous. Small wonder that life really does seem like 'one damned form after another'.

She was concerned, in a way she did little to sustain in later years, at the threat this posed to individual privacy. 'There would be produced for the first time a personal dossier about each person, on which everything would be recorded. In my view this would place far too much power in the hands of the state over the individual.'

This apprehension of the state as Big Brother was perhaps the most arresting feature, in Conservative terms, of the CPC lecture. Mrs Thatcher did make an unfashionable, if minor, reference to what later became known as monetarism, by defining the 'essential role' of government as being 'the control of money supply'. But since this essential role was combined with another, the 'management of demand', the lecture constituted no departure from orthodoxy. Lurking, half-perceived, can be seen the moralist of thrift, the prophet of self-help, the exponent of conviction politics who later became famous. But compared with the sweep and sophistication of Powell's analysis, it lacked decisiveness and self-confidence. There was something a little juvenile about the future ideologue's handling of ideology. She clung firmly to some home truths, and perhaps felt more in need of systematic moral convictions than Heath did. But she was not essentially a different political animal from him. Like him she was ambitious for office. Like him – like every politician who ever lived, in some corner of their mind – she believed that what was good for her would be good for the country as well.

If the condition of achieving both these objectives was that a flirtation with the half-absorbed economic ideas of Enoch Powell would have to be cut short, it would never have occurred to Margaret Thatcher to do otherwise. Only later could he truly be called her intellectual mentor. And even then it was a curious relationship, in which the tutor felt bitterly that he had been supplanted by his pupil without her even having to pass her first examination. In fact, she was never personally close to him, not least, according to Powell's friends, because he had a low regard for her intellect.

Certainly in these early days he did not matter. No ambitious politician would have dreamed of aligning themselves with him, unless they were exceptionally committed to his ideas. There were a few such persons of conviction, drawn to the Powellite world view. One was John Biffen. Margaret Thatcher was certainly not among them, not yet. Another few years would have to elapse before, under her, some of Powell's ideas would finally gain admission to their kingdom.

6

Public Spender

EDWARD HEATH WON the 1970 election at the head of a united cabinet. They had not all expected victory, which was achieved against most predictions and in the last days of the campaign. But the surprise of being in government increased their sense of triumphant purpose just as it increased the leader's prestige and power. The unity was directed to tasks which, as seen then, appeared revolutionary in their import. Although the challenge Heath proposed to some of the consensual orthodoxies seems in retrospect timid, it roused from him a burst of oratory so uncharacteristically resonant as to recall some of the rhetoric manufactured for President John F. Kennedy ten years earlier. He desired, Heath told the party conference in October 1970, 'to embark on a change so radical, a revolution so quiet and so total that it will go far beyond the programme of a Parliament. . . . We were returned to office to change the course and the history of this nation, nothing less.'

The role allotted to Margaret Thatcher in this revolution was not only minor but, in a sense, counter-revolutionary. The revolution was anti-collectivist and pro-business, and was therefore dependent, among other things, on a new and vigilant hostility to public spending. Mrs Thatcher, appointed Secretary of State for Education and Science, was put in charge of one of the fastest-expanding budgets in the public sector and showed not the smallest inclination to curtail its growth.

She moved into the post directly from her last shadow job, which Heath had given her barely six months earlier. Thereby hung a tale which provided some evidence of her right-wing credentials. The post had been held for some time by Edward Boyle, a conspicuous apostle of the sixties' consensus and a man who had an increasingly hard time from Conservative Party conferences for his wetly acquiescent attitude to socialist policies, especially the conversion of grammar schools into comprehensives. Heath, although a natural ally of Boyle's from the Macmillan wing of the party, was sensitive to these stirrings, especially as the comprehensive plague reached into the Tory shires. He did not actually ask Boyle to quit, but when Boyle sought the promise of a bigger job in government – he had already been Minister of Education from 1962 to 1964 – the leader demurred.

Boyle's departure from politics in 1969, to become Vice-Chancellor of Leeds University, aroused surprisingly few regrets in the Heath circle. Intellectual brilliance and past association evidently meant little. It was with positive pleasure that Heath offered his shadow post to a belligerent, hard-working performer fully in tune, as it was thought, with grass-root Tory activists opposed to the comprehensive system. She received an accolade from a Labour minister. 'She is rather a pal of mine,' Richard Crossman wrote in his diary when she displaced Boyle. 'I got on very well with her when she was at Pensions, and she is one of the few Tories I greet in the lobby. She is tough, able and competent and, unlike Boyle, she will be a kind of professional Opposition spokesman.'

There was never much doubt that Heath would send her to Education once the election was won. By sheer drive and competence she had forced her way up the shadow list during the life of the Wilson Government. Besides, a cabinet without a woman would have been deemed to lack a necessary token, and no other Tory woman was anywhere near as able as she was: in 1970, in fact, only one other woman got a job in the entire Government. But Mrs Thatcher was much more than the statutory female. At that time Heath's regard for her personal qualities surmounted his natural prejudice against all women politicians, and was yet unsullied by any particular distaste for the Thatcher style. He viewed her as diligent, reliable and fully in accord with his view of government purposes: a fit colleague, in fact, to march with him on the road to a new Conservative world.

Her time at the Department of Education and Science was her ministerial grounding, the only cabinet post she held before becoming prime minister. This was not for want of trying to escape. Aware that it wasn't a mainline political job, she began to hanker for promotion, or at least a sideways shift into a department closer to the centre after a couple of years in the job. Norman St John Stevas, her junior minister at the time, retained a clear memory of this impatience.

But Heath was as stubborn as she was and kept her where she was. He had by then become fatigued by her hectoring behaviour and was determined to corral it within a department whose business touched that of relatively few others. Her years there were therefore unbroken. They were her sole ministerial apprenticeship. The lineaments of her true political personality, later to be magnified many times over, now began to expose themselves fully for the first time.

This preparation was formative in three ways especially. The first was the discovery it permitted her to make of both the limits and the huge potential of a minister's power. A minister has to accept that certain enduring realities may be impossible to change. But a minister, equally, can sometimes gratify personal prejudices, so long as these are clearly worked out, with little intervention from anyone else. Power as a means of acting out personal convictions, especially those rooted in personal experience, has always been a Thatcher hallmark. The DES is where it was first sighted.

Much of the education agenda was already set when she arrived there. At the top of it were the comprehensive schools, and the Conservative commitment, which she wholly endorsed, to liberate local authorities from any compulsion to make them supersede the grammar schools. She observed this commitment, as Heath (and Boyle) had pledged the party to, by formally withdrawing the departmental instruction that had gone out to local authorities under the Labour Government.

But this made strangely little difference. Comprehensivisation had a powerful momentum behind it. Many schools, parents and local electors actually wanted it. The minister could not stand in their way if they came forward with sensible schemes for accomplishing the shift. In her first thirty-two months in office, Mrs Thatcher received 2,765 schemes for consideration, and rejected fewer than 5 per cent of them. It is the case, therefore, that, for all her strong prejudices against them, which continued to come out years later in her more general denunciations of the slackness of British secondary education in the 1980s, Margaret Thatcher approved more schemes for comprehensive schools, and the abolition of more grammar schools, than any other Secretary of State before or since.

Later she sought to excuse this, implying that she had been up against entrenched conventional wisdom which prevented her from doing what she really wanted to do – retain and even expand the grammar schools. Wapshott and Brock quote a recollection she offered in 1983: 'There was a great battle on. It was part of this equalisation rage at the time, that you mustn't select by ability. After all, I had come up by selection by ability. I had to fight it. I had a terrible time.' But the record speaks for itself. If she had a terrible time in this area of policy, it was because she fought and lost. She knew how much she disliked huge, all-ability schools, and yet she approved them.

Although rarely heard to praise a comprehensive, she bowed before the spirit of the age.

In other areas, she was less trammelled by fashion or commitment. Resources, obviously, were a major limitation. Before the first Heath budget, Education was widely tipped as a likely target for cuts of £300 million, a large sum in those days. She successfully resisted most of these. But more to the point was her ability, taking her tenure as a whole, to impose her own priorities within the budget, securing such agreement as was necessary but essentially taking a personal stride beyond the directives of the election manifesto. She fought, to take one small example, to preserve the Open University, which was scheduled to start up within months of the election. It had been nominated for extinction by none other than Iain Macleod, a hero in the pantheon of progressive Conservatism and Heath's first Chancellor of the Exchequer.

Macleod tragically died within days of the election, but left behind a kind of last testament which acquired a special sanctity from the untimely death of its author. He was firm that the Open University, the great socialist opportunity for the part-time student to graduate via television classes, must go. But Mrs Thatcher, who was motivated, according to George Gardiner, by 'her strong belief in giving educational opportunity to those prepared to work for it', kept it alive.

A more telling example of her personal prejudices at work was the priority she tried to give to nursery schooling. This did not appear in any early list of party promises. The Tories were pledged to raise the school-leaving age, which she tenaciously defended. They became heavily committed to building new primary schools, with plans to knock down thousands of Victorian buildings. This commitment called forth a Thatcher onslaught against public squalor that would have done credit to the best of socialists. 'A lot of these very old buildings', she told Gardiner in 1975,

> were in areas where the children tended to have a poor home background. Then you often found that these bad school buildings also had bad equipment, and that it was very difficult to get teachers to go there. So these children suffered a triple deprivation, lacking a decent home, proper school buildings and enough good teachers. If only you could give them a good school then this gave them some experience of a nice building and good conditions.

What fired the Education Secretary to still greater heights of munificence, however, was the need for pre-school education. Typically she drew on personal experience to justify this. In due course the entire national economy was to be run by a mistress of household economics. From 1970 schools policy was run by one who thought she knew all about it from the evidence of her own motherhood. 'I sent my two children to a nursery school, just a couple of hours each morning,' she said in 1972 when introducing *Framework for Expansion*, the document which made the nursery-school commitment, 'and this is something that should be available to all who want it.' While the state can never take the place of good parents, she added, 'it can help redress the balance of those born unlucky.' Her plans were ambitious – nursery provision for 50 per cent of three-year-olds and 90 per cent of four-year-olds.

Like everything else in the field of public and private finance, these plans were heavily affected by the oil shock of 1973. In fact, thanks to the quadrupling of oil prices, almost nothing came of them. But, as a preference, they throw light on Mrs Thatcher's character. This was certainly the view of her permanent secretary at the time.

He was Sir William Pile, one of the abler officials in the history of this neglected department. Pile saw the Thatcher interest in nursery schools as expressing essentially a political choice. 'She thought all children should be given a chance at the beginning of their life to prosper. If they failed thereafter, then they had had their chance.' This stark opinion was matched, according to Pile, by her lack of serious interest in expansion at the other end of the system. At that stage, elitism ruled. She was in favour of grammar schools, of the better universities, of the Science and Medical Research Councils.

To her they seemed to be the places where the best and most intelligent of minds would find themselves if the system worked. The top 25 per cent of the ability range would go to the grammar schools, the top 2 per cent of the eighteen-year-olds would fetch up in the universities, and all the best researchers in the hard elite sciences in those two Research Councils – though definitely not the Social Science Research Council or the Environmental Research Council, which she regarded as pseudo-sciences.[1]

The minister did not have an exclusive voice in expressing such biases. In the case of the Open University, a powerful departmental lobby pushed for its preservation. *Framework for Expansion*, like other white papers, was a document of ideas long in the making among official educationalists. But Mrs Thatcher was proud of what it promised. 'When it talked about expansion it meant expansion and not contraction,' she told the Schools Council in 1973. It foreshadowed a rise in spending in real terms of 50 per cent in the next decade. The Thatcher white paper was, remarkably, the last great expansionist package to issue from the DES before the oil shock and a series of public spending crises, followed by the blight of penury and then an ideology of contraction settled over Britain during the next fifteen years.

Alongside this lesson that a minister could get her way if she tried hard enough, Mrs Thatcher had a second instructive experience at the DES. She learned that there were times when people who were supposed to serve her did everything in their power to obstruct her purposes. Already nurtured at the dull old Ministry of Pensions, the notorious Thatcher hostility to the civil service, a compound of suspicion, incomprehension and sheer disregard for what they were in business to be and do, deepened into an indelible obsession.

Pile was her first adversary. He remembered combat starting early. From the moment she entered the department, she engaged in a battle for ascendancy. 'Within the first ten minutes of her arrival she uncovered two things to us,' Pile recalled. 'One is what I would call an innate wariness of the civil service, quite possibly even a distrust. And secondly a page from an exercise book with eighteen things she wanted done that day.' After years spent in mostly agreeable concord with Labour education ministers, this was a new experience for the DES: 'the beginnings of the revelation of a character that we'd have to get used to and hadn't run into before'.[2]

An elaborate minuet, halfway between a courtship ritual and a dance of death, began to be acted out. Pile knew perfectly well that the list of eighteen instant demands was a try-on. But he insisted, in recollection, that the important items were attended to immediately. Point one was the new instruction to local authorities, saying that they could disregard Labour's directive on comprehensives and retain their grammar schools. 'She had the draft of that circular on her desk that night. She said "Action this day" and she got it. We didn't stop to argue.'

On the other hand, the department declined to abandon what it saw as its duty. Seen through the eyes of a zealous minister, this was construed as a duty to obstruct. As described by Pile, it reeks of the somewhat patronising superiority which Whitehall has traditionally marshalled against an uppity minister it suspects of having half-baked ideas. His memory summons up many an acrid scene.

> We followed our old traditional course of speaking up for what the Department has always done or what we thought the Department should do, as opposed to what ministers were going to tell us to do. She thought that some of us were being obstructive. I regarded it as a necessary professional job to be done up to the point when the minister said to you that we're going to do the opposite. In which case I think we touched our forelocks and said 'Yes, Ma'am.'

The minister's problem, Pile thought, was that she didn't want advice from anyone. He recalls her 'stubborn refusal to acknowledge some facts and arguments that we put forward'. But this, naturally, was not the way it seemed to her. She thought it was all Pile's fault.

Even though he was one of Whitehall's higher fliers, a permanent secretary at the young age of fifty, she even made a spirited attempt to get him removed from the DES, citing a reason that went beyond obstructionism to much darker suspicions. At the height of one of her rows with Pile she went to see the civil service minister, Lord Jellicoe. In front of Jellicoe she broke down in tears. Not only Pile but Pile's wife were left-wing political sympathisers, she moaned to Jellicoe.

To her friend John Vaizey, a journalist–academic who specialised in education, she offered an even more fantastic view, complaining that 'it is rather difficult having a permanent secretary who is a security risk.' She insisted to Jellicoe that she be found a new permanent secretary, and pressed him to arrange this with the prime minister. But Ted Heath refused her demand, following the advice of the head of the civil service, Sir William Armstrong. His Education Secretary had to soldier on in uncongenial company, an experience she did not forget when she herself became the supreme arbiter of Whitehall postings after 1979.

Pile himself was far less bitter. Mandarins, from their lofty perch, can usually afford to be. He marked Mrs Thatcher's card quite favourably. 'She worked to all hours of the day and night. She always emptied her box, with blue pencil marks all over the papers. Every single piece of paper was attended to.' She was also a completely reliable performer. 'She was always a very good trouper, always meticulous about turning up for meetings. If she said she'd be there at two minutes past six, she'd be there at two minutes past six.'

Additionally, she had the great merit – supreme in the eyes of the department – of winning her most important arguments with the Treasury. Every spending department loves a minister who can do that.

But she did not repay the compliment. The DES never enjoyed much esteem in her eyes. Much later, she did come to value a few members of the species civil servant. The high-class officials who surrounded her in 10 Downing Street became her closest advisers, most admired associates, most intimate colleagues, closer to her, many observers noted, than all but a handful of politicians. At the DES, none entered that category. They were responsible, she thought, not only for clinging unreasonably to the wisdom they knew best but for serious lapses in their task as advisers to the minister.

The most conspicuous example of this, she thought, was the incident that first made her a truly famous national politician. It originated, in fact, in another item from Iain Macleod's last testament, which ordained that free milk should no longer be handed out to older primary schoolchildren, from eight to eleven years old. This was a welfare cut worth £8 million a year. But the damage it did to Mrs Thatcher's reputation, if this could have been quantified, must have added up to many times that figure.

It was an absurd issue on which to enter the national demonology. Plenty of free milk had already been cut by Labour governments – from all secondary schools, for example. There was much bogus talk about the damage Mrs Thatcher was personally inflicting on the health of underprivileged youngsters whom she claimed, in other guises, to care so much about. 'Thatcher the Milk Snatcher' made an irresistible taunt, appealing as much to the tabloid press as to Opposition politicians. And somehow it struck a deeper chord. It was a piece of seemingly gratuitous deprivation that conformed with the image of severity and adamant righteousness which was beginning to become Mrs Thatcher's stock-in-trade.

Lurking somewhere in this mix, both in her projection of herself and in the bitterly derisive responses she was capable of arousing, was the fact of her gender. For a woman to have taken the milk from the mouths of needy innocents was somehow especially wicked. The episode was an early instance of a continuing phenomenon: the anxieties and resentments, the over-compensation and the underestimation, flowing from her sex.

To her at the time, however, the milk row had an entirely different moral. It was proof positive of her civil servants' incompetence, and possibly their malevolence. She had plunged into the trap, she thought, insufficiently alerted to the state of feeling among teachers and local politicians, to say nothing of parents. It had burned her far more than she ever expected. She saw paid-for milk as one way of protecting the education budget for what really mattered. The department, she thought, had exposed her to being called by the *Sun* (then not the rabidly Tory newspaper it later became) 'The Most Unpopular Woman in Britain'. So exhausted was she by defending herself that this became the first occasion, though not the last, when Denis Thatcher, fearing for her health and unable to bear the insults to which she was subjected, suggested that she might even think of getting out of politics altogether. Not for the first time, she showed she was made of sterner stuff than he.

Pile's recollection is again different. He declines to accept the blame. If this was a failure at all, it was a political failure. Besides, it blooded the neophyte. 'I think it did hurt her. It was the first time she'd received stick of this kind. It did get home, but she would never reveal it in public. Like all things, it started callousing her, and she built up a protective skin. She learned that she had to.'

It was Pile's estimation, however, that this is not an experience for which she felt any gratitude to her civil servants. Her suspicion of the civil service, he thought, had increased rather than diminished in her years under his tutelage. 'We were dealing with someone who basically felt we were not on her side,' he recalled. Her own later verdict on the period was not essentially different. 'Iron entered my soul,' she said.

The third dimension of her time at the DES was to have an even more ironclad permanence. The discovery, on the one hand, of ministerial power and, on the other, of the restraints placed upon it by the civil service and their inherited ideas was important in her apprenticeship. But the experience of collective cabinet government and the sacrifices that had to be made to it was decisive. It touched many ministers in the Heath Government, to their discomfort. Margaret Thatcher was prominent among them.

The Government came in, as we have seen, with a clear programme designed to regenerate the economy. It did not eschew state intervention to achieve this, but was fired by several highly visible anti-collectivist ideas. In line with its pledges, it duly dismantled such 'corporatist' agencies as the Industrial Reorganisation Corporation and the Prices and Incomes Board. It was determined to slash government support for industry, and committed itself to letting 'lame duck' companies go to the wall. It preached with equal fervour against the iniquities of a statutory prices and incomes policy.

This policy did not survive. No sooner had the Government announced the full measure of its hard-faced industrial policy at the 1970 party conference than special reasons began to be found to justify saving special lame ducks. Rolls-Royce aero-engines' division was rescued by nationalisation in early 1971. Not long after that Upper Clyde Shipbuilders had its subsidies restored after being threatened with closure.

These rescues were entirely in line with the kind of compromises commonplace in the 1960s, in the face of economic disaster or union militancy. But from a government that had made extravagant pledges to do the opposite, they were bewildering concessions. They began a spiral back towards something close to the norms the Tories had sworn to obliterate: a process culminating in the Industry Act 1972, which created sweeping new interventionist powers for the Department of Trade and Industry to spend more on industrial projects of its own choosing. And in a parallel reversion to the past, another statute passed later in 1972 took legal powers to control all increases in pay, prices and dividends. In its search for growth and industrial regeneration, the Heath Government thereby showed itself, within two years of taking office, unable to resist the influences – convictions might not be too strong a word, even though they ran counter to the convictions of a few years before   impelling it to take central control, both over a sizeable lump of investment and over the whole of prices and incomes.

This experience, the famous U-turn which Heath was never allowed to forget, became a seminal event in the history of late-twentieth-century Conservatism. It was planted ineradicably in the minds not only of those who later displaced Heath from the leadership but, much more crucially, of the Thatcher Government itself. The U-turn took on the status of a demon, and its perpetrator was still regarded many years later as the devil incarnate: the man who had surrendered his belief to short-term expediency, caving in to pressure he should have resisted, and betraying the principles on which the election had been fought and won. During the Thatcher years, avoiding a repetition of this particular Heath disaster became a key determinant of policy, even to the extent of rendering any policy option unacceptable which Heath had ever been associated with.

Elucidating this through Mrs Thatcher's own intellectual development is, however, a puzzling exercise. Was she, as this might imply, a true believer led astray by an overmighty prime minister into paths she never wanted to follow? Was she a silent, or perhaps even an outspoken, private critic of events whose wrongheadedness later became central to her own claim on the party? Or did she support them, more or less without complaint, throughout the life of the Heath Government?

It will be the end of the century before these intriguing questions can be answered by reference to contemporary cabinet documents. Meanwhile we have to be content with fugitive strands of memories which are all prone to retrospective self-vindication. Drawn from these, however, certain objective facts are worth recording.

The Heath Government was a genuine collective. Its pre-election policies were fashioned by numerous policy committees reporting to the shadow cabinet, which produced a manifesto that conformed with remarkable precision to the collective opinion about the right way forward. There were no significant factions at that early time, as was best witnessed by the abrasive nature of Iain Macleod's last testament. Macleod, R. A. Butler's heir as the leader of the left of the party, was if anything more hard-headed than some of his colleagues (Maudling, for example) in the priority he wanted for cuts in public spending.

Once in government, furthermore, the Heath cabinet behaved as a collectivity. It has a serious claim to be called the last which respected the constitutional rules defining how British government ought to work. In public it presented a united front, something which in later years, under all prime ministers, fell out of fashion. The Wilson and Callaghan governments, just like Wilson's earlier governments so lovingly laid bare by Dick Crossman, were prone to splits and rows in pursuit of which ministers leaked against each other constantly. The Thatcher Government exhibited the same propensity throughout its first two terms, enjoying brief periods of public comity (in late 1981 and 1983, for example) which were entirely atypical of an administration that lived and often almost died by public argument. The Heath Government was never like that.

This remained true during the period of the U-turns. Such comprehensive reversals as the Industry Act and the statutory pay freeze would, in other governments, have precipitated a deluge of recriminations, if they had not been impeded altogether by well-timed leaks of sensitive documents. When the Heath cabinet agreed them, the water on the pond was barely seen to ripple. This was in spite of the devices sometimes used to secure the changes. Two junior Industry ministers did depart over the Industry Act. One of them, Nicholas

Ridley, later revealed in the House of Commons that the Act 'was not prepared in the Department of Trade and Industry at all, and no minister in that department knew about it.'[3] It was an imposition from Downing Street. But no senior minister, however close they had been to the rhetoric which had so recently said such measures should not be passed, indicated public dissent. Ridley himself, along with Sir John Eden, did leave – 'I am the only junior minister to have resigned on a matter of principle,' he told the *Observer* in December 1985, when he had risen to the cabinet under Mrs Thatcher. (This was probably a self-serving overstatement; Heath always contended that Ridley was fired.) At the time, such open alienation from the policy was considered eccentric.

There remain the private opinions of Mrs Thatcher, and those who were later her closest henchmen in discovering these years to have been a catastrophe. She herself has said next to nothing about them. As George Gardiner wrote, rather demurely: 'She still refuses to talk of the discussions that went on in Cabinet at that time, since she is bound by the rule of confidentiality.' Her own main public statement, which was made during her contest for the leadership in 1974, has the finality yet also something of the evasive inadequacy, reminiscent of the public confessions of Maoist cadres during the Chinese Cultural Revolution. 'For past errors, in Government and Opposition,' she wrote, 'I accept my full share of collective responsibility.'

We can do a little better than that. A few contemporary witnesses have offered their own recollections. One was Sir William Pile, who has described his minister as almost wholly preoccupied with her own departmental work. 'I think in the four years in the Department she showed very little interest in anything outside the Department's brief,' he said.[4]

In other words, if errors were being committed she was not involved, not even, because of the endless rush of departmental work, properly acquainted with what was going on. Apologists like Gardiner reinforce this by observing correctly that she was not a member of the key economic committees of the cabinet and thus was not in possession of 'the detail on which often fine judgments were based'.

Another snapshot produces a different angle. It is of Margaret Thatcher the public spender. The Heath Government had the conventional Tory intention to cut public spending. And when 'Thatcherism' ruled the land, public spending cuts were an obsessive annual event, the very hub around which much of the political debate turned. At the DES, however, she was a determined spender. She fought ruthlessly to expand her budget, and was very successful until 1973. Peering back in 1985, her colleague James Prior recalled a figure who, in that government, pressed the merits of neither of her subsequent economic nostrums. 'It would be quite wrong to think that she was against public expenditure,' Prior said, 'or that she made great remarks about the increase in the money supply in 1972 and 1973. In fact she and Keith Joseph were the big spenders in the Heath Administration. They were always asking for more.'[5]

In those areas, therefore, the distance between the earlier and the later Thatcher has been substantial. This was no frustrated monetarist, bleakly suffering under the whip of a prime minister insanely spending his way to growth and public service expansion. She was an enthusiastic exponent of that policy insofar as it could be expressed through her own department.

On another part of the board, she does seem to have presented some slight resistance to Heath's convoluted progress. The statutory prices and incomes policy, finally agreed by the cabinet on 6 November 1972, was the largest of all its retreats from the original plan, and the pitfalls were a source of anxiety to the Education Secretary, according to both Prior and Francis Pym. Along with some others, she warned against the dangers. But she did not actively oppose them. Nobody did. Even during its humiliation, this remained a united cabinet, in private as well as in public.

Perhaps the clearest evidence of Mrs Thatcher's true state of mind comes from a very open source. Her closest friend in the cabinet was Sir Keith Joseph. He was not as close then as he later became, but he offers some suggestive insights. To know him, one has good reason to believe, is largely to know her.

Immediately after the election defeat in 1974, they began to exchange a common analysis of what had gone wrong. It was, as they have both testified, a shared journey of discovery. Usefully, Sir Keith began performing this in public and without delay.

His assessment was radical, but significantly it proposed no recriminations. We are all guilty, he said in June 1974. Far from Heath having led anyone astray, there had been a continuum between his Government and its socialist predecessor, of which nobody in the cabinet had been properly aware. The post-war era was to be seen as a unity. 'For thirty years,' Joseph declared, 'the private sector of our economy has been forced to work with one hand tied behind its back by government and unions.' For thirty years, likewise, state spending had been too great, defunct industries had been endlessly kept alive, and social peace had been bought at the expense of economic efficiency.

Sir Keith, in short, now made a shattering discovery. He had joined the Conservative Party twenty years earlier, but had not been a Conservative. 'It was only in April 1974 that I was converted to Conservatism,' he wrote. 'I had thought that I was a Conservative, but I now see I was not really one at all.'[6]

Such public and explicit acts of repentance have not been Margaret Thatcher's style. She never made a recapitulation of error, even though much of her later career has repudiated her earlier life. And it should be said that in this respect it is Joseph rather than she who is plainly the aberrant case among professional politicians. It is safe also to say, however, that Sir Keith spoke for her, at a time when she herself said little. As he suggested, they simply had not known what they were doing when they were in government. They had ploughed on regardless, scarcely looking to see which furrow they were working.

The refinements of this process cannot be known until more of the participants break silence. What precisely became of each minister's vision as they made their compromises with events will no doubt be studied with particular relish, as the documents become available, by all who suffered from the denunciations of the Thatcherites in the later 1970s. But two conclusions already seem inescapable.

One is that if the body of liberal economic ideas later known as Thatcherism already existed in the Conservative Party from 1965 onwards, it was a puny growth. It had no roots and carried only the feeblest conviction. If either Margaret Thatcher or Keith Joseph were exponents of it in the late 1960s, they surrendered it with remarkable speed when the going got difficult.

Robert Blake, likening the Heath policies to the Thatcher policies and remarking on the failure of the former to survive, has written by way of explanation: 'Heath did not have what Margaret Thatcher had – the backing of an intellectual revolution.' It would be more to the point to observe that the intellects of the participants themselves had not then been sufficiently steeped in the revolutionary juice. It was not simply a case of Heath and Joseph and the rest of them being ahead of their time. On the contrary, along with everybody who mattered in the Tory Party, they were still committed to many of the assumptions of the sixties and were seduced within months of taking office by the attractions of sixties solutions.

It follows from this, secondly, that the images of betrayal in which these years have so often been portrayed are mostly a convenient fantasy. By his shifts and turns Heath betrayed nothing – because there was no significant body of opinion in the party that wanted him to do anything else. Least of all did he betray the cabinet colleagues who later used betrayal as a pretext for rounding on him. They acquiesced in everything he did, only discovering later, in Joseph's graphic words, how they might be 'converted to Conservatism'.

Where Heath and Joseph differed after February 1974 – and, along with Joseph, his acolyte Margaret Thatcher – was not essentially in their description of the past. It was how they analysed its meaning for the future. Here they came to the great divide of post-war Conservative politics.

7

Heroine of the Peasants

THE YEAR 1974 encompassed the long-drawn-out death throes of Edward Heath's Conservative Party. This is not the way it seemed at the time. Like all political parties, Heath's behaved as if it could win again after losing the February election. Its margin of defeat was narrow enough – Labour 310 seats, Conservative 296, Liberal 14, others 20 – to make this arithmetically credible. The commitment of party and leader was absolute, the more so given Heath's unalterable belief that he had been beaten by accident. It wasn't the miners who had brought him down by their challenge to his authority. Industrial action in the pits was the pretext on which the election was called, but in his opinion only a series of chance events and interventions during a volatile campaign caused him to lose it. He thought he could win again. When he saw the inflationary spiral Labour immediately released by giving the miners all they wanted, he thought he had every right to. So did almost every Conservative. There was no significant party pressure on Heath to resign. At least until October, when Labour won again with an overall majority of three, few could see February's destruction as the seminal event it later became.

Margaret Thatcher was no more percipient than most others about the nature of what had occurred. A year later, when she had deposed Heath, there were those who contended that she had warned in cabinet against the events which precipitated the miners' strike and hence the February defeat. As part of the attempt to discover consistency in the career of a new leader who was above all principled and undeviating, her role in many other of Heath's aberrations was depicted as distant if not downright critical.[1]

There is no evidence for this. No first-hand participant has come forward to attest to it. Of the February election she herself put forward an analysis identical with Heath's, namely that the result was a gallant misfortune. 'We went to the country on a point of principle,' she told Gardiner, 'and all the signs at the start were that the country was

81

with us on it.' What had swung things against the Government, she said, was a report from the Pay Board on the relativity of miners' pay to the pay of comparable workers, which suddenly cut the ground of principle from under the Government.

Until the documents are published, in 2004, it will be difficult to disentangle truth from special pleading about the stance ministers took at this time. That is the price of the remarkable and genuine collective responsibility the Heath Government sustained until the very end. But there is no reason to suppose that this united public stance conceals an untold story of bitter argument. Only one important difference has emerged, over the election date. Should it have been a week or two earlier? For the rest, the cabinet was dominated by events. The fact that these originated in a statutory incomes policy became grounds for recrimination only later. Well before February 1974, every member was hooked on a policy which loyalty and self-interest bound them to support, Mrs Thatcher and Sir Keith Joseph no less than all the others.

Mrs Thatcher easily held Finchley, and Heath immediately gave her the shadow Environment portfolio, charging her with the creation of a new housing policy. With rates and mortgages rising, householders had felt especially deserted by the party of wider property-ownership. Knowledgeable about local finance, she was a sensible choice. In four months she put together a radical package for shadow cabinet approval, including large tax inducements to home ownership, tenants' rights to buy their council houses, and the abolition of the rates. This was a dramatic programme, given added colour on the eve of the October election by a studiously theatrical personal pledge from the shadow minister to fix mortgage interest at 9½ per cent.

In the evolution of the Thatcher political profile, however, this marks a more ambiguous moment than at first appears. It shows how cautious was her break with Heathism, and how misleading are those accounts which present her as having spent her years in office in wretched repression, with all her deepest libertarian principles shrouded in forced loyalty. It also shows the emergence of a singularly 'political' politician, well able to depart, where necessary, from what she personally believed to be right.

For what was the mortgage-interest pledge but a naked piece of interventionism, suppressing the free play of market forces by the creation of an artificial tax device to the benefit of building societies? And how could the pledge to abolish the rates be seriously defended before any alternative had been worked out to put in their place? Both suggestions offended Mrs Thatcher's instincts. Nor was the pledge to sell council houses something she welcomed, still less invented. Heath's own recollection, confirmed by others, was of her arguing that it would not be fair to people who had already saved to buy their own homes. 'What will they say on my Wates estates?' became her cry.

The truth is that none of these were really her ideas. They were the result, originally, of Heath's own desperation. After the election, he had visited Canada among other places, and been told by prime minister Pierre Trudeau, a brilliantly successful electoral politician, that what he needed were some good populist ideas to excite the electorate. Abolishing the rates certainly qualified on that score, but his shadow spokesman demurred. Those present at Heath's house when they fought the issue out recall a hard argument in which she stood her ground, just as she did over 9½ per cent mortgages. But when he insisted – and this is what impressed the witnesses – she surrendered to his view, and led the campaign for both policies with real panache. The zest she brought to policies she fundamentally disapproved of was held to have been an important blooding: satisfactory proof that she was learning to be a real politician.

However, it was the tide of history, moving deep and only half perceived, that now propelled events in her direction. This was more powerful than any instant contributions to policy she might or might not make. The awareness of a political crisis in Conservatism may have been granted to only a small handful of people during the months of 1974. Most senior politicians, including her, were fully preoccupied with the task of positioning the party for an election they knew was imminent. But the crisis did have one prophet who strove to articulate it in a fuller way. And, in its last twitches before finally succumbing to five years of a Labour government, the party was driven by Heath into a corner from which there was no escape except by a radical break with the past.

Margaret Thatcher, picking away at the minutiae of a housing policy, was silent on the past. Keith Joseph, her friend, was not. He now embarked on a public re-examination of what the Heath Government and its predecessors had done, the process which led him after a mere few weeks' study to announce that he was now at last converted to 'Conservatism'.

Joseph was the ideal pathfinder. It was fitting and predictable that he should do the job. Recantation, with its associated endless agonising beforehand, was in his temperament. He had done it several times before, and was always ready to make it appear as though his entire career in government, which stretched back to 1959, had been a record of disasters great and small.

Joseph was a wealthy man, formerly chairman of Bovis the builders, the family firm, and he was a second-generation baronet. He was also an intellectual, and, that relative rarity in the political class, a Fellow of All Souls. But these secure props did not fortify many fixed beliefs. Rather the reverse. He was intensely interested in ideas, but unable to sustain over a long enough time the belief that any one set of them was correct. For short periods such certainties could sometimes be assembled, often with disastrously permanent results. One of the recantations he was wont to make in the 1970s concerned his role, when Minister of Housing and Local Government in the Macmillan Administration, as the political architect of high-rise council flats. These were then modish, but later became accursed by all who lived in them. Unfortunately, the buildings could not be dismantled quite so easily as Sir Keith's support for them; but, unusually for a politician, this did not deter him from publicly confessing that he had been wrong.

During 1974, the same began to happen to Joseph's opinion of his part in the Heath Government. As a man of ideas he had been particularly involved in the formulation of Heath's alternative to socialism in 1965. He was the personal creator, for example, of the welfare strategy that was designed to be based on the principle of 'selectivity' – the stage of his thinking when I first met him. Having played so formative a part in the theory, he was especially tormented in 1974 as he set about reviewing his contribution to the practice. But, as a man of ideas, he also correctly saw how modest had been the notions with which Heath entered office, let alone those he finished up with as prime minister. Joseph's denunciations of the past made no exception for Heath's early years. The 'thirty years of socialistic fashion' which he lamented in June 1974 were an unbroken continuum. When he said, 'We are now more socialist in many ways than any other developed country outside the Communist bloc, in the size of the public sector, the range of controls and the telescoping of net income,' he was offering a brutal challenge, less than four months after leaving office, to everything of economic significance the Heath Government had attempted.

This was done under the guise of attacking Labour, and in particular the interventionist zeal of the new Industry Secretary, Tony Benn.

But it was a thin cover. As befitted one of the serious men in politics, who searched to correlate all his actions with some inner impulse of belief, Joseph spared no one, least of all himself, in his quest for a new and proper synthesis. Public spending had simply become too great – and he was as responsible for this as anyone. 'We have inherited a mixed economy which has become increasingly muddled, as we tried our best to make semi-socialism work,' he reflected with evident pain. He thought agnosticism and market forces were now the only decent gods to follow. The special Heathite deity of economic growth must now be toppled. 'During thirty years we have tried to force the pace of growth. Growth is welcome, but we just do not know how to accelerate its pace. Perhaps faster growth, like happiness, should not be a prime target but only a by-product of other policies.'

Joseph has described some of the personal pressures behind this earliest contribution to the impending Conservative divide. In the last months of government, some of his friends were so disgusted with him that they sent him to Coventry. 'When I went back to pick up old friendships,' he recalled, 'I found that Alan Walters, for example, was very scornful, scarcely willing to talk to one because of what, from his understandable point of view, was a shameful failure to perceive error.'[2] Walters, a professor of economics at the London School of Economics, was one of the most prominent British monetarist theoreticians, and had been a fringe acquaintance of Joseph's during earlier years in opposition.[3] Other friends were more constructive. 'One particular friend, Alfred Sherman, kept on emphasising to me that Keynes was dead and you can make more problems by trying to print your way out of difficulties than you solve.'

There was no bitterness in Joseph's fusillade against the Government he had been a part of. Stoical mortification was closer to the tone of it. All the same, it was odd that this indictment should have come from a party officer in good standing. Joseph was still a member of the leadership team, appointed by Heath to a policy-making role. He paraded his stricken conscience, with mounting fervour, as a lieutenant of the leader he was implicitly attacking. But he did so with a special licence Heath had given him, to explore international experience of free-market policies. And it was on this slender footing that Margaret Thatcher first openly declared herself an ally, albeit a reticent one, of Joseph's emerging intellectual onslaught.

The vehicle put together to make his authorised comparative

researches was the Centre for Policy Studies, a venture at first approved by Heath but later to become a focus of vicious attack and counter-attack between the Heath and Thatcher camps. Heath permitted the CPS to exist with official blessing and with Joseph's central involvement on condition that it did not drain funds and effort away from the party proper. Joseph gave the necessary assurances. Only later did Heath discover, so he said, that the promise was breached and the CPS was touting successfully for funds among the party's traditional business sources. Instead of a harmlessly academic role – looking at the differences between European, Japanese and American economies had been Joseph's supposed purpose – it soon emerged as a hard-edged rival to the party's own Research Department. This was treachery, Heath thought. And it remained for ever after close to the top of a lengthy list of complaints against those who removed him from office, on which he spent so much time brooding for the next decade and beyond.

Margaret Thatcher was the only other shadow minister to involve herself openly with the CPS in its early days. She became a vice-chairman, thereby making her first delicate commitment against the mainline leadership. She did not write anything for the CPS. Her connection, in fact, brought to the minds of several lifelong adherents of the intellectual right just how episodic, in earlier years, her own attachment to their thinking had been.

No doubt she was at heart a rightist. In a perfect world she would favour free-market economics. She was instinctively anti-collectivist. But these 'principles' had been overlaid by the years in power. Her complete absorption with office left her little time for wider thought and no inclination for rebellion. Besides, until 1974, the hinge year for her as well as her party, she had shown only a flimsy interest in the complexities of ideology. Her own most spacious essay into the field, the 1968 CPC lecture, revealed a jejune and amateurish grasp. At the Institute of Economic Affairs, the free-market pressure-group started in the 1950s, which has a large claim to be the earliest inventor of 'Thatcherism', she was remembered as only an occasional visitor. Lord Harris of High Cross, co-founder of the IEA and justly ennobled by a prime minister much in his debt, saw more of Joseph than of her. 'We saw a great deal of Keith Joseph,' Harris said. 'It goes back to 1974 when he began to approach us about definitive advice on reading. He would go away with piles of books under his arm. Mrs Thatcher certainly isn't someone I can recall who ever came in to buy the latest Hobart Paper, as Keith would do.'[4]

To Harris it was 'entirely through Keith Joseph' that the future leader came to ponder the IEA's output, and hence to educate herself in liberal economics. And thus only thanks to him that she might have conceded as he did (if she had been the conceding type) how late it was before she, too, experienced a miraculous conversion to true 'Conservatism'.

Installed as director of the CPS was Alfred Sherman, Joseph's candid but constructive friend. He became Margaret Thatcher's friend too. For a time theirs was a most intimate and fruitful relationship, one of the key connections of the period. It flourished most after her election as leader of the Conservative Party. But already before that it mattered, not least because Sherman was so typical of the kind of people – anti-Heath by passionate conviction, and almost anti-party in their rejection of most of the post-war norms of Conservatism – already making themselves available as the clerks and footsoldiers of an intellectual revolution.

Sherman was a journalist who had drifted into the somewhat ill-defined role of an 'adviser' in the half-world between the public and private sectors. But if an interest in ideas qualifies a man for the title of intellectual, Sherman was that as well. Small of stature and insistent of speech, he had once been a Communist. Leaving the party in 1948, he first transferred to Labour but then swung, for no better reason than a desire to get into local politics around 1970, into the Conservative camp.

With part of him Sherman prided himself on not being a true party man, but he soon made the complete cross-over from far left to far right, thus identifying himself in one particular as the forerunner of many others who were to enter the Thatcher circle. He was a convert. He knew about conviction from both ends of the political spectrum. He was now as zealous in his pursuit of the collectivist demon, including its most acceptable Western interpreter, Keynes, as he had once been diligent in the defence of Karl Marx. Sherman could discourse for hours on the folly of Heath's extravagant public spending and his lunatic indifference to market laws. He also had a strong line in the rhetoric of immigration, being prepared to say and write things about the influx of ethnic minorities which most people, including most Conservatives, were not prepared to countenance.

Sherman was, in short, an extremist. What views he held, he held strongly. And since these views were all subsumed into ridicule and loathing for Heath and all his works, Sherman was in some respects well qualified to be the first bureaucrat of the Conservative revolution. Some shadow ministers, naturally, found him insufferable when he later intruded tenaciously into their lives, as the Opposition leader's principal intellectual sounding-board. For others, including Joseph and Mrs Thatcher, the clarity of his contempt more than made up for his abrasive personality and his reluctance, in any circumstances, to underestimate his own importance.

Sherman, in fact, was crucially involved in Joseph's most daring assault on his leader's orthodoxies. This was a speech he gave in Preston, in September 1974, barely a month before the election. It was Sir Keith's magnum opus to date, the most rounded and thorough cataloguing of collective guilt that he had yet attempted. Many hands took a part in this historic event, the final, considered Josephite onslaught against incomes policy, the 'imaginary' evil of unemployment, Keynesian demand-management, and the 'great havoc' caused by putting too much money into the system.

Celebrated economics editors, like Samuel Brittan of the *Financial Times* and Peter Jay of *The Times*, were invited to give helpful comments before delivery. Seemingly any available sceptic about the consensual wisdom was approached for a contributory thought. Knowing the speech was coming, the Heath circle, sensitive to electoral embarrassment, made some attempt to stop it. James Prior, one of the closest of all Heath's allies, was deputed to approach a suitable intermediary in the Joseph camp. The natural candidate was Margaret Thatcher, and Prior's account brings the intimacy of the little cabal vividly to life.

> I was asked to see Margaret to see whether she could bring any influence to bear on Keith Joseph to stop him making it, and Margaret said, 'Oh, I don't know. I think Alfred . . .' – and that I thought was significant, because it wasn't even Sherman, it was Alfred – 'I think Alfred has written it for Keith, and I think you'll find that Keith is most determined to make it, and I don't think I can influence him.'[5]

In these pre-election months, therefore, the launch-pad for a new Conservatism began to be put in place. It supplied the base for the decisive leap of Margaret Thatcher's career, although, as we shall see, the precise role of this new Conservatism at that moment was at best ambiguous. Meanwhile, a parallel development, which rendered Joseph's attacks even more jarring, sealed the fate of Edward Heath and all he now purported to stand for.

On losing the February election, Heath had briefly sought to construct a coalition government. He made overtures to the Liberal Party, but partly through the clumsy inexperience of the negotiators and partly through lack of numbers in the House, the effort collapsed and Harold Wilson was left to form his third administration. The coalition idea, however, survived in Heath's mind and came to play an increasing part as the second election drew closer. Joseph's intellectual challenge therefore posed a double embarrassment. Not only was he unpicking the record on which Heath continued to rest his claim. He was advocating a break with the accumulated inheritance of policies subscribed to by all parties for thirty years, at the very moment when Heath was proposing, in effect, a merger between these parties in the national interest.

Several strands contributed to Heath's thinking. This was a period of rising Celtic nationalism. As the Scottish National Party grew, the parties in the House looked like becoming more fragmented. The Ulster Unionists already sat as an independent party, no longer taking the Conservative whip. The Liberal revival in February placed more than six million votes behind a desire for the politics of moderation dominated by the centre. Wilson led a minority government, with no firm hope of transforming this into a safe majority at the second election. All in all, Heath could make a plausible case for the belief that since no party looked likely to be able to form a strong government, Conservatives should be looking for allies in a potential multi-party administration.

However, he went further. He began to see coalitionism not as a defensive option but as a stance with many positive virtues. It was all of a piece with the dominant motif of his 1970–4 Administration, which accorded far greater esteem to management than belief, efficiency than conviction, to the agreed common-sense of the great estates of the realm rather than to a partisan ideology ruthlessly pursued. The country, Heath thought, now wanted 'sensible' solutions. Facing runaway inflation and increased unemployment, it would welcome a programme of national unity. He was making this pitch in a speech as early as June. As the Conservatives' contribution to the new consensus, he said, they would abandon their commitment to reintroduce their Industrial Relations Act, a union-curbing measure Wilson had instantly repealed.

We do not know what every member of the shadow cabinet thought when this idea was canvassed before it. But it duly found its way, in muted form, into the election manifesto, in which the party undertook to 'consult and confer with the leaders of other parties and with the leaders of the great interests in the nation, in order to secure for the government's policies the consent and support of all men and women of good will'.

On the last weekend of the campaign, Heath, by a singular personal coup, without consulting the shadow cabinet, made the commitment more formal and explicit. He despatched a message to all Conservative candidates, saying: 'I have no doubt that the real hope of the British people in this situation is that a National Coalition Government, involving all the parties, could be formed, and that party differences could be put aside until the crisis is mastered. . . . When the Conservatives obtain a majority at the election, I will immediately set out, with this majority, to establish a government that can transcend party division, a government representing men and women of good will of all parties and of none.'

Within a week, the election was lost. But what exactly had been defeated? Notwithstanding the fact that Labour's majority was only three, and Heath's analysis of governing politics was thereby substantially endorsed, the main victim was without question the Tory leader himself and the highly visible idea which he had chosen to make the principal plank of his platform.

Already suspect among many Conservatives, the Government of National Unity or GNU became the symbol of everything the party could no longer afford to stand for. Besides the retreat from red-blooded or even distinctive Conservatism which it inherently entailed, it offered no way forward for a party now facing several years in opposition. Well intentioned though it may have been, it marked the end of a road. The Conservative Party looked like an *ignis fatuus*, kept alight by its leader's inextinguishable self-belief but no longer fuelled by the ideas that most Tory MPs imagined they had gone into politics to pursue.

The contrast with the path Joseph had begun to hack out could not have been greater. And his comrade-in-arms had herself taken another gingerly step towards open dissent. She was asked at an election press conference what might happen to her package of housing policies after the election. Would her promised 9½ per cent mortgages perhaps find their way on to the negotiating table, along with the proffered corpse of the Industrial Relations Act and any other bargaining counter Heath could lay hands on, in the interests of creating his centrist government of national unity?

'No,' she replied. 'My policies are not negotiable.'

Heath did not quit. Although he had now lost three elections out of four he had fought as leader, it seems not to have occurred to him that there was a case for instant retirement on that account.

This would have been the graceful thing to do, although grace under pressure was never Heath's conspicuous quality. Curmudgeonly silences of ever longer duration were more his style. But retirement now, on 11 October 1974, the very day after defeat, would have been more than graceful. It would have ensured the retention of the leadership in the hands of his sort of people, if not necessarily or for ever his sort of Conservatism. Had he not been leader by election, and therefore replaceable only by another election, this is certainly what would have happened. Under the old rules whereby Conservative leaders were removed and replaced by the informal alchemy of a charmed circle of elders, Heath now could not conceivably have survived. As it was, he preferred to resist every inducement from his friends, and show seigneurial contempt for his enemies, and thereby postpone the final challenge that would inevitably be made against him. Between October 1974 and February 1975, his manner of defending his position ensured that he – and, more important, it – would be swept aside.

A great deal of manoeuvring now began. It was apparent that a leadership election would have to take place at some early date, although the process was sufficiently untried for a committee to be assembled under Sir Alec Douglas-Home to determine the rules of the game. It was also clear that apart from the Heath brigade of loyalists, two lines of opinion began running strongly in the party from the moment the election result was known. One was that Conservatism now needed to move to the right, and follow roughly where Keith Joseph was pointing. The other, held by a much larger and more amorphous collection of MPs and party officials, was that a change of some kind, any kind, was now urgently desirable. Of these impulses, the second was at every stage the stronger.

Even in the savagely competitive world of contention for a party's leadership, certain rules of decorum are prudent to observe. One of these is that until a vacancy has appeared or an election has been announced, the contenders are careful to disclaim any far-fetched intentions and express only the most modest of ambitions. In autumn 1974, a kind of phony war now broke out: phony in the sense that it was formally undeclared, yet warlike in the sense that several contenders were jockeying discreetly, sometimes rather too discreetly, for the ascendancy. It proved to be a bloody contest. Yet Margaret Thatcher owed her victory in it more than anything else to the fact that it was not bloody enough at an early enough stage to hoist any of her more plausible rivals to triumph. She was, as it turned out, the tortoise, the plodding long-distance runner, the only one who lasted the course, as the hares either failed to start or collapsed long before the race was run.

The chief agent of her victory was, without doubt, Edward Heath. But for his stubbornness, his incorrigible self-belief, his refusal to release any of his lieutenants from the bonds of personal loyalty to himself, it may be doubted whether Mrs Thatcher would even have entered the contest. No reputable judge, in or out of the party, has argued that in any other circumstance than the one Heath contrived to create would she have won.

Leaving Heath's extraordinary conduct to one side, however, it was to the actions of a handful of key figures, most of them her friends, that she owed her unpredicted victory.

The first of these was Joseph. He always was driven less than most politicians by the coarser kind of ambition. This had been no impediment to his advancement. How could anyone whose cabinet career eventually stretched from 1962 to 1986 ever be adjudged lacking in political appetite? But for Joseph ambition was by this time overshadowed by ideological passion. It could genuinely be said that in thrusting himself forward, which he did instantly the election was finished, he was fulfilling a debt of honour to the ideas he had spent the past six months working out. So he did not delay to tell the right that they could say he was a candidate for the leadership. 'You have my authority to tell that to anybody who asks,' he wrote. Coming from a man so prone to torment, so conscious of office as a bed of nails which it was the duty of the believing politician to lie on, this was a curiously selfless undertaking: a rare, possibly unique, example in political history of the coexistence of powerful ambition and intense self-abnegation within a single soul.

So long as Joseph stood, Margaret Thatcher was bound to support him. This was more than a routine obligation. She saw him, correctly, as the prophet among them, and from a generation senior to hers. Insofar as she had begun to dabble in the politics of ideas, they were his ideas. After February he had led the way and she had almost invisibly followed. It appears that any doubts she may have had, and which she certainly developed later, concerning Sir Keith's judgment and even his stability were then stilled by something akin to hero-worship.

He exposed his less reliable side, however, all too soon. Within a week of saying he would be a candidate, he had effectively destroyed his credibility in a single, stunning speech.

This was another in his series of iconoclastic exposés, this time in the realm not of economic theory but of social class and, most startlingly, eugenics. Joseph was concerned, he told an audience of Birmingham Conservatives, about the quality of the British population. Too many children were being born to mothers at the bottom of the social scale who were by definition less fitted to bring children up well, and by habit less accustomed to the practice of birth control.

To Joseph's innocent eye, this line of argument was merely an extension of his overarching discourse against people's dependence on the state. To most other observers it summoned up the horror of selective breeding. And although the fell hand of Alfred Sherman could be seen in large parts of the speech, Sherman always said later that the decisive passages were Joseph's own work, uttered against his speech-writer's advice.

It took Joseph a month to face honestly his own limitations and withdraw from the contest. We may judge the bond between him and Mrs Thatcher, however, by noting that she chose the very day of his withdrawal to announce that she would be a candidate against Heath. The ideological debate, as distinct from the political contest, was not so narrowly based as to exclude the need for an ideological candidate. The right in the Commons required a Josephite to run and vote for, and Mrs Thatcher was the only credible personification of that, careful though she had been to avoid making many root-and-branch defences of it in the Joseph style. But when she entered, on 21 November, she was not generally regarded as having a serious chance of winning.

A second potential candidate came forward, entering the fray only to withdraw from it. Edward du Cann experienced a different set of hesitations from Joseph. But the political effect of his behaviour was similar. To a large body of MPs who were desperately searching for the man to unhorse Heath, he offered first promise and then disappointment.

The failure of du Cann to take part in the leadership contest presents one of the more tantalising missed opportunities of recent politics. At the least, such a contest would have been an absorbing and piquant spectacle. Du Cann was chairman of the 1922 Committee of back-benchers, and as such he played a double, not to say many-sided, role. *Ex officio* he was charged by the rules with supervising any leadership contest. By taste, habit and disposition, he was an intriguer. In the autumn of 1974, he was at the heart of the manoeuvring, first to ensure Heath either resigned or submitted to re-election, but then also to maximise the chances of a credible candidate emerging who could beat him. Many pressed this task on du Cann himself. But, true to his habitual style, at once furtive and oleaginous, smiling and ruthless, publicly smooth and privately rough, he declined openly to commit himself.

Du Cann loathed Heath, for good reason. Heath had removed him from the party chairmanship in 1967, and never offered him a decent job in government. Additionally, du Cann, who had many interests in the City of London, had been implicitly swept into range of several attacks Heath made on financiers and asset-strippers during the later part of his premiership, including the description of the international conglomerate, Lonrho, with which du Cann had connections, as the 'ugly and unacceptable face of capitalism'.[6]

While it was never wholly clear what du Cann stood for, or which wing of the divided party he would at any one time decide to support, he had a certain stature. To a party in search of a new start it might have been a virtue that he had never served in cabinet – although less so, perhaps, that there were senior Tories pledged never to permit this quintessential City gentleman to have charge of a department which had anything to do with economics.

To explain du Cann's credibility as a candidate, one must look to the lengths he always went to to remain acceptable to Conservative MPs, who elected him year after year to run the 1922 Committee, and who are the only constituency that really matters in a leadership contest. Behind his smooth exterior, there was a touch of the American political boss about him. Gliding around the corridors of the House, when he wasn't gliding about the City in his Rolls-Royce, he had a word for everybody, and an inscrutable ability to say the right thing at the right time, whatever his true feelings might have been.

He was not embarrassed to take this emollient quality to extremes. As the October General Election was beginning, he delivered himself of a spectacularly bogus encomium to Heath when the leader came to address a meeting of the Tory candidates. 'You do not only lead but command the party,' du Cann intoned. 'You command more than men and women. There is no one here who does not fully reflect your own devotion to our cause and above all your integrity. If you attack, you need never look behind. . . . We know we can count abundantly on you and you equally know that you can count on us.'

For several weeks, the most active organisers among the anti-Heath faction regarded du Cann as their most likely candidate. And he certainly manoeuvred to improve his chances, notably by exploiting the strong base he had in the National Union, the voluntary wing of the party. He even promised the National Union a share of any future leadership vote if he became leader.

He regularly took counsel among his friends. But then, rather suddenly, he pulled out, letting it be known that he would not enter the lists, at least on the first ballot. There was an opportunity for new candidates to enter on the second, but since he had given as his main reason for withdrawing the fact that his wife did not fancy being the leader's wife, still less the prime minister's, he appeared to be ruling himself out for good – although in du Cann's operations such categoric finality was never to be relied on.

By the time du Cann reached this point, Margaret Thatcher had been a declared candidate for almost two months. But she was still an unregarded one. That she moved within weeks from rank outsider and mere curiosity to winning the first ballot and triumphing on the second was due more than anything to the failure of several men to understand the situation they were in.

Heath's last bequest to his party was to make it impossible for any of his close associates to succeed him. They were in thrall to his baleful influence. Once he had decided to fight, loyalty, that deceiving virtue, bound them to his struggle. They were too close to events. None among them was brave enough to see that their man was finished, and that if he was allowed to insist on their pledges for too long he might well destroy them as well as himself. This was especially true of William Whitelaw, chairman of the party, close adviser throughout the years of government, and palpably the chief among these allies: the one who, if the normal rules of bloody combat had been observed, would have seen this as his only chance of the leadership, and struck out on his own.

But the Heathites were mesmerised. They seriously convinced themselves that not only duty but self-interest lay in backing the stubborn incumbent on the first ballot. They thought that if this was lost, the opportunity would instantly appear for Whitelaw to cruise effortlessly in on the second. Always afterwards, Whitelaw defended this decision. Still in 1985 he was unblushingly recalling his opinion at the time: 'I wanted Heath to remain,' he said. He also recalled, though, the misapprehension under which he and his friends had been labouring. They did not think it conceivable that Mrs Thatcher could do so well on the first ballot as she eventually did, rendering it politically if not quite arithmetically impossible for a second-ballot interloper to take over and build on Heath's vote. 'I don't think I'd realised quite the extent of the feeling against him in the parliamentary party,' Whitelaw said in 1985. 'They'd had enough of him.'[7]

They had not, as they saw it in 1975, had enough of his policies, his general line. They had not yet been radicalised into Josephite attitudes. For most of them that wasn't what the contest was about. Given all that has happened since, this is a little difficult to recall. But the defenestration of Heath was essentially a personal not an ideological event. And the most illuminating evidence for this is to be found in the activities of the man most commonly credited with organising the votes that made Margaret Thatcher leader.

Airey Neave has flitted into this story before. He was in Margaret Thatcher's chambers when she was a novice at the Bar. As a politician he was the kind who could be easily neglected. He was like very many other occupants of the Conservative backbenches: under-employed, frustrated and somewhat resentful of his lot. As a matter of fact, he had more reason than most to feel resentful. In the Macmillan Government, he occupied a number of junior posts and his career looked like blossoming. Since then, not always in the best of health, he had got nowhere.

Neave, however, had one talent which many of his contemporaries lacked. He was an organiser, especially well versed in undercover operations. It was for this that he had first become famous, long ago, when he escaped from Colditz and then organised other Allied escape routes across Europe. He had written books about the war, was an authentic war hero. As a barrister he had prosecuted some of the Nazi war criminals. Yet somehow none of these achievements had yet commended him for a prominent role in Conservative politics, commensurate, as he thought, with what he deserved. Now, with the party apparatus inevitably in disarray and the official whips' office no longer making its writ run in any one direction, Neave put his subterranean skills to work.

The interesting fact is that he did not do so at first on Mrs Thatcher's behalf. All Neave wanted was a winner, to displace Heath. Not a right-winger himself, he was indifferent to the political stance of his candidate. Thus at an early stage he actually offered his services to Whitelaw, who, still blindly pledged to Heath, declined them. Next Neave turned to du Cann and remained for several weeks in the thick of du Cann's plotting. Only when du Cann dithered to a halt did he switch to the least fancied candidate, Margaret Thatcher: one who had, however, the exclusive virtue of being committed without ambiguity to running against the leader.

Although Neave had known the Thatchers for quite a while, he was never an intimate acquaintance. This came later, when under his expert guidance she had won her victory. Before it happened, their relationship is better reflected in a sidelong remark Neave made to a Labour MP as the battle commenced: 'My filly is going to win,' he told Roy Hattersley.

So in no sense was Neave a conscious agent of the right. Nor was the party embarking on a rightist crusade as it approached the moment of decision. It was, instead, preparing to use the only weapon available for the purpose of destroying Heath, who was hated by some but simply rejected as a loser by many more.

The weapon was sharp and warlike. Having offered herself in the role, Mrs Thatcher became more visible in Parliament in the last front bench post Heath ill-advisedly gave her, as a spokesman on Treasury affairs. This gave her a platform for some pyrotechnic aggression against the Labour Government's tax proposals, her mastery of which impressed Neave but also many other MPs who had hitherto seen her only in a narrower field. She also collected another of the derisive sobriquets she has picked up along the way, those sure proofs of celebrity. Denis Healey, the Chancellor of the Exchequer, dignified her as 'La Pasionara of privilege' and offered what might be thought a prophetic indictment of the kind of policies with which she was indeed to become associated over the next ten years. 'She has decided to see her party tagged as the party of the rich few,' Healey charged, 'and I believe she and her party will regret it.'

In the first ballot, held on 4 February, Heath was duly demolished.

The count showed 130 votes for Thatcher, 119 for Heath with 16 for a token outsider, Hugh Fraser. In the second, a week later, the tide proved unstoppable. Whitelaw entered the field. So, in disorganised fashion, did several other Heath allies, each lured by this rarest of opportunities to put down a marker for the future. If this had been perceived as a truly ideological divide, perhaps the no-hopers – Geoffrey Howe, James Prior and John Peyton – would have restrained themselves from spoiling Whitelaw's chances. But that is not how it looked; and besides, when a party leadership falls vacant, it is asking too much of politicians to stand back from possibly the only moment when they can demonstrate the full grandeur of their aspirations.

The final vote was overwhelming: Thatcher 146, Whitelaw 79, Howe 19, Prior 19, Peyton 11.

This result has been most aptly characterised by one of the Tory Party's shrewdest internal chroniclers, Julian Critchley. He called it the peasants' revolt. There could hardly be a more evocative description of an event in which the backbenchers rose up against the leader who had scorned them, oppressed them and consigned them once again to many years out of power.

The most immediate impact of victory, however, was on the victor herself. It was the first truly astounding achievement of an otherwise fairly routine career. Everything else, beginning with Oxford and ending in the cabinet, had conformed to a pattern which, while exceptional in its success, was not a unique departure from precedent. Women had been in the cabinet before, even a Conservative woman who had not been to a public school – Florence Horsburgh, Minister of Education from 1951 to 1954, had not even been to university. Although she always started at some disadvantage, the ambitious female Tory politician was not an unknown phenomenon.

The party leadership, however, was an utterly different case. It far transcended what Margaret Thatcher had honestly thought was within her reach. She told William Pile, her old permanent secretary, about this, in one of their more amicable moments. Pile recalled: 'I can remember asking her at one point what her ultimate ambition was, and she said, "I would like to be Chancellor of the Exchequer." '[8]

When, grasping for something to say on the day she was elected, she produced a rather predictable cliché, it had a little more exactness than such tired words usually do. 'To me,' she told her first press conference, 'it is like a dream that the next name on the list after Harold Macmillan, Sir Alec Douglas-Home and Edward Heath is Margaret Thatcher.'

8

The Stepping Stone

THE WOMAN WHO became leader of the Conservative Party in February 1975 was different from her predecessors in more than gender. Her sex was crucial but her status as an outsider was more so: and in combination these two facets of her being did much to define the style she adopted and the place she took.

None of those earlier post-war leaders had been outsiders in any way. Heath, the social *parvenu* among them, had schooled himself to be the most dedicated insider of all. Margaret Thatcher emerged through no magic circle. In historic terms she was a mistake that should never have happened. Bonar Law was in this respect the antecedent with whom she could be said to have something in common, although in the pantheon of British political leaders, Joseph Chamberlain was the man whose role hers in other ways most resembled. Being little interested in the more distant details of party history, however, she would not have thought of that at the time.

The fact that she was an outsider had caused her to be elected, because it permitted her alone to run when all the insiders held back. That status, later expressed in her eccentric but persistent claim to be the leader of the opposition in her own Government, was one she embraced with unquenchable enthusiasm. In the four years' preparation for government that now ensued it did much to determine both the way she conducted the leadership and the wary, disbelieving attitude towards her of many senior people, insiders all, under her command.

As we have seen, she was not elected as a right-winger. But after ten years of Heath, the outsider's territory in the Tory Party was plainly on the right, and Mrs Thatcher, untrammelled now by office or collective responsibility, naturally belonged there. She was not an accomplished theoretician, and she never had an original idea. But she dealt in simple convictions, which had survived in some fashion even while, as a minister, she was doing and watching others do exactly the opposite of where those convictions ought to have pointed.

All politicians make their compromises. Not all politicians have much to compromise about, or remain fully seized of the principles they were originally obliged to modify or even betray. They tend to forget about them, as time changes circumstances and qualifies earlier ideals almost out of existence.

But Margaret Thatcher wasn't that sort of forgetful politician; nor did the party want that sort of politician. Although her desertion of fundamentals had been so great as to cast doubt on how strongly she was convinced in the first place, her rediscovery of them now, as leader, involved her in no discomfort, no intellectual queasiness of any kind. It was her good fortune to be propelled into the leadership when the party was ready for a return to fundamentalist Conservatism of a kind she was most at ease with. The party wanted something they could believe in, and she was only too pleased to supply it. If the defining characteristic of most items in her credo was that they should reverse the direction Heath had been taking, this was as amenable to the leader as to the party which, with the swift cruelty politics reserves for its failed men, now looked on the Heath years as a disaster.

She was, however, cautious. Even though the Labour majority was small, several years of opposition now lay ahead. She did not move at once to set her mark on the leadership, nor did she have the power to do so even had she wanted. There is a sense in which all leaders, especially of so unstructured a body as the Conservative Party, are on probation until they have won an election. In the Labour Party there are interim struggles to be won and registered, votes and manoeuvres on any number of party bodies which signify the strength or weakness of the leader. In the Conservative Party it is all much more indeterminate.

It remains, however, a necessary and formative apprenticeship, and Mrs Thatcher took to it quite easily. Culminating as it did in an election victory, it came to be regarded as quite a triumph for her. This impression did not die. In 1984, Francis Pym, whom she had sacked from her government and thus converted into a bitter enemy, still felt able to offer a generous assessment. 'She was an extremely good leader of the Opposition,' he told me in 1984. 'I think she was the best I have ever known in Parliament.'

Most of the insiders were kept on in leadership positions. The names of Whitelaw, Carrington, Prior, Pym, Ian Gilmour and the rest of the guilty men of the Heath years remained on the shadow cabinet roster. If they had not done so, there would have been nobody else of weight to pick. Besides, they were pragmatists. If they had retired hurt, they would have signalled surrender in a contest for the future of the Conservative Party which they did not believe they had a serious chance of losing if they stayed in place for long enough.

What also characterised these men was an ability to recognise that something had happened before and after February 1974 from which they could profitably learn. They drew different morals, and made varying accommodations with the new leader. But all understood that there had to be some change. It was therefore quite appropriate that the real casualties of the putsch, who now took no part in leadership, were the two men who did not see this, indeed totally rejected it. Even with a year to reflect on the events which had precipitated his demise, Edward Heath believed unalterably in the rightness of everything he had done, and so did his chief lieutenant, who ran his unsuccessful campaign to remain the leader, Peter Walker.

Behind this façade of normality, with most of the familiar names still in place, much now began to happen. In these opposition years, certain principles were laid down which had been lost in obscurity, and certain characters raised up whom Heath had cast into the outer darkness. The leader established herself as a leader, with a philosophy most people could understand. So the party which reached the threshold of government in spring 1979 looked different from the party that had been shown the door in 1974. But it was an arduous process, never certain of accomplishment, beset by rancour, and not completed when the 1979 election was won.

Philosophy was the word. What first ensued was an examination of ideas. Keith Joseph had been judged unsuitable for the leadership, but now he came into his own. The Joseph process of speech-making carried on, now not as a rebuke to the old leader but as pathfinding for the new one. He and she agreed on everything important about the most important issue of all, the economy. What they were anxious to establish – he speaking, she listening and agreeing – had more to do with first principles than specific policies. He spoke about inflation, employment, the money supply, the role of unions as monopoly suppliers of labour, the limits of government power in influencing these economic elements. From platform after platform through 1975 and 1976, Joseph expatiated on the errors of the past and the price that would have to be paid for the conquest of inflation.[1]

Government could not create jobs, Joseph kept saying. Government should not intervene on incomes. Government could not act in the public interest merely by increasing demand. The expansion of demand, as practised by successive governments, merely led to inflation, which itself soon put the stopper on expansion.

Reaching across the whole domain of politics, Joseph had another message, and it was the most evocative description of where Mrs Thatcher should lead the party, as well as the direction in which most of it was quite happy to be led. This was away from the 'middle ground'.

The middle ground 'moved continuously to the left by its own internal dynamic', Joseph contended. All parties had sought to occupy it, encouraged by the overinfluential media, so that a collectivist consensus had carried all before it. 'It created not prospects but crisis. Far from saving the public sector, it had gone a long way towards destroying it. Far from achieving social harmony and strengthening the centre, it has created resentment and conflict.'

In place of the middle ground, the new Thatcher Tory Party should seek to identify the 'common ground', the place where the real lives and aspirations of most people were in practice acted out. The only way to reach this ground, Joseph argued, was by the rediscovery of true Conservative ideas such as he himself had neglected for most of his life. Here was the battlefield. The Tory Party had to have the courage to enter it unashamed of the principles it believed in.

The Joseph speeches of this time contained everything that is distinctive about the economic and political philosophy which later became known as Thatcherism. They were very repetitive. But since their purpose was to drive home a few elementary messages, that is not surprising. They were also eloquent and deeply felt, the outpourings of the true convert who was late to see the light but aware of how soon it might go out. They remained the relevant texts ten years later, not perhaps for their detail but for the grand passion they brought to the enunciation of ideas to which, for two terms in government, Mrs Thatcher always insisted she was remaining true.

At her first party conference as leader, she put her own strident gloss on Joseph's discourses. It was the first of many conference speeches in which identical sentiments, year after year, were going to be found: 'Britain and socialism are not the same thing, and as long as I have health and strength they never will be. . . . Let me give you my vision: a man's right to work as he will, to spend what he earns, to own property, to have the state as servant and not as master: these are the British inheritance. They are the essence of a free country, and on that freedom all our other freedoms depend.'

But in converting these burning sentiments into a political programme, the leader had to deal with two kinds of problem. Which colleagues could be best entrusted with them? And to what specific policy priorities did the general principles point?

The choice of the key lieutenants was as delicate as it was crucial. A generation of politicians accustomed to running things in a certain way had been not only ousted but, in the process, humiliated. It was a question of how best to blend the new with the old. For the new Thatcher ascendancy was in effect a challenge to the entire government machine. Labour officials then in control were witness to this. One of them, who worked at No. 10, told me that the response of one senior official to the Thatcher triumph in the leadership election was to assert categorically that he would never work for her. (He was nonetheless found doing mandarin service to the 1979 Government.) Whitehall could hardly credit what had happened. Nor could some senior Conservatives. For the leader it was a question of distinguishing between those, the majority, whose public loyalty concealed a belief that any Thatcher revolution would not last, and those who could be trusted to support her.

The first of the loyalists to declare for her was William Whitelaw, who decided immediately after his defeat to accept an invitation to become her deputy leader. In time theirs became a rich relationship, with Whitelaw the key instrument for the neutering of her enemies. For now his job was to help her put together a team she thought she could rely on.

The appointment which mattered most was that of shadow chancellor. In the economic revolution she proposed, he was bound to be the decisive figure, and the obvious man for the job was Joseph, who had invented most of what she now believed in. But here the leader showed early wisdom, and some command of the capacity without which no leader survives for long – a talent for well-measured brutality. She left Joseph on the sidelines, with overall responsibility for policy and research. Whitelaw did not let her overlook Joseph's erratic tendencies. He was therefore relegated from the centre with the same despatch as party officials from the old regime were dismissed from Central Office. 'I am not ruthless,' Mrs Thatcher said, 'but some things have to be done, and I know when they are done one will be accused of all kinds of things.'[2]

Instead of Joseph she placed at her right hand Sir Geoffrey Howe, the man destined to be in all the years of power her indispensable fellow traveller on the road to what she called the free society.

Howe had many qualifications for the post. But the first of these was again that he was a convert: the first and chief of converts. Only a year before he had been a central ally not of Joseph but of Heath. As Solicitor-General, later as Minister of Trade and Consumer Affairs, he had played the leading political role in drafting some controversial statutes, including those on industrial relations and prices-and-incomes control. He had argued for the incomes policy in principle and in detail, through thick and thin, ever since November 1972. Unlike Joseph and Mrs Thatcher he did not have the excuse that he was a distant onlooker at these heretical rituals. On the contrary he was the key functionary of Heathite corporatism.

Nor was that the only unlikely element in the record of one who became early Thatcherism's senior servant. By temperament he was the reverse of an ideologue, being far more interested in the accumulation of small advances in the public interest than in great declarations of principle. Such a style, the Thatcher style, was as remote from his own rhetorical habits as it was from his way of thinking. As a lawyer, he wasn't paid to be impressed by big ideas.

In addition, he was a complete believer in the beneficial power of government. Unlike a true Josephite, he thought government was in many respects a force for good, and had given his whole political life to the service of that ideal. He had always believed strongly in an alliance between law and government as the potent agent of social change. That was why he had gone into politics in the first place. He had been active in the Bow Group in its early days in the 1950s when it was the centre of progressive Conservative thought. He had made his name by a commitment to social reform in areas which never interested Mrs Thatcher, and to which she often seemed hostile – like race relations and equal opportunities for women.

All in all, Howe was quintessentially a man of steadfast not exciting qualities: not simply a ministerial man, but one who found public life the sector of human activity in which he felt most at ease. Such an earnest establishment figure, the ultimate argument against the reputation of the Welshman as a fiery and romantic force of nature, seemed an improbable revolutionary.

But Sir Geoffrey had other credentials as well. If conversion was required, it was an experience he knew all about, for he had always been flexible. Somewhere back in the Bow Group days, he could discover that he had been a liberal on economics as well as on social policy. As managing director of *Crossbow*, the Bow Group magazine, he had published free-market articles which married well with the Josephite philosophy that now had to be given political flesh. Progressive Tories, it turned out, had always believed in the market economy alongside a dirigiste regime of improved social provision. Thus it was when he was writing Heath's statutes for state economic control that Howe had really had to swallow his principles. Only now were his deep and genuine principles – the ones he'd had to bury for all these years – like those of Mrs Thatcher, given an honest chance to express themselves. Unlike the switch he'd had to make in office under Heath, his switch back again was, in his own mind at least, a reversion to his roots.

But what of the other part of Howe's Bow Group ideas? The expansion of welfare and the drive for a fairer society through state action were plainly in jeopardy under Joseph's influence. But here Sir Geoffrey demonstrated the greatest talent he had to offer his new leader. This was his lawyer's ability to square any set of facts with the principles in vogue at the time. When confronted in later years with the discrepancy between his performance in the Heath and the Thatcher governments, he would often make a disarming joke of it. There was actually nothing in it, he smilingly suggested. It was just one of those circumstantial misfortunes that any pragmatic man of government finds himself called upon to live with.

Besides, Howe's life of dedication to the Conservative cause was seamless. A Tory is a Tory is a Tory, whatever he might think at any given point during his life. He could produce evidence of this. From time to time throughout the last fifteen years he has given lengthy disquisitions on the nature of Conservatism, and they have rarely failed to include references to how his own contributions have spanned the decades. In February 1986, for example, he welcomed straight-faced a new party study of housing policy because it consisted of a search 'for ways of obtaining the objectives set out in my 1957 pamphlet called *Houses to Let*'.

For a man with such a belief in timeless continuity, all shifts of direction seemed to be mere by-ways – day-trips there and back – off the broad, rolling road.

*   *   *

Together with Joseph, Howe was very soon the most influential politician in the most important field of Thatcherite politics: the breaking of the economic consensus. The leader occupied a kind of middle position between them. Joseph articulated ideas, Howe formulated policies, and Mrs Thatcher was the essential conduit from one to the other. The new men she brought into the shadow cabinet, notably John Biffen, a long-standing enemy of Heathite corporatism ('a glorified management consultant' is the best Biffen ever said for the former leader) helped to ensure that the impetus of Joseph's ideas was sustained.

But through the four years of Opposition, a sharp divide became apparent between the ideas that flourished and those that were resisted. One part of the Joseph analysis was accepted with little criticism. The other part was fought tooth and nail. The difference had a lot to do with the personalities who were in charge in the respective cases. They also threw light on the leader's own uneasy standing as a newcomer who had much to learn about the business of leadership.

The shape of the new economic strategy, the field Howe was directly responsible for, was agreed quite quickly. Within two years, the necessary compact between the new and the old parties, the Thatcher–Joseph disciples and the pragmatists still alongside them, was battened down. The key document, published in 1977, was *The Right Approach to the Economy*, written by Joseph, Howe, David Howell, a maverick economist without a clear label, and James Prior, the Employment spokesman and custodian of the Heath inheritance.

It put forward a distinctive programme in language that was for the most part cautious and unmenacing. A year earlier, a vaguer and more modest paper, *The Right Approach*, had for the first time set out the broad principles the new party would follow, in its determination to 'right the balance' which had for so long been tilted against freedom. *The Right Approach to the Economy* wrote down some specific priorities. These were control of the money supply, lower taxes on everything except spending, a more stable economic climate. The four authors, who boxed the compass of the party, did not make much of any commitment to spending cuts, promising merely 'firm management of government expenditure'. Their anathema against incomes policies was not especially harsh, but their sympathies were clear enough. 'Narrow deals and contracts' would be replaced by open discussion in Parliament, not merely between unions, employers and government. The document set much store by loosening up pay differentials, and it proposed the removal of 'unnecessary restrictions' on business expansion.

In retrospect what is striking about this early programme is its modesty, even its lack of self-confidence. It is far from a crusading text. Several of the policies for which the Thatcher governments became famous appear here either as distant dreams or not at all. Taking industries out of state control is referred to only as a wistful ideal, conceivably worth looking at as a long-term possibility. The case for some decisive increase in indirect taxes, to offset the promised cuts in income tax, is not canvassed. Public spending is not depicted as the curse it later became. The whole tone is a far cry from the stridency which later became the hallmark of an economic policy based heavily on dogmatic belief. Stridency, indeed, was absolutely ruled out. The document was above all rational – very much a Geoffrey Howe kind of effort. Politically its importance was to establish, with Prior as a willing co-signatory, that there really wasn't anything for Heathites and Thatcherites to disagree about.

The other half of the Joseph prospectus, however, proved much more difficult to handle. At the centre of his analysis of past error stood the failure to tackle monopoly trade unions and their excessive power. A union had broken the Heath Government. Union power collectively was bending the Labour Government. This power was an engine of Luddism and inflation. What should the new model Conservatives promise to do about it?

Here we reach one of the earliest and most characteristic paradoxes of the Thatcher approach to political leadership. There was no doubt that she shared all of Joseph's anti-union prejudices, and more. These had deep roots, planted by her father and sustained by a career that had given her no experience of trade union activity other than as an occasional inconvenience of the kind which prompted her maiden Bill ensuring public access to council meetings. She had next to no industrial experience, and had had no second thoughts about the Heath Government's union-curbing Industrial Relations Act, disruptive and unworkable though this eventually proved to be.

All her instincts, in short, converged on a hawkish position. And yet she put in charge of the union question not only a man known to disagree with her, but one who carried his opposition to her instincts to greater lengths than anyone else in the leadership. Was this cunning politics, born of caution? Or weak politics born of innocence? Whatever the explanation, the decision influenced the future more heavily than she can ever have known it would.

James Prior had been an even more important figure in the Heath Administration than Geoffrey Howe. He was a close personal friend of the former leader but had drawn different lessons from the great ousting of 1974. Unlike Heath, Prior was actually eager to think about what had gone wrong. But unlike Howe (and Joseph and Mrs Thatcher) he did not conclude that the moral of the story pointed to a resumption of hostilities. This was quite a deep disagreement. Howe, for example, never surrendered his belief that the 1971 Industrial Relations Act, which he drafted, was an excellent statute overturned only by a series of unlucky accidents. He was adamant that trade unions needed to be placed firmly within a framework of law: law which the Labour Government had swiftly undone. Prior, by contrast, doubted whether new laws were either necessary or practical. Yet this was the man who ran Conservative policy on employment and labour law for all of Mrs Thatcher's time in opposition and the first decisive years in government.

Prior was a genial fellow, and cleverer than he looked. In appearance he was the acme of a Conservative farmer, the vocation he pursued, along with many business interests, supported by a first-class degree from Cambridge in estate management. He had an engaging honesty about him, and a decent gallantry. He took some time to master his incredulity that Margaret Thatcher was now his leader, but sniped at her behind her back far less cruelly than some other colleagues on the left of the party. At the beginning he may have doubted whether she could succeed, but it could never be said that he did not want her to. It was also the case, however, that he believed with some passion in his approach rather than hers as the way of improving the chances of this success occurring.

Prior recognised that he had been put in charge of the area in which the Conservatives were more vulnerable than any other. With great energy he set about making a fresh start. Both temperament and judgment told him that this should be a smooth not an abrasive start, leading to the reconstruction of relationships between politicians, union leaders and employers such as had characterised the later, though not the terminal, Heath days. After all, Heath's policies for inflation and economic management, as Prior was fond of pointing out, had succeeded not failed, until just before the apocalypse of the final miners' strike.

Slowly he did rebuild some of these relationships. He was struck by how very little most Tories knew about trade unions and their affairs. Even Heath himself only got to know the leaders when he needed them. In the Selsdon phase and after, he had prided himself on how little contact he had with them. Prior was determined not to repeat the error. His efforts were not made easier by the fact that Heath, apparently out of sheer dislike for Joseph and Mrs Thatcher, had persistently excluded them from the cabinet committees which would have made them grapple with the union question, perhaps even come face to face with a union leader or two when these horny-handed toilers presented themselves at Downing Street meetings.

All the same, the Prior strategy prevailed. *The Right Approach to the Economy* made not a single commitment to hostile measures against union power. It promised to remove unions from the decisive consultative role the Labour Government was giving them over all legislation. But it expressed great faith in the influence and goodwill of union leaders, and their ability to move in sensible directions.

Even in the middle of a ferocious industrial dispute, this emollient Prior line triumphed. *The Right Approach to the Economy* was published while mass pickets, fighting a dispute over union recognition for a low-paid, largely Asian workforce, were conducting pitched battles with the police outside the Grunwick factory in north London, producing television pictures which aroused extreme anger among the Conservative rank and file. Keith Joseph, cutting across Prior's brief, stirred up even more fury with a denunciation of the immunities that allowed the Grunwick pickets to carry on their disgraceful campaign. But Joseph nonetheless signed the document. Prior, who was determined to promise nothing, won this point: a point which the leader made no effort to overturn.

She was not, however, happy. She was caught between conflicting pressures. Prior represented a segment of Conservatism she was neither strong nor foolish enough to exclude from senior positions. The old guard who had occupied the front line during Heath's epic confrontation with the miners, notably Whitelaw and Lord Carrington, entirely supported Prior. And yet there were mounting demands from the other direction.

The party right thought they had brought Mrs Thatcher to power, a perception as strong as it was imprecise. Men like Norman Tebbit and George Gardiner, former backbench outcasts now for the first time admitted to the fringes of a ruling circle, pressed the case for tougher commitments. When Tebbit likened Prior's softness on industrial relations and especially the closed shop to 'the morality of Pétain and Laval' it was clear enough that the leader did not entirely demur. A body called the National Association for Freedom, which made anti-unionism the main thrust of its interest in liberty, rode high in the land. NAFF, too, said that Prior was being soft on the unions, and Mrs Thatcher was attracted by NAFF. One of her intimates told me at the time: 'In emotional moments she's said that NAFF is doing more for freedom in this country than anyone else in politics.'

But the Prior line persisted. And this jarring contrast illuminates a Thatcher trait that was to be seen throughout her tenure of the Opposition leadership. While the official position, on this as on other questions, was cautiously expressed and often more pleasing to the left than the right of the party, the right gained confidence from their belief, which was rarely contested, that in her heart the leader agreed with them.

This was true of union policies, especially the closed shop. It was also true of immigration. It was a latent truth about social policy as well. In some cases, the leader supplied explicit public evidence for the truth of the right's reassuring assumption that she was one of them. In January 1978, for example, she went on television, with no advance consultation among colleagues, and delivered a powerfully sympathetic statement about legitimate fears among white Britons that they were being 'swamped by people with a different culture'. There would be four million blacks by the end of the century, she said: and 'we are not in politics to ignore people's worries, we are in politics to deal with them.'[3] These statements, regarded by the ethnic communities as shamefully provocative, were not followed by a serious policy commitment to introduce a more repressive regime of immigration control. Whitelaw, the shadow home secretary, wouldn't allow it. But the text encouraged anyone who wanted to believe that Mrs Thatcher was a repressor of immigrants, just as numerous private conversations made it perfectly clear where she would honestly stand if she didn't have political reality to cope with on such subjects as union privileges and welfare scroungers.

These tensions were never resolved. Personal caution, combined with the collective view of the shadow cabinet, inhibited the emergence into full flower of the conviction politician of later years. But the attempt was made to introduce a counterbalance to such powerful remnants of the Heath ascendancy as Prior and, to a lesser extent, Whitelaw. On two fronts, Thatcherites – at this early stage a self-appointed group, not yet so fully identified as they later became – sought to wrest more permanent control.

The first was at the rougher end of politics, well represented by

Airey Neave. Having seized upon her candidacy as a happy accident, the conspiratorial Neave became infatuated with what he saw as her uniquely heroic qualities. Once in place as leader, she soon became in his eyes 'the most gifted politician in the Conservative Party and perhaps *the* most gifted politician for 25 years . . . the first real, idealistic politician for a long time . . . a philosopher as well as a politician'.[4]

Neave was determined to protect her from what he saw as daily threats to her position. He was perhaps too much the conspirator himself, seeing threats to her position that were hardly likely to constitute any serious danger to a leader so recently elected by an unchallengeable majority. The days were past when a leader selected by the magic circle could as swiftly be displaced by it. All the same, Neave's watchfulness was a measure of something real: that those who were the victims of the peasants' revolt in some cases took a long time to adjust to the permanence of its outcome. Neave remained head of her private office as well as taking the shadow portfolio for Northern Ireland.

A circle was also put together of trusted MPs who could be relied on to form a protective fence round a leader who needed all the help she could get, even though she did not always know it. Besides Tebbit and Gardiner from the reliably hard right, another aide appeared who had worked his passage with some speed from the Heath to the Thatcher entourage.

Until February 1974, before winning his own parliamentary seat, Nigel Lawson, economic journalist and Tory backroom boy, was an important associate of the prime minister. He was in the thick of the struggle to sustain the Heath incomes policy. On one occasion of particularly emotional hysteria in the inner circle's dying days, he even reassured Heath that he was 'the greatest prime minister for 200 years'. Lawson had not been long in Parliament before he was admitted to the group of familiars who were particularly valuable in preparing Mrs Thatcher for her twice-weekly gladiatorial bouts against the Labour leader, Harold Wilson, in the House of Commons.

These politicians, however, were in a sense the less important influence. In the struggle to produce a new synthesis, something closer to a definitive break with the crypto-socialism of the past, other characters mattered more. The outsider needed other outsiders to give shape to her thoughts and a framework to her strategy, to take sides in the debate on Joseph's propositions, to counterbalance the negative instincts of so many politicians she could not afford to get rid of.

One of these was already to hand. Alfred Sherman, in post as Director of the Centre for Policy Studies, now became a man of pervasive and insinuating influence in high places. The Centre, the outsiders' foundation, effectively eclipsed the official Conservative Research Department as the source of approved intellectual activity.

Sherman's mind was appealing to the leader. He was clever, well read and multilingual, with the kind of sweepingly dismissive attitudes appropriate to the revolutionary moment. Many people found him intolerable. He infuriated several members of the shadow cabinet as time went on. Prior used to say that he did not know which was the more irritating, to be kept waiting outside the leader's office while she pursued one of her countless dialogues with Sherman, or to be rebuffed, once admitted, with the refrain 'But Alfred says . . .' Sherman, in these Opposition years, showered her with papers, and helped with the speeches, as well as taking up useful part-time activity as a leader-writer on the *Daily Telegraph*.

But there also appeared at this time an adviser of more lasting influence, and a man with particularly firm convictions about the question Jim Prior was handling: what to do about the unions? If Sherman appealed to the Thatcher taste for fancy intellectuals, John Hoskyns satisfied the presumption she often made in favour of handsome, articulate, upright men of military bearing and with a good business record. By 1978, Hoskyns was the principal, full-time ideas man in her private office.

He was an archetypal Thatcherite, one of the earliest of the breed. To qualify for membership of this select category the necessary credentials included a fierce pessimism about the past, millennialist optimism about the future and a belief in the business imperative as the sole agent of economic recovery. Hoskyns had all of these, plus that other invaluable quality so often found in this dedicated army: the experience of lurching far and wide across the political spectrum.

After Winchester and several years in the army, Hoskyns had gone into the computer business, first with IBM and then on his own account. When he sold his company for a modest fortune in 1975, he began to dabble in the political world, almost as a pastime. Exceptionally talkative by business standards, he was a compulsive communicator, with an opinion to put about the transformation of British industry and government attitudes towards it. He was obsessed by the perception that Britain was 'going down the tube', a favourite expression, and was indifferent to the party that might give him a platform to say so.

His first connection was in fact with the Labour not the Tory wing of politics, through a group of Labour-oriented businessmen whose meetings he was still attending in 1976, well after his first contacts with the Thatcher circle. He also had quite close dealings for a time with the splinter-group which broke away from Labour under the banner of Dick Taverne, MP for Lincoln until October 1974. Politically Hoskyns was rootless and restless.

He wasn't looking in some opportunistic way for a party that would give him place and power, so much as for one to listen to his ideas. Since these ideas gave great prominence to an assault on trade union power, it was perhaps surprising that he should ever have thought that progress might be made through the Labour Party. Mrs Thatcher, however, was fully receptive.

Hoskyns was another Joseph discovery. The two men first met in 1975, introduced by Sherman, and in early summer 1976 Joseph suggested that Hoskyns should meet the leader. She asked him to put in any ideas he had for speeches. But Hoskyns was not at first impressed. As a systems analyst he found the Conservative approach to policy-making woefully ill-directed. As a man with large ideas, who rejoiced in model-building and conceptualising, he thought Joseph's own piecemeal efforts to put together a Conservative strategy quite laughable. In spring 1977 he said as much to Sir Keith, and suggested a role for himself as the producer of just such a strategy statement. It would be done under the oversight of Joseph and Howe, and with the full knowledge of the leader.

Joseph was delighted. He used to say to friends that he had no idea how to set about such an enterprise. Could Hoskyns seriously gather together the multiple strands of political thinking and weld them into a coherent programme of action? Amazing. It was one more confirmation of the superiority of businessmen–thinkers, men of decision and action, over mere politicians. Joseph often thought in cricketing images, and in his mind the shadow cabinet was a Third XI for whose modest talents he felt the need to apologise to the economists and entrepreneurs with whom he now spent his time. He watched with some wonderment as Hoskyns and his colleague, Norman Strauss, until recently a corporate planner at Unilever, began to build the foundation of a long innings.

Hoskyns and Strauss produced their draft statement in the autumn

Stern taskmaster: Alderman Roberts and family, with Margaret, nineteen, on the right.

The Conservative candidate in Dartford, 1951: a solitary election defeat, until Oxford in 1985.

The Parliamentary Secretary, Ministry of Pensions and National Insurance, 1961.

With the men behind her: Sir Geoffrey Howe, Reginald Maudling and William Whitelaw.

First fame, as Secretary of State for Education and Science, 1970.

Transfigured by cameras, 11 February 1975: the new leader of the Conservative Party.

William Whitelaw, once the rival, soon the most faithful ally.

A triumph shared: with Sir Keith Joseph at the first shadow cabinet meeting.

The advisers: Alfred Sherman (*left*) and John Hoskyns.

The foreign models: Malcolm Fraser, Prime Minister of Australia (1975–83), and Indira Gandhi.

Campaign poster, 1979: Saatchi & Saatchi never looked back.

4 May 1979: into 10 Downing Street with a prayer for harmony ready on the card in her hand.

of 1977. They called it 'Stepping Stones', a title perhaps designed to emphasise the cumulative and systematic nature of any serious strategic plan but also reflecting, in this image from the nursery, the opinion the two authors held of the politicians to whom it was addressed: that they needed to be taken by the hand and led carefully through a complex world they had never shown much sign of understanding.

Hoskyns and Strauss had a lofty view of their own perceptions, but despaired of politicians. Yet, as it turned out, they were wrong. When 'Stepping Stones' was first presented, at a private dinner in the leader's room attended by Whitelaw, Joseph and Angus Maude, Mrs Thatcher was tremendously excited by what she read. Only when the text reached the hands of others, notably Prior, did the politicians live down to Hoskyns' expectations.

The 'Stepping Stones' report was never published. And the apocalyptic quality of its thinking and remedies was not reflected in the party's overt approach to the 1979 election. But it put into words many of the subterranean impulses of hard-right Conservatism, and as the Thatcher Government grew in confidence this thinking acquired greater political importance. 'Stepping Stones' is worth some examination, in particular the part of it which challenged the Prior orthodoxy about the unions.

Its essential objective was a change in public attitudes. Asserting that the election presented Britain's last chance to eliminate socialism and prepare for a world without North Sea oil – acceptable platitudes of Conservative rhetoric – it was categoric about the main obstacle lying in the way. 'The one precondition for success will be a complete change in the role of the trades union movement,' the document said. This was unlikely to come about spontaneously. Mere evolutionary change would not have a rapid enough effect. The unions' role had to be completely changed. The danger was that the Tories would seek, in traditional form, to 'get on with' the unions and congratulate themselves if they succeeded, whereas such a consensus would in fact be based on sheer ignorance about the depth of Britain's economic plight. For this, Hoskyns produced an analogy of which he was especially fond: 'Even with a radical new union role, to find a way out of our problems will be like finding a needle in a haystack. But if the unions' role and political objectives remain unchanged, then all parties would in effect be agreeing to restrict their search to those haystacks which they know do not contain the needle.'

There could not have been a more direct challenge to Prior's chosen course of not confronting the union question. 'Any strategy which does not address this problem of the trades union role from the outset ensures failure in office, even though it might, at first sight, appear to make electoral success more likely.' Somehow the union role must be changed to one of 'positive partnership', said 'Stepping Stones', and this had to be seen as a positive strategy towards both electoral success and achievement in office. There was no essential difference between these two phases. 'We cannot say "Win the election first, with a low profile on the union problem; then implement a high profile strategy when in power." The countdown for both has already begun.'

The Hoskyns plan was directed, above all, to galvanising public awareness of what was possible. The unions had to be transformed from Labour's secret weapon into its major electoral liability. To this end, communication was far more important than specific legislative proposals. People should be made to understand that 'Britain may be finished already, as far as regaining economic status is concerned,' and that the unions were central to any kind of recovery.

How was this shift to be brought about? Partly by deflecting the standard Labour charge that Tories were interested in producing confrontation between unions and government. Kick with the other boot, advised Hoskyns, and demonstrate the extent to which Labour, bonded tightly to the unions, had produced a sick, impoverished, stupid, unfair, frightened society. 'Drag every skeleton out of the union cupboard, linking it to Labour,' he counselled. Additionally, it would be helpful to raise the stakes – 'deliberately to release ideas which at first sight look half-baked, so that hasty and over-confident Labour responses can then be demolished'. By floating some extreme ideas, more modest ones would cease to look as dangerous as the public, now in thrall to the TUC, cravenly believed.

'Stepping Stones' was a heady prospectus. 'We may have to take greater political risks than we had anticipated,' it remarked, and at the time this looked like a decided understatement of the future it proposed. In part it was consciously intended to jolt all the politicians who read it, and force them to think about long-term strategies not merely about vague objectives. To most politicians, as Hoskyns scornfully told the Conservative leadership, strategy could be defined as 'the careful thinking we wish we had done two years ago, but don't have time to do today'. Strategists, he insisted, 'have at least a tendency to win, while the tacticians are almost certain to lose'.

But the document was addressed to one set of politicians in particular, those who were counselling the leader against anything more ambitious than a soothing accommodation with union leaders. Prior was not the only man in this category. Among his most conspicuous supporters was the dedicated free-market, sound-money Thatcherite, John Biffen. Biffen was as opposed as Prior to stirring up the union masses, thus revealing very early in the piece a certain independence of judgment. This always distinguished Biffen from the more slavish Thatcherites and by the start of the second term had distanced him from them almost completely.

Through 1978, therefore, a mannerly ritual unfolded in which those who took the Hoskyns view, like Geoffrey Howe, pushed forward the frontiers of the thinkable, while those who took the Prior view sought to dampen expectations and fears alike. As this took its course, the leader steadily maintained the same posture: publicly on Prior's side, privately with Hoskyns. She promised to keep the unions out of the political arena if the Tories got to power, but until the end of 1978 that was the limit of her commitment.

What changed her public stance, and Prior's as well, was the behaviour of the unions during the winter of 1978–9, Labour's last, fatal winter in power. A series of public sector strikes and the collapse of the Government's attempt at a voluntary incomes policy swiftly transformed the politics of the trade-union question. Through 1978, Prior was subjected to a constant battering from Hoskyns, who now had standing as an official Thatcher adviser. This, indeed, became Hoskyns' principal *raison d'être*. Only after local government workers and others put millions of people to inconvenience and worse during the winter, and union leaders were exposed as men who could not deliver, did Prior begin to give ground. Public opinion now imperatively demanded proposals for the curbing of union power by law.

Hoskyns continued his private campaign to get Prior sacked from the Employment portfolio. But Mrs Thatcher resisted him. She now had an Employment spokesman who was committed to some new laws, and she felt happier with him. Not for the first time, her head defeated her heart for mastery.

But looking back on 'Stepping Stones', its authors felt it played a part, even though its blood and fury were never quite replicated in the statements of any Conservative leaders. They thought it opened up a debate, and helped to clarify a consensus for specific union reforms. It had also identified the interlocking nature of the problems to be addressed in the first term: the removal of controls and regulations on the economy, the reduction of inflation, the beginnings of control of public spending, trade union law reform, public-sector pay and the consequent fighting and winning of public sector strikes.

All these were to feature centrally in Mrs Thatcher's early years in power. Each one of them would be the subject of fierce argument then as well, as the factions jockeyed and manoeuvred round different conceptions of what a Conservative government should be doing. There would come a time when the 'Stepping Stones' philosophy if not its garish prescriptions for public education became the Conservative norm, and not a radical aberration.

Out of the wider political world at this time some conflicting signals came, as judgment on the leader of Her Majesty's Opposition. How was the ingénue regarded, as her leadership developed? Incredulity eventually receded. But outside the tight circle of her friends and closest colleagues, any admiration tended to be qualified. If the nature of these qualifications could be given a single epithet, the word would be patronising. Nobody was allowed to forget that Margaret Thatcher was indeed an outsider.

Among her colleagues she attracted awe, alarm and occasionally detestation. They inevitably compared her with the man they had known, Edward Heath. She resembled him in industry and application. She worked formidably hard, sometimes at too many things. One aide said at the time: 'I found her at two o'clock in the morning rewriting a badly drafted letter to some ordinary voter in Sunderland.'

She began by writing a lot of her own speeches, and always putting other people's drafts through several versions. This was leadership without delegation: one way of asserting command, but not the way the officer class was taught to do it. Whitelaw thought these habits very questionable. He didn't like her manner with the shadow cabinet either, which he described as governessy. There was no doubt, he thought, that being a woman, added to being an outsider, imposed on her an irresistible need to assert herself at every opportunity.

Outward signs of the gender problem were also soon apparent. One was very elementary. On the over-occupied front bench of the House of Commons, no one liked to get too close to her. Whereas normally the cream of British politics are required to sit cheek by tight-pressed cheek during the great parliamentary occasions, it was noticeable that a discreet island of green leather was now left free for her sole occupation: a quarantined area, or so it seemed, which the usurped gentlemen of Conservatism did not like to violate. This exceedingly male establishment took time for a woman, even one so forensically skilled as Margaret Thatcher, to master. 'She is often formidable, but only in the afternoon,' a colleague observed. 'At night the Commons becomes a much more masculine place, and she fades.'

She strove, particularly, to be as unlike Heath as possible. In party terms, Heath had never been a very successful politician, a point on which she was determined to be different.

One of his weaknesses, although he regarded it as a strength, was his refusal in any circumstances to make political gestures to the party. She was ever alert to the opportunity to do so, on immigration for example, and through her revivalist rhetorical style. Where Heath despised backbenchers, and often did not know their names, Mrs Thatcher set about cultivating them with manic energy and involving them, or so they imagined, in the making of policy. As many as seventy-five policy groups existed at one time, many of them peopled by backbenchers. To some of her colleagues, this seemed an excessive reaction to the Heath style, deluging her with paper and only making worse the problem which her own style was always in danger of creating: an inability, through sheer overload of her personal system, to distinguish big issues from small.

In one respect, her dissimilarity from Heath was a disadvantage which she had no choice but to rectify. Unlike him she knew almost nothing about foreign affairs, and had rarely been abroad on official business. A crash course in world travel was therefore arranged to which she applied herself with customary zeal. Before her first year was out she went to France, Germany, Rumania and Turkey. By the time she became prime minister, she had visited the Middle East, made repeated trips all over Europe, and been to the Far East, including most significantly China. In China, Heath's removal from office had scarcely been noticed and certainly did not diminish the grandiose welcome always bestowed on him. Among British politicians, it had become Heath's private fief. But when Mrs Thatcher went there in the spring of 1977, she was received no less lavishly.

Innocence abroad was one of the more dismal expectations many Tories had of her. 'Can you imagine her at a summit conference?' one of the party's chief foreign policy experts mused sceptically early in her time. By the end of her apprentice years, this apprehension was not entirely dispelled; but to the extent that it had been, this was due to two particular connections she made. These were each important in themselves. But they also revealed two important aspects of the leader's persona: on the one hand her alarming capacity for something like hero-worship, on the other her determination to ensure that nobody she met should ever forget that she too possessed heroic potential.

The first of these trips was to India in September 1976. Here she met one of the few women by whom she has ever allowed herself to be impressed, Indira Gandhi, then in her first eleven-year term as prime minister. It was the first of many meetings over the next decade, most of which were characterised by an atmosphere different from the one more commonly produced on her international journeys. It was free from stridency, rancour, hectoring, lecturing and the other emanations with which the British leader was for ever striving to dominate her interlocutors. With Mrs Gandhi she had from the beginning a uniquely easy relationship, based not on ideological sympathy – the Indian socialist had many deep differences with the British neo-capitalist – so much as on the shared experience of being a woman leader.

An Indian official present at their first encounter later recalled Mrs Thatcher sitting at Mrs Gandhi's feet, most earnestly asking her how she did it. How had she made it to the top? How had she stayed there? How had she sustained her domination of her party?

There was no doubt in this witness's mind which woman, at that stage, was dominant between them. And that is how Mrs Thatcher permitted it to remain even after she became prime minister. 'They could do business together with the utmost relaxation,' a Foreign Office minister from the early days recalled. 'It became a relationship between two rather regal figures, who simply instructed their officials to reach agreements.' When Mrs Gandhi was assassinated in 1984, Mrs Thatcher's spontaneous reaction evoked something of the intimacy they had especially enjoyed. 'I shall miss her very much indeed,' she said. 'Our friendship had a special quality.' The first sealing of their bond, in 1976, marked in an important way a large step in Margaret Thatcher's journey towards belief in herself as a rising international stateswoman.

But still more significant were her visits to the United States, first in 1975 and again, to more serious effect, in 1977. In 1975 she made an instant impression by speaking to familiar American fears about the future of Britain. Breaking the conventions which are meant to restrain party politicians from pursuing their differences abroad, she described Britain as an 'eleventh-hour nation', dedicated to 'the relentless pursuit of equality'. Rebuked by the Foreign Secretary,

James Callaghan, she replied: 'It's not part of my job to be a propagandist for a socialist society.'

Not for the last time, she was a tremendous hit with Americans. It was the beginning of a relationship which never broke down: which was, indeed, to be a definitive element of her foreign policy as prime minister. Having met, among others, Secretary of State Henry Kissinger, she said after the visit: 'I feel I have been accepted as a leader in the international sphere, the field in which they said I would never be accepted.'

But two years later this process was evidently not quite complete. At the 1977 London Summit, where she first met the new American President, Jimmy Carter, she was remembered by Carter's national security adviser, Zbigniew Brzezinski, as still being somewhat tentative. She was, he said, 'very determined, purposeful, not overly well informed on the specifics of international affairs, but certainly having a rather defined world view of her own which she was quite prepared to articulate'.[5]

Later this evaporated. On another visit to the US, she was invited into the White House by Carter, conspicuous recognition for an Opposition leader which had just been denied to the French Opposition leader, François Mitterrand. It was an honour she repaid less than considerately, but in a way which scarcely indicated shyness. She took the opportunity to harangue the president in a way he was not accustomed to. According to one of his aides, he said after the meeting that it was 'the first time I've given someone forty-five minutes and only managed to speak for five minutes myself'.

Little more than a year after Mrs Thatcher became leader, something unexpected happened. Harold Wilson suddenly retired as prime minister. It was not long before James Callaghan, who was elected in his place, proved a more formidable opponent.

The new leader had done her job well in Parliament against Wilson, her command of detail and love of statistics arming her for the thankless task an Opposition leader invariably faces. Wilson was deft and experienced, but also tarnished and no longer as menacing as he used to be. Callaghan soon presented a more difficult problem. An astute manager of his weak parliamentary position, he embodied exactly the lofty arrogance best calculated to bewilder and infuriate an inexperienced opponent. Callaghan had been Chancellor of the

Exchequer, Home Secretary and Foreign Secretary. He shone in none of these departments, but it was soon the general opinion that as prime minister he performed much better than the sum of his past. Denis Healey, contemptuous of Callaghan's record in each of his jobs, now called him *capax imperii*.

One Labour politician was delighted with the Thatcher leadership. Barbara Castle's diaries are a matchless chronicle of the years she held office, surpassing in colour and accuracy those of Richard Crossman. In them she recorded her enthusiasm at the news of Mrs Thatcher's original victory: 'She is so clearly the best man among them and she will, in my view, have an enormous advantage in being a woman too. I can't help feeling a thrill, even though I believe her election will make things much more difficult for us.'[6]

Sometimes Mrs Castle would regret that Margaret was a bit too prim and perfect. 'If she would only occasionally come in with a smut on her nose, her hair dishevelled, looking as if she'd been wrestling with her soul as I do.' But mostly Barbara watched her jousting, especially with Wilson, as one woman willing another on.

This was not the general Labour view. Not that the leadership feared Mrs Thatcher. They simply despised her. Throughout Callaghan's time, they felt a mounting sense of public duty to preserve the country from her. This feeling was something more intense than the normal party political reaction. For all her caution in making specific commitments, she began to be seen very clearly as, in Labour terms, a dangerous revolutionary, especially in the challenge she was making to the unions. Although under Callaghan Labour governed only by consent of the Liberal Party, eventually propped up by the so-called Lib–Lab pact, these years were the high point of Labour's belief in itself as the natural party of government.

Callaghan himself enjoyed a remarkably long personal honeymoon with the British establishment after he had permitted the International Monetary Fund to impose rigorous disciplines on his Government's economic policies in autumn 1976. For a time, there was a general belief that he could do no wrong. Colleagues heaped praise on his ability to distinguish the wood from the trees, get the big things right, solve petty disagreements by the well-judged shuffle of a committee. Labour MPs thought him accident-proof until the election. Even Tory businessmen, recovering from the inflationary disasters of Labour's first two years, admired Callaghan for his realism, his plainspoken ideas and his reactionary social opinions.

As for the man himself, he saw Mrs Thatcher as almost beneath notice. He was extraordinarily condescending. When he survived a confidence motion, he derided her with a sneer, warning her not to believe everything she read in the newspapers about crisis in government. He gave every impression of finding her quest to displace him a piece of presumption that strained his understanding.

Younger politicians were just as affronted, recognising in her a leader prepared to challenge social norms as well as economic orthodoxies. Men like Roy Hattersley and Gerald Kaufman scorned the world they saw her as representing, especially that part of it whose views were expressed by the National Association for Freedom, and all the people who had warmed to her alarm at the country being 'swamped' by immigrants. All good people, they seriously believed, must regard the Thatcher-led Conservative Party not merely as the place to which the pendulum, in its customary way, would regrettably one day swing back. It was a positive abomination.

Thus the battleground began to be starkly laid out. The atmosphere in government, largely induced by the realism Callaghan had to maintain in order to stay in power, was dominated by consensus and compromise. But the atmosphere in politics was quite different. The sense of a fundamental challenge looming was shared by both sides. Mrs Thatcher's own rhetoric grew in fundamentalist severity, and she began to sense a response in the country. Early in 1977 she told the Zurich Economic Society that she now had reason to believe that 'the tide is beginning to turn against collectivism, socialism, statism, *dirigisme*, whatever you call it . . . It is becoming increasingly obvious to many people who were intellectual socialists that socialism has failed to fulfil its promises, both in its more extreme forms in the Communist world and in its compromise versions.'

She also ventured more aggressively into a contest between moralities. Socialism, according to her account of it, was as lacking in morality as Conservatism always sounded in the mouths of Labour politicians. 'Choice is the essence of ethics,' she instructed the Zurich bankers. 'If there were no choice, there would be no ethics, no good, no evil: good and evil have meaning only insofar as man is free to choose.' Plainly the election was not going to be a contest resembling that between Heath and Wilson in 1966, when the Liberal Party was able to make credible play with a slogan, under pictures of their two opponents, asking 'Which Twin is the Tory?'

*   *   *

For the election, the leader knew she had to be prepared with more than policies. There was the matter of herself. All elections tend towards the presidential, with voters' attention being focused on the aspirant prime ministers to the exclusion of much else. Image and chemistry can be of overwhelming significance. As the Opposition years approached their climax, this aspect of politics called forth a facet of Mrs Thatcher's personality much exhibited before, though more rarely later: her accommodating malleability. Not merely in the shaping of her profile were the image-makers important. They performed one particular service which may have had a decisive impact on the course of recent history.

The Conservatives have never been short of professional advice about their presentation in the media. Macmillan took the advertising agents Colman, Prentis and Varley seriously, and Heath employed a valued personal adviser on his image, the advertising man Barry Day. The Central Office machine had long been heavily geared to politics as salesmanship. Mrs Thatcher did not hesitate to adapt this tradition to her own purposes. A leader now so committed to an image of guileless rectitude might perhaps have been expected to be above such practices. But she was a professional. If selling the party and fashioning its leader's public profile were elementary preconditions for winning the election, she would not hesitate to do what was required. She entered with the greatest enthusiasm, according to those who helped her, into every stratagem they thought necessary.

As chairman of the party, in charge of the machine, she had appointed Peter Thorneycroft: a suitably emblematic figure, most famous for having resigned from Macmillan's cabinet over excessive public spending, but also a genuine, unthreatening veteran, who had been out of politics for over a decade and offered no sort of rivalry to the leader. Lord Thorneycroft, however, was not the man who mattered in the selling of the prime minister. Far more important was a former television producer, Gordon Reece, whom Mrs Thatcher allowed to take her in hand and adjust her public personality.

Reece subsequently acquired a sizeable reputation. He was even portrayed in some quarters as a kind of Svengali to Margaret's Trilby, being credited with persuasive powers and political command quite out of the ordinary. This overstated the matter.

Reece was a television man and almost nothing else. He had worked, mainly for Associated Television, on chat shows, comic shows, even religious shows, but rarely if ever on political shows. One of his most winning characteristics, from the point of view of a politician, was his lack of interest in the substance of political issues. All that mattered was that he was a Conservative supporter – but also one who had spotted this particular Conservative politician, and surrendered himself to her, earlier than almost anyone else. Their relationship went back to her earliest broadcasts as Education Secretary, when Reece would be on hand to help her relax in front of the cameras. He was at her side during the October 1974 election. He was behind the scenes during the leadership contest, getting her photographed in womanly pose beside the kitchen sink, and advising her not to debate with the other candidates. When she won, it was clearly to him that, sooner or later, she would turn for full-time service as her image-maker.

What he offered her was a sharp sense of television effects, and a rare capacity to persuade her that she should repose total confidence in his judgment. He coached her in lowering her voice and attended to such details as the reshaping of her hair and the clothes she wore in public. He was, in short, a valet: but one who showed that where television and high politics meet, that role has acquired an importance a thousand times greater than when it was confined to brushing down a gentleman's dress suit.

For a putative Svengali, Reece appeared to be a surprisingly nervy and insecure man. Short and dapper, and a quick smiler, he made a point of drinking nothing but champagne, as if to fulfil the cliché of what a TV-producer-turned-adman ought to be. Thorneycroft could not abide his extravagance. But he did have the talent to make his employer relax and even, occasionally, laugh. Nor was he frightened, like so many of her political colleagues, by her being a woman.

Being a woman, in fact, made her all the more receptive to his cosmetic advice. Women, he reasoned, were accustomed to being dressed and coiffured by other people, usually men. A woman was an easier product for an image-maker to work with. He once confided to me that he had been the recipient of that rarest of contrivances, a Thatcher joke. 'If we lose the election, I may be sacked,' she told him in the spring of 1978. 'But you will be shot.'

Reece, in turn, introduced into the political world a name that became even more famous than his: the name of Saatchi. The Saatchi brothers ran the fastest-rising advertising agency in Britain. Reece personally selected them to handle the Conservative Party account, and was thus responsible for forging one of the more memorable creations of the Thatcher years.

Charles and Maurice Saatchi were young men of Iraqi–Jewish

descent who made a mark in advertising well before they were thirty. They were sharp, talented and intensely ambitious, and they were to prove staggeringly successful. While no one would claim that it was the Conservative account that made them rich, Mrs Thatcher's election success certainly made their reputation. In at the beginning of the Thatcher period, they are among its ideal exemplars in a business sense. In 1978, when the Conservatives took them on, Saatchi and Saatchi's annual profit was £1.8 million. A decade later, with over 150 offices world-wide and over 60 of the world's largest 100 advertisers on their books, that figure had grown more than fifty times bigger.

The campaign they began for Margaret Thatcher, with her enthusiastic approval, made few concessions to the elevated sensibilities of politicians. Any Conservatives who imagined themselves to be embarking alongside their leader on a crusade which ranked with Gladstone's Midlothian campaign, had swiftly to revise their expectations. After interviewing Reece, the trade magazine *Campaign* put politicians squarely in their place. Saatchi's approach was going to break new ground, it reported, and 'by the time it is all finished the Tories may well have an election property which party members find difficult to recognise and the electorate finds a complete surprise.' On television broadcasting, Saatchi's instructions from Reece, acting on the leader's authority, were to 'eschew the clichés which have dominated Tory party politicals for the past decade and major [*sic*] on the selling of a brand in the most acceptable way'.

By plunging serenely into this new world, Mrs Thatcher showed a lack of fastidiousness that did credit to her commitment to victory. The agency was given a free hand. Excluded from most of the decision-making were almost all the politicians themselves. Even the most senior Conservative figures made their appearances in party broadcasts by grace and favour of the agency, often with scripts that reflected an advertising rather than a political judgment.

But the Saatchi effort during the summer of 1978 had one effect for which the politicians were grateful. 'It was the one great achievement for which they deserved credit,' said one of the party's more sceptical officials at the time. The weight and effectiveness of their advertising, under the legend 'Labour Isn't Working', began to register in the opinion polls: a factor that helped persuade Callaghan, contrary to expectations in every party, not to call an election in autumn 1978 but to wait until the following spring. If that was so – and it must have been at least partly responsible for Callaghan's retreat from early combat – it is one of the rare examples, in a field dominated by crude and baseless hype, of an advertising campaign having some demonstrable effect on the outcome of a political event.

For the delay was greatly helpful to the Conservatives, not merely in increasing their electoral chances but in resolving their main policy dispute – the great undecided question of whose instincts should prevail, Jim Prior's or Margaret Thatcher's, coupled with those of Hoskyns and Joseph, in the matter of trade union reform. The winter which Callaghan used to cling on to power delivered a series of industrial catastrophes for the Government, with destructive strikes piled upon inflationary pay claims.

These made the Government deeply unpopular. But they also removed from Labour the right to claim that it alone could hold together the social compact under which any British government was supposedly obliged to operate. Both premise and conclusion of this thesis were in ruins. It was doubtful whether the unions should any longer be seen as necessary partners in government, and quite certain that Labour could no longer rely on them. So Prior surrendered at least half his ground. From being a liability to the Tories, the union issue became through this 'winter of discontent' a potential election-winner, so long as it was properly handled.

When the election was finally called, after the Callaghan government lost a no-confidence motion by one vote on 30 March 1979, it found the leader of the Opposition well prepared but still vulnerable on a number of fronts. Both in her personal standing and in the policies to which she pledged herself, there was room for a Conservative to wonder what to expect.

She had come a long way in four years. She was indubitably the leader of her party, in fact as well as name. In her shadow cabinet were most of the leading Tories, whom she had pretty well compelled to bow the knee. Many of them still did not like her. One spoke for a good number when he told me in 1978: 'She is still basically a Finchley lady. Her view of the world is distressingly narrow. She regards the working class as idle, deceitful, inferior and bloody-minded. And she simply doesn't understand affairs of state. She doesn't have enough breadth.'

All the same, that man stayed on and climbed the ladder. Although he found her leadership style insufferably bossy, he swallowed it. Like the others, he had learned to live with her. She did, admittedly, say some very silly things by way of asserting her domination as government beckoned. For example, she, who thrived on combat and disputation, promised that she would as prime minister choose a cabinet of like-minded colleagues because, she told the *Observer* in February 1979, 'I couldn't waste time having any internal arguments.' There were to be more differences between her cabinet ministers even than in the Callaghan Government, as she must have known there would be. But still, she had greatly narrowed the credibility gap which for years persuaded many people in and out of Parliament that she could never become prime minister.

She had also come to grips with Callaghan, the man she had to beat. Her scorn was as genuine as his condescension and, as the events of winter drained him of authority, she expressed herself with ever greater self-assurance. When Callaghan tried to downplay the crisis, she argued that it was a matter of averting 'not just disruption but anarchy'. Deriding his impotence in the face of public service strikes, she declared: 'You no longer have the courage to act. Will you not at least have the courage to resign?'

But she projected this image of confidence against the grain of public opinion. Although Labour were fourteen points behind the Tories when the election campaign began, Callaghan was six points ahead of Mrs Thatcher in the personal ratings. She was seen as untried, unsympathetic and alarming. Even though the unions had become a Conservative and not a Labour issue, there was still a belief that the grappling should be done with kid gloves. People were frightened by out-and-out confrontation, and worried that she might not be able to handle the unions effectively. Gordon Reece, alert to these anxieties, said privately as the election approached that he would be happy if he could arrange for the leader to be seen but never heard on television news each night – a ruthless objective he was not entirely unsuccessful in achieving.

After all the brainstorming by study groups and the arguments between radical right and moderate centre, the policies also settled into surprising sogginess. Not for the first time, Thatcher the tactician got the better of Thatcher the ideologue. In this process, the ideologue was never buried. She always lived to reappear later. The tactician, in other words, acted as a kind of cover. But tactics, for the truly ambitious, must always take precedence, and tactics dictated a necessary vagueness in the party manifesto.

Here the influence of the Heath experience was to be seen at work.

In 1970, Heath had gone to the country with many specific and public plans. But, as Mrs Thatcher observed, he had not won the argument. She had sought to give the argument priority and, despite having the kind of lawyer's mind which is happiest dealing with the actual and the concrete, was always worried about making too many policy commitments. As early as 1976, before a visit to Australia, she mused to a colleague on the main thing she hoped to learn there. She keenly desired to know how Malcolm Fraser, the new Liberal (in British terms Conservative) prime minister, had succeeded 'without having any policy'. President Carter's embarrassment in 1977, when he was forced to retreat from a promised tax rebate, was another influential lesson.[7]

The number of specifics not dealt with in April 1979 by this most categoric of political leaders was considerable. Looking back after a third Thatcher election victory, one cannot but be struck by the mildness of what was promised and the consensual elements that survived in the leader's rhetoric. She was still paying much respect to the wisdom of the time.

The party was not, for example, opposed to an incomes policy. It disapproved of statutory pay control, but the national preoccupation with wages during the winter of discontent obliged Mrs Thatcher to concede at the time that 'pay policies are of course extremely important'.

The manifesto openly contemplated the perpetuation of the comfortable corporate state. Although it promised specific reforms of the law on picketing and the closed shop, and said unions should pay more of the costs of strikes, they were still seen in April 1979 as consulting partners in government. Public sector pay would be reconciled with cash limits 'in consultation with the unions'. Open and informed discussion was promised with unions and employers on the Government's economic objectives 'so that there is wider understanding of the consequences of unrealistic bargaining and industrial action'. The German system of round-table discussion between the economic estates of the realm was explicitly commended.

True, the shape of a distinctively Thatcherite programme was clearly picked out. There would be income tax cuts, reduced government borrowing, a more strictly controlled money supply, the sale of council houses. The manifesto proclaimed a philosophy of business and free enterprise, and promised by implication a painful shake-out of subsidised jobs in ailing firms. But it was also the expression of a philosophy only half-embraced.

The best proof of this was what it had to say about the most sacred of Tory obsessions, denationalisation. In later years this became one of the Thatcher government's central and enduring achievements. But in 1979, they weren't too sure about it. Only the National Freight Corporation was nominated for return to the private sector. There was a limit to the challenge the party was prepared to make to orthodoxy: a limit to its conviction, to its unity, and certainly to the abrasive confrontations for which it was willing to prepare the voters.

This restraint was carried into the election campaign itself. Reece didn't quite manage to prevent the leader being heard at all. But her appearances were honed for the pictorial media. The adman kept his eye on that night's television news and next day's front pages, with much photography of a harsh politician in gentle environments. Holding a newborn calf, this least agricultural of women said: 'It's not for me, it's for the photographers. They're the most important people on this campaign.'

Her speeches, while full of historic resonance about the lateness of the hour, were above all designed to diminish the fear of her as an alarming figure. 'Unless we change our ways and our direction,' she said towards the end, 'our greatness as a nation will soon be a footnote in the history books, a distant memory of an offshore island, lost in the mists of time, like Camelot, remembered kindly for its noble past.'

As every Opposition leader is entitled to do, she spent a great deal of time attacking the Government's record, less in specifying the real world Conservative policies would create. Circumspectly, she played the union card Labour had thrown away. 'Never forget how near this nation came to government by picket. Never forget how workers had to beg for the right to work.'

But what she did most and best was display her prodigious energy, racing round the country on a ceaseless exercise in self-exposure through walkabouts, factory visits, radio phone-ins and house-visiting, as well as the more routine speech-making. She ran her entourage into the ground. She also, they thought, played to her strength: the vastly better impression she was capable of making in personal appearances than usually came through her formal public work.

In retrospect, the 1979 election has been analysed as one the Conservatives were certain to win. And so perhaps it was, after the catastrophic winter and the draining away of Labour's claims to be uniquely fitted to rule. But only much later did it become clear quite how completely a socialist epoch was drawing to its close.

That wasn't how it seemed at the time, even though the Conservatives remained ahead in the opinion polls, with the odd exception, throughout the campaign. Margaret Thatcher's low personal standing compared with Callaghan's – his personal lead over her stretched to nineteen points by the end – alarmed many a Conservative candidate. The tenor of the campaign revealed a leader and a party that, for all their grandiloquence, were uncertain about the speed at which the collectivist tide was turning.

'The question you will have to consider', Callaghan told the electorate early in the campaign, 'is whether we risk tearing everything up by the roots.' At the end of it he pressed his case that a Conservative government 'would sit back and just allow firms to go bankrupt and jobs to be lost in the middle of a world recession'. Led by a thoroughly disturbing, even erratic woman, the Tories were 'too big a gamble for the country to take'.

At the time this seemed like typical politician's hyperbole. And the country rejected it, returning the Conservatives with a majority of 43. But Callaghan's words were more prescient than he knew. His predictions of disaster were false, but his imagery was apt: more so, even, than the Conservative Party itself really understood. The roots were indeed about to be dug up, and a ten-year gamble begun.

Part Two

Them and Us
1979–1983

9

Not Dogma But Reason

FOR THE CONSERVATIVE Party, the 1979 election produced an historic victory. But upon its leader the effect was still more elevated, something closer to a transfiguration. It was the beginning of a period which could later be defined as an era, in which an ordinary politician, labouring under many disadvantages, grew into an international figure who did some extraordinary things to her country. This was a large evolution. Long before it was complete, the name of Thatcher was taken for granted as one of the givens of British life. More than six million voters at the 1987 election reached voting age after 1979 and were too young to have known any government other than one under this leader. It was easy to lose sight of the politician who became prime minister in May 1979.

She had travelled a long way from Grantham. All around her were visible signs of an astonishing achievement. She had mastered, perhaps first of all, the problem of her sex. This remained the biggest psychic obstacle, the fact which she had always feared would most impair her credibility. Although she had been party leader for four years, this was not long enough to carry her into a world where she was automatically accepted. Being a woman was still a disadvantage, she was sure. In a country so socially conservative as Britain, a female leader remained peculiarly vulnerable to jibes and doubts. Who could be sure how deep an affront she offered to atavistic prejudices, both male and female? In the event, the answer was clear: not much at all. She won quite easily, as a woman. Analysis of the voting showed that the largest surge of support came from people usually reckoned to be most unsympathetic to a woman leader: the men and women of the skilled working class.

Her victory made her unique not only in the history of Britain but in that of the Western world. When she had said, years before, that the Treasury was as high as any woman could expect to get, she meant it. For her to have defeated her own prediction was, judged in historic terms, a barely credible achievement.

Nor was it the only reason for an ecstatic feeling of personal triumph. Many people, for a variety of reasons, had expected her to fail. As the election campaign reached its climax, and victory came almost to be expected, this was forgotten. But doubt and criticism of a personal kind had been her experience throughout her leadership. As leader she attracted the party's ritual loyalty, and could rely on the total commitment of her friends, some of it extravagant and some of it from supposedly even-handed journalists. 'She is going to be a very, very big success,' Paul Johnson told Tricia Murray before the election. Brian Walden, a television interviewer and former Labour MP, said: 'This country needs someone like Margaret Thatcher. In years to come great novels and poems will be written about her.' But such voices still belonged to a minority sect. In the party at large, and especially near the top of it, wary scepticism, verging on outright alarm, was the verdict. Her jarring personality was always thought to be a loser, as the opinion polls regularly confirmed. Her right-wing ideas, masked though they were by the cautious language of the manifesto, were still regarded as dangerously outlandish.

These sceptics had now surely been put to rout. The leader turned out not to be an impediment to her party. On the contrary, victory was her personal vindication. That is the truth about every modern election, conducted as it always is in presidential style. The leader dominates the scene. Victory is the leader's triumph, as defeat is the leader's fault. This election in particular was potentially the infusion of a new life-force into the body politic, and one which drew on the essence of the leader's personality. It was not a routine political shift but the assembling of a critical mass of popular support behind the Thatcherite appeal for radical change. In this it was quite a contrast with Heath's election in 1970. It was far more emphatic, not numerically but politically. Until the day of the 1970 election, Heath was not expected to win it, a fact which rendered the result politically ambiguous. This time, not only a Labour government but socialism itself seemed to have been comprehensively defeated.

At one level, an awareness of this expressed itself through Mrs Thatcher's words and actions. The occasion of her first arrival in Downing Street as prime minister was a case in point. The text selected for her, by her speech-writer Ronald Millar, exuded self-confident grandeur. 'Where there is discord, may we bring harmony,' she declaimed. 'Where there is error may we bring truth. Where there is doubt may we bring faith. Where there is despair may we bring hope.' As a promise it was misleading, and as a bid for saintly association it misfired, since, although attributed to St Francis of Assisi, the words are in fact a piece of nineteenth-century piety. But as the keynote for a leadership, it had a seigneurial ring. Here, it seemed, was a leader who knew she had entered her inheritance.

Yet that, in truth, is not an accurate depiction of her state of mind in May 1979. Although the triumph was great, it did not banish her considerable misgivings. Alongside the euphoria went anxiety. She hinted at it during the campaign, when a BBC interviewer asked her whether she doubted her ability to do the job of prime minister. She replied with thoughts few men would have spoken. 'Of course you have doubts,' she said, 'and you're tremendously aware of the responsibility. I just hope that people will take me as I am for what I can do.' A word not to be neglected in epitomising Margaret Thatcher, at the age of fifty-three, at the moment she became prime minister, is insecurity.

All her working habits belied it. Her style was built on domination. None of her colleagues had ever experienced a more assertive, even overbearing, leader. That had always been her way of doing business, and it became much more pronounced when, having defeated all her male rivals in 1975, she needed to establish a dependable ascendancy over them. With her command of facts and figures and her reluctance ever to lose an argument, she seemed so damnably sure of herself that nobody could suppose there lurked much uncertainty anywhere in her makeup. Certitude was her stock-in-trade, the commodity with which she planned to exorcise the vapid compromises of post-war politics. It was what got most of her ministers down, fainthearts that they were. It was also what the country most noticed about her. Whenever perceptions of her character were tested in opinion polls, she always scored heavily in the assertive virtues of firmness and clarity. Mirroring this, hardly anyone said they didn't know what they thought about her. There were supporters and opponents, and almost no one in between.

To an important extent, this clarity and sureness were deceptive. Her manner had become habitual. But in part it was an act, put on to convince herself and others that she really was the boss, and a cover for deeper apprehensions.

Although Margaret Thatcher was born to be a politician, she was not born to rule. She possessed no trace of the effortless superiority of the Balliol men, Macmillan and Heath, who went before her. For her, each step up the ladder was a struggle against the odds posed by her gender and her lack of any fraternity with her male colleagues. She was seen by them as an able minister: hard-working, single-minded, a fierce antagonist in argument, and an uncrackable performer in the House of Commons. She had developed and deepened these qualities as leader of the Opposition. But her experience was modest. She had held no great office. She could not compensate for this with the inner self-confidence vouchsafed to those whose great expectations began from the moment of birth. Although she knew the Tory Party well enough, she did not know much about the establishment, social or political, or about the centre of the government machine. Her position as an outsider, which she exploited to great effect in the party, was a less impressive credential in Whitehall.

She was also less than fully secure in the party itself. She did not yet possess or control it. Partly this was because, throughout her period in Opposition, she was on trial. There is a difference between the Conservative and Labour parties. In the Labour Party it is possible to dominate without ever having won an election. The more democratic nature of the party, and the tests it constantly requires any leader to undergo, can confer on anyone who passes them an authority separate from national electoral success. This is what happened for a time to Neil Kinnock after his election to the Labour leadership in 1983. By contrast, a Conservative leader who has not won is always on probation.

In Margaret Thatcher's case, this feeling of less than full-hearted consent was doubly strong and unlikely to be dispelled even by an election victory. For the Conservatives won in 1979 in an oddly disunited state, and it was by no means certain that the leader stood on the winning side of the divide. She was still there on sufferance, a fact well illustrated by her unwillingness to dispose of the leading colleagues who disagreed with her, and thus make this truly her own party. Of the probable cabinet, only two members, Keith Joseph and Norman St John Stevas, had voted for her in the secret ballot for the leadership election. The others all opposed her on the first ballot, and some of them did so still. Uneasiness pervaded the atmosphere of the collective. There was much male condescension. Irritation at being ruled over by a woman was something Jim Prior, for example, admitted to experiencing throughout his time in the Thatcher cabinet. 'I found it very difficult to stomach,' he later wrote.[1] There was also, at the beginning, a lot of private incredulity. Sir Ian Gilmour, who was despatched to the Foreign Office, never thought for a moment that the Thatcher experiment would last. The Thatcherite phase would be no more than an intermission, he thought, after which those to whom the Conservative Party historically belonged would reassume command. And Gilmour was not alone.

This was an unsatisfactory position. But because the leaders of the group of lurking sceptics – one would call them a faction, if that did not imply too high a level of organisation – included substantial names like Prior and Carrington, there could be no question of simply removing them. They were indispensable confederates. More than that, they were in a sense stronger than she was. Along with Prior, Walker and Gilmour, they remained key participants in an argument which was not yet resolved, and in which they possibly carried heavier guns than she did.

Nor could she be certain about the exact meaning of her victory. Were the voters really ready for her? The campaign, although great in its denunciations and spacious in its promises, was not very specific about what would happen next. It talked about lower taxes but not about higher unemployment. It vowed that public spending would be controlled, but there wasn't a word about cutting public services. Individual freedom was to be expanded and the role of government supposedly reduced. What had not been stressed was how uncomfortable this was likely to be for many people now cocooned in the arms of the protective State.

Personally, the leader had not thought deeply about these negative aspects of her policy either. They did not particularly excite her horror. That was part of the point of what she believed in: that it was bad for people to be cosseted and protected, and therefore unhelpful to dwell with too much anguish on the difficulties inevitably awaiting the unfortunates at the bottom of society. On the other hand, the leadership well knew that unemployment would have to rise quite steeply before, according to the optimists, it went down. Central to their plans was a scouring out of the economy of uncounted thousands of unproductive jobs. Privately they knew that, except for higher taxpayers, the immediate pain would exceed the pleasure. And yet they had not been able to say this. So a question hung over the political feasibility of what the leader wanted to achieve.

Offsetting this, though, was her great faith in her own judgment. This is what had been fortified by the election. After it, who could deny that the people felt as she did? A year after it, when her popularity was much reduced, she was entirely confident of the bond between them. 'Deep in their instincts,' she told me in August 1980, 'people find what I am saying and doing right, and I know it is because that is the way I was brought up. I regard myself as a very normal, ordinary person, with all the right, instinctive antennae.'[2] The leader who entered 10 Downing Street in May 1979 was therefore a cluster of paradoxes. She was a strong woman with much to prove: a populist who was widely unpopular: a triumphant election-winner who yet had reason to doubt how her victory could be turned to her advantage. She had strong passions she managed to moderate, held many convictions which her most powerful colleagues disagreed with. She had won the country but not yet won the cabinet. Known for her ferocious way with dissenters, she was also known for succumbing to them. She made much of her big ideas, the need for radical change and the possibility of a new world, but she was a lot less clear both in public and private about her strategy for getting there. Strategy, as is sometimes the way with politics, was more the province of chroniclers after the event, putting things together. There were plans, but was there a Big Plan? For the practitioner at the time, it was a matter of working one out on the job.

At the heart of the Conservatives' concerns was the economy. Economic regeneration was the major electoral commitment, and it included, however deceptively, a pledge to cut the dole queues. This was the major point of the leader's own attacks on the Labour Government. 'Sometimes I've heard it said', she had stated in a party political broadcast in May 1977, when unemployment stood at 1.3 million, 'that Conservatives have been associated with unemployment. That's absolutely wrong. We'd have been drummed out of office if we'd had this level of unemployment.' James Callaghan, she also said, would go down in history as the prime minister of unemployment. He could not 'run away from the fact that our policies did not produce unemployment as his have'.

Now she had to put this to the proof. She did not promise any quick fixes. 'It contains no magic formula, and is not a recipe for an easy or a perfect life,' she cautioned when the 1979 manifesto was published. 'The recovery of our country' would take a long time to begin to bring about.

The making of her first cabinet reflected this economic imperative. Conscious of her weakness in the party, she was determined not to let it compromise the central economic programme. She was not able to dispose of the old guard of Heathites and other sceptics, but she didn't need to put them in charge of the departments that mattered most to her, where the break with the past was, she believed, most necessary. Although she insisted that the policy was based 'not on a dogma but on reason, on common sense', she ensured that believing dogmatists were placed in the economic departments, where the dogma of monetarism would prove the surest defence against the siren voices of old orthodoxies.

To the Treasury she sent Geoffrey Howe, her faithful servant for the past five years. This was not a foregone conclusion. Howe had given the party some anxiety as shadow chancellor. He was essentially a man of government not opposition, and in Parliament, where shadow ministers make or break their reputations, his plodding style scored few hits against the incumbent Chancellor, Denis Healey. Indeed, so vast was the discrepancy in their public performance that an innocent visitor to the House of Commons might well have supposed that it was the brilliant and brutal Healey who was the Opposition spokesman, and Howe, with his defensive, narcoleptic monotone, who faced the daily task of defending one of the most dismal economic records of any post-war government. When Healey likened an argument with Howe to the experience of being 'savaged by a dead sheep', Sir Geoffrey was not alone in being wounded by the thrust. Many Conservatives could see the truth of it.

The leader too was worried. A measure of the desperation around her was a suggestion, seriously canvassed late in 1978, that Keith Joseph should, after all, be given the Treasury. There was even another idea. Some advisers toyed with the notion of persuading Roy Jenkins back to British politics. Jenkins, who had proved himself an excellent disciplinarian Chancellor between 1967 and 1970 in the Government of Harold Wilson, was now President of the European Commission. He was known to be thoroughly disenchanted with his old party, and had ceased to refer to himself as a member of it. Although no direct approach was made to him, there was talk, as the election drew nearer and Howe stubbornly failed to impress, of luring him back from Brussels into a safe Conservative seat. Nothing came of it. But set beside the arrogant self-confidence later exhibited by Conservative economic policy-makers, including Howe himself, this usefully recalls a period of uncertainty. Before the election, the Thatcher leadership was far less settled or sure than it usually appeared afterwards.

So Howe got the job. The inexorable tortoise of late-twentieth-century Conservatism continued on his way. Howe was not the designer of economic Thatcherism. In fact he was rather looked down on by men whose past was cleaner than his of pragmatic intellectual compromise. He did not take an automatic place in what passed for the Thatcher circle, even when he lived next door at 11 Downing Street. But he became Thatcherism's chief mechanic, the indispensable overseer of the machine, whatever direction it took.

As his closest colleague, the leader gave him someone in whom she had greater confidence, John Biffen, MP for Oswestry. To lock the Treasury tight against unsound influences, he became Chief Secretary. It would be too much to say that Biffen was Howe's 'minder' – although such a figure was placed in several other departments, where the leading minister's doctrinal soundness was felt to be in need of Thatcherite invigilation. Employment, under Jim Prior, was in that category, and so was the Department of Education, which was given, to widespread astonishment, to a noted Heathite, Mark Carlisle. Howe was never on that list. Biffen, on the other hand, was the epitome of a Thatcherite, or so the leader thought, and a reliable accomplice in the assault on Keynesian economic theories. Unlike Howe, he was a trained economist. Even more unlike Howe, he had not had to learn monetarism and unlearn what he first thought of. The faith came naturally to him.

John Biffen was the first authentic Thatcher political creation. Only two other members of the cabinet had taken no part in the Heath government. Nicholas Edwards, whom she made Welsh Secretary, was a new MP when Heath came to power, so had been ineligible. Angus Maude, now appointed to the sinecure post of Paymaster-General, was excluded from all influence under Heath long before. As Maude showed by his writings in the 1960s, he was an outspoken critic of Macmillan's as well as Heath's Conservatism: a prophet before his time, therefore, of what became known as Thatcherism. But, of this select group, Biffen was much the most important. The leader admired his intellect and liked his ideas. Though he was younger than her, she saw him as a kind of guru, and possibly one who got it right when she had got it wrong. Further, as a friend and disciple of Enoch Powell, the great untouchable of Conservatism since he bolted the party in 1974, he was the respectable embodiment of Powellite ideas, so many of which Mrs Thatcher found herself, belatedly, espousing.

Biffen's reasons for disliking Heath and all he stood for were actually the reasons which could have taken her, were she permitted some magical retrospective consistency, into the same wilderness. He had no time for state planning, did not believe in incomes policy, scorned all evidences of the corporate state, adhered unalterably to the cause of sound money. He was also an open enemy of British membership of the European Community. So even here, although Mrs Thatcher could not join the anti-Europe camp, there was a shared attitude. She was never keen on the Common Market or the importunate demands Community membership made on Britain, as she subsequently showed many times as prime minister. Once given the opportunity, she reversed the European priority which Heath, a fanatical believer, had imposed on the party. And since people like Howe, not to mention Carrington, Prior and the rest of her antagonists, remained more Heathite than Thatcherite when it came to Europe, this was an issue on which Biffen enjoyed special favour.

He entered the leadership circle, out of nowhere, as soon as Mrs Thatcher took over. Desiring to move right, she was faced with a paucity of talent among people committed to the same objective. Biffen was an obvious exception. Unlike other right-wingers, he was a man of wit and subtlety. Unlike Keith Joseph he had been, in Joseph's terms, a Conservative all his life. He was put into the shadow cabinet in charge of Energy, and survived in the leader's favour despite having to retire from the fray for a while on medical grounds. She never lost faith in him. For he had another attraction apart from his monetarist convictions. He was, like her, a self-made politician. The son of a tenant-farmer from Somerset, who still spoke with a West Country burr, he was a reassuring counterbalance to the landed gentry and other public-school men who were thrust upon her. A grammar schoolboy who won a scholarship to Cambridge was a meritocrat especially to be welcomed. This leader was as acutely sensitive to class as she was to belief, and Biffen passed both the tests.

Over his career as a whole, Biffen did not faithfully repay this besotted admiration. Although he was a believer, he was far too intelligent to be a dogmatist. There came a time in the history of Thatcherism when his role changed, and he ceased to be keeper of the intellectual conscience – and became something more like the social conscience instead. But he was part of the pattern Mrs Thatcher imposed with narrow determination: the ascendancy of like-minded men. With the exception of Prior, every minister with economic responsibility was dedicated to Keith Joseph's economic ideas, by whatever tortuous route they had discovered them.

Joseph himself was put in the Department of Industry. For such a zealous purist, it was not a happy placing. The department groaned under its massive interventionist duties. It had a budget of £2,200 million, and managerial responsibilities of precisely the kind which Josephism said should not exist anywhere in government. Joseph's brief was to work himself out of a job by winding down these responsibilities: a task which alas would be preceded, to his most painful embarrassment, by necessarily increasing them still further. His budget actually increased to £3,300 million in two years. To connoisseurs of political irony, there could be few more diverting spectacles than that of Joseph pouring ever larger sums of state money into fiefdoms he would have preferred to give away, particularly British Leyland and British Steel. But, at the beginning, that did not matter. What mattered was that, with Joseph in the post, the Industry Secretary could be relied on to speak for anything the Chancellor wanted to do.

At the Department of Trade was placed another keen monetarist theoretician, John Nott. Nott was a merchant banker, and yet another Tory whose intellectual odyssey was quite erratic. He too had served under Heath. He was actually a Treasury minister at the time when Heath's notorious U-turn towards fiscal laxity and monetary expansion – the famous 'Barber boom', named after Heath's Chancellor – was moving into top gear. Nott was not then heard to criticise the policies he was partly in charge of. There was talk of his being unhappy with them. And, after the event, he joined the ranks of those who coolly detached themselves from what they had lately been responsible for. Well before 1979, although his emotional vagaries were sometimes even less predictable than Joseph's, his commitment to the cause was beyond reproach.

So was that of the last member of the economic team. David Howell, as Secretary of State for Energy, could be described as the man in charge of the supply side of the equation. One of the gratifying certainties which beckoned was that the first Thatcher Government would coincide with the swift escalation of production of North Sea oil, the greatest uncovenanted economic blessing the country had ever enjoyed. It was important to have a true believer at Energy, and Howell was now a man of the cloth in full monetarist orders.

In his way he was an archetype. If Biffen was the prophet brought in from the wilderness, Howell was the convert who had changed his mind – had done so, in fact, rather more often than anybody could count. They are perfect examples of the two types of politician Mrs Thatcher has consistently held in highest regard.

Howell, too, was an economist, but one with a mind not so much open as permanently vulnerable to a succession of opposing certainties. In 1961, for example, he wrote that there was 'little evidence to suggest that high tax rates are a particular disincentive to mental effort and personal dynamism'. By 1965 he had decided the opposite was the case. No single change, he opined, would have 'a more dramatic, climate-changing effect' than a cut in maximum tax rates.

Tax was not the only economic variable sensitive to all the winds that blew. In 1974, as Keith Joseph was beginning to experience first intimations of his Damascene conversion to monetarism, Howell took the whole monetarist thesis apart. Writing in *Crossbow*, just before the defeat of the Heath Government of which he was a junior member, he likened monetarists to mad scientists. They were playing with the economy as if it were a structure of glass tubes through which flowed various liquids, achieving perfect balance with each other and proving that 'it was technically impossible for demand not to be curbed if the red liquid in the tube marked "money supply" began to fall.' How simple it all seemed, Howell scornfully reflected. Yet, little more than a year later, he entered the laboratory himself, pumping the magic potions around the monetarist model with quite as much enthusiasm as Keith Joseph. He became a completely trusted believer in what Mrs Thatcher herself now believed in.

Later, Howell was to undergo yet another onset of scepticism. Removed from the Government after its first term, during which he served as Transport Secretary as well as at Energy, this endlessly reflective man thought again, and began to doubt the strength of the link between the monetary aggregates and economic performance, the key connection postulated by the monetarists. Nor, for example, did he now consider the causal relationship between tax rates and revenues 'as mathematical and predictable as hitherto held'.[3]

But in 1979 Howell was an uncritical exponent of the *zeitgeist*, eloquently exploding the Heathite consensus and ridiculing the 'grandiose absurdities of incomes policies and industrial strategies'. Biffen, who had said this all the time, could not have put it better.

These four men personified and guaranteed the intellectual thrust of early Thatcherism, and particularly its manifestation in the first budget brought in by the fifth among them, Geoffrey Howe. Except for Biffen, they did not have much to do with its detailed construction. But they ensured that no veto existed in the hands of any minister less committed than they were to the monetarist idea. They were blood brothers of a prime minister who knew with unusual clarity what she wanted to do, and who soon demonstrated the interventionist habit which Sir Douglas Wass, the permanent secretary at the Treasury, found to be unique among the ten administrations he had served. This prime minister, Wass said after leaving government, was 'much more the First Lord of the Treasury than any previous holder of that office'.[4]

She brought to that post no great technical expertise, but a handful of unshakeable economic principles. As a matter of fact, she had learned a lot about the technicalities. She had taken lessons in Opposition, not merely from Joseph but from more professional hands. Prominent among these were Patrick Minford, an inflexibly ideological monetarist at Liverpool University; Brian Griffiths, a professor at City University, whose monetarism was seductively spiced with Christian morality; and a number of economists based in the City of London. One of her closest official advisers was pleasantly surprised to discover, when he began to work for her in Downing Street, how well informed she was on the details of the monetarist analysis and how rare it was for her to stumble or miss a trick. But her greatest contribution came through the clarity of her objectives and the fixity of her commitment to purposes she had identified with relentless frequency.

They were not particularly original purposes. But they were commitments made with the fire of the zealot who could not imagine she would ever become a bore. Tax cutting was one of them. In four years as Opposition leader, she had hardly made a single economic speech without alluding to the punitive rates of tax. Usually this was in reference to the upper rates. 'A country's top rate of tax is a symbol,' she said in February 1978. 'Very little revenue is collected from people in this country who pay tax at the highest rates. A top rate of 83 per cent is not much of a revenue raiser. It is a symbol of British socialism – the symbol of envy.' Restoring the morale of management, she said around the same time, was the prime requirement. 'No group is more important, and yet none has been so put through the mangle and flattened between the rollers of progressively penal taxation and discriminatory incomes policy.'

But tax at all levels was a curse. 'Considerable reductions in the lower rates of tax on incomes are just as urgent,' she said in January 1979. 'We all need incentives.' The exercise was closely bound up with the whole task of national revival, and she gave her highest commitment to reducing the standard rate of income tax, declaring at one election press conference: 'Unless someone does that, does it positively and with determination and, I might even say, with a passionate belief that it has to be done, then I see no hope and I see no change from perpetual decline.'

So tax cuts were the first objective. They were the traditional Tory nostrum, to which the leader brought her special proselytising zeal. The second was good housekeeping. It is impossible to exaggerate the power of this image, with its connotations of thrift, prudence and balanced budgets, as the guiding star of the Thatcher economic programme. She summoned it up frequently in Opposition, and it lost none of its appeal in government. For some it may have been little more than a convenient piece of populism, making economics intelligible. For her these messages – 'the homilies of housekeeping, the parables of the parlour' – were axiomatic laws of sound economic management.

The third fundamental therefore defined itself: the control of public spending. And again a kind of pietistic morality went hand in hand with a supposed economic law. Public spending could not exceed public revenue, which was based on the accumulation of wealth. 'You cannot look after the hard-up people in society unless you are accruing enough wealth to do so,' she said on BBC Television in July 1977. 'Good intentions are not enough. You do need hard cash.' But there was another dimension to this belief. The public budget was a measure of dependence on the state, itself a socially undesirable condition. Not long after coming to power, she found a quite uncharacteristically vivid way of expressing this much-repeated injunction. 'We should not expect the state', she said in March 1980, 'to appear in the guise of an extravagant good fairy at every christening, a loquacious companion at every stage of life's journey, the unknown mourner at every funeral.'

Few members of the cabinet, if any, would have dissented from these broad priorities. It was all a question of balance between them, and of the rigour with which they were to be approached.

Set against the real economy as the Tories found it on arriving in office, they were, in any case, conflicting. The most explicit electoral promises had been to cut tax and cut the public sector borrowing requirement (PSBR). The only way these could both be fulfilled was by big cuts in public spending, few of which had been openly canvassed before the voters. However, much work had been done on them in secret. The Government came in equipped with its own shadow white paper on public spending, the result of lengthy negotiation in the playground of the shadow cabinet: something on which the leader, in her efficient and organised way, had insisted, and which now paid off.

But public spending cuts were not enough to square the circle. Income tax was instantly and heavily cut: the standard rate from 33 to 30 per cent (a promise, incidentally, which Labour had also made), and the top rate from 83 to 60 per cent, the first of many massive gifts to the rich which remain one of the most enduring deposits of the Thatcher years. The cabinet as a whole was committed to public spending cuts of 3 per cent, but these did not match the tax handouts. The leader pressed for yet more off public spending. 'She wants to destroy half my programmes,' one spending minister told me at the time. She thus inaugurated early a pattern which was unusual, whereby the prime minister often took a more militant position than the Treasury over cuts. But the gap still had to be bridged.

It was done by the stunning expedient of almost doubling Value Added Tax, up to a single rate of 15 per cent. This was the major strategic decision, and it took many people by surprise. Its history illustrates both the cautious and the bold, even reckless, sides of Mrs Thatcher's character. At first she was wary of the suggestion. She would still have preferred to cut more off public programmes, and with public sector wage increases being tied to the retail price index even the most blinkered monetarist could anticipate a certain short-term danger. But the caution was soon overridden. Post-electoral euphoria was not really consistent with the cautious approach. The mandate was surely for change. One person who pressed her particularly strongly in that direction was John Biffen, something of a protector of public spending, despite being Chief Secretary, but an unapologetic liberal over the choice between direct and indirect taxation. What he said struck a sensitive nerve: 'If you don't do it now, you will never be able to do it.'[5]

The decision to raise VAT so high – indeed, the shape of the budget as a whole – was a harbinger of several truths about the Thatcher era. Some of these passed, but others endured.

The budget was decided without consultation among the cabinet as a whole. It was kept close within the economic team, and thus not exposed to much argument. By this method, therefore, the leader was able to stick, in the economic area, to the working method which she had somewhat tendentiously described before the election:

If you're going to do the things you want to do – and I'm only in politics to *do* things – you've got to have a togetherness and a unity in your Cabinet. There are two ways of making a Cabinet. One way is to have in it people who represent all the different viewpoints within the party, within the broad philosophy. The other way is to have in it only the people who want to go in the direction in which every instinct tells me we have to go. Clearly, steadily, firmly, with resolution. We've got to go in an agreed and clear direction.[6]

This was the basis on which she promised not to 'waste time having any internal arguments'. Applied to her situation, it was a fanciful statement. Her first cabinet was not merely representative of 'the different viewpoints within the party', it was dominated by men with a different viewpoint from hers. Even at the beginning, when victory usually confers some trace of comradeship, there was less 'togetherness' than in any post-war cabinet. The formation of an inner, economic cabinet was her way of achieving the kind of unity she was talking about, in support of the instincts in which she placed so much trust. The budget was the first fruit of this method of governing.

By the time it appeared, some resolution had also been arrived at of the other paradoxical promise. She said she would have no time for 'internal arguments', and yet all who worked with her knew her to be more argumentative than any leader they had ever known. Her style was entirely adversarial. Even trivial conversations had a habit of turning into a verbal contest. This was especially noticeable to ministers who had not been in the shadow cabinet, and therefore had little experience of close-quarter combat. Two of these were Peter Walker, who was amazed to be summoned from the wilderness to take up the Agriculture portfolio, and Lord Soames, who became Lord President of the Council. For them, exposure to the leader's taste for confrontation produced culture-shock. 'You mean to say you've been putting up with this for four years?', a disbelieving Walker inquired of Jim Prior after a couple of weeks of it.

But the process made it clear, all the same, what she had meant by saying she would tolerate no argument. In truth there would be plenty of arguments, but she would usually have to win them. That, at any rate, is how it was at the beginning.

Prior, in particular, soon found his place in the scheme of things. He had kept his post as Employment Secretary in the face of a determined campaign by John Hoskyns, who remained the leader's chief policy adviser, to get him reassigned. He was the only anti-monetarist anywhere near an economic job. But Prior had no influence on the first budget. Indeed, he knew less about it than people outside the Government. He was told about VAT going up to 15 per cent by the director-general of the Confederation of British Industries, John Methven. He could not believe it. Belatedly he went to treat with the prime minister, and thought he had persuaded her of the dangerous effects the rise would have on wage-claims. On the night before the budget, he gave dinner to the transport workers' leader, Moss Evans, and assured him that the rumours of 15 per cent were greatly exaggerated. VAT would go up, but not by that much.

Next day, Prior found out he knew less about what the Treasury and Downing Street had decided than either business or the unions. It was a salutary lesson. Much later, he was to reveal the depth of the ignorance in which he had previously languished, confessing that it had come as 'an enormous shock' to him that the budget was 'so extreme'.[7] Margaret and Geoffrey, Prior wrote, concocted it on the basis of a 'simple-minded' analysis: one which appeared to take him entirely by surprise. He describes the general bafflement among his colleagues at 'the scale of the changes proposed', especially the increase in nationalised industry prices which, on top of VAT, would send wages and benefits spiralling upwards. It is an interesting confession of incomprehension. All the firmness and the stridency and the rhetorical radicalism of Mrs Thatcher in Opposition, we may deduce, had not been enough to convince these colleagues that she would seriously apply the same undeviating qualities to government itself. Prior's was the incredulous umbrage taken by the dispossessed and the unconsulted.

The budget was indeed a triumph for the believers. This was another of the signals it sent. Prior was not the only one to be surprised by the elan with which it acted out the Thatcherite purpose, showing from the start what she was made of.

When her ministers actually arrived in office, there were plenty of indications that this might not be the wisest course. Opening the books, they discovered the economy in far worse shape than they had imagined. Committed to tax cuts and to reducing the money supply, they found the money supply already running much higher than they thought and the PSBR, on a forward projection, racing out of control. Already locked into the system, additionally, was future inflation of around 20 per cent, as against the 10 per cent Labour had managed to get it down to before the election.

Part of this prospective inflation was linked into public sector pay. Shortly before the election was called, Labour's efforts to create a new system for public sector pay, following the breakdown of its 5 per cent incomes policy in the famous winter of discontent, issued in a report from the Clegg Commission. Clegg produced a formula of great extravagance. It eventually led to a 25 per cent increase in the public sector wage bill over 12 months. Everything in it was anathema to the Thatcherite project. It said nothing about waste, nothing about manning, and was, in effect, an incomes policy which did not even have the merit of restraining pay. Yet, challenged to say where they stood on Clegg, as the election began, the leadership collapsed into fatal acquiescence. Although they knew it would be an albatross round all their plans, they did not dare to alienate public sector workers by throwing it out. This was the leader's own decision: a sign that she was as willing as anyone to put the short term before the long, if the election itself was at stake. Howe, the Chancellor-in-waiting, opposed it. He produced a formula that distinguished between some public sector workers and others. 'It was swept aside in the election turmoil,' said one of his advisers. 'It never had a chance.'

Clegg was not permitted, however, to deflect the radical passion behind the budget. Even though this large lump of inflationary promise was lodged in the system, it did not deter the self-confident economic cabinet, the secretive cabal at the heart of the Government, from adding another, in the form of the VAT increase. This was necessary to pay for the heavy cuts in direct taxation, which were the essential proof that a Thatcher government, whatever problems it found on taking office, would be true to its exciting promises of a change in direction.

In support of this were some early attempts to change the rhetoric. This was almost as large a shock to the system as the budget itself. In particular, a country which had lived for years as witness to government seeking to impose an incomes policy was now invited to contemplate a government that not only dispensed with incomes policy but insisted that incomes, as such, had no effect on inflation. Ministers contended that, if you controlled the money supply, you could render the nominal figures reached in wage negotiations null and void. The absence of money would, by an automatic process, impose an iron restraint on real wage deals. Precisely when and precisely how this would happen was the subject of much dispute among the theologians of monetarism. That it was indubitably the case was a message preached with fervour by the people on whose faith Mrs Thatcher depended as much as she did on her own. A particularly fervent exponent was John Biffen, the great anti-corporatist who had stayed outside the walls of Heathite Toryism on this very point. More than a year after the first budget, and well after its direct inflationary effects had become a source of something close to panic in the Administration, Biffen was still assuring the world that wages and inflation were not linked. 'Broadly speaking', he told the Commons in July 1980, he didn't think the last year's wage rises had contributed to inflation. By then inflation was running at 20 per cent, but it was 'mainly determined by the expansion in the money supply' two years earlier.

The first budget gave warning that this would not be a notably consultative government. And it was the expression of a conviction that brooked no interference from reason. But it was emblematic in another sense as well: in what it actually said about those who felt uneasy about it.

Prior, it is clear, was critical at the time. His *après*-government apologia accords closely with his private words when the budget was announced. Later he elaborated these into a wholesale assault on the quality of the people in charge. 'All through the early period of Margaret's Government,' he wrote in 1986, 'I felt the Treasury team were out of their depth.' They were all theorists. None 'had any experience of running a whelk-stall, let alone a decent-sized company.'[8] Sharing this opinion with him, in those early days, were only two of his cabinet colleagues, Peter Walker and Sir Ian Gilmour, who was Lord Privy Seal and the under-Foreign Secretary to Lord Carrington.

Some others may have privately harboured some puzzlement at what Howe and his leader were up to. But this was by no means a dominant feeling. The shared sense of crisis was much more deeply experienced. One inside observer was struck, in June 1979, by the sight of a cabinet 'seized of the scale of their task and grimly setting about what had to be done'. There was no quarrel between them about this, nor about some of the measures, especially concerning the trade unions and the nationalised industries, which had to be undertaken. Several future critics of the economic policy were very taken with the budget itself. Francis Pym, then the Defence Secretary, thought it excellent. He admired its fearless scale, and enjoyed the way it caught the City and the pundits on the wrong foot. It showed, he thought, that the prime minister and the Chancellor 'had a strategy'.

This was a time when large metaphors held the field. These had the advantage of being comprehensible to those untutored in the details of economic policy. 'Making a clean break' and, alternatively, 'breaking for the open country' were two popular images, which appeared in many a Conservative speech before, during and after the election. They were irresistibly appealing to a party that believed it had been elected to change the future. But they were effective in another way. They underwrote whatever extravaganza the Government chose to embark on: the larger and more hazardous the better. They were a convenient basis for justification by faith and not by works. They rendered thought otiose and scepticism akin to treason. They made it possible to secure a kind of unity around the proposition which nobody succeeded in dislodging for the whole life of the first Thatcher Government: There Is No Alternative.

All new political leaders peddle the promises of a new beginning. Rather like the presumption that utopia beckons, where all problems will have been solved, if only the government can be sustained in office for another five years, this belief in the abruptness of things gives definition and purpose to a politician's work. Such rhetoric, of course, also gives life to an illusion: the illusion that there is no continuity between one government and another as each struggles to master forces which are always in danger of rising beyond their control. But it is a necessary illusion. And Margaret Thatcher was in particular need of it when she came to power. It deepened the sense she had of her own mission. It also identified a prime target for her earliest attention.

This target was the machine of government itself. For ranged against the politician's claim to be breaking with the past is the belief in the civil service that it represents and personifies the seamless integrity of past, present and future government rolled indistinguishably into one. Whitehall is the custodian of the very continuity that the new keepers of Westminster think they have been elected to rupture. Never was this clash of purposes more explicit than in the summer of 1979. No government has been elected whose leader was as deeply seized as this one of the need to overturn the power and presumption of the continuing government of the civil service: to challenge its orthodoxies, cut down its size, reject its assumptions, which were seen as corrosively infected by social democracy, and teach it a lesson in political control. As Mrs Thatcher saw it, her arrival in power posed an irresistible force against an immovable object, and she set to work with quite unusual energy, as an early priority, to establish her personal dominance.

The signals to a changed world given by the first budget would lead nowhere unless the world of government itself was changed to accord with the Thatcherite ascendancy.

As a matter of fact, the need for this in the area the Government cared most about was somewhat exaggerated. Breaking with the past might be a useful concept with which to motivate the party and import a helpful element of self-dramatisation. But, as far as economic policy went, the Treasury was already well apprised of what was wanted, having experienced three years of it under the preceding Labour Government. Not only the language of monetarism but the implementation of its principal edicts were, perhaps a little shame-facedly, well established on the scene. The money supply and the public sector borrowing requirement had been talked up as crucial determinants, especially in the City and parts of the quality press, for years before they became associated exclusively, as it seemed, with Thatcherism. It was the Callaghan not the Thatcher Government which first published monetary targets as a component of its macro-economic management. It was the Labour Government, under pressure from the International Monetary Fund in late 1976, which engaged in major public spending cuts in conformity with the monetarist analysis.

So the Treasury, which had been in the thick of all this, was not quite the temple of unregenerate orthodoxy that the Thatcherites imagined. Whitehall was already easing itself into the post-socialist, post-Keynesian era. In some respects, indeed, what the Tories promised guaranteed them positive support, at least within the Treasury itself. As an institution fighting an unceasing battle to control public expenditure and observe the precepts of fiscal rigour, with part of its mind the Treasury could only look with favour on a government so evidently determined to support these priorities with more severity than any post-war predecessor.

And there was another slight misapprehension in the new government's belief that it must prepare for battle. This was not a bureau-cracy massing in blank hostility. It had just experienced several years of a government which had no working majority in Parliament, a position that may sometimes enhance the power of Whitehall, as the politicians struggle vainly among each other, but one that Whitehall on the whole does not like. 'The civil service is quite good at doing what it's told,' a senior official told me at the time. 'It just hasn't been told anything clearly for years.' Later, reflecting on the moment when it all began, Sir Ian Bancroft, who was head of the civil service when the Tories came in, described Whitehall's habitual election mood as one of 'grim relish' about the outcome. 'The relish is all the greater', he said, 'if the outgoing administration has been suffering from end-of-term palsy, the debility of no working majority. So in 1979 there was a positive welcome, on no party political grounds, for a new administration with a mandate, with firm policies and with a firm profile to it.'⁹

The Thatcherite obsession, however, transcended these particulars. And it was not all a delusion. There was a genuine clash of cultures, between a political leadership fired by an almost Cromwellian impatience with the status quo, and the mandarin world of Whitehall, in which scepticism and rumination were more highly rated habits of mind than zeal or blind conviction.

Some of the differences were purely intellectual. This is what set the limit to the Treasury's adherence to monetarism. It could cope with public spending cuts, but not with some of the contradictions that the policy contained within it. The money supply target, for example, was tightened from the figure inherited from Labour, a range of 8 to 12 per cent growth, to the absurdly precise bull's-eye of 9 per cent. To most Treasury officials this was not compatible with the rise in VAT and the jump in public sector wages implicit in the Clegg awards. The money target might be stated, and even seriously aspired to. But it did not fit reality. This fact was of little interest to ministers, who valued the new target as a propaganda weapon and proof of their long-term seriousness of purpose. Anyone who raised objections was inevitably marked down as a relic of the old school which the Government was committed to displacing.

The best that could be said for the Treasury in these early months was that it was divided. There were officials, and even economists, beginning to emerge as monetarists, disillusioned with the failures of Keynesianism. But even the more enthusiastic monetarists, mindful of the prudence, not to say the positive constitutional virtue, of backing the new political orthodoxy, shrank from the intellectual methods that drove the politicians forward. The convenient arithmetical certainties of a Treasury minister like Lord Cockfield, who told the House of Lords in April 1980 that monetarism resembled the proposition that 'if twice one is two, then twice two is four', were not for them. Their typical attitude was probably well caught by an observation of Sir Henry Phelps Brown after a few months of the monetarist experiment. Phelps Brown, a retired labour economist of considerable repute, had heard the Chancellor, Sir Geoffrey Howe, give a broadcast in which he 'treated monetarism not as one theory among others but as an incontrovertible principle like the law of gravitation'.[10]

Such certitudes were anathema to almost every mind in the Treasury. They were certainly an affront to the training, the rationality and indeed to the entire working life that had prepared the permanent secretary at the Treasury, Sir Douglas Wass, for his high eminence. Wass, as the Tories saw it, epitomised the problem and could have no part in the solution. For his part he scorned much that he was now required to become a part of.

He was the acme of a mandarin. Extremely clever, but also equable and effective, he had been in the top job for five years, after being appointed to it at the age of scarcely more than fifty. His career in the Treasury, following the normal path for high fliers from ministerial private secretary, through Washington, to a succession of senior policy jobs, framed the era of consensus politics. He was himself a born consensualist. He once told me (before the formation of the SDP) that the majority of Whitehall officials were natural social democrats: middle-of-the-road people who believed, as was only to be expected, in the benign role of government in the lives of the people. This description certainly fitted Wass himself. And for most of his life he had been permitted to act out this belief unmolested. Although the Treasury had frequently been seen, especially under Labour governments, as the enemy of progress and the flinty impediment to investment and growth, the department's power was never doubted, the influence of Wass and his fellow officials never underestimated.

All this now began to change, and Wass was dismayed. He began to be left on the sidelines. A new chief economic adviser, Terence Burns, was appointed from entirely outside the Whitehall world: a young academic who had made his mark with Howe and the others in Opposition. Treasury men more malleable than Wass began to be treated more seriously than him. After a time, he appeared to be reconciled to his fate, which was to remain as permanent secretary for another four years, keep the department functioning efficiently, look after the careers of younger colleagues he estimated highly, but as far as policy was concerned to sit in the background, a Jonah prophesying doom.

What offended Wass almost as much as the precision of the claims credulously made for monetarism was the determination with which Howe and company prevented them being submitted to wider scrutiny. He had experienced enough of this under Denis Healey's Chancellorship, especially after 1976. Healey was often attacked for not sending the main economic papers to the full cabinet and thereby stifling any informed debate on his strategy. But Howe, Wass thought, was much more secretive. 'Do you know,' he announced to a private dinner party in November 1979, 'there hasn't been a single economic discussion in the cabinet since this government came in.'

Wass was highly critical of Howe's refusal to circulate any papers reflecting the divided counsels among Treasury officials. 'We're all Keynesians round here,' he said on the same occasion. 'But we've done our best to follow the government line.' His enduring air of disbelief was precisely what the Government, and especially the prime minister, could not abide. What, under other dispensations, would have been regarded as a mandarin's professional scepticism sounded to the new regime like disloyalty. 'We're doing our best,' Wass said, 'but we don't think it will work.' This was a difference of outlook which afforded one of the reasons for a declaration of war.

There was another, more pervasive one. Of this the Treasury's intellectual fastidiousness was only a symptom. It had to do with the whole ethos of Whitehall, and was nicely encapsulated in a remark made to a friend by Sir John Hunt, the cabinet secretary, who was asked shortly before his retirement in late 1979 whether, in the real world of politics, the prime minister wasn't in fact the prisoner of the moderates rather than the leader of the zealots. 'No,' said Hunt, 'but we may be getting there.'

This preference of the official world for moderation in all things was something the leader and her associates had often discussed in Opposition, especially as the election got closer. Joseph, Howe and John Hoskyns were particularly exercised about the problem. It was, indeed, one of Hoskyns' main obsessions, as was partly shown in his 'Stepping Stones' report.[11] His early contacts with the machine, as he took his own place in 10 Downing Street at the head of the prime minister's policy unit, did nothing to make him reassess his expectations. Officials were just as negative, pessimistic and failure-bound as he had always thought. A fearsome picture was soon summoned to his mind. He saw the phalanxes of officials like American footballers, 'heavyweight line-blockers, accoutred in their padding and helmets to withstand every attack'. Every positive proposal which shook the conventional wisdom, whether for curbing the power of trade unions or setting enterprise free, was likely, Hoskyns and his leader thought, to meet with an instinctive strategy of obstruction from the blinkered asses of Whitehall. This was no time for humouring the traditional official virtues of scepticism and reserve. It was essential to go on to the offensive from the start.

For those who saw it first and at closest quarters this experience was not unlike being struck about the head by a very purposefully whirling dervish. The staff of private secretaries at No. 10, who were the cream of the middle ranks of the civil service, had grown accustomed to a different regime. Jim Callaghan was a prime minister who kept his distance from minor events. His style was very much that of the chairman of the board, concerning himself with strategic questions and issuing instructions that cabinet papers should normally occupy no more than two sides of a page. Callaghan was a good chairman, and a prime minister well suited to the compromise and permanent negotiation which is the condition of a minority government. But a leisurely air, naturally associated with a government that could do little, undeniably pervaded Downing Street.

The new prime minister was something completely different. From the first hour she established her desire to see everything and do everything. At the end of the first week, one of her officials told me: 'She reads every paper she gets and never fails to write a comment on it. "Nonsense", "Needs more briefing", "Do this again" are what she's constantly writing.'

She was, at the beginning, incurably interventionist. This was partly by calculation, for only by poking her nose into every department's work did she think she could impress upon both the politicians and the officials that she really was in charge. But it was also a matter of instinct: the tendency of an indefatigable woman to suppose that nothing would be done right unless she personally saw to it. A certain innocence infused her style in the early weeks. 'She doesn't understand how Whitehall works,' said this same official, still reeling from the change of power. 'She wants me to send out a stream of notes telling everyone what her view is. She doesn't understand how enormously influential is any note that reaches a department beginning with the words "The prime minister's view is . . .".'

As she discovered certain things, however, there was soon a change of mood. In a very short time, a process of mutual education impressed itself on her and her staff. She learned that those serving her most closely were not as she had expected them to be. Her personal experience of Whitehall being limited to the Department of Education, a ministry notoriously under-supplied with top-flight officials, she did not know until May 1979 quite how excellent and devoted a British civil servant can be.

This was not merely a matter of the civil service's inbred capacity to switch horses at the drop of an election, although the smoothness of the handover of power, masterminded by Hunt and assisted by Bancroft, took the edge off some of her suspicions. What quickly impressed her was the willingness of the young men inside 10 Downing Street waiting to greet her to 'work their backs off for her', as one of them put it.

They, for their part, learned something too. 'She is a much nicer, warmer person than I had ever expected,' said one. 'I am quite amazed.'

This was the great surprise. For anyone who knew the prime minister only through her public image, which meant virtually everyone in Downing Street except John Hunt, abrasiveness aggression and self-assertion were the only human qualities to expect from the new incumbent. And these were not lacking. But the fiery feelings also issued in human warmth, reserved perhaps for the chosen few but available certainly to those she saw every day whom she had decided were her trusty lieutenants. She was a woman, with a woman's concern for those around her and a most assiduous attention to the details of their lives: whether they missed a meal, whether their wives had recovered from flu, whether their children had passed exams. Throughout her time as prime minister she took care to establish the strongest bond with each cohort of private secretaries and other officials, as they came forward into her personal service. The contrast was much to be remarked between this attractive trait and the inability she constantly manifested to register the same quality of caring for the nation at large.

Her officials liked her for another talent too. She responded to their own concern for detail. She was good at taking a brief, even though she invariably challenged the first draft, and she was particularly admired for her attention to the footnotes. 'If she's meeting a foreigner, she'll always take on board who his wife is and how many children he's got,' said one of her familiars.

It was not long before Downing Street became the home of a mutual admiration society. The direst anticipations on both sides were found to be erroneous. Even Hunt, who as the most senior civil servant in the country might have been cast as the leading scapegoat for a reforming government, enjoyed an Indian summer of power and influence. Hunt, appointed cabinet secretary by Ted Heath, had continued at a pinnacle of importance so long as Harold Wilson remained prime minister. But under Callaghan he suffered an eclipse, being rather superseded by some of the prime minister's political advisers. Mrs Thatcher, far from victimising him as the culprit for past crimes, restored him to favour. 'John writes the most marvellous drafts,' she told a political colleague after a few weeks' admiring their urgency and polish.

Intimacy, therefore, was one of the tools of mastery. A close little group formed itself around her at the centre, bound together by more than routine loyalty. But this wasn't the only way the *parvenue* prime minister – self-conscious outsider, impatient iconoclast – reached for control.

Along with personal magnetism went the inbuilt generalised aversion, which expressed itself in various ways, all of them designed to prove that the prime minister, and no one else, was in command.

She made a habit of extreme aggression towards almost all officials who entered her presence, if they did not belong to her immediate entourage. There were many such encounters. One which lived in the memory of a man who witnessed it took place three days after the arrival in No. 10. Sir Kenneth Berrill, head of the Central Policy Review Staff, or government Think Tank, was summoned to see her. She had come across Berrill before; for most of her time as Education Secretary, he had been chairman of the University Grants Committee. He went from there to be chief economic adviser at the Treasury during the last, disastrous months of the Heath Government. He had been in charge of the Think Tank throughout the Labour period.

Whether or not the prime minister had marked his card back in UGC days, she certainly placed him now as a man of decided left-of-centre inclinations – very like many of the civil servants of his generation. Additionally, she felt that the Think Tank had some explaining to do. She took their meeting so soon after the election as an opportunity to give Berrill a ferocious working-over, which he was hardly prepared for. 'He came out wondering whether he had been told to fire all his staff and look for another job,' said the man who saw it happen.

But – and this too was characteristic – Berrill subsequently managed to establish some kind of relationship. He survived in his post for another year, and the CPRS itself remained in place for the whole first Administration. The ritual roasting was not necessarily followed by terminal immolation. The typical Thatcher performance, whether directed at ministers or officials, required a heavy argument, which often became heated, but did not always have to conclude with her victim being carried out of the room. Many times in future years she insisted that arguments be entered and blood-pressures be caused to rise before, after an hour of exhausting combat, she subsided and surrendered her point.

It was, nonetheless, a way of making her presence unmistakably felt throughout the territory of government. So was another expedient on which she soon embarked. This was the departmental visitation. Rather as Queen Elizabeth I would make a royal progress round different parts of the kingdom, Mrs Thatcher took to riding out from Downing Street to the outposts of Whitehall, to find out for herself what was being done and, more particularly, who was doing it. Other prime ministers had visited some ministries from time to time, but the systematic way in which the new incumbent set about it was without precedent.

These visits were not an unqualified success. They often had pleasing effects at the lower end of the departments. 'She went over very well with the cleaners and the filing clerks,' a junior minister at Employment told me shortly after her appearance there. 'All that glad-handing reminded one what a good populist politician she is.' But the encounter with senior officials had been disastrous.

Jim Prior, who was the Secretary of State, has described the preparations made for the visit and the beneficial effect he had naively expected it to have.[12] In fact the serious part of the meeting degenerated into a series of futile squabbles, in which she appeared determined to make the officials look silly in front of the ministers, and the ministers likewise in the eyes of the officials. The junior minister reported his observation of the Prior 'geiger counter' – the red blood-pressure line rising up the back of his neck – reaching well beyond the hair line in his fury at the way his officials were being treated. Prior himself instances an argument with a senior official, Donald Derx, 'one of the best and most dedicated civil servants I have ever met'. The prime minister evidently got too deeply into an area she knew little about, the law relating to secondary industrial action, and declined to yield to better authority, especially when an exasperated Derx volunteered the question: 'Prime Minister, do you really want to know the facts?'

Other such meetings were always likely to end in similar frustration, as the prime minister, who pretended she had come to learn, couldn't resist the temptation to teach. And yet they were undoubtedly of value to her, enabling her to accumulate a formidable dossier on the higher reaches of Whitehall, and the raw material from which these might be rearranged over the next decade. She took an intense personal interest in the faces and behaviour of the names put in front of her.

The phrase that William Pile had noted from her years before at the DES – 'I make up my mind about people in the first ten seconds, and I very rarely change it' – came into its own in these fleeting encounters, when officials had only the briefest of moments to make an impression. On the visit to the Department of Trade, one of the ministers alongside her noticed her preoccupation with people rather than policies. 'She had a list of the officials present,' he told me shortly afterwards, 'and she made marks under their names as they spoke. Some of them were noted with a dotted line, others with a solid line. I soon realised that the dots were for the goodies and the line for the baddies, as she saw them. There were only two categories, and everyone fitted into one or other.'

If these notations were also made at Employment, it is plain enough which one Donald Derx received. Despite Prior's high opinion of him, he was thereafter consistently passed over for promotion, eventually leaving the civil service several years before his time.

Within these first months, therefore, the ground began to be laid for the colonising of Whitehall with departmental leaders whom the prime minister approved of. This process gathered pace in later years. But she developed her personal intelligence system almost from the beginning. From her secure base, staffed by a corps of new-found friends, she could begin to neutralise and then slowly overcome the resistance of the bureaucracy. Perhaps she could even change the culture.

But before that, for her personal position to be fully armour-plated, certain key appointments had to be put in place.

When she arrived in office, the three most important jobs in Downing Street were either vacant or about to become so. John Hunt was due to retire as cabinet secretary in October, on reaching the age of sixty. Kenneth Stowe, principal private secretary since 1975, was overdue for promotion. And the job of prime minister's press secretary, always a more overtly personal if not political appointment, had to be filled. The Thatcher approach to each of these three appointments revealed in different ways how difficult it would often be to predict how she might behave.

Ostensibly, Hunt's successor was the most sensitive and important decision. The cabinet secretary, while nominally the servant of the cabinet as a whole, has evolved into something more closely akin to the prime minister's own permanent secretary. With Hunt's retirement date known well in advance, Mrs Thatcher had sent a message some time before the election to prime minister Callaghan requesting that no successor be named until the new government was installed – a request granted with generous alacrity.

Now the patronage was hers, and the obvious candidate was thought by some to be the one least likely to appeal to her. Sir Robert Armstrong, permanent secretary at the Home Office, had been groomed for years for the topmost job. He had risen through the Treasury as well as his own department, was a speedy draftsman, an effective fixer and an uncommonly subtle human being. But he had certain apparent disqualifications as the key official to be placed at the right hand of an impatiently reformist prime minister. He was formed a little too perfectly from the mandarin's mould, having been educated at Eton and Oxford, and he had long identified as his main leisure activity the thoroughly elitist task of secretary to the board of directors of the Royal Opera House, Covent Garden. Even more damningly, he had been Ted Heath's private secretary and had grown exceptionally close to the man whose very life-work Mrs Thatcher existed to repudiate. With this pedigree, he was seen by many people as – dreaded stigma – a centrist: the personification of consensus politics.

But Armstrong had also been busy. Not long after the change in the leadership of the Conservative Party, when he was a mere Deputy Secretary at the Home Office, he went to considerable lengths to arrange a meeting with the new, unknown woman who now had to be reckoned with. He discovered a pretext in some Home Office business, which required a visit to her room at the House of Commons. Mrs Thatcher's staff at the time noted with amusement the determination he showed in contriving the encounter. Not that this could be thought in any way to have booked Armstrong's ticket. But it showed his smooth pertinacity. Whatever the reservations of her political advisers, Mrs Thatcher duly appointed the man always most likely to succeed, and took pleasure in the surprise her magnanimity provoked. 'You thought I wouldn't have Robert because he worked for Ted,' she teased a friend. 'Well, you were wrong, weren't you?'

No less important to a prime minister than the cabinet secretary is the principal private secretary. Ken Stowe, the man in place, had been a brilliant success. One of his colleagues said that for the last six months of the Callaghan Government, when it was assailed by strikes and the threat of national breakdown, Stowe more than anyone held the machine together. The crucial dealings with Len Murray, general secretary of the TUC, for example, were handled entirely by this otherwise obscure official. He also superintended the handover to Mrs Thatcher with consummate discretion, and was among those most responsible for her early conversion to the merits of the civil servants around her.

But Stowe could not be allowed to stay. He was slotted to take over at the top of the Northern Ireland Office. He had to be replaced. And it was at this point that the prime minister displayed her curious attitude to the making of appointments. It was shot through with a paradox perhaps only explicable by feminine intuition. For although she set great store by individual character, and delighted in the personal loyalty of those closest to her, she took exceptionally little trouble to find out what they might really be like. Her most successful officials have always been those who developed an almost chemical empathy with her, not least as man to woman. But the selection of those allotted the role was left, to an unusual extent, to chance.

So it was with Stowe's successor. One of those closely involved in the process of finding him told me what happened. In accordance with normal practice, John Hunt, as cabinet secretary, presented her with a list of candidates to consider. These were the civil service's highest fliers of a certain age. She said airily that she had heard of X, who would be the right man. Hunt, somewhat taken aback, said she must look at the others as well, and particularly at Y, who was really the outstanding candidate. All right, said the prime minister, she would take Y.

But didn't the prime minister understand, Hunt persisted, what a very special job this was? The personal relationship was all-important. It would surely not be sensible to take Y, sight unseen, however good he was.

So the prime minister agreed to see Y. But she was reluctant to do so, and adamantly refused to submit herself or him to a formal interview. A working meeting had to be contrived, in which she could observe Y in action, without him knowing that he was on trial.

By this unorthodox process, Clive Whitmore, a grammar-school boy from Surrey and the Ministry of Defence, was set beside the Old Etonian Armstrong. It turned out to be a far more successful appointment than many reached by more straightforward methods. Whitmore, an unflamboyant workhorse of great dedication and a tireless capacity for getting things done, grew to be as close to Mrs Thatcher as any official or minister, before it came time for him too to move on. She utterly relied on him. He became her accomplice in many a joust with fractious ministers, an unblinking foil to her more outrageous sallies. 'Will you make up your mind,' she was once heard to inquire of Francis Pym, the Defence Secretary, in a parliamentary corridor, 'or will Clive and I have to make it up for you?' Such was the role of a man unearthed by almost recklessly random selection.

Of all these characters, however, the most important was the press secretary. In modern British government, the prime minister's conduit to the media has come to assume an ever larger place, and for Margaret Thatcher, who was not personally interested in the skills of news management, the appointment was one of exceptional delicacy. Her answer to it, produced almost as casually as Whitmore, turned out to have still more heroic reverberations.

Once again the job was filled without any direct encounter between employer and employee. The only contribution the prime minister was prepared to make, if any, was to inspect a candidate or two at a distance: spy on their performance, as it were, from behind the arras.

Bernard Ingham was in charge of energy conservation, placed there by the outgoing Secretary of State for Energy, Tony Benn. But he was by training a press officer, having arrived in Whitehall in 1967 to perform that function for the Prices and Incomes Board, an outpost of the corporate state now extinct for many years. There followed lengthy stints as director of information at both the Employment and Energy departments, before Ingham, with Benn's agreement, decided that his future lay not up the cul-de-sac of the information service but as a mainline administrative civil servant.

When, one day in late summer 1979, he was summoned from his desk to Downing Street, it was under the firm impression that he was going for an interview. He even thought he might not want the job of prime minister's press secretary, should it eventually be offered to him. On arrival in Mrs Thatcher's presence he soon realised that he was under a serious misapprehension. She immediately began to speak as though her offer and his acceptance were formalities already complete, and began to instruct him in how he should approach his new task. If she had ever caught sight of him before, it could only have been through covert glances on her visit to his department. Yet in this fortuitous manner, devoid of the normal processes of rational choice, began one of the great enduring partnerships – as consistently close as she had with any other man – of Mrs Thatcher's years as prime minister.

Ingham is a Yorkshireman, from Hebden Bridge near Halifax. He was a journalist, first on the *Yorkshire Post* then on the *Guardian*, specialising in industrial and labour affairs. Before joining the public service he had also taken an active part in Labour Party politics in Leeds, actually standing for election to the council in the early 1960s. Neither as a journalist nor as a former Labour activist did he exactly appeal to the known predilections of Mrs Thatcher. On the other hand, he had long since given up both these vices. He could be entered on the roster of welcome converts which the prime minister always kept close to her heart. She would have noted at least this much from his curriculum vitae. But it probably wasn't what set her antennae twitching positively, when Ingham was submitted to her personal twenty-second test.

Something she said to him much later gave him more of a clue. 'The thing about you and me, Bernard,' she once exclaimed after they had jointly vanquished the enemy at some particularly hostile press conference, 'is that neither of us are *smooth* people.'

For the would-be revolutionary now installed in Downing Street, her first six months in office were eminently satisfactory. The revolution seemed to be boldly in train. She had refused to be diverted, either by senior ministers or by the conventional wisdom available in endless quantity throughout the civil service.

She had also begun to establish dominance. 'The prime minister presided over the cabinet this morning, beautifully as usual,' she had told an early Commons questioner,[13] and it seemed to her to be coming true. She had her own people around her. Although years of their re-education lay ahead, the people who actually ran the country, the civil servants in charge of the main departments, were beginning to get her message. She was a presence in their lives, as the minutes and the drafts and the constantly probing interrogatories flew in a ceaseless stream to and from 10 Downing Street. Insecurity and self-doubt, which lurked persistently in the character of this woman who was always aware of the treacheries of political life, were obliterated by action.

Only elsewhere were pessimism and even fear beginning to occlude the euphoria of the election victory. Among the traditional politicians, the ministers whom she had mostly kept away from the making of economic policy, there was little disposition to share the leader's uplifting excitement. Even those who had been quite happy with the budget were, by the autumn, steeped in apprehension, brought on by rising inflation, by another oil-price shock in the summer, by the discovery that real life was a great deal harsher than it could be made to sound in an election campaign against a demoralised and defeated government.

Jim Prior was a bellwether figure. On 11 September, which fixes a mood at a particular moment, he disclosed his feelings to a journalist. He was not, I noted afterwards, a man exuberantly carrying out a revolution. He was appalled by the seriousness of the situation, sceptical about the Treasury's extremism, highly aware of the possibility of failure. His targets for success in the first five years were very modest. 'There is a fatalistic air about him,' my notebook reads. 'He says, roughly, that nothing else has worked in the past, so we must try it our way. But he adds that we are sober people who can see real collapse staring this country in the face.'

10

La Fille d'Epicier

THE EARLIEST DISCOVERY which new prime ministers make is the extent to which foreign affairs dominate their lives. In May 1979, issues of foreign policy were as prominent on the agenda as those of economic and domestic policy. But they were there for a different reason, and called forth different responses from the newly installed mistress of 10 Downing Street. Whereas she and her party had defined the economic crisis in their own terms and devised their own priorities to meet it, circumstance not choice dictated that Rhodesia and the European Community should require a parallel surge of involvement in the foreign field. Without a day's delay, the prime minister began to be tested in the international arena: one for which she was less well prepared, and to which she brought far fewer certitudes.

Her formation in diplomacy was woefully slender. As we have seen, the journey from Grantham to Finchley was, for the first dozen years of her political life, about as far as she had ever travelled. It accurately defined the limits of her outlook. She was not as other Tories of the fifties and sixties, and certainly not as other Tory leaders. Nothing in her past gave her a trace of Macmillan's instinct to scan the far horizon, or of Heath's natural interest in consorting with the leaders of other countries. As Education Secretary she had been obliged to travel, and absorb what she saw and heard. It wasn't that she resisted this. On the contrary, she had a voracious appetite for experiences of every kind and the inexhaustible interest of a kind of super-tourist, often to be witnessed on her frequent journeys as prime minister, in the lives and artefacts, and also the politics, of every country she visited. What she did not have was global vision or any well-tutored feel for the subtleties of foreign affairs.

Her ignorance, when she became leader of the party, was startling, but also remarkably unembarrassed. An official sent from the Foreign Office to brief her for her first trip to Italy was among the first to come across it. He discovered that, as far as she was concerned, Italy was as remote as Outer Mongolia. She had no idea how Italy was governed, or what Italian political parties were really like. She seemed to imagine that the Christian Democrats were simply an Italian version of the Tory Party, instead of being a federation of rival barons who found it convenient from time to time to elevate one of their number to a brief tenure as prime minister.

John Davies, then shadow foreign secretary, who was with her at the briefing, sought to instruct her with an analogy. 'It's rather as if I were the party potentate in North-west England,' he said, 'and you had to bargain for my favour.' 'You mean the party leader isn't really the party leader?' she asked. Those present nodded slowly. 'How simply terrible,' she said.

In the four years that followed she filled in some of the lacunae, concerning Italy and many other countries. She went to West Germany for the first time. Systematically boxing the compass, she built up a reasonable network of acquaintances in leading positions, who, like President Carter, took her more seriously the closer she moved towards power. But to the conduct of foreign affairs, when this responsibility was thrust upon her, she brought no deeply pondered set of priorities. Her principal contribution was a world view of powerful simplicity – but of limited relevance to the untidy problems that first confronted her.

This view was determined, above all, by anti-communism. She had formulated her position about communism and given it prominence from her earliest days in politics. Her election address in 1950 contained sentiments she was repeating almost word for word thirty years later. 'Every Conservative desires peace,' she wrote in 1950. 'The threat to peace comes from Communism, which has powerful forces ready to attack anywhere. Communism waits for weakness, it leaves strength alone. Britain must therefore be strong, strong in her arms, strong in her faith, strong in her own way of life.' In June 1979, her keynote speech before the first direct elections to the European Parliament cast these in eerily similar light. 'Communism never sleeps,' she said, urging Europe to come together for its own defence. 'It never changes its objectives. Nor must we. Our first duty to freedom is to defend our own.'

By the time she became leader of the Opposition, prejudice was enriched by reading and a certain amount of experience. She had read Solzhenitsyn's novel, *The First Circle*, when she was Education Secretary and been riveted by its horrific depiction of the absence of human rights in the Soviet Union. Driven by events, she first began to think hard about her policy rather than her instincts in the summer of 1975, in anticipation of the forthcoming Helsinki conference on human rights and East–West detente.

Hastily, with Helsinki looming, a speech was put together. She had cold-bloodedly set about trying to educate herself, one of her chief tutors being Robert Conquest, noted historian of the Stalin Terror and a scholar with clear-cut views about Soviet intentions. Conquest's was the main hand behind this first essay in Cold War oratory. 'Detente', Mrs Thatcher told Chelsea Conservatives in July 1975, 'sounds a fine word. And, to the extent that there has really been a relaxation in international tension, it is a fine thing. But the fact remains that throughout this decade of detente, the armed forces of the Soviet Union have increased, are increasing, and show no signs of diminishing.'

Her education proceeded. Rumania, as chance would have it, played a large part in crystallising her hawkish attitude. It was one of the countries she had visited as Education Secretary, and also a place she happened to go to again, in September 1975, to attend a conference in the Carpathian mountains. An aide who accompanied her recalled later that the four-day harangue on the virtues of Marxism–Leninism to which she was subjected, coinciding with Helsinki, had the important effect of concentrating her mind.

This issued in another speech, in January 1976, in which she laid out her philosophy more fiercely. The Russians, she said, were bent on world domination and were well placed to achieve it. 'They put guns before butter, while we put just about everything before guns. They know they are a super-power in only one sense – the military sense. They are a failure in human and economic terms.' If Britain didn't understand this, then 'we are destined, in their words, to end up on "the scrap-heap of history".'

This single speech did more than any other to define the personality, in its international aspect, that arrived in power in 1979. It was made at a time when the Wilson Government was cultivating its relations with Moscow, having recently negotiated a new Anglo-Soviet trade agreement. It contained unfashionably strong language about Soviet iniquities. But, most of all, it provoked a counter-attack from the Russians. Tass, the official Soviet news agency, immediately labelled Mrs Thatcher the 'Iron Lady', a sobriquet which did her several favours at once. It established her importance: for nobody unimportant would be worth the Russians' while to attack. It gave her an identity as an international, and not merely a domestic, politician. It also neutralised the danger still seen to lurk in the fact that she was a woman, completely unversed in the male world of high diplomacy. Nobody could be too disturbingly feminine who was now presented as being made of iron. No wonder the image is one Mrs Thatcher was to return to, with pride and pleasure, many times during her prime ministership.

In a national leader, nonetheless, it had drawbacks as well as merits. It suggested a one-dimensional approach to foreign policy. It was the single bias for which Mrs Thatcher was known when she became prime minister, and yet it seemed to lack sophistication. Flung into the complex worlds of African and European politics, she plainly needed a more rounded and experienced adviser. Fortunately she found one in Lord Carrington, her first Foreign Secretary.

As a matter of fact, an imitation of Carringtonesque skills had once been available to her, and she had abruptly dispensed with them. At the beginning of her leadership, she made Reginald Maudling, former Chancellor and Home Secretary and, despite a few ups and downs, a pillar of contemporary Conservatism, her chief foreign affairs spokesman. Maudling, an experienced if somewhat idle figure, had once been quite a friend. But his approach was traditional, by comparison with the leader's own. He was seriously vexed by her anti-Soviet fusillade, and especially by the Iron Lady speech, of whose contents he learned only two days before it was due to be delivered. As shadow foreign secretary, he felt he should have been consulted; and had he been so, he would have advised against, as he made clear in a letter reeking of the patronising world weariness by which Mrs Thatcher, even at that early stage, was unimpressed. 'No doubt a violent and sustained attack upon the Soviet Government may have some political advantage within our own ranks,' Maudling wrote. 'But I am doubtful as to what long-term purpose it is intended to serve, not only in Opposition but, more important, in government.' As he read the speech, it implied an 'immediate and massive' commitment to rearmament, something he thought should only be contemplated after lengthy consideration by the whole shadow cabinet.

Maudling was disposed of in short order. It was 'rather a shock', he confessed in his memoirs, 'to be summoned and dismissed without any prior criticism or warning from her of any sort whatsoever'. Yet Peter Carrington was in some respects another Maudling: from the same wing of the party, and steeped in the same inherited attitudes to foreign policy, which were the attitudes of the Foreign Office rather than the Conservative rank and file, of the mandarin not the zealot. His appointment, for that very reason, was critical to the entire conduct of foreign policy by the first Thatcher Administration, and in particular to the different course it took from economic policy.

By 1979, Carrington was the only serious candidate for the job. He was known to covet it extremely, although the shadow post was then filled by Francis Pym. The one job he did not want, and would have rejected, was the leadership of the House of Lords, in which shadow post he had dutifully performed, while maintaining his business interests, ever since 1974. So he became Foreign Secretary, and one half of the most improbable and yet successful partnership Mrs Thatcher formed with any of her ministers in the first term.

It was improbable because Carrington was a toff. He was a genuine aristocrat, the sixth baron of the line, and had a whiggish disposition. When asked at the time, he called himself 'a Macmillan Conservative' – not normally a recommendation to the leader. He had 800 acres of land, which also placed him on the wrong side of the tracks. But, to set against these bad marks, he offered some of the better aristocratic virtues. He was unfailingly civil, effortlessly charming, unexpectedly witty. He was without side of any kind and, at least in her presence, never by a blink or a smile revealed anything other than respect for her authority. She liked him as a man, which was important – and distinguished their relationship, for example, from that with Geoffrey Howe. Carrington gave himself a licence to joke with and even tease the lady. Because the chemistry was good, he always got away with it.

By the objective test of experience and success, he was not so obviously qualified for his job as later became taken for granted. He had certainly been a minister a very long time ago. Churchill made him parliamentary secretary for Agriculture in 1951, but he was not a success. In 1956, Lord Home, who was Commonwealth Secretary, made him High Commissioner in Australia, his only apparent qualification being a family connection with the country. He did better at that job, and later called it the most useful political training he'd had.

After Australia, he rose fast through the Macmillan and then the Heath governments. He was First Lord of the Admiralty, then leader of the Lords. Under Heath he was Defence Secretary and, briefly, Energy Secretary but, more important, became a member of Heath's inner circle. He was chairman of the party at the time Heath met his Waterloo, in February 1974. Despite his charm, he was among the least suited of men to hold such a post, being ever willing to explain to visitors to his room in the House of Lords how much he loathed the party activists and dreaded the occasions, which he had happily reduced to a minimum, when he was obliged to visit local Conservative Associations.

For a man who was later deemed indispensable – indeed, who at the nadir of Mrs Thatcher's fortunes in late 1981 was seriously mentioned as a credible replacement for her – Carrington's career was oddly clouded by error and doubt. He was at Agriculture in 1954 when the Crichel Down scandal, over the handling of military land, brought down his minister, Sir Thomas Dugdale, with Carrington himself being criticised in the inquiry report. When he was First Lord, the Admiralty spy, William John Vassall, was exposed, and the shadow of negligence hung for a while over the ministers in the department. Later, when the party crashed to defeat during the 1974 miners' strike, the chairman could have been badly burned – except that Carrington let it be widely known that he would have held the election three weeks earlier, when it was commonly believed the Tories would have won.

What gave him most credentials to be Foreign Secretary was, oddly, not so much his political record as his business experience: that plus his ability to impress Mrs Thatcher as a man of the world who knew what he was talking about. In Opposition he spent a lot of time travelling around as a director of Rio Tinto-Zinc, the international mining conglomerate. Throughout Africa, Asia and the Middle East, he collected a vast repertoire of contacts. Although a member of the shadow cabinet, he was often prevented by these journeys from attending: a habit continued in government, often to the prime minister's convenience. When ministers opposed to the economic policy wished to raise their stifled voices and needed Carrington's support, he was usually missing. His absence became a by-word: 'Whenever we want Peter, he's in Australia.'

They were pleased, all the same, that he was Foreign Secretary. He was one of them. The Foreign Office was equally pleased. He was one of them as well. After an abrasive two years under his predecessor, David Owen, who challenged their advice as often as he offended their belief in good manners, the members of the foreign service were looking forward to a return to order and decency.

Yet this was not quite what the prime minister wanted. She saw the Foreign Office no less than the Treasury as a bastion of complacency. What she lacked at the beginning was the same confidence in dealing with the raw material of the subject, or the same determination to give it the full Thatcher treatment. This was why she was content to put Carrington in charge. There was also the not

unimportant fact that her most trusted lieutenants, the true believers
in the rage for change, were few in number; they could staff the
economic ministries, but otherwise there weren't enough to go round.
Yet even if there had been, Carrington's appointment, while presaging
some frightful rows as the prime minister grew in self-confidence,
would doubtless have seemed to her the right one.

Certainly her first experience of foreign affairs at the highest level
failed to impress her that it was a subject meriting her most diligent
attention. A few weeks after the election, an economic summit of
world leaders was due to take place in Tokyo. Mrs Thatcher flew
there via Moscow, taking the opportunity for a meeting with the
Soviet prime minister Alexey Kosygin who, going beyond protocol,
came out to the airport to inspect this new phenomenon, the Iron
Lady, while her plane was refuelling. In Tokyo she aroused similar
interest. Here for the first time was a female among the men, who,
if nothing else, stood out in every photograph. Some years later,
Geoffrey Howe, who accompanied her as Chancellor, could still
recall the impression she made. 'There we were,' he said,

> amongst these great established figures – Giscard, Schmidt,
> Carter – and emerging for the final press conference, I noticed
> that the curiosity of the large Japanese audience, including many
> Japanese women who were amazed to see a woman assuming
> primacy in male company, was enormous. She spoke last in the
> statements they all made to the press conference. She was the
> only one to do it without notes. She was the only one who
> achieved a spontaneity and a sparkle that justified the curiosity
> with which she was first greeted.[1]

But she was less impressed by what she found. In fact she was not
much engaged by the main argument at the summit, which concerned
the new energy crisis induced by the leap in oil prices. With Britain
in sight of oil self-sufficiency, the rows about imports and quotas
mattered less to her than to the Germans and the Japanese. More
than that, she did not readily enter into the jocular camaraderie with
which the world leaders helped persuade themselves they were friends
beneath the skin. For her, Carter was still Mr President, never
'Jimmy', and Schmidt Herr Chancellor rather than 'Helmut'. 'First-
name terms can lead to artificial familiarity,' she noted in her best
governessy style.

When she got home, she candidly told her staff that she had no real idea what the point of it had been. She expressed some contempt for the agreed statements the summit produced at the end, which were in most cases drafted before the leaders even reached Tokyo. She was, it seemed to one of her private secretaries, pleasingly unseduced by the red carpets and high living and other appurtenances of the global power game: but also, less realistically, tempted to excessive impatience with a necessary part of her job. She wanted to get on with running Britain, and not be bothered with diplomacy – work for which her mind was not naturally fashioned.

Foreign affairs, however, set their own timetable. The press of events imposes an agenda no prime minister can control. An issue in this category awaited the new occupant of Downing Street which put her skill and judgment to an early test: her skill in the international field, and her judgment of the Conservative Party. For it involved a country of particular sensitivity to the party.

For the past fifteen years, Rhodesia had been an anomaly on the international scene. In 1965, under the leadership of Ian Smith, the minority white Government made a unilateral declaration of independence, and this settler territory, while theoretically still a British colonial responsibility, became an increasingly painful irritant to every British government thereafter. Various efforts had been made to end the rebellion and reach a settlement. Economic sanctions were imposed by the Wilson Government, when UDI occurred, and were maintained by the Heath Government throughout its time in office. But it was at that time that Conservative backbenchers opposed to sanctions and friendly with Smith became a vocal, and occasionally menacing, political force. Year after year, a hard core of them, known as the Rhodesia Lobby, opposed sanctions and did their best to embarrass Heath into breaking with world opinion, which insisted that, however little damage sanctions were doing to Rhodesia, they must be kept in place until Smith surrendered.

Margaret Thatcher had never been part of the Rhodesia Lobby even during the Opposition years. She was far too busy penetrating, and then retaining her position in, the upper echelons of the party. As Secretary of State for Education, the provision of nursery education and the expansion of the comprehensive schools were preoccupation enough, without her having to bother with the further reaches of foreign policy. But this did not prevent her being seen as a sympathiser when she came to power. The forces that placed her in the leadership included the right-wingers in the Lobby, so that among the many factions and interests who expected her Administration to smile on them were certainly Ian Smith and his friends at Westminster.

Rhodesia, however, was in a desperate state. In the past seven years, more than 20,000 people had died in civil war, and significant voices around the world were clamouring for an end to it. Rhodesia's neighbours were suffering, the Commonwealth was divided and Washington's awakening interest in southern Africa had already, under the Labour Government, added to the pressures for a diplomatic solution. Lord Carrington, therefore, identified Rhodesia as a problem demanding most urgent attention. The new man at the Foreign Office gave it a natural priority, even if the new woman in Downing Street did not; and he drew her along with him. What followed was a double-act between the two of them, in which their contrasting styles each played a decisive part. It was a fortunate conjunction. The episode permitted Carrington to launch his leader into the world arena with an uncovenanted diplomatic triumph, completed within the year.

The route towards it was far from smooth. Earlier in the spring, Rhodesia had held its own election which, by African standards, was a roughly democratic exercise. The latest in a series of grudging responses by the Smith regime to the demands of world opinion, it produced a black prime minister, Bishop Abel Muzorewa. Moreover, according to a team sent out by the Tory leader to observe it, it was conducted fairly. When she became prime minister, there were strong temptations to accept the result and recognise the Muzorewa Government, even though the electoral process had excluded the leaders of the main African elements in the civil war, the veteran black nationalists Joshua Nkomo and Robert Mugabe. Having no sympathy for black nationalists, nor any interest in the dubious abstraction known as the Third World, Mrs Thatcher had few personal reasons not to give Muzorewa a fair wind.

The election, however, was in important ways bogus. It was fought on a constitution which entrenched white power, even while giving blacks the vote. Muzorewa was in part a front man for a Smith regime in different guise. For this reason, the result was not recognised by any of the nations that counted. Rhodesia continued to be a pariah, and the civil war continued with renewed ferocity.

Mrs Thatcher showed her natural instincts early. On her way back from Tokyo, she stopped over in Canberra for talks with her admired role-model, the Australian prime minister, Malcolm Fraser. In fact, although there were similarities between these two Conservatives, and Mrs Thatcher had sent emissaries to discover how Fraser won his election in 1975, they differed strongly in their opinion about African emancipation. A little later, Fraser was to be influential in pushing towards a Rhodesian settlement. But in Canberra Mrs Thatcher made a point of noting that she would not, this year, be able to drive through Parliament the annual vote to renew economic sanctions. It sounded as though she would not even try: first strike to the Rhodesia Lobby.

She was, however, prepared to be open-minded. Rhodesia did not fall under the unblinking gaze of the conviction politician. The history of the settlement is to an important extent the history of her own conversion to the need for a solution along lines which the Foreign Office, under Carrington, now invented.

A Commonwealth Conference in Lusaka, Zambia, was fixed in the calendar for early August. It, the Foreign Office thought, should be the catalyst. Through a series of conversations during July, Mrs Thatcher was persuaded at least that the opportunity should be kept open. As usual, personal chemistry came into this. According to Patrick Cosgrave, one of her advisers at the time, she had met Muzorewa and thought little of him, whatever the merits of his election.[2] When it was suggested that she should definitely not endorse the Muzorewa election and the so-called internal settlement ahead of Lusaka, she agreed – to the chagrin of the Tory right.

There was to be a Commons debate on Africa on 25 July, and she opened it with a speech of uncharacteristically Delphic opacity. She was generous about the internal settlement, said it represented a major advance, urged nobody to write it off, castigated those who remained determined to see no progress whatever in Rhodesia. She was also scathing about the warring nationalists, insisting that there could be no solution 'which seeks to substitute the bullet for the ballot box'.

But, at the same time, she laid the ground for something different and better. The election may have fulfilled the six criteria which had long been posited as the British test for any settlement, but she now added another. 'Because it is in Rhodesia's own interest to be accepted into the international community,' she said, 'we must have regard to the views of other governments.' Nor would she say formally that the recent elections were decisive. 'We have not yet decided on the matter, because we have wanted to go another way – a way that we believe

177

will be better for Rhodesia in the longer run. It is a way that we believe will bring more countries along with us, and if we go along that consultation route it will be to the benefit of Rhodesia.'

This speech was written in the Foreign Office. It seemed to mark a considerable change in her position. But a Foreign Office minister told me at the time that it was necessary to have been present in the House to understand how far she still had to go. He noted how unenthusiastically she read out the speech, 'so that no one could take it in'. She kept interpolating her own off-the-cuff lines, somewhat contradicting the text, with far more enthusiasm. When Foreign Office spokesmen were on their feet, on this and other Rhodesian occasions, she often gave them a hard time, 'constantly kind of barracking us from behind'.

She arrived in Lusaka, however, committed more for than against attempting a new settlement, although totally averse to having one forced upon her by a body of leaders, the Commonwealth, for whom she had no real respect. And the Foreign Office had a plan. Its officials, led by a deputy under-secretary, Sir Anthony Duff, and the head of the Rhodesia department, Robin Renwick, reckoned that the time had come for Britain to take some risks in the search for a final resolution, and that a heavy squeeze could be applied to the Smithites. The intensifying military pressure from the Patriotic Front forces of Nkomo and Mugabe, combined with the desire of all outside parties for an end to the war, meant that now was the time and place from which to advance to a new constitutional conference.

The Foreign Office put this before the prime minister with a certain psychological insight. Their plan appealed alike to her boldness and her chauvinism. Britain, they suggested, should control the whole independence operation. Earlier proposals, under the Labour Government, had contemplated an international solution; Dr Henry Kissinger, the US Secretary of State, had become briefly involved, and the United Nations hovered expectantly in the wings.

Mrs Thatcher had no time for the United Nations, and was much attracted by the idea of Britain assuming full and sole responsibility, hazardous though this might be. Britain would hold a constitutional conference, Britain supervise a fresh election, Britain police the transition to legal independence. This deal, if it came off, would be Britain's deal, which meant her deal. Once anything was agreed at Lusaka, it would necessarily enlist the formidable weight of her personal commitment.

There was another important precondition, the atmosphere in

which the Lusaka conference convened. Plainly the chances of success would improve if the other national leaders arrived expecting the talks to break down on the rock of British intransigence.

Achieving this required nothing of Mrs Thatcher. What was known of her character, and what had been read into her speeches, guaranteed the worst reception imaginable. Kaunda thought she was obsessed with the idea of Soviet influence dominating the region through an independent Rhodesia, and said he hoped she hadn't 'lost her reason'. He accused her of prejudging the outcome of the conference by deciding in advance to lift sanctions. The government-owned *Zambia Daily Mail*, comparing Mrs Thatcher unfavourably with the Queen's 'extraordinary loving heart', said the prime minister was a racist.

It would have been difficult for any leader to live up to the images of viperish monstrosity which the Africans conjured up of Mrs Thatcher before she arrived among them. When she did so, the effect was predictable. She turned out to be less appalling than they imagined. And she particularly pleased them by her directness, whether sweeping fearlessly into crowds or describing candidly her intentions. Carrington, too, was amazed by her methods on this, the first big international expedition when her quality was put to the test. 'Peter would have been devious,' one of his ministers told me at the time, 'but she sailed into the other prime ministers. She was quite undiplomatic. She cut out all subtlety. She was very candid about her problems with the Tory Party, and they loved that especially.'

But she was not at first prepared to do what the Commonwealth wanted. Kaunda and President Nyerere of Tanzania were the principal voices of these demands, and they were not people for whom she had much personal respect. In particular she reacted badly to the smallest sign that she was being bullied. She was not, at first, prepared to denounce the existing constitution nor to acknowledge that, following a ceasefire, Nkomo and Mugabe and other military leaders should be present at a new conference and all Africans be entitled to vote in a genuine independence election. It took persuasion from Carrington, and all the pressure the Commonwealth could muster, to persuade her to go the whole way: to say the constitution should be scrapped, not merely amended, and to acknowledge the indispensable part which the Patriotic Front leaders had to play.

For their part, the Africans had to make a few concessions. They did not like the idea that this would be a British operation. Eventually the British conceded that there should be a token Commonwealth involvement in policing the transition, but at every stage of the independence process, the British were to assume their ancient responsibilities as the decolonising power. This was what made it palatable to Mrs Thatcher. There would even be a British governor for a few months, while the Rhodesian Army was held in baulk and power was handed over.

But at the end it was a wrench. An eye-witness has recorded the prime minister's demeanour when, in the middle of the Lusaka conference, she finally succumbed to the collective demand that the Muzorewa government be offered no crumb of support. She read out a statement drafted, fittingly, not by one of her own officials but by Sir Anthony Duff. She read the statement at speed. 'Her head was bent over the paper; her voice, for once, lacked its usual timbre. Defeat had been unpleasant, but Duff's skill enabled the public relations campaign to get under way.'[3]

The aftermath of the Lusaka decision, to set up a constitutional conference in London with the hopeful purpose of bringing Rhodesia to independence, well illustrated two facets of Margaret Thatcher's prime ministerial personality. It was a kind of warning, both bright and salutary, of things to come.

The first was her commitment to a cause, once she was converted to its merits. Having arrived in Lusaka sceptical, she left full of optimism and determination. She was hugged on the dance-floor by President Kaunda, who now declared that 'the Iron Lady has brought a ray of hope on the dark horizon'. The *Times of Zambia*, which a week earlier had called her a racist bigot, now decided that 'inside the iron casing is a soft heart'. According to the *Daily Telegraph* reporter, the conference was, in Zambian eyes, the 'apotheosis of the Blessed Margaret', and if her homeward plane had been 'drawn skywards by cherubim', few Zambians would have been very surprised.

When she returned home, these acclamations fortified her in preparing to do battle with the Conservative right and the hard-core Rhodesia Lobby. She had not been half-heartedly converted to Kaunda's analysis; she was absolutely convinced it was correct. Asked to explain her refusal to recognise the Muzorewa regime and her willingness to submit to Commonwealth opinion, she was characteristically adamant. 'This way offers a very much better approach for the people of Rhodesia,' she insisted. 'I feel that very strongly indeed.' Such fixity of view, combined with her credentials as a born-again right-winger herself, meant that the fire of the right never had much chance of shifting her. A Rhodesian settlement was now her personal objective. She was convinced of its merit and necessity. Her reputation as an emerging international figure was entwined in the successful transition that had to be accomplished from Rhodesia to Zimbabwe.

This unflinching aspect of her character, once it was set on course, heavily influenced the process through which the transition was now undertaken, a constitutional conference held at Lancaster House in London. Her direct part in this tortuous event, lasting from September almost to Christmas, was kept to a minimum. Although she involved herself closely in redrafting the Rhodesian constitution to make it provide for genuine majority rule, she rarely met with the participants, that motley gathering of every member of the famous cast who had fought over the future of Rhodesia for two decades. The patience and the cunning required to inch the contending parties towards a final resolution were supplied by others.

Nonetheless, she played a critical strategic role. This was the first time a significant Rhodesian negotiation had been supervised by a straight and not a devious politician. Harold Wilson, Mrs Thatcher's main predecessor in the field, had seen all his considerable wiles come to nothing in successive attempts to force Ian Smith to surrender. The Thatcher approach, by contrast, achieved much more by its adamantine simplicity. She made it clear that she was not available as a court of appeal before which the Smithite remnant could hope to reverse the concessions extorted from them at Lancaster House. They always thought she was their friend, but she proved in the end to be their most effective opponent.

Allied to her clarity was her political courage. When the talks reached what might have been their most fateful impasse, she took the large gamble of sending a British governor, in the person of Lord Soames, out to Rhodesia as proof that Muzorewa was not to be allowed to remain as prime minister and that the talks would not be allowed to fail. With the civil war still raging and no ceasefire in sight, the governor could easily have become a victim of the violence and the whole enterprise been abruptly aborted. It was a big risk for Lord and Lady Soames, but a scarcely smaller one for the prime minister. Not all politicians would have taken it. To Mrs Thatcher its inherent danger was exceeded by the imperative need not to retreat from the objective she had set herself: an objective Soames saw through to the end, supervising an election at the end of February and formally transferring power to an independent Zimbabwe on 17 April 1980.

At the time, the prime minister took due credit for this. 'We are once more a nation capable of action rather than reaction,' she told the Scottish Conservative conference three weeks later. 'Zimbabwe has now embarked on nationhood in circumstances more favourable than many had dreamed possible.' But there was a darker side to her assessment. And this too reflected a habit deeply embedded in her political character. Just as important as the completion, once embarked on, of the project in hand was the capacity to doubt, in some different time-frame and another corner of her mind, the true validity of the exercise in the first place. Mrs Thatcher often employed this intellectual device to reconcile herself to compromises and deviations from instinct which she was obliged to make on domestic as well as foreign policy. To a politician who had special need at all times to believe that her true convictions had never changed, it offered much reassurance.

In respect of Zimbabwe, moreover, her deeper doubts were not entirely baseless. Compared with what she hoped would happen, quite a lot went wrong. Robert Mugabe, the more militant of the nationalist leaders, was not meant to win the election. While the Foreign Office team, led by Duff and Renwick, later claimed they always thought he would get the most seats, because he had the tribal majority, they didn't expect his ZANU party to get overall control. The British expectation, and certainly their hope, was for a more malleable independent government, formed by an alliance between Joshua Nkomo and Bishop Muzorewa. 'We did want Nkomo very badly,' a Foreign Office official told me later. 'He's not as intelligent as Mugabe, but he's bigger. He's a conciliator and a compromiser: in fact a good, old-fashioned Tory politician.'

This was what the Foreign Office assured Mrs Thatcher she would get. They could rationalise it, of course, when she didn't. Soames had a particularly trenchant line in retrospective justification. Within a month of returning from Zimbabwe, he was fond of saying that Mugabe's victory was the best thing that could have happened, since Muzorewa was 'useless' and 'Josh would have let the Russians in'.

Notwithstanding this merciful release – from the fate, after all, which had originally most inclined her against having anything to do with the Commonwealth plan – Mrs Thatcher later tended to sound displeased with her handiwork. Ministers and officials heard her say from time to time, as inter-tribal warfare intensified, that the Rhodesian whites had been sold out for the sake of short-term advantage.

In fact, independent Zimbabwe made remarkable strides. When

Soames returned there for a visit six years after Mugabe's election, he was impressed by how few of the worst fears had been fulfilled. With the civil war at an end, communal black farmers were able to feed the entire population, leaving the big commercial farms to supply the export market. Infant mortality had been halved, the number of children in secondary schools quadrupled. Although Mugabe talked a lot about Marxism, not an acre of land had been sequestrated and not a business compulsorily nationalised. Soames saw in front of him a mixed economy thriving in a multi-racial society.[4] It seemed a mildly triumphant justification for a rare diplomatic success.

But for Margaret Thatcher this was never wholly convincing. She had been instrumental in creating another Third World country, ready to line up against her and the West, as she saw it, in any international forum, but especially in the Commonwealth. She had helped to push the whites out of power, their entrenched protections as a minority due to expire in a very few years. Across the border in South Africa, a graver struggle loomed which threatened British interests much more materially. When this came to a head in 1986, with a Commonwealth demand for international economic sanctions against South Africa, Mugabe was the most implacable of all opponents of her anti-sanctions stance. It did not escape her recollection that he was a man whom expediency had prompted her, of all people, to legitimise.

Addressing the Parliamentary Press Gallery in early December, at a moment when the Lancaster House conference seemed on the verge of collapse, the prime minister offered a rare complaint about her lot. 'I want to spend more time on the economy,' she said, 'but foreign affairs have taken over.' Wistfully she reflected on the impossibility of putting political tasks into separate compartments.

Even more pressing than Rhodesia was another diplomatic question: the cost to Britain of the European Community. The Rhodesian intervention was a conscious choice, an initiative that could, at a price, have been withheld or delayed. The Community budget, on the other hand, was an inexorable reality demanding urgent attention. It was also an issue on which Mrs Thatcher knew exactly where she stood. It appealed perfectly to her sense of justice, of economy and of British nationhood. The net cost of British membership was spiralling upwards: £800 million in 1978 and, according to Treasury figures

prepared just before the election, heading towards £1,000 million in
1979. This had to stop. Within days of her arrival in Downing
Street, her first foreign visitor, Helmut Schmidt, the West German
Chancellor, was told as much. Their meeting inaugurated one of the
major continuing themes of the first Thatcher term which only reached
its conclusion in the second: the process whereby, in the interests of
saving what she termed 'our money', stubbornness and a most startling
aggression were revealed as the style Mrs Thatcher would bring to
her dealings with the world.

Europe and all it stood for in the imagery of post-war Conservatism
presented another opportunity for a challenge to the past. Harold
Macmillan had tried to take Britain into the Community. Ted Heath
had finally succeeded. Both of them lived and breathed the air of
Europe, believing in Britain's European destiny and placing entry at
the top of their agenda, despite all rebuffs. Both, likewise, had
delivered speech after speech filled with incantations to the European
dream and suchlike elusive ideals. Entry, when it came, was seen by
Heath as unquestionably his greatest achievement, the quintessence
of Conservative internationalism.

His Education Secretary went along with this. But, as with so
much else, revisionism set in when she displaced him. His Euro-
rhetoric turned out never to have appealed to her. She cultivated the
more populist line, which regarded all Europeans with suspicion and
the machinations of the Community bureaucracy in Brussels with
outright hostility.

She was not against a concert of Europe, but she saw it in quite
different terms from Heath. The major speeches she gave in Opposition depicted European unity as something desirable as an arm of
anti-Soviet policy rather than economic co-operation. The Community
needed to be strengthened, she told an Italian audience in June 1977,
'to keep alive in the Eastern as well as the Western half of our
continent those ideas of human dignity which Europe gave to the
world'. Moreover, with the first direct elections to the European
Parliament looming in two years' time, it was the need for right-wing
unity in the struggle with the left that mattered: 'If we look on Europe
as a whole, it is clear that the present fragmentation of the centre and
the right gives to the left an advantage which the rest of us cannot
afford.'

Speaking in Brussels a year later, she clothed herself even more
completely in the armour of the Iron Lady. The Soviet threat posed
the greatest challenge to Western Europe and the greatest motive for

unity. Her new hero, Alexander Solzhenitsyn, should be the inspiration for a collective stance against Russian expansionism. The Community, she thought, should have a closer association with Nato and develop much more interest in defence policy. The coming accession of Spain and Portugal was, from a defence point of view, 'essential'. Yet 'who is there in the EEC deliberations to speak up for defence? I feel no assurance that all these connected matters are being looked at together. Where there is so much at stake we cannot tolerate confusion of purpose in the West.'

This was not the perspective that presented itself in May 1979. Instead it was a matter of money, or, more precisely, how large a subscription Britain was prepared to continue paying for the doubtful privilege of merging her identity and sovereignty with richer European partners. Here the leader was quite clear that the answer should be nothing. Posed in that way, the proposition saw her Iron Lady-like idealism crumble before the Micawberesque rigour of household economics. Her differences with the Heathites were beautifully summed up in a phrase much cited by one of them, Lord Soames, a fanatic European long before he had been anywhere near Rhodesia. 'She is an agnostic who continues to go to church,' Soames said, rolling the metaphor pleasurably off his tongue. 'She won't become an atheist, but on the other hand she certainly won't become a true believer.'

In charge of the operation, under Carrington, was a man who also had a non-believing disposition. But Sir Ian Gilmour, Lord Privy Seal and second minister in the Foreign Office, scattered his non-belief far and wide. Sceptical by temperament and training, he certainly did not believe in the kind of anti-Europeanism now necessary to carry out the Thatcher plan of attack. If there was a polar opposite to the Thatcher style in the Cabinet, Gilmour embodied it. Where she was aggressive he was emollient. Her impatience he met with languor, her ferocity with disdain, her zeal with withering contempt for zeal. He was, in short, the perfect Foreign Office man; and it was over the Foreign Office that, in this matter at least, she was determined to have her victory.

She laid the ground for it with the assistance of the Foreign Office's great rival for power and influence, the Treasury. The Treasury had long been bothered by the costs of the EEC, and not least by the impossibility of discovering exactly what these added up to. Shortly before the election, in fact, it started its own inquiry into this, which was put in the hands of its brightest under-secretary, Peter Middleton. The results of the Middleton inquiry leaked into the press, and along with them the hitherto obscure name of Middleton himself: from which almost chance event began another of the personal relationships that particularly characterised the Thatcher way of government.

Soon after the election, Middleton was summoned to Chequers, the prime minister's country residence. With a Foreign Office man in tow, he spent the weekend delivering a seminar on the EEC budget, at the end of which, in the absence of hard data, it was decided to send to the European Commission a set of figures representing Britain's best guess at what the Community was costing her. These figures, adding up to the £1,000 million, were 'virtually invented', according to one official. But they smoked out the 'real' figures, which Brussels yielded up for the first time. From these figures derived Britain's negotiating position in the abrasive series of meetings that now began with the European partners. But from them also sprang the youthful Middleton's rather special relationship with the prime minister. He regarded himself, with some justice, as the architect of the case Mrs Thatcher made for the return of 'our money'. For her part she regarded him with sufficient favour to promote him in 1983, above several more senior candidates, to be permanent secretary, the top official in the Treasury.

Armed with the Commission's own figures, she embarked on a round of private and public harangues designed to exhibit her adamant belief that the British contribution was both politically and economically indefensible. She had one powerful negotiating weapon. The Community looked certain to exceed its own budget in 1981 or 1982 largely because of the excesses of its common agricultural policy. The prime minister made plain in Strasbourg and Luxemburg, Bonn and Rome, and anywhere else she could find a platform, that Britain would not agree to any increase in the Community's own resources until satisfied on the British contribution.

But it was in Dublin, at the end of November, that the depth of her commitment finally became clear to her fellow heads of government on the European Council: here that her unique diplomatic style, in all its reckless ferocity, was first unveiled before the disbelieving eyes not only of the other leaders but of her own supposed advisers in the Foreign Office. Absolutely unwilling to compromise on her demand for the £1,000 million reduction, she pursued her interlocutors with the confidence of someone who thought she was on a winning streak and the zeal of a leader who positively relished destroying the shibboleths of quiet diplomacy. So grating was her language and so inflexible her demand that the summit almost collapsed without a result. One eyewitness, Christopher Tugendhat, a European Commissioner at the time, has recorded the near-terminal effect of her refusal to see the EEC budget as anything other than the felonious theft of British money – 'my money', as he has her calling it. 'As the vehemence of her arguments increased,' Tugendhat writes, 'Schmidt at one point feigned sleep, and when she refused to give in, the French party's cars were drawn up outside with their engines revving in order to emphasise the take-it-or-leave-it nature of what was on offer.'[5]

At the last moment, a minimal agreement was struck. Mrs Thatcher would have nothing to do with the paltry £350 million reduction the Community offered her on next year's contribution, but she did finally agree to another meeting. Schmidt said afterwards that, 'until literally the last five minutes', it seemed likely that even future talks would be ruled out. The Thatcher style, without subtlety or finesse, at least carried the clout of a fearlessly single-minded negotiator.

The experience crystallised some of her international relationships, notably those with Schmidt and the French president, Valéry Giscard d'Estaing. In Giscard's case, the Dublin summit confirmed the already poor state of the connection. Although they were both Conservatives, they had extraordinarily little in common. It was mostly a social thing. He was insufferably grand, as well as clothing himself in all the natural perquisites of a head of state. A few months later, in conversation with me, she made a nice distinction. 'Giscard is olympian, not patrician,' she said. For 'la fille d'épicier', as he contemptuously called her, neither state made for a natural friendship.

With Schmidt there were none of these social barriers nor, despite his being a socialist, many political ones either. She would often tell him, looking enviously at his market-oriented economic policies, that he was more right-wing than she was. It was said only half in jest.

But Schmidt also kept his distance. There was a serious gulf between their views of Europe. Later, after the Chancellor had left office, I heard him expatiate on their differences. By then he had become fully seized of the scale of the global crisis, and even more given than when in power to a grandiose, sometimes apocalyptic, view of the world. In this mood he looked back on the Thatcher attitude to Europe by way of an original, but telling, analogy. The person he thought she resembled most, in her inability to understand any point of view but her own, and her short-term desire to see the Community as an arena of struggle in which she should invariably be seen to 'win', was Harold Wilson. Although Schmidt, in office, preserved the courtesies and sometimes evinced quite an admiration for Mrs Thatcher's political muscle, he never imagined he was in the company of a true 'European'.

This personal coolness, indeed, was a key to the problem. The new British leader knew that, quite apart from the budgetary dispute, she was potentially an interloper between friends. The Franco-German bond was very close but doubly hard to penetrate, in her opinion, because it was an axis between Schmidt and Giscard personally, who were on the telephone to each other constantly, sharing judgments and exchanging ideas. It worried her, in line with her primordial view of the EEC as a defender of the West, that one of these intimates should have no part in Nato. She knew well enough that she was an outsider at the gates. And the knowledge did nothing to encourage her towards the more conventional approach.

Nor, for their part, were these great established Europeans very diplomatic either. Christopher Tugendhat, watching from the inside, noticed this. He saw them treating the European Council as 'a private fief', and thought they were alarmed by the arrival in it of another strong leader with an unassailable five-year parliamentary majority behind her. They were unstatesmanlike, Tugendhat judges, in refusing to assist the solution of the British budget problem before it got out of hand. Instead they promoted 'a derisory offer', at Dublin, and drove Mrs Thatcher into a corner from which she had no choice but to come out fighting as 'la Dame de Fer de l'Europe'.

Whoever was to blame, negotiations were now bound to be protracted, and also narrow. It was the narrowness that gave the Foreign Office such anguish. Their traditional métier was set at almost nothing by a leader who refused to contemplate any of the linkages or compromises by which the budget quarrel might be mitigated. Oil, fishing and the export of British lamb were all bargaining chips they wanted to play in the search for some solution to the biggest problem. The leader would not countenance any such suppleness, constantly denying that she had any room for manoeuvre, and at one stage publicly contemplating an open breach with Community law. If Dublin had ended in complete breakdown, she said immediately afterwards, 'I would have called a cabinet meeting in London to discuss what to do, and that would have precipitated a crisis.'

Instead, a series of 'last chance' meetings took place under her menacing eye, culminating in Luxemburg at the end of April 1980. Here the European offer to Britain was doubled, a tribute no doubt to her vexatious but effective methods. Even this, however, she rejected. Although now worth about £760 million, the cut in the

British contribution remained defective in her eyes because it was only a two-year deal, and the probable payment in the second year looked as though it might be a little higher than in the first. 'We must look after British interests,' she nervelessly insisted after the Luxemburg breakdown. And she exulted, as she told radio listeners, on discovering that the Europeans talked of her as a 'she-de Gaulle'. Giscard, among others, was almost inexpressibly furious. 'I will not allow such a contemptible spectacle to occur again,' he said as he departed.

Fortunately, the Frenchman was not put to the test. The scene of hostilities was now transferred to the British cabinet.

On 30 May 1980, an outline agreement between Britain and the European Community was finally reached in Brussels. Significantly, the prime minister was not present. This was the moment at which the Foreign Office took over, securing, somewhat to their surprise, an advance on the Luxemburg offer. The balance between the first and second year was adjusted and, crucially, the formula was extended into a third year. This, however, was not quite the end of the piece.

The Foreign Secretary and his lugubrious colleague, Gilmour, returned from Brussels pleased with what they had achieved. While willing to grant some credit to the Thatcher obduracy over so many months, they were quietly relieved that Foreign Office methods had finally produced a result. Their leader was less impressed. From the moment they set foot at Chequers to acquaint her with their triumph, she insisted that it was an unacceptable disaster. She thought it worse than Luxemburg, not better. It was still only three-quarters of the cake, and it would put up the Retail Price Index – a totem before which, as the monetarist John Biffen drolly observed around this time, 'she bows like some primitive Saxon on his knees before the great god Thor'. The fight between Carrington and Gilmour on one side and Mrs Thatcher on the other at Chequers that weekend, as she struggled to deny them and herself a considerable success in economic diplomacy, deserves a prominent place in the annals of political perversity.

On the Monday it adjourned to full cabinet. Still the prime minister continued the fight. To several of those present it became apparent that she was ready, indeed thirsting, for yet another acrimonious sortie round Europe, and that there was a more overtly political reason for this than they had previously understood. What she could not bear to lose, they realised, was the populist appeal of the anti-EEC card. At a time when economic problems were piling up at home, the leader who was seen as struggling to the death against no fewer than eight foreign powers made much of her image of patriotic valour.

The cabinet, however, did not agree. The decision to endorse the 30 May Brussels agreement was one of the quite rare instances during the Thatcher era when the cabinet collectively gathered sufficient will to divert the prime minister from her favoured course. Hitherto, as sole negotiator at successive summits, she had sole right of decision on what to reject. On this occasion – and it irked her deeply – she was faced with something close to a *fait accompli* which she might overturn only at her peril. It was essentially because Carrington informed her that he would support no other course, knowing that at least half-a-dozen colleagues and seventy Tory MPs would side with him and split the Government, that she finally gave her assent to what the Nine had agreed.

This was the end of a phase: one which occupied a substantial portion of the first Thatcher year. The 30 May Agreement, however, did not end the argument, nor conclude the deforming domination by the budget question of all Britain's relations with the EEC. Another interim deal was needed in June 1982, and it took another two years, well into the second term, for a permanent arrangement finally to be concluded, at Fontainebleau in June 1984.

But already in the first year a pattern was established, which was often discernible later, whereby the Thatcher character became the single most important factor in assessing a diplomatic position and forming a policy to deal with it. In its very rejection of the conventional smootheries of diplomacy, this character produced advantage for Britain. It was certainly good for Mrs Thatcher, since her stand on the EEC well reflected the feelings of the British people. And its value to the narrow negotiation is not denied, even by men of different political persuasion. Roy Jenkins, who was President of the European Commission in her time, while deploring her methods, conceded their merits. 'As a proponent of the British case, she does have the advantage of being almost totally impervious to how much she offends other people,' he said in 1985. 'I have seen her when she was a new prime minister surrounded by others who were against her and being unmoved by this in a way that many other people would find difficult to withstand.'[6]

But she made her mark in another way as well. By articulating the British sense of distance from Europe, she reinforced it. She was not interested in expanding the European idea beyond the narrow ground

of Britain's greater economic advantage, where she was quite successful, to getting the EEC more interested in defence, in which she
completely failed. The scenes of a decade earlier, which some of her
colleagues could remember, when Edward Heath, Willy Brandt and
Georges Pompidou sat together sharing their dreams of a more united
Europe, were gone, never to return. She simply did not think like
that. To her, the epithet *communautaire* was a term not of commendation but of abuse, even though there was never any serious question
of her attempting to lead Britain out of the Community.

Many Europeans regretted this. Schmidt was very disappointed.
European leaders were insular about their continent, he thought in
his retirement, and Mrs Thatcher was exceptionally insular even
among them. That is what the Foreign Office thought as well. So did
the old Heathite wing of the Tory Party, many of them still in power
and now preparing to abandon such faith as they ever had in her
economic policies. On both matters, Ian Gilmour, for example, was
beginning to doubt her capacity for rational behaviour. But nobody
denied that they could tell, on the evidence of a year, what kind of
international figure she was determined to cut.

11

The Capture of the Cabinet

FEW GOVERNMENTS HAVE had as short a honeymoon as Mrs Thatcher's. Disharmony flared not with its voters but among its members. The anger was within it. The period when it was bliss to be alive did not last much beyond the first summer recess. On the central issue that defined its purpose, economic and industrial reform, euphoria soon gave way to grimness, and ministers fell to fighting among themselves. In this process the leader's naturally belligerent tendencies played a part. Mastering her colleagues, like trouncing the Europeans, was a task in which she felt justified by the scale of the challenge confronting Britain. When the election's afterglow gave way to grinding reality, she cast herself in a heroic role. Restoring sound money, she told the Lord Mayor's banquet in November, was the first objective. 'It is a Herculean task,' she said. 'But we are not faint-hearted pilgrims. We will not be deflected by a stony path.' The difficulties that faced her, she suggested, were 'greater, perhaps, than any faced in time of peace by Disraeli or Churchill'.

On this analysis all ministers were agreed. Jim Prior was saying something very like it in September. As the year closed, the objective facts held no grounds for optimism. Inflation was forecast to reach 18 per cent, minimum lending rate was at an unprecedented 17 per cent, and business confidence, according to the Tories' friends in the CBI, had collapsed since the election, with demand and output weak and investment seriously lagging. Already since the budget, the public sector borrowing requirement had had to be revised upwards, from £8,300 million to £9,000 million. A 5 per cent cut (£3,600 million) was ordered for next year's public spending. The dreaded 'Clegg' award, so rashly endorsed as an electoral necessity, meant that public sector wages alone, in the current year, would rise by £1,500 million: and in 1980–1 perhaps by £2,000 million.

What ministers even now could not agree was what to do about this multi-faceted crisis. 'As usual, the cabinet was united this morning,' the prime minister said when goaded at Question Time on 15

November, indicating by her very insouciance that most people knew the opposite to be the case. She survived these occasions by tireless repetition of the need to cut public spending and stop printing money, and fluent recall of the consequences of Labour's extravagance. But acceptance of the Thatcherite remedy – savage cuts in spending, fearless rises in interest rates, unshakeable resolution exhibited as a virtue in itself – was only in its early stages. Jim Callaghan, leader of the Opposition, still remained incredulous. Labour MPs were quite sure she would have to bend, and introduce an incomes policy. Some of her cabinet colleagues were already beginning to draw from the depth of the crisis the opposite lesson from the one she regarded as axiomatic.

The stage, in short, was set for the central internal struggle of the Thatcher years: the one she saw the whole of her leadership hitherto as preparation to undertake and win. But it was preceded by another which, for the time being, indicated that old ascendancies were not entirely dead.

In parallel with the budgetary shifts in taxes and spending was always meant to be a second urgent exercise in radicalism: the reform of trade union law. Although Prior, who was in charge of this, had no illusions about the need for legislation, his tenure as shadow spokesman on Employment was marked by a persistent unwillingness to promise extreme measures, and a determination, which to him was not even worth debating, to foster good relations with union leaders. For this he had been called a 'Quisling' by one backbench MP, John Gorst, as well as likened to Pétain and Laval by Norman Tebbit. But Prior had won the argument, and had also survived the effort by Thatcherite ultras to have him replaced. He now set about putting his moderate package, to which the party was committed in its manifesto, into practice.

His efforts to do so, reaching a climax in the autumn of 1979, afforded an early glimpse of one of the more persistent traits Margaret Thatcher was to show throughout her prime ministership, but particularly in her first term. This was her capacity to distance herself from the policies of her own Government, even to the point of undermining them: not exactly to veto or even openly oppose them, but to encourage anyone else who might want to do so. Some might call this the promotion of open debate: the fostering, even, of a version of 'open government' by a leader otherwise entirely opposed to this commonplace nostrum. To others, especially the ministers involved, the style smacked more of a novel form of disloyalty.

Prior's strategic objective was to secure a law that would be obeyed, his political tactic to persuade moderate union leaders to acquiesce in what he was doing. It was an undramatic approach. He looked for the least controversial initiatives, beginning with the provision of public money for union ballots on strikes and leadership changes. His Bill curbed coercive union recruitment tactics and, more combatively, made it much more difficult to introduce a closed shop. This would now require approval by 80 per cent of employees in the workplace, with a conscience clause for anyone wishing to escape its impositions. Additionally, and most hazardously, Prior proposed a first curb on the violent picketing seen by millions on television the previous winter. Secondary picketing, away from the picket's place of work, was to be outlawed.

This was a sizeable package, but not adventurous enough for some. They were looking for outright abolition of the closed shop and far more ruthless treatment of picketing. Anti-union feeling went deep and wide in the Tory Party, and even a natural Prior ally like Ian Gilmour reckoned he was being too cautious. Gilmour and others thought that if Prior was going to stir up union fury, he might as well do it for a more ambitious cause than he was contemplating. But the real hostility came from the right. Prior's fiddling restraint offended all the leader's own gut instincts, and those of her closer colleagues, some of whom were remarkably public in their lack of sympathy. As Prior was in mid-negotiation with the TUC – this was still an era when talks with TUC leaders were thought a helpful accompaniment to policy-making – the Chancellor, Sir Geoffrey Howe, unleashed a quite indelicate philippic against unions and the entire 'dreamworld' in which they lived, sheltering, Prior later wrote, behind the tendentious claim that Prior agreed with him.[1]

The leader herself rarely engaged in such open warfare. But when the creative tension thus induced favoured the argument she wanted to make, she did nothing to discourage it. Although she had kept Prior in place, she never really trusted him. Nor did she do much for his credibility. She was quite open about her scepticism, as he has recounted. In the bargaining over the junior ministries in his department, she told him with winning candour that she was determined to put *'someone* with backbone' there. The designated junior, Patrick Mayhew, turned out to be more Priorite than Thatcherite, an essential ally of Prior's careful approach. But the insult stuck, and the wariness was mutual.

Howe's public disruption of the Prior emollience was only the first of the onslaughts it had to survive from exponents of more full-blooded Thatcherism. Events themselves conspired against it. On 2 January 1980, a national strike began at the British Steel Corporation. This destroyed Prior's hopes that his lengthy haggling over the precise measure he was going to introduce would take place against a background of industrial peace. But it had a more direct effect on his plans. It was the first setpiece confrontation between the forces of the Thatcher Government and the forces of labour. As such it was soon designated as an event of mythic portent for the party that had never forgotten the circumstances in which it was last unseated from power. The steel dispute was to be prosecuted to its bitter end to achieve, as one minister told me with grim relish at the time, 'a demonstration effect'. Prior's union reform was in danger of becoming hopelessly enmeshed in that more congenial endeavour.

In fact, the steel strike had rather more complex origins. The 'demonstration effect' was a somewhat belated government commitment. BSC was already pursuing a harsh closure policy under Labour in an effort to convert the dinosaur into an effective international competitor, and of its own accord fixed on a 2 per cent pay rise as the 1980 offer. It did this, however, at a time when the prime minister was already applauding the 'realism' of the National Coal Board in offering miners nearly 20 per cent, and of the engineers for settling at less than 15 per cent. Alone among the big battalions, BSC was sticking to a tough line, in which task it was at first hindered not helped by the politicians. Only when the steel strike began did the prime minister pay it much attention.

Pressure to gratify the Thatcher instincts – which in the union field were the instincts of the majority of Tories – now mounted inexorably. Following a court case, Prior was pressed hard to extend his Bill far into the realm of union immunities in every kind of secondary action. Once again Howe pushed in cabinet committee for a much tougher line. And when the steel strike spread to the private steel-makers, with picketing at their works and blacking of their supplies, Prior was again obliged to contend with his party and his leader, all of them sympathetic to the plight of the private steelmen and conscious that less than a year before they had been railing at Labour for precisely the kind of thing that was now going on: one damaging strike after another.

He was not, however, defeated. Great efforts were made to force him to narrow the immunities and accelerate the part of his Bill dealing with secondary picketing. Mrs Thatcher, according to his account, was behind them. 'Her own instincts were to respond to events,' he writes.[2] But by mobilising support in the economic, or E, committee of the cabinet, and with the threat of resignation in his pocket, he saw off the hardliners and kept his Bill intact – much to their fury.

A number of truths emerged from this early episode about what it might mean to have a government presided over by this particular prime minister. The first was her marked indifference to the normal protocols of collective responsibility. While always driven in the end formally to side with Prior, she lost few opportunities to diminish him. For example, after finally losing the argument in E committee, she took the chance on that same afternoon, 19 February, to announce a piece of retaliation on which she had privately decided. Without a word to the Employment Secretary, she used a parliamentary question to declare that plans would shortly be unveiled to strike a new blow at union privileges: in future, strikers claiming social security benefit would be deemed to be receiving strike pay from their union.

This concept of 'deemed strike pay' had been in the manifesto, but wasn't yet part of the collective agenda. Prior writes: 'Margaret hated the fact that she had been thwarted from taking tougher action and was determined to announce an initiative of some kind against the unions. The right wing loved it.'

They also loved another of her ventures in the gentle art of public humiliation. At a private meeting with journalists, Prior had made some critical remarks about the conduct of the steel dispute by the British Steel Corporation's management. After his attack on their inflexibility leaked out, the leader agreed to give an interview on BBC Television. In the course of this she was invited to sack the minister. You do not sack a man for a single mistake, she sweetly murmured. In any case, she added, 'we all make mistakes. I think it was a mistake, and Jim Prior was very, very sorry indeed.'[3]

A second message could be picked up from the whole government posture towards the strike. The 'demonstration effect' was to be achieved whatever the cost – but always under the pretence that the Government wasn't really intervening. This was Thatcherism in action: the new style that a new government would prove it could bring to public sector disputes. Keith Joseph, the minister responsible for steel, contorted himself with masochistic rigour in the cause of preserving the fiction that management had to manage. It was in the end a fiction because government and not management decided what money was available, and government paid the price for the job losses its financial constraints on this ailing industry brought about.

In fact, the dispute was by conventional standards a defeat for government, and something of a farce. It dragged on for thirteen weeks, ending with a 16 per cent pay award as against the 2 per cent originally offered: at least 4 per cent more than the steel unions would have accepted at the beginning. But this apparent absurdity was not the point. Or rather, it simply added to the lesson the Government wished unions everywhere to learn: that the market must rule, and let the devil take the hindmost – no matter how great the social cost, how bloody the factory-gate fighting, or how nonsensical the final price of settlement.

The leader experienced occasional apprehensions about this. Prior describes how, compared with the fanatical Joseph, she did not entirely lose sight of the consequences of a long strike. In the early days she inquired whether the independent arbitration service, ACAS, was involved; and she allowed herself one meeting with the union leaders. She was 'torn between the pragmatic politician wanting an end to a damaging strike, and the doctrinaire economist'. But, says Prior, the doctrinaire won. And the Government's greatest triumph, as one minister said at the time, was that 'we didn't settle it with beer and sandwiches at No. 10.'

A third lesson in the politics of Thatcherism was also available out of Prior's experience with his measure. Potentially it was the most instructive: the one which, if its full import had been appreciated and applied elsewhere, might have had an impact across the broad field of economic as well as industrial policy. For the point about the 1980 Employment Act was that it was in its final form the measure Prior had always wanted. It made no concessions to extreme opinion. At the price of much public slanging, and despite numerous manoeuvres designed to divert him, he overcame the prime ministerial instincts which, had he not resisted her, would have been ineluctably converted into the prime ministerial will. As late as July 1980, when the Bill was going through the Lords and facing renewed attack from the right, Mrs Thatcher was still to be found egging the ultras on. Prior recounts her offering no criticism to a group of rebel peers, led by Lord Orr-Ewing, who persuaded her to listen to their attacks on his measures. But it was passed all the same, to the gratification of the man who had shown what results might be achieved by standing up to her.

There was a moral in this. Clarity and firmness, when pitted against the prime minister's similar clarity and similar firmness, might on occasion overcome them, provided that rational pragmatism plainly belonged on one side rather than the other. Unfortunately none of these qualities were so manifest in the debate at the centre of the Government's strategy, concerning its economic policy. And here, in the main business of government, the outcome was entirely different.

As the designation for a group of Conservative politicians, 'wet' is a term of uncertain origin. But as a word epitomising the attitudes she most scorned, it entered the mind and the vocabulary of Margaret Thatcher early in her time as party leader. Latently it was there long before. The first sighting in my own notebooks is during a conversation with Jim Prior in the summer of 1976, when he reported that he was being accused of 'wetness' because he did not wish to reduce trade unions to impotence. Around that time, the word already seems to have been a favourite among the denunciations scrawled by the leader in the margin of papers submitted to her. Then, however, it was still several years from being recognised as a term of art with not only a clear meaning but an identifiable collection of men to whom it could aptly be applied.

So 'wet' was probably not a conscious or specific coinage. It seeped into the language, reaching full public visibility some time before the Conservative Party conference in autumn 1980. It signified moderation, caution and the middle-minded approach to politics which most of its exponents had learned under the aegis of Macmillan and practised as ministers in the Government of Heath. To be a wet was to be paternalistic and speak the language of One Nation. It was also to be fearful of extreme measures, such as severe anti-union laws, and unfamiliar conditions, such as high unemployment. This aspect of wetness was what Mrs Thatcher most disliked about it. Although often described by her intimates as a cautious politician, she set great store by her own fearlessness, a quality to be cultivated, it often seemed, for its own sake and regardless of the objectives to which it might be directed. Conspicuous displays of bravery were one way she would distinguish herself from the men around her and the discredited regime they personified. 'I hope that one quality in which I am not lacking is courage,' she told the Commons on 20 November 1979. This self-regarding tribute, so expressive of her personal scale of values, was to be heard many times.

Although not classified as such until the middle of 1980, the wets were beginning to disclose themselves late in 1979 as people with serious reservations, sometimes amounting to apocalyptic anxiety, about the economic policy which the inner 'economic' cabinet, from which they were excluded, was intent on pursuing. Prior, as already noted, feared a complete economic collapse. Around the same time, William Whitelaw, the Home Secretary, although always distancing himself from wetness in public, was voicing similar apprehensions. Peter Walker, at the Ministry of Agriculture, viewed the doctrinaire contortions of the Chancellor with mordant ridicule. Francis Pym, the Defence Secretary, soon abandoned his initial satisfaction with the budget, as he records in the book which he published in 1984 after being removed from office. 'The second explosion in oil prices in the summer of 1979 triggered the world recession', he writes, 'and radically altered economic conditions.' Business was put under intense pressure. 'The wets felt that this pressure should be relieved by Government action.'[4]

To speak of the wets as a collective is, however, misleading. There were, among all the critics of the economic policy, what may be termed inner wets and outer wets, although even that distinction conceals divergent tendencies within each category.

The inner wets, who after Howe's second budget had come to the conclusion by the summer of 1980 that the policy was fundamentally misguided, were Prior, Walker and Sir Ian Gilmour, supported by Lord Carrington, and, with increasing irreverence, by the leader of the House, Norman St John Stevas. But they were by no means all of the same mind, or similar political purpose. Carrington's constant absences exonerated him from grappling with issues which, in any case, he did not really understand. Prior, while gloomy about the policy's chances of success, had his own preoccupations to consider. Too overt a challenge to the remorselessly deflationary Treasury could well have brought upon him demands for a far more stringent line with the unions, which it was naturally his highest priority to avoid.

The outer wets were a still more fragmented class. Pym was one of them. He was experiencing his reservations, but also fighting to master the Ministry of Defence, and on the rare occasions when an opportunity appeared to voice an economic opinion in cabinet he is not remembered, in the early years, for displays of forthright eloquence. Michael Heseltine, Secretary of State for the Environment, was another candidate-dissenter, but of quite different stripe from anyone else. Heseltine was an unrepentant Heathite, in that he believed passionately in an interventionist government exercising strategic industrial leadership; but he was the reverse of wet in that he considered the Thatcherite purge of extravagance and waste was proceeding far too slowly. Other outer wets, unpersuaded by the new ideology but unable or unwilling to do anything about it, were to be found in the House of Lords. Lord Hailsham, now Lord Chancellor but once an architect of post-war Tory reform, found it difficult to get the point. Lord Soames would have been part of the same faction, had there been one.

The components of the wet position, insofar as anything so definite could be said to exist, were twofold. One was the belief that a policy combining high inflation, accelerating unemployment, indiscriminate cuts in public spending, all held together by an ideology called monetarism which nobody could understand, presaged an electoral disaster. This opinion, a matter of covert gossip for months, was first publicly expressed by Gilmour in February 1980.

The speech in which he did this, under cover of a quasi-academic lecture at Cambridge, was an unusual exercise for a minister to undertake. It inaugurated a year of ever more outrageously public debate which set at nothing the most famous promise Mrs Thatcher had made, that she would not tolerate arguments. Gilmour was a political theorist of distinction, who had written two substantial books devoted to the thesis that the Conservatives were not the party of dogma. He now set forth an argument applying this analysis to the Government of which he was a part.

It was a performance of some effrontery, which began with an assault on the prime minister's own favourite political thinker. 'In the Conservative view,' the Lord Privy Seal suggested, 'economic liberalism à la Professor Hayek, because of its starkness and its failure to create a sense of community, is not a safeguard of political freedom but a threat to it.'

The prevailing ideology, Gilmour thought, was a threat to social order. People wouldn't feel loyal to the state unless they received protection from the state. 'Lectures on the ultimate beneficence of competition and on the dangers of interfering with market forces will not satisfy people who are in trouble.' He accepted the need for reform, but counselled unambiguously against the danger of subordinating political to economic considerations. 'While I agree that we are embarked on a programme that could well take the best part of two Parliaments to carry through,' he observed, 'I also note that between the first Parliament and the second the electorate will have its chance of a say.'

Gilmour spoke for the cream of the party, although not all of them thought it prudent for a minister to put such opinions into words. His incredulity, however, was effaced by a consoling thought. Alongside one wet opinion that the policy was crazy went another that it was certain to be changed.

Some, indeed, thought it already was being changed. The chief proponent of this was Peter Walker, an experienced politician but one with a single deforming intellectual habit: that of luring the facts in any given situation towards the judgment he had made of it and the hypothesis he desired to verify. Whereas any visit at this time to the offices of Gilmour or Prior or Stevas tended to provoke monologues of gloom and despondency, Walker received callers with the gleam of triumph in his eye.

He would deride the monetarists and pour scorn on the ideologues who apparently did not mind Britain becoming a de-industrialised country. So profound was his contempt for them, however, that he was certain they would soon be seized of their own bottomless folly and start changing the policy. In particular, with a wage round chasing up towards 20 per cent, they would be bound to embrace Walker's own pet belief in an incomes policy. It was only a matter of time, he told me in May 1980. Clinching evidence that, after a first year of dalliance with monetarist lunacies, sanity was taking over could be found in the decision, by the monetarist guru Keith Joseph himself, to save British Leyland from bankruptcy and closure. 'The theory said you shouldn't pay,' Walker said jubilantly. 'But they paid the cheque. They looked at the employment consequences and the balance of payments and they were absolutely horrified.' The preservation of BL, at a first cost of £450 million with at least another £1,000 million likely to be required, was the first of many conversions, Walker seemed to think.

Many wets felt this way by the beginning of 1980. They did not believe that what they saw around them – collapsing businesses, high interest rates, devastated jobs – could go on being allowed to happen as a conscious choice of government policy. Yet the people who made this judgment were the same people who had constantly feared, and sometimes reviled, the leader precisely for her stubbornness. Perhaps they did not completely believe their own propaganda on this point. Whatever the explanation, their first rather than their second assessment now proved to be correct. Any belief that this stubborn woman might bow before political facts which they considered incontestable proved to be a serious illusion.

In February she survived a no-confidence motion with an unflinching defence of the importance of controlling the money supply. In March she lectured the nation in a party political broadcast, likening her position to that of a tightrope walker poised 'between the need to face economic facts and the claims of common humanity'. The message was sternly didactic, making a virtue of the extreme measures the Government had been obliged to take. 'After almost any major operation, you feel worse before you convalesce. But you do not refuse the operation when you know that, without it, you will not survive.' Nor was there anything to be said for a policy of appeasement at home. We were only, it seemed, at the beginning of the famous 'demonstration effect' the steel strike was meant to have. 'The result of buying off trouble', the prime minister said, 'was simply "decline on the instalment plan".'

In March, too, the budget also offered no concessions to the wets' anxieties. It maintained the pattern whereby every major economic decision was taken without consulting them. In the previous November, when exchange controls were abolished overnight, the first Peter Walker knew of the decision was when he heard it on the radio. Now, when the Medium-Term Financial Strategy, supposedly the guidebook to all future economic decision-making, was set in place beside the budget itself, no wet was permitted to take part in its formulation. It was seen at the time as a seminal document, setting forth monetary targets for the years ahead which were to be the guiding light for all other economic policy. This was the signal that a real break with the past was intended, with government abandoning employment or output targets, the traditional tools of Keynesian management. A Bank of England official cited by William Keegan[5] said, 'It was after that budget that I began to take them seriously. They meant it. This government was different.' And against such deviation from old norms the wets proved themselves powerless to act.

However, this was not yet a tribute to the prime minister's strength. Strange to say, it told rather more about her comparative weakness vis-à-vis her critics through most of 1980: a weakness they were entirely unable to exploit.

Fear of their reaction determined a crucial element of the MTFS's presentation. Having successfully manoeuvred for almost a year to prevent cabinet discussion of economic policy, Mrs Thatcher and the

Chancellor steeled themselves to admit their colleagues to a full preview of the MTFS before its details were unalterably fixed. A date was set for the momentous encounter, but at the last moment it was cancelled. The duumvirate lost their nerve, fearing that the wets, once they had seen the targets, would insist that they should not be published – something Howe and his leader had always wanted for its salutary disciplinary effects, but which other opinion, led by Chief Secretary Biffen, opposed on the (prescient) grounds that the targets laid down in the Strategy would not be met and hence would make the Government an object of ridicule. At this stage apprehension was as important as contempt in defining the Thatcher approach to her opponents.

Nor was the monetarist policy immune from attack in its own terms. Although control of the money supply was placed at the centre of the strategy, it proved impossible to achieve. Having failed actually to control money, how could the proponents of this policy convince anyone of its therapeutic properties? For 1980–1, when the MTFS set target growth at between 7 and 10 per cent, the actual growth was 18.8 per cent; and next year the discrepancy was only slightly smaller.

After leaving office, Ian Gilmour termed monetarism 'the uncontrollable in pursuit of the indefinable'. Yet when he was still there, its prophets suffered a highly visible embarrassment which partly accounted for these startling figures, and which in other circumstances he and his friends might have exploited to devastating effect. A mere four months after the target was set, it was suddenly found to have been hugely exceeded when the Bank of England loosened the so-called 'corset', a mechanism to restrain lending by the banks. This released a torrent of credit, sending the growth-rate of M3, the monetary measure, to nearly double that prescribed by the MTFS.

This had one predictable effect. It dealt a shattering blow to the prime minister's confidence in the Bank of England. She took it out on the Governor, Gordon Richardson, who had opposed publication of the MTFS and was in any case, as the appointee of a Labour government, regarded with suspicion – although anybody less vulnerable to criticism for political deformities it would be hard to imagine.

'She's vitriolic about the Bank, absolutely vitriolic,' said one close observer at the time. 'Richardson has been having a very hard time.' And no wonder. The huge escalation in the figures, carrying monetary growth even above the inflation rate it was supposed ineluctably to curb, made the policy look ridiculous and its prophets incompetent.

But the other consequence did not occur. No political price was exacted for this bungling. Given the strength of feeling on the other side, the farce of the monetary figures might have become the basis for a root-and-branch attack in cabinet on the small cabal that set such overriding store by them as the determinant, come what may, of an economic policy which appeared to bring with it only higher unemployment and deep industrial depression.

That this did not happen is a measure of the demoralisation that was now endemic. The wets' pessimism got the better of their political sense. In truth, although willing privately to tell anyone who would listen how deeply they deplored what was going on, they never assembled their criticisms into a single statement of united resistance. Not only their separate departmental interests and distractions prevented this occurring. There was also a deep fastidiousness about appearing in any open or organised way to be working against the leadership. This is the obligatory Conservative pattern. Although the party can be wholly ruthless in despatching leaders who have failed, it looks with loathing on treacheries against them before that general judgment has been made. Unlike the Labour Party, where factionalism exists by custom and practice, Tories like to pretend that any such tendency is alien to their politics. This is especially true of cabinet ministers. Jim Prior's explanation in his book echoes those offered by Gilmour, Pym and several others: 'We felt that it would be dangerous for us to form ourselves into a cabal, since we would run the risk of being castigated immediately as conniving together against the leadership.'[6]

Behind these niceties of protocol, however, lay a still more fundamental flaw in the wets' position. It was that they did not really have a position for which they could persuasively argue. They could explain, in terms of unremitting gloom, how catastrophic were the consequences of monetarism, but they were not able to put together an alternative which fulfilled the requirements of the day. They wanted, roughly speaking, less of everything from monetarism to unemployment, in keeping with their instincts as moderate men who mistrusted dogmas and feared for the social fabric of their country. But this was not satisfactory as An Alternative, of the defined and rounded simplicity the age demanded. That was the meaning of TINA, a famous acronym that became a beautiful propaganda weapon. There Is No Alternative grew from a conventional piece of impudent bravado on the part of the monetarists into an assertion that mesmerised the anti-monetarists, terrorising them into spellbound if curmudgeonly acquiescence. They could think of alternatives, but no Alternative. They escaped, at best, into agnosticism. 'I don't have a view about it,' Stevas told me early on. 'I don't know whether it will work or not. Why is there no critique of it? Because no one has any alternative. There is nothing else to try.'

This was not a state of mind prepared for battle, as monetarism went through its first crisis during the second half of 1980, the middle of a seemingly unending deterioration in every relevant indicator. Manufacturing output was in steep decline. Unemployment that year rose by 836,000, the largest rise in one year since 1930. In addition, the exchange rate rose by 12 per cent on average, another uncovenanted squeeze on export competitiveness, which throttled more businesses to death. What faced the cabinet was what faced the Confederation of British Industry: 'As gloomy a picture as it is possible for anyone to paint', said the chairman of the CBI economic committee in his July survey of business opinion, 'and I fear things will get worse before they get better.'

The wets were not alone in being disoriented by the encircling gloom. With only one real exception, so were the people on the other side of the argument. For them, in a sense, it was worse. They had prescribed the drastic remedies, and these were apparently not working. Mechanistic relationships between money supply, borrowing, wages, the exchange rate and inflation were proving to have been inexactly described by the professors, and the vibrant economy they were meant to produce was not even in sight after eighteen months.

A glimpse of the collective psyche could be caught at a cabinet meeting on 30 October. An official who was present described the scene to me. It was the first of a series of meetings to discuss a further round of public spending cuts for 1981. The mood, said the official, was dominated by crisis and low morale. The worst of it was that the Treasury seemed to be losing faith in the policy it was in charge of, and the Chancellor could not conceal it. 'Howe's performance was pathetic. He seems to have no conviction any more, and this permeates the Cabinet as a whole.'

The Treasury forecasts for the next four years, moreover, were beginning to show something very ominous. There would be some economic improvement by 1983, but it would be shortlived. A year further on, the picture looked black again. The light in the tunnel was there, but then the tunnel took another bend and the light disappeared. The 1981 unemployment forecast, additionally, was black. At first the prime minister could not believe it, and a typically Thatcheresque scene occurred. When the forecast, required by the Government Actuary for the management of the National Insurance Fund, was presented to her, she resorted, in the words of a witness, 'to the familiar posture of prime ministers, asking furiously why no one had told her'. In order to persuade her, the humble forecaster himself was brought in to show how he reached his figure. 'After she cooled down, she became engaged in the process and took an intellectual interest in it. But she finds the figure appalling.'

She did not, however, lose her nerve, as Howe was beginning temporarily to lose his. Howe, after all, was a bit of a latecomer to the policies he now presided over; and although this was true of his leader as well, in his case the experience had left him not so much with the zeal of the convert as with the less durable commitment of the politician who has grasped at passing fashion. Sir Geoffrey was at heart a pragmatist, and the position in late 1980 was enough to disturb anyone with even the smallest tendencies in that direction. Margaret Thatcher was at heart a believer and a missionary, to whom beckoning disaster was cause only to redouble her faith. It was that difference, a matter of character and not of wisdom, which both sustained the policy's wavering friends and routed its paralysed enemies.

She was now a maturing leader. She had gained in experience without losing in fire. Far from crushing her with their leaden, insoluble weight, problems and crises seemed only to expand the sense she had of fulfilling a personal destiny. In later years, and especially towards the end of her second term when questions began to be posed about exactly how long she would carry on, she became ever more shamelessly candid about her belief that nobody else could be expected to do her job as well as she was doing it. But this powerful sense of self was getting quite well developed much earlier.

Several moments bore witness to this. I was present at a small lunch for her on 9 July. In the previous twelve months prices had risen by 22 per cent, wages by 20 per cent: figures which, had they been forecast a year earlier, might have been enough to mobilise hesitant wets against the policy. The leader, I noted at the time, was undismayed. She talked like someone observing the economy from afar. Believing as a matter of ideology in the limits and not the power of government, she could view without embarrassment the short-term failure of things to come right. She sounded positively serene about the failure of particular firms to survive, or even that of particular nationalised industries to make sensible wage settlements. Ultimately this was their problem. Government's job was to set the context within which economic operators did their business, a task not yet complete. 'My job is to let the country begin to exist within sensible and realistic economic disciplines,' she said.

Unlike almost everyone else in government, of every persuasion, she therefore found no difficulty in sticking to the policy. She expressed surprise that anyone could think otherwise. Conviction was in her bones and in her mind: to take any step backwards would be 'absolutely fatal'.

I noted her demeanour. 'Far less shrill than ever in living memory. Cool, quiet, confident, rather more galleon-like in appearance. Sharing certain facts with us, rather than indicating, like Wilson used to, that we poor fellows knew nothing, and then blinding us with his own cleverness.' The language of the good housekeeper was still in place during any discussion of public spending: 'I've got so much here . . . I've got so much there.' The large planks of her political strategy were identified with starker clarity than usually emerged in public. 'The two great problems of the British economy', she said more than once, 'are the monopoly nationalised industries and the monopoly trade unions.' But what came over more than anything was the self-belief. Not merely a rock-like confidence showing that the apprentice years were over, but a belief that duty and rectitude coalesced uniquely in her person.

This was not a private sentiment. Around the same time, her public statements showed an increasingly explicit preoccupation with the ego – and with the seamless continuity of its thinking. She said, for example: 'Deep in their instincts people find what I am saying and doing right. And I know it is, because that is the way I was brought up. I'm eternally grateful for the way I was brought up in a small town. We knew everyone, we knew what people thought. I sort of regard myself as a very normal, ordinary person, with all the right, instinctive antennae.'[7]

On the same occasion she also said: 'I really am trying to bring into British life everything I deeply believe about democracy.' And: 'If I give up, we will lose. If I give that up, I just think we will lose all that faith in the future. We'd lose the justification. I hope that doesn't sound too arrogant.'

Many thought it did. Her closest colleagues could not manage anything like that kind of language. Nor did it silence her opponents. The Conservative party conference in October 1980 was like none that had been held before, featuring ministers on and off the platform engaged in disagreements that managed to be at the same time subtly expressed yet unambiguous in their import. Peter Walker used his position as Minister of Agriculture, the most dirigiste of departments, to deliver a self-congratulatory homily clearly intended to suggest that what was good for Agriculture would be good for Industry as well. Prior talked about the desirability of 'help to the youngsters', 'harmony of wills' and 'reasoned political discussion': bromides and banalities converted by the times into explosively daring challenges to the leadership. Stevas delivered a lecture, piously entitled 'The Moral Basis of Conservatism', which dwelt upon the need for 'flexibility' and 'positive measures' and cautioned against 'theoreticians living in an abstract world'.

Everyone knew, as they were meant to know, what these words meant. They were intended to undermine the case for the Thatcherite ideology and summon the Tory Party back to its paternalistic traditions. And because they were so out of line with the conduct good Conservative ministers are meant to exhibit at party conferences, they dominated the week. They were indeed splendidly irreverent.

Yet, in retrospect, what is more striking than their impudence is their timidity. Here were ministers who believed that a disaster was being visited on their party and their country by a leader whose credulity before the 'theoreticians' was exceeded only by the blindness of her refusal to examine the evidence of eighteen months' work or consider the consequences for the next election. Coded murmurings were the best they could offer against the deluge they could see around them. These quite mistook the nature of their situation. As Prior says pathetically in his book: 'Those of us who were out of sympathy with Margaret's views grossly underestimated her determination. . . . We didn't appreciate the degree to which the party was becoming more doctrinaire in its approach. . . . We made a number of fundamental mistakes.'

She saw them off with a single phrase. She has uttered few memorable phrases in her time, and most of those, like this one, were composed for her within the fraternity of speech-writers and other wordsmiths who struggle to impart rhetorical elan to her naturally pedestrian efforts. The chief of these was Ronald Millar, playwright and gag-man, a genial soul who had, unusually, transferred his allegiance from Heath to Mrs Thatcher and more than survived the experience. Millar became a worshipper and minor confidant, who occasionally even managed to make the leader laugh.

Now he came up with a good line, to bring the conference to a climax. It was plainly addressed to the fainthearts who thought they'd had enough. 'Turn if you like,' she sonorously declaimed. 'The lady's not for turning.' And that was only the beginning.

On 5 January 1981, Mrs Thatcher sent for the Leader of the House, Norman St John Stevas, and removed him from office. Her first move against a serving wet came as a surprise to the world and a thunderbolt to him. She assured him at their interview that the decision was not prompted by incompetence on his part, either as Leader of the House or as the minister responsible for the Arts.[8] But she did not say why else he had to go. So the suspicion gained currency, assisted by inept official briefing, that he was probably sacked for having dangerous habits and unacceptable ideas.

He was touchingly ill-cast as victim. He had thought he was doing so well. One of the only two cabinet members known to have voted for her leadership, he felt he had a special intimacy. When he called her the Blessed Margaret, his little joke was only faintly brushed by irony. Personally, he was a complete Thatcher loyalist, however much he disliked the economic policy.

He had also been a remarkably successful reformer, if not in a way she approved of. For a government self-consciously bent on radical change, the Stevas reforms of the House of Commons should have been a badge of seriousness. He got them through very early in the Parliament's life. As a result, Commons select committees shadowed the Whitehall departments almost from the start of the Thatcher years: a major innovation which ensured that a government which showed great resistance to all forms of openness and accountability was sometimes invigilated quite uncomfortably. Before long, the appearance of ministers and officials testifying to these committees became a commonplace spectacle. The leader had not really wanted this. Stevas pushed it through cabinet when her mind was on larger matters in 1979, and got a second major procedural reform through in October 1980 which made it possible for these expert committees to act not merely as policy investigators but as legislative committees as well. He also did a lot for MPs' pay, getting it almost doubled from the pittance of £6,890 at which it stood when the Conservatives came in.

Neither of these initiatives exactly endeared him to his leader. But they did not appear on the charge-sheet in January 1981. Nor did anything else, explicitly. It was rumoured that he had gone because he was thought to be indiscreet, but this too was a canard. As perceived by the more penetrating observers on either side of the cabinet divide, Stevas' main role was sacrificial. He went because a wet was required to go. Mrs Thatcher would occasionally disclose in the future how little she cared for sacking people. One thing she wasn't good at, she conceded, was butchery. Yet she did it often enough, not because the minister in question was exhausted or even incompetent, but more in quest of a cabinet she found personally congenial. Norman St John Stevas was the first in quite a line.

He was the victim, also, of an interlocking pressure: another dimension of the great contest with the many-limbed beast of wettery on which the prime minister was now embarked. A little earlier she had, to her great discomfort, been worsted by the Defence Secretary, Francis Pym. In the ceaseless search for spending cuts, Defence had gone into the last ditch to resist the demand, even to the point of exercising the right customarily enjoyed by the Chiefs of Staff to a personal hearing from the prime minister when they consider an issue sufficiently grave. Pym himself became the first minister in the Thatcher Government to threaten resignation (which he did in mid-November 1980) and one of relatively few to do so with effect. Defence got very nearly all the money it was asking for.

Pym, therefore, was moved sideways to be Leader of the House. He could call himself nearer the centre. Prior, for example, thought 'Francis has been immeasurably strengthened': quite a coup, he felt, for a minister who, while completely unwilling to enter any joint enterprise with colleagues against the economic policy, thought the prime minister 'a walking disaster'. But, from the Thatcherite perspective, the operation looked rather different. Into Pym's seat came John Nott, the double-dyed monetarist now thought eligible on that account to deal ruthlessly with the MoD. To Nott's seat at Trade, Biffen was transferred from the Treasury. Into the Treasury as Chief Secretary came a junior minister from the Home Office, Leon Brittan.

For Brittan it was a climax to a meteoric career in which, having reached the Commons only in February 1974, he had become the closest of friends with Chancellor Howe, as well as a protégé for whom William Whitelaw and the prime minister vied in affection and admiration. In the balance of the cabinet, Brittan-for-Stevas seemed a satisfactory swap.

From the viewpoint of the ideologues, it needed to be. They were not unaware of history, and in particular the history of the Heath Government. Although history never does repeat itself, politicians are more prey than most people to thinking it might: perhaps because they see themselves as history's vessels. In the Thatcherites' historical demonology, Heath's U-turn in 1972, away from free-market and towards corporatist policies, was the moment to which this aversion always directed itself with most spit and venom. Now, in March 1981, the danger-point of repetition approached. Two years in, there were parallels between the Heath and Thatcher experience: the same wasting of industry, the same failure of the economy to respond to a government's benign neglect, the same belief in parts of the Conservative Party that the experiment should be ended. Would Mrs Thatcher also buckle?

The comparison, in fact, was facile. There was no particular reason why two years, rather than two-and-a-half or three, should be the moment to go into reverse. Nor were the two situations closely analogous, especially in relation to the relative power then and now of organised labour. But the fact that this fear of a repeat performance did quite widely exist among the hardline monetarists – they had now, after an uneasy linguistic interval, become the 'drys' – recalls how imperfect public understanding still was of the prime minister's character.

Her intimates had already put the question in private. John Hoskyns, the head of her policy unit, was one of those who thought it needed to be asked in the winter of 1980. With others he went to her and said, 'If there is ever going to be any sort of U-turn on policy, you absolutely must think about it now.' He was concerned that any significant change which had not been prepared for would make them look ridiculous. But she said to him: 'You know, I would rather go down than do that, so forget it.' Later, Hoskyns recalled the impact this made on him: 'There was very impressive readiness to look right through to the end and say, "That is what we'll do." '[9]

The test was now upon them. Pym's autumn victory over the defence budget had been accompanied by another Treasury defeat over welfare payments. The Treasury had proposed to reduce the annual uprating of benefits and save £600 million. The Social Services Secretary, Patrick Jenkin, to widespread amazement, chose not to fight like a departmental minister should, and apparently accepted the cut. Later, to still greater astonishment, he summoned the nerve to read out to the prime minister a pledge she had made at the election not to cut benefits. The full uprating was smartly restored. But this brief display of muscle by spending ministers left the Treasury £1,000 million short of the cuts demanded by the monetarist diagnosis.

Meanwhile, there was a new arrival at 10 Downing Street, well prepared to stiffen the sinews for the last battle: a battle against economic orthodoxy, against conventional political wisdom, even, in the end, against the instincts and opinions of the Treasury itself. Even though the economy was contracting fast – gross domestic product down 5.5 per cent in two years, unemployment at 2.7 million and still rising – a budget was produced in March 1981, in obeisance to the new wisdom, which had every chance of making the catastrophe deeper still.

Early in January, Mrs Thatcher took on an economic adviser, Alan Walters, who secured more influence in less time at the heart of government than anyone in a comparable position before him. For a relatively brief period – he served full-time for only two years – he became her trusty guru on the matter she felt to be at the heart of her purpose. He was one of a line stretching back through Alfred Sherman to F. A. von Hayek, who in different relationships and varied ways served a similar function. But, given his particular time and place, none perhaps fulfilled more completely than Walters the role she required of such people: which was to provide for her, who was not an intellectual, a thorough and expert intellectual superstructure for the instincts she was so sure were right.

Walters was a monetarist from long ago, before the term was heard in political society. A professor at Birmingham University at the age of thirty-five, and later at the London School of Economics, he had published a paper as early as July 1972 predicting, on a monetarist analysis, the 15 per cent inflation that disclosed itself two years later.[10] In the death-agonies of Heathism, Walters it was whom Keith Joseph produced as counsel for the prosecution during a post-mortem between the 1974 elections on where the economic policy had gone wrong. To natural self-confidence and a bluff northern contempt for lesser mortals he was therefore able to add an ingredient Margaret Thatcher found particularly congenial in anyone who served her. If they were not converts, they should preferably be people who could furnish proof that they had been right all along. Walters sometimes concealed this behind outward signs of diffidence and simplicity. 'I'm just an academic economist,' he was fond of saying. But the humility was bogus. On the big questions he was certain he had always been right: and right in the same sense that the prime minister, his new pupil, was now certain she was right as well.

He came to his new post from the United States, where he had lived part of his life for the previous twenty years. He was only an intermittent observer of the British economy at first hand, and had decided to leave for good in 1975, judging a choice between Wilson and Heath to be 'no choice at all'. Only rather late was he drawn into the Thatcher circle, on visits from his chair at Johns Hopkins University in Baltimore. His ultimate willingness to accept a post at No. 10 was due not least to the ministrations of Alf Sherman, the old intriguer now mainly displaced from influence.

When Walters arrived he was plunged into a complex struggle. This was taking place inside the economic cabal, not between them and the wets.[11] The monetarist course of events had given rise to puzzlement and dispute, mainly about the exchange rate and the double-bind in which a high exchange rate and high interest rates placed British business. The prime minister, always the politician as well as the zealot, was extremely worried. Why was the exchange rate so high? Was it all due to North Sea oil? Or perhaps to some mishandling of monetary policy? Where did interest rates fit in to the cycle of cause and effect? She summoned another professor, Jurg Niehans from Bern University, one of a number she had met on Swiss holidays in the past and, with the insatiable appetite of the autodidact, invited to fill her vacation days with economic seminars. Niehans produced a paper throwing doubt on several aspects of the way monetarism had been managed, and, according to William Keegan, even felt compelled to ask the mortifying question: 'Tell me, who are your monetarists in this country? You don't seem to have any.'

Within the closed economic community, therefore, raged an argument about whether recovery, on the back of lower interest rates, would be better assisted by loosening or tightening the reins on M_3, and loosening or tightening still further the general economic stance. At one level, it was a technical discussion, between worshippers in the same Church who were troubled to discover that their fundamentalist catechism did not answer all the questions. But the heart of the matter was political. Did the leader and her Chancellor have the nerve to turn the screw one more time by cutting borrowing and raising taxes, even when the economy was still in a downward spiral?

Professor Walters had no doubt that they should, and Hoskyns was his ally. These, the 'unofficials' and non-politicians, with their power-base at the prime minister's side, now assumed critical influence. They made a telling argument. The Treasury, led by Douglas Wass, was contending that public spending was under control; and even the more committed monetarists there, like Peter Middleton and Terence Burns, argued that a drastic cut in the targeted public sector borrowing requirement was no longer necessary. Howe, aware of the political turmoil awaiting him if he announced yet another squeeze, was with them. But Walters and Hoskyns made precisely the pitch designed to stiffen the prime minister. Having assured Hoskyns personally a few weeks before that she would rather leave politics than preside over a U-turn, she was now faced with their fearful prognostication that any sort of 'soft' budget now might lead to disaster in the markets by the autumn – even to the point of putting her own position in peril.

To Walters it was partly a matter of credibility. The Government had to establish that they were not going once again to move forward 'with enormous unsupportable borrowings'.[12] It had to convince the financial markets once and for all that it was a reforming government, determined to get inflation down. This was entirely in line with the leader's basic beliefs, but he thought it was 'rather useful for her to have someone like me to talk to about this major decision'. He saw himself standing against the tide of received opinion, in the civil service and in politics and in his own profession,[13] all of which was demanding some economic relaxation.

Because it took something of this line, the Treasury too became a kind of enemy. Even Mrs Thatcher herself wasn't easy to persuade. At one point, as Walters relentlessly pressed his case for taking £4,000 million out of the public sector borrowing requirement, she shouted at him: 'You're just an academic. You haven't got to go to the House of Commons and see this through.' But he stood his ground, and she joined him. Unwise to the ways of politics, he was taken aback by how long Howe resisted. He thought it was all settled at a final meeting at the end of February, only to be told that Howe was still undecided. 'Geoffrey says it's impossible,' the incredulous professor was told by a Downing Street official, and he instructed his wife to pack their bags in readiness for a swift departure. But Geoffrey, it turned out, had also been told that his job was on the line if he didn't find an answer. Next day he came up with a package worth £3,500 million, which Walters advised was enough; and the key budget of the Thatcher years went forward.

The leader was well aware of the enormity of the thing. The squeeze was tightened by increases in personal tax, petrol and other indirect taxes. The package produced a forecast that output would be down 1 per cent from its already diminished level, and unemployment would rise above three million in 1982. Walters ran into the prime minister outside the Commons chamber, as she went in to hear the budget speech. 'You know, Alan,' she said, 'they may get rid of me for this.' But, she added, it would be in a worthwhile cause. 'At least I shall have gone knowing I did the right thing.'

Outside the hothouse of government, this never seemed a probable eventuality. What it reveals is the inner frailty of political leaders, their natural proneness to watch their backs, their necessary and understandable awareness that their first duty is to survive against the odds. Margaret Thatcher, although afflicted with little doubt about what she thought or what was 'right', remained always conscious of her possible impermanence. Yet in March 1981 the objective evidence of danger was scanty, as anyone could see who was privileged to enter the minds of those best placed to inflict it on her.

There were a few menacing noises in the House. But these were directed entirely at the Chancellor. A senior backbencher from the City, Peter Tapsell, rotundly announced that Howe should go. The prime minister, Tapsell said, 'owes it to the country and to the Conservative Party to find a Chancellor who will command confidence and offer hope'.

The cabinet wets, however, by whom any assault on the prime minister would presumably have to be led, put on their final show of impotence. When Prior heard the budget details, twenty-four hours before they were announced, he was beside himself with anxiety and rage. When Howe gave him a preview, he has recorded, 'I couldn't say anything bad enough about it.'[14] Encountered at a party on budget night, he said he had thought about resigning but 'didn't want to give her the satisfaction of just getting rid of me'. He didn't object to the petrol tax, but found incomprehensible – 'criminal folly', he said – Howe's refusal to do anything for industry.

Next morning, he had breakfast with Walker and Gilmour to consider what to do. This, according to more than one participant, was the closest any wets ever came to conduct that might have been recognisable as plotted and collective action. It did not come to much. For one thing, nobody else seems to have thought the budget was too bad. Carrington, Pym and Whitelaw, according to Prior's account, said in cabinet that they weren't terribly pleased. But they had been persuaded by Howe the night before, and now argued that the Chancellor must be supported. Walker and Gilmour were not men of real weight, whose departure could have had any decisive effect. Prior himself thought he should carry on fighting from within, rather than 'sacrificing myself unnecessarily'.

So ended the first and last consideration of a putsch against the leader and her policies by the wing of the Conservative Party to whom she had thrown down the gauntlet. Subsequently, both Prior and Gilmour expressed regret that they did not in fact resign at this time. It was a moment for instantaneous action, or none at all. If it hadn't been done before the budget speech, it would have lost much of its impact. Understandably but fatally, they hesitated and pulled back, and thus consigned themselves to a client role for the foreseeable future. For them this ended, after different spans of time, with more or less enforced departures from the scene. Walker, however, survived unscathed his little flirtation with matters of principle and conviction, and remained free to preach about them intermittently from the security of office for many years yet.

The economic consequences of the budget remained to be seen. But its political effect was immediately felt. Although greeted with incredulity by her critics and not a little anxiety by her friends, it produced in Margaret Thatcher a resurgence of almost messianic commitment.

The private hesitations she had expressed to Walters were eclipsed by her conviction that the budget was right: not only right in that it conformed to the arithmetical sums and economic laws she regarded as axiomatic, but right at some deeper level which had to do with the moral condition of the people. Her political style, as it developed while she was prime minister, always depended to an unusual degree on this search for 'rightness'. She was a woman with a low quotient of cynicism, about herself if not about her opponents. She believed that, being so absolutely and incontestably right, she could communicate her own convictions in the matter to a wide audience and eventually persuade them that any discomforts and disappointments were but minor pitfalls on the road to recovery. Now, when this message was hardest to believe, she set about delivering it with redoubled passion.

To the Conservative Central Council, at the end of March, she spoke of years of decline 'brought on ourselves by self-deception and self-inflicted wounds'. Britain was no longer competitive because of the neglect of her predecessors. She was a different sort of leader altogether, she said. Addressing the party's Scottish conference a few weeks later, she said Britain's plight wasn't really the Government's responsibility. The Government was grappling with global forces, as well as past cowardice and folly. Public spending was up, so it had to be prudently paid for. That was the reason for the tough budget. The pain, she implied, was good for you. And it was already showing its therapeutic effects. The stock markets were beginning to turn round. Although (as she did not say) Britain's largest company, ICI, had recently dismayed the City by cutting its dividend, business confidence was returning.

She was particularly scornful of her economic critics, who apparently lived in Cloud-cuckoo-land:

> Oh yes, I know, we have recently been told by no less than 364 academic economists that such things cannot be, that British enterprise is doomed. Their confidence in the accuracy of their own predictions leaves me breathless. But having myself been brought up over the shop, I sometimes wonder whether they back their forecasts with their money. For I can't help noticing that those who have to do just that – the investing institutions which have to show performance from their judgment – are giving us a very different message.

No other minister was able to emulate her passion. Howe and others were later to look back on the 1981 budget and deem it the turning-point in the Government's and the country's fortunes. For the eight years that followed, by overlooking the steep collapse in the previous two, they could point proudly to an unbroken record of growth. But at the time, nervous doubt and incipient heresy were much more pervasive among the colleagues. It was as if, having backed the budget as a climactic expression of the monetarist analysis, they could stomach no more. They had, after all, been given studiously little opportunity to influence the course of economic policy in free and open cabinet debate. When the chance did arise, it was against a background of mounting national as well as political discontent with rising unemployment. Several cities had seen outbreaks of civic disorder. The dominant mood around the country remained one of pessimism, even depression. In the Conservative Party, still unconvinced by the therapeutic properties of the budget, it was close to panic.

The moment when this was given its most potent expression occurred on 23 July, the date scheduled for the last cabinet meeting before the summer recess. It proved to be an extraordinary occasion, perhaps the most memorable meeting of the cabinet in the whole decade of the Thatcher Government. It was certainly a time when outright disagreement, amounting almost to open rebellion, reached a climax never attained before or after.

The main item on the agenda, a reminder that in managing the economy every battle won is only a prelude to the next, was Howe's first projection of the economic balance-sheet for the next year, 1982–3, and his anticipation of the public spending cuts that would be required if targets were to be met. After a swingeing budget, and against a background of apparent civil breakdown – even as the cabinet met, the Toxteth district of Liverpool was recovering from another night of highly publicised violence between police and unemployed youths – he presented a paper which solemnly announced a preliminary demand that next year's projected spending should be cut by £5,000 million.

Now, for the first time, the wets' unease at the economic strategy spread far beyond the usual dissenters. Heseltine was one of the first to speak. As Environment Secretary, he was especially close to the urban consequences of the economic squeeze, and he said that Howe's proposal would cause despair in the cities and electoral disaster for the Tories. If the situation demanded rigour, he inquired, why didn't the Chancellor consider a pay freeze: a remarkable suggestion for any Thatcher minister to put forward but one which others took up.

Peter Walker, likewise, reached for remedies that smacked of the dreaded days of Edward Heath. He, too, thought that rising incomes were the problem, and also suggested more planning of production and investment by government. Pym declared that employment not inflation was the issue, and a political rather than an economic strategy the prime requirement. Gilmour quoted Churchill: 'However beautiful the strategy, you should occasionally look at the results.' Britain was already experiencing heavier deflation than other countries, said

Gilmour, and was entering a cycle of hopeless decline: more spending cuts producing an increase in the PSBR through rising unemployment, which in turn would require more cuts.

Heavy guns from the House of Lords then turned on the hapless Chancellor. Lord Soames backed Heseltine's proposed freeze. Lord Hailsham's verdict was perhaps the most apocalyptic of all, invoking the memory of Hitler's Germany, in which unemployment gave birth to fascism, and the America of Herbert Hoover, whose restrictive policies, Hailsham said, had destroyed the Republican Party for thirty years.

More appalling to the leader, however, were the contributions of her chosen loyalists. Biffen openly jumped ship for the first time, saying that public spending had already been heroically held down and enough was enough. Demanding yet more cuts for the sake of future tax cuts was a profoundly destructive policy, Biffen thought. So, perhaps even more painfully, did John Nott, who delivered a withering assault on the intellectual quality of the Treasury paper.

The mood, in short, was one of utter consternation. Piecing the day together, from the accounts of several men who have never forgotten it, one finds minister after minister speaking in the most lurid terms of the need, before all else, to save the party and save the country. Whitelaw, weighing in with an attempt at cross-factional bridge-building, opposed the freeze but did say that it would be preferable to exact higher taxes than to be responsible, as he put it, for breaking the tolerance of society. By the end of the exchanges, only Joseph, Brittan and Howe himself spoke up for this next stage of the Thatcher-ite economic plan, with Howe vainly seeking to impress his colleagues that there was no true comparison with the 1930s – either German or American style – because in the 1930s there was no inflation, the great curse of the 1980s.

The prime minister herself was shattered by what had passed, and contributed her part to the extremely heightened tension. She spoke pitifully of those who believed in spending their way out of recession. Did they want another 'Barber boom', she derisively asked, referring to the later, detestable, inflationary portion of the Heath years. Were they honestly prepared to give a higher priority to jobs than inflation, when 20 million Building Society investors, many of them Tory supporters, wanted above all to see their savings protected from the ravages of being devalued? To the majority's panic-stricken contention that the party would be destroyed if Howe's plans went through, she defiantly replied with a counter-prophecy: her Government would be finished if they didn't.

She closed on a prudent managerial note, rather than face a decisive showdown. Howe was asked to produce another paper, setting out both sides of the argument. All present were especially instructed not to disclose that a pay freeze had even been discussed. Quite apart from the blow this revelation would strike at the Government's credibility and the scorn it would attract to a prime minister who was publicly opposed to an incomes policy, it would, she knew, immediately start a new round of pay demands. And this piece of obedience she did at least exact from her ministers. No rumour of a freeze leaked out.

The rebellion, however, had a powerful influence on the prime minister: not, at first, in persuading her to moderate the rigours of the economic policy, although that did happen, but in pushing her to make changes in the cabinet. Sacking is the ultimate weapon in any prime minister's hand, and this meeting persuaded Mrs Thatcher that she had no alternative but to use it. All cabinet reshuffles, of course, have to be carefully calculated. Some ministers are strong enough not to be removed with impunity. But after more than two years in office, the season of reshuffling already beckoned. And the experience of those two years had hardly suggested that any collection of wets, even wets embittered by loss of office, would be capable of summoning the will and the method to damage the Government from the back-benches. At any rate, it was a gamble worth taking, for a prize that would be great: a cabinet, at last, dominated by people she could call her own. The event of 23 July hardened her purpose, and probably extended the range of her butchery.

The new cabinet was announced on 14 September, after all concerned had had a summer holiday to think about it. The mordant Gilmour was the first target, sacked from the Foreign Office. He was accompanied into the wilderness by Mark Carlisle, the Education Secretary, and Lord Soames, so recently the hero of Zimbabwe, now despatched from his position as leader of the House of Lords. Carlisle and Soames, although not major figures, were to be found on the wrong side of most of the arguments she cared about. Unlike Gilmour, who came stylishly out of 10 Downing Street to tell the waiting reporters that the Government was 'heading for the rocks', their public responses were meek. But Soames did not go quietly. When summoned to be sacked, he turned upon Mrs Thatcher all the fury of the dispossessed grandee. Her private secretary, Whitmore, was dismissed from the room, while Soames assailed her for twenty minutes for her various shortcomings, including the way she had treated him as minister for the civil service, handling a very bitter civil service strike. He had never been spoken to by a woman, he told her, in the abusive way she had spoken to him then. His thunderous curtain-lines, it was said, could be heard out of the open window halfway across Horseguards Parade.

A rather different case was Jim Prior. He was held not to be so dispensable, but was, on the other hand, ripe for moving. He was allowed to know in early August that he might be offered a very particular move, to the post of Secretary of State for Northern Ireland. This signal was conveyed, as became a regular Thatcher style with reshuffles that were going to hurt somebody, by nods and winks from Downing Street. Prior chose to respond with a bold tactic, letting it be known by signals of a similar kind that he would not accept the post. He was determined to stay where he was, close to the centre of economic power. He would not accept demotion and exile, and he made this clear in many public ways.

Somehow it was fitting that the leader's final act in this completion of her ascendancy, after a thirty-month passage of arms with the Conservatism she was determined to uproot, should be to call Prior's bluff. And it was equally appropriate that he, a decent and well-meaning man, should let this happen to him, as he had let quite a lot happen before. He decided, when she did formally offer him the Irish post, that in all honour he could not refuse it. To do so would have looked like running away from gunfire. Besides, perhaps his particular qualities of goodwill and sweet reason and political ingenuity would be more welcome in the benighted province than they any longer were in Whitehall.

Prior would have made a good Industry Secretary. It was the job he was qualified for, having actually worked in industry, unlike most of his colleagues. He passionately wanted to be there, at the productive end of the economy; and, under a leader more interested in forming a ministry of all the talents than in marginalising or excluding those that caused her trouble, he would have got it.

Instead, Belfast was, in all the circumstances, a natural terminus for this apostle of the old paternalism. The men of the future now entered cabinet in the seats that mattered more. Nigel Lawson, clever architect of that great totem the MTFS, became Secretary of State for Energy. One Cecil Parkinson, a junior Trade minister, replaced the ageing Thorneycroft as party chairman, with a place at the top table. Norman Tebbit, last seen to best advantage as a parliamentary street fighter during the Opposition years, became the Employment Secretary. Jim Prior, meanwhile, could now be found in Stormont Castle, his days spent bleakly surveying life and death in the Bogside and along the Crumlin Road.

12

Those Poor Shopkeepers!

ONE DAY IN early May 1978, Margaret Thatcher was driving across Teheran with the British Ambassador to Iran, Sir Anthony Parsons. Much later, Sir Anthony was to serve her in a close personal capacity, but this was the first time he had met the leader of the Opposition, and she gave him a taste of her political philosophy which he found memorably startling. 'Do you know,' she said, briefly diverting the conversation from the Shah's prospects of survival as Iranian head of state, 'there are still people in my party who believe in consensus politics.'

Parsons was taken aback. 'I think most people in the country, including me, believe in consensus politics,' he replied.

'I regard them as Quislings, as traitors,' the leader of the Opposition said. And when Parsons remarked that this was strong language, she did not demur. 'I know,' she said. 'I mean it.'

This anathema was not withdrawn when she got into government. Consensus is another word for agreement, and in the normal way of politics prime ministers may be expected to seek the maximum national agreement for the policies they wish to pursue. As national leaders, they usually set some store by the need to coax and cajole and deviously educate the people towards some species of consent, especially, as was the case with the Thatcher Government, when they see their purpose as being to change the course of history. Consensus methods, if not the old consensus policies, would have seemed to most politicians appropriate to the case.

From the beginning, Mrs Thatcher rejected this proposition. Although she finally captured her cabinet in September 1981, it took longer to capture the hearts and minds of the nation. Spurning consensus, she repelled consent. Her apprentice excursion into political philosophy, back in 1968, had first tentatively canvassed the dangers of consensus as a political axiom, and she now repeated the theme. For the cabinet was only the first bastion to fall. Outside the cabinet, some of the resistance proved a good deal more resilient.

She was disinclined to bow to it. This resistance – to high unemployment, cuts in public services, the deflationary stranglehold – produced many demands that she should return to 'consensus policies'. Edward Heath, at the peak of choleric abomination of his leader, used the very phrase shortly before the 1981 Conservative party conference. She was in Australia at the time, and quite unrepentant. Consensus was achieved, she replied, only by 'abandoning all beliefs, principles and values'. And, she derisively inquired: 'Whoever won a battle under the banner "I Stand for Consensus"?'

As a matter of fact, her approach was not invariably so combative. She did occasionally think of herself as a persuader, doing something more than vanquishing the enemy. Her style veered between the trenchant summons to arms and rather more cloying orations which seemed to be feeling their way towards the language of consensual appeal.

One of these which she considered important was a sermon delivered at the church of St Lawrence Jewry in the City of London, on Ash Wednesday 1981, just before the budget. Speaking 'as both a Christian and a politician', she entered a plea for more personal moral responsibility, and argued a familiar theme: 'We must always beware of supposing that somehow we can get rid of our own moral duties by handing them over to the community; that somehow we can get rid of our own guilt by talking about "national" or "social" guilt.' Individual freedom and social good were intermingled not contradictory, she said. Inflation was an insidious moral evil, she claimed, and deeply though she cared about unemployment, everything must first be subordinated to the defeat of that evil.

But she also began to grope for a more ecumenical vocabulary, placing herself at the head of a nation that was, she said, 'but an enlarged family'. She identified four characteristics of this nation – not perhaps the same ones Heath would have chosen, but still indicative of some wider ambition than merely the defeat of the factions ranged against her. Britain, she thought, valued 'the acknowledgment of the Almighty, a sense of tolerance, an acknowledgment of moral absolutes and a positive view of work'. She could not resist the opportunity for taking a dig at churchmen for failing to distinguish between 'defining standards and descending into the political arena'. But this was, by her standards, an emollient address. 'We need to establish in the minds of young and old alike a national purpose,' she said. 'I want this nation to continue to be heard in the world and for the leaders of other countries to know that our strength comes from shared convictions as to what is right and wrong, and that we value these convictions enough to defend them.'

In the end, though, it was not emollience that mattered, or fitted the purposes of this leader. The words weren't spoken insincerely. But they had more to do with clothing Conservatism in elevated language which made her and her Conservative audience feel good, than with changing the minds of people who were not Tories and could see little benefit for them in what was now happening. These people had to receive their education in Thatcherism by more direct methods. For were not consensus politicians Quislings? And if you were an anti-consensus politician, didn't you carry a stick and not a carrot?

One group which had to be taught a lesson were the trade unions, especially those in the public sector. They were not willing pupils. No more than the wets in the cabinet were they able to perceive the wisdom of the economic policy. Nor, of course, did they like what Prior was doing to their powers and privileges with his new law. But they had more muscle than the wets. The 'demonstration effect', which in the Government's judgment had strategically justified its holding out against the 1980 steel strike, had yet to make its mark on all unions. It had to be produced again and again.

Such militant obstinacy was not deployed without discrimination. In February 1981, the prime minister, who was on all important occasions of this kind the decisive strategist, gave a public exhibition of her capacity for caution. The National Coal Board, under pressure from the stringent borrowing limits placed on them by government, outlined plans to close twenty-three pits and lose 13,000 jobs. The miners' union called for government intervention to stop the closures, increase the subsidy to the NCB and block cheap coal coming in from abroad. In each particular this was a direct challenge to the Thatcher strategy of exposing the nationalised industries to market competition.

Memories of 1974 were still raw, and the prospect loomed of a repeat performance, since it was clear that the miners were united and would strike if instructed, with support from seamen, steelworkers and transport workers. In conformity with what he understood to be the strategy, the Energy Secretary, David Howell, supported the Coal Board plan and declined to intervene. But the matter was swiftly removed from his hands. It wasn't easy for a government which had made so much of the need for financial discipline to climb down. Watching from his post as a junior minister at the Department of Employment, the Earl of Gowrie, for example, noted that two or three cabinet ministers wanted to make a fight of it, not least because they suspected collusion between the Board and the union – still fighting a joint battle for the featherbedding of their industry. But for once the leader was not among the hawks. Gowrie admired the swiftness of her action. 'The decision was very much hers,' he said. 'She made a rapid, decisive political judgment.'

Some ministers were remarkably candid about the climb-down: a reminder that they did not yet by any means carry all before them. Chief Secretary Biffen said on television: 'The spectre that frightened the Government was the very clear evidence that there would be massive industrial action. . . . I do not deny for one moment the acute embarrassment this means for the Government.'

The prime minister, while unwilling to go as far as that, made a rare virtue out of her flexibility, reporting with a straight face to the Commons that the Government was willing 'to discuss the financial constraints with an open mind and also with a view to movement'. Even more unusually, she sought to lighten her embarrassment by essaying a little joke. When the Labour leader, Michael Foot, crowing over the miners' victory, offered to take the prime minister out to dinner 'every time she turns', Mrs Thatcher responded: 'Doubtless he will not need reminding that on occasion it is a lady's prerogative to say "No".'

Public sector pay had already breached the theoretical superstructure of monetarist Conservatism, in that a benchmark incomes policy had been laid down as a control mechanism both for public spending and for the 'external financial limits' (or borrowing) of nationalised industries. This centrally determined figure, 6 per cent for 1980–1, 4 per cent for 1981–2, stood far below inflation and would give the Government plenty of opportunities to exert the demonstration effect it was seeking.

A nationalised industry, however, was not the ideal vehicle for this effect. In theory, at least, government operated there only at one remove. Bent on restoring to management the right to manage, and on lifting from its own back the direct burden of making painful decisions about unemployment, it usually sheltered on those occasions – the state-owned car-maker, BL, was the classic example – behind the managerial decisions of the industrial bosses. With its own employees this was not possible, and after the fiasco of the miners, which appeared to demonstrate the virtues of old-fashioned union militancy rather than the efficacy of new government rigour, it was a happy chance that the pay and conditions of the most inviting targets among all these groups should fall for settlement.

Civil servants were unambiguously the government's responsibility. They also represented, at two different levels, a suitable case for treatment. One was the conventional industrial level. The civil service unions were demanding 15 per cent, and had to be clearly defeated if government policy was to retain any credibility. But there was also the political – better, the cultural – challenge they presented. They embodied from top to bottom a class for whom Mrs Thatcher had little time. Their dispute engaged the prime minister very personally. So did its wider outcome, in the institutions of Whitehall. It was in many ways the emblematic struggle in the leader's long war for domination.

The Government's response to the 15 per cent demand was to offer a 7 per cent pay rise, which was already above the norm it had laid down. But as well as curbing pay, it was committed to reducing civil service numbers by over 10 per cent in five years. The atmosphere was already tetchy and untrusting when Lord Soames, the minister in charge, was instructed to put his offer on the table, with a codicil to the effect that there would be not a penny more. Within days, the unions began a series of selective strikes, particularly concentrating on the computer installations which controlled the payment of welfare benefits. This action, beginning in March 1981, soon began to have painful repercussions for hundreds of thousands of pensioners, and mothers in receipt of family allowances, as well as a major impact on government revenues through the non-collection of income tax.

On the leader these proliferating effects had no visible influence. Week after week, when questioned in the Commons, she intoned the same litany. Civil servants, in common with other public sector workers, had got 50 per cent more pay in the past two years, she said. They were now being offered 7 per cent, which many private sector workers might envy. The 'cash limit', the instrument used by the Government to control expenditure generally, was fixed at a 6 per cent increase. There was no more money.

The dispute lasted twenty-one weeks. It was eventually settled at the end of July with a formula which gave the civil servants a 7.5 per cent rise. This was a small concession, but it by no means measured the cost of the dispute, nor the portion of that cost which was attributable to the personal judgment, or lack of it, of the prime minister.

For it subsequently emerged that the same deal could have been achieved seven weeks earlier, at the beginning of June. Soames wanted to do such a deal. He judged that the unions had had enough, and would settle for 7.5 per cent. The head of the civil service, Sir Ian Bancroft, had reached the same conclusion. Thanks to the employment pattern of civil servants, moreover, a 7.5 per cent rise could be fitted into the 6 per cent cash limit.

But the leader would not hear of it. When the cabinet looked ready to grasp at the opportunity during the first week in June, she took the most drastic course open to her, mobilising Whitelaw, her deputy, to ensure that the cabinet did not do what it wanted to do. She told him quite crisply that she would resign if the civil servants were given 7.5 per cent. This Whitelaw was told to convey to each member, which he duly did.

There were at this point some members of the cabinet who would have been glad to see Mrs Thatcher depart. This was before the big reshuffle, and she was close to the nadir of her popularity. Two years after the election, she was not yet secured in place as part of the permanent furniture of British life, and there were senior colleagues who could envisage a better future without her. But none would have been happy to see her departure occur in precisely this way: or, as it turned out, in any other way which imposed on them the burden of taking concrete action to achieve it. Besides, as Whitelaw sagely reminded them, if the cabinet tried to override her wishes, she could take the issue to the parliamentary party and be certain of a massive vote of confidence. So the deal was not done. The prime ministerial will achieved its necessary mastery. The dispute, with all its attendant inconveniences, dragged on – until being settled, under the thinnest of face-saving disguises, on the very terms against which the leader had staked her position seven weeks before.

Reflecting on this episode later, Whitelaw thought it revealed more about the prime minister's character than simply her desire to register her own unbreakable determination. He thought it a regrettable business. It would have been far more sensible to give the civil servants the extra 0.5 per cent at the earliest moment. But he judged the failure to have been due as much as anything to a very personal matter, which had nothing to do with great principle or grand strategy. This was Mrs Thatcher's dislike of Christopher Soames. Somehow or other, Soames got across her, got on her nerves. He had, it was said, 'mishandled' the civil service strike. Perhaps more unforgivably, he had got it right when she had got it wrong.

This was certainly the conclusion to be drawn from a calculation about the cost of the dispute, which was published by the Treasury in February 1982. By that date, the Treasury said, £500 million had been paid in interest charges as a direct result of the non-collection of taxes during the strike. Further, at least another £1,000 million remained uncollected, with interest accruing. Tax on unemployment benefits, due to start in April, was delayed until July: cost, £120 million. Several millions of VAT were lost for ever.

But the interesting figure covered the last seven weeks of the strike, for this afforded a rare opportunity to count the cost of a specific government decision. Given the compound rate at which interest accrued, the last third of the period – the money that could have been saved by a June settlement – accounted for at least £500 million.

Was this, however, a blunder? The Thatcher view of the matter was reflected, as ever, by her press secretary, Bernard Ingham, who on 30 October epitomised for the journalists of the parliamentary lobby what the Government's policy towards public sector workers was all about. It was not, primarily, about sensible deals rationally arrived at, although those might be desirable. Nor was it about paying the right price to keep necessary operations flowing smoothly. 'It took the steelworkers thirteen weeks and the civil servants twenty-one weeks', said the abrasive Ingham, speaking in the middle of one of the periodic crises at BL, 'to realise that we meant business.' A demonstration had been given, a seat of opposition put down, and £500 million was possibly not the point.

This 'victory' in the strike was the prelude to another. For Soames had, in Ian Bancroft, a man the leader perceived as a co-conspirator against her policy for the public service. Bancroft, the permanent secretary at the Civil Service Department, was pained by the dispute. Not so deeply pained, however, as Mrs Thatcher was by him.

Their mutual suspicion went back some little time. Bancroft, the quintessence of a seventies mandarin, had never been regarded by the Thatcherites as 'one of us', nor had he sought enlistment in the ranks. He was not a member of the inner cabal of her closest servants, who were able to assure the prime minister within six months of taking office that she was surrounded, against her expectations, by friends. Bancroft was rather of the opposite school, and he had plenty of clout. Formerly permanent secretary at Environment, he was as head of the civil service second only to cabinet secretary Hunt when she came in. He saw himself, out of inclination and duty alike, as a custodian of the Whitehall culture and the public service tradition. In that role, it wasn't long before he began to understand the depth of her determination to challenge these once eternal verities.

She could not take them apart in one fell swoop. And to begin with, under Bancroft's guidance, Whitehall fairly readily collaborated with what it saw was coming to it. Professional civil servants in Britain are well accustomed to trimming to new winds. This capacity, indeed, was the proudest boast of the world in which Bancroft himself grew up. So when, as a dramatic opening gesture, word went out that all departments should undertake studies of the impact of cuts in their own staffing of 5, 10 and 15 per cent respectively, Whitehall responded in the knowledge that every new government tended to favour this kind of exercise, and in the belief that the Thatcher Government, like its predecessors, would soon discover that even cuts of 5 per cent posed impossible problems. Similarly, Bancroft and his men co-operated in a series of departmental 'efficiency audits' run by the noted management expert, Sir Derek Rayner, on part-time secondment from Marks and Spencer.

But these were only partial accommodations. They did not address the change in political culture which the mandarins could discern as being one of Mrs Thatcher's objectives and of which they had the darkest forebodings. A clammy air of mutual mistrust, as unsatisfactory to the mandarins as it was to the politicians, hung over the early dealings between Thatcherism and the government machine, which Bancroft felt it his duty to do something about.

His chosen method was to arrange a dinner-party, to be held at 10 Downing Street, at which the prime minister could have an exchange of views with her restive senior bureaucrats. The overt purpose would be to clear the air between them, the more covert perhaps to persuade her that it was she not they who suffered from misunderstandings about their role in the conduct of government. The occasion was designed, in short, to teach her a polite lesson or two and restore at least a portion of pride to the scions of the public service.

Every permanent secretary was invited, and they duly appeared on 6 May 1980 to press their case. But what followed was one of the more splendid social disasters of the Thatcher years, a catastrophe not least for Bancroft himself. A continuous thread can be traced from this event, though the civil service strike next year, to the winding up of the Civil Service Department and his own enforced early retirement in November 1981.

This was not entirely Bancroft's fault. Indeed, the episode shows better the combustible effect which chance and personality may sometimes have on the best-laid schemes of even the most sagacious civil servants.

As luck would have it, a critical event intervened long after the date for Bancroft's dinner was fixed but before it took place. The Iranian Embassy in London was seized by gunmen, and a siege ensued which was covered live on nationwide television before being raised, to enormous national excitement, by the daring intervention of the crack soldiers of the SAS. The climax was reached on 6 May itself, as the permanent secretaries were changing into their dinner jackets.

The prime minister arrived late for the dinner. The aftermath of the siege detained her, and she arrived among the mandarins directly from a congratulatory visit to the new military heroes. Somehow, as one who witnessed it later recalled, the clash of cultures was intolerably jarring to her. There she had been, sitting at the feet of the boys in black being instructed in the successful detonation of stun grenades. And here she found herself, half an hour later, among a class of people whose style she thought at best oblique, at worst evasive, and who now seemed to her feminine eye quite effete. By comparison with the SAS, this all-male collection of watchful officials in later middle age, who did not always look her in the eye, was positively unmanly.

From an unpromising start, the evening did not improve. Bancroft opened in defensive mode. When the prime minister got up and said, in effect, that together she and they 'could beat the system', Bancroft offered the true but imprudent retort: 'But we are the system.' Several of those present insisted in different language that they didn't want to be obstructive, but then, as she thought, made it quite clear that they were more interested in criticism than support. The permanent secretary at the Ministry of Defence, Sir Frank Cooper, by temperament the least stuffy of mandarins and a natural Thatcheresque smasher of icons, got into open and bitter argument with her.

The fall-out from this occasion was felt in Whitehall for many months. Emerging from it, the prime minister told a member of her staff: 'It will be etched on my soul.' And nowhere was the impact more traumatic than on Bancroft and his department.

There had long been an argument about abolishing the CSD and returning its duties to the Treasury. But Bancroft had staved off the switch, and the proposition was in any case quite finely balanced. It had the merit of bringing back together the department that recruited civil servants and the department that paid them. It risked, on the other hand, the morale of the service and the sense that a single hand was entirely devoted to running it, rather than the cabinet secretary giving it a small part of his time.

In that dispute it was perhaps never likely, under the hand of Mrs Thatcher, that the CSD would win. But the twenty-one-week disruption clinched its demise, because of the suspicion in high political circles that Bancroft could not sort out his loyalties. After he left, he spoke mordantly of his inability to do quite what was required of him. The Thatcher Government, he felt, demanded more zealous fealty than it was customary for civil servants to supply. 'What is called in the jargon the grovel-count . . . was a bit higher than it had been in some others,' he said.[1] Certainly his own departure closed a chapter in the process of forceful persuasion by which the Thatcher writ was being made to run through the land.

There were to be other strikes in the public sector. The lesson was not altogether quick to take effect. In summer next year, 1982, a long rail dispute culminated in an all-out strike. Hospital workers, including nurses, also took prolonged disruptive action, which followed the same pattern as the civil service dispute. These harrowed or infuriated the nation, for a while. But the Government, its stance dictated by the leader's, profited from the new norm it had established: that it should never be expected to surrender. This rule was reinforced by another: that trade union leaders were to be regarded with indifference verging on contempt. Mrs Thatcher did occasionally meet them, notably when she chaired the National Economic Development Council. But she was never impressed by their contributions. 'When about forty of them come to see me,' she told a questioner in the House of Commons, 'the difficulty is to persuade thirty-seven of them to say anything at all.'[2] In the first five years of the Thatcher Government, Len Murray, general secretary of the Trades Union Congress, Poobah of the Wilson–Callaghan period and a permanent presence in the inner councils, entered 10 Downing Street only three times.

The unions, however, were only one agent of dissent. A less calculable enemy lurked on the horizon. This was the country at large. A uniquely painful experiment was being made on it. By the date of its second anniversary, the Government had presided over the biggest fall in total output in one year since 1931, and the biggest collapse in industrial production in one year since 1921. Unemployment, up by a million in the past twelve months, was rising towards the once unimaginable total of three million. And therein lay the weight of the case which the wets were singularly unsuccessful at making in the cabinet. They feared a social breakdown. They thought the fabric of Britain could not stand the strain.

That this was an anxiety over which the leader herself did not lose much sleep was revealed on the first occasion when the delicate mesh of social order was torn asunder. One weekend in the middle of April 1981, serious disturbances occurred in Brixton, south London, a multiracial area with a long history of poor police–community relations and high unemployment, especially among young blacks. At the height of the violence, on the Saturday evening, 279 policemen and scores of members of the public were injured, and twenty-eight buildings were damaged or destroyed by fire. Nobody, fortunately, was killed. But as a manifestation of consent withheld it looked like a fearful harbinger. According to a subsequent report on the riot, commissioned from a senior judge, Lord Scarman, the nation witnessed that weekend, often on live television, scenes of violence and disorder 'the like of which had not previously been seen in this century in Britain'.

From Margaret Thatcher, however, this epochal event elicited a response that hardly did justice to its complexity, still less to the hazards it apparently portended as a consequence of her economic policy. It touched her on one of her least sensitive nerves. As she had sometimes shown before, she possessed no delicacy, such as other politicians of all parties had learned to cultivate, when dealing with black or brown people. Rather the reverse. Permanently on her record, and permanently lodged in the memories of leaders of the ethnic minorities, was the remark she had made on television in January 1978 about the legitimate fears of the white community that it was being 'swamped' by non-whites. On immigration she had always belonged instinctively, without effort or much apparent thought, on the hard right of the party.

After the Brixton breakdown, she offered an instant analysis which came straight from the same natural root. It was to remain a cardinal axiom, pressed and defended throughout her time as prime minister, in the social perspective which she advanced.

She insisted that social disorders, whether in the form of riots or crime, had nothing whatever to do with the policies, and least of all the economic policies, her Government was pursuing. Asked in the Commons whether social deprivation, high unemployment and bad housing might not have contributed to events in Brixton, she gave her questioner a magisterial rebuke. 'If the hon. Gentleman considers that unemployment was the only cause of the riots, I disagree with him. If he considers that it was the main cause of the riots, I disagree with him. Nothing that has happened with regard to unemployment would justify those riots.'[3]

They were, in other words, not a problem for the Treasury. They raised no awkward questions for the wizards of monetarism and fiscal squeeze, who prescribed high unemployment and lower public spending with the liberated insouciance of people whose task extended no further than an examination of abstract mathematic equations. Brixton was strictly a problem of indiscipline, motivated by nothing more complicated than human wickedness. It was therefore a matter for the Home Office, and the man who had by now become Mrs Thatcher's closest and least dispensable ally in the Government on everything to do with the state of the nation – including even the economy, which he did not pretend to understand.

William Whitelaw's instincts, left to themselves, would have been different from hers about an event like Brixton. The Home Secretary would have shown more of the old, hand-wringing paternalism; and to some extent the noises he made, the inimitable sound of Whitelaw barking up several trees at once, offset her abrasive certitudes. Lord Scarman, for example, was a typical Whitelaw man, and the antithesis of a Thatcher man. A law reformer with obviously centrist leanings, he appealed to Whitelaw as the natural investigator of Brixton. They were of an age and time. Both were sixties people, reaching into the early but not the later seventies. They were the very epitome of Consensus Man. The verdict of Consensus Man would always be less against human wickedness than against social evil. The Scarman Report, which so found, was thus a rare artefact of the Thatcher years couched in pre-Thatcherite language. By assigning Scarman to the task, Whitelaw helped produce this effect – though the final outcome was more Thatcherite: almost all that Scarman had to say about strengthening the police, and almost nothing he had to say about social reform, was put in train with Whitelaw's blessing.

Quite apart from having run against her for the leadership, Whitelaw was different from Mrs Thatcher in many ways. He was a rich landowner, who had never needed to work for a living: almost the last of that class of Conservative who could give their lives to the party in the certainty of financial independence and with every hope of preferment.

Whitelaw had received preferment in abundance, briefly from Macmillan and then substantially from Heath, to whom he became an intimate friend and counsellor, as chief whip in Opposition and later in a succession of cabinet posts. Power and its management were Whitelaw's forte: acquiring it, maximising it, deploying it, ensuring as far as possible its retention. Although a graduate of Cambridge University, he was not in the smallest degree an intellectual, or even, in the academic sense, clever. But as chief whip and beyond, he established himself as a man of judgment. That is why he was valued by a succession of Conservative leaders for an unbroken period of nearly thirty years. Willie knew what was on, and what was not on. He could smell it in the wind, feel it through his toes. He could tell you at twenty paces whether any particular Conservative MP was straight or crooked, and he was usually right. He could also detect the scale and durability of a majority opinion, and here he was usually right as well.

This particular faculty, however, he quite consciously put into cold storage after Mrs Thatcher became leader. Other considerations became more important. Whitelaw nurtured as many doubts about monetarism as Prior and the others but, unlike them, had closed his mind to heresy, let alone rebellion, by the time monetarism came to be put into practice. He had an anterior commitment, sealed with a kiss, which excluded doubt as a permissible condition. Those who witnessed it reckoned that the night of the 1979 election was the date this pledge was made between the leader and her deputy. At a moment of uncertainty, when the projections failed to show her winning, Whitelaw gave her a sudden, comforting hug, and she did not forget it.

He bound himself completely to her. At one pit of her unpopularity, in the winter of 1980–1, he declared to a visitor, like a man who had put all impious temptations aside: 'I shall stand by her to the end.' When pressed on the point, he would admit that he still didn't like every aspect of the economic policy but he was completely prepared to believe that there was no alternative. In a sense, this didn't matter to him. He was operating on a different plane, making his own analysis, which told him that blind obedience, punctuated by sage advice on matters outside the economic realm, was the only rational course of conduct.

This greatly disappointed the more active wets. Whitelaw was, after all, supposed to be one of them. But he gave them no comfort. When they still thought the policy was bound to change if they gave it a push, they retained fleeting hopes that he would be in their side against the Treasury. 'Willie has almost but not completely collapsed,' one of them confided lugubriously in March 1980. But within six months he was, according to the same colleague, 'a burned-out case': a pathetic Thatcher bootlicker, blind to the economic crisis, the once acceptable face of Conservatism who was now reduced to providing the cover behind which every kind of depredation was being attempted. Some of the language was very strong.

This wasn't how Whitelaw saw his function at all. Even in the wets' own terms, he thought he was right. They were not being realistic, he thought. For better or worse, Thatcherism was now Conservatism, and the party's future was entirely bound up with the lady. His thinking was wholly political. 'Whether we win the next election depends completely on how she is regarded,' he had concluded well before the 1981 budget.

For all that, their relationship was far from tranquil. A point on which they regularly differed concerned the meritorious qualities of the Conservative party conference. The leader was both the child of the conference and its mistress. These were the grass-roots Tories with instincts like hers. Whitelaw, on the other hand, detested them, and continued to do so even after becoming a Thatcherite. He mistrusted the adulation the conference regularly gave the leader. 'It's indulging in the cult of personality, and getting worse every year,' he once said.

He was also bruised by the repeated encounters he had with it as the party's leading spokesman on Home Office affairs. Late in life he retained a strangely exact memory of each onslaught the conference had made against him, whether about hanging or immigration – and how he had seen it off. He particularly remembered the conference of 1981, when, as he struggled against tidal waves of applause for every attack on the Government's weak-kneed approach to law and order, he noticed the prime minister repeatedly clapping his opponents. His fury was incandescent. He ushered her into a room behind the platform, and, enraged male to inconsiderate female, delivered a rebuke which was said to have chastened even her. That was the other thing about Whitelaw. He was a proper man, with a wartime Military Cross to prove it, and the manner, behind a great deal of charm, of a well-born country gentleman accustomed to being in command of any room he entered.

From this base he thought he was in a strong position. He was able, for example, to argue with her without being misunderstood.

In no way would she suspect him of undermining her or intriguing to displace her. In no way did he do so. By his own account, he argued with her constantly, curbing her impulses and reminding her – his famous talent – to distinguish between folly and common sense. These arguments rarely extended to the economic policy, the heart of her political existence, on which Whitelaw freely confessed that he was baffled by all the figuring. On the economy, indeed, his dialectical role was the opposite: to explain to the wets with the considerable weight at his command that there was indeed no alternative. But he sometimes influenced her on other matters, against doing exceptionally reckless things.

One example, showing her to be as impetuous as he was level-headed, occurred late in 1980. A murderer, known as the Yorkshire Ripper, had been at large in the environs of Leeds and Huddersfield for more than five years, and had claimed the lives of thirteen women. The police seemed to be incompetent and the tabloid press was full of it. So vexed was the prime minister by yet another murder that she summoned the Home Secretary and announced her intention of going to Leeds that weekend to take personal charge of the investigation. Nobody but her, she thought, really cared about the fate of these wretched women. Certainly no man could care enough.

Whitelaw managed to restrain her, but only after heavy argument. He told her that her presence would merely distract the police effort. It would look as though she was overreacting. Above all, it would quite gratuitously associate the Government with the failures of the West Yorkshire police and, if the Ripper wasn't caught immediately, make people think ministers were to blame for the next murder. All this he carefully spelled out to her. It was the kind of question on which she actually wanted Whitelaw to use his pacifying skills with her, while being galvanised to action himself. (Not long afterwards, working through the Inspectorate of Constabulary, he quietly got the Ripper investigating team changed, and an arrest eventually followed.)

On the complex of issues that surrounded the Brixton explosion, Whitelaw's influence was less pronounced. He was certainly more sensitive than she was to the problems afflicting young blacks. He had deplored her 1978 reference to 'swamping' by coloured immigrants, and was convinced at the time that this was no accidental phrase, uttered in the heat of a television interview. As a direct result, Whitelaw was obliged to announce tighter policies and include in the home affairs section of the manifesto a pledge to set up a register of all New Commonwealth citizens entitled by family connection to settle in Britain in the future.

He regarded the register as quite impractical, and by the time of the Brixton riots had succeeded, with Home Office assistance, in removing it from the agenda. But otherwise he was no longer seen, either inside or outside politics, as a force to be distinguished from Mrs Thatcher herself. He was the chief operative of a policy that laid heavy emphasis on the enforcement of law and order, to the exclusion of most other subtleties. Police pay was the first and central plank in this. Almost the first decision the Government took, within a week of reaching office, was to meet an inflationary police pay award in full, and commit itself to steady rises thereafter so that, in the life of the first Thatcher administration, the pay of a police constable rose by 25 per cent more than average earnings and 30 per cent more than prices. The police were a favoured class under Mrs Thatcher, even more conspicuously than in previous Tory times. Cynics, not all of them anti-Conservative, saw this as prudent preparation for the civil breakdown that seemed implicit in high unemployment and anti-union policies.

Whatever the reasons, Whitelaw was the man in charge of this favoured class, presiding over a swift expansion of recruitment and an improvement in morale. But it was not his voice that was heard most loud when even this expanded police force turned out, at first, to have no answer to the localised outbursts of rebellion. Brixton in April was followed by Toxteth in July, along with lesser troubles in Moss Side, Manchester, as well as another outburst in Brixton itself.

The country briefly felt as though it was aflame. What Lord Scarman called, in Brixton, the worst disturbances of the century were exceeded by those in Toxteth – 'the worst experience we have yet had in this country,' the prime minister told the Commons. At the time, the riots seemed to be endless and uncontrollable. It was a frightening few weeks for anyone with a television set, still more so if they had an imagination.

It wasn't really like that, of course. The riots did have a termination, and the country soon turned a more languid eye on the wedding of the Prince of Wales. But that was the contemporary, night-by-night impression. And it struck alarm into the heads of many conventional politicians, not only the cabinet ministers who took this as the moment to rise up against Howe's plans for more cuts.

The prime minister's reaction, however, was different. It helps explain her refusal to be impressed by the united apprehensions of her ministers. These civil disorders, a spectacular demonstration that important parts of the population felt sufficiently oppressed to break with the democratic norms, did not seem to her a reason to re-examine her policies. As was often the case in adversity, she returned with redoubled assurance to the instinct she first consulted. It was essentially a police matter, she said each time she had to answer in the Commons. 'We have increased the police force in England and Wales by about 6,000,' she said after Toxteth, 'and thank goodness we did. We must support them to the hilt.' She conceded that it would be necessary to discover the causes of the violence, but insisted that nothing was more paramount than bringing home to each citizen 'his duty to obey the law'.

That was her public stance, and it was supported by a party political broadcast[4] specifically excluding unemployment as a contributory factor. In private, what she said to her personal staff was not inconsistent, but it was more revealing. 'Oh, those poor shopkeepers!' she cried, on seeing the first pictures of riot and looting in Toxteth.

A lot of Margaret Thatcher's character is expressed in that single phrase. It was a perfectly intelligible reaction. It just wasn't the first response that most people might have made when they saw rioters and police in pitched battle, and watched the disintegration of a run-down city. Later, seeing looters walking away with armfuls of merchandise, they may have felt for the shopkeepers too. It was interesting that this should be the first and overriding reaction expressed by the prime minister, speaking eloquently for the priorities rooted in the Grantham grocer's shop and the party which, for the first time, had one of nature's shopkeepers at its head.

Throughout 1981, Britain was a country nowhere near to being at peace with itself. And nor was the Conservative Party. The cabinet reshuffle in September claimed the heart of government for Thatcherism. But this victory did not take immediate political effect. Although it was ultimately seen as the decisive event it was intended to be, it did not still the combat or conclude the argument. The wets, perhaps because some of them had been so brutally routed from their jobs, now became rather less wet in pressing their cause.

The party conference opened in a continuing atmosphere of strife and doom. For the previous three months, the Government had scored no more than 30 per cent in opinion polls of voting intentions, eight points behind Labour. John Biffen, the party's resident Jeremiah, and about the only man whose judgment was regarded with equal seriousness by wets and drys alike, openly reminded the faithful that the party might be on the verge of destruction. It might be, he told a conference fringe meeting, 'within touching distance of the débâcles of 1906 and 1945'.

He, a Thatcherite once pure as driven snow, sought in fact to reinterpret what was going on and steer the language away from the crusading militancy in which the leader preferred incessantly to couch her purpose. Biffen, who a year earlier had horrified some Conservatives by warning the nation to prepare for 'three years of unparalleled austerity', now said the Government was being seriously misunderstood. For all the ferocious rows and rhetoric about cutting public spending, this had not in fact happened. 'The statistics show that in the first two years of the life of the Government, public spending has risen by two per cent,' Biffen said. This was far from being the kind of 'Chicago revolution' proposed by Professor Milton Friedman. The Government, if it could only admit the truth, was showing itself to be part of the great all-party consensus in favour of the welfare state and the protective role of public spending. 'We are all social democrats now,' Biffen impudently concluded.

It was a valiant effort, but it wasn't widely heard or believed. Biffen's was a solitary voice, drowned out by the fratricidal viciousness which attended this, the final phase of serious factional warfare. The sacked Gilmour, at a fringe meeting, spoke of Treasury ministers as if they were soulless primitives incapable of reciting the two-times table. Sir Geoffrey Howe, winding up an economic debate in which a lot of sincere anguish had been expressed by grass-root Tories, could not remove himself from the bunker of his mind sufficiently to acknowledge the merit of a single one of their arguments. Mrs Thatcher, addressing what she presumptuously termed 'the grand assize of the nation', was obliged for once to praise it for its disagreements. 'There has been strenuous discussion and dissent,' she said. 'I welcome that.' She even said that 'there would be no question of sticking doggedly to so-called dogma.' But, she added, 'I will not change just to court popularity.'

There was, in short, nothing here for wets. Before the conference, a group of younger wets had published a restrained but pointed pamphlet, entitled 'Changing Gear', which argued for moderating the speed of the monetarist juggernaut. Their purpose, wrote one of them, Chris Patten, was to halt the decline of the economy, to make the re-election of Mrs Thatcher's Government more likely and 'to rescue the moderate Tory cause from the broom cupboard to which it has been consigned'. He could not then know just how long postponed this rescue was to be.

Not all the available devices, however, had been exhausted. There remained the possibility that the leader might be obliged to depart. For most of the second half of 1981, the idea that she could not last was current. It never took any purposeful shape, but it existed at least at the dinner-tables of the wets and was open for retaliatory discussion among the drys. No plot even began to get under way. The possibility of an enforced resignation never became more than a talking-point. But it was toyed with, wistfully meditated, and in some quarters longed for. It reflected the wets' incredulity, more than anything. After Brixton and Toxteth, they did not see quite how she could carry on without a change of tack. One good judge, asked around that time what chance he gave her of leading the party into the next election, pondered for a while and then said 85 per cent.

The friends of Francis Pym, for example, reported him to be sunk in a pessimism lightened only by the possibility that she might have to go. He steadfastly refused to say in so many words that she would or even should stand down, but also declined to rule it out. Pym was a real Micawber. He always believed that something might turn up.

Prior too was heard to canvass the possibilities. Suppose, he mused, that a handful of the great and good – Whitelaw, Carrington, Hailsham, Pym – waited upon her and said they could no longer support the policy. She would have to change or go. But she might call their bluff. And then where would they be? It was Prior's suspicion that one of the emotions lurking inside her was a 'Joan of Arc complex'. He felt that in some ways she would not be entirely averse to bringing the whole show crashing down around her. Certainly when Biffen suggested in cabinet in October 1981 that tax rises rather than spending cuts would be a better way of balancing the budget, she said in terms that she would rather quit there and then than entertain any such idea.

These were unrealistic thoughts. Wets whose collaborative tendencies baulked at taking breakfast together were, as conspirators, incredible. That this kind of talk went on was nonetheless a measure of people's desperation. An opinion poll published in December 1981 recorded that only 23 per cent of the voters thought she was doing a good job. She was as unpopular as any prime minister since polling began.

This was a standing low enough to alarm most prime ministers. But the present incumbent was different. She almost seemed to relish it. Douglas Hurd, Foreign Office minister and part-time novelist, decided after extended exposure to her on a foreign journey that she was at her happiest when she was up against the wall. When she wasn't actually embattled, she needed to imagine or invent the condition: embattled against the cabinet, against Whitehall, against the country, against the world. 'I am the rebel head of an establishment government,' she had once startlingly announced to a private party in Downing Street, kicking off her shoes and standing on a chair to give an impromptu speech.[5] Never did this self-image barricade her more securely than during the dark months, the middle period, of her first Government.

If the wets' pathetic expectations had ever come to anything, she always knew she had a secure line of defence, the party itself. The party was the one institution she never saw as embattling her. On the contrary, she was its instrument. This was certainly true of the party in the country. But it was just as true of the party in Parliament, as everybody on all sides of the argument knew. One aspect of prime ministership she never allowed to fall into disrepair was her control of the backbenches. As Heath had found, omitting to do this could cost a leader dear when times got hard. His successor did not make the same mistake.

She maintained her domination partly by sheer forensic competence. She was not an inspiring orator, possessing no natural felicity of phrase or command of the unexpected thrust. Throughout her time as prime minister she did not make a single speech which anyone would place in an anthology of great parliamentary occasions, or even a speech that would stand out in the memories of those who heard it. But she was rarely, if ever, embarrassed, and never for want of thorough briefing on the facts. She made her mark not by elegance but combat. She was a fighting speaker who always liked to win, preferably leaving a corpse rather than taking hostages.

She did not lose this relish for battle. At difficult times, the little triumphs it made available were a pleasurable distraction. Michael Foot, the Labour leader at this time, gave her opportunities she did not miss. On 10 December, to take just one example, he obviously thought he had cornered her on a detail about the latest cuts in welfare.

Could she confirm, he asked, 'that a married man on average earnings with two children, who becomes unemployed, will be £13 a week worse off than he would have been had the Government not cut the value of benefits?'

The prime minister instantly demonstrated her command of detail. 'Would the right honourable gentleman, in giving me that figure,' she replied, 'tell me how he has dealt with earnings-related supplement?'

Foot was clearly unprepared for this, and began to bluster. The lady had done the cutting. She should answer his question. Didn't she know that the real value of unemployment benefit would soon be lower than it had been for fifteen years? Wasn't that a scandal?

'I see the right honourable gentleman is not absolutely sure of his figures,' Mrs Thatcher gloatingly replied. Perhaps she could assist him. Since only a minority of unemployed claimants had claimed the earnings-related supplement a year before, the unemployed generally could not now be said to be £13 worse off. The supplement was £11.20 so Foot should knock that much off his figure, and what's more didn't he know that the entitlement in November 1980 affected only 23 per cent etc. etc. etc. Game, set and match. This kind of show made worried backbenchers feel better to be alive.

That was the public face of her attentiveness. But she also took a lot of care with her private relationships. Not only was she usually prepared to talk to any MP with a serious point to make to her, she was always oiling the machinery of party management: a task in which she had the assistance of an oddly matched pair of mechanics.

If, at the nadir of her popularity, a serious rebellion had begun, the 1922 Committee of Conservative backbenchers would have been involved. The chairman of the '22 was a man who mattered to every Tory prime minister. He could make trouble or keep the peace, though he usually saw the latter as his duty.

From 1979 this preference could not be absolutely relied on. The chairman was Edward du Cann, briefly a candidate for the Heath succession, briefly a kingmaker when he didn't stand himself. He had run the '22 since 1972, being reinstalled there by the backbenchers year after year, often unopposed. Naturally, throughout the Opposition years, he had made himself useful to the new leader. He was a man of experience, although not of high office. He was also a man of puzzling ambiguity.

By now du Cann had become first and foremost a businessman, with a number of City interests, including his big job with Lonrho. But he retained in parallel not only the backbench leadership but the chair of the influential all-party Select Committee on the Treasury and Civil Service.

As his long survival testified, he was always an adroit politician. With his Rolls-Royce ticking over at the Members' Entrance to the Commons, ready to depart for the City at a moment's notice, he always had time for the small gestures more humble backbenchers valued: the elbow squeezed, the shoulder patted, the whips' office sick list regularly consulted and messages of good cheer despatched to the missing. Yet it wasn't always very clear whose side du Cann was on at any given moment.

His chairmanships raised a conflict. The Select Committee, as was its job, invigilated government economic policy, and from 1979 to 1983 issued over the signature of its chairman a series of critiques, some of them quite damaging, of monetarism in all its aspects. He even permitted a draft report, highly critical of the state of the economy, to be published in the middle of the 1983 election. At the same time he was *ex officio* important to the leader, and made a sufficient number of unctuously loyal statements to confuse, if not entirely efface, the signals he seemed to be sending out from under his other hat. No backbench rebellion did occur, and had it broken out he would probably have felt it his duty to act to quell it. But, cordially ruthless and brazenly smooth, he was not, on the whole, as helpful a backbench leader as Mrs Thatcher might have thought she could expect.

To sound the pulse and take the temperature, she therefore fell back on someone closer to her. Ian Gow, MP for Eastbourne, acted as her eyes and ears in the House of Commons. It is improbable that any prime minister's parliamentary private secretary in modern times has been quite so influential.

Gow, a solicitor by profession, was a complete Thatcher loyalist. He admired her to distraction. Questioned once about her character, and particularly any passages of self-doubt, he indicated that this was a somewhat academic hypothesis. 'The truth of the matter', he said, 'is that in my experience she was almost always right and therefore there wasn't a great necessity for her to admit she was wrong.'[6] Other loyal Thatcherites saw in this man the complete master of fawning subservience. 'I am prepared to do my duty and stand up and applaud after Margaret's made a speech,' one of them once told me. 'But Ian is blubbering before she's even begun.'

For four years Gow put this faith and devotion at her service wherever she went. Up and down the country or across the globe, Gow was always at her side, smartly tailored and discreetly masterful, like every man should be. But above all in the Commons his activity never ceased. Backbenchers called him, not unaffectionately, Super-grass – for his qualities as a two-faced informer. During his leader's regular excursions round the Commons, looking for Tories to lecture and persuade, Gow went before her, gathering the flock, a process the decidedly non-Thatcherite Tory Julian Critchley once memorably described:

> I have on occasion sat at a table which she has joined for lunch, a table shall we say of five rather cheerful Members of Parliament drinking rather bad claret and gossiping. Suddenly you look up and the first thing you see is the sight of Ian Gow with the sunlight glinting in a sinister fashion from his spectacles, and you knew that this was the harbinger of trouble. And then in she would come, she would sit down and everybody would stop talking and she'd look at you and say, 'Julian, what are your views on the money supply?'[7]

But it was through Gow that the prime minister kept in touch. His intelligence network was as valuable as the whips', and more personal to her: a comforting guarantee that, if trouble loomed, at least it would not take her unawares.

Serious trouble, however, never really surfaced. That was the truth which began to dawn through the winter of 1981–2. At the Guildhall in November, Mrs Thatcher made an economic speech registering cautious optimism. 'We are at last becoming more competitive,' she told the City. The worst of the recession was over, exports were improving, retail sales were rising. But, she added, 'do not throw it all away.' The Government was determined to stick to its strategy, although in a limited way it could be flexible in its tactics. 'It is sometimes said that this Government has stuck to a rigid statistical plan, regardless of the consequences,' she said. 'Well, anyone who says that simply has not looked at the facts.'

Therein lay the basis for an emerging concordat, which could now begin dimly to be perceived in the reshaped cabinet. Howe did not get the £5,000 million cuts he had demanded in July. The 1982 budget marked, at last, the cautious beginning of a little economic relaxation after more than two years of extreme rigour. Although the fiscal stance was only marginally eased, some totems of monetarism receded into the distance. Sterling M3, the chosen measure of money supply, had grown in 1981 by 30 per cent more than was provided for in the supposedly axiomatic Medium-Term Financial Strategy. Now, rather than trying to retrieve this and get back on course, the Chancellor simply revised the MTFS target – the first of many such revisions. The national insurance surcharge was cut, which industry had demanded, and tax allowances were increased by 2 per cent more than inflation. The budget received a remarkably good press, and heartfelt cheers from the backbenches.

It was in the run-up to the budget that a change in the political atmosphere became gradually discernible. For one thing, the prime minister and the Chancellor found the confidence, for the first time, to open up discussion of the budget strategy to the whole cabinet. When this took place, on 28 January, the unanimity was remarkable. 'Apart from five minutes from Keith Joseph arguing for another dose of deflation, nobody said anything silly,' one wet minister told me next day. The leader, it was noticed, rarely talked about M3 these days, and even the public sector borrowing requirement was much less prominent. When Peter Walker, always the most forthright wet, said that the budget must take account of huge rises in the cost of living through escalating rates and gas prices brought on by government decision, Nigel Lawson, a durable dry, was his most vocal supporter.

Here was the time, in fact, when the rebalancing of the cabinet began to pay its dividend. No longer feeling that she was among enemies, the prime minister, said one of her closest allies, 'has less need to come out fighting'. She was less prone, at least in these private meetings, to make every policy discussion a virility test. There was, said another participant, 'a strange sense of amity'. The party managers, moreover, had done a precise calculation of how many serious rebels actually existed in the House, who might be prepared to convert the tumult of words into purposeful action. Their conclusion, according to the chief whip, was that the 'deep waverers' amounted to 'twenty-three or possibly twenty-four MPs'. From which it followed, reassuringly, that 300 MPs in the end agreed with what the Government was doing.

Outside the party, and outside the country, events were stirring which held great menace. The Government was deeply unpopular, and millions of Conservative voters appeared to be deserting it. British territory, the Falkland Islands in the South Atlantic, was being targeted for invasion even as the 1982 budget was announced. But the party itself, from top to bottom, could now be relied on, whatever happened next.

13

The Falklands Guarantee

FOREIGN AFFAIRS ARE the least visible preoccupation of a prime minister's life. They dominate the daily business, with sheaves of telegrams filling the boxes and foreign visitors commanding an obligatory place in the diary. But only when there is a crisis or an argument, or when publicity is for some reason positively cultivated by the government, does the British political system these days raise its head above domestic obsessions. The time is long past when more than a small handful of MPs took seriously Parliament's role as a cockpit of global debate.

In 1981, for example, Mrs Thatcher, while answering Prime Minister's Questions twice a week for the nine months the Commons sat, faced fewer than thirty which had an international dimension. Even adding European Community questions into the count, the number was a derisory fraction of the total. Compared with unemployment, factory closures and the future of neighbourhood hospitals, such global crises as the Soviet occupation of Afghanistan or Israel's attack on an Iraqi nuclear installation received only fleeting attention from the parliamentarians. Meanwhile, however, the diplomatic demands on the prime minister continued intensely, as she dutifully reported to the House.

Through the year, she was variously visited by Shagari of Nigeria, Schmidt of Germany, the Sultan of Brunei, the Kenyan foreign minister, the prime minister of New Zealand, the American vice-president, the Rumanian foreign minister, King Hussein of Jordan, and others – and that was only on Tuesdays and Thursdays, the days she answered questions. Only on the rarest of matters, such as the future of a Gurkha battalion in Brunei, did these glimpses she volunteered into the submerged part of her routine elicit a probing interrogation.

At the beginning, such insularity matched her own temperament. When she addressed foreign affairs, she did not instinctively do so like a diplomat. A Foreign Office official who admired her more than some of his colleagues remarked that 'she doesn't think in the supple way of someone who is occupied with foreign affairs a lot of the time.' She had difficulty adjusting to an 'ever-shifting context'. She preferred to see the business as 'a set of finite, setpiece problems, which raise the British interest in a fixed way, which she has to sort out and solve once and for all'.

This preference for the concrete was revealed at an extreme of self-parody quite early on, in preparations for her first visit to Washington as prime minister. One irritant in relations between Britain and the US was the Americans' refusal to sell arms to the Royal Ulster Constabulary. The RUC felt strongly about this, and Mrs Thatcher was determined to put it high on the agenda of her talks with President Carter. But merely setting this as a diplomatic target wasn't enough. She had to get closer to the facts. On the eve of her departure she had specimens of each of the weapons – both the ageing pieces then used by the RUC and the high-calibre armaments they wanted – brought to Downing Street for her to handle and examine personally.

Over time, her appetite for travel grew. Significantly, this became apparent for the first time in 1981. It was the year, with the budget as its climax, when her domestic position was at its lowest. This is a condition when, in many times and places, political leaders become suddenly receptive to the pleasures, the distractions, the relief, the sheer eye-catching publicity available from journeys far and wide. Thus in early April this once reluctant traveller rattled off her year's itinerary with pride: Washington in February, the Netherlands in March, India in April, followed by Saudi Arabia and the Gulf States. Then Ottawa for a world summit in July, Melbourne and the Commonwealth prime ministers in September, Mexico in October.

On these visits, she did not adjust with great sensitivity to the norms of diplomatic conduct. Her willingness to engage with abstractions and acknowledge that the diplomatic context must always be infuriatingly fluid did not noticeably increase. Her temperament, some would say her temper, remained proof against the demands of convention. Most of these journeys, rather than broadening her mind, resembled more closely a transportation of the manners and teachings of Downing Street across the globe.

The visit to the Gulf, typically, revealed her unusual strengths and weaknesses, as an inside eye-witness recorded on his return. It was essentially a sales trip, clinching arms deals with the United Arab Emirates and pushing negotiations along for more missiles and tanks to be bought by Oman and Qatar. The prime minister was vexed by the progress made by Germany, France and Japan in this supposedly British sphere of influence. Keen to rectify the position, she insisted that her visit be extended beyond the time originally planned by the Foreign Office.

The public side of the tour was a success. She was judged spectacularly good at the quasi-regal aspects – 'far better than the Queen and infinitely better than Ted Heath'. She performed impeccably when meeting the various heads of state, having briefed herself down to the last detail. 'She didn't put a foot wrong in public,' the witness said.

But her private behaviour was more problematic. She could be imperially inconsiderate to lowly embassy officials and their wives, 'going on and on in a very public way if they hadn't done things in exactly the way she wanted'. And she had yet to learn the art of diplomatic discretion. She thus showed herself, in Foreign Office terms, to be 'unreliable'. They cautioned her against a plan to make a fulsome speech about Gulf leader X, on the grounds that he was known to be amassing an illicit personal fortune. Before long X's associates were furious, having learned that the Foreign Office had been defaming him to the prime minister. What had happened was that Mrs Thatcher, characteristically, had sounded off about the Foreign Office advising her to moderate her enthusiasm, and this was relayed back to leader X. 'This is the way she operates the cabinet,' said a colleague. 'It makes it very difficult to have a private conversation with her.'

Such niceties of conduct did not matter much to her. Insofar as her behaviour was conscious, it was one more way of distancing her from the style, as from the ethos, of the Foreign Office: an intention, rooted in deep suspicion, which she had already made plain enough in handling negotiations with the European Community, and which was to burst forth still more incandescently later in her Administration.

Besides, the Gulf visit was unimportant by comparison with the first journey she had made that year. If 1981 was a watershed in domestic unpopularity, it was no less epoch-making in international uplift. In January, Ronald Reagan was inaugurated president of the United States, and the foundation was laid of the most important foreign relationship Margaret Thatcher formed as prime minister. The Reagan–Thatcher axis was the most enduring personal alliance in the Western world throughout the 1980s. From Moscow to Pretoria, from Tripoli to Buenos Aires, no theatre of global conflict failed to feel its effects. It eclipsed, where it did not determine, many of the details of Mrs Thatcher's performance in the diplomatic field.

Historically, the Reagan connection with British Conservatism predated the Thatcher leadership by several years. In origin it was more than a purely personal affair. Ronald Reagan had come to the notice of Conservatives soon after becoming governor of California in 1967. His ascent to state power, on the back of a radical right-wing programme, coincided with Edward Heath's attempt, as the new Tory leader, to reform the Conservative Party in somewhat similar style. At the Conservative party conference held in Blackpool in October 1970, in the wake of Heath's election victory, 'the governor', although not present, featured much in private conversation, his identity and importance fully recognised without any need to mention his name.

But the governor's connection did not survive Heath's swift retreat from ideological politics. As a name to conjure with, Reagan soon faded, to make his return only when he was forsaking the governorship for the Republican presidential candidacy and the Conservatives had a new leader. The two became firm personal allies, when they met in 1975 on one of Reagan's visits to London. 'We found ourselves in great agreement about a number of things that had to do with international situations,' the president later told me, recalling his first meeting with Mrs Thatcher. 'She was extremely well informed, but she was firm, decisive, and she had targets in mind of where we should be going. I was just greatly impressed.'[1]

There was therefore an apt symbolism in Margaret Thatcher being Reagan's first visitor, among all the allied leaders, after his inauguration as president. It was not only apt, it was calculated. She was determined to go, and he was as keen to receive her. As the day approached, at the end of February, she was getting more and more excited. One colleague described her as 'intolerable'. She was 'on a complete high', and 'tremendously worked up about seeing Reagan alone'. At the least, the visit promised to be a blessed escape from the sniping and pessimism that defined her daily life at home.

But it was far more than that. Washington greeted her as a heroine of pan-Atlantic conservatism. She had been in power for eighteen months before Reagan's election, proving in the eyes of Reaganites not only that an ideological conservative was electable but that the tide could actually be turned against the collectivist consensus which, despite the vastly different politics and economics of Britain and the United States, was seen to have had both countries in its grip for at least the previous twenty years. To an important extent, Mrs Thatcher was a kind of Baptist to Reagan's Messiah, and was welcomed amid scenes of festivity and pomp never laid on for anyone during the pious austerities favoured by Jimmy Carter.

At this time, there was almost nothing that divided the Thatcher from the Reagan view of the world. What typified and infused it was, above all else, a wonderful measure of certainty. After the agonising and compromises of the Carter years, what Reagan promised was a simple analysis which accorded closely with the analysis Mrs Thatcher wanted to make but was being constantly cajoled by the Foreign Office to modify and complicate. The public words with which they greeted each other would not necessarily have been unspoken by a Carter or a Callaghan, but when uttered by these two new conviction politicians they took on a meaning that lifted them well above the level of cliché. Anticipating 'a decade fraught with danger', the president pledged that Britain and the United States would 'stand side by side' in defending freedom. The prime minister said: 'We take the same view in the United States and Britain that our first duty to freedom is to defend our own, and our second duty is to try somehow to enlarge the frontiers of freedom so that other nations might have the right to choose it.'

So their view of the Soviet Union was identical. Although Reagan had yet to coin the phrase 'the evil empire', as his description of the place, it would not have been disputed by the Iron Lady. Nor did they disagree about the immediate evidence of Soviet imperialism, to be seen at work in Cuban support for guerrilla operations against the rightist government of El Salvador.

Similar mutual reassurance was available on economic policy. Washington received a lengthy lecture on Thatcherite economics, as the lady's response to receiving an honorary doctorate from Georgetown University. It was remarked that long tracts of it could have been painlessly inserted into any one of Reagan's campaign speeches promising to set the economy free and insisting that a combination of deregulation and sound money, together with an expansion of 'individual freedom', were 'the springs of our prosperity as well as the foundations of our moral order'.

Not all these similarities of economic philosophy continued to be observable in practice. Reaganism gave a higher place to deregulation than sound money, and permitted itself a scale of borrowing that Thatcherites came to view as positively orgiastic in its recklessness. Even in February 1981, there were Reagan people disposed to argue that Thatcherism had been far too cautious in implementing tax cuts. But this hardly detracted from the general impression of solidarity, of a shared crusade, of affection already far deeper than the normal run of international relationships, that was the residue of this first encounter.

The prime minister returned from it ecstatic. She felt she had established an even greater closeness than she had expected. Lord Carrington, who accompanied her as Foreign Secretary, was rather less overjoyed. As she made her regal progress round Washington and through an incessant round of television interviews, he was engaged in quieter diplomacy, which included efforts to modify some of the unconsidered commitments she was prone to make. She had made it sound, for example, as though Britain might participate in one of Reagan's new pet ideas, for an American Rapid Deployment Force which would be available to respond to events such as had recently occurred in Iran and Afghanistan. Part of Carrington's job was to neutralise such rash effusions.

He also viewed the whole operation with the kind of patronising astonishment which, had she been aware of quite its full extent, would surely have redoubled the feelings of suspicion which she tended to experience whenever she contemplated the sort of mind that chose to make a career out of professional diplomacy. When a colleague inquired of Carrington how the Washington visit had gone, he replied: 'Oh, very well indeed. She liked the Reagan people very much. They're so vulgar.'

If this was meant to be a serious evaluation, it was wide of the mark. Perhaps it was merely a demonstration of Carrington's incorrigible, upper-class frivolity: or at worst the scornful *mot* of a scion of the old order as he watched the barbarians taking over. In truth, however, the Reagan–Thatcher relationship did have its puzzling aspects, which continued through the 1980s to confuse more sympathetic observers than the first Foreign Secretary of the period.

What chiefly bemused rational inquirers was how such intimacy could exist between two such utterly different characters. Mrs Thatcher had all the important qualities of a high-flying American business executive, being hard-working, single-minded, fascinated by detail and a swift master of every brief. She was fierce, impatient, sharp, fearless and inexhaustible. Reagan, by contrast, had most of the vices of a languid upper-class Englishman, of the type Mrs Thatcher spent years trying to exclude from her cabinet.

Time magazine, after several years watching him, produced a portrait of the Reagan presidential style which in almost every respect described a character with whom the prime minister ought to have nothing in common.[2] Reagan, said the magazine, was often called serene, instinctive, visionary, determined and eternally optimistic. But these words were a cover for less satisfactory traits. He could as well be called intellectually passive, unreflective, oblivious to troubling details, rigid and detached from reality. The detachment was particularly worrying. The president wasn't interested in detail, however momentous the job in hand. On the way to a summit meeting with the Russians, according to *Time*, 'to get himself into the right frame of mind, he read Tom Clancy's *Red Storm Rising*, a potboiler about a non-nuclear war between Nato and the Soviet bloc'. On any plane trip he was more likely to pass the time chatting to Secret Service agents than reading his briefing papers. He favoured 'a kind of Zen presidency', which meant 'the less he worried and prepared, the more popular and effective he would be.'

His daily schedule was studiously undemanding. Whereas Mrs Thatcher habitually rose at 6.30 a.m. and was rarely in bed before 1 a.m. next morning, with little or no recreation in between, Reagan rose at about 7.30, watched the morning talk shows, looked at newspapers and then attended staff briefings to which his typical contribution was not to ask about the issue at hand but merely inquire, 'What do I have to say?' Most Wednesdays the president took the afternoon off, and most Fridays he packed up by three o'clock to fly to his weekend retreat at Camp David. Even the full working days usually ended around five.

His working methods matched this leisurely pace. He read little. Memos submitted to him were kept to one or two pages, and his aides reported that he rarely asked them questions. He did not enjoy hammering out difficult decisions, preferring to wait until others had reached a consensus. When, in his second term, his chief of staff, James Baker, arranged to swap jobs with the Treasury Secretary Donald Regan, they initiated and carried through the crucial switch without the president's intervention. Reagan, according to *Time*, merely looked on 'like a bemused bystander'.

In every particular this way of life would have been incomprehensible to Margaret Thatcher. As her premiership matured, she required to be in command of ever more detail, not to mention an ever wider span of public jobs. Moreover, she had few illusions about Reagan's personal limitations. At times, especially as her second term moved into her third, and a new Soviet leadership was presenting a more urgent challenge to the West, she expressed private concern about the president's mental slowness and his inadequate command of specifics especially in the disarmament field. But these were puny reservations, beside the large fact of their ideological accord. There had probably been no more striking example of this between a president and a prime minister in the whole history of the relationship.

Previous instances of conspicuous personal intimacy – Churchill and Franklin Roosevelt, for example, or the brief paternal liaison of Macmillan with John Kennedy – were not accompanied by such agreement on all important matters of philosophy, domestic as well as global. The Thatcher–Reagan bond was unique and, although not a woman who ever showed any profound awareness of history, she knew it. 'Your problems will be our problems, and when you look for friends we will be there,' she told Reagan before she left Washington. From the beginning, a watchword she constantly presented to her ministers when things looked bad in Washington was: 'We must make sure that Ronnie never gets isolated.'

For although there were these huge differences of temperament and application, the intellectual formation of the two leaders did bear a striking resemblance. Both consciously looked back to their childhood and the lessons learned at their parents' knee. The long years of office imposed no patina of forgetful sophistication on the grocer's daughter. What the *New York Times* once wrote about Reagan could almost as exactly have been written about her. 'The President's ideas about the world', wrote Leslie H. Gelb, 'flow from his life, from personal history rather than studies. He developed not so much a coherent philosophy as a set of convictions, lodged in his mind as maxims.'[3]

Reagan, according to Gelb, 'grew up with a strong sense of right and wrong, with a view of the world as a battleground of good and evil'. This, too, was identical with the self-portrait Mrs Thatcher has often supplied of herself, the only difference being that in her case the mentor was her father whereas in Reagan's it was his mother. Reagan's father, however, took on a different aspect of his son's formation, which also rose to the surface of the Thatcher personality – if only after many years of being suppressed during her ambitious ascent into the Conservative Party establishment. The experience of growing up as the son of a down-at-heel New Deal Democrat in a small town in Illinois conferred on the future president 'populist instincts, including nationalism and anti-elitism'.

Anti-elitism, in Reagan's case, expressed itself as anti-intellectualism, which Mrs Thatcher could not so obviously be accused of. Both, on the other hand, saw themselves as engaged in a crusade to rescue their countries from the dead hand of an unrepresentative establishment that had ruled too long, whether its power was rooted on the East Coast or in the corridors of Whitehall.

This crusading, missionary spirit was what they especially shared, and they applied it to the global plane as much as the domestic. Obviously it was an unequal partnership, as would become apparent on several occasions when Britain, as the smaller power, could do little but meekly comply with American requests. But Mrs Thatcher did have one advantage. She had got there first. This gave her a seniority in the ideological struggle, which slightly compensated for Britain's comparative inferiority. As did the tenacity with which she held to her basic ideas.

This habit she certainly shared with Reagan. It is often the most potent of all political weapons. The two leaders might have different intellectual strengths. 'Does he get the right answer?', one of Reagan's economic advisers rhetorically mused to Gelb, and responded: 'In my experience, he fails the essay questions but gets the multiple choices.' Mrs Thatcher wrote the essays as well. But whether on tax cuts or national defence or market economics or personal choice or individual freedom, each clung to a handful of elementary axioms which they did not tire of consulting. Because these axioms were the same axioms, believed by members of the same Church who saw themselves defying the infidels without, their intimacy withstood many pressures over the next eight years.

It was put to the test before the end of 1981 by a major disagreement which showed that there were limits to the British leader's anti-Soviet militancy, or at least to what she was prepared to do about it. Reagan was hurt and surprised by this defection of his most reliable friend in the world. But not for the last time in their history together, this supremely Atlanticist politician showed that on some occasions she put Europe first and on all occasions she would put British nationalism, as she construed it, before most other considerations.

On 12 December 1981, martial law was declared in Poland and the regime headed by General Jaruzelski declared itself to be a military government of national salvation. The trade union, Solidarity, was suspended and many of its leaders and other dissidents were arrested. A fortnight later Washington announced a list of sanctions against the Soviet Union, including the end of Aeroflot flights to and from the US and the suspension of a great deal of trade and technical exchange. This included, in particular, the revoking of licences for gas and oil equipment, including pipelayers.

The American embargo directly and intentionally cut across a massive European contract to build a gas pipeline from Siberia to the West German border. This would run 3,300 miles and eventually supply between 20 and 30 per cent of Western Europe's natural gas needs. It was a colossal project, entirely financed from Europe but incorporating some American technology, and a lot of equipment built either by American companies or European subsidiaries and licensees thereof. The embargo affected all this, with retrospective effect. Not merely were new contracts banned, but existing contracts were to be cancelled, at the cost of hundreds of millions of dollars and hundreds if not thousands of jobs. The European allies were given five hours' notice of these draconian sanctions: a procedure, as the US Secretary of State Alexander Haig later characterised it, 'that transformed the perfunctory to the curt'.[4]

The British could hardly believe it. One British firm, John Brown, stood to lose more from the pipeline ban than the entire value of American industrial exports to the Soviet Union. German and French companies were equally at risk. Yet the Americans, for all their anxiety to hurt the Russians, were not proposing to suspend their own huge wheat exports to Moscow. Naturally, Margaret Thatcher desired to support the Polish people against Moscow and against their own regime. But she was not about to ratify a wholesale assault on European sovereignty from her friend in Washington.

She opted, instead, for the role of interpreter. General Haig has supplied an account of her performance as Reagan's candid friend.[5] Haig was invited to lunch at Downing Street on 29 January 1982. He already knew the prime minister as 'a most intelligent and courageous and politically gifted leader, utterly devoted to the West', and also as being 'among the Reagan Administration's best friends in the world'. She was in a strong position to deliver a few home truths. The continentals, she said, deeply believed they needed the pipeline. France and Germany would never be persuaded to give it up. She had heard rumours, moreover, that Reagan was contemplating a policy which would put Poland into default on its massive international debts. Had he considered the likely spread of this to other East European countries, and the consequences it might have for the entire Western banking system?

Haig replied that the rumours were correct. It was possible that Reagan would impose a total embargo on the Soviet Union, and call in the Polish debt.

'At these words,' Haig writes, with a fidelity that shines through his convoluted syntax, 'a silence fell over the luncheon table. Mrs

Thatcher gasped: There would be nothing left to do were we to go the whole hog at once, suggesting that in such circumstances the Soviets might as well go into Poland.'

'I profoundly agreed,' Haig continues. To him the episode was one among many in which misguided people all over Washington were preventing the State Department from operating a sound foreign policy. He saw the British leader as an ally. 'With her usual perspicacity', he decided, she had identified the problem that was to trouble the alliance for years, well after Haig's own time, namely that of 'the United States expressing its policies by gestures instead of actions'.

But to Mrs Thatcher herself the moral was more direct. Several months passed before a face-saving formula was found to neutralise the Reaganites' zealotry. To her, student of Solzhenitsyn though she was, no measure of detestation of the Soviet Union could sensibly justify a set of policies that did no damage to Moscow, while inflicting massive harm on the West's own interests. It was an important moment on the learning curve towards a foreign policy which, unlike affairs at home, was usually driven more by pragmatism than prejudice or ideology.

Nor did it damage by one iota her personal relationship with her admired co-religionist in the White House. That was the most important point. There were to be a number of differences during Reagan's eight years. The personal connection survived and transcended them. Reagan gave me his own explanation for this. 'I don't think any of the disagreements have survived as disagreements,' he said, 'once we could talk to each other. Some of them might have been the result of distance and not having heard the entire story, and when it is told then everything is just fine.'⁶ Mind-joining and even body-contact – Reagan was the only leader Mrs Thatcher invariably greeted with a kiss – always worked the magic. Whatever their differences, and whenever they found themselves separately in crisis, they presented each other with irreplaceable draughts of personal reassurance.

Besides, they agreed far more than they disagreed, each taking risks for the other in regular expressions of their joint enterprise. Early in 1982, the United States sponsored an election in El Salvador. Few people thought it would be fair, and it was boycotted by Salvador's own leftist groupings. Every country except Britain declined to send observers, because they didn't want to be seen legitimising an American puppet government. The Foreign Office organised a British team. Carrington privately regarded the election as likely to veer between 'farce and semi-farce', and warned Haig that the British observers would probably report unfavourably. But Haig said send them all the same. What moved Mrs Thatcher, and Carrington as well, was the fear of what Reagan might do if he was isolated.

This was a small favour, which in Thatcherite terms had as much to do with the interests of the West as with those of the president. It was soon matched by a much larger one, donated by Washington to London, which could again be categorised under the heading of Western solidarity, but whose most specific and immediate effect was more momentous: nothing less than the preservation of the Thatcher Government from ruin and collapse, fewer than three years after getting into power.

The war to reclaim the Falkland Islands from Argentinian occupation was the result of a great failure in the conduct of government: arguably the most disastrous lapse by any British government since 1945. Precipitated by Argentina's aggression, it was provoked by Britain's negligence. While nobody can be sure of the circumstances in which Argentina might have desisted from invading the islands to assert her historic claim to them, what is incontestable is that British policy offered no deterrent to her doing so. Britain's indifference, indecision and lack of foresight were accessories before the fact of Argentinian aggression, which produced between 2 April and 14 June 1982 the loss of 255 British and over 650 Argentinian lives.

In the political history of Margaret Thatcher the war played the part of an unqualified triumph. Because it ended in a great victory, eight thousand miles from home, it made her position unassailable, both in the party and in the country. It guaranteed her what was not previously assured: a second term in office. Yet the message it conveys about the Thatcher style and record – about her stewardship of the total conduct of government, for which a prime minister is alone responsible – is more ambiguous. The Falklands war showed her qualities of decision and fortitude at their most brilliant, but only after a certain fallibility had been exposed which originated, paradoxically, in indecision. The war was the culmination, if not necessarily the product, of a fatal unwillingness to grasp a diplomatic nettle and a parallel failure to decide whether her Government was more interested in maintaining defence commitments or in cutting defence expenditure.

The Falklands were and are British territory, but have been re-cognised by all British governments since 1966 as an anomalous possession which should, if the right conditions could be arranged, be negotiated into a different status. The prime condition was that any settlement tampering with British sovereignty should be acceptable to the islanders, who numbered few more than a thousand souls. The Thatcher Government did not exclude itself from this continuing, though only intermittently active, process. It carried it on, as a low priority among the myriad Foreign Office preoccupations it inherited from Labour in 1979. A junior minister, Nicholas Ridley, was put in charge, and he made two visits to the South Atlantic as part of this bipartisan effort to resolve an anomaly that could be simply described: the Falklands were a very small territory, occupied entirely by British families, which could not be defended against any serious attack the neighbouring mainland power chose to launch in pursuit of its historic claims.

The solution Ridley proposed could not be described as entirely his own. It was a Foreign Office solution, in line with propositions put and haggled over by previous governments. But it was a solution which Ridley, a combative character on the Thatcherite wing of the party, put his name behind after due consideration. He proposed a transfer of sovereignty to Argentina, with an immediate long-term leaseback to Britain. This was designed to satisfy Argentinian claims while maintaining British protection for the Falklands way of life. It seemed to Ridley to be the only policy with a chance of being accepted by the Falklanders, oppressed as they were by many years of British vacillation and Argentinian sabre-rattling.

It was at this point, autumn 1979, that the Falklands problem first crossed the desk of the prime minister. Foreign Secretary Carrington, who thought the Ridley scheme 'right but rash',[7] later described her first reaction to it as 'thermo-nuclear'. She was embroiled in the much more visible negotiations to decolonise Rhodesia, and the spectre of an enraged Conservative right was already fully formed before her eyes. She was appalled at the thought of giving the Falklands away, whatever the fancy terms. But she did not prevent Ridley from continuing his mission. He got collective authority from the overseas committee of the cabinet to refine the leaseback idea and take it to the Falklanders, among whom he arrived for the second time in November 1980. With more vigour than finesse, he sought to persuade them of the merits of leaseback. A month later he sought to do the same in the House of Commons, and received a mauling so vicious and extreme that there were those who (falsely) predicted the imminent end of Ridley's political career.

This was the first point at which a better-organised deployment of government energy might have produced a result that avoided ultimate war. The Falklanders were by no means all opposed to leaseback, and the Falkland Islands Committee, a London-based pressure-group, was evenly divided on the point. But Ridley's parliamentary inquisition, which he was left to endure unaided and without any prior massaging of the parliamentary party, effectively made progress impossible. In a single half-hour, a handful of the Tory right, with support from the Labour and Liberal front benches, was able to render a negotiated change in the status of the Falklands politically impossible. There were, in the end, more commanding priorities to consume the limited resources of senior ministers. And besides, wasn't the Falklands impasse something Britain could continue to live with in the knowledge that all Argentina's threats had proved to be quite empty?

Here the failure to mobilise any high-level political will in support of the Ridley scheme met the simultaneous ambivalence of the Thatcher Government, and most notably the prime minister herself, about defence spending. The logical corollary of rejecting Ridley's plan was at least to consider strengthening the Falklands defences in face of a mounting barrage of threats from the military government in Buenos Aires. But far from this being considered, such defence as the islands enjoyed was designated for cutting, with an announcement on 30 June 1981 that the survey ship, HMS *Endurance*, would be withdrawn from the South Atlantic.

The Government came to power committed to a steady increase in the defence budget. This naturally conformed to a traditional Conservative priority, and it took shape with a pledge, in line with a general Nato policy, to increase defence spending by 3 per cent a year in real terms, which was implemented for five successive years. But the political reality was more complex. The instincts of the Iron Lady had clashed with those of a would-be Iron Chancellor. Oddly for a defence-minded government, Mrs Thatcher's first Defence Secretary, Francis Pym, had been obliged to threaten resignation in November 1980 to protect his budget.[8] Even more oddly, he had been removed from his post six weeks later, on the grounds that a 'tougher' minister was needed to knock the military lobbyists into line. Although Pym had appeared to be fulfilling to the letter the defence imperative, his successor, John Nott, was expected to combine his background as a former Gurkha officer with his intellectual prejudices as a fervent monetarist, and make defence cuts which contrived to be consistent both with the desire for better defences and with the demands of the Treasury.

In this, Nott might have succeeded, had it not been for the extraordinary eventuality of his plans being subjected to examination in real warfare. His 1981 Defence Review did grasp the nettle. It took the brave strategic decision to reduce the size of the Navy and limit the role of the surface fleet. The decision rested on a critical choice: to lower British capacity outside the Nato area and focus naval power mainly on submarines. This was a decision taken by Nott and ratified by Mrs Thatcher and other ministers. Indeed, it was approved more by them than by other Defence ministers. Keith Speed, who was dismissed as the Navy minister for raising a public question about the plan, wrote later, in a striking comment on the limits of collective decision-making, that he had been effectively excluded from the Defence Review. Of the background to it, Speed said, 'I do not know how these financial decisions and air, military and naval force directives were arrived at,' adding that he was 'certainly not consulted in any detail about these important matters'.[9]

HMS *Endurance* was a peripheral casualty of the Defence Review, but a far from accidental choice as such. Although *Endurance*, which carried guns, helicopters and twenty marines as well as hydrographic equipment, cost only £3 million a year, she was judged a suitable candidate for cheese-paring, but only over Foreign Office objections. Having lived long enough with the bluff which was essentially all that the Falklands' defence consisted of, the Foreign Office wanted *Endurance* retained. But Nott was adamant. He was carrying out the agreed policy. This disagreement was later documented in the Franks Report, produced after the war by a committee of Privy Counsellors chaired by Lord Franks, who were charged with investigating its origins. According to Franks, Carrington minuted Nott on 5 June 1981, 22 January 1982 and again on 17 February, each time urging that the vessel's removal be reconsidered because it would be construed in the Falklands and Argentina as a weakening of British commitment.[10]

On 9 February, the prime minister herself defended the withdrawal of *Endurance*, answering a parliamentary question put by James Callaghan, who had lived with the Falklands conundrum longer than she had. As late as 29 March, four days before the Argentinian invasion, Nott was telling the Commons, during a debate on the

Trident II nuclear missile system, that there was no relevance in the comparative cost of this future nuclear deterrent (then £8,000 million) and the £3 million it would cost to keep the *Endurance* on patrol against a present danger. 'I do not intend to get involved in a debate about the Falkland Islands now,' Nott said. 'These issues are too important to get diverted into a discussion on HMS *Endurance*.' On the same day, according to the Franks Report, another of Nott's juniors was still minuting the Foreign Office that the Ministry of Defence 'could not justify' paying for *Endurance*'s retention.

Intelligence reports, meanwhile, had indicated the Argentinian response ever since the ship's withdrawal was announced. From this and other signs, even before General Leopoldo Galtieri seized control of the junta government in December 1981, conclusions were drawn in Buenos Aires as to the firmness of British purpose in the South Atlantic.[11] Even the Franks Committee, which is studious in its efforts to absolve the Government from all significant blame for the Argentinian invasion, allows itself to conclude that it was 'inadvisable' to withdraw *Endurance*, and that, in view of the situation developing in the second half of 1981, the decision to pay off the vessel should have been rescinded.

Franks chronicles, in fact, the kind of failure in the machinery of government which deserves to be judged according to its outcome. Although hindsight is often the last refuge of the instant historian, scorning hindsight is always the first resort of the evasive politician. Ministers are responsible for the results they preside over, whether or not these could be foreseen. The fact is that, until almost the moment of invasion, the Falklands suffered a remarkable measure of neglect at the centre of government. Franks supplies the evidence. Between January 1981 and 1 April 1982, there was no meeting of the Defence Committee of the cabinet to discuss the Falklands. Nor was there any reference to the Falklands in full cabinet until 25 March 1982. Additionally, in the intelligence community, although the Latin America Current Intelligence Group met eighteen times between July 1981 and March 1982, it did not once discuss the Falklands on those occasions.

A crisis was therefore gathering around a leader who was singularly unprepared for it. A few voices, all in the Foreign Office, had been trying to put the Falklands on the agenda. Intermittently the issue had attracted senior ministerial attention. But when it did so, the outcome was invariably to endorse the existing non-policy and thrust the islands back out of sight. In the panoply of matters within a government's responsibility, there are at any one time many which necessarily suffer a similar neglect. Time does not allow every issue to be at the top of the agenda. But it is government's job to get the priorities right, and government's fate to be abominated when events oblige other people to pay for its bad judgment. Unlike James Callaghan, who always claimed to be particularly conscious of the danger lurking in small imperial relics, Margaret Thatcher was not adequately sensitive to the danger in the Falklands until it was too late.

When the danger finally became obvious, she did begin to move. Franks charts some of her interventions. On 3 March, having seen a telegram from the British ambassador in Buenos Aires indicating threats of some unilateral Argentinian action against the islands, she wrote on it, 'We must make some contingency plans' – although Franks notes 'no immediate response' from Whitehall. On 8 March she spoke to Defence Secretary Nott and asked him how long it would take to send Navy ships to the Falklands. No doubt, as diplomatic activity intensified and Argentinian action escalated with a landing on the Falklands dependency of South Georgia on 19 March, the prime minister was kept informed of the mounting debates within the Foreign Office and the Ministry of Defence about what should be done. It is notable, however, that her next positive intervention, as recorded in Franks' detailed account of what happened each day, occurred only on 28 March. Franks (in paragraph 212) seems to be describing a minister in less than daily touch with events that were on the verge of engulfing her:

> Later that evening the prime minister, prompted by the most recent telegrams, telephoned Lord Carrington expressing her concern that the Government should respond effectively to the critical situation on South Georgia and worsening relations with the Argentine Government. Lord Carrington said that a message had been sent to Mr Haig [US Secretary of State], and that Mr Luce [Minister of State, Foreign and Commonwealth Office] was to hold a meeting with officials the next morning, and would report to them at midday in Brussels, where they were due to attend a European Community meeting.

But if this suggests a leader catching up with events rather than riding eagerly alongside them, it was the last such moment in the history of the Falklands war. When the Argentinians did invade, on

1 April, the first reaction in official London was of utter disbelief. When a BBC radio producer, having heard rumours of an invasion, rang the Foreign Office in the middle of the night, the duty officer reassured her. 'Believe me,' he said, 'if anything was happening, we would know about it.' A woeful failure of communications with the South Atlantic left it unclear for several hours whether an invasion had in fact occurred. The prime minister's transformation from diplomatic onlooker to warrior queen, however, had already taken place.

When she met the Commons on 3 April, a rare Saturday sitting, preparations for war were already well advanced. Before ever Parliament had been consulted, a naval task force was being assembled. She had met the military and, on advice from the Navy that the job could be done, instructed that it should be. But in truth a momentum was building up that was virtually irresistible, as belated recognition of what the Argentinians might be up to had seized the Defence Ministry and its officer class. If Phase One of the disaster, the unrecognised build-up towards it, cast the prime minister as an accomplice in collective negligence, Phase Two, the assembling of a war machine, saw her as the instrument of decisions that were in reality forced upon her. It was after another month had passed and Phase Three, the fighting itself, was on the brink of starting that the choices were made which really entitled this war to be called Thatcher's War.

Phase Two presented her with great but inescapable risks. She would be damned if she did not get the Falklands back. But she would be double-damned and destroyed, probably alongside her Government, if she tried and failed. Yet these facts could not be altered. They required of her not a choice but a submission to fate. What remained was for her to handle her fate with as much strength and finesse as she could muster.

At its start, the war wasn't Thatcher's war but Parliament's. This became stunningly apparent on 3 April. The Commons, after hearing incredulously that British territory had been occupied, met in a mood of bulldog outrage. In the memory of those present, including this writer, that scene survived as an occasion of terrifying but irresistible power. The Conservative right, and not only the right, snarled and fumed its way through the three-hour debate. The old imperialist, Julian Amery, said the Government 'must wipe the stain from British honour'. Sir Bernard Braine, the leader of the Falklands lobbyists, who had played a decisive part in killing off the Ridley initiative, said there must be no dealings with the 'fascist, corrupt, cruel regime' in Argentina. The chairman of the 1922 Committee, Edward du Cann, forswearing his usual silken ambiguities, contemptuously swept out of existence practical considerations such as time and distance, declaring with unsmiling self-importance: 'I don't remember the Duke of Wellington whining before Torres Vedras!'

The Labour Party, with few exceptions, was almost as militant. The party leader, Michael Foot, spoke of Britain's 'moral duty and political duty and every other kind of duty' to expel the Argentinians.

Margaret Thatcher herself was, by comparison, unexultant. Apart from the two backbenchers, one on either side, who dared to puncture the balloon of warmongering hysteria, hers was the most moderate voice in the House. She was a chastened woman. Although the Commons had now rendered it certain that the task force would sail, and that any negotiated peace would be subjected to the most unsympathetic scrutiny, she had had longer than most people present to contemplate the risks, political as well as military, which now attended any course of action.

The political damage wasn't long in making itself apparent. Carrington felt obliged to resign on the Monday after the debate. She made strong attempts to dissuade him. And he, in fact, did not believe that the doctrine of ministerial responsibility absolutely required him to go. Although, in an interview on the day of his departure, he described what had happened as 'a national humiliation', he was not convinced that the Foreign Office was uniquely culpable. He could have pointed with justice to his numerous attempts to persuade the Ministry of Defence to retain HMS *Endurance* on station. And John Nott, who also tendered his resignation, had had it rejected and been persuaded that it was his duty to stay.

Carrington's reason for going was different, and he stuck to it despite many efforts by the great and the good of post-war Conservatism to get him to change his mind. He felt mortally wounded by the attacks made against him on the floor of the House of Commons and later, in an upstairs committee room, when many Tory backbenchers vented their rage against the Whitehall department they most enjoyed to hate. The noble lord, for all his eminence and his thirty years of service, had always despised the party and not always troubled to conceal its unimportant place in his priorities. Now, in a sense, the backbenchers exacted their revenge, displaying Carrington's scalp on a pikestaff. He went because they wanted him out, and he thought he could not carry on.

In fact this brought certain political benefits. It would have been a little bizarre if, after such a catastrophic event as the Falklands invasion, no minister had paid for the blithe negligence that had contributed to it. The evidence, particularly following the Franks Report, does not really identify the Foreign Secretary as the appropriate minister, except as the man who failed to persuade the rest of Whitehall, especially the Ministry of Defence and Downing Street, that his diplomatic strategy should be supported. Nonetheless, his departure was a bloodletting. The war could be carried forward over the bodies of its first sacrificial victims — Richard Luce and the deputy Foreign Secretary, Humphrey Atkins, resigned as well — without other ministers fearing for their positions. Additionally, the anomaly was averted whereby this major exercise in gunboat diplomacy was being carried forward without the Foreign Secretary being present to answer for it to the House of Commons.

There was another advantage in Carrington's resignation. It pre-empted any question about the prime minister's own position. An impending war was not a moment to labour the point, but any rigorous definition of ministerial accountability could hardly have left her outside its sweep. By taking an axe to himself, Carrington made the forest a safer place for the leader. She, for her part, greatly missed his sagacity and experience — and called on it informally in later years, particularly over lunches at Chequers, which is close to Carrington's own country seat — but she could see that his going left her more secure.

Not, however, entirely so. For there now slid into Carrington's place a man whom the leader was decidedly unhappy to have there: a man, moreover, of whom, if she had had to name one reason why she felt uneasy having him anywhere near her, she would have said it was his manifest and hostile ambition. By a rich accident of politics, Carrington, with whom she had a more respectful relationship than any other minister in her first term, was replaced by the man she least respected and least liked, Francis Pym.

As a former shadow foreign secretary, Pym was the easy and obvious choice to fill the gap. Now Leader of the House, he could be moved into the Foreign Office with relatively little disruption to other ministries. Whitelaw was the only other candidate with sufficient seniority, and probably could have had the job if he had pressed for it. Much later, when it was all over, Whitelaw mused on how foolish he might have been not to seize the moment. It had been such an impossible relationship! Francis cannot stand her. And she cannot stand him. Can there ever have been a worse relationship between prime minister and foreign secretary? Oh dear, oh dear, Whitelaw groaned to his friends.

Pym was, of the many available candidates for such an accolade, perhaps the most perfect epitome of the kind of Conservative politician Mrs Thatcher detested. It went without saying that he was one of the old 'wets'. He disapproved of the economic policy, from a time very soon after the first budget, which he had greeted with enthusiasm. In his opinion, the world oil shock in the summer of 1979 changed both the politics and the economics of what it was sensible to attempt. He clung to this judgment, and went about propagating it in a way the Thatcherites found distasteful and also threatening.

For Pym was entirely a party politician. A former chief whip, he was an adept manoeuvrer with the well-justified reputation of being better able than most to detect the mood of the party and, whatever this was, to present himself as its discreet and loyal spokesman. Unlike Gilmour and Prior and Stevas, he rarely, therefore, made dissenting speeches, even in coded language.

Also, according to some colleagues – although he later vigorously contested this – he rarely dissented in cabinet either. Some said he did not really have the confidence to tangle with the prime minister over the details of monetary policy. Instead, he would simply let it be known by private murmurs in the corridors how little he took responsibility for the mess. And this was one of the habits the Thatcher people, both politicians and officials, most disliked. Unlike Walker, who brought a certain futile bravado to his open disagreements, or Prior, who never minded having a blazing row, or even Gilmour, who at least made elegant speeches on the subject, Pym's style was covert. He seemed to be a mole, but one who never for a moment lost the acuteness of his vision.

In spring 1982, as it happened, Pym's reputation was even lower than usual in Downing Street. Just as the economic clouds appeared for the first time to be lifting, he had made a lugubrious speech counselling against unseemly optimism. This was in February, immediately after a meeting at which the newly Thatcherised cabinet thought it had for once been able to discuss economic policy before the budget without any leaks occurring. This unique triumph for the collective was, in the hyperbole of the prime minister's office, 'shattered' by Pym's effusion. Even though his words accorded with cabinet policy, which was to discourage excessive expectations after the long monetarist winter, his crime was to include nothing optimistic of any kind. Not for the first time, he was thought to be playing a nefarious game.

As a credential for becoming the prime minister's most omnipresent colleague, which the foreign secretary is bound to be even in time of peace, this did not help. It reminded the prime minister that she had been obliged, as she saw it, to take a viper to her bosom.

Nor did Pym's greatest talent make up for this. On the face of it, his skill at the despatch-box deserved recognition as one of the key political anchors of the Falklands expedition. His manner had always been firm and fluent. During the war, on numerous testing occasions, his parade-ground bark and military bearing produced a more incisive impression than some of the prime minister's own appearances. But recognition rarely came. His skills, indeed, were turned against him. Pym's behaviour in the Commons is quite misleading, said the snipers at No. 10. He may sound clear in public, but in private he's a bundle of wittering indecision, always looking for peace where peace is not available, always deceiving himself that war might be avoided.

If that is the way he was, Pym was not alone. And that made another dimension of mistrust. For although the Navy was sent to the South Atlantic with deafening huzzas from the Conservative Party, confidence and solidarity were by no means universally sustained before the fighting began. Throughout April and for much of May as well, every Conservative MP, beginning with the leader herself, was aware that she might not survive. That was the political undertow, soon forgotten afterwards, of the tide to war. Until victory was in sight, Mrs Thatcher had become a conditional leader, supported out of loyalty and the vital need to stand shoulder to shoulder with our boys in the South Atlantic, but sustained on sufferance, pending the outcome. If she fell, moreover, the man most likely to succeed her, it was commonly agreed, was the one with hands unsoiled by the scandalous catastrophe, who had done his best, thrust into the role of emergency Foreign Secretary, to pick up the pieces.

She took sensible precautions against that eventuality. On 2 April, before the decision was made to send the task force, she held a full cabinet meeting at which each member was asked by name whether he supported the decision. This bound in the Government as a whole, making it less easy for her to be a solitary scapegoat. The warrior cries from the House of Commons next day assisted in this collectivising of responsibility. All the same, she could have no illusions about the consequences of failure to re-establish Britain's Falklands sovereignty by whatever means: and the still worse results of deciding to do so by military means, but then losing the war.

To run the operation she formed an inner cabinet. It was the only time in her first two terms when she formally resorted to this familiar device; at other times, although there might be an inner group, its membership was informal and subject to constant shifts. The Falklands war cabinet consisted of four politicians alongside the prime minister, but none, as they agreed after the event, was more important than the representative of the military who always sat with them: Admiral of the Fleet and Chief of the Defence Staff, Sir Terence Lewin.

Two of the politicians, Whitelaw and Pym, were veterans of the Second World War and therefore knew what war and killing meant. The other two, Nott and Cecil Parkinson, the new chairman of the Conservative Party and a protégé in whom the leader reposed much hope, had not seen war but were, on the other hand, Thatcher creations. Pym and Nott, as Foreign and Defence Secretary respectively, were there ex officio. Whitelaw, as deputy prime minister, was an automatic selection. Parkinson, a former junior to Nott at the Department of Trade, was there partly to balance Whitelaw's supposedly natural alliance with Pym, but partly as one more symbol through which the party collective could be locked into the outcome, whatever it was.

Whitelaw and Parkinson, however, had something else in common: a particularly personal relationship with their leader. During both the preparations and the war itself, they could offer her a special kind of solace. They felt a desire to protect her. For all her command of supposedly male virtues such as coolness and fortitude, they remembered also that she was a woman and admitted to certain feminine frailties. Whitelaw, with his Military Cross as proof of sometime gallantry in the Scots Guards, saw it as part of his job to remind this inexperienced lady, who had no first-hand knowledge of gunfire, that she must steel herself for casualties, prepare for bloodiness, not imagine that it could be a painless victory. Equally, there were moments when Parkinson, seeing the fraughtness in her face, felt that what he really ought to do was put a manly arm around her.

With Pym and Nott, the relationship was different. They carried the departmental responsibilities, and in a perfect Thatcherite world neither of them would have been in those posts at that particular time.

Nott, having been sent to Defence as a loyal monetarist with instructions to bring the military budget under control, had lost his faith and was failing in his task. At the famous cabinet meeting in July 1981, he had shockingly withdrawn support for more spending cuts. Through the winter, he had lobbied for his department and used the press to help him. Downing Street was not amused. Two months before the Falklands invasion, the prime minister's office was putting it about that Nott would soon be on the way out. He was too flashy, too febrile, definitely unsuited to the long, slow grind of taking on the Ministry of Defence and forcing it into a managerial regime that would succeed in reconciling its commitments with its resources.

Nott continued to reveal his mercurial temperament when the Falklands enterprise was under way. His intellectual brilliance and complex mind counted for less than his almost Josephite capacity for agonising. He was deeply worried, as any sensible Defence Secretary would be, about the fate of the task force. He knew that the further south it sailed, the more ineluctably it was moving towards a war that could not be avoided and landings on the Falklands that were extraordinarily hazardous. To his fellow ministers, meeting daily and sometimes more than once, Nott could be a disconcerting colleague. Quite often he would spend the time persuading them of the feasibility of a particular course of action, only to pause as he was going out of the door and wonder aloud whether he was right after all.

For the prime minister, however, the Nott problem was trifling compared with the Pym problem. Nott's private frailty was offset by the unfailing robustness of his department, personified by the military leadership. Pym's public ambiguities, by contrast, were not similarly tempered. As Foreign Secretary, and the leader of the peace party in the cabinet, he expressed the typical Foreign Office instincts which Margaret Thatcher had come to loathe.

The contest between a peace policy and a war policy was, in fact, no facile argument. Sending a task force on its way was seen at the beginning, by almost everybody involved in the policy, as essentially a negotiating gambit. Negotiation, Pym's job, was meant to proceed in parallel with a military build-up. It continued to be the assumption of most Conservatives and most of the war cabinet for at least a month, before the bulk of the task force was despatched from its staging post in mid-voyage at Ascension Island, that the Argentinians would be persuaded not to fight.

Secretary of State Haig was the principal agent of the peace process, and Pym, acting on behalf of the collective Government, was his main British interlocutor. During the process, at least five variants of a peace proposition were batted via Haig between London and Buenos Aires. Haig's account of his exhausting shuttle makes plain beyond doubt that the Argentinians were the main obstruction.[12] The Galtieri junta were too weak to make concessions, could never agree among themselves, and repeatedly undermined the diplomatic efforts of their civilian foreign minister, Nicanor Costa-Mendez.

The British position was at first extremely tough. Haig eventually produced a plan calling for Argentinian withdrawal from the islands and the halting of the task force 1,000 miles north, to be followed by joint control under American supervision and a negotiation about sovereignty which safeguarded the wishes of the islanders for at least five years. It was badly received in both capitals. Later, however, after the first major action of the war, the sinking of the Argentinian cruiser, *General Belgrano*, Britain took renewed interest in a very similar package, this time promoted under the aegis of President Belaunde of Peru. Again, Pym took this up with the authority, in fact under the instruction, of the war cabinet which at that juncture thought it had dealt Buenos Aires a fatal blow and was concerned to appease world opinion.

So the disentangling of peace and war strategies is complex, and the division of the war cabinet into fixed camps misleading. Just as the armed menace of the task force was meant to assist negotiations, so the peace talks had at times a calculated effect on the war effort. Thus it was the judgment of one member of the war cabinet, speaking after the war was over, that taking up the Peruvian plan, besides being directed at world opinion, was directed at British opinion also. Such a deal would have been hard to sell in mid-April, when Haig first touted it, and the Argentinians might have bought it if the British had first. British war-fever would hardly tolerate such an outcome with the task force steaming massively south. But when the British relented, post-*Belgrano*, it was at a time when they could be certain that national pride would debar Galtieri from even looking at it. The offer therefore served a different purpose. It was partly done, said this minister, 'to make the British understand why they had to go to war'. Such a generous offer having been rejected, the voters at home would the more easily tolerate the casualties that were sure to come.

In the formal record of the lead-up to the war, the Pym and Thatcher contributions will thus be seen to be intertwined. But the formal record is not the whole truth. Behind this picture of prime minister and Foreign Secretary acting out their allotted roles were differences that penetrated every bone and fibre of their political being. Pym saw war as something which should at almost any cost be avoided. Mrs Thatcher, while growing more conscious by the day, under instruction from Whitelaw and the generals, of what war meant, came to see it as a probable necessity, in a noble cause, for which she felt her nature to be supremely well equipped.

Her different temper was apparent from the start. Haig has left some first-hand snapshots. Before he left Washington on the first leg of his shuttle, he was told by the British ambassador, Sir Nicholas Henderson, that Britain was entirely behind their leader, and 'we wouldn't mind sinking the Argentine fleet.' When he got to London, the relevant historical analogy was immovably fixed in the prime minister's mind. As their talks began, Haig writes, 'She rapped sharply on the tabletop and recalled that this was the table at which Neville Chamberlain sat in 1938 and spoke of the Czechs as a faraway people about whom we know so little.' Recalling that this omission had lead to 'the death of over 45 million people' she identified the Argentinian challenge as a repeat performance. If they got away with taking the Falklands by force, this would 'send a signal round the world with devastating consequences'.

Later Haig records a painful clash between prime minister and Foreign Secretary. 'At one point, during a discussion about the capabilities of the British task force, Pym murmured, "Maybe we should ask the Falklanders how they feel about a war." Mrs Thatcher heatedly challenged him: Aggressors classically try to intimidate those against whom they aggress, saying that things far worse than the aggression itself could happen.'

This was Pym's difficulty. Every time he ventured a word of caution, he exposed his deficiency in the spirit of machismo. When not crossing the Atlantic, he moved from studio to studio giving the wrong impression on television. He never broke with the collective line. But his hangdog air and insistence that all options remained open were seen in Downing Street to reek of appeasement. Well before the British finally landed at San Carlos Bay – and therefore while the peace process was still overtly the British priority – the view of the Thatcher camp inside the war cabinet, available to anyone who inquired, was that Pym was variously 'not very clever' and 'a quitter'. Her most faithful acolyte confided: 'She thinks nothing of him whatever.'

Her own public appearances were the antithesis of Pym's. She had a nation to keep on side, as well as a cabinet and a party, and she had to preserve the appearance of balance. The search for peace had to remain as apparently high a priority as the voyage to war. Sobriety and seriousness, neither of them contrived, were therefore the hallmark of her parliamentary appearances. The Commons remained essentially supportive through all the losses and gains, and she did not have to fight it. But to the wider public, and especially when the cameras were in evidence, she issued more resonant summonses to arms. When South Georgia was recaptured on 25 April, in the first encounter with the enemy, she strode regally into Downing Street and instructed the nation: 'Rejoice, just rejoice!' Addressing the annual conference of the Scottish Conservative Party on 14 May, she noted: 'When you've spent half your political life dealing with humdrum issues like the environment, it's exciting to have a real crisis on your hands.' The struggle, she said, was between good and evil. It went far wider than the Falklands and their 1,800 British people. It was a challenge to the West. 'It must be ended. It will be ended.'

She received a wild, stamping ovation, which did not please everybody. The Secretary of State for Scotland, George Younger, was appalled by the spectacle. It was not merely his local Conservatives who shocked him, but the prime minister's demagogic desire to exploit the occasion. 'It reminded me of the Nuremberg Rally,' he told a friend on returning to London.

But politicians, including her inner cabinet, mattered less to her than another group. Her most important relationships were with the military men. In an official photograph taken after the war, at a Downing Street dinner for seventy of the leading officers, officials and ministers involved in the Falklands campaign, the man placed at her right hand wasn't Whitelaw, her deputy, but Lewin, the Chief of the Defence Staff. This was correctly symbolic of their relative importance. During the war, according to a deputy secretary at the Ministry of Defence, Lewin was 'the most powerful man in England'.

When war preparations were suddenly thrust upon them, an unusually personal connection already existed between Lewin and Mrs Thatcher. It wasn't a relationship that had to be suddenly established. A naval man, he had been CDS throughout her prime ministership, waiting upon her more than once in exercise of the right of the chiefs of staff to a personal audience. Botched assaults on the defence budget had called this right into play, but also persuaded the prime minister that she needed a personal defence adviser with direct access to her. From January, as it happened, this desire was formalised and Lewin occupied the post, which put him in a subtly different relationship from all his predecessors with the Secretary of State for Defence.

Already elevated to being a genuine, single defence chief, rather than chairman of a body of equals, Lewin now occupied a position in No. 10 which clouded the lines of accountability and sharply qualified John Nott's authority as the departmental leader.

This had happened before the Falklands. When the campaign began, it was natural that Lewin should become the most trusted of all the advisers the prime minister had to depend on. He was a reassuring, thoroughly professional presence. He, too, had seen action, and, like Whitelaw, he assumed a tutorial role towards the neophyte. A large man with an unflappable mind and a distaste for the lower forms of inter-service politics, he proved to be the perfect intermediary between the military planners and a prime minister who wished, without ambiguity, to satisfy their wishes. Of the men who attended the meetings of the war cabinet, he was by common consent the one to whom she most often listened.

Lewin was an initiator not a responder. That's how military chiefs like to be during times of war: men of action, pushing forward, dragging the politicians with them. In this case, he had a politician at the top whose natural wish was to be compliant. But his own account of the first military action of the war aptly illustrates the leading role he saw for himself.

He told two early historians of the Falklands enterprise: 'We just about got the war cabinet to agree that we should repossess South Georgia on the way down.' There had been a lot of political opposition to this, he recalled. Ministers were afraid it would be a distraction and absorb forces that should be devoted to the Falklands. But, he said, the military were 'quite keen to have a go because we thought we could do it and also felt we needed a success. We hadn't had many successes politically. We also needed a success militarily to get ministers to believe in what we could do because a lot of my job was trying to give the cabinet confidence that the services would deliver what they said they could deliver, because we hadn't had a war for a long time.'[13]

Of these ministers, the leader, unlike others, always tended towards the military's persuasion. She was not recklessly looking for war, but she perceived with greater clarity and speed than anyone else the case which Lewin insistently put before them: that war required decisive action, that a task force far from home could not hang about, that the whole gamble depended upon a calculation that made no provision whatever for delay.

Lewin was not alone in the circle of military influence that revolved

The first assault on Europe: France's Giscard d'Estaing (*second left in front*) and Germany's Helmut Schmidt (*behind his left shoulder*) eye their new friend in Dublin, November 1979.

The wets: Sir Ian Gilmour and Christopher Soames (*above*), in 1980, thought their time would soon return. As Foreign Secretary, Lord Carrington (*below*) played a different hand.

The wets: Jim Prior (*above*), who warmly disagreed and then surrendered. Francis Pym (*below*), who despaired and was then removed.

Ted Heath's last throw: the 1981 Party Conference.

Sir Geoffrey Howe, Chancellor of the Exchequer 1979–83, Foreign Secretary 1983–: faithful purveyor of Thatcherism at home and abroad.

A particular fondness for men in uniform: with our boys in the Falklands, January 1983, and with some of the brass on the first anniversary of the war.

The men who mattered: Denis Thatcher, husband, (*left*), Bernard Ingham, press officer, Charles Powell, private secretary (*above*), and Sir Robert Armstrong, cabinet secretary.

The most special relationship: with President Reagan.

around this unresisting target. The First Sea Lord, Sir Henry Leach, was a man of different stamp but of hardly less importance. Whereas Lewin satisfied Mrs Thatcher's admiration for avuncular calm, Leach's ferocious executive qualities were most responsible at the earliest stage for persuading her that the task force could, against all the odds, be assembled. He remained a prime exponent of the mood she felt and wanted the British to feel as well: that this was a gallant expedition for the worthiest of causes.

But Leach had another motive for unquenchable exuberance. He saw in an instant that a Falklands campaign could be the saviour of the Navy, which Nott had already made clear he intended to cut. Of all the responses to the 1981 Defence Review, Leach's was the most unwaveringly hostile. He roamed freely round Whitehall and Westminster calling it 'the con trick of the century', because it pretended Britain's security would be unaffected by naval cuts that were twice as heavy as those on the Army and, he said, *seven times* bigger than anything visited on the Royal Air Force.

In campaigning to get these cuts restored, Leach was unsparing in his dissection of his minister's personality. After the Falklands war was over and the First Sea Lord ('First', to his admiring subordinates) reopened hostilities in Whitehall, he obliquely made apparent some of the hidden difficulties facing any politician at that time who displayed a cautious or even mildly apprehensive reaction to the military imperative, whether this involved the landing at San Carlos Bay or the restraining of exponential growth in the defence budget. Although the Defence Secretary had never fought in a real war – 'a few months in Borneo', First snorted to anyone who would listen – he presumed to know what the defence of Britain required. In more reflective moments, surrounded by his aides, First would muse, 'I don't think I actually *hate* John Nott – but then perhaps I am not a hater.'

For Mrs Thatcher, on the other hand, Leach felt nothing but admiration, even though he had called on her twice to try and stop the Defence Review and, as he dolefully recorded, 'She obviously agreed with Nott.' This presented him, he acknowledged, with a problem. But it was swept aside when the bugle sounded for the task force to depart. Although Leach and his fellows had themselves not fought often, they were agreed that as a leader of the warrior class Margaret Thatcher could not have been improved upon.

They liked her, first of all, because she was decisive. She didn't hesitate to send the task force, but also didn't shrink from any of the implications of this: the resources it would consume, the massive mobilisation, the exceptional powers of requisition, the huge distortion of the defence budget. Leach thought that if the task force had not sailed, 'we would have woken up in a different country'. She, the military were pleased to note, thought the same. They were quite unused to such clarity in a politician. Because they warmed in general to her decisive mien, she was able to rebuke them over details and they would take it. At the first breath of inter-service rivalry, over the use of Vulcan bombers to incapacitate Port Stanley airfield, she was very sharp with the air marshals she thought were keen only to get their own people in on the show.

But equally, because she respected them, the military brought out the best in her. Throughout the war she listened with far more sympathy to the admirals than the diplomats. Diplomats invariably had a hard time, and not merely because Pym was in charge of them. Admirals and generals, on the other hand, could rely on getting a decent hearing. She knew she depended on them for her own survival. In the long years of her prime ministership, the two-month Falklands crisis is remembered by insiders as a time, uniquely, when she listened more than she spoke. Here was a cause which, unlike the trade unions or the economy, exactly matched the simplicity of her temperament. And here were the people, with similar tunnel vision, who could tell her how to make that cause triumphant.

They liked her, secondly, for her executive courage. On 2 May, when the *General Belgrano* was sunk by the British submarine *Conqueror* and 368 sailors drowned, this drastic act hugely escalated a war which, until then, had been almost without casualties save those lost in helicopter accidents. The order to perform it had to come from her. She did not hesitate for long. Later, a reliable source gave his account of the circumstances of this decision, which involved ministers authorising an attack outside the designated Exclusion Zone round the Falklands. Rear-Admiral J. F. Woodward, as the commander of the task force, naturally could not be present when the decision was made. But Lewin was there, pressing for an immediate attack on the *Belgrano*. His request was immediately acceded to, and, in the absence of Pym, without a dissenting voice from the politicians. In a lecture after the war, Woodward, briefed by Lewin and other naval colleagues, suggested that this occurred in an atmosphere almost of insouciance. 'I sought a major change in the Rules of Engagement', he recalled, 'to enable the *Conqueror* to attack *Belgrano* outside the exclusion zone. This was achieved in remarkably short order, reputedly in the entrance porch at Chequers.'[14]

The decision to sink the *Belgrano* was to have an enduring impact on Margaret Thatcher's reputation. It marked her career more deeply than she can ever have imagined it would at the time because, as we shall see, it threw the first serious doubt on some people's assessment of her character. Simple and correct as it seemed at the time, to men consumed by the most hazardous operation most of them had ever been engaged in, it later cast a blight over the Thatcher reputation which lasted as long, in a smaller way, as the golden aura of the victory.

But none of these subsequent estimations cut any ice with the military. To them the decision to sink the *Belgrano* showed what the prime minister was made of, as did her unapologetic demeanour when discussing it in public. It certainly alienated world opinion as well as nullifying any possibility of an early peace. But whether it was completely necessary or completely wise were questions she declined to entertain. Even in her private moments she continued to place it on the heroic rather than the catastrophic side of the ledger. Next Christmas, among those she entertained at Chequers was David Puttnam, the newly famous British film-maker who received a Hollywood Oscar for his celebration of British grit and decency, *Chariots of Fire*. There was much talk in the Thatcher circle about the desirability of something similar being put on to celluloid to celebrate the Falklands victory. Although the leader herself decently refrained from putting this into words, the guided tour of Chequers that Christmas, enjoyed also by Andrew Lloyd-Webber, the composer of heroic musicals, included an obvious idea for some location shooting. 'This is the chair I sat in when I decided to sink the *Belgrano*,' the prime minister told her visitors.

Another quality she needed beside decisiveness was fortitude. And this too she displayed in abundance. Two days after the *Belgrano* was sunk, HMS *Sheffield* became the first major British casualty of the war. The destroyer was hit by an Exocet missile with the loss of 21 lives and many more sailors grievously injured. For the war leader it was a testing moment. Until then, after the exhilarating launch of the task force and the slow build-up as its vanguard reached the South Atlantic, all that the British knew of this unfamiliar business of war was a series of successes.

After the *Belgrano*, one member of the war cabinet told me, with only faint intimations of concern, that it was all looking uncannily easy. *Sheffield*'s fate changed this opinion. Quite apart from suddenly reawakening the cabinet's interest in Pym's continuing peace initiatives, it hit the prime minister very hard. Despite Lewin's tutelage, nothing had prepared her for the shock of losing young British lives, nor for the apprehension this drove home of how close the entire fleet was always going to be to a similar disaster. She did not conceal her feelings, or her tears. But nor did she wilt. She knew she could not possibly afford to. Throughout this entire, extraordinary episode, an awareness of the possibility of her political destruction was never far away. Her fate was absolutely bound up with the need for a victory that nobody could doubt.

And this called forth another important quality, which was patience. Until 21 May, when troop landings finally commenced at San Carlos, cabinet deliberations took place in an atmosphere of feverish anxiety. The peace process continued, but as the large troop carriers bore down upon the Falklands their deployment became ever more inevitable. What would then happen was, as seen in London, imponderable. Quite apart from the running danger of either aircraft carrier, *Hermes* or *Invincible*, being hit, or the troop carriers *Canberra* and *QE2* going down with all hands, nobody was sure how a landing could be safely effected. The tensions between ministers and military were often great. 'Are you willing to risk your troops, yes or no?', Lewin kept demanding of the politicians, playing on their worst apprehensions. If they said Yes, they stood accused of an unfeeling betrayal of their duty to the soldiers. If they said No, they were invited to follow the logic from this conclusion to such drastic preventive measures as an attack on mainland air-bases in Argentina. Equally, the fate of task force and Government alike seemed to some of them to rest on the incalculable genetic makeup of the typical Argentinian conscript. 'We just don't know whether they will fight,' a war cabinet member said to me at the time. 'There's no precedent. They're half-Spanish and half-Italian. In my judgment, if the Spanish half is uppermost, they'll fight, if the Italian they won't.'

Through weeks of turbulence and political fear, Mrs Thatcher behaved like the best kind of soldier. She was calm and, having identified her objective, clear-sighted in separating the risks she was prepared to run from those which she rejected. The acceptable risks were always, in the end, those of military action, the unacceptable those that might flow from a settlement which fell short of a complete Argentinian surrender. In this she was much assisted by the Galtieri junta which, as General Haig has recounted at first hand, proved unable at every important moment to accept any proffered concessions. The most important of these, however, were put forward after the *Belgrano* went down and therefore at a time when all diplomatic wisdom would have said that Buenos Aires could in no circumstances have accepted them.

She maintained her patience and nerve to the end. The three weeks of fighting on the islands imposed, at times, severe strains. Awaiting the final assault on Port Stanley, ministers were conscious of their lack of control over their own destiny, even though victory was by then virtually assured. But the prime minister, as ever, supported the military judgment that delay was necessary for the preparation to be complete. Whatever the rank and file might feel about the point of the war they were fighting or the political incompetence that had preceded it, to the admirals and generals at the top, who can never have expected to be running such a tremendous operation, Margaret Thatcher had proved herself to possess every quality they least expected in a politician.

The Falklands war was a seminal event in the life of the Thatcher Administration. Its triumphant end, effacing the many tribulations on the domestic scene, was what guaranteed the Conservatives' political triumph at the next election, and on into the measureless future. But its darker side also prefigured something. In the aftermath, Mrs Thatcher's reputation began to suffer in what had always been thought its strongest aspect: her guileless passion, so different from most other politicians, for telling the British people the truth.

The theme that ran through the war, as it ran through her first two terms as prime minister, was luck. She was in all sorts of ways a lucky leader: lucky that opposition parties were in such disarray during the early years, lucky in the accidental prominence taken by foreign affairs at the very time when the domestic economic squeeze was at its tightest, lucky that the Galtieri junta provided such incompetent political and military leadership at the time she became forcibly engaged with it. But nothing was more crucially fortunate than the failure of Argentinian shells to explode on at least three occasions when they had buried themselves in task-force vessels. Minor pieces of greater technical efficiency by the enemy could have gravely damaged both the moral and material resources on which a British victory depended. For all Britain's military superiority once the landings were made, the air and naval war was a close-run thing. So far from home, the task force, and with it the Thatcher Government, needed all the luck that was going.

A triumph was a triumph, however. Just as defeat would have destroyed her, victory elevated Mrs Thatcher to a new level of public esteem, hitherto untouched. It was an event of stunning political impact all over the world, and not least on her personal reputation. This was true even in Argentina. Not long after the war was over, an unnamed woman in Buenos Aires told a reporter from the *New Yorker*: 'Thatcher deserves a statue in white marble here on the Plaza de Mayo.' She had broken the hated junta, at whose hands thousands of people, including the woman's son, had disappeared. At home, the prime minister's rating in the opinion polls, which stood at rock bottom in late 1981, soared to 44 per cent in June 1982.

Within a month of the Argentinian surrender, one of her ministers, reflecting on what he had lived through, remarked how personal a victory it had been. The risk she had taken had been hers alone. No one else would have been destroyed by a failure to regain the islands. But when every colleague dithered, she acted. And now victory, he said, 'fortifies her conviction that she is right on every subject'. This fact was crucial to everything that would now happen, as the Falklands event seeped into every decision. There was a nagging pay dispute among the nation's health workers, for example. It was going on and on, causing widespread inconvenience. Very well, she said at a cabinet committee in July. It was a great nuisance. But on no account would the health workers get a bigger pay rise than our boys coming back from the South Atlantic. Over her dead body. As the committee meeting ended, a supplicant Third World leader was waiting outside to press his case for more British aid. He would get short shrift. She was going to tell him he could have nothing more, she said as she swept out of the room.

The Falklands spirit, this minister noticed, had already induced in her a new lordliness which would not be denied. He was not the only one now reconciling himself to the adamant instructions he knew would be assailing him with redoubled vigour from Downing Street.

This pride in victory, which seemed to justify her limitless conviction, reached into the public realm as well. Not for her the decent self-effacement of a typical gentleman–politician. She openly took tremendous pleasure in what had been achieved. 'This nation had the resolution to do what it knew had to be done, to do what it knew was right,' she told an ecstatic party rally at Cheltenham on 3 July. 'We fought to show that aggression does not pay and that the robber cannot be allowed to get away with his swag. We fought with the support of so many throughout the world. . . . Yet we also fought alone.'

It was obvious that she thought her own leadership, personifying all these virtues, had played a major part in victory. 'There was a feeling of colossal pride, of relief that we could still do the things for which we were renowned,' she told an interviewer a few weeks later.[15] But greater than that was her desire to transmute the experience into something larger. The Falklands factor was the spirit of a new age, she told the Cheltenham Tories. What the country had done in war, with unprecedented displays of solidarity and civilian as well as military effort, it could surely do in peace. A rail strike, then due to begin, 'didn't match the spirit of these times'. Union leaders set to bring the trains to a halt were 'misunderstanding the new mood of the nation', and were duly spurned by a quarter of their own members who loyally turned up for work. Thus did they show they understood that the battle of the South Atlantic had not been fought to defend manning levels dating from the First World War.

There was, in her opinion, an important link between the Falklands and everything else the Government was attempting. The record, she thought, was made of whole cloth. 'We have ceased to be a nation in retreat. We have instead a new-found confidence, born in the economic battles at home and tested and found true 8,000 miles away.'

Not everyone was prepared to scale the same heights of triumphalist rhetoric. On 26 July, a service of thanksgiving for the victory was held in St Paul's Cathedral, and the Archbishop of Canterbury, Robert Runcie, delivered a sermon which, while welcoming the outcome and thanking God for the courage and restraint of the task force, also asked the congregation to share the grief of both British and Argentinian mourners alike. The service was fully ecumenical, and reflected the pacifist as well as the patriotic strand of religious observance. 'Onward Christian Soldiers' was not sung.

The prime minister did not approve. Although personally obliged to maintain a diplomatic silence, she could not prevent the infuriated right of the party from saying what they thought of Runcie. Privately, according to an aide, she agreed with Edward du Cann, Julian Amery and other Tory MPs who saw the Runcie sermon as proof that the Government still had many enemies who deserved denouncing. 'She doesn't really see what damage they are doing by making the Falklands a party matter,' this aide reported. Besides, her husband Denis had spoken for her, being reliably reported as saying that while Runcie's sermon was 'better than expected', this was 'more than could be said for the rest of the bloody service'. Not the least of the Falklands after-effects was the start of a long, sometimes venomous distancing, which continued through the 1980s, between the leading representatives of Church and state.[16]

Any insufficiency of jubilation at St Paul's was soon made up for. In October a march was held in the City, followed by a 'Salute the Task Force' lunch at the Guildhall. This was perhaps the pinnacle of the prime minister's self-glorification. Unusually, no member of the Royal Family was invited to be present at this great ceremonial occasion. In the 1945 parade celebrating victory in the Second World War, Churchill and Attlee were positioned at a discreet distance from the saluting base. But now Mrs Thatcher herself, along with the Lord Mayor, took the salute and also supplied the somewhat regal benediction. 'What a wonderful parade it has been,' she told the lunchers, 'surpassing all our expectations as the crowd, deeply moved and sensing the spirit of the occasion, accompanied the band by singing "Rule Britannia".' And once again there was an association to be made between what had been achieved on the battlefield and what beckoned for the country. It had been a triumph unalloyed. 'In those anxious months the spectacle of bold young Britons, fighting for great principles and a just cause, lifted the nation. Doubts and hesitation were replaced by confidence and pride that our younger generation too could write a glorious chapter in the history of liberty.'

In the aftermath of victory, no other sentiments were much heard. The political exploitation was virtually complete. And as a political event, the Falklands war had an unsurpassed importance. To some ears, nevertheless, the prime minister's megaphone sounded altogether deafening. There was a discrepancy between her perception and theirs, although this did not often surface for a long time.

The people in question were some of those who had gone to war. However grandiloquently she might cite the young men who won the Falklands as proof that Britain, Thatcherite Britain, was great again, they did not always agree. As time went by, their more ambiguous attitude to what they had done became apparent. Some of the things they said as they looked back hardly matched the public oratory of 1982. On the fifth anniversary, bewilderment and even cynicism were more prominent than pride. Invited to describe their memories on television, paratroopers and marines were far from nostalgic.[17] Major Chris Keeble, of the 2nd Battalion the Parachute Regiment, said,

'The whole affair is one of tragedy. We should never, ever allow ourselves to go to war.'

Brigadier Julian Thompson, second-in-command of the land forces, was even less inclined to accord the Falklands campaign a Churchillian aura. To him, on reflection, it certainly hadn't seemed a heroic episode. 'You don't mind dying for Queen and country,' he said in the same film, 'but you certainly don't want to die for politicians.' His thoughts on the battlefield did not square with the prime minister's depiction. They were, as he recalled: 'I'll win the war for these buggers, and then I shall go.'

The source of this scepticism was obvious. It went back to the origins of the war, which fighting soldiers had reason to contemplate with a more pitiless eye than armchair generals or triumphant politicians. Those who put their lives at risk find themselves thinking quite hard about the difference between heroism in defence of their country and heroism demanded far afield as a result of political incompetence.

As soon as the war was over, that question was necessarily put to the test. Even in victory it had to be addressed. Why had the Argentinian invasion occurred, and why therefore had the colossal enterprise of retaking the islands been set in train? It was a question Mrs Thatcher did not enjoy discussing, and she worried what the answer might be. She was right to be worried, but not perhaps for the reason she anticipated. The report of the Franks Committee, which was set up to examine it, found her not guilty, which was a great relief. But the way Franks reported came to be seen as the first, albeit the lesser, of two outgrowths from the Falklands war which did her reputation more harm than good.

Lord Franks, the high priest among post-war British mandarins, was seventy-seven when summoned back to the colours. He was a veteran of numerous inquiries, and was supplied with a cross-section of Conservative and Labour dignitaries in order to conduct this one. The terms of reference were 'to review the way in which the responsibilities of Government in relation to the Falkland Islands and their Dependencies were discharged in the period leading up to the Argentine invasion of the Falkland Islands on 2 April 1982, taking account of all such factors in previous years as are relevant'.

The report is among the most revealing of public papers. It describes in considerable detail the tortuous course of the Falklands' pre-history: the various efforts to negotiate the islands away, the run-down of resources for their defence, the diplomatic manoeuvrings over many

years and, unusually, the policy advice submitted by named Foreign
Office officials. When it enters the period of the Thatcher Government,
it itemises one unfortunate misjudgment after another, producing a
catalogue of errors and missed opportunities which provide the raw
material for a formidable indictment.

But the Franks Report is revealing in another way too. It was a
classic establishment job. It studiously recoiled from drawing the
large conclusions implicit in its detailed findings. There had been
mistakes, it said. But they were the mistakes of reasonable men. With
hindsight they might look bad, but hindsight, above all, must be
eschewed. Indeed, it appeared to be the Franks doctrine – a doctrine
visibly at work in much of the contemporary governing culture – that
as long as politicians and officials had behaved reasonably at the time,
no error, however great, was capable of attracting blame. On this
basis, the Franks Committee saw fit to conclude in the 339th and
final paragraph of their report that 'we would not be justified in
attaching *any criticism or blame* to the present Government for the
Argentine junta's decision to commit its act of unprovoked aggression
in the invasion of the Falkland Islands on 2 April 1982' (italics
supplied).

Subsequently, many glosses were offered on this startling verdict.
It was said from within the committee to be more subtle than people
appreciated. The precise terms of the conclusion should be closely
studied, we were told. It meant only what it said: that an invasion
on 2 April, although not necessarily on any other day, could not have
been predicted and therefore wasn't the Government's fault. Lord
Franks' admirers saw the report as his last flawless exercise in mandarin ambiguity. But this was not its political impact, and nor, one must
surmise, was it intended to be.

What the Franks Report was really addressing was another imperative familiar to mandarins, that of political reality. The fact was that
the war had been won, and nothing could be allowed to interfere with
this great event. Had the war been lost, the same set of facts would
have been produced as devastating proof of negligence. But, as was
again later conceded from inside the committee, Lord Franks' strategic
objective was to ensure that Mrs Thatcher's reputation should not be
damaged. He could see no possible need, in the circumstances, for
any other course of action.

Thus the report finds defective machinery but no defective men or
women. It soothes and reassures, by performing the ultimate trick of
appearing to be so candid. It offers the grace of exoneration without

the stain of a cover-up. But it also offers the first important spectacle of Margaret Thatcher securing that history is written the way she would like it written. A carefully hand-picked committee – including, in such former close associates of Labour prime ministers as Harold Lever and Merlyn Rees, Opposition politicians who would not rock the boat – conveniently masked the truths that might have been more rudely driven home.

A more resonant example of the same phenomenon haunted her, tiresomely, for longer. Franks, after all, was soon forgotten. That was the point of it. It did the job required, which was to bury unpleasant questions in the afterglow of military victory, leaving only pedants to marvel at the prime minister's allotted role of escaping scot-free. The sinking of the *Belgrano*, and more particularly the lengths the Government was prepared to go to in order to prevent the truth of it emerging, left a more lasting doubt about Mrs Thatcher's vaunted name for straight dealing.

In a sense, the precise circumstances of the *Belgrano*'s sinking, on 2 May 1982, were of merely academic interest once the war was won. As a political fact, it was subsumed within the great victory. But if that were a rule of universal application, the notion of ministerial accountability, already under permanent pressure in late-twentieth-century Britain, would vanish altogether. Within general triumphs there can be particular errors and valid controversies. The *Belgrano* was a controversy kept alive partly by its own intrinsic interest but more by the persistent refusal of the Government, for years after the event, to tell the truth about it.[18]

The central contention of the Government's critics may be briefly stated. They say that the sinking of the Argentine cruiser, on the afternoon of Sunday 2 May, was ordered, whether recklessly or with malice aforethought, at a time when it was certain to destroy the last best hope for a negotiated peace, which had been tabled that very day by President Belaunde of Peru. The fiercest critics, notably the Labour MP Tam Dalyell, argued that the prime purpose of the sinking was to sabotage the Peruvian peace plan. Dalyell contends that, if the prime minister had accepted the plan, 'she knew that she would be deprived of the "military victory" which is what the Falklands War was all about from an early stage.' He says that she is guilty of 'gross deception', and 'sustained, calculated lying' to the House of Commons: a charge for which, when he made it in the Commons itself in May 1984, he was suspended from the House.

Others make a lesser charge. The Labour members of the Commons

Foreign Affairs committee, when they looked into these events, were not so adamant. They found merely that 'the possibility of a link between the Peruvian peace initiative and the sinking of the *Belgrano* is still an open question'. But they chronicled a history of public deception which served as a reminder that this prime minister, apparently so open in her operations and so pious in her scorn for duplicity, would collaborate in any misinformation strategy if she judged the situation to demand it.

Several key deceptions were officially perpetuated about the *Belgrano* long after there was any operational need to do so. The impression given at the time of the sinking – an impression necessary to justify the shock it administered to British and world opinion – was that the decision was taken by a submarine captain on the spot, that the *Belgrano* presented an immediate threat to the task force, and that for this reason the captain was quite correct in his action. Defence Secretary Nott informed Parliament that the cruiser was 'closing on' elements of the task force. Questioned on television a year later, during the 1983 election campaign, the prime minister persisted with this story. It was an encounter that became famous, because it ranged Mrs Thatcher against an 'ordinary' viewer, Mrs Diana Gould, rather than a professional interviewer, and Mrs Gould, to the prime minister's visible irritation, would not be deflected. When she asked why it had been necessary to sink the *Belgrano* when it was in fact steaming away from the Falklands, Mrs Thatcher replied, 'But it was not sailing away from the Falklands.'[19]

It emerged by degrees that many of these details were entirely misleading, and that, well before the end of 1982, ministers knew they were misleading. Far from being a decision of the submarine captain, the sinking had been approved by the war cabinet, in the circumstances described by Admiral Woodward.[20] The *Belgrano*, moreover, had not been sailing towards the Falklands but away from them, towards a position where none of the task force was deployed. Whereas Nott had said it was converging on the task force, his deputy, Peter Blaker, was obliged to concede on 29 November 1982 that at the time the cruiser was torpedoed it was on a course almost due west, away from the islands and the task force. Piece by piece, the edifice of the Government case was slowly dismantled, including the contention, also vigorously made for more than a year, that when the decision to sink was set in train the Peruvian peace plan was not known to London. Cecil Parkinson, a member of the war cabinet, later said on BBC Television that they were aware of all the peace proposals when the decision was made, and 'primarily those of President Belaunde'.

If the war had been lost, all these matters would doubtless have been the subject of bitter argument. Every decision taken by the cabinet would have been open to legitimate scrutiny, and those involved could have been expected to fight tigerishly in their own defence. That this should have occurred, over one episode in the war, after great victory rather than humiliating defeat, was a signal. It revealed a government and prime minister determined, if possible, to justify every particle of their actions, even if this required the persistent misleading of Parliament and the public.

The full extent of their determination became apparent only in 1984, after the election victory which followed the Falklands triumph. A senior civil servant in the Ministry of Defence, Clive Ponting, felt driven to expose the deception and misinformation of which he, as it happened, was invited to become an instrument. A new Defence Secretary, Michael Heseltine, decided to acquaint himself with what had really happened over the *Belgrano*, because he was under pressure from post-Falklands inquiries being undertaken in the Commons, Ponting was assigned the task of gathering the highly sensitive material, and subsequently witnessed the discussions between Heseltine and his officials which determined that Parliament should continue to be misled.[21]

For Ponting it was too much to stomach. He resolved to send the incriminating papers secretly to Parliament, via the hand of Dalyell. After being identified as the source, he was prosecuted under section 2 of the Official Secrets Act.

As a commentary on both the style and the reputation of the Thatcher Government, the trial of Clive Ponting was a significant coda to the Falklands war. The war was an event of indestructible importance to the Government, and especially its leader. But the trial was also of moment. It derived from an attempt to cover up the truth. It was prosecuted by a government which was determined that its prerogatives should not be challenged by Parliament. It concerned events from which ministers could not bear to see the heroic aura removed. It put in the dock a civil servant who did not actually deny that he had transmitted classified information, but who pleaded that in doing so he had answered the call of a public duty higher than that of obedience to his minister.

The judge at the trial, Mr Justice McCowan, strove hard to undermine this defence. He committed himself to the doctrine that the interests of the state were indistinguishable from the interests of the government. Ponting could claim no higher duty than to do what ministers told him. 'The policies of the state were the policies of the government then in power,' said McCowan, in words even a minister, were he sensitive to constitutional niceties, might recoil from.

But Ponting was acquitted. The jury would not have it. Rather like Brigadier Julian Thompson, they withheld their jubilation from the onward march of government after the Falklands war. For Margaret Thatcher they laid down a marker that would be returned to, when the same kind of thing continued to happen, far into the future.

As the Falklands war was reaching its climax, two world leaders paid visits to Britain which had been scheduled for many months. Together they came to be seen, along with the British leader, Margaret Thatcher, as proof of the existence of a new order in the West. Each was a cornerstone of the conservative decade which was now establishing itself. That all three should have been on British soil in the first week of June 1982, the month in which the British prime minister finally acquired a reputation as a global figure of the first importance, should somehow have been more symbolic than it turned out to be.

The first was His Holiness Pope John Paul II, a Pole whose fierce anti-communism and instinctive rejection both of social permissiveness and left-wing politics put him squarely in the Thatcherite camp – or possibly put her in his. His visit to Britain, one of a continuous series of foreign journeys, was planned many months before. But the war put it in question. Argentina was a Catholic country, and the Vatican did not want to be seen taking sides. The British visit, it was thought, could be a severe embarrassment, and not only to Rome. London was worried that great manifestations at papal masses, possibly accompanied by sermons lauding peacemakers before warriors, might compromise popular support for a war which, at the precise moment John Paul II was due to arrive, was itself due to enter its triumphant final passage.

In the end, the visit went ahead, but in strange circumstances. It may be doubted whether, even without a war, Mrs Thatcher would have particularly relished a meeting with the head of the Roman Catholic Church. It was an organisation to which her very British Methodism felt entirely alien.[22] Their solidarity as anti-communists might not have provided a sufficient meeting of minds. But, as it was, they did not meet at all. A compromise was struck whereby the Pope fulfilled his commitments, but had no formal talks with a single British minister: which made this potentially historic visit unusual for a different reason – it was the only foreign tour the Pope made in which he actually avoided seeing the local head of government.

Hard on John Paul's heels, however, came a less complicated conservative hero, President Ronald Reagan, on his way to a world summit at Versailles. The Washington love-in of February 1981 was resumed on home territory, and with more passionate intensity. This time, mere days before a Falklands victory that was already in sight, Britain had been unarguably the gainer from the close relationship. As Mrs Thatcher knew, but the world did not, Washington was supplying massive military assistance to the British effort. Nicholas Henderson, Britain's ambassador in Washington, later wrote from first-hand experience: 'It is difficult to exaggerate the difference that America's support made to the military outcome.'[23] The support included everything from transport aircraft to Sidewinder missiles and, most crucially, a measure of collaboration on signals and intelligence that was quite indispensable. Truly did the president deserve to be received as the prime minister's most supportive ally. Whether saddled up for an early-morning ride with the Queen at Windsor, or accorded the full ceremonial of an address to the two Houses of Parliament, Reagan was royally saluted, and he repaid the compliment.

He saw the war exactly as his friend, the prime minister, saw it. The task force were freedom-fighters with a message for the world. 'Voices have been raised', he told Parliament, 'protesting their sacrifice for lumps of rock and earth so far away. But those young men are not fighting for mere real estate. They fight for a cause, for the belief that armed aggression must not be allowed to succeed.'

It was one of Reagan's most spacious speeches, linking Britain with his own anti-communist crusade, and duly invoking Churchillian memories and their relevance to modern times. Later, he gave a considered verdict on the performance of the leader he was talking about, which put in a few words what other leaders round the world, imagining how they would have managed, might well have thought. 'I don't know how it could have been improved,' Reagan said. 'I think she was faced with a very grim necessity, and I think it was well handled. But I think it also was the result of her ability at decision-making and firm action.'[24]

Certainly that was her own opinion, for better or for worse. Although straining for outward modesty, she could not exclude a new resonance from her language. In the months after the Falklands, she sounded surer of her place in the world. Her speeches were not cheaply self-congratulatory. But they strove to point the moral and broaden the lesson. 'The spirit of the South Atlantic was the spirit of Britain at her best,' she told the Tory party conference. 'It would be no bad thing if the feeling that swept the country then were to continue to inspire us.' At the Lord Mayor's banquet in November, she said: 'The 1970s were racked by doubt. Few thought that the qualities which made this nation great still lived in its people today. . . . Those years are over. Doubt whether we shall resolve our problems is giving way to knowledge that we can, and to resolve that we will. A task force showed the way last spring.' In the Rathaus Schöneberg, Berlin, she proffered the Falklands as earnest of wider purposes. 'You have a special need to know that Britain honours her obligations,' she told the Berliners. 'I come before you as prime minister of a country which has recently proved that.'

She went before other audiences in the same spirit, but with rather more ambiguous effect. I had an opportunity to observe Margaret Thatcher at her post-Falklands zenith, and take stock of her at close quarters, on her visit to Japan and China in the autumn of 1982.

It was the first foreign journey in three and a half years as prime minister which she was not at all reluctant to undertake. Her aides often commented on her dislike of travel. This time she was eager to go. Maybe she took some private pleasure in anticipating the extra interest she would attract as the leader of a military venture which must have seemed, in the East as much as anywhere, incomprehensibly eccentric. But the more public reason for her keenness was that the journey wasn't a goodwill mission or some purposeless excursion into the lesser summitry. There was an agenda to be followed and work to be done.

In Japan, the task was trade promotion. Tokyo, the scene of her first world summit where her directness and femininity had shone luminously through her fundamental boredom, continued to be a little dumbfounded. She sailed stately as a galleon through the small Japanese, among whom female politicians scarcely exist. The Falklands had plainly given her a new dimension. English women resident in Japan now complained of being regarded as immensely strong, because they were assumed to be exactly like their leader. In a recent United Nations vote urging a negotiated settlement of the Falklands,

Japan had inexcusably crossed the floor into the Argentinian camp. Mrs Thatcher grandly ignored the slight, and delivered reproving lectures about the Japanese place in the world as one of the 'Western' democracies and therefore under a duty to open the frontiers to British trade.

It was not a very successful visit. Japanese leaders, while remaining scrupulously polite, gave little ground. The greatest excitement concerned whether or not the board of Nissan could be induced to build their next European car factory in Britain. In the event, this decision wasn't made for another year, but its great importance in the scheme of things showed what British diplomacy, the Falklands notwithstanding, was now essentially about. Trade and jobs had to be the height of any travelling prime minister's ambition. She bent to her task with a will, selling her country in words infrequently heard at home. Come to Britain, she urged the Japanese, a place now strike-free, inventive, eager to work and guaranteed to make your investment pay.

Her task in China was different, and less amenable to her character. Coming straight after the Falklands, it was unfortunately timed. The British lease on Hong Kong and its associated territories was due to expire in 1997, and this visit to Peking was to inaugurate the process of negotiating a settlement with the People's Republic. 'Our people' in Hong Kong were perforce to be treated rather differently from 'our people' in the South Atlantic: a fact for which the leader was psychically not well prepared.

To begin with, she played her hand according to the book. There were many subjects on which she and the Chinese prime minister, Zhao Zyang, could agree. When talking about the Soviet Union they were united in extravagant condemnation of hegemonism. Poland, Afghanistan and the Middle East also elicited complete accord. In addition, the British leader had absorbed perfect oriental manners, entering with enthusiasm into the agonising small-talk which preceded the meetings, and lacing her public speeches with grace-notes from Chinese proverbs and the appropriate dabs of history.

Over Hong Kong, however, she could not keep it up. An agreed statement was issued which was studiously non-committal, saying simply that talks would now continue, with the aim of maintaining the stability and prosperity of the colony before and after its change of status. Eastern opaqueness required that no further elaboration should be given. But at a press conference dominated by the Hong Kong media, the largest ever held in Peking, the fearless gladiator of

Prime Minister's Question Time could not restrain herself from giving an impression of belligerence and proclaiming a determination to defend British treaty rights. Deviousness and low cunning were the tools she needed. But they did not sort well with the spirit of the South Atlantic. And besides, she had never had much time for the talents of her sinuous predecessor, Harold Wilson.

Already, however, the imprint of the events of summer 1982 was indelibly marked on her future fortunes, and not least on the way she would run her Government. Her visit to the East was eloquent proof of it in one particular. Although it was directed to important matters, including a most momentous colonial disengagement, it was conducted without the assistance of the Foreign Office. Remarkably, no Foreign Office minister was present on the trip. This was partly, the leader's aides candidly suggested, because she found it hard to be in the same room, let alone the same cramped aircraft, as Francis Pym. But it also expressed her extreme disregard for Foreign Office procedures and the Foreign Office mentality, which she continued to see as inimical to her own. They might be acceptable, even valuable, as local intermediaries; and the embassies in both Tokyo and Peking, both of which awaited her arrival with an apprehension better directed at some avenging Visigoth, had scurried around preparing her way. But on the big things, she thought, the Foreign Office was invariably likely to be wrong. It was wrong on Europe. And, she decided, it had really been to blame for the Falklands, the worst crisis she had ever had to face, which could easily have pitched her into oblivion.

So that was one piece of the aftermath of war: the greater imposition of the Thatcher effect, unmediated by the sybilline modalities of professional diplomacy, on British foreign policy. It was a shift which had mixed effects. But no such ambiguity attached to the other major consequence: the creation of a prime minister whose position at home was suddenly as invulnerable as the Great Wall of China.

14

Elected Unopposed

IN THE WEEK in January 1981 when Ronald Reagan was inaugurated president of the United States, an event occurred at home which had a still more formative influence on the character of the Thatcher prime ministership. A group of influential politicians took the first formal step towards leaving the Labour Party and irrevocably splitting the opposition to the Tories. To the survival of Thatcherism, both the phenomenon and its heroine, this proved to be among the most decisive contributions.

It had two conspicuous effects, both of them highly therapeutic. The first was to add another distracting political story to the headlines. Almost since the day she became prime minister, Mrs Thatcher had been fortunate enough to contend for prominence in the media with a Labour Party which was carving itself to pieces. Jim Callaghan retired from the leadership in October 1980, and Michael Foot was elected to replace him; but that divisive process was almost civilised by comparison with the subsequent struggle of the hard left to seize control over both the policies and the structure of the party. For the Conservatives, these ruthless and bloody contests coincided most conveniently with the darkest days of the economic squeeze. So did their natural outcome: the departure of elements of the right wing of the Labour Party and the formation, under the leadership of four former cabinet ministers, of a new party, the Social Democrats (SDP).

The second consequence went more directly to the heart of the political system. Not only did Labour's turmoil supply a gory diversion, it ensured that the parliamentary Opposition was effectively neutered: a feature of the Thatcher years much magnified and doubly confirmed by the creation of the SDP. For the party in power, with an overall majority of 44, a formal split among the anti-Conservative forces, combined with a first-past-the-post voting system lacking all proportionality, offered considerable reassurance.

This split began to become permanent on 25 January, when the ex-ministers Roy Jenkins, David Owen, Shirley Williams and William

Rodgers issued the Limehouse Declaration and launched what they called the Council for Social Democracy. They were leaving the Labour Party on a constitutional point: it was the day after a special Labour conference voted to remove the election of the leader from the exclusive power of the parliamentary party, and place it in the hands of the unions and the rank-and-file members as well. But the Declaration proposed itself as an attempt to re-express social democratic principles and organise around them, the Labour Party, in the view of the four authors, having entirely abandoned that part of its ideological inheritance. The pillars of Limehouse consisted of policies on which Labour attitudes were now either ambiguous or openly hostile. It supported British membership of the European Community. It favoured a nuclear defence policy. It defended private enterprise and the mixed economy. It described a party in which democracy would be genuine – based on one person, one vote – and not corrupted by the block votes of trade unions or the manipulation of unrepresentative constituency activists.

The connection between this initiative and what Margaret Thatcher thought she was trying to do was not entirely empty. There were similarities of perception. The Social Democrats were also moved, in part, by an apocalyptic vision of the state of the country. Although they were inevitably cast as centrists, they were determined from the start to renounce the milk-and-water caution that might be associated with that designation. They, too, had great dreams, or thought they did, and were even capable of depicting recent history in the very language Mrs Thatcher adopted. 'The last twenty-five years', David Owen said on the radio at the time Limehouse was launched, had been 'a failure'.

At the same time, the nascent party seemed to speak to a national yearning for some remission from the Thatcherite winter. Its timing was impeccable. It could present itself as somewhere between sensible socialism and humanised conservatism. After Limehouse and well before the SDP was formally launched, the Marplan poll reported that 38 per cent of the electorate would support some kind of new alignment between these refugees from the Labour Party and the party already occupying the radical middle, the Liberals.

To begin with, Mrs Thatcher was remarkably unmoved by this development. It was the period when, having renewed her vows of constancy, she was preparing for the 1981 budget in a spirit of highly self-conscious determination. Mainly this was directed against the weaker spirits in her own party, the wets who were calling down all sorts of lamentation about electoral disaster and demanding the end of the economic squeeze. The emergence of the SDP, and the instant electoral support it apparently enjoyed, entered the same category of siren voices which the leader must ignore.

The new party also failed to impress her for another reason, one that went to the heart of her political nature. She simply did not believe its claims to be something different. On 26 March, in answer to Commons questions, she gave two replies conveying a point of view which essentially never altered throughout the six years the SDP remained a significant force. In the first, she noted that she had heard on the radio that morning a discussion about whether the SDP would be a new centre party. 'I heard someone say that such a centre party would be a party with no roots, no principles, no philosophy and no values,' she went on. 'That sounded about right, and it was Shirley Williams who said it.'

The second reply epitomised this disbelief in centrism more positively. She said of Labour, the Liberals and the SDP: 'There may be three parties but they are all divisions of socialism.'

This was a genuine opinion, and indeed it could have been no other. Guile and artifice, not to mention the instinct of a more traditional kind of Conservative, might have suggested an opposite response: to welcome these apostates from socialism, make some kind of common cause with them, curry favour with their obviously numerous supporters. At that time, most senior Tories, if pressed, would probably have agreed that there were substantial differences between the policies of Roy Jenkins and those of Michael Foot. That is not how it appeared to a born-again believer of the school led by Keith Joseph, which had discovered itself to be 'truly' Conservative only in the spring of 1974.

Linking Jenkins and his friends with their past became Mrs Thatcher's invariable habit whenever she was under pressure from them in or out of the House of Commons. There was hardly a question they could ask which was not susceptible to this treatment, reminding the world of their part in the creation of the collectivist society which a visionary government was now struggling to dismantle. The only variant in the prime minister's response was to chide the Social Democrats for ever having left Labour in the first place: conduct, she implied and sometimes said, which revealed a regrettable spinelessness, an unThatcherlike refusal to stand their ground and fight their corner.

Morally and ideologically, therefore, the agents of the new fragmentation failed to excite Mrs Thatcher. But politically they could not be forever ignored. They continued to attract a great deal of popular support, scoring a steady average of between 30 and 35 per cent in opinion polls through the summer and palpably cutting away the soft Conservative vote. It became necessary for the leader to modify her policy of lofty disdain. She herself, after all, seemed so plainly a contributor to Liberal–Social Democratic support. In October 1981, before the party conference, the Mori poll showed that only 28 per cent were 'satisfied with Mrs Thatcher as prime minister' as against 65 per cent who said they were dissatisfied, a position only slightly mitigated by the fact that Foot, the Labour leader, stood even lower in public esteem.

At the conference she began to acknowledge for the first time that the third party was worth seriously attacking. The wordsmiths and phrase-makers were set to work. The Liberal leader David Steel, she said, had a passion for pacts and associations: 'a sort of man for all fusions'. Against the manifold threats to freedom, the new party of the soft centre provided 'no shield, no refuge and no answer'. But her main thrust, passionately meant, was against the errors of the past. It was, she said, to 'those nice Labour moderates' now in the SDP that we owed the nationalised industries and numerous other socialist excrescences.

She also went to work more quietly. In November, a by-election in the Conservative stronghold of Crosby, on the Lancashire coast, produced a swing of 25 per cent to the Social Democrats and the return of Shirley Williams to Parliament. Alarm in the ranks of the party spread very wide. Even its leader, behind her resolute sangfroid, felt the need to soothe her critics as well as encourage her friends. Around this time, she began to attend the occasional cosy soirée at which intellectual blandishments were on offer which may or may not have been convincing. For example, the sceptics were informed that Keynes had really been a monetarist and therefore should be counted among the mentors of Thatcherism. By the same token, the critics were slyly chided with being more right-wing than she was. The word flexibility was even heard whistling sibilantly through her teeth.

What was most striking about this period, however, was that she did not lose her nerve in spite of the most imperative demands that she should do so. Although the polls were terrifying – Gallup once put the SDP and Liberals at 55 per cent – and the party far from passive, the September reshuffle had given a sounder political base to her blind economic convictions. When Roy Jenkins took another Tory seat, in a by-election at Hillhead, Glasgow, at the end of March 1982, it was a victory over a party whose leader had shown extraordinarily little sign of flinching.

It was upon this desolate scene that the Falklands victory worked its magical political effect. After the war, it was often pointed out, especially by Conservatives, that even before it the Government was recovering in the polls and the SDP–Liberal Alliance beginning to go down. And that is true enough. But the shift was not so great, nor were the reasons for it so clear, that any sensible Tory could have counted on it being maintained. As a basis for discounting the Falklands effect on the fortunes of the Thatcher Government it seems singularly inadequate. While nobody can be certain what would have happened if the war had never taken place, there is no room for disputing that the victory started a steady process of decline in Alliance fortunes and abruptly lifted the Tories on to a plateau of public support which, six months earlier, would have seemed quite unattainable. It removed all hope the other parties entertained of improving their situation.

In Labour's case, admittedly, such a hope looked fanciful. When the war began, it had staunched some of the bloodiness of 1981. The contest for the deputy leadership between Denis Healey and Tony Benn, having been the focal point for extremes of bitterness, went to Healey by the skin of his teeth, whereupon the party right embarked upon attempts to purge and modernise. The Militant Tendency, a Trotskyite party within the party, came under attack. The promise to get out of the European Community was diluted into irrelevance. Optimists like Healey began to talk as though they could see their way through towards a new credibility.

However, the objective realities argued against them. Quite apart from the divisions, there was the leader. Yet another advantage for Mrs Thatcher, a very personal one, in her early years as prime minister was that the peculiarly symbiotic connection between her office and that of Opposition leader was established on a footing which favoured her in every particular.

Michael Foot, Labour's compromise choice in 1980, possessed no qualities which could disguise or compensate for the fundamental weakness of his party. He was a very decent man, affectionately regarded by the great majority of socialists. But he offered no serious forensic challenge to the prime minister's sharp-taloned technique, with which his long-winded expressions of general indignation were regularly gouged to pieces in the House of Commons. Nor had time improved him. His bulldog style during the war, besides being an embarrassment to one section of his party, never concealed the fact that he was and would always remain a weak leader.

After the war, the third party was in scarcely better case. It began to be steadily swept aside. By August its opinion-poll support was reduced to 23 per cent. Less than six months earlier, when I put it to Roy Jenkins that the Alliance would get no more than seventy seats at the next election, he expressed disbelief in such a modest expectation. But now the trend-line made that figure look ambitious. Although there was one other spectacular by-election triumph, at Bermondsey, south London, in February 1983, the quarterly average of all published polls for the second half of 1982 and the first half of 1983 never showed the Alliance higher than 25 per cent.

There was nothing in the nature of Thatcherism, nor any brilliant stratagem in the mind of its leader, which brought these propitious circumstances about. Socialism, certainly, was presented with a frontal ideological challenge, which would grow more irresistible through the 1980s. This, as we shall see later, was a durable mark and one of the tests by which the lady herself wished to be judged. It was no necessary part of such an evolution that Labour should first be split apart. That happened by a series of chances and blunders, in which chronically weak leadership and a steadfast refusal to modernise were the decisive factors. Its origins, moreover, lay in the pre-Thatcher era. Neither Margaret Thatcher nor the Conservative Party had much to do with the crack-up. It was a largely uncovenanted blessing. Yet it produced among the forces ranged against the most unpopular British leader of modern times, on the one hand a party that was unelectable, on the other a grouping destined merely to be a vote-splitter. No radical visionary, now beginning in the aftermath of war to raise her historical sights, could have asked for more.

At the time, the future did not seem anything like so predetermined. To practising politicians it rarely does. What seems obvious later – what was, indeed, in this case objectively and irrefutably true – is obscured in the fog of anxiety which clouds the judgment of people in this vulnerable trade, especially when they are within sight of being put to the test at a general election.

On 10 September 1982, the prime minister chaired a meeting

of what was known as the Liaison Committee. This body, which concerned itself with the presentation of government policy, was mainly composed of ministers and party workers, and included, for example, the marketing director from Conservative Central Office as well as the head of the Conservative Research Department. But sitting with them, significantly, was a civil servant, Bernard Ingham, the prime minister's press secretary, his presence a testimony to the intimate linkage, even beyond the bounds of Whitehall propriety, between party and government machines. The papers prepared for this committee reveal the decidedly uncertain mood of the party less than three months after the recapture of Port Stanley.

'Few voters have a clear view of the government's overall economic strategy, its objectives and how it is meant to work' was one summarising verdict. There was evidence that 'half the voters think the government is deliberately making unemployment high to curb union pay demands.' Several key aspects of policy were simply not understood in the way they should be. For example, while nationalisation had always been unpopular, privatisation 'has not yet had time to acquire much positive electoral support'. It was now vital, this paper concluded, 'to convince people that we have a strategy and that it will in due course deliver the goods'.

There followed some helpful hints on how to set about rectifying this deplorable situation. Ministers should emphasise that there were no quick fixes, that unemployment and inflation were not alternatives but blood brothers, that the Government was 'tackling the long-term problems' and 'reversing the long-term decline'.

Other policies were also being sadly misrepresented. The great achievement of protecting the National Health Service in a period of recession needed more powerful exposition. Spending on education was perceived to have gone down when in fact it had gone up. Bernard Ingham, for his part, weighed in with a paper identifying miners' pay, the Common Market budget and the next round of anti-union legislation as issues which posed especially acute presentational problems.

What emerges from the minutes of this meeting, as it did from almost every conversation with a Government minister at that time and well into 1983, is the reverse of confident triumphalism. The prime minister herself, on the other hand, chafed at the spirit of caution.

A few days before the Liaison Committee met, and unknown to most of those present who were worrying about the Government's inability to get across even what it had done so far, a giant leap forward, far more challenging to conventional pieties, was proposed in a paper circulated to the cabinet on the prime minister's authority. It was an event of much symbolic moment in the history of the first Thatcher term, throwing light not least on the balance between the prime minister's reckless radicalism and her openness, in extreme circumstances, to correction by her ministers.

The paper was prepared by the Central Policy Review Staff, or government Think Tank, as a contribution to long-term thinking about public spending. It was addressed to a forecast that seemed likely to blow much of the Thatcherite enterprise out of the water: namely, that on the assumption of economic growth at less than 1 per cent a year public spending, on current projections, would consume 47 per cent of gross domestic product by 1990, or 6 per cent more than the share inherited by the Thatcher Government in 1979. Sponsored by the Treasury, the paper arrived with a lugubrious commentary by Chancellor Howe, suggesting that it should form the basis for a six-month study to determine a public spending strategy for the decade.

The Think Tank's proposals were hair-raisingly radical. Education cuts could be usefully achieved, it suggested, by ending state funding for all institutions of higher education. Student loans should replace grants, with a limited number of state scholarships provided after a means test. The massive welfare budget could be slashed by stopping all benefits rising in line with inflation. On the health service, the Tank suggested its complete replacement with a system of private health insurance, which could save £3 billion on the 1982–3 budget of £10 billion. Additionally there should be charges for doctors' visits and higher charges for drugs.

When they received this paper, out of the blue, many cabinet ministers were horrified. They could not see the economic, let alone the political, sense in it. The wets, in particular, wanted it to get no further. So they devised a double-sided strategy.

The first part was to stop cabinet discussion in its tracks. The wets wanted to signify that the Think Tank's startling programme was deemed not worthy of further consideration. On 9 September, in a rare display of unity, they succeeded in forcing it off the agenda, against the wishes of the prime minister as well as of Howe and his Treasury sidekick, Leon Brittan, the Chief Secretary. But this would not necessarily be enough. So the second device was to leak the contents of the paper to *The Economist*, action commonly believed to have been undertaken by the Agriculture Secretary, Peter Walker, the most unrepentant if not always the most reliable of all wets.

It was this unauthorised act of open government that finally killed the CPRS proposal for a six-month study in thinking the unthinkable. The prime minister was furious, but chastened. Various exercises in damage-limitation were undertaken, including the pretence that the whole thing had been an error not by her but by the cabinet secretary, Sir Robert Armstrong, who had mistakenly circulated the paper and put it on the agenda. This contention was greeted with ridicule by those who heard it, aware, as one of them put it, that 'not a fly moves on the wall without her knowing'. Newspapers were briefed to the effect that she opposed the Think Tank report and really had nothing to do with it.

This was not the case. She had clung on to it until, following the *Economist* story, the majority of ministers told her she had made a terrible blunder. Lord Hailsham said in cabinet: 'It is the worst mistake the Government has made since it came to power.' When the voices were collected she said, in what one minister called a petulant huff, 'All right then, shelve it.'

They each had their own opinion about why the blunder had occurred. Jim Prior probably came closest to the truth. He put it down to the Falklands effect. 'Does anyone imagine she would have dared to circulate the paper if it hadn't been for Falklands euphoria?' he privately inquired. That euphoria, together with the opinion polls which were its temperature gauge, was inducing in the prime minister a quite false sense of confidence, thought Prior. And he was not alone.

This, perhaps, was the point of the Think Tank episode. It agitated nerve-ends in circles well beyond the shrinking band of wets. Few ministers at the time were more imbued with radical aspirations than they were with apprehension. For most, the need to do something severe about public spending ranked rather less prominently than the need not to frighten the natives any more than they were frightened already. (And as it turned out they were right. Well before 1990, economic growth had accelerated far past the CPRS's niggardly predictions to a rate as high as 4 per cent in 1987–8, which naturally put public spending, as a proportion of gross domestic product, on a reducing path.)

There was no enthusiasm for an attack on social spending, in short, because every minister outside the Treasury, with the single exception of the eccentric, apolitical and unelected Trade Secretary, Lord Cockfield, remained more or less unsure of the Government's political

301

standing. They could not judge with confidence how the tides of three-party politics would move. After three years of intense unpopularity, they could not persuade themselves there was any wisdom in even privately discussing a serious assault on such sacred parts of the British way of life as the health service and public education.

The talk at that time was not of victory but of a phenomenon last seen in the Callaghan days, the 'hung Parliament'. This was how it seemed to the likes of John Biffen and the Employment Secretary, Norman Tebbit, on the right, just as it did to Jim Prior and Francis Pym, not to mention Whitelaw. It was a period when publishers thought it worth producing academic studies of the implications and modalities of minority government.[1]

What worried the politicians, and inspired the academics, wasn't the Labour Party but the SDP and the Liberals. Even on a downward path of popularity, they looked capable of menacing most of the old calculations. Elaborate and alarming sums began to dominate the lives of ministers, computing the ratio of votes to seats the third party might win: seats which, as they all observed, were almost all held by Conservatives.

Although Tebbit was disposed to marvel at the Government's high standing in the polls, he could not quite reconcile this with the unrelentingly high level of unemployment, now standing at over 3 million. Although Whitelaw took comfort from a private prediction he had heard Jim Callaghan make, that Labour could not win, his own opinion was that the Alliance would do better than now seemed likely from the polls. If there was an end in sight to his own political career, he once reflected, it would certainly be reached if he saw any prospect of serving in a coalition cabinet cheek by jowl with the Liberal MP Cyril Smith. Until well into 1983, Biffen, who had some claim to see himself as the most realistic man in the cabinet, thought a hung Parliament not merely possible but the most likely of all results.

What they all agreed on, however, was that there could be no change of course. While it was elementary politics to avoid the trap set by the Think Tank, it was equally important not to be seen to deviate the other way. Whitelaw was particularly clear about this. The Government was stuck with its record and must make a virtue of its rigour. The worst thing, he said, would be a giveaway budget. It would lose the party all credibility. Unemployment was terrible – 'nobody has ever won an election with three million unemployed before,' he dolefully ruminated – yet there was nothing for it but to hope that the other parties were severally and collectively unelectable.

But what he placed most hope in, as did all the wets and drys alike, was the contest that would inevitably dominate the election, whenever it came: the comparison between the leaders. Partly this rested on a negative assessment of the Opposition. The most widespread fear gripping senior ministers between autumn 1982 and spring 1983 was that the Labour Party would summon itself to dispose of Michael Foot and replace him with Denis Healey. Healey, well aware that this would be his last opportunity, was wholly apprised of the circumstances in which it might be accomplished. If it were done near enough to the election, the whole elaborate machinery of the new electoral college could be circumvented on grounds of time. Even until a late hour Healey had hopes that the party would see its situation to be so dire that the deed might be done. For just as long, Tories feared that Labour would shoot their fox, the aged and uncharismatic Foot, and expose their leader to more equal competition.

But there was a positive side as well. This leader was now an asset. It was a great contrast with 1979, perhaps the biggest one of all. With politics rooted in a long pre-electoral phase, one development that was scarcely disputable was how far the leader herself had come. Most of the reservations which weakened and damaged her in 1979 had now been set aside, and not least the largest one, billowing round her name, generating doubts among all conditions and classes, adding a whole troublesome dimension of difficulty which none of her predecessors had experienced. This had now been disposed of. Margaret Thatcher had proved it was possible to be a woman and be prime minister, and live to fight for a second term.

In the 1979 election, she ran far behind her party, and even further behind her chief opponent, James Callaghan. At the end of 1982, with 1983 certain to be the next election year, her popularity remained, after its brief post-Falklands resuscitation, well behind the party's. But her situation was nonetheless transformed. She was established in political leadership. Around this burgeoning personality, nothing wove a more complex web than her femininity.

Its importance was then, and has remained, a matter of some dispute. This is not surprising. There were competing and contradictory aspects of her gender, as it related both to her rise to the top and to the way she handled herself when she got there.

One school of thought, perhaps the most voluble, held that she actually discarded most of the significant gender traits and became, for all practical purposes, an honorary man. This was an intelligible analysis. Politics is a male world, and nobody can succeed in it without some of the qualities commonly associated with masculinity. In one sense, she could not help becoming an honorary man from the moment she became leader of the party, a condition aptly symbolised by her admission, after considerable grumbling among the baffled clubmen, to honorary membership of the all-male Conservative stronghold, the Carlton Club. Since all previous party leaders had belonged, there seemed no way of excluding the present one, although her installation was not followed by any further concessions to female Tories.

Some of this leader's most prominent characteristics were not obviously womanly. She set great store by domination and executive command. In public she rarely showed emollience. Her approach to most situations turned them into a struggle which she had to win. In peace and war, she prided herself on her toughness. Her speech was often harsh, her demeanour self-consciously severe.

At best, on this view, while plainly remaining a woman, she used womanhood merely as a helpful device. 'She shows how much femininity is a production,' Beatrix Campbell writes. 'Femininity is what she wears, masculinity is what she admires.'[2]

Campbell distinguishes between gender and sexuality, judging that while the former is important the latter, the real heart of the feminine, is concealed to the point of conscious insignificance. 'Is this a function of age?' Campbell inquires. 'That a middle-aged suburban woman is not represented as sexual in white Anglo-Saxon culture? Is it because she is a married woman and a mother, facts which both express sexuality and make it inaccessible? Is it because the arsenal of criticism fired at Margaret Thatcher, surely one of the most personally disliked politicians since the war, de-eroticises her?' A condition summarised in one common verdict: 'She's not a real woman.' Or, as Jimmy Carter's national security adviser, Zbigniew Brzezinski, once said: 'In her presence you pretty quickly forget that she's a woman. She doesn't strike me as being a very female type.'[3]

Campbell's preferred explanation is the lady's preoccupation with maleness and manly virtues. This, according to the inquiring feminist, made itself clear in some of her favourite reiterations. 'It is not femininity but buccaneering masculinity which is evoked in her celebration of Victorian values, of the prime ministers who came before her, of "merchant venturers".'

Another, subtler, feminist perspective is offered by Marina Warner. Warner notes the role of the media, especially the cartoonists in the tabloid press, in conferring on this female leader an intimate identification with Britannia.[4] Especially after the Falklands war, the traditional allegory, which casts queen as country, attached itself in popular mythology to the person of the prime minister: a device which did not deny femininity but exalted it.

Warner also emphasises a de-eroticised quality. The sexual woman, she suggests, has been replaced by the nanny, the matron, the governess. 'Margaret Thatcher has tapped an enormous source of female power: the right of prohibition.' Her toughness, her 'flintiness', her 'piercing' quality are not designed, according to Warner, to prove that she is as good as a man 'but that she is not under the governance of Venus, that she is a stranger to the exactions and weaknesses of the heart, that her most private organ is her gut'.

What is certainly not disputable is the reluctance of this controlled and controlling woman to treat women, politically, as any different from men. She was against this on principle, apparently seeing nothing in her own rise to power which might prompt her to single women out for special attention, or consciously single out herself and her sex and the special effects this might have on her political strategy. Women as a separate category of voters were not of special interest. Patrick Cosgrave, who worked for her, once proposed to do some private polling to investigate this relationship with a view to seeing how it could be further exploited. He later recorded her put-down: 'Since my draft idea for a poll depended on an emphasis on her sexual identity, she turned the scheme down flat.'[5]

A woman whom some fondly expected to give women and their advancement priority in fact did exactly the opposite. Although she had always had a job herself, whether working for Joe Lyons or reading for the Bar or becoming an MP, she led no sort of crusade for others to do the same. Before she got anywhere in politics, she was, as we have seen, strident in her assertion that women were as entitled as men to succeed in public life. She was saying this as early as 1952. When she had reached the top, a change came over the balance of her rhetoric. She became a lot more ready to praise the Conservative model of the housewife and mother. As for positive discrimination or anything which smacked of feminism, she was derisive.

Both prejudices were epitomised in a lecture she gave in July 1982, commemorating, rather oddly, a revered Liberal feminist, Margery

Ashby. First there was praise for domesticity. Contemplating the women's suffragettes, Mrs Thatcher noted that 'they had the inestimable privilege of being wives and mothers and they pursued their public work against the background of full and happy domestic lives. They neglected no detail of those lives. . . . The home should be the centre but not the boundary of a woman's life.' But then there was the assertion that nothing more was needed to change the condition of women. 'The battle for women's rights has largely been won,' she said. 'The days when they were demanded and discussed in strident tones should be gone for ever. I hate those strident tones we hear from some Women's Libbers.'[6]

Even to less demanding feminists, her attitudes actually looked worse than that. Never mind her incomprehension of women's liberation, she declined, they thought, to be sensitive in more elementary matters. Barbara Castle, who as a Labour cabinet minister in the 1960s preceded her as leading woman in this male world, thought she could have been far more perceptive about the particular difficulties ordinary women faced. Her attitude to the social services, Mrs Castle contended, showed that 'she's had no compassion at all for the working woman struggling to deal with a home, earn a wage, deal with an elderly parent, perhaps a mentally handicapped child, and sickness in the family.'[7]

So several outward signs, from the severity of her manner to the aggression of her anti-feminist ideology, argue for taking her at what seemed like her own valuation: as a woman in a man's world neither demanding nor receiving concessions to her femininity. Yet that account left a gap in her manifest personality. It might have quite aptly described some other women politicians. Shirley Williams, Social Democrat and near-contemporary, was free of these disabling prejudices, being a healer not a warrior by temperament and more of an egalitarian feminist by conviction. In Mrs Thatcher's case, leaving sex out of the picture became, as time went by, a steadily more misleading violation of the truth.

First, it so obviously mattered very much to her. What Campbell diminishes as a femininity concerned merely with 'what she wears' was, nonetheless, very feminine. Barbara Castle noticed this from the beginning. Her diary at the time the Thatcher leadership started is full of private solidarity with this amazing opponent who had risen to the top ahead of every man. At an early Question Time, Mrs Castle noted her appearance: 'She sat with bowed head and detached primness . . . hair immaculately groomed, smart dress crowned by a string of pearls.' At the same time, the diarist writes, she brought out a kind of male gallantry which she obviously enjoyed. 'Margaret's election has stirred up her own side wonderfully: all her backbenchers perform like knights jousting at a tourney for a lady's favours, showing off their paces by making an unholy row at every opportunity over everything the government does.'

Throughout her public life, she gave the greatest care to her appearance. Mrs Castle used to find that Mrs Thatcher's wardrobe had virtually taken over the lady MPs' room in the Commons. 'The row of pegs was always filled with her clothes,' she recalled. 'There would be half-a-dozen garments hanging up there and underneath them a tidy row of at least eight pairs of shoes. I can only assume that she slipped there from the opposition front bench, nipped into this little room and did her quick-change act between great parliamentary scenes.'[8]

The only woman to be admitted to her cabinet, Janet Young, who was leader of the House of Lords from 1981 to 1983, noted how attentive she was to her skin and complexion. 'When you meet her, you know this is a woman,' Lady Young once remarked to me. Nor did she trouble to conceal her detailed interest in these feminine concerns in the interviews she gave to women's magazines, which appeared so frequently, year in and year out, as to indicate that behind her refusal to permit Cosgrave's scientific inquiry there in fact lay a shrewd understanding of her particular female constituency.

She sometimes did the same on television. Only someone at least partly a woman's woman could have agreed to show her wardrobe to the viewing masses, as Mrs Thatcher once did on the BBC.[9] She had arranged for the cameras a rack of favourite clothes, and went through them with quite innocent pleasure. 'This black one came through the Falklands war all right,' she enthused over one suit. 'Clothes should be a background not a foreground,' she decreed as a general rule of public dressing. Black and blue were best, because brighter colours tended to distract attention, and frills should always be avoided. Her underclothes, she announced, came from Marks & Spencer.

Only a woman, surely, would have enthusiastically collaborated in such an invasion of her privacy, and by no means every woman at that. Certainly it would be hard to imagine any of her predecessors in Downing Street publicising the name of his tailor, still less the supplier of his hosiery.

It was not just by her keenness on womanish things, however, that she showed herself to be different from a male prime minister. There were other outward signs. For example, she wasn't ashamed to weep in public. This could happen on occasions devoid of sentiment. 'I once saw Margaret Thatcher weep. It was in Lusaka in 1979,' wrote Owen Harries, at the time an adviser and speech-writer to the Australian prime minister, Malcolm Fraser. It happened, he said, when she failed to get her way over a detail in the preliminaries to the Rhodesian settlement.[10] But more usually the tears flowed in moments of personal emotion: when bad news came in from the Falklands, or after an IRA atrocity. When her son, Mark, disappeared during a trans-Sahara motor rally in January 1982, she spent six days in a state of extreme anxiety, frequently weeping, sometimes in public. Reporters who caught her off guard before she addressed a lunchtime meeting at a London hotel found her in the foyer crying quite openly when there was still no news.[11]

Nor was she above deploying such emotion in what seemed a more calculated way. Once, on television, the very memory of what happened to her father was enough to summon it up. She was describing how Alfred had been thrown off the Grantham council when the office of alderman was abolished. Plainly this had eaten into her heart. She recalled how he had laid down his aldermanic robe. 'I remember when my father was turned off that council, including his speech for the last time. Very emotional. "In honour I took up this gown and in honour I lay it down." That's how he felt.' Almost theatrically, she produced a handkerchief and brushed away a tear at the thought of it.[12]

But tears weren't the only manifestation that she was indeed a woman and, as a woman, different. There was also her role as hostess, pursued with as much tireless dedication on small occasions as on large. After her trip to China she held a small reception for everyone on her plane, including cabin staff and journalists as well as officials. Arriving late, I was immediately led on my own private journey round the public rooms. Number 10 Downing Street had been 'a furnished flat to rent' when she took it over, she briskly chattered: nothing on the surfaces, other people's choices on the walls. She'd changed it all. Here was the silver from Lord Brownlow (descendant of Alfred's aldermanic colleague), there the portraits she'd personally chosen: a good Nelson, a better Pitt, a special corner for scientists including a bust of Grantham's own Isaac Newton, one or two Turners, one or two Romneys, and only one solitary foreign painting, a small Corot landscape. Now it was more like the public home she wanted. Obviously she had given hundreds of visitors the same tour, the tour of a house-proud tenant which few people had enjoyed from Callaghan, Wilson, Heath, Douglas-Home, Macmillan or Churchill.

Her sex, however, went beyond her private consciousness and instinctive behaviour. It was an unavoidably important element of her relationship with her public, noticed by all and commented on by many. We have seen, for example, how awe-struck she rendered the male-dominated society of Japan. But the French, more sophisticated in such matters, were hardly less ready to speak of her in tones of submissive adulation, for her femininity if not her political behaviour. Before a visit to France, in March 1980, she was interviewed for French television. The interviewer emerged from Downing Street and told *Le Figaro* that he kept the memory of a woman 'full of charm and seduction whose radiating presence conceals a great authority and a deep-seated desire to infuse some warmth into the climate of Franco-British relations'.

Le Quotidien de Paris, still more lyrically, permitted itself to speak of this political leader in terms it could not have begun to employ about a man, even one it admired to distraction. Mrs Thatcher, it said, should not be called the Iron Lady, 'for that metal is too vile, too obscure'. She was, instead, 'a woman of uranium, with peculiar irradiations. Compared to her, how leaden appear most of our leaders, opaque masses of flesh, austere fortresses without windows, save for the loopholes of deceit and the skylights of hidden pride. Power corrupts a man but liberates a woman and reveals her for what she is.'

Not all foreigners were so enchanted. The closer they got, the more vexed they often became. 'You must tell your prime minister', a German official told EEC Commissioner Christopher Tugendhat, after the interim settlement of the British budget contribution in May 1980, 'that she hurt my Chancellor [Helmut Schmidt] in his male pride. If things are to be put right between our two countries, she must find a way of making it up to him.'[13]

To European statesmen, the female in their midst presented a double problem. It evidently hurt them in their maleness if she beat them. But she also to some extent disabled them before the issue was determined. Viscount Davignon, a vice-president of the European Commission from 1977 to 1984, observed the process as a man of the world. 'They felt it was more difficult to be rough with a woman than with another man,' he said. 'And so being challenged by a woman disconcerted them. If it had been a man they could have said "Shut up".'[14]

By 1985, Davignon thought, it was no longer a problem. The Europeans had got used to her, and gave no quarter. Whether the same was ever true of the Conservative Party is another matter. There the gender factor came up against the indestructible psychic conditioning of the English middle-class male. This was not well adapted to dealing with an aggressive woman. Julian Critchley, discussing the received opinion that the best way to deal with their leader was to 'stand up for yourself, shout back, argue the toss, and then she will respect you', also noted the drawback to this course of action. 'We've always been brought up to believe that it's extremely rude to shout back at women,' he said.[15]

Critchley, who was never a minister, spoke somewhat theoretically. Jim Prior saw things at close quarters and confirms the difficulties he could never surmount. The Thatcher method, he reports in his doleful autobiography, the confessions of a beaten man, depended heavily on challenge: seemingly incessant confrontations based on detailed briefing and a desire to press her antagonist, who could be any minister or official, to the limit. Prior found that such constant aggression exposed his own weaknesses. 'It is not a style which endears, and perhaps even less so when the challenger is a woman and the challenged a man,' he writes. 'I have to confess that I found it very difficult to stomach and this form of male chauvinism was obviously one of my failings.'[16]

But there was another side to the virago, her capacity to allure. Visitors calling on her for the first time attested to the sex appeal she could project in a private conversation. She was reckoned by her ministers to have a particular weakness for handsome men of a certain age, who stood up straight and wore well-cut suits: a preference of which the most conspicuous beneficiary was widely agreed to have been Humphrey Atkins, chief whip throughout her leadership of the Opposition and later Northern Ireland Secretary. Robert Armstrong had a small encounter which he never forgot. At a cabinet meeting her earrings were obviously pinching her. 'As the meeting went on, she removed one of them,' he once told me, 'and as she did so she gave me a sidelong look of total amused complicity. It was a completely male–female moment.'

Jim Prior, equally, records one moment when he was not being beaten about the head. A newspaper had commented on the 'sexy' voice she had developed on a radio programme. In fact this was the result of a cold. When Prior next saw her, he said, 'Margaret, I read in my paper that you have developed a sexy voice.' Back came her reply: 'What makes you think I wasn't sexy before?'[17]

The fact is that sex, if not sexiness, was incontestably a conscious part of the Thatcher personality as a political leader. It always had been, and could not have been otherwise. She couldn't fail to be acutely aware of the disability under which it placed her, especially in her early days – as the constant references in her speeches showed. 'If you want something said, ask a man. If you want something done, ask a woman,' she trumpeted to the Townswomen's Guilds in 1965. At the 1969 party conference she quoted Sophocles: 'Once a woman is made equal to a man, she becomes his superior.'

When this woman had become superior to the men, she remained a woman. If she was best known for male qualities, such as aggression and domination, these were doubtless explicable by her feminine predicament: they were necessary, in large quantity, to combat the aggression and domination to which the surrounding males would otherwise subject her. Has any woman deficient in hardness ever succeeded in politics, anywhere in the world? Has any man, come to that? Margaret Thatcher possessed this universally necessary ingredient, but it coexisted with attributes men could not in fact lay claim to.

Janet Young, sensitive to the woman's strange place in this circle, thought there were two particular ways in which femininity and political leadership intermingled. 'Being a woman makes her decisive,' she reflected, when still observing Mrs Thatcher at close quarters in government.

> Women have to make instant decisions, admittedly of a minor kind, like what shoes to buy for the children and what to have for supper. This gives them a natural decisiveness which applies itself to larger fields. But there is also a great caution, again very feminine. An anxiety in human terms about the effects of an action. It could be seen in Mrs Thatcher during the Falklands. The men were discussing the casualties in cold figures, but you could see that wasn't the way she was thinking about them. This made her cautious.

Caution, in fact, was not the quality most commonly associated with her as the first electoral test of her leadership approached. Strength and lack of compassion were much more widely perceived. And as for anxiety about the effects of her actions, cold indifference to the misery of unemployment was an essential accompaniment to the economic policy, and the evidence suggests that she possessed more of this than any prime minister of the twentieth century. But her ratings had risen on most of the measures that mattered, and she was now judged predominantly as a leader and nothing else. Without discarding womanhood, she had transcended it. A Mori opinion poll told the story of what had changed between April 1979 and April 1983. Four years before, only 34 per cent of voters thought she 'understands the problems facing Britain'. Now the figure was up to 40. Then, 30 per cent thought she 'has a lot of personality' and 21 per cent that she was 'more honest than most politicians'. These, too, had now risen to 41 and 30 respectively. Where 26 per cent used to think her 'a capable leader', four years' experience put this up to 56 per cent. As for being 'rather inexperienced', the figure was now statistically insignificant, down from 28 per cent in 1979 to 3 per cent in 1983.

Her most glaring weakness was a strange one. It showed perhaps the limitations of a feminine nature when hoisted into the highest place: not its lack of central importance but the way in which it was seen by many people to elevate the prime minister too far above the masses. She did, after all, make great play with her role as housewife. The image was used repeatedly to illustrate how the national economy should be run and how this woman, unlike any man, could apply the household economist's down-to-earth experience of making ends meet. It came out in many an interview: repeated tales of making Denis his morning cup of tea, tidying the kitchen in her private flat, sorting out her linen. But for some reason these bids for ordinariness stubbornly failed to reflect themselves in her reputation with the voters. On her rating as 'down to earth', the Mori poll showed a decline from 24 to 18 per cent. Her tendency to 'talk down to people' was noted by 53 per cent where only 31 per cent had mentioned it before.

This worried her handlers, now readying themselves for the most expensive sales campaign in the history of British politics. Maurice Saatchi, salesman in chief, saw a flaw in the product and it bothered him. Every poll said in one way or another that she was 'out of touch with real life', he told me in early 1983. She had most of the other virtues. But somehow her very uniqueness had caused her to ascend inconveniently towards the stratosphere.

At Chequers, early in the first week in January 1983, the prime minister held her first serious discussion about the date of the election. It consisted mainly of a concerted argument by three or four of her intimates in favour of waiting no later than June: a case which she resolutely declined to concede. A week later, however, she arrived out of an empty sky in the Falkland Islands. Her journey, arduously cooped up in a military plane, was a complete surprise, her arrival a brilliant *coup de théâtre* engineered chiefly by cabinet secretary Armstrong, who later remarked, not entirely in jest, that getting the prime minister to the Falklands without anyone knowing she had gone was the proudest of his achievements to date. To other observers it was immediately apparent that the election was now unlikely to be long delayed.

In Port Stanley, the freedom of the Falklands was conferred on Margaret Hilda Thatcher, and she responded with a speech reliving the dire days of war. Everyone had their own memories, she said, adding, with small concession to modesty, that 'somehow history is something that happens to other people, and then all of a sudden we found ourselves making history here in these islands.' A select group of reporters had been let into the secret and was on hand to record her journey through the battlefields. So was the BBC, to whom her press secretary, Bernard Ingham, issued fearsome threats of retribution if they did not hand over all their film to the rival network. Although the new Falklands honorand was to reiterate for months that she had far more important things to think about than the election, it was as obvious as it was appropriate that she should open her campaign in the location where its outcome, for all the professional pessimism of many ministers, had in fact already been determined.

Presiding over preparations for this campaign was a new star in the Tory firmament, the brightest jewel of Mrs Thatcher's personal creation. Cecil Parkinson had been one of those present at the little New Year's gathering at Chequers, saying like the others that June looked the best bet. But of those there he was already the most intimate of all with the leader: the very first of her protégés, unheard of until she picked him out, who achieved maximum national prominence. Socially as well as politically, Parkinson personified a kind of fulfilment of the Thatcher ideal.

The son of a railwayman, he had graduated through grammar school to Cambridge and then become a chartered accountant. As an accountant he built a large variety of business interests, notably in the construction trade, and grew quite rich, though not as rich as he would have liked. Proud of his upward mobility from working-class origins, Parkinson nevertheless had a clear idea of the limitations they might impose on an ambitious politician. Financial independence was the key, and as he saw it there were only two ways it could be achieved: either by being born into great wealth or by a swift and purposeful escalation from the very bottom to the very top. Too many Conservatives, Parkinson observed, were marooned somewhere in the middle, deprived by politics of the chance to become seriously rich, and driven frantically to keep up to a standard of living they couldn't afford. For him it was going to be different. But when he got into Parliament, at a by-election in November 1970, he still had some way to go.

He continued on a rising path, however, up to and including his first preferment. He was, fleetingly, a junior whip during the last two months of the Heath Government, and remained in the whips' office after the change of leadership. It was now, he would later recall, that he had his greatest business successes, 'doing it all on Fridays'. By the time Mrs Thatcher became prime minister, he had duly reached a state of considerable prosperity. He also satisfied a number of familiar Thatcher tests. He was self-made, could read a balance-sheet, and he had had nothing to do with Heath. In addition, he was a clean-limbed-looking fellow, plausible on television and smartly presented.

Even so, his elevation from Minister of Trade, where he travelled much and was rarely seen, was one of the more surprising features of the 1981 reshuffle. At his first party conference, he cut a somewhat cardboard figure and was widely construed to be a featureless Thatcher puppet, so assiduously did he smile and applaud from the chairman's seat. This impression was misleading. Their relationship, as later appeared, was far more complicated.

By 1983, after eighteen months in the job, he had made quite a mark on the Conservative Party. When he took over from the aged Thorneycroft, the organisation was depressed after forty staff redundancies and no pay rise for two years. Parkinson imported glamour, as well as a natural interest in the most modern marketing skills. The Saatchi advances in 1979 had by no means exhausted the possibilities available in the commercial salesman's methodology. The new chairman showed his hand by appointing an old friend, Christopher Lawson, as the party's marketing director[18] and introducing British voters to the wonders of direct mailing.

What pushed Parkinson into a new league, however, was the Falklands war, when he was brought into the inner cabinet, much to the envious disgust of his contemporaries. The war supplied Cecil with a quantum leap, in the eyes of friends and enemies alike. It also made him think even better of himself. He was always somewhat resentful of the common assumption that he had come from nowhere into the chairmanship, and would point out with an edge of indignation the richness of his earlier *cursus honorum*. Had he not been the youngest chairman of the Hemel Hempstead Conservative Association? Won power on the local council there? Scored the highest vote ever recorded by a Conservative in a parliamentary election in Northampton, even though he hadn't quite won it in 1970? People had tended to forget his diligent record. But now it mattered less, because he was helping to run a war, something no modern politician could ever have expected to be involved in. Moreover, he was no patsy in that war. He talked, as all would testify, toughly to the generals, especially at moments when they voiced their doubts about whether the recapture of the islands was actually a practical proposition.

But the chief legacy of the Falklands for Parkinson was the link it solidified between him and Mrs Thatcher. He possessed a quality that eluded the great majority of his colleagues: a talent difficult to explain, impossible quite to trace to its origin, but crucial to the mutual respect in which they held each other. He was able to make her stop and listen. Somehow she liked him and came to respect him. It had something to do with his willingness, although younger than she was, to treat her as a woman. It also grew in part out of his well-tuned political judgment. He turned out to have excellent instincts for assessing any situation, and going straight to the heart of the Conservative interest in it. He had an unerring eye for the important message in any opinion poll. Unafraid of journalists, rejoicing in every last detail of media manipulation, he was a chairman in whom the leader reposed a comfortable confidence as together they faced the electoral test. He made a fussing, worried, preoccupied woman feel rather luxuriously at ease.

He needed to. For what song did they have to sing, what message to convey? All ministers were aware that by most conventional tests it was deeply uninspiring. If you took the pieces apart and looked at the record, it could be faulted for many things: promises unkept, results unachieved, consistency unattained. If you pretended, for a moment, that the Opposition was a real opposition, rather than being divided between a demoralised rabble and an unconvincing third force, any clear-headed analysis would confirm that the Conservatives' popular appeal rested so heavily on future assurances rather than on past performance as to be wide open to destruction.

To begin with, unemployment continued quite inexorably to increase. It rose from 1.2 million in May 1979 to 3 million in May 1983. If there hadn't been several changes in the basis on which the figures were calculated, another 300,000 would have appeared in the latest total. Yet another 350,000 were accounted for by special employment measures which kept them out of the headline tallies. The number of long-term unemployed, without a job for more than a year, was very nearly as great as the total number out of work when the Tories took over.

They weren't short of explanations, but not all of these were creditable. The vertiginous collapse in national output, of which unemployment was the direct consequence, wasn't entirely due to rational policies rationally arrived at. Gross domestic product fell by more than 3 per cent over the whole period, but by 5.5 per cent in the first half, during the relentless squeeze from 1979 to 1981. Output in manufacturing industry up to 1982 fell by more than 15 per cent. All this was happening far more sharply in Britain than anywhere else in the industrialised world, partly because monetarism implied a number of brutal choices but also because the value of sterling was permitted to surge to such a height as to make industry even less competitive than it had been already.

For a long time, the exchange rate was seen as beyond the proper reach of monetarist politicians. It was what William Keegan calls 'an act of God about which the Government could do little'.[19] Belatedly, ministers recognised the terrible damage it was doing. Patrick Jenkin, who succeeded Keith Joseph as Industry Secretary, was often critical of what he had inherited by way of a philosophy which said that the cold draught of competition, however unnecessary, was a therapy that justified maintaining the high pound. Joseph, characteristically, would admit the terrible havoc it had wrought, wiping out businesses by the thousand. But he continued to attribute it to forces out of the Government's control, notably the relentless currency pressures imposed by North Sea oil. Much later, and again in character, he reflected upon the handiwork of the first term with the detached bemusement of the laboratory technician who has found the materials at his disposal failing to behave according to the textbooks.

'We hadn't appreciated, any of us,' he said, 'that an oil-strong currency, and hence a strong exchange rate, coupled with intense world competitiveness, would lead to such rapid and large demanning.' Unemployment, he went on, 'had not been considered a huge problem'. Ministers had assumed that the trade unions would see the need to get unit costs down and would co-operate. 'Alas, they didn't.'[20]

No matter what the reason, the record on output, and with it unemployment, was an electoral politician's nightmare. No end to it was in sight. There were repeated promises of corners being turned and lights in tunnels. As early as December 1980, when John Nott was Trade Secretary and one of the inner cabal of economic ministers, he spoke of the recession now 'bottoming out'. In April 1981, the Chief Secretary to the Treasury, Leon Brittan, said recovery would come 'naturally, just as day follows night'. A year later he was sure that dawn had broken. 'Those who still refuse to see that the fruits of recovery are on the way', he said, 'should open their eyes and look again.'[21] But little of this was apparent in 1983.

Although the deep depression of 1981 was behind them, working politicians would have been hard put to demonstrate to millions of voters, had circumstance obliged them to do so, that the recovery was either fast or permanent. In many parts of the country, things were still getting worse. One Tory backbencher returned from a visit to Hartlepool, in North-east England, with the intelligence that according to the town's director of education it was now statistically more probable that a young person would get to university than get a job. Another thought four years of policy had epitomised particularly Thatcherite characteristics: 'masochism and bloody-mindedness, necessary in the Falklands but hardly enough to run a sensible economy'.

In the Treasury, too, the pockets of scepticism remained very deep. As election year began, a senior official was expressing amazement at how much ministers had got away with. 'I'm astonished how little they've really been pressed on what happens after the recession,' he said. 'Where is this great engine of growth coming from? They simply won't face up to the consequences of the recession, which will be permanent.'

Another count on which ministers were vulnerable was their detailed failure to achieve what they said they would achieve by the methods they said they would use. Reducing tax was the major promise, the motor that would release energies and get the state off people's backs. But between 1979 and 1983, the tax burden rose sharply, from 34 per cent of GDP to almost 40 per cent. There had been the promised shift from direct to indirect taxes, thanks to the near doubling of VAT in the first budget. But despite that, only people earning a lot more than twice the national average wage paid less income tax in the fourth year than in the first. At the bottom end, the tax burden had risen with special severity.

A parallel failure in the practice of the promised revolution was obvious in public spending. This, too, grew when it was meant to fall. It finished lower than Labour had projected, but still far higher than intended, consuming 44 per cent of GDP in 1982–3 compared with the 40 per cent originally planned by Chancellor Howe and the 42 per cent inherited in 1979. The wets, of course, welcomed this. Had the target been hit, the recession would have been even deeper. But as the evidence of a purposeful government which knew which sacred cows it wished to slaughter, it was not overwhelmingly persuasive.

There were spectacular examples of this, especially in the industrial field. The refusal to prop up lame ducks with public money was one of the most aggressively stated of Tory policies, but large exceptions were made in practice. None was more visible than what happened to the car firm, British Leyland. At the time, Joseph, the responsible minister, sweated with embarrassment as he came to cabinet to secure the necessary millions of subsidy.[22] Reflecting at leisure in 1987, he reckoned it his biggest personal failure, saying: 'I didn't have the conviction and moral courage to assume that, had I put successfully the argument to de-subsidise, the investment and risk-taking to absorb many of the jobs would have been forthcoming.' He pleaded in defence that his conduct in respect of British Aerospace, British Telecom and even British Steel was more satisfactory, but conceded that this might not be enough. 'British Leyland may wipe out all of those.'[23]

Nor had monetarist theory itself, as a doctrine, survived the length of a Parliament. Here, too, there were deviations which critics could have ridiculed, had it been in their interests to do so. By early 1982, the retreat had begun from the monetary targets once considered the linchpin of an anti-inflationary economic policy. The figures bore out Ian Gilmour's description of monetarism as 'the uncontrollable in pursuit of the indefinable', with the targets for monetary growth being missed by a wide margin in every year until 1982–3. Sterling M3, the much-trumpeted measure of money, grew by 65 per cent between 1980 and 1984, as against the range of 24–44 per cent projected in the original statement of strategy in March 1980. Yet at the same time, inflation showed an impressive fall, from a high of 21.9 per cent in May 1980 to 3.7 per cent in May 1983. This seemed to destroy the axiom declared to the Treasury Select Committee by the American monetarist guru, Professor Milton Friedman, in 1980, to the effect that inflation is 'always and everywhere a monetary phenomenon'. At the same session, Friedman had said the anti-inflationary process would have 'as an unavoidable side-effect a temporary retardation of economic growth'. He had certainly not predicted the depth of the recession or the doubling of unemployment. Asked in March 1983 to explain these discordances, he told a BBC television interviewer that they were attributable to the 'gyrations' in monetary control. 'It's gone down, it's gone up, it's gone down, it's gone up,' the professor said, and that was why 'you've had a much more severe recession than would have been necessary.'

Six months after coming to power, Mrs Thatcher had told a conference of Conservative trade unionists: 'It is my ambition to face the next election with the slogan – No U-Turns.' As the election approached, not only had some such turns plainly been effected, but, to the extent that they had not, the ground on which the leader and her chairman had to work for a second term seemed to be a desert of pessimism and unemployment.

It was offset, however, by other factors. The chief of these was herself. In her post-Falklands incarnation, she was not only in unassailable command of government, she also bestrode the country. Circumstance neutralised most of these powerfully negative facts; indeed, it almost turned them to advantage. The rigour underlying them, and the unpopularity they mightily deserved to bring, became for this leader at this time a badge of honour – but one craftily obscured, when the occasion demanded, by concessions to political orthodoxy which made a virtue of the inconsistent deviations. Mrs Thatcher approached the election as a righteous radical, glorying in a highly self-conscious brand of toughness, but also as the prophet of a new consensus – dreaded word! – within which, for the first time, old household gods could be claimed for her side of the argument.

In February she began a series of interviews in the press and on television. It was another sign that politics was speeding towards settlement day. To conduct one of these interviews was to confront the full spaciousness of the claims Mrs Thatcher posited against the awkward facts ranged all around her.[24] To no interviewer, including me, did she display a scintilla of doubt about the rightness of her course. That was the word. Rightness, in the sense of conformity with fundamental truth and economic logic, meant that any apparent failures would be only temporary.

Take employment, she said. It was inevitable that there would be a shake-out in the old industries, but just as inevitable that these would be replaced as job-providers by others. 'When I came into politics,' she said, 'there were 700,000 jobs in mining. Now there are 200,000. But who's suggesting that mining would be more flourishing if you put 500,000 people back into it?' The probability that other industries would emerge could be taken for granted. 'It isn't an act of faith, it's an act of *experience*,' she insisted. Just as industry had replaced agriculture and domestic service as the major field of employment in the early part of the century, the service sector would colossally mushroom to take the strain from industry.

All this would happen, she went on, by observing the rules she had made famous, of which two were particularly important. Inflation must be kept down, and socialism must be extinguished. Ending inflation would utterly transform the country. 'You're going to change the whole of your life, the whole of the nation's life, the whole of the attitude to honesty and integrity, if the pound you put in and save out of your earnings is still there for your retirement. You're going to alter the whole attitude towards investment if a building costs the same when it's finished as when it was started.'

But socialism was the real curse. It had created the habit of looking to the state for everything, and gravely impeded the natural forces of economic growth by discouraging the small entrepreneur. There was no longer any such thing as democratic socialism of the old Fabian variety, in her opinion. This was her answer to those who accused the Tories, with all their cuts, of whittling away the welfare state. In her view the welfare state had reached the end of the road. 'When we took over the basic welfare state, socialism had nowhere to go except to go marxist. There is nothing else.'

The Conservatives, by contrast, had begun to correct the balance. 'We've *got* the basic welfare state,' she unflinchingly asserted, 'but now we've got the opportunity as well.'

This was only part of the message, however. By this time, she felt sufficiently confident – or perhaps apprehensive – to make a claim to continuity as well as a promise of unceasing change. The traditional household gods of Conservatism, once the target of this self-proclaimed iconoclast, now became the object of her piety. Harold Macmillan, under whom the inflationary rot was always said to have begun, was now brought forward as something of a hero. 'It was from him that I learned how to deal with industries in difficulty,' she recalled. 'Don't put in subsidies unless they put their house in order.

He did it with cotton. It's what we continued to do with British Leyland.'

Ideologically, as the election loomed, the wheel began to come full circle. Thatcherism, far from breaking with the past, had, according to her, a seamless connection with it. This even stretched, most impudently, as far back as John Maynard Keynes. Keynes, the very prophet and inventor of a form of macro-economic management which four years of economic policy had affected to repudiate, was now enlisted on to the side of the revolution. Keynes, too, we were to understand, was a monetarist not a Keynesian. 'You'll find he says that if your money supply is below your production one or two years, then you've got to bring it up. But taking one year with another, you've got to keep the balance. People forgot about keeping the balance, one year with another.'

'I would say', she concluded, 'that I really am the true Keynesian, when I'm taken as a whole.'

And, without going quite as far as that to defame a great icon of the twentieth century, there were others who noted the conservative rather than the radical aspect of what had been achieved. According to *The Economist*, one of her most urgent supporters in the upmarket press, Mrs Thatcher's first government had not honoured 'its promise of structural radicalism'. Its reputation for austerity derived more from the recession and from the leader's rhetoric than from bold and deliberate decisions by the cabinet. It had run away from reforming welfare. A lot of its micro-economic policies, the on-the-ground evidence of reform in transport and industry and energy and the rest, had received no strategic attention but had instead been afflicted by 'demoralising criticism and constant juggling of ministers'.[25]

To take the shine off the record, it could also be said that much of the British Government's performance was unexceptional. Not only did domestic recession do more than detailed policy initiatives to reorder the national life, international recession put many governments in the same boat. Although greater in Britain than anywhere else, the rise in unemployment was universal throughout the developed economies, and the policies to meet a perceived economic crisis spread with remarkable similarity through many Western nations. Britain was not alone in cutting public borrowing, deregulating the private sector, reducing income taxes and pursuing financial prudence before every other goal.[26]

Britain, in fact, was only one among many countries in which the right held sway. Among major powers, the United States and West

Germany had moved the same way; among lesser countries, Canada, Denmark, Norway, Belgium and the Netherlands also had right-wing governments. Even Sweden, the home of social democracy, saw the upholders of that great consensual creed ousted from office, briefly, in 1981. Parties of the welfare left were everywhere losing their traditional political base. Later, Thatcherite ministers were to make increasingly large claims to have fathered and exported round the world the economic philosophy they believed in: claims which, in the limited area of privatisation of public industry, had some plausibility. In 1983 it was truer to describe Thatcherism as the British response to a global phenomenon, and thus to look with an unexultant eye on some of the more fantastic insinuations that this Government was engaged on a project that was unique.

The election, however, would not be about global comparisons. It was a test of the British mood. And there was evidence that, irrespective of the absence of any Opposition fit to put it to the test, four years of government had seen some change in that mood. One minister put it in a very simple way. He thought the Thatcher years had already reclaimed the country from the grip of the modish tyrannies of the sixties which had endured through the early seventies. 'We've latched on to the great middle mass of the British,' he told me in November 1982. 'They're ordinary people who want to own things, make choices, live decently and free from being beaten up. They also like to see us bashing the trade union barons.' This was the 'new consensus', a phrase already being given currency in the forward thoughts of men like Norman Tebbit: a phrase, also, which did not depend on the patchy economic record but crystallised an attitude – the attitude Margaret Thatcher herself could trace directly back to Grantham.

'To the public,' Robert Blake wrote of Stanley Baldwin, 'he seemed to embody the English spirit and his speeches to sound the authentic note of that English character which they so much admired and so seldom resembled.'[27] At least in her own eyes, this came close to describing the condition Baldwin's latest successor had by now attained.

She hesitated before putting it to the test. Unpersuaded by Parkinson and the others at Chequers in January, she still wasn't sure in April that an early election, in June, with a year of the mandate unexpired, was the proper thing to do. And propriety, as she saw it, was what mattered as much as anything. The choice of date could not be determined solely and exclusively by the advantage it gave the Tories. There was another dimension, wrapped up with the Thatcher self-image. According to this construct, everything she did had to accord with a larger rightness. It had to be in all respects correct. 'She won't call an election until we can convince her that it is in the national interest,' one insider said in March. Another thought until a late date that June would not satisfy this stipulation. It looked too opportunistic, too incongruent with her sense of personal destiny. 'It would not sit well with the successor to Evita Peron,' he added unkindly.

The condition, however, was duly met. The need to end uncertainty became a satisfactorily overwhelming reason to go to the country on the date, 9 June, which all Conservatives, moved by more mundane considerations, believed the likeliest to maximise their victory.

The leader began her campaign on an almost elegiac note, half-concealing her vaunted destiny behind words of anticipated regret. 'If you feel you've been responsible', she told the *Observer*, 'for a major change of direction in your country, which you feel you managed with a combination of yourself and the people of this country – you feel it would be sad for both of you if this relationship came to an end.'

But she had no intention of letting that happen. She summoned her people to the colours for a battle against not merely the enemy but the Antichrist. 'This is a historic election,' she told the Scottish Conservative conference. 'For the choice facing the nation is between two totally different ways of life. And what a prize we have to fight for: no less than the chance to banish from our land the dark, divisive clouds of Marxist socialism.'

It was an election she ran no risk of losing. The authors of the Nuffield Study, a series going back to 1945, declared it to be, of all post-war elections, the one whose outcome was least uncertain. She performed, as ever, under tight control. Parkinson, her most trusted intimate, took personal command of her itinerary, spacing out the speeches and lifting her as majestically as a sophisticated salesman could manage above the futile scuffling of the various oppositions. In the middle of the campaign she took time to attend a world summit meeting in Williamsburg, Virginia, a forum which Michael Foot and David Steel, the Liberal leader, could only dream about. Throughout, the Tories had no difficulty in controlling the agenda, whether this was their own claim to have begun the British recovery or their effortless dissection of a Labour Party more deeply split and chaotically disorganised than at any election it had ever fought. Having been high in the opinion polls since the Falklands war, the Conservatives began the election itself exactly where they ended it: fifteen points ahead.

In fact they secured fewer votes than they had in 1979. Now they got just over 13 million; then there were nearly 700,000 more. But their parliamentary majority was up by a hundred, to 144. This discrepancy was resolved conclusively, as it always is in the British system, in favour of the latter figure. The landslide victory totally concealed the drop in national support, and ordained that the new consensus had indeed established itself. That's the way people saw it. So that's the way it was.

What they also saw was a victory secured this time through the person of the leader, if not entirely because of her. No longer could she be called an obstacle. She bestrode the political scene. The collective wisdom of the polls, including the party's private polls, suggested that it was precisely her personal qualities which enabled the party to transcend unemployment and the rest of its poor economic record. Toughness was in, likeability was out. Masochism and bloody-mindedness, the man said. There could have been no more perfect embodiment of it than Margaret Thatcher.

She had always said hers was a two-term prospectus. Now she had got her second term, and in conditions which approximated to one of her secret wishes. She once told her most senior official adviser, in a moment of speculative candour, that the position she really fancied was that of president not prime minister. There was nothing she would like better than to take on the Labour leader, head to head, and beat him into the ground on a national vote. After that, how much more efficient it would be if she exercised something like presidential powers. It would be a presidency with a difference, of course. A president below the monarch. But in a perfect world it might enable her to hasten the expunging of socialism and the remaking of Britain.

Now she had just about achieved this position. Foot had been routed, in what amounted to a presidential campaign. As prime minister she led a party with an impregnable majority, certain of putting through Parliament whatever she could get through a cabinet of her own people. Viewed from the mountain where she stood, the land of opportunity stretched towards a very distant horizon.

Yet this was not how everybody saw the prospect. Contemplating her victory, one of her staff, a blunt, far-seeing man, vouchsafed a doubt. He thought she had done a wonderful job in her first term as prime minister. By diligence and firmness and attention to the smallest detail at home and abroad, she had hauled Britain back from disaster. But what had not been tested was her imagination, even her vision. The second term, he thought, would ask a more challenging question. 'She has proved herself a wonderful managing director of UK Limited,' he said. 'But is she a chairman of the board?'

Part Three

One of Us
1983–1987

15

Trouble with Friends

THE PROSPECTUS FOR this great national corporation, UK Limited, was most notable for its extreme sobriety. The next five-year programme, it promised, would be little different from the last. Extravagant commitments were few, and lunges forward in the new radicalism were hardly adumbrated at all. The manifesto to which, whether as chairman or chief executive, the leader could be relied upon to cleave was curiously shapeless. If it had a single thrust, this was directed more at the extirpation of another cohort of enemies than at the fashioning of a new society. It was not, however, an unfaithful guide to the future. Anyone who read the manifesto carefully could foresee conflict looming larger than creativity in the years ahead. And so it proved. Well before the end of 1983, the electoral triumph had been eclipsed by personal calamity, disorderly decision-making and renewed doubts, in and out of the Conservative Party, about the prime minister's capacity for survival. To some extent, these set the tone for the second term of the Thatcher Administration.

The programme was not always intended to be so unadventurous. By mid-1982, nine policy committees had been assembled, with a view to identifying the next leap forward. They began to examine the frontiers of Conservatism as it might be applied to family life and the inner cities as well as to such old faithfuls as trade unions and unemployment. Sir Geoffrey Howe was in charge of the exercise, with the leader's personal policy adviser and draftsman, Ferdinand Mount, stationed alongside. Mount, journalist, novelist and social historian, had made himself, among other things, an expert on the family; and a policy for family enhancement was meant to be one of the new syntheses of Thatcherism – one which would simultaneously announce its renewed originality and its human face.

But in the event neither this nor any other novelty emerged in the manifesto. The concern, instead, was above all with continuity. The work of the policy committees had virtually no place in the programme. This directed itself, on the one hand, to a further reduction in inflation, controlling public expenditure and the rest of the familiar economic litany: and, on the other, to more onslaughts against key sources of anti-Conservative power and agitation, principally trade unions and local government. Several wars of attrition loomed, of an essentially negative character. The Greater London Council and six metropolitan authorities would be abolished. Rates would be capped. Union immunities would be removed, and so, perhaps, would be union members' payment of political levies to the Labour Party. On the positive side, the only promises calculated to raise a radical's adrenalin were those that had hardly featured in 1979, concerning the privatisation of several public industries.

The prospectus, in a word, was anodyne. It took no risks, canvassed no excitements. And this was a conscious choice. According to one involved in drafting it, ministers viewed with distaste the habit of previous governments to make lavish promises and raise false expectations. 'We felt . . . a desperate need to get away from such childish pandering to fashion,' he said.[1] Equally to be avoided were ideas themselves. This was not a period, it seemed, when bold thinking was encouraged. Labour had proved that, according to this same Tory official. The fate handed by the electorate to Labour's 'cornucopia of new ideas', he said, clearly showed that no other party should indulge itself in a similar excess. This is why the programme had no freshly radical impulse, no obvious momentum that might sweep aside the little local difficulties which all governments are heir to, and which increasingly, as time went on, dogged this Government in particular.

On the morrow of the election, however, that is not how it seemed to most people. At that moment, there was every reason to believe the body politic had finally been captured by Margaret Thatcher and all its extremities infused with her priorities. In victory, she was suitably restrained in what she said. After all, since it had never been in doubt, it gave no cause for unseemly ecstasy. 'Power is a trust,' she intoned when the votes were in. 'When you get a big result . . . you have to be even more careful the way you use that trust and the way you use that responsibility.' But these were to some extent token pieties. With a parliamentary majority of 144, she could at last arrange the body of which she was the head exactly as she wished.

For another thing she had said concerned cabinet reshuffles. She wasn't a good butcher, she claimed (not for the first time), but had 'learned how to carve the joint'. She now set about the task with voracious appetite.

Throughout her first term, she had been obliged to content herself with a cabinet that did not entirely satisfy her. Although she expelled some of her opponents, the process of submissive unification was far from complete. Of those remaining, one man in particular had remained the focus of her ineradicable displeasure.

The counts against Francis Pym were many and long-standing. Some of them were to do with his views on policy. Pym had never been in any sense a Thatcherite, and did not care who knew it. For fully two years he had been making speeches shot through with a lugubrious brand of gloom and despondency, and delivered, as the prime minister and her circle read them, with the kind of posturing gravitas still peculiarly available to the possessor of an Etonian pedigree and a Lancers tie. Time and again, but most memorably in early 1982 after the first official intimations of economic recovery, Pym seemed to be going out of his way to kill off the frail plant of public confidence that Treasury ministers were starting delicately to nurture. Time and again in cabinet, he was to be found not openly arguing with the Chancellor but sitting there in a posture the prime minister detested even more than stubborn disagreement: broodingly silent, exuding dissent from every pore, with the dark countenance of a man only waiting his moment to strike from behind the arras.

There was more than policy between them. Each had left wounds on the other at especially sensitive points. Pym it was who, when Secretary of State for Defence, had been the butt of one of the leader's crudest shafts, when she publicly jeered his indecision and announced that if he didn't make his mind up quickly she and her private secretary would have to make it up for him. But Pym himself, gentleman though he was, wasn't lacking in corridor savagery. 'The trouble is,' he once murmured to a receptive backbencher, 'we've got a corporal at the top, not a cavalry officer.' The line was duly fed back to Downing Street. Instead of enraging the leader, it merely confirmed her natural suspicions. 'Francis is just a snob,' she said to her informant. Another way of saying it would have been that he epitomised, in manner and class and cunning habit and squireish paternalism and innumerate dedication to the feel of politics rather than the facts of economics, everything that she wanted to defenestrate from the Conservative citadel.

In June 1983, however, Pym remained a force to be reckoned with. As Foreign Secretary since the beginning of the Falklands war, he had placed her considerably in his debt. She was not grateful for this.

On the contrary, it pricked her irritation further; and the more so since it had always been clear who would be her successor if the Falklands expedition ended in disaster. Nor did she respect anything he had done during the war, or since. The leader's verdict reported from inside the war cabinet – 'She thinks nothing whatever of him' – was like other verdicts on other men: it was never open to revision. All the same, objective facts seemed to make Pym immovable from his high position. Surely he was just too eminent for any reasonable leader to displace?

She began by thinking so herself. So a stratagem was devised, and deployed even before the election. Should Pym not become Speaker of the House? This would indeed be a grand climax, fitting for a Foreign Secretary, especially one whose ancestor in Cromwellian times had filled the same position. The plan took no account of Pym's absolute rejection of the idea, conveyed the moment it came to light. Nor did it show much sensitivity to the Commons, which was unlikely to tolerate a Speaker thrust upon it by the executive. Undaunted, the prime minister continued to manoeuvre for a solution which, as Whitelaw and others began to see it, obsessed her.

Even though it failed, the rumours of her intentions were enough to settle Pym's fate and render thinkable what in normal times would have been hard to contemplate. What finally sank him was the colossal size of the majority. This left the leader free to do whatever she wanted, immune from credible danger on the backbenches. But worse than that, Pym himself, as his final contribution to the wisdom of the age, publicly ventured the opinion, at the height of the election campaign, that a large majority was a dangerous thing. Such an implied invitation to the nation to give something less than full-hearted assent to a second Thatcher term appeared to the party's high command as a piece of treachery which could have only one purpose.

Pym himself has recorded what followed. 'Francis, I want a new Foreign Secretary,' the reluctant butcher told him on the day after the election.[2] And the departure into the wilderness of this pillar of the old Conservatism, a man who had held many offices and displayed in all of them some formidable political and parliamentary abilities, marked another change in the old order. He went without anyone making a whisper of protest. There was a time when his power would have saved him. But the politics of interest, of faction, of groupings and collaborations within the party, which a leader might ignore at her peril, had entirely vanished. Now it was every man for himself. Francis Pym became the unlamented centrepiece of a reconstruction which brought new men to the top, who owed their place to this leader and to her alone.

For the first time, she succeeded in filling the three most senior positions in the cabinet, and not just the economic ones, with ministers who were her unreserved supporters. To replace Pym she moved her faithful Chancellor, Geoffrey Howe, into the Foreign Office, thus opening another stage in the most enduring ministerial relationship of the Thatcher years.

She still found Howe a bore, but a plodding, industrious bore, loyal to the point of submissiveness. He would never let her down. 'Geoffrey is like a cruiser,' a senior Treasury official once said, in tribute to Howe's years of hard labour defending an unsuccessful economic policy. 'He never sinks, he enjoys the flak, he doesn't get pushed off course.' The Treasury also thought him chronically indecisive. 'He wants to talk about everything for a long time. He'll listen to everyone from the permanent secretary to the man in the lift. God knows what would have happened if he had been running the Falklands war.'

But it wasn't the Treasury opinion that counted. To the leader he offered the rare advantage of utter reliability and a proven reluctance to challenge either her opinions or her position. He was also, she once publicly noted with the patronising air which her ministers learned not to wince at, 'an excellent negotiator'. With Britain's contribution to the European Community budget as far as ever from settlement, and negotiations with China over the future of Hong Kong still at an early stage, the presence at the Foreign Office of such a master of fine print was, for her, a reassuring prospect – even though, as we shall see, this was not the arrangement she originally intended, and Howe was only second choice for the job.

Howe's replacement at the Treasury was Nigel Lawson, who had been Energy Secretary since the 1981 reshuffle. It was a natural but also a disputed succession. 'Margaret was always determined to have Nigel at the Treasury,' the doleful Whitelaw ruminated shortly afterwards. For Whitelaw, still the keeper of what he liked to regard as Tory pragmatism, this represented a defeat. Of his myriad managerial tasks, keeping Lawson out of high places had not been the least important. Whitelaw tended to regard him as ideological and thoroughly unsound – although once the promotion had occurred it was equally consistent with Whitelaw's pragmatic instincts that he should take on the role of the Chancellor's protector. 'Nigel Lawson is unfortunately almost entirely without friends,' was a regular Whitelaw refrain within six months of the election. 'I have therefore made a very conscious effort to become his friend. People tell me this is a doomed enterprise.'

The reason for Whitelaw's suspicion, as for Mrs Thatcher's determined enthusiasm, was that Lawson possessed many qualities missing in Geoffrey Howe. He was intellectually brilliant and politically inexperienced.

He had not always been an exponent of monetarist economics. A journalist and editor before he became a politician, he did his time in service of whatever Tory orthodoxy was in command at the moment. This was first, fleetingly, that of Harold Macmillan, whose speechwriter he agreed to become in 1963; then of Alec Douglas-Home, Macmillan's successor. Although the Conservative Government was in decline, there was no talk then, from Lawson or anyone else, of the doctrinal errors into which it had fallen. In 1962, when City editor of the *Sunday Telegraph*, Lawson wrote scornfully of the American obsession with old-fashioned fiscal conservatism: 'the Eisenhower school of economic commentators who see mystical significance in an overall budget balance', producing, as Lawson thought, 'a muddled amalgam of Gladstone and Keynes without the logical consistency of either'.[3]

All monetarists, however, had been through such a phase. It induced in them little humility before the new dogmatism they now thoroughly embraced, and Lawson was no exception. An aide to Edward Heath in the last days of Tory corporatism, he became, from the beginning of the Thatcher ascendancy, one of the most creative and committed exponents of its successor doctrine. When he was in his first government job, as Financial Secretary to the Treasury, it was to him rather than to Howe that officials went to be instructed in its finer details. He was the intellectual architect of the Medium-Term Financial Strategy, although Howe was its public face. Their qualities, indeed, were complementary – but also different. Where Howe plodded, Lawson sped ahead; where Howe seemed always to be learning what the policy was all about, Lawson saw it effortlessly. Where the leader had hitherto tolerated a willing servant she now placed a man of dangerous zeal, but one whose congenial support for her own thinking she had no reason to doubt.

Still less could she doubt the loyalty, even the subservience, of the third member of the senior office-holding trio. Whitelaw, it was jointly decided between them, should give up the Home Office and move to the House of Lords in order to impart to this increasingly dissident branch of the legislature his special brand of adroit parliamentary leadership. In his place, to general astonishment, she put Leon Brittan.

Brittan was at that time the prime example, after Parkinson, of a complete Thatcher creation. An able barrister, he had for long been unsuccessful in his efforts to become a politician. To seat after seat he tramped in search of a comfortable nomination. Eventually it was offered him in a place not noted for its affinity with London-based Jews, Cleveland and Whitby in north Yorkshire, which sent him to Parliament just a year before Mrs Thatcher took over the party. Under her patronage, his rise was swift. A friend of Howe's, and latterly of Whitelaw's, he prudently eschewed a factional label. It was clear by 1979 that he could not fail to secure preferment, which duly followed in the departments of his two sub-patrons. First Brittan became Minister of State in Whitelaw's Home Office; then he leaped with a single stride into the cabinet, as Chief Secretary to the Treasury, and thereby into the closer affections of the leader.

But he had always been there or thereabouts. The first time she took a holiday as prime minister, in August 1979, she went, as if drawn by an atavistic compulsion, to the Scottish estate of the Morrison family, party grandees in the Macmillan era. They were hardly her sort of people, but they had entertained many leaders before her. Besides, she took her own company. In the photographs from a windswept moor, whose was the unexplained face lurking in the background? Why, that of the new Minister of State at the Home Office.

What Mrs Thatcher admired about Brittan was his brain, which was quite formidable. He did something to compensate for the sad fact that most of the brains of Conservatism were still to be found on the left rather than the right of the party. She warmed to this fluent young practitioner of all that she believed in, and he found himself filling such lacunae and resolving such doubts as he found in his own thinking by aligning it with what he perceived to be hers. At the Treasury he was held to have done an excellent job as Chief Secretary, especially by comparison with his predecessor, the sceptical and unrigorous Biffen. While, as with the Foreign Office, the final choice would not in a perfect world have been the first – and as with the Treasury, there arrived in place a politician with no personal following in the party – Leon Brittan looked like the right sort of Home Secretary for an administration intended to mark the rise to power of Mrs Thatcher's friends.

There were others in this category. One already in place was Parkinson, now sent to the Department of Trade, with a brief to amalgamate it with Industry. Another was Norman Tebbit, retained at Employment but playing an expanded role, which again derived from a very personal relationship with the only Conservative leader he had ever admired. Some of the old hands from a more distant era were retained. Jim Prior remained at Northern Ireland, Peter Walker was handed the Department of Energy. But each had cause to reflect on political vagaries that required them to show every last scrap of their resilience. To be outdistanced by a Chancellor and a Home Secretary neither of whom was even a Member of Parliament when they, great pillars of the last Conservative Government, were already in the cabinet, fairly put them in their place.

So the leader controlled the cabinet without serious fear of contradiction. Seemingly, the balance of power had been tilted conclusively in her direction And by the time the second Thatcher term was beginning the civil service, too, was oiled and retuned, ready to do its duty with fewer grinds and curses than were often heard, to the prime minister's fierce displeasure, after 1979.

Experience in office had not much modified her suspicion of the civil service, save those members of it who worked personally for her. Not long before the election, she was still retailing, as if it were freshly minted in her mind, the key story which she appeared to regard as typical of Whitehall but which better exemplified her stubborn incomprehension of what officials regarded as their natural way of life. In a television interview with Sir Laurens van der Post, she described her first experience as a junior Minister of Pensions more than twenty years before. She had served, she recalled, under three ministerial bosses. It had been an instructive experience. 'You see how the civil service works, because of the advice they gave,' she told van der Post. 'I saw it vary from minister to minister. And I used to sit there and say, "That's not what you said to the last minister. You're giving him totally different advice. Why?" And gradually they said the last minister wouldn't have accepted that advice. And I said, "You're now trying it on the present one." '[4]

This kind of memory plainly infused her dealings with the civil service. It was repaid in part by determined attempts to cut the service down to size. Reducing Whitehall manpower by 10 per cent in four years was one of the more concrete achievements of the first term. But the most important impact was on appointments. Mrs Thatcher devoted a great deal of time to cultivating personal knowledge of senior civil servants and a personal relationship with those who took her fancy. 'She probably knows the top hamper of the civil service better than any prime minister I've known,' Sir Douglas Wass said shortly after his retirement as permanent secretary at the Treasury.[5] Wass had reason to know. Apart from being badly rated by the monetarists, he had just seen his personal advice on his successor, the customary *envoi* of the departmental head, roundly rejected. It was, said one who saw it, a consummate piece of mandarin analysis. But it pointed towards a man whom the prime minister, in her determination to have the right machine in place, did not want to have.

With the abolition of the Civil Service Department, control over top civil service jobs now lay unambiguously in Downing Street and the Cabinet Office, since the cabinet secretary, who was the closest thing the prime minister had to her own permanent secretary, acquired the parallel role of head of the civil service as well. *De facto* power was thereby coupled with *de jure* responsibility. And the opportunity beckoned, as it happened, to deploy them both.

No fewer than eight heads of Whitehall departments reached retirement age between mid-1982 and the end of 1983. There was a wholesale clear-out of the wartime generation: men who had entered Whitehall together fresh from the services and were now all reaching sixty at the same time. For a conviction prime minister, such a feast of patronage offered the rare possibility of creating something a little closer than usual to a conviction civil service.

The nodal case was Wass's job. The customary norms of selection suggested a number of senior candidates, whom age would have qualified for half a dozen years in the post: or, alternatively, one or two men with international experience and a traditional mandarin style such as had previously found favour. Instead it went, at the prime minister's express insistence, to Peter Middleton, then a deputy secretary and not yet fifty, whose ability was universally recognised but whose superiority to other candidates lay mainly in the measure of his perceptibly unmandarinlike commitment to the policy. Middleton understood the importance of monetary policy, had been present at its creation under the Labour Government, was relatively unmarked by the sceptical deformities of his colleagues. Besides, for this and other reasons, Mrs Thatcher liked him. He was unstuffy, a doer not a talker, and he had been especially helpful as an ally against the Foreign Office during her quest to get 'our money' back from the EEC.[6]

There were other appointments in the Middleton vein. Clive Whitmore was sent from the private office at No. 10 to run the Ministry of Defence. Michael Quinlan, another character more gritty than smooth, moved from Defence to take over Employment. It was the opinion of more than one insider that each of these appointments, while being given to able men, would not have happened at that time under a different prime minister.

Middleton, Whitmore and Quinlan had other things in common besides the surprising irregularity of their promotion. Each went to an unfashionable school – Sheffield City Grammar, Sutton Grammar and Wimbledon College respectively – and not only Middleton had done the prime minister valuable personal service. With Whitmore, it consisted of his entire time as her first principal private secretary, the civil servant on whom she came to depend perhaps more than on any other before or since. As for Quinlan, he had come to notice as a brilliant expositor of the case for Britain's independent nuclear deterrent. A practising Catholic, he was able to bring a moral force to the argument which the prime minister found especially appealing. As a tough-minded stylist, he was wheeled in to strengthen a key speech she made to the United Nations disarmament conference in June 1982, the Foreign Office version having been judged woefully unmuscular.

By such services would civil servants be remembered. This did not produce bad appointments. Like almost all ministers she especially favoured, these officials were clever men with a penchant for action. But they became some of the larger tributaries in a network of personal connections through which Whitehall power flowed, with less and less of it permitted to bypass the prime minister. They and others like them were proof, at least in the leader's own mind, that the Whitehall culture was beginning to change, and was now in the hands of some senior people each of whom could justly be described as 'one of us'.

Not everyone saw them this way. At the same time as Thatcherism, loosely defined, began to seep into the thinking of the regular government, some Thatcherite irregulars were taking their leave of the great experiment. They did so with a certain acidity about the system they were leaving behind. While faithful to Mrs Thatcher and all she wished to do, they expressed some doubt about the capacity of the civil servants on whom the prime minister was now choosing to rely. These, the radical ultras, even wondered whether she had not already become trapped inside a system which did not understand how radical she, or at least they, understood Thatcherism to be.

One such was John Hoskyns, the first head of her policy unit. Late in 1982 he began making a series of speeches attacking the entire political system as he had found it on entering government service and continued to find it now. Because of their professional formation, he suggested, civil servants were incapable of working wholeheartedly for a Thatcher government. They could only function, he said, 'by cultivating a passionless detachment, as if the process they were engaged in were happening in a faraway country which they service only on a retainer basis'.[7] How could you have a radical government without radically minded officials? Hoskyns' scathing diatribes, so soon after leaving his post and receiving a knighthood for services rendered, attracted no echo from the radical in Downing Street. Instead, he was seen as a caution against ever again granting the accolade so soon.

Hoskyns' partner, a management consultant named Norman Strauss, also cast doubt on the ability of the machine to behave as required, and even on that of the prime minister to understand what was needed. 'It seems that even – or perhaps especially – our current prime minister', he later wrote, 'will not address the problems of civil service reform and strategic leadership at the level of change and complexity that their seeming intractability demands.' 'Surely,' he insensitively jeered, 'she of all people is not "frit"?'[8] A painful jibe, calling up the very word, a unique descent into Lincolnshire dialect, with which the prime minister had shriekingly derided Labour's terror of an early election during one of her Question Time performances.

Another ultra on the way out of the circle was Alfred Sherman. He too was prone to despair of the government machine, although unlike Hoskyns he had never been a part of it. Unlike Hoskyns, too, he had to wait until the election for his knighthood. In his case, departure from some species of influence consisted of resignation, in a typically complicated personal quarrel, from the Centre for Policy Studies, the research body he had helped Keith Joseph and Mrs Thatcher found in 1974. After leaving, he wrote an apologia protesting, not without a certain palpable pride, at the common fallacy which drove people to present him in his relations with Mrs Thatcher 'as an amalgam of Père Joseph, Svengali and the Elders of Zion'.[9] All the same, their connection was close enough for her to take an interest in his retirement. Even in the middle of a post-election journey round North America, she took time on the transatlantic telephone to try to sort out dear Alfred's pension arrangements.

The serious point Sherman made was about the difficulty of thinking through radical ideas in a governmental environment. Although Margaret Thatcher went to a lot of trouble to look after her old friend and mentor, she had not necessarily made her escape into a new intellectual world. The old one had made its adaptations, and now offered her its embrace: a shift well summed up by a remark of Robert Armstrong's. Before and during the election, it was Armstrong's traditional duty, as secretary to the cabinet, not only to prepare for any eventuality by studying each party's manifesto and positioning Whitehall to respond, but also to present himself as entirely agnostic about the outcome. There was a certain punctilious wit about the way he carried out this obligation. 'The prime minister, whoever she may be' was the formula he drolly used throughout the campaign. But it also symbolised the cosy acquiescence with which the machine and its mistress had come to understand each other.

Within a few months, there were others besides Hoskyns and Sherman who, judging the radical thrust of Thatcherism to have faltered, believed that the supplanting of iconoclastic outsiders by a reformed official orthodoxy was partly to blame. The studied caution of the election manifesto was now reflected, they thought, in the renewed ascendancy, albeit behind fresh faces, of a cadre of public servants deeply imbued with the unhelpful habit recently upheld by Douglas Wass himself as a prime function of the civil service: 'the duty of officials to ensure that ministers are fully seized of the obstacles, the pitfalls and the dangers of their initiatives'.[10]

Whatever the weight of that, it hardly alters the objective fact: that from behind an impregnable parliamentary majority, the prime minister was in command of all she surveyed. And yet very soon she looked like a leader marooned.

With extraordinary speed, accidents and mistakes began to reveal a government rather different from that which ought to have been propelled magisterially forward. Some of these were in the field of economic reality: huge though the victory was, it did not obliterate the fact that the recovery was still tenuous. Others happened in the realm of personal conduct, a common Conservative weakness from which the first Thatcher term had been unusually free. Another crisis was precipitated in foreign affairs, which by its very oddity caused the government which had won the Falklands war particular and agonising embarrassment. In all these setbacks the prime minister was personally involved in the dual role of protagonist and, to some extent, victim.

The months before the election had seen the beginnings of recovery make themselves felt in voters' pockets. A consumer-led surge, coupled with sterling devaluation of around 15 per cent, produced a spurt in growth and the colourable contention that Britain was at last on the way back. But immediately after the election the bad news began to roll in. Within two weeks, mortgage rates were increased by 1.5 per cent – 'I am disappointed,' Mrs Thatcher coolly told the Commons – and both investment and output in manufacturing industry were shown to be down. In early July, the new Chancellor was obliged to call for emergency public spending cuts. Momentarily this sort of crisis measure produced an atmosphere reminiscent of Labour governments in the seventies.

Lying behind it was a still unsolved equation: how to reconcile promises about spending with promises about tax cuts, or make either of them credible in an economy where the immediate post-electoral prospect was for another slow-down in the rate of growth. No matter how large the majority, inflated as it was by division and incoherence among the opposition parties, this problem would not simply go away.

The first attempt to address it occurred at a meeting of the cabinet on 23 July. This took place against the background of pessimism first sketched in by Chancellor Howe during the notorious row precipitated the previous September by publication of Think Tank proposals for curtailing welfare. The proposals were swiftly buried, but Howe's confidential observations accompanying them had reappeared during the campaign. These centred on the spectre of a future growth rate of possibly less than 1 per cent per annum. Simply to maintain public spending programmes at present levels, Howe wrote, would in that event produce a £15,000 million deficit before 1990. The only way to avert this would be by either putting VAT up to 25 per cent, raising the basic rate of income tax to 45 per cent or abolishing virtually all tax allowances. 'I invite my colleagues to agree', he concluded, 'that we need to take a new and fundamental look at levels of public spending.'

On 23 July, the cabinet met to consider public spending levels for 1984–5. Its analysis was utterly unexultant. The mood, according to one member, was grimly realistic. Four great obstacles lay in the path of all would-be radicals. Pensioners were living longer, unemployment was still going up, the National Health Service was in greater demand than ever, and there was an unreviewable commitment to higher defence spending. All the same, some discussion took place on what were then known as the 'unmentionables'. More than one minister canvassed the possibility of a cut in unemployment pay. The idea was rejected without delay, as one whose political cost far outweighed its economic value. Yet its appearance on the agenda served to emphasise the air of stony pessimism, verging on permanent anxiety, which surrounded the conduct of economic policy. The argument about the merits of any tax-cutting whatever continued to rage, with Jim Prior leading the depleted forces of the old wets arguing for a lower dollar exchange-rate and a higher priority for growth. There was no better measure of the gloom than the appearance in the *Daily Telegraph*, then still the unwavering voice of High Conservatism, of a leading article urging the Chancellor to increase public borrowing lest he 'fall into the trap of trying to dig a hole in soft sand which fills as fast as it is cleared'.[11]

To this atmosphere of struggle and, in some cases, alarm, Mrs Thatcher was able to supply no counterblast of euphoria. At one level, naturally, the election produced in her enormous satisfaction. Her sense of personal triumph rendered her even more impossible to deal with than before. One minister found her 'in a state of mind where she thinks she can do literally anything she wants'. But she was also exhausted. The election had drained her to the bottom. She went into hospital in early August for a minor eye operation. To those who saw her every day and were therefore in a position minutely to inspect her outward condition, the famous Thatcher stamina seemed for a time to be cracking.

If this was so, there was a reason for it which none of them knew. Throughout the summer, she was burdened with a nasty little secret of a kind to which prime ministers have sometimes in the past been made privy but which can never before have been disclosed in quite such piquant circumstances as those in which this secret was inflicted on this prime minister.

On election day itself, the party chairman who had organised the victory went to the leader, who valued him above most other men, to confess to her that he had a mistress, who had once been his secretary, and that this mistress had lately informed him that she was expecting his baby. In their very hour of triumph, a blighting shadow was laid across it. For plainly Cecil Parkinson, who was already married and had adolescent children, was about to become a rather different sort of political commodity.

He told the prime minister that, as a consequence of the pregnancy of Sara Keays, he was probably about to divorce his wife, Ann, and remarry. He thought this would be the decent thing to do. And in the public ruminations following the disclosure of the affair in the autumn there were many who agreed with him. These included a number of his political colleagues. After all, it would be no singular disgrace for an avowed adulterer and *divorcé* to take up a cabinet seat. There would be plenty of others beside him.

Mrs Thatcher's instincts were different. Her first question, Parkinson told a journalist later, was 'What about Ann?' Her second reaction, which had to be decided on the instant, was to withhold from him the office she had intended to give him, which was none other than that of Foreign Secretary. When this story was later put about, many Tories could not credit it. But subsequent inquiries among several sources confirmed it as a fact. The original intention was to send Howe to the Home Office, with Parkinson and Lawson, two thrusting and unambiguous Thatcherites, in the two key posts flanking the prime minister. With a messy divorce pending, Cecil, alas, was no longer eligible for one of them.

But aside from politics, the affair posed a tricky challenge to Mrs Thatcher's famous set of values. Victorian rectitude might have pointed either way, in favour of the fatherless child or the deserted wife. But the prime minister's instinct proved very clear. Not only were her first thoughts for the wife, but, even after making her initial political choice and sending Parkinson to the DTI rather than the Foreign Office, she persisted in trying to persuade him of his first duty. Her parliamentary private secretary, Ian Gow, Parkinson later recalled, took him to dinner not once but twice to argue him out of the planned divorce.

Eventually, after extended deliberation culminating in a Caribbean holiday with his wife, the errant minister complied. When he notified the prime minister, she replied: 'Thank God for that.' Ever the politician, he reminded her at their meeting that when the affair became public there might be held to be some conflict between it and the Tory attachment to Victorian and family values – even though, as he noted, he personally had never been known to make a speech about Victorian values. Mrs Thatcher, brushing such quibbles aside, replied: 'What is more Victorian than keeping the family together?'

All this, until that point, was private between them. It was a little burden she shared with almost no one. Whitelaw, her closest ministerial lieutenant, was left completely in the dark. Only later was he in a position to reckon how much the Parkinson business took out of her.

It certainly exposed her human strengths and weaknesses more clearly than they had been before. She showed herself, as she would at other times, to be no prude. She did not demand Parkinson's resignation, only his demotion from an office he never held. She might be a voluble critic of the moral decay of society, and point as evidence for it to the waning of the idea of self-help. She certainly disapproved of the *social* damage done by sexual aberration as projected, for example, on television. But she also believed in individual liberty, and was not disposed to cast the first stone against a friend or colleague in personal moral difficulties.

Secondly, the Parkinson affair showed the loyalty she was willing to extent to people she regarded as close to her. Anyone not so close invariably received the opposite impression. There has never been a prime minister more openly disloyal to ministers she disagreed with or disliked or was preparing to sack. For most of her first two terms, she practised a version of open government which consisted of making quite clear through her intermediaries how frequently she dissented from the Administration of which she was head and in what low esteem she sometimes held its members. But Parkinson was different, as she showed when the affair did become bloodily public.

At first this had no effect. Parkinson's public admission to the affair and to paternity of the impending child made no difference. He even survived a BBC interview with sufficient dignity to preserve his position with the woman who really mattered most to him. Miss Keays, however, would not be denied. The minister's refusal to marry her, followed by the prime minister's refusal to sack him, and his own blithe continuance in office as if nothing could deflect his political career, eventually induced her to provoke a public uproar timed to coincide with the Conservative party conference. But still the prime minister declined to dismiss her favourite, only deciding to do so when they both agreed that Miss Keays could not be relied on to bring her child to birth in obscurity.

Such personal loyalty was in one way admirable, in another way utter folly. Although Parkinson was a man of unusual political talent, the episode showed that, with certain men, this leader could permit sentiment to overcome prudence without normal regard for the consequences. Perhaps it was attributable to her belief, in the hour of victory, as the minister said, that she could do anything she wanted.

344

Certainly the result was a period of strain she could have done without, as her second Government struggled for momentum.

Within a week, another crisis, which was similarly marginal to what she liked to regard as real events, briefly but destructively engulfed political London. Although its focus was a long way away, its impact could not have been closer to home. For it challenged the prime minister at her most vulnerable point, which was precisely that on which her reputation most depended.

Grenada, a small island in the Caribbean, had for some years been ruled by a Marxist regime and for the same period been regarded by successive United States governments as a possible threat to security in the region. Grenada was also a member of the British Commonwealth, and successive British governments, insofar as they were aware of Grenada at all, had had reason to be grateful that the Americans never did anything to destabilise the Grenadan regime, despite a growing perception that, together with Cuba and Nicaragua, it could be seen as part of a triangular communist presence to the south of the US. On 19 October, an event occurred which was to change all that and make Grenada more famous than it had ever been before. The existing Marxist leader, Maurice Bishop, having first been deposed, was murdered by a still more left-wing faction. To the alarm of other east Caribbean governments, and the greater alarm of Washington, law and order in Grenada appeared to be collapsing.

Moves immediately began in Washington to respond to the crisis. There were 1,000 American nationals on Grenada, whose lives it was thought might be at risk. Other Caribbean countries, notably Barbados and Dominica, feared that the contagion of disorder and Marxism might spread through the region and sought outside assistance to restore normality, whatever that might mean, to Grenada. Among the 'friendly states' to whom such a request was intimated were both Britain and the United States. But there was a vast discrepancy in the way these two friends of Grenada responded. In Britain it was received on a dozy weekend, when the Foreign Secretary was in Greece, and it was understood to be merely an informal probing of British opinion. In Washington, it excited intense interest and, after swift deliberation, the readying of plans for a benign invasion of the island. With little further delay, the invasion was duly carried out on 24 October and law and order, with the possibility of democracy, restored. It was one of the quickest and cleanest American military operations of recent times.

The only trouble was that the British, supposedly America's closest allies, were kept in the dark about American intentions. So was the Queen, Grenada's head of state. Indeed, the Foreign Office had been cold-bloodedly deceived. Even as the invasion was about to commence, the Foreign Secretary went to the Commons and said that the only reason why a large American naval presence was in the Grenada area was in case the need arose to rescue the sizeable American community there. Asked specifically about invasion rumours, he said: 'I know of no such intention.'

That morning, a cabinet committee chaired by the prime minister had decided that, if a formal request for British military intervention was received, it should probably be turned down. Ministers thought any invasion, even at the invitation of other Caribbean states, would be against the rule of law. They were uneasy about the logistics and other practicalities, but in particular they declined to see Grenada as resembling the Falklands, or as calling on British solidarity with the Washington hawks in return for America's invaluable assistance to Britain in the South Atlantic. Rather, they thought the boot was on the other foot. Would not any invading force, on that analogy, be more akin to the Argentinians than the British?

More would be heard of these rational arguments, but for the moment they were as nothing by comparison with the affront experienced in London on discovering that the Americans had been engaged in a charade of which the British were not the least conspicuous victims. Close to midnight, the message came from the White House that the final order to attack had been signed and the invasion was under way. Mrs Thatcher was infuriated: had rarely been more so, according to people present that night. She did not hesitate to vent her rage on the president, and a record of their conversation survives from the American end of it.

It took place shortly after Congressional leaders arrived at the White House to be briefed on the invasion. In the course of the discussion, Tip O'Neill, the Speaker of the House of Representatives, remarked to the president that Grenada was part of the British Commonwealth and asked what Mrs Thatcher thought about the news. 'She doesn't know about it,' O'Neill recalls Reagan replying.[12] O'Neill concluded that in its excitement the White House had simply forgotten to tell London. But they soon learned how the prime minister felt. 'Sure enough, as we left the meeting,' O'Neill writes, 'the president was already on the phone with Margaret Thatcher. We could hear Reagan's side of the conversation, and from his fumbling and his apologies it was obvious that she was enraged.'

The rage did not abate next day. John Biffen, arriving for a cabinet committee meeting, came across her ripping through the piles of telegrams on the Grenada invasion with an air, as he recalled, of 'haughty disgust'. She simply could not understand why she had not been taken into Reagan's trust. Anglo-American relations, she declared to anyone in hearing distance, would never be the same again.

And now her rationalisations for the British position grew more strident. Arguments which had pushed ministers half-against intervention became, under the influence of this treachery on Washington's part, root-and-branch attacks on the entire enterprise. Not only was the invasion in plain breach of international law, it was a gross affront to British dignity, in particular that of Her Majesty the Queen, whose governor-general on the island had been compelled to accept invasion as a *fait accompli*. There was also the security of British citizens to be considered; and, as the decisive argument, the question of moral propriety. How would this look, the prime minister inquired, to a world which the Americans had been trying to convince of the iniquity of the Soviet invasion of Afghanistan?

But Washington, for its part, was a little baffled. It admitted to the secrecy, which Reagan later explained to me as follows:

> It was unfortunate at the time. My situation was not one of lack of trust in her or on your side of the ocean, but in this city of Washington, the walls seem to have ears. I felt it was so important in the limited time that we had to plan and move after the decision actually to send the troops on their way that I put it on close-hold, because there were so many lives involved. I was so fearful of a leak from our side. And the minute we could, I explained to her what our situation had been and why I had made the decision I made.[13]

Besides, he had made his decision on the basis of a clear assumption: that Margaret Thatcher's staunch anti-communism would lead Britain to support decisive action against this odious Marxist regime, whenever it was taken. This, along with the favour London owed Washington after the Falklands, made the Americans grossly underplay the British problem: a piece of negligence for which the lady repaid them with her incandescent rage.

In public she eventually picked a more measured way out of her humiliation. After the private lectures she gave the Americans, her first public responses were made in a phone-in programme on, appropriately, the BBC World Service. By the end of Grenada week, with the mission accomplished, it was easier to support the outcome while still dissociating from the method. She maintained her anti-communist credentials by noting that 'the people in Grenada will be delighted to be free of an oppressive rule' and showing a little more sympathy for the Americans' entitlement to look after their own regional security. But she also stood up for fundamental rules of conduct. No country was entitled simply to walk into another country. 'Many peoples in many countries would love to be free of communism, but that doesn't mean to say we can just walk into them and say now you are free.'

Among the accidents of politics illuminated by the Grenada affair was the way in which events, especially international events, can interlock with each other and thus capriciously influence what happens. For the Americans, perhaps the key to the invasion lay not in Grenada but far away in the Lebanon. On the Sunday before the invasion, while Reagan was conferring on a golf-course in Georgia, a car-bomb was driven into an American compound in Beirut and 241 American marines were killed. With news of the casualties mounting hourly, the political ramifications of this catastrophe pressed on the policy-makers more acutely than events on a minor Caribbean island. Tip O'Neill contends in his book that the invasion was ordered purely to take Americans' minds off the Beirut massacre.

But there were also other events playing on Mrs Thatcher's mind. The weekend when Grenada first came to public attention happened to be the same weekend of massive demonstrations in London against the imminent arrival of Cruise missiles in Britain. On the Saturday when the possibility of invasion was first rumoured, the *Guardian* published information, based on a leaked government document, revealing the date the missiles would arrive and the security arrangements to be enforced at the Greenham Common air-base where they would be located. On the Tuesday when Mrs Thatcher was sighted explosively fulminating over the Grenada telegrams, she should have been chairing a meeting with Howe and the Defence Secretary, Michael Heseltine, to decide how to respond to the leak. Throughout the period, she was preoccupied with the problem, long anticipated but never fully resolved, of how best to handle the presentation of the missile issue. Not the least of her concerns when raging at Washington's high-handed insensitivity was what this seigneurial assertion of territorial interest in the Caribbean would do to anti-American feeling in Europe, and in particular to the credibility of insisting that the Cruise missiles were not an extension of the American imperium.

The most telling accompaniment to Grenada, though, wasn't any one policy, however well that might illuminate the complexities of a prime minister's life. The most damaging counterpoint was with a mood, which was already beginning to overtake her world. This mood was of drab pessimism, dominated by a lack of confidence that this Government could in fact succeed. It reached across the economic sphere. It looked gloomily upon the parliamentary programme, which appeared to be dominated not by exciting new strides forward but by an interminable and possibly futile struggle against local authorities. And now it had been taken aback by some very confusing signals, which appeared to suggest that the heroine of the Falklands was, after all, just as seriously flawed as other political leaders by the habit of contradictory vacillation when confronted with a matter of diplomatic complexity. The election victory seemed to be thoroughly deceptive. The opposition parties had been routed, and were even less satisfactory voices for the country's discontents than they had been between 1979 and 1983. But what they failed to do began to be taken up by others.

Now, for the first time in her career as prime minister, she began to experience what most other British leaders had learned to suffer much sooner in their time. In the first term, although fiercely criticised by her opponents, she had remained free from the disillusionment of her friends. Brought to power by zealots, she was sustained by them through every difficulty. The great majority of the press, in particular, had accorded her more unswervingly loyal support over a longer period than any prime minister in British history had probably ever enjoyed.

When the message changed, as it did in some quarters in late 1983 after the Grenada affair, it did so with peculiar savagery. And this was of an exceptionally personal nature, expressed by men about a woman in terms they might have hesitated to use about another man.

One such man was the newspaper tycoon Rupert Murdoch. An Australian who spent much of his time in aeroplanes, and who never remained in Britain for long enough to find out much about it, Murdoch was an early Thatcher admirer. He had access to Downing Street, and friends such as Woodrow Wyatt, a right-wing newspaper columnist and former Labour MP, in common with the prime minister. His papers, from the *Sun* to *The Times*, were among her most slavish supporters. But in November 1983, it seems, Murdoch had

had enough of Mrs Thatcher. Her attitude to President Reagan, he said, was 'just childish'. It was due to a more pervasive condition: 'She has gone out of her mind,' Murdoch volunteered. He wasn't quite sure why this had happened, but part of the problem was that she was 'desperately overtired'. Also, 'she's not listening to any friends – so I'm told.'[14]

Among these friends, who had certainly pressed his advice upon her in the past, was Paul Johnson, historian, newspaper columnist and a famous convert from socialism, which he had once upheld as editor of the *New Statesman*. Around this time, Johnson apparently underwent yet another conversion, from gushing admirer to patronising critic of the prime minister.

Ever since she became the Conservative leader, Johnson had offered hardly a word against her. Week after week, this admirable historian, so scholarly and punctilious in his books, put his journalism at the service of the only serious politician he could discover in all of British politics. During the Falklands war, under a headline calling her the best man in the cabinet, he had particularly praised her male qualities – 'a robust lady, morally as well as physically' – and even likened her performance to the 'gigantic and leonine spirit' of Winston Churchill.[15]

But now, for some reason, everything had changed. The decision not to accompany the Americans into Grenada was a 'huge failure of judgment, by far her worst since she took office'. Johnson said it had shattered his confidence in Mrs Thatcher 'as an intuitive politician'. Her feelings of umbrage at being excluded from Reagan's confidence revealed a fatal flaw. 'She felt spurned, slighted, ignored. For the first time, one was conscious she was conforming to a female stereotype.'

'I have given her a degree of loyalty and support I have accorded to no other politician,' the affronted Johnson concluded. 'But if her judgment can no longer be trusted, what is left? A very ordinary woman, occupying a position where ordinary virtues are not enough.'[16]

Fortunately, Johnson soon recovered himself. Another quick somersault returned him to his old allegiance. And the Murdoch papers, notwithstanding that the proprietor judged Mrs Thatcher to be off her head, continued to favour her with their support. But these were unexpected verdicts to confront her within six months of a second glorious victory. Along with the critiques of the departed ideologues, they were a reminder that every politician, however garlanded with tributes from sworn champions, must always be prepared for periods of treachery and desertion when they have to soldier on regardless. Re-election was a necessary but hardly a sufficient condition for political triumph.

16

Vanquishing Lucifer

THE QUALITY WHICH distinguishes politicians from most other people, and good politicians from bad ones, is resilience. The politician can never afford to be crushed by disaster, or to lose hold of the inextinguishable optimism which says that vindication lies only a few months, or perhaps a few years, in the future. Surrounded by opponents and critics and sceptics and other deriders merely waiting for the fall, every political leader must develop their own defences. Often this lies in the kind of consolation to be derived from the crude fact of office. I am in power, says the leader privately to himself. I have been elected for several more years. My business is to act and, whatever the critics may say, they do not have the power to act. In the end, they don't matter as much as I do. If I stand firm and sit tight, I can see them off because until the next election I am inside the gates and they can never do more than hurl insults and occasional bricks through the bars.

In Margaret Thatcher's case this would always have been an inadequate account of her state of mind. No doubt she occasionally took comfort from her guaranteed security of tenure, as these treacherous friends began so publicly to reassess her. But, unlike some of her predecessors, she wasn't prone to despair about the condition of the country or her capacity to improve it. She was propelled into this state of confidence by an inner force, to which no British prime minister since Gladstone had laid claim with quite such unembarrassed clarity. As she once told a journalist during a particularly difficult period: 'I am in politics because of the conflict between good and evil, and I believe that in the end good will triumph.'[1]

This sense of mission had many aspects to it, none more passionately felt than the part of it which related to the powerhouse of the economy – industry, coupled with the enemies of industry which were trade unions. Here were the perfect exemplars of good and evil, the complete epitomising reason for a politician to devote herself to ensuring the victory of the one over the other. And if there was one theatre in which this great moral drama would necessarily be played out, it was where the worst of the bad met the worst of the good and had already come close to gaining the victory of Lucifer.

Mrs Thatcher had always said, when asked to crystallise the essence of the British disease, that the nationalised industries were the seat of it: where monopoly unions conspired with monopoly suppliers, to produce an inadequate service to the consumer at massive cost to the taxpayer.

They were, she thought, two sides of the same debased coinage. The industries, which should have had virtue on their side, were hopelessly distorted and confined by state control and the absence of market competition. The unions, who were the beneficiaries of these monopolies, were accomplices to the most scandalous inefficiencies, and had to be stripped of their power.

Through all the hard times, this moral vision contributed greatly to Mrs Thatcher's personal brand of resilience, but the part of it with the longest pedigree concerned the bad rather than the good: the unions, which the Tories reckoned they knew what to do with, rather than the industries, about which they began by being considerably less certain. In respect of the unions, the boundaries of the unthinkable had been significantly redrawn during the first term. The Employment Act 1980 restricted picketing, weakened the closed shop and curtailed union immunities for secondary action. The Employment Act 1982 further weakened the closed shop, greatly increased the rights of individuals against unions, outlawed political strikes and exposed union funds to liability for unlawful industrial action. In addition, several public sector strikes had been permitted to last much longer than they might otherwise have done had the Government not been determined to produce the famous 'demonstration effect' – that is, a demonstration of who was boss, whatever the short-term consequences. Thus, a steel strike had lasted thirteen weeks; health workers, civil servants, water workers and the rail unions had all been seen off.

This was only the beginning of a continuous process. The process was directed towards establishing an irreversible shift of power away from trade unions. This required, as a preliminary, something else: the overturning of an assumption that had lasted for decades, which said that certain principles and also certain unions composed a kind of 'no-go' area where sensible governments did not dare to tread. Such an overturning was congenial to the Thatcher vision, according exactly with her need for the presence of good and evil in all her major political undertakings. The prospect of it at the beginning of 1984 transcended the difficulties which, to the outside world, seemed already to have tarnished her. Its fulfilment a year later, with the least mistakable demonstration effect of all, was the most positive event of the entire four years of the second term.

It was preceded by a lesser event in the same apparently impassable territory. If the National Union of Mineworkers was the last enemy, the right of workers to be trade unionists at all was the last sacred cow. Each was sent to the slaughterhouse with a firmness of purpose that owed a lot, and in one case everything, to the adamantine personal opinions of the leader herself.

On 25 January, the Foreign Secretary announced without forewarning that the Government Communications Headquarters, a Whitehall outpost for which he was responsible, would henceforth cease to permit trade unions to operate inside it. No employee of GCHQ would be allowed to belong to a union. The reason, he said, was that the possibility of industrial disruption at GCHQ had now to be excluded. It was a high-security listening-post, a vital link in the chain of such places which allowed the Western world to eavesdrop on Soviet and other communications. Between 1979 and 1981, the civil service unions had selected GCHQ as a suitable target for selective industrial action in pursuit of broader union objectives, with the loss of a total of 10,000 working days. This sort of disruption in service was, in the Government's view, intolerable. The unions must go, and every member would be offered £1,000 in exchange for the sacrifice of what were customarily regarded as fundamental rights.

The announcement caused uproar in the still not entirely demoralised ranks of trade unionism. There was some consternation among Conservatives as well. Curbing trade union immunities was one thing, abolishing the right to belong was quite another, especially when it was done on a pretext which another minister had already discounted. As long ago as April 1981, shortly after the main 'day of action' at GCHQ, the then Defence Secretary, John Nott, had issued a statement saying that 'this dispute has not in any way affected operational capability'. Now the Government was apparently countermanding that assessment, and taking the largest stride it had yet attempted towards the beginning of a union-free state. The TUC, after years on the defensive, girded for action.

Suddenly though it was announced, it was not in fact a hasty decision. Ministers, led by the prime minister, had thought about banning unions at GCHQ before the 1983 election. The 1981 disruption horrified security chiefs, and compromised the confidence of the Americans with whom GCHQ secrets were closely shared. Further American disquiet had been caused by the arrest of a GCHQ employee, Geoffrey Prime, and his conviction in 1983 as a Soviet spy. All in all, the eavesdropping agency, from being an establishment whose function no government had formally acknowledged and which had an almost invisible public profile, became a major focus of ministerial concern. The decision to ban the unions finally elevated it from obscurity to daily tabloid prominence. Institutionally, indeed, GCHQ was one of the great discoveries of the Thatcher years, its new and universal notoriety a rare contribution to more open government.

So fierce was the row and so inept was Howe's first defence of the action that the search for a compromise was immediately set in train: at the heart of it, one of the more ambiguous characters in the Thatcher entourage, who himself, rather like GCHQ, was soon driven from behind the veil of a cherished privacy to become one of the most highly and damagingly publicised men of his time.

As cabinet secretary, Robert Armstrong occupied a post which all its previous incumbents had succeeded in keeping shrouded in mystery. In the persons of Norman Brook, Burke Trend and John Hunt, the cabinet secretary was the mandarin of mandarins, a high priest of administration, endowed with power and influence he took care to maximise by the device of being neither seen nor heard outside the most secret places of government. But Armstrong had been saddled with other duties, of a more public nature. As head of the civil service, he was in charge of all civil service management and pay negotiation: also, more elusively, of such matters as the morale and professionalism and even the ethical dilemmas of a service which ever since 1979 had been made to feel more like the enemy than the valued ally of the elected politicians. Naturally it fell to Armstrong to hear the passionate objections of the employees at GCHQ, supported by most of the trade union movement. While it was not the most arduous of the public duties he did the prime minister – two far more searing experiences awaited him, which to his great discomfort made him more famous than at least half the cabinet – it rather exposed his ambivalent position. For while, as head of the civil service, he needed to keep civil servants happy, as cabinet secretary he was both the senior agent of their chief tormentor, the prime minister, and her principal adviser on security, the imperilling of which was supposed to be the reason for the ban on unions at GCHQ.

But this is the kind of conundrum which senior mandarins are paid to resolve, and Armstrong duly did so. After lengthy negotiation, he appeared to be on the verge of extracting agreement from the civil service unions that, in exchange for retaining union membership, they would offer binding guarantees against any further industrial disruption at GCHQ. A unique threat seemed to have produced a unique concession. It attracted, moreover, a lot of ministerial support. For many ministers, including some like Howe who were involved in the original decision, now felt that this was a quite unnecessary crisis which cried out for compromise.

They reckoned without the prime minister's willpower, which had the capacity to harden inflexibly when it was crossed. The greater the fury over GCHQ, the more obsessive became her determination to see the decision through. Some of the dissidents, Whitelaw prominent among them, mobilised support for compromise while she was on a foreign trip and presented her with the case for it on her return. Maybe it was the place she had been to which hardened her belief that anything less than total victory would be a concession to the forces of darkness. A visit to Moscow, for the funeral of the Soviet leader Yuri Andropov, was hardly likely to have set her musing on the possibility that Geoffrey Prime's trade union might have a place in Britain's defences after all.

Whatever the cause, on returning from Moscow she was in no mood to accept the Armstrong compromise. Even had she been tempted, there were people around her who knew how to return her to her natural instincts. At one point, when the cabinet secretary seemed to be making some headway with his case for peace and a quiet life, eye-witnesses were struck by the crucial intervention of her press secretary, Bernard Ingham, supported by her private secretary, now Robin Butler. After all, the subtle course would have been to wait for the union conferences to overturn the menacing deal their GCHQ members had accepted. Or to see whether individual employees would reject it. In either event, the Government would be seen to have made a gesture and not be responsible for de-unionising part, perhaps only the first part, of the civil service. But Ingham moved in with the decisive line. 'It will look like a U-turn,' he told the prime minister. 'It will *be* a U-turn.'

'The Tsarina has returned,' one minister remarked when she delivered the final rebuff to Armstrong's efforts. Although the verdict of Denis Healey, the shadow foreign secretary, would normally be dismissed by Conservative backbenchers as vitriolic hyperbole, on this occasion it struck some of them as a credible rendition of the facts. 'Who is the Mephistopheles behind this shabby Faust?' he inquired, referring to Howe. 'The answer is clear enough – to quote her own backbenchers – the great she-elephant, she who must be obeyed, the Catherine the Great of Finchley, the prime minister herself.'

The consequences of the GCHQ decision dribbled on for months, and then years. Although 95 per cent of the staff complied with the decision, the grievances of the rest were aired in several court cases and the principle of the Government's right to act in this way had to reach the Court of Appeal before receiving judicial approval. As late as 1988, action was still being taken against individual GCHQ employees who declined to accept their new conditions of employment.

But the political message emerged far sooner. There were two very clear signals. One was that when the prime minister had taken a public stance she would not be deflected from it merely by universal outrage. Indeed, she found particularly rich nourishment in the insults of her enemies. Their defence of old shibboleths merely confirmed the necessity of her mission to destroy them.

Secondly there was the union signal. From the point of view of the system, this was the more significant. For these events coincided with what the trade unions, and especially the general secretary of the TUC, Len Murray, regarded as the beginning of a process of almost revolutionary generosity on their own part. After four years of battle fiercely fought but always lost, the TUC's response to the 1983 election was to gear itself for what Murray called the 'new realism'. Ever so gingerly, Murray himself began to construct a strategy which he hoped might bring the unions and the Government into some kind of collaborative dialogue with each other about matters of common interest.

He had had difficulty in persuading some important members of the TUC General Council to go along with this approach. To them it sounded like treating with the enemy. But they had acquiesced. Now the GCHQ affair rendered his efforts null. Before it was finally closed, he led a TUC delegation to Downing Street to press the unions' case. It was only his third visit there since 1979: a poignant sign of the times. The prime minister's attitude was worse than uncompromising. It was, thought Murray, profoundly insulting. What she told him, in effect, was that trade union members could not be trusted with national secrets. Their union membership, in other words, was not compatible with their patriotic duty.

This was the epitaph on the new realism. It was also the end of

357

Murray. Two months later he announced his premature retirement from his job, ostensibly on the grounds of ill-health but as much, so his friends said, because he believed the Government's attitude left him with no purpose to serve.

It was as a harbinger, however, that the GCHQ decision could later be seen for what it really was. It expressed an attitude, announced a determination, and enforced a priority which previous governments shrank from. In this way it set the stage for a larger struggle, across ground not confined to a recondite branch of government but encompassing the whole industrial nation.

The map of this terrain was drawn a long time earlier. The hazards it threw up in relief had been contemplated since almost the first days of the Thatcher leadership. It was apparent to those most committed to that leadership that the portion of the capitalist integument commanded by the state was too large, and that sooner or later the trade unions associated with it would have to be confronted.

The principal map-maker had been one of the few men removed from the Heath Government for overtly ideological reasons. Nicholas Ridley had the wrong social pedigree for a natural Thatcherite, having been educated at Eton. But he burned with zeal for the free market and the diminution of the state; and as a Heath reject his appeal to the early Thatcher was beyond doubt. In the late 1970s, he set to work on some unthinkable thoughts about tackling the nationalised industries, and produced a report which, along with 'Stepping Stones', John Hoskyns' analysis of how the unions might be broken,[2] provided a blueprint for the more adventurous Thatcherites to contemplate and, some day, act upon.

Ridley believed that the nationalised industries were from every point of view deplorable. Over-subsidised, uncompetitive and monopolistic, they could not but be inefficient and under-productive. His report[3] proposed a strategy for dismantling them, or at least for removing their offensive dependence on subsidy from the taxpayer's bottomless purse. They should be set 'totally inflexible' financial targets, which they could meet only by the wholesale closure of unprofitable plants. Their managers should manage, free from ministerial interference. Managers not ministers should determine how far the workforce at British Leyland, British Rail and the rest would be reduced, and should also be responsible for their own prices and pay rates. Government finance for their investment programmes should be gradually cut to zero over a ten-year period. Eventually, the state corporations should be split into smaller entities. At all times, the ending of subsidy would be the ultimate object of the exercise.

Noticeable by its absence from the Ridley plan was, significantly, privatisation. Even for him that was a thought too far, in 1978. But the regime he proposed would to some extent mimic the virtues of private companies, including tough-minded management, reduced union power and the creation of competition.

Ridley also thought about how this revolution might be imposed. For it was more than a revolution of ideas. It would challenge vested interests and almost certainly provoke a massively disruptive response. So he suggested a series of tactics with which to buttress the strategy, to be applied before any challenge was undertaken. These were cold-bloodedly pragmatic. For example, if one of the most sensitive industries was involved – which Ridley identified as water, sewers, electricity, gas and the health service – he recommended that the figures in the accounts should be massaged so as to appear to justify payment of an above-average wage claim. He urged that the greatest deterrent to any strike would be 'to cut off the money supply to the strikers, and make the union finance them'. There should also be strong, mobile police reinforcements available to prevent violent picketing, and 'good, non-union drivers' recruited to cross the picket lines.

These ideological preparations were, needless to say, concealed from view during the 1979 election. Truth to tell, they exceeded the anticipation of most ministers as to what might be regarded as possible during the first term. But they closely reflected the opinion of the leader about the collectivist assumptions that ought, one day, to be smashed and the forward thinking any prudent politician would need to do beforehand. Accordingly, during the first term, little of the Ridley plan was called into service. The steel strike and the civil service strike, together with trouble on the railways and at British Leyland, had all been canvassed by him and duly met an obdurate government response. But the onslaught against the very structure of state industry and the unions that went with it began only in modest vein. Some British Rail assets were sold, British Gas lost some of its monopolies, British Telecom was exposed to competition on equipment supplies; but full conversion from public to private sector was limited to the National Freight Corporation, some of the docks and the radio-chemical centre, Amersham International.

Such tentative beginnings, however, were not meant to signify a departure from the Ridley scheme. As time went on, ministers became more solidly convinced than they had been in 1978 that the wholesale removal of state control, rather than tinkering with the financial regime imposed on state industries, was as politically popular as it was economically necessary. In September 1982, Nigel Lawson, who as Energy Secretary had several of these industrial baronies under his command, said that this could not be allowed to continue. 'No industry should remain under state ownership unless there is a positive and overwhelming case for it so doing. Inertia is not good enough. We simply cannot afford it.'[4] In so saying, Lawson was by now speaking for the whole Government.

Besides, while not yet ready to act out her own ideological imperatives, Mrs Thatcher had intervened aggressively on a different front, that of appointments. She might, for the moment, be stuck with the industries, but she was determined not to be stuck with all the industrial leaders whom she had inherited from the earlier age. Industry was no exception to her general belief, which she held and deployed with a peculiarly feminine mixture of tenacity and intuition, that personality – the right personality, a personality to which, above all, *she* could give her unfettered admiration – was the key to successful change.

As usual, her ideas about these personalities, the good and the bad, the 'one of us' and the 'one of them', were unnervingly decisive.

Business people had been high in her estimation for many years, beginning with the keeper of the corner-store in Grantham. She grew up with a natural understanding that business made the world go round, and she married, to her inestimable advantage, into the business community. Through her earlier career, she was never less than an orthodox practitioner of Conservative faith in the link between business and politics and a thriving economy. But it was perhaps only when she became leader of the party that her admiration of a certain kind of business leader reached its full flowering.

The kind she really admired were not the captains of industry but, rather, freebooting entrepreneurs who had built something from nothing. A representative case was Frank Taylor, who in 1921, when he was sixteen, founded a small building firm called Taylor Woodrow. Over the decades, Taylor Woodrow grew into one of the half-dozen largest construction companies in Britain and had a world-wide presence. To Margaret Thatcher the story of Frank Taylor had an inextinguishably romantic appeal. She saw his as an example of the

most worthwhile kind of life imaginable, and in 1982 raised him to
the peerage.

At times, indeed, it seemed as though no other way of life was truly
virtuous, including her own. Certainly a journalist's did not compare.
One of my own encounters with her, at a social occasion far from
home, consisted of a harrying inquiry as to why I didn't abandon
journalism and start doing something really useful, like setting up a
small business.

Surveying her inheritance by reference to this set of prejudices, she
was soon dissatisfied with the men through whom she was supposed
to carry out her task as the ultimate owner of public industries. Some,
like Sir Peter Parker, the chairman of British Rail, were seen as the
embodiment of the old consensus: a correct perception in the case of
Parker who, although a manager of proven talent, had devoted a
remarkably large part of his life to the incomprehensible perversion
of actually believing in nationalised industry. Others, like Sir Derek
Ezra, chairman of the National Coal Board, had long since been
marked down by the Thatcher people as a disposable asset. In Ezra's
case, the die was cast at a meeting Mrs Thatcher had with a group of
nationalised industry chairmen quite soon after she became leader
of the Opposition. A witness, Sir Monty Finniston, who was present
as chairman of British Steel, recalled the moment: 'She virtually
roasted poor Derek Ezra alive. She said that, when she got into
power, he wouldn't get away with what he was doing in the Coal
Board with the miners, she'd see to that.'[5]

Others again were marginally more acceptable. Sir Michael Edwardes, chairman of British Leyland since 1977, had proved himself
in a number of tough battles with the car workers, although BL was
still consuming immense sums of taxpayers' money. He later recounted
a somewhat spiky relationship. The first meeting was not auspicious.
At lunch with the BL board in January 1979, the leader of the
Opposition 'had scarcely taken her seat before she fired the first salvo.
"Well Michael Edwardes, and why should we pour further funds into
British Leyland?" She glared stonily around the table at each of us in
turn.'[6]

Later, when the BL problem had become her problem, requiring
further large injections of funds, Edwardes found her resenting both
it and him. He also experienced a taste of the kind of interventionism
which even Mrs Thatcher – especially Mrs Thatcher – could not
resist. In public she would say, in accordance with Tory orthodoxy,
'We have to back Michael Edwardes' judgment. He's the manager,

I'm not the manager.' In private it was a different story. Downing
Street insisted on being constantly involved, to the exclusion of other
ministers. 'Everything of any conceivable political consequence was
referred to Number 10,' Edwardes found, 'not only the strategic
decisions on funding but even matters such as the chairman's
remuneration. Moreover this was no rubber-stamping process. Recommendations on other matters were frequently overturned.'

The truth is that Edwardes could never have expected to find
unalloyed favour. Nor, it would seem, did he particularly want to.
He was associated in the prime minister's mind more with a problem
than with a solution. And besides, he came from the past. He owed
nothing to her.

This was still truer of Arnold Weinstock. Managing director of
GEC, Weinstock had made himself into one of the great icons of
late-twentieth-century British industry. But he was just the kind
of industrialist to whom the great romancer of entrepreneurship was
least likely to warm. For years, GEC had grown fat, in part, off
cost-plus defence contracts and monopoly supplies to such captive
customers as British Telecom. This made Weinstock a powerful and
much-consulted figure under previous governments, but his relationship with the Thatcher Administration was more adversarial.

He lobbied intensively against the privatisation of British Telecom,
thinking wrongly that the sale would be a failure, and predicting
rightly that it would increase the power of BT to bargain with his
own company. But this was only the beginning of his critique. In
1985, he took a prominent part in the most carefully orchestrated
attack made by industry on the entire thrust of the Government's
economic policy. This emerged, of all places, from the House of
Lords. Numerous ennobled company chairmen past and present
testified before a Select Committee to the effect that, owing to the
decline in manufacturing industry, the country faced disaster when
North Sea oil dried up. The report, doom-laden in its pessimism, was
scathingly rejected by the Government – a 'mixture of special pleading
dressed up as analysis and assertion masquerading as evidence', said
Nigel Lawson. But Lord Weinstock's contribution was not forgotten.
He ridiculed the claim that service industries could fill the gap left by
manufacturing decline, and asserted that, while the standard of
management in industry had improved, 'the standard of management
in government has not'.[7]

So Weinstock was yesterday's man, a symptom of times past. Others
supplanted him in the salons and antechambers of political power.

Two of them in particular achieved great prominence as the kind of managers of public industry whom the leader could really believe in.

John King, who became chairman of British Airways in 1980, was the perfect model of a Thatcherite. Like Frank Taylor, he began from nothing. The son of a private soldier, he left school having passed no examinations and got jobs in a variety of engineering workshops. At nineteen he had his own business, making components for Rolls-Royce; at twenty-eight he built a factory on derelict land in south Yorkshire and proceeded to make his fortune out of ball bearings. 'I wondered whether one was grand enough for the Tories,' he later recalled of that time. 'I was certainly too grand for the Labour Party. So I had a look at the Liberal Party, and when I discovered that it was nothing more than a convenient attitude of mind, I got on with being a Tory.'8 And thirty years later, with the Thatcher leadership beginning, Tories were a lot less grand than they used to be. The fact that King himself had become very grand indeed, master of the Belvoir Hunt and owner of 2,000 acres in Leicestershire, in no way rendered him ineligible for membership of the Thatcher circle of acceptable faces of capitalism. Entirely to the contrary.

King's first service, alongside his position as chairman of the engineering company Babcock International, was as chairman of the National Enterprise Board, with a brief to wind up a body which Tories regarded as the quintessence of corporatist folly. This was achieved in short order. Next, again while remaining in charge of Babcock, he accepted the British Airways job and the much more difficult task of ending its monstrous overmanning and returning it to profit. In three years he had done it: a brilliant achievement. He sacked 23,000 of the 57,000 staff and turned a loss of £140 million a year into a profit of £214 million. In a nice union of Thatcherite stars, King, the favourite businessman, and Saatchi & Saatchi, then the favourite advertising agency, projected British Airways as the world's favourite airline and propelled it eventually into the private sector.

But King, duly ennobled in 1983, was more than a hard manager. He became a Whitehall operator of formidable influence, which derived at bottom from the blessing he was known to have received from Downing Street. This wasn't enough to win all the battles. He didn't get the privatisation through as soon as he wanted. But he did succeed, through the ruthless deployment of his clout with the prime minister, in brushing ministers aside and preventing some BA routes being handed over to the rival airline British Caledonian. And through it all a barking, posturing arrogance proclaimed a man quite certain he was 'one of us'. Did Mrs Thatcher admire him, he was asked on television in 1986. 'Well, she didn't say she didn't,' he riposted with a complacently dismissive smile.[9]

King was one of a handful of business people whose names kept cropping up for any number of state industry chairmanships. At an early point he was canvassed for British Steel. But in this group his ubiquitous presence was exceeded by that of one other man, named Ian MacGregor: a different character, with a very different temperamental connection to the Thatcherite enterprise, yet the man destined to take the most important part of all in grappling with the beast she had identified as the most fearsome of her enemies.

MacGregor was a Scots-American. A metallurgist by training, he had built a prosperous career not through ownership but through management. After a few years with metal-bashing companies in Scotland, he emigrated to the US and led a long, successful business life rising through the ranks of the mining conglomerate Amax Inc., of which he was chairman from 1969 until 1977. By then he was sixty-five, but by no means ready to retire. So he embarked on a new career as a New York banker, first with Lehman Brothers and then with Lazard Frères. Except for a small number of businessmen, nobody in Britain had ever heard of him.

Those few, however, had good connections. The first was Ronald Grierson, a merchant banker with Warburg's, a colleague of Weinstock's on the GEC board, and a man with a considerable finger in the corporate state. These were the old ante-Thatcher days. In 1975, through Grierson, MacGregor was approached to take a big job in British Leyland, but at that time was only able to be a part-time board member. He became deputy chairman in 1977, after leaving Amax.[10]

Thus did MacGregor place himself for the first time on the British map. But hardly anyone would have known it. At the time the only name associated with BL was Edwardes': a perception largely unchanged until several years later, when MacGregor published his autobiography and the world learned at last that it was in fact he who persuaded Edwardes to take the job, and he who, as deputy chairman, headed the 'unique quartet of board members' who were instrumental in keeping Edwardes up to the mark.

MacGregor's second fruitful encounter occurred six months into the Thatcher Government, with a member of the newer business establishment, Sir Hector Laing. Laing, the chairman of United Biscuits, was a friend more of Jim Prior than of Margaret Thatcher, but he was an energetic performer at the interface of business and politics, and apparently a self-appointed head-hunter for the top jobs. At any rate, when Laing ran into MacGregor in New York and heard from the latter about his struggles at Lazards with the US steel industry, he said, according to MacGregor's own account: 'My God! You may be the person we need. I was talking to the prime minister the other day and heard her concern as to how she could find someone to get British Steel into better shape. Maybe you're just the man she's looking for.'[11]

Prior himself in fact takes credit for MacGregor being offered the chair of British Steel. He was one of the few people who did know him, for the old-fashioned reason that David Prior, his eldest son, worked for MacGregor at Lazards. But at the time the man who felt the heat was the Industry minister, Sir Keith Joseph. The heat derived from some unusual financial arrangements, by which the British Government undertook to pay a total of £1.8 million over three years for the chairman's services, if he managed to turn British Steel round. It was this fee, offered to an unknown Scotsman now well past retirement age, which finally thrust MacGregor into the British con- sciousness, where he arrived in the wake of an unpropitious question posed to Joseph after he had announced the appointment. The Labour front bench brutally inquired of the Industry Secretary: 'Is the Right Honourable Gentleman well?'

At British Steel, however, MacGregor did a successful job. He took over just after the debilitating strike, and in three years laid the basis for a much-shrunken but much more efficient British steel industry. Just as important, he came fully into the sights of the prime minister. Before he started the steel job, she had been as ignorant about him as everyone else. The moment of their first meeting, when she gave him his brief, evoked a homely response from the old Scotsman. 'Most families have one like her,' he wrote afterwards. 'She didn't beat about the bush. In some ways she was like my mother – who always had a clear idea of what she wanted to do.'[12]

For her part, she came to admire MacGregor to distraction. Quite soon he became, although never so committed as others to dining out on the political circuit, a member of an extremely select elite, as Prior later noted in a sentence which is as graphically descriptive of the Thatcher self-image as it is of MacGregor's reputation. 'She once went so far as to say he was the only man she knew who was her equal,' Prior recorded.[13]

What more could there be for such a paragon to set his hand

to? Only one answer impressed itself: the largest, most obstinately recalcitrant Conservative enemy, the National Union of Mineworkers.

No name was scarred more deeply on the Conservative soul than that of the NUM. For Margaret Thatcher the miners were where she came in. If they hadn't humiliated the Heath Government into fighting an election which it lost, she would not now be party leader and prime minister. But this mattered less than the memory of that bloody defeat itself, and the apprehension that it might always be capable of happening again.

Nor was bitter recollection confined to 1974. There had been a more recent exchange of fire. In early 1981, another pit strike had been averted only by a swift climb-down on the Government side, promoted by the prime minister but resented by her all the same. Above all she was impatient with the man who, as she saw things, had let it happen, the chairman of the National Coal Board, Sir Derek Ezra.

He had survived the threat which Monty Finniston remembered her making in the 1970s. But now his time had come. There was more than a suspicion in Whitehall that Ezra may have helped to provoke the 1981 dispute, letting it be known how many pits would shut and hoping by that means to create trouble enough to induce the Government to relax the limits on NCB borrowing.

On the morning after the 1983 election, Mrs Thatcher appointed a new Secretary of State for Energy. She told him that some time during the course of the next Parliament the miners' leader, Arthur Scargill, would mount a challenge to the Government. This would be an essentially political assault. He would, she said, try to use the industrial clout of the miners to achieve his Marxist objectives.[14]

Peter Walker was the politician chosen to prepare for this confrontation. His industrial counterpart, although not yet in place, was already selected. Ezra had left the board in July 1982, but the Government, and above all its leader, were determined that no trace of Ezra-ism, playing footsie with the union and squeezing endless subsidy out of government, should survive.

Ian MacGregor, it seems, took a little persuading. He recalls advising the prime minister to find somebody younger for the task.[15] Others, by contrast, said at the time that MacGregor didn't want to leave British Steel and was actually suggesting that he should run it and the Coal Board at the same time. Either way, it was into the hands of this transatlantic veteran, schooled in the business environment which she passionately wished to replicate in her own country, that the prime minister happily entrusted what would be the defining event of her second term in office.

The Government's belief that the miners would present it with a frontal challenge was made good within four weeks of the election. Arthur Scargill, president of the NUM and, as the prime minister correctly observed, a Marxist, said that the election result was 'the worst national disaster for a hundred years'. He particularly insisted that it was 'undemocratic', since a parliamentary majority of 144 had resulted from the votes of only a minority of the electorate. This intolerable propensity of the British voting system made Scargill the most left-wing member of the Labour Party to favour electoral reform. But more immediately it validated, in his eyes, his thirst for revolutionary action. 'A fight-back against this government's policies will inevitably take place outside rather than inside Parliament,' he told the union's conference on 4 July. 'Extra-parliamentary action will be the only course open to the working class and the labour movement.'

For this action the Government had made a number of preparations. It was an example, a fairly rare one, of the leader's capacity for strategic planning. She was not by habit a strategist. Although she had pictures in her mind of the kind of place she would like Britain to become – a vision, even, of what it would take at least two terms in office to bring about – the common experience of those who worked closely with her was that she did not instinctively relate present problems to some grand conceptual plan. Because of her vivid personality and emphatic way of speaking, she was usually depicted otherwise: as a politician whose ideology was so complete that all the answers were preordained, and whose presence was so commanding that everything she did had a kind of interlocking consistency, with all the details correctly in their place. But this was propaganda, put about not so much by her staff as by an adoring press. At close quarters, it all looked rather different.

In the case of the miners, however, she had thought ahead. Tribal memories required it. So since the 1981 débâcle the NCB had been given every financial and other encouragement to produce more coal than anyone could consume, and the Central Electricity Generating Board given similar inducements to pile up the stocks at power stations.

This procedure conformed with the Ridley battle-plan of 1978. Ridley had in fact identified coal, along with the docks and the railways, in an intermediate category of risk, less terminally sensitive to the life of the nation than water and gas. But any coal stoppage meant possible cuts in power supplies, so the maximum contingency planning would be needed. Thus, Ridley also recommended, as well as the heaviest possible stockpiling, readying the electricity grid for more oil-fired generation. This, too, became a crucial aid to survival once the strike began. And finally there was the preparation of the police. Here, circumstance had obliged the Home Office to move a very long way since 1981. The riots of that year, in London and Liverpool, had found both cities' police forces seriously under-equipped for crowd control, and lacking any satisfactory system of national co-ordination. In the aftermath, police vehicles, weaponry, communications devices and protective body armour were all expensively refurbished. The police National Reporting Centre, based at Scotland Yard, became a permanently available facility – to provide some of the benefits of a national police force without the odium of establishing one.

All in all, it was not surprising to hear the opinion of Lord Whitelaw at the height of the strike – a judgment on his own time as Home Secretary. 'If we hadn't had the Toxteth riots,' he told a group of journalists, 'I doubt if we could have dealt with Arthur Scargill.'

So this was a well-anticipated event. And the Government's stance towards it was equally well considered. As Scargill edged his juggernaut forward, first into an autumn ban on overtime and then, in the new year, towards an all-out strike, ministers positioned themselves for two purposes. The first was positive: to justify pit closures in the name of an efficient coal industry, and keep emphasising the generous terms – no compulsory redundancies, early retirement on better terms than any other industry, large redundancy payments to younger miners. The second purpose was more negative: once the strike began, which it did on 6 March 1984, ministers would for public purposes behave in conformity with the tenet they had always preached – that managers should manage. As the prime minister said often and righteously, alluding to numerous Labour governments of hated memory, there would be 'no beer and sandwiches at Number Ten'.

This was an accurate, but deceptive, promise. Only towards the end of the strike, when it was virtually all over, did a union official cross the threshold of the prime minister's residence. But no government as aware as this one of how much depended on the defeat of

Scargill would sensibly subcontract the task to an industrial manager without political experience. In the record of Margaret Thatcher, therefore, the miners' strike of 1984–5 is an episode which reveals certain dual capacities. Naturally it called on her famous firmness, falling perfectly into the moral mould where good and evil could be identified without ambiguity. Her most conspicuous contributions were of this kind: denouncing, hectoring, challenging, fighting, defiantly glorying in the bloody combat. But there was also another side to it, which was less prominent but almost as important, namely the practice of a shrewd dissimulation. For the sake of the greater good, she was prepared to go on insisting for months that government was merely a spectator at Ian MacGregor's battlefield when in truth government was never more interventionist – not least because of the conclusion, drawn by her and others quite early in the piece, that MacGregor, 'the only man who is my equal', wasn't entirely to be relied on.

The minister in charge of the operation, Peter Walker, himself had an ambivalent relationship with her. He was the one great survivor of Heathite Conservatism. She had retained him through the first term, but mainly as a kind of statutory court jester of the consensus politics she loathed. The only old wet who was regarded as rather too dangerous to release on to the backbenches, he did a competent job as Minister of Agriculture, and was now, she felt, the ideal candidate to handle a pit strike. Here, after all, was something they could agree about. Whatever Walker thought about the economic policy, with his mincing little coded speeches which hardly anybody now listened to, he would be entirely at one with the leader about the defeat of Scargill. He was also well endowed with the darker political skills that might be necessary. He was very experienced. He knew what he was doing. He had a record of maximising every public position in which he ever found himself. Above all, he was an expert manipulator of the media, having spent a fair amount of his political life attending to the way things would play on the nine o'clock news.

These talents proved to be more necessary than anyone anticipated. From the moment the strike began, Walker became the substitute for MacGregor's own helpless shortcomings in the area of presentation, while at the same time contriving, as best he could, to hold to the misleading contention that the politicians were standing aside.

The first time this involved the prime minister in the kind of deception which used to be graced with the epithet 'Wilsonian' concerned the decision not to deploy some of the legal remedies against strikers which were created by the 1980 and 1982 Employment Acts. As the strike got going and intimidation by flying pickets became steadily worse, the NCB did secure an injunction against them. But it consistently chose not to pursue the union for contempt of court when the injunction was flagrantly ignored; and other public sector industries declined to take their legal opportunities to get secondary action banned. Since these were Tory laws, their non-use on this most perilous occasion was the subject of much goading from the Opposition benches in the Commons. But the fiction was maintained for months that this had nothing to do with the Government. As late as July, Mrs Thatcher was still perpetuating it. Why hadn't the employers taken advantage of the legislation? she was asked on television. 'I have said in the House that if they wish to take action we certainly would not override them,' she replied. Pressed to instruct them to do so, she claimed only a limited role for government in the conduct of the strike. As far as the NCB was concerned, all she did was 'set them financial targets'.

Only later did the full measure of this deception become clear. A senior official at the Department of Employment gave me a graphic account of the calculations. British Steel, in particular, had pressed hard to go to court. But government, at the highest level, was adamant that this should not happen. The strategy, which had to be a political strategy, was to do nothing that might unite workers from steel or the railways or the docks with the miners, and nothing that would undermine the commitment of around 25,000 miners, mainly in Nottinghamshire, to defy the union and carry on working.

This decision to avoid unnecessary provocation was a classic piece of political generalship. So was an episode early in the strike which found ministers taking the closest interest, contrary to their professions of detachment, in negotiations over railwaymen's pay. A leaked letter from a Downing Street private secretary hardly reveals a prime minister recoiling from the detail of industrial management. 'She agrees that BR should increase its pay offer,' the letter specified. 'She accepts that the offer can be increased along the lines suggested. . . . She would be concerned if the offer were improved beyond this point. . . .'[16] When she still insisted that the Government was not intervening in the coal strike, Michael Foot, now speaking from the backbenches having resigned the Labour leadership, said that she had 'lied to the House' and the Speaker, unusually, did not require him to withdraw the accusation.[17]

Declining to give the railmen a pretext to join the miners was,

within the strategy, plainly a sensible initiative. But, even in the teeth
of the evidence, it somehow could not be admitted. At the managerial
level a myth had to be preserved. Partly this was to deprive the
miners' union of the full and open satisfaction that they were taking
on a deeply unpopular government, and doing so, at least in Scargill's
fevered imaginings, on behalf of the country as a whole. But also it
maintained the line. It was a piece of duplicity that revealed Mrs
Thatcher to be a rather more Machiavellian leader than many people
took her for.

Even so, it was in her more familiar role, of Amazonian scourge
and moralist, that she performed most convincingly. After sitting
tight and mostly silent for the first ten weeks of the strike, she found
plenty of targets for her wrath and numerous occasions when she
felt the need to show it. The more fastidious souls, like Jim Prior, deplored the extent to which the strike had been allowed to become a
matter of man-to-man combat with Scargill. Prior's temperamental
allies also tended to see the thing in rather fearful terms. John Biffen,
for example, would reflect dolefully on the inconvenient paradox that,
while it had become extremely important to the Tory Party to dance on
Scargill's grave, it was just as important to the Government, which had
to carry on living with the miners, that this should not occur.

Few such hesitations afflicted the prime minister. Through the
summer she delivered a series of broadsides against the union which
appeared to become steadily less judicious. Once again, as if to echo
1981 when the economic policy was under attack from a similar angle,
the point at issue became not merely the policy but the faint-hearts
in the party who were disposed to run away from it. They needed
stiffening. On 19 July, at the high point of her rhetorical onslaught,
she told the 1922 Committee of Conservative MPs that the striking
miners and their violence were 'a scar across the face of the country'.
Their shocking intimidations ought to summon from the nation the
spirit which had recently vanquished another enemy. 'We had to fight
an enemy without in the Falklands. We always have to be aware of
the enemy within, which is more difficult to fight and more dangerous
to liberty.'

'There is', she said, in a peroration of blazing grandiloquence, 'no
week, nor day, nor hour when tyranny may not enter upon this
country, if the people lose their supreme confidence in themselves,
and lose their roughness and spirit of defiance. Tyranny may always
enter – there is no charm or bar against it.'

A week later she pulverised the new Labour leader in the Commons.

Neil Kinnock, she said, had given aid and comfort to the NUM, and the party had 'allied itself to the wreckers against the workers'. Once again she was able to call upon highly personalised categories of moral righteousness. Kinnock she saw as the embodiment of the bad – 'there is only one word to describe his policy when faced with threats from home or abroad, and that word is appeasement.' She, by necessary implication, stood for everything that was good.

This atmosphere did not abate as autumn began. Momentarily, the beginnings of a dock strike looked like widening the crisis. The prime minister was due to spend a fortnight in Malaysia, Singapore and Indonesia. To carry out the commitment would exhibit a proper coolness, but to cancel it would proclaim that she was indispensable at home. She cancelled, while still maintaining the straight-faced fiction that this wasn't really the Government's strike at all.

Into this acrid climate was now pitched another drama, far more horrific in scale. On the night of 11 October, a bomb exploded at the Grand Hotel, Brighton, where she and the rest of the Tory leadership were staying for the Conservative party conference. Planted by Irish terrorists, it was plainly intended to murder the prime minister herself, and it very nearly did so. The terrorists misjudged by only a few feet where the seat of the explosion would be in relation to the movements of its main target. But five people were killed and many, including two of her most valued ministers, Norman Tebbit and the chief whip, John Wakeham, were seriously injured.

Nothing like it had ever happened before in Britain. The scenes at the hotel, shown on breakfast television, gripped the nation. The pictures of Tebbit being manoeuvred out of the rubble, terribly injured on his stretcher, brought home to people, perhaps as never before, the direct and constant danger to which British politicians are exposed by the IRA. None more so, though, than the British leader.

Upon her, two effects were visible or became known about. One, the visible and public effect, was to summon up her sangfroid. She, too, was inevitably seen on television, reacting and commenting. She showed extraordinarily few outward signs of shock, and still fewer of fear. Moving through crowds of reporters, she registered an unreal but impressive calm. It was as if such terrible deeds were only to be expected from her wicked enemies, and they must not be seen, by even so much as the flicker of an eyebrow, to have touched her. She was determined to enter the conference hall on time for a prompt beginning to the day's proceedings, which were to culminate with her speech. When she did so, no hair out of place and the picture of exaggerated insouciance, it was as if she almost relished this most extreme of challenges to fortitude. When she made her speech, she seemed to be showing that the atrocity only redoubled the sacred duty which fell to her as the vessel of democracy. 'It was an attempt not only to disrupt and terminate our conference,' she said. 'It was an attempt to cripple Her Majesty's democratically elected government.'

But that wasn't the whole story of her reaction. Privately, she was as terrified, according to friends, as any human being would expect to be. How could anyone shake off the knowledge that she, she in particular and above all, was the target? The event moved her far more deeply than her somewhat routine public expressions of contemptuous bravado might have indicated. When she returned to Chequers and a beautiful autumn weekend, she was said to have wept copiously, on reflecting that 'this was a day I wasn't meant to see.' Quite naturally, also, the iron entered still more deeply into her private, as well as public, attitude to terrorism. When, in future years, one inquired of her people why she was utterly obdurate – far more so than the leaders of most other governments – in her refusal to contemplate dealing with or talking to foreign 'terrorist' organisations, which included, according to her, the African National Congress as well as hostage-taking factions in the Lebanon, the unique personal experience at Brighton would be cited as one explanation.

It was also analogous, in some sense, to the miners' strike. Although that was far less of a human atrocity, it posed the same kind of social threat and demanded from the leader a similar sort of language. She did not take long to make the comparison explicit. Addressing the Carlton Club in November, she said: 'At one end of the spectrum are the terrorist gangs within our borders, and the terrorist states which finance and arm them. At the other end are the hard left operating inside our system, conspiring to use union power and the apparatus of local government to break, defy and subvert the laws.'[18]

Before the strike could be settled, however, there needed to be one more demonstration of her Machiavellian rather than Amazonian persona. The fiction of ministerial detachment was finally destroyed by the untimely irruption into the dispute of the pit deputies' union, Nacods. Nacods members occupied an overseeing role at all pits; it was against the law for any underground work to begin without a Nacods overseer present. With the Nottinghamshire pits remaining open, and a slow trickle back to work beginning at other pits, Nacods clearly had an importance which MacGregor and the board needed constantly to bear in mind. But instead of continuing to massage the union and its officials, the board decided in late summer to threaten members with the sack unless they undertook to cross NUM picket lines. By a majority of 82 per cent, this previously unmilitant union voted in favour of strike action.

If Nacods had struck, the entire government strategy would have been put in the gravest peril. The Nottinghamshire miners would have been forced to stop producing, and the trickle back elsewhere would have dried up. Much of September and October unfolded against a background of failed negotiation between the obdurate MacGregor, determined to drive an inflexible closure policy through the entire industry, and Nacods officials who knew they had a lot of power in their hands.

What MacGregor declined to see, however, Peter Walker and the prime minister were finally obliged to address. When the union named the day for the strike to start, 25 October, the myth of non-intervention was finally abandoned. The ministers moved in to insist that Mac-Gregor climb down.

MacGregor himself was disposed to blame Walker for this. Unable to believe that, left to herself, the heroic leader would surrender, he chose to conclude that she had been led astray. She was evidently persuaded that the public wouldn't accept that the board was entirely blameless if Nacods went on strike. 'Clearly the enormous anxieties of her ministers had been passed on,' MacGregor later wrote. And he recalled the words the prime minister said to him: 'You have to realise that the fate of this government is in your hands, Mr MacGregor. You have got to solve this problem.'[19]

The chairman obeyed his orders. A formula was found to buy off Nacods, and from then on the trickle back to work became a drift and eventually a flood. Scargill, characteristically, failed to exploit the Nacods climb-down and make a settlement which he could quite plausibly have described as victory. Had he done so in October, he might have deprived the Government of much political advantage, because the Nacods deal involved a substantial backing-off from the original pit-closure programme.

As it was, when TUC leaders made their way into Downing Street after more months of impasse, it was not as the defiant messengers of the working class, sent to lay down terms to exhausted ministers, but as accomplices of government in the search for procedures by which Scargill's struggle could finally be laid to rest.

The conclusion, however, was not quite as clean or simple as that. There was an odd disjunction between people's perceptions of what exactly had happened. Who should take the credit was also a question which somewhat blurred the outcome.

For months after the strike was over, ministers often alluded in conversation to the strange ingratitude of the British public. These ministers saw themselves as having engaged in a struggle for the very soul of democracy, in which they were conclusively victorious. People should understand what this meant, and see how triumphantly the balance of power between unions and politicians had been shifted closer to its proper alignment. Yet, as everyone could sense, there was no such consensus. When the strike ended, there was no full-throated roar of approval of the kind which had been heard, almost universally, when the Argentinians surrendered in Port Stanley.

One could speculate about the reasons. Certainly, the ending was messy. More and more miners went back to work, but Scargill was determined not to sign a surrender document and never did so. When the NUM executive split 11–11 on whether officially to recommend a return to work without an agreement, he declined to exercise his casting vote against it. But he was determined not to make any agreement either, or do anything to heal the divisions in the mining community.

And this was another reason, perhaps, for the ambiguousness of the public response. There had been a sense throughout the strike that the contest was, on both sides, something less than a heroic endeavour. While the scenes of violence and intimidation were appalling, and were mostly blamed on the union, not the police, these people were in no sense to be compared with the Argies of the Falklands war. They were our own people. Towards the end, a palpable feeling existed that the Government was as responsible as Arthur Scargill for the impossibility of reaching a negotiated settlement, mainly because, in the words of a minister sceptically observing the scene from afar, 'our leader will not be satisfied until Scargill is seen trotting round Finchley tethered to the back of the prime ministerial Jaguar.'

But ingratitude was felt in another quarter too. Throughout the strike, MacGregor's own relations with government had not been easy. With Walker they were frankly acrimonious, as he later revealed in his book, which speaks frequently of 'unpleasant sessions' with the minister and charges him with everything from ignorance and inexperience to near cowardice in the face of the enemy. For his part, Walker was no more enchanted, as finally became apparent from a review of this book written by his parliamentary private secretary,

Stephen Dorrell, faithful voice of his master. 'The government had quite simply come to doubt his competence,' Dorrell wrote, itemising six important moments at which MacGregor had got things badly wrong. 'Ian MacGregor had ceased to be part of the solution and had become part of the problem,' Dorrell-Walker witheringly concluded.[20]

But Walker was not the only source of the old man's feelings of rejection. Walker he could handle, because he so despised him. Mrs Thatcher was a different matter. She had shared the misgivings about both his tactics and his presentational skills. Now, with the strike over, she seemed to become more not less critical.

For the strike, in one sense, had ended nothing. Coal still needed to be dug, MacGregor was still in charge of the Coal Board, and in the summer of 1985 the Coal Board was obliged to announce a record £2,200 million loss. There still had to be relations between the owners and the chief manager of this inglorious enterprise. They did not go well for the manager. At one Downing Street lunch, the prime minister was reported to have been 'extremely relentless' in her criticism of the management, and MacGregor to be extremely peeved that she should give him a dressing-down in front of his subordinates. 'I have weals all over my back, which I would be happy to show you,' he complained to a reporter.[21]

Presumably to save some face with the reporter, he fell to pulling rank over the prime minister. Being at least half-American, he had plenty of contacts in Washington and was close, it seemed, to the president himself. Might he be looking for a big job over there? Might ministers be trying to ease his passage? MacGregor was scornful. 'Mrs Thatcher's the only one who has any sort of entrée in Washington,' he said, 'and she hasn't seen Ronnie for six months.'

Within a few more months, MacGregor's own entrée to Downing Street was nil. Contact with the prime minister ceased altogether. A sad demise for one of the business titans in whom she had once invested so much hope: but not one which actually affected her in the least.

For the truth was that, however muddy the surface waters, the deeper currents flowing out of the miners' strike carried her in the direction she wanted to go. The effect of it might not immediately penetrate the minds of the electorate, or surge with unqualified admiration through the pens of the opinion-forming classes. But certain quite profound political tendencies had been reinforced.

The first was in the Conservative Party. At last the catastrophe of

1974 had been avenged, and the revolution in attitudes towards trade unions, somewhat tentatively broached in 1979, nailed firmly into place. The miners, as everyone knew, and none knew better than Arthur Scargill, were the last redoubt of the old attitude. Some time there had to be a confrontation. And for the Conservatives defeat was not an option. Although the victory was nothing like a victory over foreigners, Scargill's own imperishable extremism successfully placed him in the folk-memory alongside the Argentinian leader General Galtieri as an important accessory to the Tories' continuing political domination.

The second useful tide which the strike set flowing was in the Labour Party. For Labour it was yet another divisive disaster. Scargill played Kinnock and the leadership of both party and trade unions like fish on the end of his line. Unable or unwilling to denounce him, they became passively associated with every offence he gave to the opinions of middle England. This was the line of least resistance. But in the end they paid for it, by slipping further and further out of the political reckoning.

In theory there was another way to look at these events, and the simultaneous war the Government was waging on local government in general and left-wing councils in particular. Both in the miners' strike and in penal assaults against Liverpool, Lambeth and other notorious concentrations of left-wing power, the Conservatives could have been said to be doing Kinnock's work for him. By eliminating Scargill from the board, they removed not only an enemy of the state but a major embarrassment for the middle-of-the-road brand of socialism which Kinnock was seeking to advance. But that is not the way the public saw it, or the way Kinnock was able to exploit it. He was left with the memory clinging to his name of violence inadequately rejected, and with a party in which significant numbers continued to see Scargill as he saw himself: the only one in all that multitude who dared to stand and fight against the evil of Thatcherism.

But thirdly there was the reinforcement in herself. This was as powerful as the others. She knew her second term had not started particularly well. As was always the case with her, challenge and struggle were the best way of reconfirming her purpose – as long as they were followed by victory. The method appealed to her sometimes alarmingly powerful sense of destiny. In the future, as things turned out, the second term would continue in all but one respect – the not inconsiderable matter of economic progress – to be fraught with domestic trouble. But Scargill's scalp was a permanent trophy, available for exhibit at any time. The woman who said, when driven to the bone of her belief, that she was in politics 'because of the conflict between good and evil' was in no doubt that good had triumphed.

17

Small World

IN THE CONDUCT of foreign affairs, good and bad may present themselves, to a leader with a disposition to moralise about the world, as clearly as they are manifested on the domestic scene. After all, good and bad people, pursuing good and bad causes, exist all over the globe, and are a permanent challenge to any politician who prides him or herself on knowing the difference between right and wrong. But there is a problem. International politics is more complex than domestic politics, which means that the weight of a moral attitude cannot usually be driven home with the same fervour applicable to an event like the 1984 miners' strike. This was one reason why foreign policy was never so congenial to Mrs Thatcher's personality as the constant struggle for economic reform at home. From time to time, it threw up demands for rectitude and moral courage, the commodities of which she saw herself as having a bottomless supply, but many issues were more subtle and all involved the interests of other sovereign states which usually, by their own lights, had as great a claim on justice as she did. The foreign policy of the second term consisted, in the main, of different kinds of compromise with this awkward fact – with some spectacularly different kinds of outcome.

It began with a rearrangement at the Foreign Office, a department which she held in considerably greater contempt even than she had visited on the rest of Whitehall, but which until June 1983 she had been able to do considerably less about. Now, as well as sacking the Foreign Secretary, she moved to try and exert over it greater personal control.

This initiative, which in the end did not really succeed, had its origin in the Falklands war. Of all the officials who came to her notice during the war, the one who had impressed her as much as anyone was the ambassador to the United Nations, Sir Anthony Parsons. It was, as he remembered better than she did, a renewed acquaintanceship. Parsons, when ambassador to Iran, had been graphically favoured with the then leader of the Opposition's opinions on the

379

iniquity encompassed by the phrase 'consensus politics'. Now the moment of his re-entry into her consciousness was almost as startling. In the middle of the war she telephoned him in New York and said: 'The Foreign Office has given me some advice which I don't accept for a moment. I want your opinion.'

Parsons, a sardonic and unstuffy character, was somewhat taken aback. 'But, prime minister,' he began, 'I must remind you that I am a member of the Foreign Office.'

She brushed this aside, in a rejoinder that somehow encapsulated all she felt about the department that had given Parsons employment for thirty years. 'I know, I know,' she said. 'But I don't consider *you* to be one of *them*.'

From this beginning, Parsons established a relationship which identified him as the man to become the prime minister's personal foreign policy adviser, a post that had not hitherto existed. There had been an economic adviser, Alan Walters, and fleets of other advisers on social and trade union and business policies, each of them selected as a counterweight inside Downing Street to the regular civil service. But the Foreign Office had escaped this kind of invigilation. When Mrs Thatcher plucked Parsons back from the brink of retirement in late 1982 and installed him beside her, Francis Pym, for one, descended even deeper into the gloom that had become his inescapable condition.

It could have been worse. Once the prime minister's intention became known, a strong rumour circulated that the appointee would be someone quite different: the incorrigible interferer Alfred Sherman. Among his many talents, Sherman reckoned mastery of foreign affairs to be not the least impressive. Although his own diplomatic faculties seemed to be deployed more consistently in the making of enemies than friends, he had still managed to resist complete exclusion from the prime minister's circle. Later, he served as her personal emissary on a tour through Central America to see what the Nicaraguans were up to, which ended with his being received at the White House. Had he been appointed to her office, he might have brought to bear on the Foreign Office something of the same uncomfortable dogmatism Walters applied to the Treasury. On the other hand, it must be doubted whether the orderly conduct of British diplomacy would ever have survived the shock.

Parsons, by contrast, was a Foreign Office man through and through, as he had reminded the prime minister. He reminded her of it again on being appointed. Visiting Downing Street to settle his terms and conditions of employment, he told her he wanted to discuss them with his old friends across the road. She was taken aback. 'Why?' she asked. 'It's got nothing to do with them. You're becoming *my* policy adviser.'

All the same, he went to the Foreign Office, and that is where his spirit remained for the year he served. It was the opinion of those best placed to witness it that he did rather more to interpret the Foreign Office to the prime minister than to communicate her imperative demands to them. He was a smoother of channels rather than an agent of control. Control, in the sense of daily intervention in the minutiae of policy-making, came later and by a different route. What now obtained was much greater wariness about everything that was presented to her, as Parsons later recalled: 'She would go through everything that came over from the Foreign Office, all the documentation, with a microscope and examine every single sentence, and test each sentence for the power of its reasoning and the clarity of expression. Nothing sloppy or woolly would escape her.'[1]

In place of Pym, moreover, she had Geoffrey Howe, as soon as the election gave her the opening. Howe might not be a soul-mate. There wasn't a trace of excitement between them. But she didn't actually detest Howe. He might disagree in private, and stubbornly press his case. But he would bear her roaring counter-attacks with practised resilience and never, but never, give the slightest hint in public that there was a difference between them. Nor in fact would he give obvious offence to the Foreign Office, since his diligence and discretion and distaste for anything resembling a drama mirrored the working habits of most professional diplomats. He would see that her writ ran among the infidels, without rousing them to rebellion.

Another of Mrs Thatcher's Falklands heroes, Sir Nicholas Henderson, ambassador in Washington at the time, once attempted to instruct a journalist in what he had seen at first hand of her attitude to diplomacy. 'You see, she doesn't really believe that there's any such thing as useful negotiation,' Henderson said. 'She doesn't see foreign policy as it is, which is a lot of give and take.'[2] Nowhere was the truth of this, and yet also at another level its deceptiveness, more visible than in the major piece of unfinished diplomatic business left over from the first term. In dealing with the European Community, the Thatcher style showed itself to be inflexible – that is, not interested in negotiation as most other European leaders understood it – and yet also, by this very indifference to normal procedures, successful. It would therefore be false to call her a non-negotiator: truer to say, with Roy Jenkins, that she succeeded by bringing to the task the rare quality of being 'almost totally impervious to how much she offends other people'.[3]

The Community problem, which to her consisted primarily if not quite exclusively of the British contribution to Community funds, was left in uneasy peace by the budget settlement of May 1980. After a great deal of bitter argument,[4] Community heads of government agreed a rebate to Britain of part of her vastly excessive contribution. For 1980 and 1981 this amounted to £1.4 billion, and a further haggle in 1982 produced another tranche. But the system was plainly unsatisfactory. Britain secured relatively small receipts, mainly because the small size of its agriculture qualified it for less of the immense subsidy handed out to European farmers; and Britain paid out more revenue than anyone else in the form of levies and duties on non-European imports. An annual argument was bad for the British and worse for the spirit of constructive collaboration. But above all it was intolerable to the British leader, who had brought a new spirit of combat to the Euro-dialogue without as yet securing her objective. Armed with a new mandate, she marched out to battle, in which she was determined not to relent until a whole new mechanism, securing the British position indefinitely and removing the need for annual exercises in supplicancy, was in place.

She began with certain advantages. The cast of characters ranged against her had significantly changed. The German Chancellor, Schmidt, whom she respected but was unable to dominate, had been succeeded in 1982 by a Christian Democrat, Helmut Kohl, who was not only a conservative like her but less formidably equipped than his predecessor. Kohl, as she was to find, could be stubborn, and he was very political; rather like her, he wasn't weighed down with Schmidtian visions of some new world order, preferring to look after his domestic interests. But in the highly personal arm-wrestle that Community negotiations on this matter had become, Kohl was somebody she might expect to get the better of.

An even more favourable shift had occurred in France. On paper, the replacement of a conservative, Giscard d'Estaing, by a socialist, François Mitterrand, might have been expected to make for difficulties. But Mitterrand, as he quickly proved, was a special sort of socialist: pragmatic, far-sighted and uninterested in doctrine. And Giscard – 'olympian but not patrician', as she had scornfully judged his patronising air – was an entirely unhelpful ally to the new British prime minister when she took her first steps on the European stage. Mitterrand later spoke of her with a flattering hyperbole which, for all its extravagance, can only have made her feel good. Briefing his new European Minister, Roland Dumas, he reputedly counselled him thus: 'Cette femme Thatcher! Elle a les yeux de Caligule, mais elle a la bouche de Marilyn Monroe.' More significantly in the short term, Mitterrand had less command of the mundane budgetary detail than she did. Whereas Giscard's time as Finance Minister had given him a grasp of the figures, the new French president had not learned them so well.

This was her other advantage. Although the details of all budget negotiations were fearsomely complicated, and every summit was prepared by armies of experts, the heads of government met largely alone or with one accompanying aide, their foreign minister. As things came to the crunch, they were on their own. And once Schmidt and Giscard had departed none of the other leaders could match Mrs Thatcher's personal capacity to be her own expert, nor any longer compensate for this with overriding displays of grandeur.

The process, none the less, took a long time. No fewer than four summits over twelve months were dominated by the British problem. It was a weakness of the Thatcher approach to these that, while most European politicians and Community officials accepted the merits of her case, she did nothing to make the most of this latent support but instead continued to take the offensive, in both senses of the word. Her strength, on the other hand, was that she won.

The preliminary failures were spectacular. The Stuttgart summit in June 1983, which was supposed to take a large stride towards cutting food surpluses and increasing revenue, was the first to founder on the new British position: that nothing would be permitted to happen until the British overpayment problem was permanently solved. The Athens summit in December ended without even a communiqué, the first time this had happened. The British leader was pleased with the impasse, and especially Howe's part in creating it. 'For the first time I've got a Foreign Secretary who understands the tactics as well as the strategy,' she told her staff afterwards.

The next summit was due in Brussels, on 19 March. A few days before, Mrs Thatcher, wrenching her mind from the miners' strike which had begun the same week, tried to raise Europe's sights. 'I am tired of this being described as a British problem,' she told a dinner of Strasbourg parliamentarians. 'The problems are Europe-wide.' They weren't merely to do with equity for Britain, but with the

Community failing to live within its means. 'I want an agreement, but I don't want to paper over the cracks. I want to get rid of the cracks. I want to rebuild the foundations.' She said roughly the same to Mitterrand, now running the French six-month presidency of the Community, who decided to try and solve the problem by a painstaking series of bilateral meetings with his nine fellow heads before the summit proper. What he learned from this was that the basis of her negotiating position remained unchanged: she was unmoved by the prospect of a major crisis.[5]

This summit, too, however, ended in failure, with a great deal of mutual recrimination. The figures on the table were not actually too far apart. Mitterrand's diplomacy had not been unfruitful. Working in the back room, French and British officials were also able to put together the formula for a permanent mechanism that would finally remove the British problem from the agenda and pave the way for an all-round increase in resources which the Community needed if it was to stave off bankruptcy.

But it did not get anywhere. The atmosphere degenerated as time went on. The Germans put in an impossible alternative scheme, and the Irish walked out. At dinner, Mrs Thatcher showed that she had lost none of the capacity to destroy a good meal with hectoring and harangue which she had first revealed in Dublin in 1979. Some of those present were reported to have looked rather frightened. 'One felt that if an argument was sufficiently silly in her eyes, she would pick the culprit up by the collar and shake him,' a Community official said. When they broke up without agreement, the Italian prime minister, Bettino Craxi, said that 'la signora Thatcher carries the entire and grave responsibility for the failure.'

This wasn't in fact quite true, at least in the sense he meant it. Other leaders, especially the Germans, were still stalling on a fair and honest mechanism. But in another sense Craxi was correct. One consequence of the Thatcher style was to raise the political threshold against anyone making concessions to her. By now she was famous throughout Europe as 'La Dame de Fer'. While some Europeans might confess to a sneaking admiration for her, no leader thought he could easily afford to be seen making concessions to her. Opinion polls showing her falling popularity at home were prominently published in newspapers throughout the EEC. She was a bogywoman, who at the same time exerted a horrible fascination. When, after Brussels, in a retaliatory spasm of outrage, the British cabinet was reported to have discussed withholding all payments to the Community pending a solution to the problem, the temperature was raised still further.

Mitterrand did not give up. While Mrs Thatcher, at bottom, was indifferent to the crisis, other leaders, in countries where Europeanism was a more naturally accepted condition of existence, could not afford to be. They knew, moreover, that British money was more than ever necessary to the Community. A solution simply had to be found, and preferably before the presidency left the French, who had a powerful presence and a sophisticated bureaucracy, and passed to the Irish, who had neither.

The final 'French' summit was to be held at Fontainebleau on 25 June. Meanwhile other events touching upon it distracted from the preparations. At the beginning of June, a world, as distinct from European, economic summit was held in London: as futile an event as all the previous such exercises with which Mrs Thatcher had shown herself thoroughly impatient, but which on this occasion, being the hostess, she was obliged to term a great success. Next, the week before Fontainebleau saw the quadrennial election to the European Parliament, an event which made it more than ever necessary for the participating leaders to emphasise how little they had given away to the hated Iron Lady. Indeed, the French in their turn upped the ante and began to talk about a 'two-speed Europe', by which they meant a Community divided between enthusiastic collaborators in the first division and reluctant slow-coaches in the second.

Mrs Thatcher was not impressed. She thought there could be no question of any further speeding towards a United States of Europe. 'I do not believe in a federal Europe,' she said, 'and I think to ever compare it with the United States of America is absolutely ridiculous.' As for a two-speed Europe, she added, 'let me tell you what I mean: those who pay most are in the top group and those who pay less are not.'[6]

The Fontainebleau summit was laid on with more than the usual grandeur. The national leaders arrived in the Cour des Adieux, where Napoleon made his farewells before leaving for Elba. The appearance of each was staged with some solemnity at meticulous intervals, and a special roar of excitement greeted the arrival of La Dame de Fer.[7]

Once again, the early signals were very negative. The French, with the European Commission, made a proposition which set a time-limit on future British rebates and sought to hustle it through in two hours before dinner. Much time was wasted beforehand in the kind of indulgence which only heads of government permit themselves, with Mitterrand briefing the others on his recent trip to Moscow and Kohl offering them an interminable account of a journey to Hungary which he had lately returned from. Sensing a lack of purposefulness, the British prepared for failure. Bernard Ingham, speaking for Mrs Thatcher, made such a point of ridiculing Kohl's performance as to persuade the audience of journalists that the British were not interested in keeping the Germans or anyone else sweet. Here, it seemed, one more tableau of bitchery and farce was being played out in the fraternity of Europe.

This time, however, the signs were false. Or rather, at the eleventh hour, the heads of government managed to assemble a serious momentum towards agreement. A mechanism, one of more than a dozen that had done the rounds, was finally settled for the British contribution: the rebate would consist of a fixed percentage of the difference between what Britain paid into the Community and what the Community spent in Britain. What remained to be settled was the figure. After some last-ditch resistance from Kohl, Mrs Thatcher got what she had come for, the figure which on this occasion had not been a negotiating figure but was, throughout, her top and bottom line: 66 per cent.

It was a matter of immediate dispute whether this deal was better or worse than the one available in Brussels. Because of the complexity of the fine print, each side could make a case. Certainly it wasn't a giant improvement of the kind which one might suppose would have been necessary to justify the extraordinary amount of wear and tear endured by all concerned through these four summits. At the same time, it satisfactorily laid an argument to rest.

But the gritty details, although they had been the subject of all the argument, were not perhaps the point. The point was about perceptions.

On one side stood the Europeans, and their more committed friends in Britain. They thought that while Mrs Thatcher had certainly 'won', in the sense that she had moved far less than her opponents from the base-line they each occupied, she had also lost a lot, beginning with her remaining friends in Europe. Her rapacious demands, together with the insulting manner in which she pressed them, carried this price. Further, they thought, she sacrificed to this narrow national demand the chance of progress towards other European reforms, particularly in agriculture, and delayed the evolution of the Community. Christopher Tugendhat, a British Commissioner in Brussels for eight years, regretted the 'ghetto' mentality of the Thatcher Government. Why didn't it find ways of proving its commitment to the Community? Tugendhat asked. 'It should have launched initiatives of its own unconnected with the budget and responded to those of others in a manner designed to attract sympathy and understanding.'[8] Quite apart from being unfortunate for Europe, this narrow struggle, it was further argued, delayed the day when Britain could be received alongside France and Germany as one of the three co-equal leaders of Europe. This should be Britain's objective. Why didn't Mrs Thatcher have the breadth of mind to grasp this priority? In the wet and whiggish salons of sophisticated London, as in some of the chancelleries of Europe, such had been the despairing question ever since she pronounced the Common Market guilty of the theft of 'my money'.

To the British Government, the verdict on Fontainebleau looked rather different. First of all, they had no doubt that without Mrs Thatcher's anti-diplomatic style Europe's concessions on the budget would have been much smaller. On this point few people, even in the Foreign Office, offered any convincing counter-argument. But secondly, they saw the process not as a series of messy and futile collapses, followed by a last-minute recovery, but more as a step-by-step vindication of the British approach.

Howe was especially seized of this. Later he would look back on the 1983 4 summits, the first he was in charge of as Foreign Secretary, and see in them a pattern, of which he and the prime minister, and perhaps nobody else, were the masters. It went back to the superior skill and knowledge which the two of them brought to those intimate negotiating sessions. The prime minister and he, he would modestly aver, had become very experienced at the business of working through texts: building from one to another, carrying structures and paragraphs and concepts over from one summit to the next, identifying the key phrases which could change meanings.

Fontainebleau, it seemed, had been like that. The Brussels summit, far from being a disaster, had in fact started a text-building process, partly achieved by himself and Roland Dumas, in the course of three private meetings at the Foreign Secretary's country house, Chevening. The logic of the thing, indeed, had a still broader sweep. Taxed with the suggestion that Fontainebleau was really no better than Brussels, he replied: 'Yes. But the basis on which we concluded it was remarkably close to the original objectives we set ourselves five years before. As with all these things you came to a moment of decision, of making the last move and the last counter-move. There was no doubt in her mind, no doubt in our mind, that that was the moment to make that choice.'[9]

Nor were the British disposed to see this as merely a matter of national interest. They entirely rejected the charge that they were somehow anti-European. Immediately after Fontainebleau, Mrs Thatcher began to utter sentiments that were impeccably *communautaire*. 'The way is now clear for the completion of the Common Market in goods and services,' she said in her report to Parliament on the deal. Visiting Paris in November, she praised the French presidency as well as taking the first diplomatic steps towards Anglo-French agreement to build a tunnel under the Channel. Speaking to the Franco-British Council, she cast herself, in rare obeisance to a Labour politician, as the heir to Ernest Bevin, echoing his description of the aims of foreign policy: 'To go down to Victoria Station, get a railway ticket and go where the hell I like without a passport or anything else.'[10] She listed a series of European objectives: 'Greater unity of the Community market, greater unity of Community actions in world affairs, greater unity of purpose and action in tackling unemployment and the other problems of our time.'

This did not actually signal much change in her well-known prejudices. She was still highly resistant to what she thought of as Eurofroth. She did not warm to abstractions like the Idea of Europe. She continued to have difficulty thinking of negotiation as a process that did not need to have a winner, preferably herself. Foreign policy, to her, was still best seen as the resolution of finite problems rather than the maintenance of blurred conditions of existence. But Europe was evidence for rather than against this view. A problem had been solved and everyone was happier.

Later, it was Howe's mature analysis that, far from casting him and his leader as their enemies, Europe owed them a debt. Britain's strategic determination had made Europe think straight. In the span of the Thatcher years, three big things happened in the Community. The budget question was finally settled, farm prices finally began to be reformed, and progress accelerated towards the full common internal market. All this, in the opinion of the British, from which the Foreign Office would not now dissent, was down to Europe's most realistic friend.

The European policy was notable for its iron consistency. Europe's friend was ready to drag the Community towards a possibly terminal crisis if that was necessary to secure the objective she had fixed five years earlier. But in parallel with this, another policy was being developed which moved in the opposite direction. It was not only a rare example of a genuine U-turn – the favoured image of contemporary jargon – in Mrs Thatcher's prime ministerial journey. It is the only known example of this being openly confessed to by a politician who set exceptional store by never being seen to perform such a discreditable manoeuvre.

La Dame de Fer had originally earned this appellation by taking an attitude of uncompromising hostility to the Soviet Union. Suspicion of Soviet intentions was the motive behind the first speech which had identified her foreign-policy position, back in 1976, when she rejected the euphoria then fashionably surrounding the Helsinki accords on human rights. The Russians and their evil empire roused all her righteous instincts; Soviet dissidents were high among the heroes most regularly remembered in her rhetoric. 'Solzhenitsyn could not be ignored, nor could his quiet disappearance be arranged,' she said in 1978. 'In some ways the pen is still mightier than the sword.'[11]

This deep anti-Soviet conviction was often reinforced by events, the invasion of Afghanistan most memorably among them. It was also the cornerstone, of course, of a defence policy to which she had always given the highest priority. Defence spending in general and the modernisation of the British nuclear deterrent in particular were justified by reference to the Soviet threat. The Soviets were the enemy, they were constantly building their offensive power, they were not to be trusted. These themes, which underlay the telling contention that Labour's non-nuclear policy would leave Britain naked before a hostile power, made more contribution than most to winning the 1983 election. For virtually the whole of the first term, Moscow played little more part in the prime minister's thinking than that of the useful idiot whose manifest wickedness and incompetence supplied the butt she needed.

Before the term had quite ended, however, a sea-change began to overtake her natural prejudice. It did not involve, as she saw it, any concession to Soviet incursions or illegalities, and certainly did not mean that her solidarity with dissidents was weakening. In late May 1983, after the election was called, she had time to receive Alexander Solzhenitsyn himself, and the two of them discoursed in mutual agreement about the pernicious power of fashion to impose on the Western world a form of intellectual censorship which was in its way as odious as the state censorship in the East. But the change of tack was already imminent. Later she pinpointed it to the period immediately after the election. 'I think it is an important change,' she reflected in January 1984, and it happened 'over the long summer recess'.[12]

In fact it had begun rather earlier. The first signal of an adjustment in the British stance came with a visit to Moscow by the junior Foreign Office minister Malcolm Rifkind in January 1983, which was followed by a cautious but systematic reassessment of the frozen impasse into which British policy, alongside that of Reagan's Washington, had sunk. The man most responsible for this, as he struggled to survive, was actually Francis Pym. His efforts finally issued in a post-election seminar, long prepared for, which the prime minister chaired but a new Foreign Secretary, alas, had the pleasure of addressing. From then on, this 'opening to the East' became one of the more carefully cultivated features of the Thatcher–Howe foreign policy.

Naturally it involved more of a conversion for Mrs Thatcher than for the Foreign Office. It was the kind of thing the Foreign Office had despaired of getting her to undertake. But she had what sounded like quite a sudden awakening. 'In a very dangerous world, the thing is not whether you agree with the other very powerful bloc's political views,' she reasoned. 'The important thing is that you simply must make an effort the more to understand one another. . . . We've got to do more talking.'[13]

In this opinion she was apparently echoing another convert, President Reagan. Reagan, who was famous for calling the Soviet Union 'the focus of evil in the modern world' and once said that Soviet leaders were not worth negotiating with because they were liars and cheats, was now proposing arms talks. He made a public speech calling for 'constructive collaboration' to reduce the nuclear stockpile, insisting that his remarks of previous years had been 'overplayed and over-exaggerated'. It was upon this speech that Mrs Thatcher was driven to rationalise the experience she had begun six months earlier. And she was shocked by the cynicism which greeted the president's own change of line. People had suggested, she noted, that the speech wasn't sincere and was meant strictly for domestic consumption. 'I am convinced it was much, much deeper than that,' she said. 'Convinced because Ron Reagan and I think very much the same way, because I had come to the same conclusion.'[14]

Once reached, this conclusion, like many Thatcherite conclusions, was adhered to with an emphatic clarity which at times seemed as bewildering as it was imprudent. Shortly after the new pragmatism had become a matter of transatlantic solidarity, the prime minister paid a visit to Hungary, her first to Eastern Europe (except for funerals) since the 1979 election. She arrived in her new guise as peace-maker and arms controller and protagonist of 'dialogue', and was received like a conquering heroine. She completely won over the Hungarians, her people reported. Hungary, already the most market-oriented state in Eastern Europe, was ripe for further, sub-Thatcherite developments, they suggested. But what struck less ecstatic observers was how little she now stressed the downside of communist society. She said not a word in Budapest about the Helsinki Final Act or the Madrid conference examining the post-Helsinki human rights record. For the moment what was on the agenda was a new problem – detente and arms-talks – which meant that the old problem, of repression in an anti-democratic society, was not to be mentioned. Did elementary politeness demand such silence? Even if it did, there was a time when the old Thatcher would have brushed the demand aside.

Her theme now was practicality. 'She wasn't interested any more in changing the Russians, or recovering Eastern Europe for the Western way of life,' recalled one minister closely involved at the time. 'She might detest their system, but she didn't even want to talk about anything except the strictly practical.'

One practicality that impressed her was the sheer poverty of experience of the typical Soviet leader. These leaders were people who hadn't been anywhere, and didn't know anything about us, the West, the countries they supposedly wished to have relations with. 'It shakes you just a little bit,' she once told an American magazine, with the characteristic ingenuousness of one who has only recently thought about it, 'when you read that Mr Andropov has never set foot in any country which is not a Communist country.'[15] This was a terrible limitation. It meant that they didn't understand, let alone talk, our language. 'They really do not understand what a free society is all about.' Or, with eyes still wide: 'Sometimes when you use the same words, they may not have the same meaning.'[16] So you mustn't expect too much too soon. 'You just have steadily to work away at it, getting, I think, contact with far more of them.'

However, contact with one Soviet leader, Andropov, and then with his successor, Chernenko, was impossible. Quite apart from the unfavourable political climate, they were sick and old, and each was to be encountered only in the tomb. If contact were to happen and be significant it had to be with a younger man, who might himself venture some of the way across the immense cultural gap dividing this particular British leader, with her straight-backed provincialism and intolerance of opaque diplomacy, from the double-dealing silences of the Kremlin.

It is to the credit of the despised Foreign Office that they managed to discover this man before anyone else in the Western world laid a hand on him. Mikhail Sergeyevich Gorbachev had been a member of the Soviet Politburo since 1980. A protégé of Andropov's, he was far younger than most of his fellow members – born 1931, six years after Margaret Thatcher – and it seemed to a good many observers unlikely that the procession of the elders through the general secretaryship of the Communist Party of the Soviet Union would end up with the promotion of quite such an aberrant figure in their place. For the Foreign Office, like everyone else, it could be only guesswork.

In December 1984, at Britain's invitation, Gorbachev led a thirty-strong delegation to London. It was the first visit to Britain by a senior Soviet leader for seventeen years, and, more important, the first serious visit Gorbachev himself had ever made to a leading Western nation. It proved to be a most providential occasion. Within three months, Chernenko was dead and Gorbachev had succeeded him.

He made a powerful impression on all the British ministers who met him. The lunches and dinners were long, so several of them had the opportunity for extended conversation. They found him sharp, wide-ranging and a good listener, who exuded power and the pleasure of using it. He was quite different from other Soviet leaders they had met. His reactions were personal, his demeanour was confident, his mind was relatively open. 'He was very ignorant, but tremendously interested,' said one minister. He was especially amazed by the English countryside and the prosperous villages he drove through, an even greater contrast with life in the steppes than London was with Moscow. 'We didn't give him the usual treatment – Sainsbury's superstore at Nine Elms – but took him to Oxfordshire instead, to the ICI research centre,' the minister recalled. 'He was astonished.'

He was also less dependent on aides than anyone expected. The Gorbachev trademark, ministers noticed, was a personal notebook, written in his own hand, to which he would refer at moments of factual disagreement and in which he kept writing during conversation. When they saw him in later years he was still using exactly the same kind of notebook in just the same way. It looked like a sort of proof that in the end there was often no substitute for personal opinions personally recorded.

Upon nobody, however, did he make a stronger impression than on Mrs Thatcher. Having opted for dialogue, she found that here, miraculously, was somebody she could talk to. They covered a great deal of ground, including both arms control and human rights. At the end of the visit, she told BBC Television, in a phrase that famously registered the new dimension of the Iron Lady, 'I like Mr Gorbachev; we can do business together.'

They had, she added, two great interests in common. They wanted to see that war never started again, and were therefore determined that disarmament talks should succeed. But they also believed that what mattered was a growth in mutual confidence, 'and therefore we believe in co-operating on trade matters, on cultural matters, on quite a lot of contact between politicians from the two sides of the divide'.

Later, she reflected more personally on the shock of this first encounter. 'He is totally out of the normal pattern of what we have come to regard as a typical Communist,' she said. 'They tend to read from a very tightly prepared paper, and when you ask them questions they never answer them. They still go on with the prepared paper. He did not have a prepared thing. . . . We were able to discuss for hours, which is totally refreshing, totally refreshing.'[17]

She then described the basis of the discussion, which disclosed an unfamiliar emollience. In effect, she said, she was saying this to him: 'Please understand that everything I say is only to try and have a genuine discussion. There are some of our things that you do not like; there are some of your things that we do not like, and, of course, I will mention some of them. Of course, you will mention some of them to me, but that is not to try to get a battle going on who can score the most points. It is trying to find the basis on which we can go forward.'

All this was part of the new realism. 'You are much more likely to be able to do business with someone else', she explained, 'if you have a realistic assessment of their approach, their strengths, their fears, and you do not go starry-eyed thinking that one day Communism will collapse like a pack of cards, because it will not.'

She had, she said, enjoyed their talks, found them refreshing. They were such a contrast with the normal run of foreign business. 'Some of these diplomatic minuets you have to go through I cannot stand,' she said. Gorbachev was different. He came to the point. 'That suits me much better.'

He, for his part, acknowledged a special personal warmth. After he became General Secretary, he sent a personal greeting to his new friend on 13 October 1985, her sixtieth birthday: a cordial message, in which he and his wife, Raisa, expressed their good wishes. This might have been seen as a routine gesture, were it not for the fact that, only weeks before, relations between London and Moscow had momentarily cooled, following the defection to Britain of the top KGB man based in London, Oleg Gordievsky, and the expulsion of Soviet Embassy officials which resulted from Gordievsky's information. Even these reminders of Cold War realities – Gordievsky, after all, turned out to have been a double-agent since 1966 – were not permitted by the Soviet leader to damage the personal relationship he had struck up.

The 1984 meeting was an important landmark in Mrs Thatcher's evolution into something of an international operator. She did not particularly lust after that role in the way of her predecessors – whether those with some power, like Macmillan, or those with almost none, like Wilson. Unlike her, they positively adored the diplomatic minuets. But, in one important area of operation, the Gorbachev visit was the beginning of something quite big, which endured until the end of the Reagan presidency. It inaugurated a relationship which, while obviously never so close as the Reagan connection, enabled the prime minister to act as an interlocutor between the super-powers. Reagan, an obtuse and waffling character, provided little stimulus to Gorbachev. Gorbachev, from the outer darkness of Soviet Russia, aroused no empathy in Reagan. Mrs Thatcher, politically on Reagan's wavelength and intellectually on Gorbachev's, had some of the qualities required to interpret the one to the other – which, for a second-division European power, was not a role entirely to be despised.

Her first venture into communication between them, however, began with unfortunate auguries. Gorbachev, as she noted, had the habit of coming to the point. And the point he returned to most insistently during his visit to London was the unalterable opposition of the Soviet Union to Reagan's Strategic Defence Initiative, also known as Star Wars. This subject dominated the London agenda, as it had dominated both Western and Eastern strategic debate ever since the president, without warning either his allies or most of his cabinet officials, had announced the SDI in March 1983. Reagan was persuaded that laser-systems and other weaponry based in space could provide the final and complete defence against nuclear attack. The SDI, he said, would 'give us the means of rendering nuclear weapons impotent and obsolete'.

The theory of nuclear deterrence, in other words, would be superseded. Massive retaliation and all the other immoralities of the nuclear age could be forgotten, once this perfect system for eliminating all nuclear missiles the moment they left the ground was in place.

This prospect horrified the Russians, who saw it as inevitably escalating the arms race. They could not conceivably stand by while space was militarised by one side only. And Gorbachev's argument to this effect made its impression on the British leader, not least because she was already halfway to accepting it before he arrived. No West European country had said it approved of Star Wars. They agreed, broadly, first that it would not work and second that it would grossly destabilise the delicate balance of deterrence on which the whole European defence system had rested for forty years.

In her comments after their meetings, Mrs Thatcher, as well as deeming Gorbachev a man she could do business with, echoed some of his sentiments, repeating obliquely what she had said more ex- plicitly in relation to Star Wars in a speech at the Guildhall a few weeks earlier. 'One does not want to go into a higher and higher level of armaments,' she said. The sentiment was picked up in Washington, but coincided with a Pentagon announcement that, from the United States' point of view, Star Wars continued to have the highest priority. Indeed, while Gorbachev was still in London and his new acquain- tance was discovering how much they had in common, it was announced in Washington amid great fanfares that a fresh round of contracts had been let to ten defence corporations in an effort to accelerate the project.

But there was another coincidence of timing. By long arrangement, Mrs Thatcher had a date in Washington at what turned out to be the confluence of these swirling developments. She left London while Gorbachev was still there, on a journey that would take her round the world in six days, dropping off to do major business here and there. One of these stopovers was Peking, to complete what was probably the most momentous piece of bilateral treaty-making Britain undertook in her time, the surrender of the lease on Hong Kong. The last was in Washington. A week after her brilliant conversations with the greatest enemy of Star Wars, she would be sitting round the fire with its most determined friend.

They had remained close. In her second term, Washington continued to be the foreign city where she was happiest, as it had been in her first.

When I interviewed him in January 1985, Reagan called Margaret 'one of my favourite people' and said how much he enjoyed talking about her. In her presence, official Washington seemed to find it more difficult, as time went on, to restrain itself from a posture of drooling effusion. No matter how often she returned, Americans never seemed to tire of extending to her a greeting couched in terms of wonderment that she was a woman, a *strong* little woman, a woman like no other English person since Winston Churchill.

Within weeks of the election she was over there to collect the Winston Churchill Foundation Award. 'Like Winston Churchill, she is known for her courage, conviction, determination and willpower,' the citation read. 'Like Churchill she thrives on adversity.' As Washington gathered ecstatically at the British Embassy, George Shultz, Secretary of State, called her 'steadfast', Paul Volcker, chairman of the Federal Reserve Board, said she had 'backbone', and Bernard Ingham swore that she had been offered the American presidency three times including once on television.

The contretemps over Grenada followed shortly, but did not sour relations for long. Reagan personally seemed unmoved by her criticisms, putting them down in his folksy way to an unfortunate failure of communication. Where possible, he continued to ease her passage as long as it cost him little or nothing. It was thanks to Reagan that Britain had secured the Polaris successor, Trident D-5, on the cheap – an unusual bargain. Having originally negotiated with President Carter to secure the Trident C-4, Britain briefly stared at the possibility of being without any nuclear weapon at all when the Americans decided to upgrade the C-4 to the D-5, a more expensive and much more powerful weapon. Mrs Thatcher, unlike her Defence Secretary, John Nott, was desperate to secure the D-5 when the Americans announced the switch at the end of 1981. Possession of the independent nuclear weapon, no matter how excessively large or expensive it was, remained, of all the aspects of her inheritance, the one about which she countenanced least argument. It barely occurred to her to entertain a second thought when Reagan offered it to her at cost price, with virtually no charge for research and development.

Reagan also helped with an irksome little domestic matter. British Airways was embroiled in anti-trust suits in the American courts, and looked certain to be indicted for price-fixing and carving up the American market in the months leading up to the collapse of a cut-price interloper, Laker Airways. The suits, which had dragged on since 1982, were having a damaging effect on British Airways' privatisation prospects. To the relief of Downing Street the president used his executive power, in November 1984, to quash the actions before they got to court.

Clearly the Star Wars difficulty would put the relationship to more of a test. But first, there was Peking to be revisited and an agreement signed.

Since her first visit in 1982, when she was breathing post-Falklands fire, the process of disengaging from Hong Kong had been handed over to the diplomats. Britain's legal rights over the island and its associated territories ended in 1997, whereupon they reverted to China in perpetuity. In crude terms, this gave Britain only a modest negotiating position, well removed from the grandiose stance of never surrendering with which Mrs Thatcher preferred to be associated. But at the moment of completion she made the best of it with a characteristic burst of hyperbole.

The conception behind the deal, she said, was 'an idea of genius'. This referred to the promise that Hong Kong would remain a capitalist enclave within the Republic of China for the next fifty years. She also alluded to 'moments of tension' in the final phase of negotiations, and reported without shame that the Chinese leader, Teng Hsiao-ping, had found her an almost impossible woman to deal with. But when Teng attributed the success of the talks to 'the dialectical and historical materialism of Marxism', the new international realist did not contest his opinion. Indeed, she flatteringly said, both governments had followed the axiom of Chairman Mao: 'Seek truth from facts.'

No one could guarantee, of course, that the deal would stick in 1997, or even last until then. Would the idea of two systems in one country continue to be sustained by Teng's successors? Quite soon there was reason to doubt it. As the detailed negotiations proceeded through the 1980s, the prospects of any genuine political freedom surviving in post-colonial Hong Kong seemed remote. When it came to pinning down the Peking Government, the British, never having introduced Hong Kong to the democratic process, became impotently vulnerable to the communist Chinese contention that the colony had been 'occupied' by Britain: an indignity from which it would soon be liberated, thus 'fulfilling the long-cherished common aspirations of the entire Chinese people'.

But in 1984 this looked like a rather academic point. As an exercise in constructive diplomacy, the Hong Kong deal would be reckoned a success in most people's language. Besides, by the measure often set up as the crucial test of Thatcherite enterprises of every kind at home, the reunification treaty was an instant success. On receiving the news from Peking, the Hong Kong stock market leaped overnight to a record peak.

When Mrs Thatcher arrived in Washington, on 22 December, the mood seemed likely to be rather less cordial. But she had taken some steps already to modify her perceived opposition to Reagan's most cherished programme. She wanted to make it clear, she said en route, that while opposed to deployment of Star Wars hardware without far more super-power negotiation she had never been against continuing research into it.

Nevertheless, on arrival at Camp David, the presidential retreat, she did not hesitate to deliver a lecture which drew in part on her meetings with Gorbachev. She spoke for an hour and a half, with a directness which no other leader, it was said from the Reagan side, would have been permitted. She claimed it was a mistake to continue saying that Star Wars defence was attainable. It might well not be; indeed, 'as a chemist' she said she knew it wouldn't work. Meanwhile the whole edifice of public support for nuclear deterrence, she suggested, was being undermined by Reagan's reiterated dream that it would soon be obsolete. One of the Americans said: 'It was a great Thatcher performance.'[18]

Out of it grew what the British soon hailed as a diplomatic triumph, justifying the whole journey and proving, at Christmas 1984, that Mrs Thatcher's presence was now making itself felt on a global stage. For Reagan, if not persuaded by what she said, saw the need for a formula which could be composed into a public statement. And the British duly obliged, with a four-point statement which someone on their side had already put together. The first point said that the West wasn't looking for nuclear superiority; the second that the production and deployment of SDI-related systems would be a matter for negotiation; the third that the objective was to 'enhance, not undercut, deterrence'; the fourth that none of this should get in the way of continuing arms-control talks.

The Camp David accord became a celebrated document, the basic text of the Star Wars debate among the allies. Although the Thatcher people made much of it as a kind of victory for the British–European position, an American official described its catalytic function to me more subtly. Washington, he said, was a bureaucracy in permanent turmoil, very badly organised and always full of feuding power-centres. The job of the president was normally to prevent the place falling apart, by hammering the table. Reagan, this official went on, was incapable of behaving like that. If decisions were to be made, he needed help. On this occasion, Mrs Thatcher at Camp David provided that help. By imposing herself, she managed to get US policy defined in a way it had not been defined before, and against the wishes of the Pentagon, which opposed the limitations the document contained. Camp David might not have stopped the Star Warriors in their tracks, but it had provided a frame of reference: order where there was something like chaos.

From the Thatcher viewpoint, of course, it had another purpose: to rectify any appearance of an imbalance that might have been created by her talks with Gorbachev. Momentarily, it had looked as though there were serious differences between Washington and London. Camp David provided some evidence for the correction the prime minister was anxious to get across. 'I told the president,' she said to the press before leaving Washington, 'that I had made it absolutely clear to Mr Gorbachev that there was no question of the Soviet Union being able to divide the United Kingdom from the United States on these matters.'

That, in fact, is how it was from then on. But more on Reagan's terms than on hers, or certainly than on Europe's. The Germans and the French, more categorically alarmed by Star Wars in any guise, looked to Britain to exploit a still quite special relationship and continue to chip away at Reagan's dream. But having established the four points, the British prime minister spent far more time thereafter chiding the critics of Star Wars than reinforcing Washington's anxieties about European solidarity. For one extraordinary moment, breaking with everything that was known of his quietist character, Foreign Secretary Howe seemed to be rejecting this line. He called SDI 'a new Maginot line of the twenty-first century' of which the risks 'might outweigh the benefits'.[19] But this was not the official position, and Mrs Thatcher hadn't seen the final draft before Howe delivered it.

Her own line was by now solidly in favour. On yet another visit to Washington, in February 1985, she addressed a joint session of Congress, the first British prime minister to do so since, inevitably, Churchill. 'Winston', as she familiarly termed him, was constantly invoked on all sides. In between twenty-four interruptions for applause, she seemed to place herself behind the very doctrine which previously she had challenged. To maintain nuclear deterrence, she told Congress, it was essential to ensure that 'our research and capacity do not fall behind the work being done by the Soviet Union'. 'That is why', she went on, 'I firmly support President Reagan's decision to pursue research into defence against ballistic nuclear missiles – the Strategic Defence Initiative.'

While the flirtation with Gorbachev wasn't over, it had been put in its proper perspective. After the speech to Congress, the Reagans turned up at an Embassy dinner to mark the 200th anniversary of diplomatic relations between Britain and the US after the War of Independence. Relations, all agreed, had never been better than now. 'I think you are a wonderful president,' said the one to the other. 'We are inspired by your leadership,' he replied.

All the same, the Gorbachev conversations had opened a new phase in Mrs Thatcher's global odyssey. Without discovering any greater taste for diplomatic minuets, she understood more about the value of personal contacts whenever they might be made. Going round the world in six days in December 1984 was an experience that stuck in her mind. 'I had no idea it was such a small world,' she said later, 'and that you could get round it in six days while seeing so many people. It's a very small world – except for the Pacific, which is rather a big place.'[20]

18

Treason of the Intellectuals

IN THE WEEK when the British leader was circling the globe to settle these international matters, an announcement appeared in the *Oxford University Gazette*. It listed the names of seven people on whom the university's ruling executive, the Hebdomadal Council, had decided to confer honorary degrees. Four of these were eminent academics, one was an opera singer, Sir Geraint Evans, and two were politicians: President Pertini of Italy and prime minister Thatcher, eighth in the line of post-war holders of her office to be so nominated.

There was already something singular about her position on this list, nearly six years after coming to power. Of her predecessors Attlee, Macmillan, Heath and Wilson all received honorary doctorates from Oxford within a year of taking office. Douglas-Home and Eden had received them before they became prime minister. Like all these men, Margaret Thatcher was an Oxford graduate, but she had to wait. In 1979, the first year when she might have been thought automatically eligible, the university had just gone through an acrimonious row over a proposed honorary degree for President Bhutto of Pakistan, and it did not seem appropriate to hazard another rejection, of a new prime minister primarily remembered in educational circles not for protecting the Open University, which she did against much cabinet opposition, but as the Secretary of State for Education who snatched milk from the mouths of impoverished children.

Twice more, between 1979 and 1983, consideration was given to continuing Oxford's tradition. But each time the awards committee, fearing repudiation by the 2,500 Oxford dons who all had a vote, judged the time to be unripe. This repeated delay was expressive tribute, of course, to the power of the prime minister's personality and the strength of the reactions she tended to generate from the moment of her installation as leader of the Conservative Party. But its resonance was slight by comparison with what happened when the degree was at last recommended in the annual list. An event was in the making which, more than any other, crystallised the Thatcher effect on the intellectual culture, and the struggle of that culture, long after the political world had made its submission to a new orthodoxy, to cling to the world and the values which this leader was crusading to overturn.

The announcement produced an immediate eruption of feeling in Oxford. Furious dons formed themselves into a committee which produced an unprecedented tally of 275 objectors, ranging across all faculties and disciplines. Through January, the issue became a national controversy, with the leader's familiar supporters in the press publishing some majestic philippics against the professors' folly. Conservative Oxford past and present rallied to the prime minister, and counselled the university, in the words of Daphne Park, principal of Somerville, to consider 'what the rest of the country is feeling'. Lord Goodman, master of University College, wrote that 'it would be entirely wrong to regard the question of an honorary degree for the prime minister as one involving any political implications.'

But the dons were spectacularly unimpressed. By 738 votes to 319 they refused to grant the degree, thereby inflicting on the prime minister her first defeat in an election of any description since she failed to take the Dartford constituency in the 1951 General Election. She issued a dignified response. 'If they do not wish to confer the honour, I am the last person who would wish to receive it,' it was said on her behalf. Perceptive observers noted an undertone of contempt rather than bitterness. The vote confirmed quite a lot of what she already thought about the amply tenured and wholly uninvigilated members of Oxford University.

Why was this unique rebuff administered? At one level it was defended as a respectable, indeed necessary, retreat from the questionable practice of conferring academic honours on any serving politicians. 'As an active politician, she should never have been considered,' two dons wrote, citing the Bhutto precedent but also noting this particular politician's inability to attract a consensus round her nomination.[1]

This was an elevated but misleading explanation. Closer to the mark was the direct attack made by the 275 leading objectors on Mrs Thatcher's record as it pertained to this and other universities. Her Government, they wrote, had 'done deep and systematic damage to the whole public education system in Britain, from the provision for the youngest child up to the most advanced research programmes'. This damage, they thought, might be irreparable. Because Oxford was 'widely perceived to stand at the pinnacle of British education', it would be especially inappropriate for Oxford to accord such a wrecker its highest token of approval. By withholding it, Oxford would be acting for the entire academic world.

The power of this argument was particularly felt by scientists. In sheer numbers, it was the scientists who surprised. Deprived, as they contended, of vital research funds, and increasingly denuded by emigration to America, Oxford's scientists proved rather more important than Oxford's predictably hostile sociologists in ranging universities against the prime minister. In fact, Oxford had actually escaped the worst of the cuts, but the scientists saw the issue on a wider canvas: and, seeing it that way, they could hardly have been expected to bow before the arguments from convention or propriety.

Underlying this hard-nosed rationality, however, was a less definable but perhaps still more powerful feeling, which went back to the opinion expressed by Lord Goodman as he sought to salvage the university's reputation for fair play. It was a strangely obtuse remark to come from fashionable London's most sagacious *homme d'affaires*. In urging that the degree be shorn of all political implications, Goodman did not seem to understand that by now the years of Thatcherism had rendered it difficult to identify any area of national life which was free of its political penumbra. A government so committed to reform as this one, and particularly reform of the most ancient institutions, could not shelter behind a plea of political neutrality when the institutions fought back.

It could certainly make no such case in respect of the universities, and least of all could the prime minister herself. Not only the cuts but the philosophy that lay behind them were a challenge to many of the traditions which academics thought inviolable. Universities could not show a profit, prove they were cost-effective, demonstrate a ruthless employment policy penalising inferior work, or argue the merits of Sanskrit and Philosophy as contributors to the gross national product. Mrs Thatcher's way of talking rarely offered the reassurance that she had any deep sympathy with what universities thought they were about. And so it should have come as no surprise that, when offered a rare opportunity to reply in kind, a representative body of dons lifted their puny fists and shook them at a powerful leader whom they had reason to regard as their enemy.

The Oxford decision, however, had a wider meaning. Oxford spoke, if not for the country, for a number of institutions sacred and profane. What Oxford said, others also said – or were perceived as saying. This continued to be true to the end of the Thatcher decade. Aligned most closely with the dons were the bishops, but the feeling extended into many reaches of what were loosely termed the chattering classes: social London, higher journalism, civil servants in private, the arts establishment, even the softer corners of the City. What they said, and continued to say throughout the period, was that Margaret Thatcher was no friend of their world, being variously a philistine, a better friend of Mammon than of God, an anti-intellectual.

This was an enduring but in several ways a curious verdict. An unresolved paradox presented itself. A leader who particularly prided herself on her grasp of matters close to the intellectual realm was yet unable to say that she had succeeded in taking over the citadels of the intellectual world.

At one level, the political, the takeover was almost complete. Not only had she won a second, and would later win a third, election, but by 1985 there wasn't much left of socialism as an alternative creed or the Labour Party as an alternative government. Over the important territory of economic management the battle had been fought and won, in the sense that growth had been continuous for three years and massive unemployment accepted as a necessary condition of existence. For want of an organised, politically credible alternative, the intellectual argument in favour of Thatcherite economics had carried the day – and yet it could not be said that intellectuals, considered as a class, now rejected the post-war consensus in which most of them grew up.

This was a different pattern from previous eras. Robert Blake has noted that in the past there was usually a close congruence between political tides and intellectual fashion. 'One can compare the anti-Conservatism of the intelligentsia in the 1930s and early 1940s,' he writes, 'the swing the other way in the late 1940s and early 1950s, and the reversal in its turn of that trend in the early 1960s.' Looking further back, Blake cites the predominantly Liberal sentiments of the intelligentsia as underpinning predominantly Liberal governments from the fall of Peel to the early 1870s, and the subsequent disenchantment with Gladstonian Liberalism, mainly over Ireland, as the precursor of a new Conservative ascendancy.[2] Although, as Blake also cautions, such tides are marked by eddies and cross-currents, the decidedly limited nature of Mrs Thatcher's intellectual hegemony after fifteen years of political leadership sets her somewhat apart from precedent.

This is puzzling for another reason. Of all post-war prime ministers, she both used intellectuals and exhibited a studied interest in political ideas to a greater extent than any other.

From the beginning, she felt an uncommon need to link politics to a broad, articulated philosophy of life. She told me that she read Hayek's key work, *The Road to Serfdom*, when she was at university. Asked by another questioner[3] who met her in the mid-1980s what was the most important single book she had ever read, she replied without hesitation that it was *A Time for Greatness* by Herbert Agar. A revealing choice. Agar, an American thinker and propagandist, wrote his book to justify American intervention in the Second World War, in the most high-flown terms. Hitler had succeeded, Agar said, only because of the moral sickness of the West. What was needed now was not merely military victory but moral regeneration, an end to 'the long wail of pacifism and self-depreciation in which the democracies have indulged for 20 years', and a resurgence of human courage. 'We must fight inner weakness at the same time as we fight the enemy in the field,' Agar proclaimed.

A Time for Greatness[4] does not prefigure in every detail what came to be known as Thatcherism. Agar quoted R. H. Tawney and was in favour of equality: 'To whatever extent we make the concept of equality come true, to the same extent we fulfil many of our deepest political and moral ambitions.' He was also scornful of the business culture – 'The lives of many businessmen are pathetic because their emotional and imaginative range is so immature' – and had a passionate mistrust of naked individualism, which he contrasted with the idea of society based on community and mutual support. But Agar was a preacher and, above all, what he called a conservative. 'Power follows property,' he wrote. All good men must defend constitutional government against 'that cruel abstraction, the State'. Choices could be made and redemption found. 'We are not subject to a doom, whether proclaimed by Marx or Spengler, or the old dark gods of the northern forests.'

It is not hard to imagine the impact this might have made on an undergraduate searching for belief. Evidently Margaret Roberts never forgot it. It appealed to a craving she often revealed for fundamentalist texts, which wasn't entirely obliterated when her later preoccupation with office and ambition came to dominate. Bryan Magee, a writer on philosophy, was a Labour MP in the seventies and later recalled her holding him in conversation in the Commons cafeteria on the subject of Karl Popper, perhaps the greatest living conservative thinker. Magee found himself more impressed by her enthusiasm than by the exactness of her knowledge. He even wondered how much of Popper she had read in the original. But it is undeniable that some of Popper's axioms concerning the open and free society – though fewer of his sceptical injunctions against ideological certitude – eventually found their way to the centre of her rhetoric.

Once she became party leader, the early appetite for thought – or at least for the thoughts of selected great men – vigorously reasserted itself. If Herbert Agar had been alive in 1975, he could have expected a ready invitation to the Conservative Philosophy Group, a dining-club she adorned almost from the moment it came into being after the fall of Heath.

This Group was founded and run by a collection of younger Conservative zealots, among them Jonathan Aitken MP, and presided over by a distinguished Tory elder, Hugh Fraser MP. It saw itself as a source of ideas at a time when ideas were thin on the ground, as the barren Labour years began. Conservative academics such as John Casey, from Cambridge, and Roger Scruton, from London University, were regular attenders, along with more senior dons such as Hugh Thomas, the historian, and Anthony Quinton, the philosopher. Selected journalists and politicians would attend on these or other thinkers, listen to a paper presented by one of them and engage in sometimes lively disquisition about the new Conservatism.

Margaret Thatcher came when she could, and Aitken recalled two particular uses she made of these people, apart from casting them as a butt for her unquenchable love of argument. At an early meeting, she crystallised at least one of the reasons she thought it useful to consort with intellectuals. 'We must have an ideology,' she declared. 'The other side have got an ideology they can test their policies against. We must have one as well.' The Philosophy Group played its part in providing what she wanted. But it also, Aitken remembered, answered to the highly practical requirements of a professional politician. The leader was constantly on the look-out for new phrases. Borrowing or stealing or otherwise taking over other people's language was as regular a quest of Mrs Thatcher's as was the plundering of their ideas.

The relationship with philosophers, therefore, was more utilitarian than speculative. It was a new dimension of Conservative leadership. If Edward Heath engaged in similar discourses, it would have been with businessmen and foreigners who knew how the world worked. At the other extreme was Arthur Balfour, who had actually written a philosophical treatise before he became prime minister. Somewhere in the middle was Harold Macmillan. But it would never have occurred to Macmillan to *use* intellectuals. He dined with them at high table as a part of his natural way of life. As a user of intellectuals, Mrs Thatcher was unequalled, although Harold Wilson's deployment of a handful of them in Whitehall in his 1964 Government offered a faint antecedent.

For her the chosen elite were her teachers as much as her agents. They were heavily concentrated in two areas: primarily economics but also, not insignificantly, international affairs. Alan Walters, who became her personal economic adviser, was perhaps her leading instructor.[5] Others included Ralph Harris, founding father of the Institute of Economic Affairs, and two well-known City intellectuals, John Sparrow, later to run her policy unit, and Gordon Pepper, a monetarist guru from Greenwells. Around these close advisers was ranged a constellation of sympathetic irregulars, from Milton Friedman and Arthur Laffer in America to a variety of Swiss bankers who came and went. Behind them all loomed the contentious but revered figure of Hayek – described by house philosopher Quinton, as recently as 1967, as a 'magnificent dinosaur'[6] – who, while always insisting he was a liberal not a conservative, had such a formative part in shaping the Thatcherite vision. On the foreign side, meanwhile, it was to scholars such as Hugh Thomas and the historian of Stalin's Russia, Robert Conquest, that the leader turned first for advice, rather than to the diaspora of the Foreign Office.

These people had their limitations. But they were certainly intellectuals, employed and exploited precisely for the intellectual challenge they were capable of mounting to the world which prime minister Thatcher would inherit. In the tenth year of her Administration, the Conservative Philosophy Group could count six of its number promoted to the House of Lords.[7] Their presence in or near her circle, both in Opposition and in government, was testimony to an attempted revolution of the public mind which nevertheless, oddly, failed to capture more than a fraction of the intelligentsia.

Nor was the private mind at the heart of this revolution entirely to be despised. Neither the culture nor the intellect of Mrs Thatcher explained the contempt in which the high priests of art and academe continued to hold her. Compared with Wilson she was an aesthete, compared with Callaghan a personification of the higher sensibilities.

She was not herself an intellectual. Upon that all close observers were agreed. She was not a ruminator or a speculator; hers was not the kind of mind eternally troubled by the uncertainty of things. Both by temperament and training, she was almost the opposite of an intellectual. The life of the mind was directed not to the pondering of problems but to the discovery of solutions. She once described her mental processes, as they derived from her education. First she was a scientist, where 'you look at the facts and you deduce your conclusions'. Then she was a lawyer, where 'you learn your law, so you learn the structures. . . . You judge the evidence, and then, when the laws are inadequate for present-day society, you create new laws.'[8] This was not the mental instrument that might rejoice in an evening's gentle discourse on the comparative merits of Burke and Disraeli.

Similarly, she was impatient with what she regarded as pretentious intellectual language. One reason she mistrusted the Foreign Office was its habit of employing a 'frenchified' vocabulary. In her mind, English nationalism seemed to have a close link with plain English usage. When a commentator charged her, in a phrase that was remembered, with the dangerous vice of 'bourgeois triumphalism', she ridiculed the propagator of this expression. 'Dear Peregrine,' she told an interviewer, 'why does he talk about "*boo-jhwha*"? *Boo-jhwha?* Why can't he find a plain English word for the plain people of England, Scotland and Wales? The *boo-jhwha* live in France.'[9] One of the counts against consensus was that it wasn't really an English word. She once told me she had forced a Commonwealth Conference to remove it from the communiqué, in favour of 'agreement' or 'consent'. Good, firm words instead of a muzzy one. 'I am in favour of agreement but against consensus.'

It is also true that her leisure pursuits hardly bespoke a person who placed great importance on enriching the mind. She was not ill-read. One long-serving member of her staff contended that she knew more English poetry than anyone he had met. Certainly she was in the habit of producing verse quotations to fit the conversation. But these tended towards the same narrow mode of didactic couplets that might have been learned at school, with Kipling the acknowledged favourite and Rossetti a constant companion, especially for one quatrain which was produced on numerous occasions: 'Does the road wind uphill all the way?/Yes, to the very end./Will the day's journey take the whole long day?/From morn to night, my friend.'

In prose, she had lower tastes than Macmillan, who never let anyone forget that he turned in fraught moments to Jane Austen, or sometimes Livy. When Mrs Thatcher wanted to relax it was with the thrillers of Freddie Forsyth and suchlike – 'At the moment I'm

re-reading *The Fourth Protocol*,' she told an interviewer in 1985[10] –
although the educationalist John Vaizey, quite a close private friend
from her favourite community of former socialists, was struck by how
much she enjoyed 'exciting herself with books about the horrors of
Marxism'. These, plus improving works by selected moral theologians, formed the main pabulum of her off-duty reading. But the
truth was that she did not take much time off duty. She would as
soon go to bed with a fat government report. Over Christmas 1984
she let it be known that her holiday reading would be the 3,000-page
report of a planning lawyer on the siting of the third London airport.
Christmas 1986 was celebrated in similar style, with an equally long
report from an equally scintillating author, on the siting of a nuclear
power station in Suffolk.

As a rounded intellect, therefore, she suffered from limitations. She
was almost as different as it was possible to be from her contemporaries
across the English Channel. Giscard d'Estaing, in his last days in the
French presidency, spent serious time involving himself in passionate
debate about the contents of the new Musée d'Orsay in Paris. The
museum was to be a grand celebration of the totality of French culture
of the nineteenth century. But when did the nineteenth century begin?
That was the question which had Paris in ferment. The president was
ablaze with a passion which would have been unimaginable in the
British leader. Nor would she have cared how Giscard's successor,
Mitterrand, resolved the matter: that the century began with the
Revolution of 1848 and ended with the First World War. Such
engagement with history and aesthetics was beyond the reach of
Margaret Thatcher – although she had the merit of not pretending
otherwise. 'She sees Mitterrand as a philosopher,' one of her advisers
told me in 1987. 'She would like to be a philosopher, but she knows
she isn't one.'

Even so, this could hardly be counted a decisive mark against her.
It did not grossly distinguish her from many, indeed most, of her
predecessors. They were not philosophers either; and it has never
been the English way for prime ministers to enter the artistic debate.
If British politicians are philistines, it is partly because British voters
prefer them that way. Besides, this leader was at least adequately
cultured. She collected porcelain. She went to the opera. Before an
Austrian holiday in 1984, it was announced that she planned to attend
five concerts at the Salzburg Festival.

And she was also clever. No intellectual could ever doubt the
quality of that part of her intellect. It could work almost anything

out. Give it a problem and it would be oriented entirely towards a solution, and the more complex the problem the better. Grappling with complexity was what it really enjoyed. 'She may not be the very cleverest person in politics,' said one of her policy people in 1988, 'but she's got the most intense intellectual curiosity I've ever come across.' Walters, the pedagogue, could not fault her. 'She asked most searching questions,' he said, 'which as a teacher I've often wished for but rarely seen and rarely heard.'[11]

This, then, was a leader whose relationship with intellectual currents was not entirely distant. She saw her struggle as partly a struggle of ideas. She enlisted on her side academics and thinkers in greater number than her predecessors. Eventually it came to be agreed that she had won a part, perhaps the most important part, of the intellectual argument. She was also in herself a quite adequate exponent of most of the qualities that the intelligentsia, whether broadly or narrowly defined, have been accustomed to expect from British political leaders.

Yet none of these attainments was enough to grant her the acceptance, let alone the support, of this influential, hard-talking community. The world of fashion and of intellect continued to disparage rather than exult in her contribution. What the Oxford dons said in 1985, Oxford University as a whole seemed to repeat in March 1987 when all its graduates voted for a new Chancellor and gave the job, by a wide margin, to Roy Jenkins, the politician who more than any other might be said to epitomise the era and the values which Mrs Thatcher stood against. The contest was complicated by the presence of Edward Heath and the absence of an avowedly Thatcherite candidate, although Lord Blake attracted the pro-Government vote. All the same, by electing Jenkins – corporatist, consensualist, man of culture, of permissiveness, of Europe – Oxford was stating that as far as it was concerned the 1960s were not to be forgotten.

Charting the reasons for this disjunction between the thrust of politics and the resistance of intellectuals takes one quite close to the heart of the Thatcherite project. But the journey begins on terrain that is all too familiar.

One of the most readily discernible issues between these two worlds was a matter of social snobbery, laced, on the part of the dissenting intellectuals, with a special tang of indignation deriving from the fact that their antagonist was a woman. From the beginning, Mrs Thatcher attracted strong feelings for her or against her; in opinion polls, she always scored lowest among the Don't Knows. But when people from the academic or cultural world spoke, their words often revealed an intensity of feeling rarely deployed against her recent predecessors – with the possible exception of Macmillan in his last days. 'She terrifies me, she repels me, and I think she's ruining everything that is best about this country,' wrote Carmen Callil, a publisher, before the 1983 election. On the same occasion, Melvyn Bragg, novelist and television producer, expressed revulsion for 'gloating incantations from a woman dangerously in love with her own publicity'.[12] Angela Carter, another novelist, offered an analysis in terms which it would not have been easy to imagine her using about a man. 'Of all the elements combined in the complex of signs labelled Margaret Thatcher,' Ms Carter wrote, 'it is her voice that sums up the ambiguity of the entire construct. She coos like a dove, hisses like a serpent, bays like a hound.' It was a voice from the past, 'a form of "toff-speak" now reminiscent not of real toffs but of Wodehouse aunts'.[13]

Time did not abate such attitudes. In 1988, Sir Peter Hall, director of the National Theatre, opined that 'well over 90 per cent of the people in the performing arts, education and the creative world are against her'.[14] Their reasons for this stance revealed something more than mere political disagreement. Dr Jonathan Miller, theatre director and polymath, said he found the prime minister 'loathsome, repulsive in almost every way', and specified 'her odious suburban gentility and sentimental, saccharine patriotism, catering to the worst elements of commuter idiocy'. Baroness Warnock, a philosopher who was given a peerage in 1985, returned the compliment with a withering attack on the entire prime ministerial persona. She considered Mrs Thatcher to be inadequately cultured and, when it came to the academic world, incapable of understanding what it was all about. Again the voice came in for particular scrutiny. Lady Warnock did not like the 'patronising, elocution voice' or the way the prime minister 'shouted people out' (in fact a false description of her private demeanour). But there was worse. The baroness had once seen Mrs Thatcher on television choosing clothes at Marks & Spencer, and there was, she found, something quite 'obscene' about it. The clothes showed a woman 'packaged together in a way that's not exactly vulgar, just *low*'. Lady Warnock confessed to 'a kind of rage' whenever she thought about her.

Scarcely less remarkable than such sentiments, which sounded as though they sprang from something deeper than the well of pure reason, was the willingness of these intellectuals to express them. It was as though the passions of the age had lifted all restraint from the canons of public conversation. Nothing, it appeared, was unmention-able, no depth of condescension need be left unplumbed. This very performance was in its way a tribute to the potency of the hate-object it was all about.

These feelings, however, were not an isolated growth. Lady War-nock wasn't the only person to experience a kind of rage. Shortly before the 1983 election, the longest-serving adviser at 10 Downing Street stated, in a tone of fiercely vindictive passion, that he hoped the prime minister would be re-elected in order to 'show the sneerers'. The sneerers were the Warnocks and the Millers but also the Gilmours and the St John Stevases, and assorted outriders in the media, including at that time the *Financial Times*, some of whose writers persisted in taking a notably disrespectful attitude. These people, he felt, had always underrated the prime minister because she spoke not only for a different sex but for a different class. She wasn't one of *them*.

The Warnock rage, in short, was predated by a Thatcher rage. Her own fury at the condition of the stables she was sent to cleanse derived not least from an opinion about the Augean elite who had permitted them to get into the state they were in. Fashionable London, with its outposts in the older universities and cultural quangoes and moribund public bodies of every description, stood for values which she had come to loathe. They were, as she saw them, anti-business, anti-merit and even anti-British. So for her, too, there was a strong class element to her analysis: which was not so much an analysis, more a collection of instinctive feelings arranged around her favourite self-image, that of the outsider. She was prejudiced against inherited wealth and whiggish paternalism, class symbols as potent as the suburban classlessness revealed by a woman buying her blouses at Marks & Spencer. Her challenge was directly to that whig world. Although she was in the habit of saying, when asked which side she would have taken in the English Civil War, that she was a natural cavalier,[15] this was entirely misleading. In the matter of British institutions, she wanted to be a reformer of Cromwellian proportion.

What faced the intelligentsia was a painful disinheritance. It was plain from the early days that they would not be courted but chal-lenged. As the repositories of the conventional wisdom, they were the enemy. An important symbol of their declining status slowly became apparent in one particular prejudice of the new leader, against the age-old British habit of dealing with difficult problems by establishing weighty committees of inquiry. The Royal Commission was part of the standard armoury of post-war prime ministers, but also a source of patronage for propitiating the thinking classes. The Royal Commission and the departmental committee were traditional power-bases for middle-ground intellectuals. But no longer. As the years passed, Mrs Thatcher contrived to avoid establishing a single Royal Commission. The idea passed into the museum of political dinosaurs. In a climate in which everything was political, detachment was held to be a chimera and objectivity a fraud, and the classes who claimed these virtues lost their foothold in public life.

That was one count against Mrs Thatcher. She took away the children's toys. She also declined to worship in their cultural church. Although not unusually philistine, she was reluctant to make the usual deferential noises of approval for public sector art. Public spending on the arts did not go steadily down; there were years when it more than held its own. But over the decade, the great arts institutions like the Royal Opera House and the National Theatre were made to struggle harder. Private patronage was encouraged, state support made to sound more and more grudgingly like a regrettable extra.

Anything that depended on the public purse, in other words, started at a disadvantage in the Thatcherite scale of priorities. It had to justify its existence against ever stiffer presumptions of guilt. Since Dr Miller was largely that kind of artefact – producing operas and plays for state-funded houses, performing ubiquitously on state-funded television – it was perhaps inevitable that he should begin to understand that he no longer belonged to a favoured class, and take reprisals. Plenty of Jonathan Millers had been spawned in the sixties, although few so talented as he. A sizeable group, in fact, could be gathered within what American sociologists have identified as the 'new class': a pejorative term meant to describe the kind of people who have successfully made it by riding on the back of state institutions with taxpayers' money. This 'new class' was being downgraded, if not displaced, in the world designed by Mrs Thatcher. To that extent, the alienation between Conservative politicians and mainstream intellectuals was an almost conscious product of political choice, unmediated by any serious attempt on the part of Thatcherites to seduce rather than denounce these apostles of anachronism.

Nowhere was this more visible than in the universities themselves. Here the disinheritance appeared to be most threatening of all. Assaults on the very home of intellectual life ensured a state of something like continuing war, which transcended any auguries that might have foretold a certain mutual trust and toleration.

The Thatcher years began with cuts in higher education and continued in the same vein. In 1981, universities were given a month to plan an 18 per cent cut in budgets over three years, and 3,000 posts were eliminated. At the 1983 election, the Tories promised no more cuts, but within a year, well before Oxford took its revenge, further cuts of 2 per cent all round were demanded. The whole atmosphere in which intellectual life was supposed to be conducted was dominated by parsimony.

But cuts were not the only problem. There was also the question of the Government's attitude. This appeared to accord a low value to intellectual activity as such. Instead, an economic ethic was pushed to the fore, reaching its purest expression in a 1985 green paper, *Higher Education into the 1990s*.[16] This called frankly for higher education to serve the national economy 'more effectively'. Cost–benefit tests were in, the leisurely pursuit of learning for its own sake was on the way out. Further, the whole context of relative freedom within which dons pursued their research interests was in course of being replaced by a regime of financial rigour controlled by central government through research councils and the like, all of them steadily colonised by more reliable supporters of the new ethic.

Mrs Thatcher herself was wont to put university people firmly in their place. 'Why is it', she rhetorically inquired of an interviewer in 1984, 'that a lot of the people who want to build up a business never get to university, don't want to go to university, but will employ a lot of university people?'[17] The answer was implied, but obvious. There was no serious point in securing a degree unless it opened a door to productive employment in the private sector.

These aspects of Conservatism in the 1980s made a distancing between politicians and many intellectuals probable, and perhaps inevitable. In the mass, the latter were so little respected by the new orthodoxy of the former. This conflict, moreover, had a self-perpetuating quality.

The biases of the academic world might be expected to change somewhat, as the occupants of academic posts came and went over the years. Not only would inherited bitternesses tend to diminish, but there would surely arrive in the universities a growing number of academics of a new breed, more representative creatures of their age, less purblind exponents of the kind of intellectual life that the politicians were prepared to finance. If political norms really did march with the prevailing opinions of the intelligentsia, one could look to significant growth in the number of political scientists who were of the right, of natural scientists who disclaimed a preference for pure research, and of professors in general who understood that universities should cease to be such a massive charge on the public purse.

For this evolution to occur, however, it was necessary that there should be a steady turnover of personnel. And this was to an important extent impeded by the Government's own policy. By cutting funds and cutting posts, the policy ensured that the infusion of fresh blood was limited, and in some university departments non-existent. As the dons clung to their shrinking world, their colleges and departments tended to embody with greater concentration than before the age from which they sprang. Appointed in the 1960s, during the period of massive expansion in the universities, they remained as stubborn relics from that era, and obstructions to the intellectual revolution.

This did not, of course, lack its devotees. Alongside the Millers and the Warnocks, a faithful band of Mrs Thatcher's supporters could be wheeled out of the libraries and common rooms. Kingsley Amis, the novelist, wrote that she was the only leader he could trust. A. L. Rowse, the historian, was always to be found among her vigorous supporters. Goaded, perhaps, by the language of revulsion on the left, a few more writers and artists began to come out in her favour.

But it remained the case, late as well as early in her time, that if this was a revolution of ideas it was the property of only a minority of intellectuals. They were well placed, sometimes near the heart of government. They had the supreme advantage of being listened to by Mrs Thatcher. But that was all. Perhaps the problem was that theirs, and hers, was not a rounded philosophy. Conservatism has never pretended to be a system of thought, or to offer a completed vision of the earthly paradise. Conservatism has been against things rather than for them, sceptical not missionary, the enemy of zeal and the stoic friend of imperfection. At the centre of Mrs Thatcher's attempt to repudiate some of this tradition, moreover, was a fundamental division which was bound to flaw any serious effort to overturn and eradicate the post-war liberal consensus: the division between Hayekians, who regarded themselves not as conservatives but as liberals, and the young bloods of the Conservative Philosophy Group, whose greater passion was for order – 'I myself believe neither in traditional liberalism, nor very much in democracy,' Dr Scruton said[18] – and whose interests lay more in deriding liberal shibboleths on such matters as race relations and the punishment of crime.

This minority, it is true, gave Mrs Thatcher what she wanted. 'We should have an ideology as well,' she had said. Functionally, this was provided. But culturally its guarantees were limited. The world from which it came remained dominated by a surly, alien class, unenamoured of the role they were supposed to play – and they were not the only ones that could be so described.

As 1985 drew to a close, an event occurred which ensured that Mrs Thatcher's year would end as it had begun: in a state of war with established institutions. This phase of the conflict, moreover, involved a continuous exchange of fire between Conservatism and former friends rather than incorrigible opponents. Even at moments of wildest optimism, the Conservative Party would hardly have laid claim to a safe constituency among university teachers, but the Church of England and its bishops were different. Although it was many years since the party could truthfully be called the Church of England at prayer, atavistic expectations lived on. And like other old fashions of that kind, it was the destiny of these to be subjected, during Mrs Thatcher's time, to considerable strain – the more so, in this case, because the nature of the argument often touched with special intimacy on the deepest spiritual affiliations of the leader herself.

Early in December, a report entitled *Faith in the City* appeared under the aegis of the Archbishop of Canterbury, Dr Robert Runcie. Two years previously, the Archbishop had set up a commission, composed of churchmen and lay-people, to examine the conditions of urban life in Britain and suggest what the Church and the Government, in their different ways, might do to improve them. The report was highly critical of the Church, suggesting that many of its clergy were out of touch with life as it was lived in inner-city slums; a Church Urban Fund was recommended, through which by private subscription and with money from the Church Commissioners the urban Church could be strengthened. But the other half of the report attacked various aspects of government policy, and urged what amounted to a reversal of some of the Conservatives' most cherished priorities: more money for job-creation, higher welfare payments, a sharp increase in child benefit. It also offered a general verdict, which proved to be still more provocative. The problem with the inner cities, said the Archbishop's investigators, was that they were victims of the overall philosophy of modern Conservatism, which gave too much emphasis to individualism and not enough to the collective obligations of society.

Faith in the City stimulated an immediate political uproar. Even before it was published, government spokesmen denounced its sentiments as Marxist and its members as predominantly Labour Party hacks. Conservative MPs from both the godly and the ungodly wings of the party lined up to protest against its collectivist bias and its apparent neglect of the central Christian emphasis on individual salvation. Dr Runcie, undeterred, insisted that it was in no way Marxist – a term of abuse whose wide currency nonetheless illuminated the degree to which traditional socialism was by now considered inadmissible in a democratic society – and termed it merely 'a Christian critique with political implications'. As he pointed out, some sections of the report spoke with enthusiasm about small business and local enterprise, the very stuff of Thatcherism. But this did not satisfy the prime minister. She read the report, she said, 'with the greatest possible interest'.[19] But she had found in it no recommendations to do with individuals and families, who were the source of all standards in society. The Church should be preaching to families in that vein. In this report it had failed to do so, she said. 'I must say I was really absolutely shocked at that.'

This was not the first time she had experienced such critical astonishment. *Faith in the City* touched a particular nerve, and acquired a special place in the pathology of Church–state relations in these years. But there had been several earlier episodes in which the Conservative Party found, to its mounting indignation, that certain bishops were able to command the headlines with utterances running wholly against the new political orthodoxy, not to mention old and, as most Tories thought, eternal theological truths.

Runcie, as they saw it, had already shown his colours in an excessively even-handed sermon after the Falklands war.[20] The newly appointed Bishop of Durham, Dr David Jenkins, riled them still more. By questioning both the doctrine of the Resurrection and the pit-closures at issue in the miners' strike, he showed himself, to them, to be a many-sided incarnation of the devil. Dr Jenkins accused the Government, on this and many future occasions, of 'not caring' about poverty and unemployment. Making miners redundant, he said, revealed an 'insulting determination' to ensure that the under-privileged bore the heaviest burden of economic change.

Other bishops also wrung their hands over the miners, some even imprudently offering themselves as mediators between Scargill and Mrs Thatcher. They joined, in the Tory mind, those of their number who in 1982 contributed to a Church working-party report which came out in favour of British unilateral nuclear disarmament. Although this never became the official Anglican position, it was one more count against the Church. Whether on the cities or the Bomb, the Archbishop and his friends were entirely unreliable acolytes at the service of elected politicians.

This rendered them unsatisfactory, more so perhaps than they had seemed to any previous twentieth-century government. Part of this was due to a sense of affronted disappointment among Conservatives in general. The old feeling of proprietary affinity still infected some quarters of the parliamentary party. And the old sense of tolerance, even respect, for men of the cloth had largely vanished. In the 1920s, bishops opposed government policy over the General Strike and later attacked cuts in dole, without being impudently anathematised by hooligans on the Tory backbenches. In the 1980s, equivalent positions could be taken only at the cost of being charged not merely with error but with transgressing the rules of clerical silence. Whereas Disraeli thought the Church 'the best, if not the only, agency for evangelising the masses', modern Conservatives preferred it to keep quiet unless it spoke for an identical morality to their own. Besides, with the tabloid press to hand, who needed bishops to preach the word?[21]

But a more potent influence was at work on this complex, sensitive relationship. The fact is that it engaged the personal attention of Mrs Thatcher more closely than that of any of her predecessors. She thought about religious questions more than most prime ministers have publicly admitted doing, although Macmillan went often to church and Heath played church organs. What interested her, admittedly, were the issues of behaviour rather than belief; but these interested her very intensely. In them she saw what should have been a happy marriage between the personal values she most passionately believed in and the values for which, as she saw it, vicars and bishops should be standing with unambiguous clarity.

She was born, as already reported, a Methodist. And, in one sense, a Methodist she never ceased to be. Having married in Wesley's Chapel, she gradually evolved, at least in terms of religious observance, into an Anglican. But, as with many others who have drifted along the same path, the shift was more informal than formal, and probably happened more for social than spiritual reasons. She was never confirmed into the Church of England. On the other hand, the upwardly mobile Conservative Methodist is a rare species outside Wales, a place where Tories of any type are thin on the ground. Overt Methodist practice would have required more conscious and systematic commitment to a Church, as distinct from a set of precepts that appeared to conform to the divine will, than Margaret Thatcher could easily give.

A minor sign, though, of her ineradicable Methodism was her attitude to the Church of Rome. The non-conformist tends to find Roman Catholicism considerably less comprehensible than does the Anglican. To Mrs Thatcher, if one judges by the outward signs, it usually seemed like a strange presence, and Cardinal Basil Hume, the senior Catholic bishop for most of her time, like a man floating mysteriously outside the reach of earthly things. Perhaps this sense of something alien began in childhood when she, the daughter of a fiercely Methodist house, lived opposite a Roman Catholic church 'and a Roman Catholic manse', as she once inexactly termed it.[22]

There were more positive signals that the Methodism had never really been supplanted. Even considered as an Anglican, she was firmly of the evangelical persuasion. She believed in simple verities simply and repeatedly stated, and the common thread running through these invariably had something to do with the importance of personal responsibility. 'The values of a free society like ours come from religion,' she told her friend Sir Laurens van der Post, the traveller and semi-mystic. 'They do not come from the state.' The key value was the right of personal choice, the free will that linked the earthly and the heavenly kingdoms. It was all summed up, she told Sir Laurens, himself a considerable exponent of ethereal moral uplift, in the hymn 'I Vow to Thee, My Country', which included, as she reminded him, the verse: 'soul by soul and silently her shining bounds increase, and her ways are ways of gentleness and all her paths are peace'. 'There is the message,' she triumphantly insisted, ' "soul by soul".'[23]

This interest in personal salvation was, without doubt, genuine. Reading the kind of books that might assist it, whether for herself or for others, was a consistent adjunct to the heavier stuff of official papers. I once asked her without notice what she was reading, in February 1983. While she might re-read Freddie Forsyth for relaxation, this time the re-reading was different. 'Right now I'm re-reading *The Ten Commandments*, by the Archbishop of York.' This was then Dr Stuart Blanch. 'I'm always trying to read a *fundamental* book,' she went on. 'I read quite a lot of theological work.'[24]

A later favourite in the same line was the work of Dr Graham Leonard, Bishop of London from 1981. Dr Leonard was not, in Church terms, an evangelical but quite the opposite – a high priest of the Anglo-Catholic wing. But perhaps this further demonstrated Mrs Thatcher's distance, in her heart, from true allegiance to Anglicanism. As a Methodist she had possibly learned that bishops were not to be taken seriously anyway. But if a bishop like Dr Leonard, although prone to smell of incense, delivered fundamental truths about human conduct that she could warm to, that was enough for her. Certainly by the mid-1980s she was in the habit of saying to anyone within earshot that the Bishop of London was the only man in the Church of England who made the kind of sense that she was looking for.

This brand of good sense was, at bottom, political. Or rather, it conformed with some precision to the message in which she, as a politician, was seeking to instruct the country. This meant that, for her, it was not merely one version of Christianity but the only version that anyone of integrity could conceivably believe in. Once again we confront a mind that was religious without being speculative, just as it was clever without being, in the proper sense, intellectual. Dogmatism reigned. Religion was put to the most useful service it could perform for a crusading politician of the late twentieth century. It reduced to simple issues of personal morality highly complex questions of social and economic behaviour.

Thus, it was because a religious idea had been misunderstood that egalitarianism had taken root, to Britain's great disadvantage. For far too long, Mrs Thatcher thought, the British middle class had been made to feel guilty about success. 'How are we to explain this British guilt-complex?' she wondered. 'Perhaps it is a misplaced non-conformist conscience, a misunderstanding of people like John Wesley.'[25]

Wesley, she thought, didn't remotely preach that sort of negative conscience. He was a High Tory. 'He inculcated the work ethic, and duty. You worked hard, you got on by the result of your own efforts. Then, as you prospered, it was your duty to help others to prosper also. The essence of Methodism is in the Parable of the Talents. All that helped to build up a middle class in this country, a middle class with a conscience.' So the founder of Methodism marched side by side with the founder of Thatcherism.

Similarly, the moral standards of society depended on individual behaviour, which in turn was the proper object of episcopal attention. In her opinion, this was where the Church had most conspicuously failed. Indeed, she seemed to see the rise of the state and of dependency on state solutions as a direct result of the decline of the Church. Interviewed in 1987 on the subject of the Aids epidemic, she was prompted to some spacious contentions on this theme. 'Parliament isn't the great institution of life,' she said.

> Churches are your great institutions, as are your great voluntary associations. And you are entitled to look to them and say 'Look, there are certain standards and if you undermine fundamentally these standards, you'll be changing our way of life.' When the authority of these institutions is undermined because they haven't been forthright, it is then that people turn too much to the State.[26]

Asked directly whether the Church should have been more outspoken about the moral laxity which ensured the spread of Aids, she replied that it should. Some bishops had spoken out, but not enough. Translated by the popular press into another chant in the litany of Conservative complaints against Dr Runcie, this did not mislead. His eye for moral complexity, coupled with his staunch refusal to espouse an extreme position on any part of the agenda with which the Tories presented him, marked him out as a man destined for ever to irritate them.

There were, however, limits to the effects of this irritation. Although Mrs Thatcher experienced it personally, she was more careful in this area than in some others to restrain herself. She made her opinions known on every controversial subject on which the Church intervened. Parliamentary Question Time provided a forum in which opportunities to do so were unfailingly made available by her more boorish backbenchers. But she rarely indulged, herself, in the most venomous attacks. Some kind of gut respect, for the Church if not for churchmen, held her back. The knife tended to be wielded instead by successive chairmen of the party, in which role John Selwyn Gummer, who believed in God and belonged to the Church synod, played hardly less aggressively than Norman Tebbit, whose relationship to organised religion was altogether different.

By the same token, the Thatcher hand on appointments, so palpable elsewhere, was here strangely absent. The rules for filling vacancies in bishops' sees, revised in 1976, left her the opportunity to intervene. Two names went forward for each vacancy from the Church's own appointments commission, and were recommended in the order of the Church's preference. On only two occasions did the prime minister disturb the recommendation. In 1981, she ensured that Leonard was appointed to London, when the Church couldn't make up its mind. In 1987, when Birmingham fell vacant, she insisted that the Bishop of Stepney, who was known to be a Labour sympathiser. should be supplanted by the Bishop of Kensington – who did not look like one, but who turned out to be a committed nuclear disarmer. For so vigilant a scrutineer of the moral stance of bishops, this was neither an offensive nor a very successful record of intervention.

Although she had to live with the Church of England, however, she did not need to depend on it for her spiritual succour. Alternative traditions were available. As well as the Methodism to which she was born, there was the faith thrust upon her from the moment she became MP for Finchley. As the guiding light of this Conservative politician, it in many ways took the place of the cradle Anglicanism which constituted the alpha and omega of her predecessors' religious formation.

When she was elected in 1959, a reasonably careful count showed that 20 per cent of the Finchley electorate were Jewish.[27] The local MP was bound to develop a close association with this segment of the constituency; and, as a Conservative, Margaret Thatcher had special need to do so, since shortly before her first election Tory forces had combined to exclude Jews from membership of the Finchley Golf Club. This presented her with no difficulty. For, quite apart from the obvious political incentive, a close similarity existed between the values she most admired and those which are upheld in one part – albeit only one – of the Jewish tradition. Her thirty years of courting the Finchley synagogues deepened this affinity to the point where the Jewish priority, by the end of the 1980s, penetrated many aspects of Mrs Thatcher's life, as could be seen alike in the lifestyle she advocated, the friends and colleagues she particularly favoured and the staunch support she gave to the State of Israel.

It was the Jewish belief in self-help which she found most telling. Ambition and self-advancement are more explicitly blessed in Jewish teaching than they are by Christianity. In parallel runs the Jewish tradition, again more passionately acted out than in some Christian communities, of social action and support. But, as a moral code for upward mobility of the kind the MP for Finchley never ceased to preach, Judaism embodied many useful precepts and could produce many shining exemplars, some of whom found their way into the prime ministerial circle and thence into public positions including the cabinet itself.

Not the least among this number was a man who wasn't a politician but became an important influence at roughly the same speed as the Anglican leadership slid into contumely and disregard. Immanuel Jakobovits, Chief Rabbi since 1967, first met Mrs Thatcher when she was Education Secretary. They discovered they had much in common. He told her that she should be called Secretary of State for Defence, since education was what really protected the future of society. They shared an appetite for conversation of a fundamentalist kind, he the teacher, she the learner. When she became prime minister, Jakobovits was first knighted and then, in 1987, elevated to the peerage. It was rare to come across anything he said which did not chime harmoniously with some aspect or other of the new Conservatism. Indeed, his speeches became a valuable source-book for Mrs Thatcher's own, and the nourishment she gained from them did not wane over the years. As late as 1986, she went to hear a speech he gave at the opening of a new Finchley synagogue, and was so struck by a metaphor he had deployed that she immediately asked his permission to borrow it.

The Chief Rabbi had spoken of man, on life's journey, having left some important baggage behind in the 'spiritual left-luggage office'. His most important listener was enchanted. Could she not apply the phrase to the enterprise culture, another lost commodity languishing in a store-house at the other end of the line?

But even if Jakobovits had not previously been a friend, he would have entered the pantheon in a high place after his most valued service, his reaction to *Faith in the City*. He attacked it for both its underlying philosophy and its detailed prescriptions.

It was based, he thought, on a mistaken view of work. Work, rather than welfare, should be the prime object of policy. 'Cheap labour', he argued, 'is better than a free dole.' Although he warmly endorsed much of the welfare state as an essential safety-net, he did not like the Anglicans' reiterated emphasis on the Government's obligations. A Jewish contribution, he observed, 'would lay greater emphasis on building up self-respect by encouraging ambition and enterprise through a more demanding and more satisfying work-ethic, which is designed to eliminate human idleness and to nurture pride in "eating the toil of one's hands" as the first immediate targets'.

He went on to attack two of the major unspoken premisses of the report. First, he offered an argument rooted, startlingly, in racialism. Blacks in the inner city, he insisted, should learn from the Jewish experience, especially in the United States. There the Jews worked *themselves* out of destitution: educated themselves, built up their own charitable institutions, put down demagogues, cultivated a 'trust in and respect for the police, realising that our security as a minority depended on law and order being maintained'. Further, the Jews never demanded that they should set up a culture separate from their host country. From all this the British blacks should take inspiration, instead of being encouraged by muddle-headed Church people to look to the state.

The Chief Rabbi was even more scathing about trade unions. Why, he asked incredulously, did the Anglican report make no mention of them? Why did it have nothing to say about the morality of strikes in the public utilities and services, which most especially harmed the inhabitants of the inner city? He concluded: 'The selfishness of workers in attempting to secure better conditions at the cost of rising unemployment and immense public misery can be just as morally indefensible as the rapaciousness of the wealthy in exploiting the working class.'

This uncompromising challenge came as a shock to the leaders of the Church of England. It seemed so deeply unfraternal. But to Mrs Thatcher it had the ring, at last, of true moral leadership. It marked out the Chief Rabbi as, in effect, the spiritual leader of Thatcherite Britain, a role for which Dr Runcie was plainly ineligible.

This dichotomy did not correct itself. The two sides remained locked in their opposed positions about the priorities of politics, even perhaps about the meaning of life. The leading bishops continued to announce themselves as critics of Conservatism. As each budget loomed, sometimes Dr Runcie and sometimes Dr John Habgood, the Archbishop of York, and always Dr Jenkins from Durham would denounce the promised cuts in taxation and urge the case for a less divided society, which they continued in an old-fashioned way to define as one which was more equal. When a new issue presented itself, the question of applying economic sanctions against South Africa, the bishops again took up the torch against the prime minister's determination that nothing should be done. They were, in their way, a modest twentieth-century version of the old Christian martyrs, returning with unflinching, perhaps pleasurably masochistic, fortitude for another dose of punishment. When the 1984 Conservative party conference, riled beyond measure by Dr Jenkins' defence of the miners, gave a standing ovation to a turbaned Indian elder who delivered a ferocious attack on the established Church, it said something definitive about the way Church–state relations were changing in these years.

For the Government remained unmoved by the bishops' pleas. Mrs Thatcher continued her religious explorations, the ceaseless quest for the texts which might link ever more closely her political project to what she thought of as the higher purposes of existence. In May 1988, in a speech largely written by herself and strewn with biblical quotations, she explained at length to the General Assembly of the Church of Scotland the indissoluble link between Christianity and individual responsibility, including the responsibility to make money. 'How could we invest for the future,' she asked, 'or support the wonderful artists and craftsmen whose work also glorifies God, unless we had first worked hard and used our talents to create the necessary wealth?'[28] One of the clergymen present denounced her sermon as a 'disgraceful travesty of the gospel'.

Dr Leonard and Lord Jakobovits continued to be sure of an eminent audience for anything they wrote, although even Dr Leonard fell somewhat from favour by opposing, on religious grounds, the utilitarian thrust of the 1988 Education Reform Bill. Like the so-called intelligentsia, the so-called moral leaders in their palaces and pulpits were deposited outside the walls: a discardable class whom government found it could easily do without.

With the political wind behind it, it could afford to ignore these excrescent bodies, save only to flatten them with outrage whenever they dared speak for different ideas. Its leader went back to her roots. The mind first captivated by Herbert Agar and then enriched by the lofty axioms of Hayek turned its attention to higher things. In 1988 she determined to read the Old Testament from cover to cover, and gave daily reports to her staff about how she was getting on. It was a typically systematic performance, vacuuming up the facts. What was the only book in the Bible that did not mention God? she challenged them one day, and beamed with pleasure when nobody else knew it was the Book of Esther. But her eye was caught mainly by biblical accounts of vengeance. 'It is a very *gory* book,' she noted.

19

Economy with the Truth

ALTHOUGH IDEAS WERE important to Margaret Thatcher – more important than to any of the predecessors she had known – political leadership is about more than thinking. It calls for a collection of talents, public and private, light and dark, whether growing out of character on the one hand or artifice on the other. These, which might be called the technical skills of politics, can be broadly grouped into two categories. There are the skills of persuasion, whether exhibited in rhetoric or salesmanship or myriad facets of self-presentation as the politician chooses to deploy them. And there are the skills of management: the methods by which the leader assembles the necessary support, arranges the way decisions are taken and gets the business done.

Mrs Thatcher had an idiosyncratic approach to both these aspects of the art of politics. But she paid rather more serious attention to one than to the other. Early in 1986, reckless inattention to the processes of political management brought about the most serious personal crisis of her time as prime minister. She made a series of mistakes, and was driven to more and more unorthodox expedients in order to avoid the consequences. These revealed her as the kind of politician she had striven mightily to appear not to be: a politician of the old school, a fixer and manipulator and, when the system forced her to the point, a person capable of being an accessory to outright deception if this was necessary in order to preserve her position. She possessed, it became clear, the willingness if not quite the natural talent to dabble in the darker political arts.

As a persuader, she was more orthodox. But her performance, it must be said, was largely the creation of artifice. Her natural rhetorical abilities started low and did not improve. In Parliament, her command of the House of Commons did not depend on mesmeric oratory or any conspicuous parliamentary skill. Nobody looked to her for instinctive eloquence, still less for disarming shafts of humour. Granted substantial majorities in three successive Parliaments, she relied on their dependable loyalty rather than on any winning brilliance of her own to traverse the difficult passages. Between Edward Heath and Margaret Thatcher, the Conservatives were led for the quarter-century from the mid-1960s by people with tin ears and negligible capacities for inspiring any but audiences of the already converted. For Mrs Thatcher was no more compelling outside the House than in it. Indeed, such were the demands of both security and news management that almost never did she allow herself as prime minister to be placed in front of a neutral, let alone a hostile, audience with a view to moving them by the power of her speech.

She made up for this pedestrian style with capacities she could acquire by dogged learning. While rarely approaching eloquence, and never the irresistible fluency of the born parliamentarian, her efforts in the House were usually as effective as they needed to be because she prepared for them meticulously. Age did not stale her almost infinite attention to detail. Her rehearsals for the twice-weekly Question Time were as thorough in her tenth year as in her first. Her big speeches were subjected to intensive planning, far into the night. Only on the most informal occasions did she trust herself to speak extempore. What was required was a battery of facts and figures, assembled in the most persuasive order, coated with the appropriate veneer of righteousness or indignation, and seasoned – although this rarely applied to speeches in the House – with an occasional vivid image contrived for her by a hired hand. No British leader had ever been in power for so long and left so little in the depository of the English language. None, on the other hand, was so infrequently worsted in a parliamentary argument.

Contrivance was more conspicuously at work in the most important medium of political communication, television. To this she paid as close attention as she did to Parliament, but with more copious resort to subterfuge. From the beginning she willingly submitted to the image-makers, principally Gordon Reece and the Saatchis' televisual maestro, Tim Bell, both of whom stayed with her, through several vicissitudes of their own, for the duration. It was not only a question of looks and makeup and dress, all of which, in Bell's opinion, made it much easier for a professional in his line of business to work with a woman than a man – a woman being well accustomed to manipulation for cosmetic effect. Speech itself was subjected to radical change. An academic authority on the techniques of political oratory, Max Atkinson, even managed to measure the change Mrs Thatcher achieved. In his esoteric excursion down this little-travelled by-way of political science, *Our Masters' Voices*, Atkinson notes that she took voice lessons from a tutor at the National Theatre, and began a programme of special humming exercises to lower her natural pitch level. By making her speak more deeply and also slowly, this would enhance the statesmanlike character of her talk. The experiment was successful, Atkinson judged after listening to tape-recordings of her speeches before and after. 'When these are played through an electronic pitch and intensity analyser,' he solemnly reports, 'it emerges that she achieved a reduction in pitch of 46 Hz, a figure which is almost half the average difference in pitch between male and female voices.'[1] Moreover, she had done it at an age when the natural pitch of women's voices apparently begins to rise. None of this assiduous effort made her voice attractive. Its grating, relentless monotone drove half the nation into paroxysms of irritation. Atkinson concluded nonetheless that the Thatcher way of oratory had probably created 'behavioural precedents' for female politicians of the future.

By suchlike devices, the fruit of hard work and serious study, she made herself a tolerably effective performer. She knew her limitations, wanted to minimise them, and did so by the means within her capacity. She wished, still, that she could have been better at it. For communication, as time went on, became one of her most pressing ambitions. What she admired above all about Ronald Reagan, compensating for some of his obvious areas of incompetence, was his matchless power to get his message across. She envied that. To emulate it she was willing to try almost anything the media-men came up with. The so-called 'sincerity machine', an electronic gadget which reflects a text on to discreet transparent screens in front of a platform-speaker, thus enabling them to appear to be speaking extempore and direct to the audience, was an American invention she eagerly seized on, putting it to intensive use in the 1983 election and for all her major televised speeches thereafter.

All this was part of the self-improvement, even the self-creation, which is one of the continuing necessities of political leadership. It wasn't unique to Mrs Thatcher. Like others before her, she simply sought to make the most of a limited talent to enthral. But on the other side of politics, the managerial, it was a different story. Demosthenes might be an elusive role-model, but Machiavelli was closer within her grasp than she liked people to know. To leadership of a collective government she brought habits and prejudices which marked her out as different from most of her predecessors. Dangerously so. It was a style that nearly led to her downfall.

Some of these differences were organisational. From the beginning, the cabinet met less frequently than under many previous prime ministers. It was a rare week when it gathered more than once. Additionally, the system of cabinet committees was less richly byzantine than at any time since the war. Whereas Attlee, in six years, accumulated 148 standing committees of the cabinet and 313 ad-hoc committees that came and went with single issues, the Thatcher tally for a similar period was 30 to 35 and 120 respectively.[2] As the leader made plain, she did not want government by committee but government by herself in concert with selected ministers, who were often brought together only semi-formally under her aegis and outside the structured dockets of the conventional system. Ad-hoc groups were a way of maintaining her control, bypassing rival interest-centres in the cabinet and narrowing the circle of decision. Some ministers complained about them. They imparted a certain looseness to a governmental machine that was in any case, like such conveyances the world over, constantly in danger of running out of control. But it certainly assisted the process of prime ministerial domination, and the weakening of what the textbooks call the British system of cabinet government. 'Temporarily we don't have cabinet government,' one anonymous Whitehall figure told Peter Hennessy. 'We have a form of presidential government in which she operates like a sovereign in her court.'[3]

But this was not manifested solely by the downgrading of formal cabinet business. Temperamental factors also played their part. One of the earliest commonplaces of the Thatcher style was that she was a chairman who invariably led from the front. Not for her the preference of Wilson and Callaghan, and also Heath, for silently listening to the voices before exercising the prerogative of summing up. Within this leadership method, however, other habits also emerged which did not make for collegial harmony.

Ministers' tales of misery at the hands of Mrs Thatcher's standard forensic technique were legion – and consistent. One senior man told me, after years of exposure, that the leader wasn't seriously interested in rational discussion. Although she thirsted for argument, 'arguing with her is an extremely unsatisfactory experience.' It had never changed, he went on. 'She doesn't have discussions, she states opinions.' This did not mean that she would never change her mind. In fact she would sometimes change it quite suddenly. But this rarely happened after a deep process of reflective reasoning, and invariably involved unpleasantness. He instanced two decisions he had been involved in: the surrender of Hong Kong to China in 1997, and the formulation of a British response to Star Wars. Over Hong Kong, it took 'many long and very bitter sessions to get her off her line' – which was that she could not contemplate 'giving in' to China when the lease over the colony expired. On Star Wars, her initial reaction, tenaciously clung to through several abrasive meetings with Foreign Secretary Howe, was to offer far more strident support for Reagan's dream than Britain eventually gave.

A characteristic of this method was often its futility. It was as though she simply needed to blow off steam. Ministers found it insufferably time-wasting, not because they lost the argument but because, win or lose, the argument had to take place, and often on a point which was far from central to the decision. This was another propensity that didn't change with age. 'These battles are totally exhausting,' a minister reflected to me, an hour after enduring one in July 1986. 'They can't be good for government. They're a quite unnecessary expenditure of energy. They almost never result in any clarification, mainly because of her habit of going off at a wild tangent and worrying away for half an hour at a minor detail.'

This was not the most orderly of governing methods. It was personal and headstrong, permanently straining at the seams of the collective. Because Conservative politicians are usually better than their Labour counterparts at preserving a united front and concealing the chaos that is sometimes called government, few public glimpses were afforded of the costs of these reckless emanations from 10 Downing Street. After the first two and a half years, the Thatcher Government, with occasional exceptions, was not one which featured a great deal of ministerial leaking and counter-leaking. But the prevailing style was, nonetheless, dangerous. It could lack strategic foresight. It risked things being overlooked. And nemesis lay in wait.

It arrived, improbably, by helicopter.

Among the problems confronting government halfway through 1985, the future of Westland plc, a small private company in the West Country, did not rank high. It was not entirely off the agenda, because the company was Britain's only maker of helicopters and, facing bankruptcy, had gone to the Government for assistance. Meetings took place, including meetings with the prime minister, as the leaders of a government which was powerfully committed against public sector solutions for private sector business failures grappled with the prospect of maintaining Britain's defences, to which they were equally committed, without the capacity to build these crucial aircraft. But there were larger matters on the leader's plate: Ireland, Europe, crises in local government, continuing bitter discord in the Conservative Party.

So Westland did not look like an issue of great substance. Nor was it. It was one among many middle-grade problems swirling through Whitehall, which every now and again wafted into Downing Street on the breeze. But it embroiled a large personality, the only man in Mrs Thatcher's cabinet whose fearlessness and ambition came close to matching her own. And it cast a searching light on the central question of the Thatcher style of political management, coupled with the Thatcher reputation for straight dealing: matters which far transcended balance-sheets, helicopters, jobs in Yeovil (where Westland was located) and even British defence policy.

Michael Heseltine had always held himself at a distance from Margaret Thatcher, as he had from all other senior colleagues. In the early years of faction, when most ministers were identifiably either wet or dry, he could not be firmly located in either camp. This made him an unsettling figure. Strong enough in 1979 to reject the Energy portfolio in favour of Environment, because it was the more important, he possessed qualities that tend always to alarm prime ministers: he was independent and he was unpredictable. 'She doesn't trust him further than she can spit – which, being a lady, is not very far,' said one of Mrs Thatcher's staff six months after they came to power.

Part of Heseltine's capacity to alarm stemmed from his wealth. After public school and Oxford, property and publishing made him seriously rich. He could make far more money outside politics. Indeed, by the time he entered the Thatcher Government it was commonly said that he didn't need to make money ever again other than by prudent management of his investment portfolio. But wealth was not, in fact, the chief identifying feature of Heseltine's politics. This was, instead, his contemptuous rejection of both the main strands of Tory economic thinking from 1979 onwards.

He wasn't, on the one hand, a wet. He had no time for the Priors and the Pyms and the other hand-wringing paternalists who, he considered, merely wanted to slow down and soften what the Thatcherites were doing. On the other hand, he despised the Thatcherite philosophy especially as it related to industry. To the suggestion that Mrs Thatcher was a radical he would reply sharply: 'Oh? And in what respect?' He said she was an old-fashioned reactionary liberal, whose abiding folly was not to believe in government intervention to achieve industrial reform. Pressed further, he always contended that the mistake had not been going too fast but too slow. If he'd been in charge, he told me in 1980, he would have shaken out employment, imposed the squeeze, throttled uncompetitive businesses, all far more harshly than occurred under the hand of Chancellor Howe – but as a prelude to rebuilding British industry with the open and dominant assistance of the Government.

Heseltine, in other words, was that most loathed of specimens, an unreconstructed believer in the Conservatism of Edward Heath. He regarded 'corporatist' as a pejorative term for a benign activity. He sincerely believed in one-nation policies, involving the unions and business and government together. Given the huge opportunities offered by North Sea oil, he regarded it as a form of insanity to deny that these would be best exploited by a government prepared to make the key strategic choices. A man of some Celtic passion, he did not regard such an extravagant word as hyperbole.

At the Department of the Environment, as it happened, he had the opportunity to put some of this thinking into practice. Charged with local government reform and inner-city revival, it became a kind of ghetto, quarantined off from the excesses of free-market ideology. Heseltine did not make much of a fist of local government at this early stage, when his main task was to control its spending by a succession of ever more complex financial formulae. And he opposed more drastic measures. But his reputation burgeoned with a personal crusade for the revival of Liverpool after the 1981 riots: an effort which enabled him to conduct a kind of laboratory experiment in the politics he believed in. How much could be achieved by business and local government and even some trade unions, under the inspirational leadership of a Secretary of State who devoted 20 per cent of his time for a whole year to this single problem? Heseltine proved that the answer was quite a lot. Mistrustful though she was of this least supplicant of ministers, the leader could see that he had his uses.

His next job put these to still more acute effect. In January 1983 she moved him to the Ministry of Defence, to perform tasks closer to her own heart. One, the reorganisation of the ministry with a view to increased efficiency and closer scrutiny of its massive budget, called on his managerial skills. At Environment, Heseltine had always seen himself as manager. With his interest in 'systems' and lack of interest in small-printed paperwork, he was sometimes felt to be better at management than policy, and the MoD with its service rivalries and its cosy cost-plus contractors certainly needed managing.

But the other task was more urgent. Heseltine arrived at the ministry at a time when support for the 'peace' movement across Europe was reaching its peak. In Britain, national membership of the Campaign for Nuclear Disarmament grew from 2,000 in 1979 to something close to 100,000. With American Cruise missiles scheduled to arrive within months, the nuclear issue needed major attention from government propagandists, which Heseltine duly provided. He flung himself into the work with brio and ruthlessness. This again called on instincts that were far from wet. He might be sensitive to hard-luck cases in Liverpool, but he did not scruple to deploy foul means as well as fair against the enemies of the state, as he defined them to be, who constituted the one-sided disarmers of CND. If evidence was needed, he would get it from any source, including MI5, as was later revealed by the security operative who was required to transmit it to the party politicians, Cathy Massiter.[4]

These efforts brought Heseltine closer to central ground that mattered to the Tory Party. So did his handling of the Ponting case which, although it ended in Ponting's acquittal on a secrets charge, did the minister no harm. He was picking up the pieces from other people's war. He defended the deceptions surrounding the *Belgrano* affair, and made a sonorous case for all-encompassing *raisons d'état*. A week after Ponting's acquittal, he secured the Government's revenge by assembling one of the most brutal ministerial attacks on a named civil servant ever heard in the House of Commons.[5] In this field, he did the leader's business for her without doubt or contradiction.

But theirs was never an easy relationship. Michael was always a potential menace. Whenever he got up at the party conference, he managed to rouse the audience to peaks of ecstasy only marginally lower than those she more ritually provoked. He was completely dedicated to self-advancement, as long as it didn't require him to curry too slavishly her grace and favour. The virulence of their disputes retained, it seems, a special savour. He continued to oppose her more radical expedients for demolishing the power of local government. Jim Prior has recorded what happened after the 1983 election when Heseltine persisted, from the MoD, in criticising the plan to abolish the Greater London Council. His opposition 'led Margaret to deliver him one of the most violent rebukes I have witnessed in cabinet'.[6]

It was not, therefore, an emollient or naturally compliant Secretary

For cameramen alone, the conviction politician submits.

The Westland connection: Michael Heseltine (*above*), who was feared, and Leon Brittan, who resigned two days after enjoying this joke.

Ambiguous friendships: Cecil Parkinson (*above*), who resigned and was reinstated, and Norman Tebbit, from whom affection was withdrawn.

The Evolution of a Public Person

The new MP, 1959.

The junior minister, 1961.

The clothes horse, 1975.

The dowd, 1979.

The Evolution of a Public Person

Gloriana Imperatrix, 1983–8.

The Iron Lady and the new man: Mikhail Gorbachev, 1987.
The Tsarina meets the peasants, Moscow 1987.

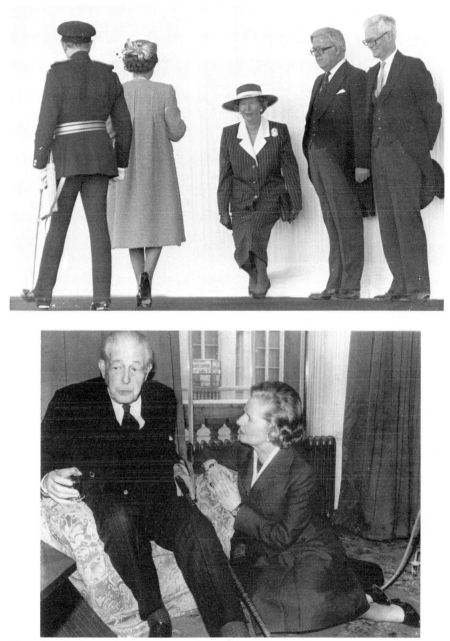

Two forms of genuflection: the loyal, to Her Majesty the Queen, 1988, with Sir Geoffrey Howe and Douglas Hurd looking on; and the ambivalent, to Harold Macmillan, 1979, with whom the problem had begun.

The new generation in their place: Conservative Party Conference, 1988.

of State for Defence who began, rather late in 1985, to take an interest in the fortunes of Westland plc. Discovering that the solution which appeared to be most favoured was the purchase of the company by an American corporation which included one of Westland's rivals in the helicopter business, Sikorsky, he determined, in a spirit which escalated over a period of days from cool, quizzical rationality to burning messianic zeal, to challenge that proposal and have it supplanted with another: purchase by a consortium of European firms to guarantee the European identity of a vital defence industry.

The argument followed many twists, drew in a large variety of rival interests at home and abroad, and displayed before the British public a bewildering assortment of names and companies they had never heard of.[7] As in many crises which sprang out of small beginnings, the question at issue seems even more trifling after the event than it did at the time. But politically it was explosive. And its explosive quality resided, more than anywhere, in the personalities of the participants and the style they brought not so much to a decision about this defence industry as to the very business of politics.

Ranged against Heseltine was a politician as different from him as it would be possible to find. Where Heseltine was loud and charismatic, Leon Brittan gave every impression of being publicly insecure. He was now the Secretary of State for Trade and Industry, and therefore in charge of decisions about rescuing industrial lame ducks, decisions which even in the Thatcher era could not be entirely avoided.

Brittan had recently had a nasty shock. Summoned to Chequers early in September, with a cabinet reshuffle in the offing, he confidently supposed that the prime minister would be wanting to seek the advice of her sagacious if youthful Home Secretary on a delicate matter then troubling the party managers: namely, whether or not it was wise to invite Cecil Parkinson back from exile and return him to a senior job in government. In the end, caution and Lord Whitelaw prevailed, along with the dire forebodings of the influential chief whip, John Wakeham. But distinctly more noticeable than Parkinson's non-return was the sudden demotion of Brittan to the DTI. It was to hear this news rather than to deliberate on Parkinson's future that Brittan had been summoned to the country. He was shattered. The fell hand of Wakeham was at work here too. Leon's fealty to the leader had taken him round several uncomfortable bends on the issue of capital punishment, a one-time abolitionist searching for common ground with her opposite opinion. Similar instincts had persuaded him to take on the BBC, challenging its right to broadcast an interview

435

with an IRA terrorist.[8] But this was to no avail. Somehow his handling of these constant efforts to do right by his leader was judged to have gone more wrong than right. A Home Secretary widely thought to be a fine administrator – Douglas Hurd, at one time Brittan's junior, thought he was the ablest minister he had ever worked for – was despatched to the less sensitive territory, as it seemed, of the DTI.

When he got there, Westland was still low among the department's priorities. He was soon ensnared in the more complex, and ultimately abortive, endeavour of selling the Austin-Rover motor group, formerly BL, to an American buyer. But Westland, seeking its marriage with Sikorsky, hove into view. The DTI, while not committed to the Sikorsky solution, was committed to letting Westland and its shareholders decide what to do. Since Westland's first preference was this American option, Brittan's ministerial line, while initially pretending to be detached, in effect became diametrically opposed to Heseltine's. The terrain was laid out for powerful combat between a hardened operator, steaming with ever less controllable passion, and a relative newcomer who evinced little passion about anything and had no experience of the political killing-fields. It was the carnivore against the herbivore: by the law of the jungle a decidedly unequal contest.

Brittan, however, was not on his own. The prime minister, although dimly aware of earlier rescue efforts, caught on late to the full dimensions of the space that Westland suddenly seemed likely to occupy. When she did so, it was to side with Brittan. By this time, which was early December, several developments had sent a second-order private drama well on its way towards a first-order public crisis.

One was that Brittan's attitude, under forcible external pressure, had by then become significantly clearer than it was at first. While the Commons Defence Committee later established that he had indeed 'held the ring' between Westland's rival suitors and, as Heseltine requested, had urged the company to keep the European option open, this formal aloofness could not survive for ever in face of the second development, which was Heseltine's increasingly frenzied and public campaign to mobilise the Europeans and present them as the only acceptable partners. With his extensive European contacts, he personally put together the consortium of businesses that would bid for Westland. He also got the relevant national arms procurement chiefs not only to give it their official blessing but implicitly to denounce the possibility of a Sikorsky takeover. Thus, one minister was lobbying and manoeuvring with increasing abandon to displace another minister, the one who was supposed to be responsible, from his turf. The time was overdue for an assertion of prime ministerial control.

It came, even then, only slowly. With the company itself enraged by Heseltine's efforts to deny it its chosen objective, Mrs Thatcher stepped in to chair three successive ministerial meetings in early December to resolve the issue – which eventually they did, or so most of those present thought. First, two ad-hoc groups of ministers met to determine whether the Sikorsky option really should be ruled out, as the arms procurement chiefs, lobbied by Heseltine, had implied. Then a meeting of the full economic committee of the cabinet, called in response to Heseltine's continuing pleas that in the national interest his European consortium should be given its chance to make a formal bid, was held on 9 December. It, also, decided that time was about to run out for the European option.

But here we come to the first moment in the saga which exposed the weaknesses of the Thatcher style of management. Her preference for doing business through semi-formal groups of ministers left these occasions open to challenge by malcontents. The Heseltine camp later said that the Thatcher version of what happened simply wasn't true. Contrary to her contention, they said, there was no majority against Heseltine on 9 December or before. Instead, his colleagues were still waiting to see what he could come up with to keep Westland in European hands. Which leads immediately to Heseltine's other, still more outraged, complaint, that on 9 December it was agreed to assemble a few days later for one more time the smaller, ad-hoc group of ministers before whom he could lay his completed case.

This meeting, scheduled for 13 December, was never held: a non-event which became the initial *casus belli* of the Westland affair. Again what is striking, some years afterwards, is the triviality of this detail. Yet this was the moment, according to Heseltine, when he 'knew that something very wrong had happened':[9] indeed, it attested to 'the emergence of what I consider to be the breakdown of constitutional government'.[10]

Mrs Thatcher, by contrast, asserted that no such meeting was ever fixed.[11] There might have had to be a meeting on 13 December 'if unforeseen developments required one'. But no decision to hold one was taken or recorded.

How could so gross a discrepancy of perception have come to exist? Until the year 2017, when the papers should be available in the Public Record Office, it will not be possible to know who was correct about this petty detail on which so much was made to turn. What can be said without much doubt, however, is that in a system which allowed so much business to be conducted at the informal whim of the chief minister, one man's meeting could quite easily, and even honestly, become another woman's meeting-that-never-was.

But Heseltine was far from finished. The struggle now was not with the lawyerly and somewhat bewildered Brittan. It lay directly between the two largest beasts in the jungle. And it exposed, at each stage of the combat that followed, some crucial shortcomings, to put it no lower, in the prime minister's conduct of a situation once it had broken free from the reassuring norms of political behaviour.

First, she exhibited strange weakness. Having been deprived of his 13 December meeting, and seen the time-limit for the European option apparently expire, Heseltine carried on as though these setbacks had simply not occurred. While the Trade Secretary told the Commons, on 16 December, that the arms directors' impediments to the Sikorsky bid no longer obtained and that Westland was therefore free to do what it wanted, the Defence Secretary only redoubled his efforts to undermine this collective decision. Between Christmas and New Year, he lobbied British Aerospace and Lord Weinstock of GEC, continued to threaten that an American-owned Westland would be excluded from European defence contracts and corresponded intensively with the consortium's bankers, Lloyds Merchant Bank – all with a view to keeping the European solution alive.

Heseltine, in short, was now openly flouting the elementary rules of collective responsibility. By the turn of the year he had sheared off and was clattering like some displaced cog around the government machine. Yet the leader did nothing to stop him. Other ministers, St John Stevas for one, had been fired for mere indiscretion. Heseltine, whose disruptive influence now exceeded that of poor old Stevas ten times over, carried on with apparent impunity.

In fact one attempt to curb him was considered. In the first week in January, an inner cabal which included Whitelaw, Wakeham, Brittan himself and the Cabinet Secretary, Robert Armstrong, in discussion with Mrs Thatcher, got quite close to persuading themselves that the errant Defence Secretary should be sent a letter telling him to mend his ways, return to the embrace of collective responsibility or face the sack. Only when Bernard Ingham entered the room and was asked his opinion did they apparently pull back. Ingham pointed out that Heseltine, in his present mood, would only seize on such a feeble missive and exploit it. The sack or nothing was Ingham's opinion: a view they took as a welcome excuse for doing nothing.

A few weeks later, Mrs Thatcher was challenged on why she had not confronted Heseltine much earlier in the affair. She gave a winsome, but unpersuasive, explanation. The media, she said, would have jumped on her. 'Had I done that . . . I know exactly what the press would have said: "There you are, old bossy-boots at it again." '[12] This was not a charge which she had previously shrunk from inviting. It was extraordinary that, at a moment when her authority was more than ever called for, she failed to assert it: testimony, perhaps, to the fear, which she accorded few other politicians, of what a martyred Heseltine might do to her.

If this was an influence on her, it was a misjudgment. Or, rather, if she assumed that by taking a different course she might avert damage to herself, she was seriously mistaken.

We now enter the second stage of Mrs Thatcher's personal Westland crisis. If the first was marked by weakness and lack of control, the next took her into the realm of plain chicanery. It was as if the system, having been thrown out of gear by one minister's impropriety, could recover itself only by descending to a similar or even lower level of dubious conduct. While her own precise involvement in this remained hard to determine for sure, the episode required her to forfeit for ever what the *Belgrano* affair had already compromised: the image of a political leader whose unfailing integrity and flawless honesty and disarming willingness to tell the truth made her different from all the others.

Although she didn't send Heseltine the letter she was cooking up when Ingham stayed her hand, letters from several quarters became the chief exhibits in the case.

First, in an effort to reassemble the authority of collective government, the prime minister herself sent a letter to the Westland chairman, Sir John Cuckney, designed once more to clarify what the Defence Secretary had muddled. While it was true, she wrote, that some European governments and companies might find it difficult to carry on with certain Westland contracts if the company was sold to the Americans, it was equally the case that Britain, as a main collaborator in these contracts, would always work hard to stop any discrimination against Westland. This letter, delivered on 1 January, was cleared with all relevant ministers. Cuckney said that the company was 'considerably heartened' by it.

Heseltine, however, again raised the ante. Two days later another pair of letters were published, both of them his own work. One was a letter from Lloyds Merchant Bank, acting for the European consortium, the other his reply to this letter, stating with considerably more emphasis than the prime minister had that a Westland–Sikorsky link would render 'incompatible' any further involvement by Westland with certain European military projects. This exchange was manifestly a ruse: yet another artifice devised by Heseltine brazenly to challenge the prime minister's authority. For the first letter was solicited by Defence Ministry officials, simply to provide a pretext for their minister to say what he wanted to say, and what he had been stopped from inserting into Mrs Thatcher's own letter to Cuckney.

As the Commons Defence Committee later observed, the effect of this letter, which was of course immediately published by Heseltine, 'can have been nothing short of incendiary'. Certainly the prime minister had had enough. It was decided to secure the writing of yet another letter, this time by the Solicitor-General, Sir Patrick Mayhew. A law officer would be the man finally to lay down the law.

But it wasn't quite so simple as that. Mayhew's opinion had first to be informally ascertained. Was Heseltine right or wrong in the clarity of his insinuation that all relevant European governments and companies would withdraw business from Westland if it didn't remain in European hands? It wouldn't be much use if Mayhew thought Heseltine was correct. So Brittan was deputed to telephone him. On discovering that, in Mayhew's provisional opinion, Heseltine's letter contained 'material inaccuracies' the prime minister, as she later told, asked him 'to consider writing to the Defence Secretary to draw that opinion to his attention'.[13]

Later, there was much discussion about why she had done that, if not in order to ensure that Mayhew's opinion was thrust into the public realm without delay. Had she really suggested the letter so that Heseltine himself could be apprised? Or was there not some nefarious plan, laid that weekend at Chequers, where Whitelaw, Wakeham and others of the core-group gathered? We do not know. But it soon turned out to be an academic question.

Mayhew did not immediately decide to comply. He thought about it until Monday, but then, having consulted the files, did set cautious pen to paper, and suggest to Heseltine that he had gone too far. His sweeping assertions about the Europeans could not all be sustained as faithful interpretations of the contractual position. Mayhew stressed that he hadn't seen all the documents. But on the basis of what he had seen, there were indeed 'material inaccuracies' which the minister should correct.

This letter arrived in Heseltine's office at midday, with copies to the prime minister and Brittan's DTI, which reached them an hour later. It was swiftly apparent to officials in both places that parts of what Mayhew said were extremely damaging to the minister who now daily tormented their lives. Here was a law officer, most respected of counsellors, stating that this minister was putting about falsehoods: falsehoods, moreover, which had a bearing on an important matter of possible commercial sensitivity due to be transacted that very afternoon, namely a Westland press conference fixed by chairman Cuckney for four o'clock. The opportunity was too good to miss – if, indeed, it had not already been anticipated, whether at the Chequers meeting or inside the DTI itself, where the information officer, Miss Colette Bowe, was very early on the scene when the Mayhew text arrived. By mid-afternoon the relevant words had been leaked to the Press Association, with much the desired effect. They turned out to have little bearing on the Westland press conference, the deadline later offered as the reason which made these manifold unorthodoxies essential. But the *Sun* occupied much of its front page next morning with a picture of Heseltine, alongside their largest available two-word headline: *You Liar!*

For the first time, Heseltine, who had conducted much of his campaign through use of the calculated leak, found himself leaked against to apparently devastating effect. The devastation, however, proved to be quite undiscriminating. And thereby hangs the main political tale of Westland: a story which came close, in Mrs Thatcher's opinion as well as in many other people's, to terminating her prime ministership.

It was no ordinary leak. In the annals of leaking, law officers' letters had rarely featured. A special sanctity attached to them, which was no doubt part of the contagion with which English lawyers have long succeeded in infecting British society at every level not excluding the political. Under this baleful influence, the British have often tended to treat both lawyers and their utterances as specially privileged. So it was with this particular leak, which provoked a response no less outraged than if the cabinet minutes themselves had been published in full on the front page of the *Daily Telegraph*.

Slightly less extraordinary, but no less enraging to the Solicitor-General, was the fact that the leak had apparently been perpetrated by another minister. Ministers have done this to each other in the past, although not often with such crudity. When he saw a carefully edited version of his opinion published that same day in the evening newspapers, Mayhew was furious. He did not then suppose that a minister had done it. What privately concerned him was the selectivity of the leaker's approach, which distorted the balanced judgment he had given Heseltine. What publicly infuriated him was that any particle of his opinion should have escaped into the open air. Violation of this sacred bond between lawyer and client was *lèse-majesté* of the grossest kind.

So that was one troublesome aspect of the Westland affair. It sprang from a leak of very special quality. But this was only a preliminary detail, the *hors d'œuvres* before the feast of scandal. The more complex and dangerous circumstance arose from a question. Who, precisely, had been responsible for authorising such a departure from all the known rules of engagement between ministers of one government?

When the text arrived at the DTI, Brittan himself was on his way to lunch. His private secretary telephoned him, read the Mayhew letter out and asked him what he wanted done with it. Brittan gave, by his own account, an ambiguous response.[14] He said it should go into the public domain, but only 'subject to the agreement of No. 10'. In fact he would have preferred it to come out direct from Downing Street.

But, whatever words he used, his caveat about No. 10's agreement was not permitted to get in the way of selective release of specific verbatim passages from the letter. He was understood, in the course of that telephone call, to have given the necessary ministerial authority – without stopping to think about matters of propriety, or the special status which one lawyer might be particularly expected to give to another lawyer's letter, or the entitlement of Sir Patrick Mayhew to be consulted before his letter was made public. It was Leon Brittan's tragedy, one of several, that whatever others understood he did not fully understand. When he put the phone down, he told friends later, he had no idea of the momentousness of what had just occurred.

No. 10 was thereupon consulted. And No. 10 said that disclosure of the letter by its officials, rather than the DTI's, was out of the question. Again, we do not know precisely what words were used, and the major participants in this great saga have continued their self-denying ordinance of silence from the time of the inquiry by the Defence Committee until the present day. But the committee concluded that it was well understood on all sides that disclosure in this way and without Mayhew's permission 'would be a wholly improper course of action'.[15] Nonetheless, despite this knowledge, the leak would go ahead. Downing Street – through the person of Ingham, who was telephoned for advice by Ms Bowe – said it would not leak the letter. But it did not openly disapprove of the DTI, through the luckless Ms Bowe, doing the dirty work. And when Ingham subsequently reviewed his own conduct in the matter, which he retained an ability to do for years with photographic recall of every twist and turn, he could usually find only this to reproach himself with. In the heat of the moment, he had not stated with sufficient firmness to Ms Bowe that she should have nothing to do with such an unorthodox procedure.

Whoever leaked it, however, there is no doubt that the prime minister herself wanted Mayhew's opinion, if not his exact letter, in the public domain. She said so on numerous occasions. She first of all encouraged him to write it. Then she stated firmly in the Commons: 'It was a matter of duty that it should be made known publicly that there were thought to be material inaccuracies which needed to be corrected in [Mr Heseltine's] letter.'[16] Then, questioned further on that statement, she reaffirmed that her purpose was 'to get that accurate information into the public domain'. She even made reference to that purpose as the reason why 'I gave my consent.' An astonishing revelation, uttered on 23 January in the context of a statement saying that she was in no way to blame. 'It was to get that accurate information to the public domain that I gave my consent.'

Was this a sudden accidental glimpse of the truth? That she had in fact been the one to authorise the disclosure, even though it was effected by the DTI rather than her own officials? Possibly not. When the Defence Committee interrogated Armstrong, the cabinet secretary, about the whole affair, he explained this phrase away as 'a slip of the tongue'. But for a woman whose tongue had slipped less often than that of any contemporary politician this seemed like an accident as rare as it was unfortunate. Nor did her own explanation sound much better. Questioned four days afterwards, she contended that the 'consent' she had referred to was not consent to the disclosure but to the inquiry Armstrong held into how it had come about. This was a lame apologia, which fell far short of her normally watertight cogency. How could it possibly make sense, since consent to the Armstrong inquiry had nothing whatever to do with getting 'accurate information to the public domain'?

Nevertheless, however puzzling these confusions, it is improbable that she personally gave consent to the leak, for the simple reason that she wasn't asked to. Brittan had made No. 10's agreement a condition, unenforceable though it was, of his assent to leaking. 'No. 10', for this purpose, did not mean the prime minister but two of her officials. At the heart of the Westland affair, as it reached this near-fatal climax, were these two men, who were by now, with the exception of her husband, the closest of all men to Margaret Thatcher, and long accustomed to acting in her name, on her behalf, fulfilling her best interests as they saw them, especially when these involved her not being kept informed of every detail of what was going on.

Bernard Ingham, after six years as her press secretary, was the master of all he surveyed in Whitehall. He was in charge not merely of the prime minister's press office and the lobby briefings through which it incessantly dominated political news but, in effect, of government information. He held weekly meetings of departmental press officers, many of whom were people he had trained in his own office and placed in strategic posts around the civil service. All governments including this one had striven for ways of co-ordinating public information and managing the news. Among those charged with this elusive function under Mrs Thatcher had been both Whitelaw and John Biffen, both of whose efforts passed without notice. In the expanding empire of Ingham, six years on, the first seriously business-like information policy was to be found.

But Ingham was more than a powerful co-ordinator. He had become famous in his own right, better known than any previous holder of his post. This was partly because of the things he was willing to say. He cordially despised most of the media he had to deal with. Lecturing the Guild of British Newspaper Editors, he called some media treatment of the Falklands war 'disgraceful', and whether in person or at the end of a telephone often used language so coarsely dismissive that its origin could easily be identified behind the veil of Downing Street's conventional anonymity.

Ingham was particularly fond of castigating what he saw as the determination of journalists and editors to see only sinister motives in public officials.[17] All the same, he acquired a reputation for precisely such manipulative power himself: one in which, even as he disclaimed it, he gave every sign of revelling. 'I only wish I was as sophisticated, as devilishly clever, as Machiavellian, as some make out,' he told the editors. 'Not even a combination of Einstein backed up by the world's most advanced computer could achieve the presentational coups with which I have been credited.' Ministers, too, sought to reduce him to size, with images which served mainly to enhance his reputation. After a Commons debate had been devoted to the Government's, but especially Ingham's, multiple attempts allegedly to seize control of the media, John Biffen chose to epitomise the press secretary with a form of hyperbole that never entirely detached itself from his name. 'One would begin to imagine', said Biffen dismissively, 'that we had here some sort of rough-spoken Yorkshire Rasputin who is manipulating government and corroding the standards of public morality.'[18]

But Ingham's greatest strength continued to be his closeness to the leader. He was seen at home and abroad to know her mind, speak for her, even on occasion exceed her in the zeal of his commitment to the cause. This closeness had helped him survive one particularly difficult passage before anyone ever heard of Westland. In January 1985 Ingham cost the country rather a lot of money. Sterling appeared to be in free fall, and he gave a briefing to the Sunday press which conveyed the impression that there would be no intervention to prop up the currency. It was put about that the prime minister, in conformity with her belief in market power, would not object to a 'one-dollar pound'. This was an unsophisticated effort, venturing into territory that Ingham probably did not understand, and he was arraigned next day before a Treasury court consisting of Chancellor Lawson and his senior officials. It might have been a tricky moment for him. His words could plausibly be said to have cost the Bank of England several hundred million pounds in support for sterling. But he escaped scot-free. He had taken the precaution of securing the prime minister's absolution, which effectively took the wind out of Lawson's indignation. A few days later, she was steering him round a drinks party in the Commons, saying 'This is Bernard. Bernard is the *greatest.*'

Such intimacy gave Ingham a special place in the Westland imbroglio. And he had a partner, less widely known in the world, but of comparable stripe. Among her private secretaries, the case officer on the Westland affair was Charles Powell. Powell and Ingham between them were the people who shielded Mrs Thatcher from direct culpability: a function she later repaid by shielding them in turn, when the Defence Committee came knocking at the door and demanding their testimony.

Powell was nearly two years into his service as the Foreign Office man on the prime minister's staff, and had already established himself in her particular affections. He was a man of great ability and great industry and also, more exceptionally, had developed close personal rapport with the leader. Westland was not strictly a Foreign Office matter. It would normally have been handled by her principal private secretary, Nigel Wicks. But Wicks was a newcomer. Powell, although the junior, eclipsed him, and was to continue doing so for several years more, retained in post long after the normal tour of duty: proof, as he became, of the indispensability certain of the Thatcher entourage acquired for her. No politician enjoyed such status. Some civil servants did. They were the replacement for what previous leaders might have called a kitchen cabinet. Charles Powell – intellectually and half-emotionally too, some said, the son she never had – rose high in their number.

In the eruption of Westland, Powell played the part of loyal servant to a fault. He was in at the beginning. According to the Defence Committee, he was the one official who knew before anyone else that Mayhew was actually going to write the famous letter.[19] He told no one else either in Downing Street or in the DTI. He was also a key player in the middle game. For he it was, according to Armstrong, who, in the euphemism that was developed, 'accepted' that the DTI should leak the relevant parts of the letter.[20] And he was particularly crucial to the central and greater euphemism, invented to cover everything that passed between Downing Street and the DTI on that fateful lunchtime: that there had been 'a difference of understanding' over who exactly was seeking and who was granting the authority to disclose, without the permission of either man, the legal advice given by the Solicitor-General to the Secretary of State for Defence.

At any rate, the deed was done. But it was the prelude only to further uproar among the colleagues. It was now Heseltine's turn to feel enraged. He knew, or thought he knew, they were out to get him. However, he continued to believe in the substance of his case for a ncn-American helicopter company. He thought it could still be argued through. He took steps, so his friends said at the time, to calm himself and settle the atmosphere. He did discuss quite openly with Whitelaw and chief whip Wakeham the possibility that he might need to resign, chewing over with them and others his dissatisfaction with the whole conduct of the Westland decision. But his last talk with Wakeham, before the regular cabinet meeting on 9 January, three days after the leak, suggested to him that there would be no need to go. Like the vast majority of cabinet ministers in the whole of history who have been exasperated by the behaviour of their leader, he would stick it out.

At that meeting, however, he suddenly departed. The prime minister, striving yet again for mastery of the collective, produced a new ruling which Wakeham had not prepared him for. From now on, she said, all future ministerial statements about Westland would have to be cleared with the Cabinet Office. Gathering up his papers, Heseltine said quite quietly: 'I cannot accept that decision. I must therefore leave this cabinet.'

It was a faintly ambiguous curtain line. Did 'this' cabinet mean merely this meeting of the cabinet? Only when it was ascertained that the minister had left Downing Street and announced in the street that he had resigned were the colleagues absolutely sure what had happened. Even then, sangfroid did not desert them. The novelist's eye of Douglas Hurd, the Home Secretary, recalled a few days later how amusingly British the whole scene had been. The cabinet carried on almost as if nothing had happened. There was a discussion about Nigeria and, after a coffee-break, a perfectly sensible round-table debate on rates reform.

For long after Heseltine's resignation it was the object of a great deal of speculative inquiry. Had he, perhaps, always intended to go, notwithstanding the pacifying efforts of Wakeham? Certainly he was letting it be known as early as autumn 1985, before Westland became a political issue, that he was increasingly discontented.

The statement he was able to make within hours of leaving Downing Street was suspiciously well drafted, as if it had been long in preparation. It chronicled the entire saga from his special point of view, with all the slights and improprieties to which he had fallen victim. It was an intricate, detailed account of meetings held and cancelled, letters hurtling around Whitehall and the City, international dealings done and undone, two ministries in a state of open war. The whole affair, said Heseltine, immediately locating it as close as possible to the constitutional high ground, showed that the prime minister's methods were 'not a proper way to carry on government and ultimately not an approach for which I can share responsibility'.

The thoroughness of the diatribe caused some of the Thatcher camp to see the resignation as a highly calculated act. They thought it was cover for a bid to unseat her, now or later. Alternatively, some of them even decided that it was all about money. Michael, they reckoned, had a massively expensive lifestyle, and needed to devote himself to financing it. To anyone who knew about Heseltine's political ambition, this seemed a preposterous explanation: rather more so than the view which said he was out to destroy her – although even that soon came to seem improbable, in view of the emollient and helpful stance he chose to adopt after the first abrasion.

Equally subject to scrutiny was the possibility that calculation had come from the other side. Just when, it was asked, was the new formula dreamed up, which was finally designed to silence the errant minister? Was this, perhaps, the fruit of the Chequers meeting? Was it coldly identified by the Thatcher people as the provocation most likely to induce the outcome they wanted: which was the departure of Heseltine without the fateful need for the prime minister to sack him? Certainly this was the story the Heseltine camp told. But we were now in a period when nobody could be relied on to tell the truth.

At her Christmas party, which seemed a lot more than a fortnight before, Mrs Thatcher had discussed with the select company there present the possibility of giving Heseltine the sack: indeed, of sacking both the ministers who were now at such loggerheads that they were undermining her credibility. 'But that would be terribly unfair on Leon,' she concluded. Now that Heseltine had gone, however, a reassessment of Brittan's position was gradually forced upon her.

If Heseltine had shown too much nerve, Brittan showed too little. For every insensitive assault the Defence Secretary made on the conventions, the Trade Secretary showed such hypersensitivity as to make him, for opposite reasons, just as difficult to deal with. Although he was privy to many of the meetings that were supposed to settle Heseltine's hash, he proved a prickly colleague ever watchful lest he, too, was being got at. He seemed to know that, beyond the prime minister and a few men like Howe and Whitelaw, he wasn't widely popular; and in any case he had lately suffered the indignity of losing the Home Office. There were signs, disgracefully, that even his Jewishness was an object of scornful comment among some Conservative backbenchers. He could hardly help being sensitive about this, and it kept showing. At one of the New Year meetings, when one of the bolder officials present likened the Government to 'a warring tribe', Brittan drew himself to his full height and called on Mrs Thatcher to bring the official to heel. 'Prime Minister,' he fulminated, 'I must object in the strongest possible terms to the use of such language.'

While this lack of touch was sustainable in private, public performances were another matter. Immediately Heseltine had departed, Brittan began a series that became steadily more catastrophic.

Again the issue focused on the question of pressure. Who was pressuring whom? With Heseltine it was a case of pressure persistently applied on one set of combatants, the Westland board itself, to force them to act his way. With Brittan it was a case of different pressure applied to different people for the same purpose: in particular, attempts he allegedly made to induce British Aerospace, a company heavily dependent on DTI sponsorship, to have nothing to do with Heseltine's European consortium. Through several parliamentary occasions, this, of all the many possible aspects of the Westland affair, turned out to be what the Commons most keenly addressed, with particular reference to the propriety or otherwise of Brittan's conduct.

First, it fell to him to make the first government statement on Westland after the hair-raising machinations of the recess. He did not want to do so. He was firmly of the view that it was the prime minister's job, but she wouldn't hear of it. So on 13 January he rose reluctantly to his feet to offer a dry account of events thus far, and to be questioned about the latest sensation, which had already surpassed Heseltine's resignation in the headlines: namely, the contention that he, Brittan, at a meeting with the chairman of British Aerospace, Sir Raymond Lygo, had virtually ordered him to withdraw from the consortium 'in the national interest'. Brittan denied doing any such thing. But he added another twist to the tangle of deception in which the cabinet was all too plainly trapped. In the middle of the session, he was asked from his own side, all innocent, whether the Government had 'received any letter from British Aerospace giving their views on the matter'.

This was the backbencher Heseltine speaking, who had not yet entered his emollient phase. It was a lethal question because, of course, Heseltine knew perfectly well that such a letter had been sent. Brittan, who knew of the letter but did not want to talk about it, produced a series of smart lawyer's responses that proved decidedly unsmart. So unsmart were they that he was obliged to return before nightfall to apologise to the House for misleading it: an admission which, as Mrs Thatcher knew all too well, damaged not merely her most favoured young minister but the Government as a whole.

Two days later, Brittan ventured forth for his next parliamentary triumph. This time, the prime minister herself could not avoid accounting for what she had done, and she made the opening speech, explaining in as anodyne a manner as she could the turmoil of the last month. But Brittan was the man the vultures, sniffing blood, had come to hear. After his apology, he had a lot to make up for.

The British Aerospace text, almost the last in this tale of many letters, had meanwhile been published. It did not seem to support the Trade Secretary's version of events. But, from a state of extreme and manifest anxiety, he quickly retrieved the forensic confidence of a good Queen's Counsel. He called in aid his officials. Anyone who challenged his version, he said, was fouling the name of these honourable men who had taken a faithful record of what happened. Did anyone dare to impugn the reputation of three distinguished civil servants who could not defend themselves? Let them try, said Leon. And he had something of a triumph, at least by comparison with what was generally expected. Even the prime minister was relieved. 'You were superb,' she reportedly told him, in the heat of the moment. 'No one could have done it better.'[21]

But this was a premature verdict. It probably did not reflect her cool judgment, and it certainly didn't reflect the opinion of the mass of Conservative backbenchers who, for good reasons and for bad, and not excluding some of the reasons subsumed in the odious prejudice which had long made Brittan a man with few parliamentary friends, were now moving towards the collective opinion that he ought to go. At the same time, the prime minister's own opinion began to crystallise. The decisive date was 22 January.

On that day, Armstrong submitted the report of his private inquiry into how the Mayhew letter had been leaked. This itself had had its origins in the reek of cordite that clung day after day to so many aspects of the affair. It was set up in response to the intervention of the Attorney-General, Sir Michael Havers, who, rising from his sickbed to come to the rescue of his affronted colleague, Mayhew, had descended on Downing Street and said that, unless he got satisfaction, he would call in the police to investigate the leak, with the possibility of criminal proceedings to follow. Havers needed mollifying, and the Armstrong inquiry was the result: an inquiry, however, into events whose details were very well known to most of the participants and all of the witnesses he examined.

Yet one person who apparently did not know all these details, and who insisted from beginning to end that she did not know, was the prime minister herself. This always seemed incredible to most politicians, of all parties, who kept abreast of the matter. How was it conceivable that Charles Powell, sitting right outside her office for eighteen hours a day, could have failed to acquaint her with what was going on from minute to minute? How could she have insulated herself in a cocoon of such self-created ignorance about the very matter that was tearing her Government apart? Surely she did not need Sir Robert Armstrong to inform her, after solemn inquiries among the five civil servants involved, that Brittan had authorised the leak, and that each of these civil servants had in different ways been implicated in what was a flagrant breach of Whitehall rules?

There is evidence, of a kind, which brings such speculations at least one step closer to hard reality. On the day after the leak, when it had made its helpful impact through the media, she was witnessed in Downing Street airily remarking to her staff that the exercise had gone well. Heseltine's misinformation had been successfully countered. She was pleased.

But this does not quite clinch the case for saying that she was personally implicated in the leak. There was nothing inconsistent about observing that the outcome had been satisfactory, while at the same time remaining in ignorance as to how it had been accomplished – although the general level of ignorance which she claimed, both before and after the Armstrong report, continues to strain belief.

The scene when Armstrong presented his report, and she read it for the first time, refines the picture of her state of mind. One reliable witness described what she said. 'You mean Leon *knew*!' she exclaimed, on reading the account of how Brittan had behaved on the telephone that Monday lunch-time. This appeared to be an honest reaction. For the first time she discovered that this unfortunate minister, beside whom she had sat as he sought to box his way out of several corners in the last few days, was more deeply involved – and she more deeply ignorant of his involvement – than she had hitherto appreciated.

If this was her reaction, it was, of course, perverse and unfair. For if Brittan *hadn't* authorised the disclosure, then who had? It could only have been something helpfully arranged by her own trusted staff, for whose actions the only authorising agency was herself. Her rational mind ought surely to have alerted her to the possibility, long before she read the Armstrong report, that Brittan was not only the minister in question but was the essential bulwark between herself and a lot of awkward questions about the role of both Bernard Ingham and Charles Powell.

But that was apparently not the view she took. Instead, Brittan's involvement, hitherto unmentioned, added to the mounting case against him. And this now began to broaden, as consideration was given to how the Armstrong report should be presented to the public. Originally she hoped to keep its contents secret and make no statement. But this was now plainly impractical, not least because of the number of interests that needed to be satisfied. Brittan and Mayhew, the officials at the DTI and at No. 10: all had a stake in what Armstrong said he had found, and what she would say about it to a world now thoroughly sceptical of almost everything any minister said.

Brittan, however, proved an awkward customer. He had to be invited to discuss the draft of the statement she was due to make next day, 23 January. Were he publicly to attack her version of events – even without making any new revelations of fact – he had the power to destroy her. He could lay the blame entirely at the door of her officials, and hence on her as their superior: who would then be charged not merely with the original leak but with having persistently misled Parliament about it for nearly three weeks. From that charge there would be absolutely no way back. So Leon certainly had to be propitiated. When he objected to the statement as drafted, because it did not categorically admit that Downing Street had given 'clearance', he had to be paid attention. When Wakeham or Whitelaw began to suggest that he ought to resign, he said he had no intention of doing so and that the officials – her officials – were the ones who should go.

This display of truculence paid off, for the moment. But it wasn't forgotten in calmer times, when Brittan was again seeking preferment.

The negotiated statement was duly made. The prime minister delivered most of it in a low, fast blur. She presented herself as not only innocent but almost completely ignorant. 'An enormous number of facts were not known to me until yesterday when I received the results of the inquiry,' she said. She admitted that her own officials had been involved, but found words to exculpate both them and herself. On the one hand she would have instructed, had she been consulted, that 'a different way must be found of making the relevant facts known'. On the other hand, insofar as her officials thought they were speaking for her when they told the DTI that the contents of the Mayhew letter should be put into the public domain, 'they were right.' As for the reason why the whole unfortunate affair had occurred, this was entirely comprehensible. It was to do, she said, with the overriding demands of commercial reality. A business decision was at stake. Westland were holding a press conference at four o'clock. They absolutely had to know what the legal opinion of Heseltine's view was.

It was probably the most unconvincing statement she ever made to the House of Commons. One of its themes was that every person involved, official or politician, had in fact behaved impeccably at every stage. All the right people had communicated in the right way and received the right authorisation for what they rightly did. But few who heard her were convinced by the picture she gave, still less by the impression they were invited to accept of a prime minister they had never hitherto caught sight of: one who did not, after all, know and see everything, however distant and pettifogging its detail, but whose relationship with the world more closely resembled that of a Trappist monk.

When Neil Kinnock, the Labour leader, spoke of her 'heavy and inerasable guilt', it did not at the time seem like Opposition hyperbole. The question from a Conservative backbencher, Alex Fletcher, was left hanging, unanswered, in the air. 'Are you satisfied', he asked, 'that the statement you have made this afternoon has enhanced the integrity of the Government?'

Many people thought not, especially many Conservative MPs. They needed a sacrificial victim, and one was readily to hand. For although Leon Brittan, having dug in his heels, had got his way and obliged the prime minister to acknowledge that 'cover' – a talismanic word of his, much repeated – had been supplied by Downing Street for his authorisation of the disclosure, her statement had actually done him no good. It did not diminish, but rather confirmed, his responsibility. At a meeting of Tory backbenchers that evening, there were repeated calls for Leon to fall on his sword. The message was conveyed to him, to the prime minister, and quickly to every minister who mattered.

Brittan did not immediately answer the call. Nor did Mrs Thatcher press him to. Indeed, when he finally concluded next day that, having lost the confidence of his party, he should go, she spent some time persuading him to stay. 'It was my wish that you should remain a member of the Cabinet,' she wrote in the post-resignation exchange of letters. This was a decent thing to say. It doubtless reflected the feeling, in one part of her mind, that to lose another minister, however much of a liability he had become, would only add to the impression of a government falling apart. Yet his resignation, as she must also have understood, made it easier for her. It was rather like Carrington's resignation over the Falklands invasion, with the difference that Brittan, while permanently scarred by the confession that he had lost the party's confidence, never admitted he was to blame for anything. It lanced the pent-up balloon of party anxiety.

Further back in her mind, moreover, there was a great deal of resentment against Brittan. He, after all, had got her into this. If he had had the wit to stop the leak of his brother lawyer's communication, there would have been much less trouble. And later, when he was cavilling and complaining about every last word of her statement, defending his own corner rather than seeing that hers, above all, was the reputation that mattered, he planted himself unfavourably in her memory. 'I hope that it will not be long before you return to high office to continue your ministerial career,' she wrote in her parting letter. To Brittan's utter chagrin, this optimistic intimation proved to be insincere. 'He was awkward and ungracious,' one of her close advisers recalled in June 1988, when Brittan still had no job. 'She got extremely disenchanted with him.' And when a job was eventually found, it was not in her Government but involved exile to Brussels as a European Commissioner.

With Brittan gone, and her 23 January statement clearly having failed, the prime minister was now as rattled as she had ever been. Douglas Hurd, confirming the feverish state of things, said on television: 'The worst thing for the country would be to lurch into some kind of discussion of the leadership.' Not a helpful remark. Such discussion was already intense, and Hurd seemed to be legitimising it. Moreover, yet another parliamentary occasion beckoned which would put the Thatcher leadership, shorn now of all props and distractions, squarely on the line. Labour had called an emergency Commons debate for Monday, 27 January.

Mrs Thatcher was profoundly apprehensive. All the great men of modern Conservatism were summoned to give aid to the speechwriter, herself. Besides old Westland familiars like Whitelaw and Wakeham, Foreign Secretary Howe and Home Secretary Hurd were invited to lend their counsel and their phrase-making. Additionally there was Havers, the Attorney-General. And there was, once again, Brittan, somewhere in the wings, his capacity for detonation not yet exhausted: the need, therefore, to keep him sweet still a matter of pressing importance.

Before she left Downing Street for the House, Mrs Thatcher said to one associate: 'I may not be prime minister by six o'clock tonight.'[22] That was the measure of the disillusionment she knew to be present in the Conservative Party.

The day ended, however, in bathos if not quite in triumph. Labour did not take its opportunity. Rarely has so inviting a target been so easily missed as when Neil Kinnock failed to pin the prime minister to the questions she needed to answer. Bombastic and blustering, he managed the extraordinary feat of making these events sound, after all, almost unimportant. Verbosely ranting about the prime minister's incompetence, ruthlessness and dishonesty, he never succeeded in rendering these generalities precise or freshly lethal. Before he sat down, she could know that she had escaped, as the Tory backbenches, shaking off their gloom, rejoiced in his discomfort.

Her own speech therefore was easier to make. But it was still important, and it contained at last some admissions that verged on candour – of a strictly limited variety. She acknowledged her role in getting the Mayhew letter written in the first place. She admitted that she knew about the leak 'some hours after it occurred', but said she hadn't inquired into it. She confessed, unprecedentedly, to having made mistakes. The way the leak occurred was regrettable, she said. 'Indeed, with hindsight, it is clear that this was one, and doubtless there were others, of a number of matters which could have been handled better, and that too I regret.'

For the moment, this settled the Westland crisis. Heseltine, seeing which way the wind blew, made a supportive intervention. He knew well enough that the rump of Tory wets were keen to make common cause and see him do what they had never managed to do, hole the leader below the water line. He wanted nothing to do with them, although it remains a moot point what he would have done if Kinnock had made the speech he should have made. Next day, Whitelaw, ever the touchstone, privately pronounced his leader to be 'just' in the clear. And so it proved. But Westland was not without its residue of political detritus.

First there was the insight which this saga afforded into the Thatcher style of government. For Heseltine appeared to have been vindicated on that point. He had accused her of being party to the breakdown of cabinet government; and although his own conduct was hardly a model of collegiality, the scenes half-witnessed by the public through the month of January 1986 certainly attested to that kind of breakdown. Manipulation, vicious division, hole-in-the-corner dealing: this was the governing mode which Westland put on display.

Heseltine may have depicted his position with excessive grandeur. To talk about the failure to hold the 13 December meeting as 'the breakdown of constitutional government' put one in mind of E. M. Forster's response after reading a review of a first novel which was couched in terms of unqualified ecstasy: 'And what is there left for *Anna Karenina*?' The same could be said of Heseltine's self-serving roll of drums. Later, in fact, he somewhat reduced such pretensions and, when accosted about what really happened over Westland, was in the habit of saying: 'It was narrower than Westland. It was about cheating. No one ever cheated me in business and got away with it. I won't be cheated.'

Nor, perhaps, was his experience in the Thatcher cabinet as exceptional as he imagined. When George Brown resigned as Foreign Secretary in the Wilson Government in 1968, he blamed Wilson's 'dictatorial' methods and said that Downing Street was 'trying to maintain a private Foreign Office in exactly the same way as the White House'. Richard Crossman, a minister in the same Government, wrote two volumes of diaries dedicated in large part to the same kind of thesis. 'If ever I was to resign,' he mused at one point, 'it would be precisely because I can't stand the way the cabinet is run. It is because of Harold's inability to create a firm inner group with whom to work consistently, and his determination to keep bilateral relations with each one of us.' By this measure, nothing much had changed under Margaret Thatcher.

For her, all the same, it was different. Wilson was the last model to whom she would have chosen to liken herself. She had long been presented as the opposite of Wilsonian: strong, leading from the front, and disliking very much to lose a single argument – but a leader who ran a tight ship and steered a straight course. Westland proved to most people's satisfaction that the furniture was crashing round the cabin as the vessel tacked and gybed through every breeze that blew.

But, secondly, there was something a little more personal. It was after Westland that her staff, and especially Ingham and Powell, became most indissolubly associated with her, almost as if they were her praetorian guard. They became linked, as it seemed, for ever in a society for mutual protection.

The officials had protected the leader, letting her know only what she needed to know, and associating themselves with blind loyalty in the increasingly frenzied attempts to unhorse Michael Heseltine. For this, Powell in particular came in for some heavy private criticism among his colleagues in the Whitehall mandarinate. They thought his involvement in such political savagery quite reprehensible. One permanent secretary told me that he considered Powell should have been severely punished for exceeding his proper function.

But that would have been to challenge the other member of the protection society. Margaret Thatcher remained devotedly loyal to the people who had done her such service. She trusted them as she trusted almost nobody else. Ingham was already part of the permanent furniture of the Thatcher decade. Plainly he would survive as long as she wanted him to, which was a very long time. But Powell also now remained her long-lived servant, apparently unblackened by passage through this rite of fire: a passage which showed that his patron, while not exactly at ease in the nether world where politics is dirty and accountability a rather private matter, could operate there.

Nor was this, actually, the first or last time when that capacity in her was tested. Nothing quite like Westland occurred before or after. On the other hand, another aspect of her responsibilities already put her closely in touch with the duplicity which even a conviction politician must come to grips with. It raised rather similar questions, and evoked from her very similar responses, about secrecy and openness and what it was proper and/or necessary for the public to know about the workings of government. It also enlisted, in an unusually personal way, some of the same servants most involved in limiting the damage done by the Westland affair.

After the Commons debate and after Kinnock had let her off the hook, one more performance was required in order to ensure her permanent escape. This burden fell not on her but on Robert Armstrong, the man whose career, bracketing hers for her first eight years, was so closely bound up in the second term with her survival. Armstrong was her faithful ally and stealthy guide through the jungle of covert, as distinct from conviction, politics.

Over Westland he performed what looked at the time like his most signal service. He conducted the inquiry, and was deeply shocked by a lot that he discovered in the behaviour under pressure both of the officials and of the politicians. But he was nonetheless called upon to make the trickiest defence, not of everything that had occurred but at least of the prime minister's part in it. Unusually, the Select Committee on Defence had kept fairly close scrutiny of the government decision-making process as it unfolded, interrogating at least some of the Westland participants since before Christmas. Having failed to secure the presence of all of them, however, it was obliged to accept a portmanteau substitute for Ingham, Powell and the others, in the person of Armstrong.

The day of his testimony was keenly anticipated, as a moment when hostile MPs could make a last attempt to inculpate Downing Street in all that had happened. For the cabinet secretary to appear anywhere in the House was a rare occurrence. And Armstrong seemed apprehensive when, on 5 February, he duly sat down in front of the Defence Committee.

In fact the occasion was transformed from an ordeal into a forensic triumph. All Armstrong's mandarin skills were placed at the service of the prime minister. His silky word-play and years of Whitehall committeemanship left few crevices in the case for her defence. In discussing the precise nature of Downing Street's involvement, Sir Robert managed to find great chasms of difference between the meanings of the various verbs proposed. Did it 'accept', or 'agree', or 'acquiesce in', or 'authorise', or merely 'not object to' the DTI's nefarious transaction? After toying with each of these semantic possibilities, he rejected all of them, except perhaps the last, as inappropriate to the case. Similarly, when No. 10 gave 'cover' for the leak as Brittan insisted, this was in no sense, Armstrong smoothly averred, 'covering authority'.

For nearly three hours, he conducted the fencing-match without dropping his guard. There was an irony in this which went beyond the delicious spectacle of the supreme mandarin proving that his hallowed methods, once axiomatically regarded by the incoming Tory Government as suspect, could be of use to it. The thing went further. In a sense, the balance of power had been reversed. Armstrong's testimony had become indispensable. What he was doing, from his unimpeachable height, was surveying the prime minister's behaviour and giving it the seal of official approval. Instead of the minister being responsible for the conduct of the civil servant, here was the chief civil servant solemnly assuming responsibility for the integrity of the prime minister. Normally it would be the minister up front, and the civil servant in the back room. That was what ministerial accountability to Parliament was all about. But this time it was the civil servant who, along with his numerous confidential duties, had to face the public heat on the entire Government's behalf.

And it wasn't the last time the prime minister required him to perform this irregular task. The constitutional innovation was taken a stage further. Westland had a postscript which, at least as it affected Armstrong's life and thrust him into a politician's role, was larger than the imbroglio that kept Westminster alight throughout the opening weeks of 1986.

As well as taking the cabinet minutes, and organising the network of cabinet business, and attempting to keep track of the prime minister's informal way of doing her own business, and running the civil service, Armstrong had another job. He was her principal security adviser, and thus in charge, on her behalf, of a murky corner of government which came to distract her more than she would have wished from her central project – and which wrote an unwanted epitaph on Armstrong's glittering career.

From far back in the opposition years, Mrs Thatcher took a keen interest in the secret world. Guided by Airey Neave, she felt this was a necessary priority, and almost over-compensated for her total ignorance by gathering around her a network of briefers and other shadowy experts, some of them offering their services while full-time government employees. She made a point of getting to know the security chiefs, and formed, for example, a close and mutually admiring relationship with Sir Maurice Oldfield, head of the Secret Intelligence Service, MI6, from 1973 to 1979.[23] In government, she maintained this interest and connection more assiduously, it was said, than many of her predecessors.

Ideally, this would have remained part of her private work. In her time, however, it had a lot of public manifestations, rudely thrust on her by some unusually public events. They revealed some shifts in her own approach, as well as an evolving relationship with the man who drew together the threads of MI6 and MI5 and the rest of the secret apparatus.

These events included a number of discrete disasters. There was the union trouble at GCHQ. There was the conviction in 1982 of Geoffrey Prime, a GCHQ employee, on charges of spying for the Russians. In 1984, an MI5 agent, Michael Bettaney, was similarly convicted in circumstances that indicated a serious crisis of management in the security service. But what mainly brought security matters into the light, exposing the Thatcher attitude to this world, were certain accidents of history: or, rather, the very large accident that history itself, concerning the most contentious security scandals of the post-war era, began to be rewritten in Mrs Thatcher's first months of office and was still the subject of literary disputation ten years later.

When this process began, it seemed to reveal her as the exponent of an unusual candour. In November 1979, she made the longest and most revealing statement any prime minister had offered to Parliament on a security matter, when she confirmed that Anthony Blunt, the former Keeper of the Queen's Pictures, had admitted as long ago as 1964 to being a Soviet agent.[24] This cleared up quite a lot of lies that had been told, publicly and privately, by both Blunt and a succession of government spokesmen over the years. It was read as announcing a determination on the part of the new prime minister to some extent to demystify the secret world, or at least to take her own responsibilities seriously as its accountable minister before Parliament. The question of how much penetration there had been of the foreign service and the secret service in the 1940s and 1950s seemed to have taken a large stride towards closure.

Armstrong advised against her making the Blunt statement. He had spent quite a lot of his professional life close to high security matters, and believed in the old maxim 'Least said, soonest forgotten'. Literally anything out of the mouth of an informed minister was likely to shine a ray of light into corners best left publicly dark. And what the prime minister had to say about Blunt, his treacheries, his denials, his interrogations, his non-prosecution and his maintenance *en poste* in high society certainly revealed a lot about the methods and the psychology of British security.

But her hand had been forced by a book.[25] This wasn't a voluntary opening of the shutters, so much as an effort to close speculation on a matter which had been so heavily discussed for so many years that the repeated denials of the truth could now be judged to do more harm than good. This pattern, whereby an insinuating publication managed to extract from the authorities some kind of prime ministerial apologia, was to be repeated several times. In 1981, she made another major statement, following a book by the noted security specialist Chapman Pincher, which charged that a post-war head of MI5, Sir Roger Hollis, had also been a Soviet agent.[26] This statement, likewise, gave an absorbing glimpse into the procedures and paranoia of the security service. Even though Mrs Thatcher refuted Pincher's allegation, the evidence she adduced permitted the public once more to penetrate behind the veil normally drawn across every detail of this class of work.

Anyone who imagined from this early record, however, that she was seriously motivated by a desire for greater public discussion of security matters was badly misled. On the contrary, she soon out-Armstronged Armstrong in her passion for silence. From being a subject on which she thought the air should be selectively cleared, it became in her mind one that ought never to be written or spoken about, whatever the cost this might exact from her reputation as a truth-seeking politician, or as a prime minister who could be relied on to keep a sense of proportion.

She personally vetoed publication of a number of books on the intelligence services, including some serious tomes written over many years by respectful historians working under official auspices.[27] It was entirely fitting that a book, which became a very famous book, should mark an apotheosis – or, as some would say, a kind of Armageddon – not only for her policy of silence but also for her tortuous relationship with her most senior official.

The history of this book, *Spycatcher*, epitomised the worst aspects of this prime minister's approach to government management. The work of a discontented former official of MI5, Peter Wright, it gave an exceptionally thorough account of a lifetime spent in espionage and deception, revealing large amounts of MI5 tradecraft, the details of surveillance and interrogation techniques, and reinforcing the case for believing that Roger Hollis had been a Soviet agent. Plainly, from any government's point of view, it should have been stopped. But the pass had long since been sold. Wright had gone to live outside British jurisdiction, in Australia, and being deeply bitter about the inadequacy of his pension arrangements was not amenable to suggestions that he should keep quiet. These suggestions were in any case made far too late. Extreme bureaucratic pettiness failed to measure the extent of the threat Wright posed, and therefore the sum it might be appropriate to offer him to desist.

But there was another problem, which involved the prime minister directly. During the Government's efforts to stop *Spycatcher* in courts around the world, it emerged not only that Wright had been the main source for Chapman Pincher's allegations but that, knowing this and having the opportunity to stop Pincher publishing, another little group of ministers – so reminiscent of the informal band who ran the Westland crisis – had decided not to go to law. Pincher, in other words, had virtually published with government approval. This revelation fatally undermined the case, certainly in the Australian courts but also elsewhere. It led to wholesale publication of *Spycatcher* in many countries, so that when the case finally wended its passage to final hearing in the highest British court, the House of Lords, the judges found themselves unable to uphold the obligation of confidentiality on which the Government depended. They decided that the obligation could be extinguished by prior publication or outweighed if disclosure were in the public interest.

As the affair unfolded, over a period of three years between 1985 and 1988, the Government's efforts to stop publication came to seem as absurd as they were desperate. Again, it emerged, the exact identity of the ministers and officials responsible for a particular decision was a matter of vexed dispute. Again the Attorney-General, and the ignorance in which he was kept concerning matters that affected him, became the subject of much contention, with charges being flung about between government officials about exactly who knew what. And, presiding over this unseemly spectacle, was a prime minister who, having failed to control the original crisis, posed by the Pincher book, stood firm on her conviction that, however many courts might find against her, she had a duty to fight the case until the last drop of taxpayer's money had been expended to defend the principle that spies should not talk. What some called stubbornness, even vanity, she referred to as her bounden duty.

Once again, however, she had a proxy defender to hand. Robert Armstrong was propelled into the front line to do work which no previous prime minister had ever asked the cabinet secretary or any other official to perform. The scene this time was not the House of Commons but the Supreme Court of New South Wales, to which Sir Robert rather than a minister was despatched to argue from the witness box that, as a matter of national security and the public interest, *Spycatcher* should be banned for ever.

In this forum, he didn't do so well. He was obviously a reluctant witness. At London Airport on his way out, he showed his apprehension at being flung into such irregular work by actually striking a press photographer: conduct far removed from that normally found within the portals of the mandarinate. Up against a disrespectful Australian interrogator rather than the scattered fire of divided MPs, he wilted. But he did, in his way, the duty demanded of him. He put himself on the rack, at considerable personal cost, for the sake of a prime minister who was determined to exhaust every remedy against Peter Wright and his vile book, and would continue doing so after more than a million copies of it were on the market. Sir Robert, from his backroom post, became the front man for a policy which, as in the Westland case, made sheer prime ministerial will the substitute for orderly decisions logically arrived at.

In the course of his odyssey round the *Spycatcher* courts, Armstrong also uttered one of the more memorable locutions of the period. He remarked at one point that it was necessary, in his job, to be from time to time 'economical with the truth'.

It wasn't his own phrase; the original authorship was ascribed to St Thomas Aquinas and Edmund Burke, to name two of several proffered names. It may also, if one looked at it in the context of Armstrong's job as a senior mandarin, have been given excessively sinister connotations. After all, it really only described what went on every day in any bureaucracy. It was almost a truism. And yet nobody could deny that, coming from those lips at that particular time, after Westland and in the middle of a host of revelations of the way business was done in the secret world, it had peculiar resonance. The moment it was said, it tied itself to the man who said it — but also to the woman he served. It struck such a jarring chord with the protestation she had so often made that she, unlike most others of her kind, always told the truth, the whole truth and nothing but.

20

The New Diplomacy

A FEW WEEKS before Westland finally emerged from the chrysalis of obscurity into full-blown crisis, and while her cabinet was still intact, the prime minister's public life was dominated by something completely different. On 15 November 1985, she and the Irish Taoiseach, Dr Garret Fitzgerald, signed an Anglo-Irish Agreement which provided, for the first time, for the joint management by Dublin and London of certain aspects of a problem they had in common.

For Margaret Thatcher, the Agreement marked an epic shift of her perceived public attitude towards the incurable excrescence on the British body politic, the province of Northern Ireland. But it illuminated something wider. It was a good example of the hold she personally exerted over a quite unusually high proportion of the policies her Government pursued. What she supported tended to happen. What she neglected or opposed tended not to happen. What she permitted, but did not support, might happen, but only in a context where she had openly distanced herself from the consequences and therefore assisted in the enfeeblement of what she allowed others to do.

All these stances were visible at one time or another in her attitude to Northern Ireland. Each in its turn was a determinant of what happened. Such personal influence, in fact, was observed to be decisively important in foreign policy even more than in domestic – and Ireland, for these purposes, was part of foreign not domestic policy. All post-war prime ministers have been eager to establish an ascendancy over the conduct of foreign policy; most of them have had larger pretensions than Mrs Thatcher to consort with world leaders more powerful than themselves in fashioning grandiose global visions. In attention to concrete detail, however, their successor in the eighties kept a tighter grip than any of them. Personal vetoes matched personal commitments in their fateful reach. This was especially so in 1986, the nodal year of Mrs Thatcher's second term.

In her view of Ireland, she was and remained an instinctive

Unionist. A minister who served for some time in Belfast judged her to be the most Unionist politician in Downing Street since the war, a position which could be attributed to several root causes. She belonged, after all, to the Conservative and Unionist Party, a title which proclaimed the historic connection. In her case this was fortified by special factors, not to be overlooked. As well as being a Conservative she was a Protestant, of the breed which scarcely comprehended Catholicism and would certainly experience no natural sympathy for a Catholic minority living in part of an otherwise oppressively Catholic island. Religious preference, therefore, reinforced political habit. And then there were her friends and mentors. One of these, Airey Neave, close to the Unionists in his role as shadow spokesman on Northern Ireland until 1979, instructed her in the Orange perspective before being murdered, unforgettably for her, by terrorists from the other side. Another, Enoch Powell, was a Unionist MP whose baleful eye she could never entirely escape across the chamber of the House of Commons.

These Unionist instincts, however, were qualified by other traits, deriving not from doctrine or prejudice so much as from professional considerations. Habits of a different order overlaid the habit of Unionism. They were the habits exhibited by a number of prime ministers, born of the demands and the hazards of the office. On the one hand was an executive compulsion to act: the can-do philosophy, as Americans admiringly term it, which every competent political leader needs to cultivate. On the other hand, Northern Ireland always tended, sooner or later, to bring out in mainland leaders an opposite set of emotions: of indifference, boredom or the kind of despair which makes all action seem futile. Mrs Thatcher's Irish attitudes were no exception.

She began in the former mode. Like everything else, Northern Ireland would submit, she thought, to the vigour of a new and businesslike government. 'We will listen for a while,' she told the *New York Times* in November 1979, giving one of her earliest comments on the advice being showered upon her. 'We hope we will get agreement. But then the Government will have to make some decisions.' There was a time when the talking would have to stop. London would impose 'whatever we get most support for'.

This was not immediately successful, but it was an approach which appeared to receive support from an almost simultaneous change across the water. Six months after the arrival of Margaret Thatcher, another leader reached the centre of the stage, who was also fired with a will to act. Charles Haughey was elected Taoiseach, and there ensued a gradual warming of relations between London and Dublin. The most Orange leader seen in Downing Street appeared capable of making some kind of common cause with an unrepentant proponent of united Ireland, in an alliance based as much as anything on a certain roguish mutual admiration. For a time, Haughey worked hard to charm his counterpart, and for a time he succeeded. In December 1980, Mrs Thatcher took to Dublin the most high-powered collection of ministers ever seen at an Anglo-Irish summit. The Chancellor and the Foreign Secretary, along with the Northern Ireland Secretary, were all in attendance. The communiqué spoke of 'extremely constructive and significant' discussions, and committed the leaders to devoting their next meeting to 'special consideration of the totality of relationships between these islands'.

This was a resonant phrase: too resonant, in fact, and the beginning of the end of this period of ingenuous optimism. It had been drafted by the Irish, and when Mrs Thatcher raised a sceptical eyebrow Haughey was seen by an Irish official to dig his foreign minister furtively in the ribs as if to acknowledge that their little game had been rumbled. But 'totality' remained in the statement, and Haughey was ecstatic. In an off-the-record briefing, he described it as 'an historic breakthrough', much to Mrs Thatcher's fury. Other Irish ministers went even more public, with the opinion that references in the communiqué to 'possible new institutional structures' were a harbinger of major constitutional reform and a changed relationship between the North and the South.[1] At the next meeting between the leaders, a European summit in Holland in March 1981, Mrs Thatcher showed her displeasure. The two leaders met for only five minutes, and when Haughey emerged he remarked sullenly that she was very upset.

This was the end of her first flush of activism. It had been a painful education, but in truth it was already overshadowed by a larger event which drew the British leader into a world rather different from the diplomatic, and closer to ground on which she would know exactly where she stood. For the Haughey courtship had proceeded in parallel with an intensification of Republican pressure brought about by selected hunger strikes in Long Kesh prison. By spring 1981, these were reaching a grisly climax in which London was supposed to submit to IRA prisoners' demands rather than see them die. But London did not submit. It was the kind of pressure which this leader had few if any qualms about resisting. In any challenge to the authority of the state, where naked moral blackmail was assembled in order to extract decisive political concessions, she had no doubt where duty lay, and seems to have experienced no countervailing anxiety about the consequences of calling the blackmailers' bluff. She saw out one IRA leader, Bobby Sands, who starved himself for sixty-six days and died on 5 May. 'Mr Sands was a convicted criminal,' she told the Commons that day. 'He chose to take his own life. It was a choice that his organisation did not allow to many of its victims.' Nine more hunger strikers followed at intervals through the summer. She sat tight, unmoved, as they dropped.

By this time, after the initial promise of vigour, Ireland had fallen far down her agenda. It was an impossible problem, which any 'solution' could only make worse – the standard Unionist case for preserving the status quo, however unsatisfactory. But she now did something, for other reasons, which actually made this position unsustainable. She made Jim Prior Northern Ireland Secretary, a change which, although it saw him satisfactorily bowing the knee to a calculated demotion,[2] also placed in the office a man who was certain to try and do something about it. She paid this price – but then sought to avoid its impact by engaging in irregular activities of a kind she had already made one of her trademarks.

True to form, Prior was moved to act. After taking over in September 1981, he decided to devise a new expedient to wrench the province halfway back to a condition of self-government, thus alleviating direct rule from London. He opted for a form of 'rolling devolution', whereby a local assembly might evolve from small beginnings into a forum of genuinely devolved power-sharing.

Prior has left an account of what happened to this initiative. It affords a diverting insight into the Thatcher style of government. The prime minister, he recalls, was 'very much against the whole idea'.[3] She didn't like any species of devolution, mainly for fear of reawakening the appetite for devolution in Scotland, writes Prior. Nor would she tolerate a chapter in his proposed white paper which discussed Anglo-Irish relations as though these might be the key to peace. This was abruptly excised. However, the white paper was published. It became government policy to legislate for rolling devolution. And this is where the prime minister's behaviour broke the usual rules. She continued to oppose the measure. When the cabinet discussed guillotining the Bill to save it from Unionist filibustering, she made her position quite clear. Prior describes a petulant scene. She said 'that she thought it was a rotten Bill and that in any case she herself would not be voting for it because she was off to the USA'. Moreover, when the Bill reached the floor of the House, a further irregularity was plain to anyone looking down from the gallery. Ian Gow, her parliamentary private secretary, could be seen moving among the anti-Prior forces on the Tory benches and encouraging their opposition. Prior saw Gow's manoeuvres as 'tipping the wink to the Official Unionists that the prime minister was not in favour'. He thought it disgraceful. But through other eyes it might be regarded as rather skilful: one of relatively few devices which showed the prime minister to be capable of low political cunning. For if the initiative succeeded she could claim credit as the leader in whose time it happened, whereas if it failed her hands would be clean.

In fact it failed. The Assembly was established, and devolution ready to roll, by autumn 1982. But the SDLP, the moderate Republican party whose support was crucial if politics was to supersede terrorism as a credible way forward, declined to join. In any case, it was probably blighted from the start, at least as far as Mrs Thatcher was concerned. Not only was the white paper published on 2 April 1982, the weekend when the British consciousness was beginning to be engulfed by the prospect of a war in the Falkland Islands, but the politician who was, as it were, the proxy leader of the people supposed to benefit from rolling devolution, Charles Haughey, came out against Britain and its pretensions in the South Atlantic. There was plainly no business to be done with Mr Haughey.

Another period of impasse therefore ensued. The Assembly met, but did not get anywhere. It was Prior's plaything, which failed to distract the prime minister from numerous heavier tasks which she really cared about.

Yet this could not go on for ever. Sooner or later, given Mrs Thatcher's leaning towards hyperactivity, and her genuine irritation at the sight of unsolved problems within her territory, the craving for executive action and the can-do philosophy were bound to reappear. Once again, an injection of the democratic process in two countries helped supply it. After June 1983, when the prime minister received her overwhelming second mandate, the condition of Ulster remained a running rebuke to her reputation as a problem-solver. It was hard for her to resist the conclusion that so powerful a leader had a powerful duty to try and act. Six months earlier, moreover, the Irish scene had changed, with the expulsion of Haughey from office and his replacement by Dr Fitzgerald. Perhaps the time would soon be ripe. That, at any rate, is how it was seen in the Foreign Office, the engine-room of most of the schemes and interests at home and abroad which, it was hoped, might conduce towards 'progress'.

The new relationship was not, at first, any more harmonious than the old. A long time elapsed before Mrs Thatcher and Dr Fitzgerald became working partners. Indifference and uninterest continued to hold the field at No. 10 throughout the disastrous first six months of the second term and while the miners' strike dominated political London. When a greater closeness began to develop, it was in the most improbable of circumstances: an event which helped to demonstrate the colossal insensitivity which the British leader brought to Irish matters and at the same time the shrewd magnanimity of the very different character on the other side of the table. Together, and rather bizarrely, these qualities bore fruit.

The event was the second summit between them, held in November 1984. This had been preceded by publication of the report of a body called the New Ireland Forum, one of many well-meaning think tanks endlessly circling round the intractabilities of the Irish question, but a more serious and representative one than most. The Forum report had been long anticipated by politicians on both sides of the Irish Sea and, admittedly, was received with more enthusiasm in Dublin than in London. None of this prepared them for Mrs Thatcher's own reaction, delivered at a press conference after the November summit. Reducing a long and earnest document to its three suggested alternative 'solutions' – unification, confederation or a joint authority to run the province – she dismissed each with a contemptuous flick of the wrist and the same curt incantation: 'That's out. . . . That's out. . . . That's out.'

The Irish media, and a fair number of Irish politicians, were furious. The headmistress appeared to have been slapping down the product of childish minds. Barely a month had elapsed since the IRA bomb created infernal mayhem at the party's conference hotel in Brighton, and perhaps she should have been excused the abruptness of her attack on a report which, although produced months before that atrocity, could be construed as going too far towards Republican objectives. Equally, however, she showed little appreciation of Fitzgerald's own delicate political position. This was what made ministers in the Northern Ireland Office despair. Fitzgerald had backed the Forum report, and she imagined that to be his final and complete position, as simple as hers was. 'She can't see what Garret has to be seen to be doing for the sake of ancient rituals,' one British minister told me at the time. When Fitzgerald rebuked her in the Dail, as he had to, she told a group of colleagues that she simply didn't understand what he was talking about.

Subterranean movement towards a new deal was, however, already under way. And it did not come to a halt because of her outburst. This was the point about Fitzgerald's undemonstrative shrewdness; although obliged to reject what she had said, he did not let it interfere with the real business that was slowly proceeding, and which issued a year later in the Anglo-Irish Agreement. Nor did she, which was the greater surprise. Some of her ministers thought she would never see it through. In late 1984, with the process at a relatively early stage, they knew that all would depend, in the end, on her personal commitment. Whatever could be put together by officials as a form of words to entrench greater co-operation between London and Dublin in managing the myriad problems of Northern Ireland, especially over security, her commitment would be irreplaceable. The question, at bottom, would be whether she was prepared to take on the Unionists. 'She is terrified of their plantation extremism,' one minister judged, who was closely involved. 'I don't think she will.'

He turned out to be mistaken. But the struggle to persuade her was arduous. She was someone who took a great deal of persuading whenever the object was to carry her mind away from her gut, otherwise known as her political instincts. The achievement was to the credit of three men in particular.

The principal deviser of the Agreement on the British side was a Foreign Office official then seconded to the Cabinet Office, David Goodall. Goodall, a serious Catholic as well as an accomplished diplomat, had already seen service close to the prime minister during the Falklands war. He got on particularly well with the Irish, but was credited with a well-rounded appreciation of what could and could not be made to work in the North. He was also a deeply reflective man. He once published an essay on Fortitude, which showed how singularly well equipped he was to be associated with the Thatcherite project – how much, perhaps, he had drawn from being close to the lady. A part of fortitude, as Goodall worked it out, consisted of the will 'to follow through, to press ahead in the face of misrepresentation and the ebb and flow of public opinion'. Fortitude also had 'less to do with conduct than with character'. Without it, moreover, there was 'no achievement, whether in the intellectual or the spiritual life, in politics or in ordinary human relationships'.[4] These were unexpected effusions from a civil servant. They might have been written by the leader herself. They were masked by

Goodall's chirpy humour, but they singled him out as an unusual man
– who also had the unusual satisfaction, for a Whitehall official, of
seeing a project through from conception to completion.

The second key player in Downing Street, slowly edging its occupant towards a concordat which nobody, least of all the Ulster
Unionist politicians, expected her to accept, was the cabinet secretary.
This was one of Armstrong's finest hours. A man who had much to
put up with, and quite a lot to regret in his last years, he took a crucial
role in the diplomacy which Goodall began. Armstrong was a man of
subtle disposition, his own prejudices, if any, so deeply concealed as
to be irrelevant, his hooded demeanour and pragmatic instincts ideally
suited to the game that had to be played. It was never lost on
Armstrong that, at the end of the day, the Orange politician who was
his mistress would need to be persuaded that there was virtue in
excluding from the table the Orange veto which, from time imme-
morial, had blocked political change in Ulster.

The third contributor was a new Northern Ireland Secretary. Prior
had finally departed, after three years in the job he tried rather
humiliatingly to avoid but which he described in his resignation letter
as 'the most challenging of my political career'. Although he had
come to look, during the Thatcher ascendancy, like something of a
burned-out case, the prime minister's published reply was careful to
state that he need not have left. There would have been another
cabinet post for him after Northern Ireland, she said. She wanted it
to be quite clear that Prior was not being pushed out: a telling
reflection, in September 1984, of her continuing insecurity.

Prior's replacement now brought fresh talents to the post. Douglas
Hurd was a diplomat by training and a Heathite by political origin.
He had done his time as junior minister in the Foreign Office and the
Home Office, but he was exceptionally able, far more so than many
of the dedicated Thatcherites who rose earlier than he did. Arriving
in Northern Ireland, he had the right combination of talents to carry
the Foreign Office initiative forward. Not least of these was his
in-born social confidence: the straight manner, the upright mind, the
humorous intelligence, the necessary mastery, all of which contributed
towards convincing the person who most needed to be convinced that
this diplomatic effort was worth pushing to completion.

As the prospect of an agreement grew more real, she began to apply
herself closely to it. One of the officials involved said that, for a
period, she gave Northern Ireland more attention than any British
prime minister had ever done. What began to reassure her, ironically,

was her warm relationship with Garret Fitzgerald. She came to see him as a man to trust, a man also to admire. She was greatly impressed, for example, by the quiet professor's ruthless defence of Irish interests against the European Community's assault on milk surpluses on which Ireland's agricultural economy depended. Here was an Irish leader who seemed to be straight, and who spoke the language of national interest which she could understand.

The fiasco of November 1984, moreover, now paid a dividend. It lowered Dublin's expectations. Her coarse rejection – 'out . . . out . . . out' – meant that the deal agreed a year later came to sound rather more important than it otherwise would have done. Fitzgerald looked to his own people more like someone who had won something. Certainly, no one close to the Anglo-Irish Agreement denied that in the end it grew directly out of the personal chemistry between the two leaders.

It was indeed a fairly modest document. It began by affirming that there would be no change in the status of Northern Ireland without the consent of the majority of the people there. So the Unionists' central demand was acknowledged, even as Dublin, in effect, surrendered its claim to a united Ireland. But it allowed, for the first time, a consultative role to the South in the governance of the North. There would be a regular inter-governmental conference to discuss security matters, political matters, legal matters and cross-border co-operation. A joint secretariat would be established. The apparatus of a collaborative enterprise, though without any infringement of sovereign rights, would be set in place.

The Unionists were enraged, and their fury carried a particularly personal venom. Here, they felt, was a Unionist who had betrayed the Union. They never seriously expected that this leader would ever parley in so treacherous a way with Dublin. It was in such a belief that they had steadfastly declined to co-operate with other forms of political evolution. They thought their veto was permanent. When it turned out not to be, they rounded on Mrs Thatcher with unrestrained bile. Enoch Powell, whose eye she had now stared down, was especially bitter. Fitzgerald, he said, was 'smarmy and ingratiating', but Margaret Thatcher was another Jezebel. 'There you have it', Powell ranted, deriding a Christmas visit she paid to Ulster, when she defended the Agreement, 'straight from Jezebel's own mouth.'[5] This was a slanderous comparison which had, from Powell's point of view, a certain apposite precision. Margaret Thatcher was not a painted lady, and could never rival Jezebel as a symbol of female wickedness. But the source of Jezebel's offence was a dynastic marriage which caused strict Israelites to brand her a harlot. To strict Ulster Unionists, the Agreement seemed to be in the same lineage of cynical betrayal.

Once Mrs Thatcher was committed, however, it was in her character never to be shifted. The ministers who had laboured to persuade her knew this, exploited it, rejoiced mightily in their triumph. She was locked in, as a matter of pride if nothing else. Besides, this was an inter-governmental agreement which could not be taken apart by merely personal intervention, capricious or otherwise. And it carried considerable advantages for the British, whether or not its impact on security, which was its strongest practical purpose, came to be noticeable. At small cost it gave London what is called 'presentational cover' round the world. Any ignorant foreign politician who chose to belabour Britain with its record in Northern Ireland could be shown the Agreement as proof that constructive processes were now afoot.

To Britain's most Orange prime minister this represented change, and yet also no change. She did not accept that she was any less of a Unionist than she had ever been. When challenged with the suggestion that the Agreement contained traces of the formula to which she had three times said 'out', she utterly denied it. 'We have none of those things in the Anglo-Irish Agreement, and I was very careful not to get them,' she told the BBC.[6]

It was also the case that her own language and attitudes did not really change. She did not become permanently seized of the importance of Ireland or infused with the spirit of Irish comradeship. She still tended to use 'Unionist' and 'Loyalist' as if they were synonyms, likewise 'Nationalist' and 'Republican'. In future, there would be constant attacks on the Agreement, and plenty of evidence that it had neither solved the security problem nor ended the terrorist threat. Her own interest in maintaining the momentum it was supposed to begin was not great, partly as a result of the security failures. But the Agreement existed: the most durable shift any recent British prime minister had brought about in the handling of their most intractable legacy.

But the Irish problem was part of a larger crisis. The overwhelming reason why this leader made what looked like an uncharacteristic surrender of prejudice to pragmatism was, in the first place, because it seemed to offer a better answer to the terrorist menace. Even though the security effect was at best patchy and at worst counter-productive, that was the main object. As well as offering presentational advantage, the Anglo-Irish Agreement was Britain's contribution to the efforts of the Western powers to control and then defeat terrorism of many kinds. Its signing coincided with a burst of terrorist outrages from a different quarter: directed by Middle East factions, usually Libyan or Iranian, against Western targets, usually American. These posed for Mrs Thatcher a more sensitive problem even than Ireland, and one where the famous Thatcher consistency, placed under still greater strain, was subject to more complex resolution.

She was, it went without saying, utterly opposed to terrorism, and to making any surrender to terrorist demands. She was in favour of the sternest measures against known terrorists, and during her first two terms pushed forward a whole range of measures, from massively increased police pay to greatly enhanced police powers, which spoke for that priority. She would watch British hostages rot in the undiscovered cells of the Hezbollah with as much indifference as she permitted Sands and his fanatic friends to die in Long Kesh, her determination fortified by the certainty that what she was doing was right as well as proper. She stood shoulder to shoulder – except that hers usually seemed the more aggressively positioned – with other leaders who saw their solemn duty in protecting the legal entity of the state against the violent assaults of lawless gunmen.

Legality, however, was a seamless concept. It reached far beyond the terrorist problem, and this genuinely seemed to trouble her. Perhaps it was her legal training, perhaps her need always to see herself as immaculately in the right, but she believed more than most of her contemporaries in the importance of that elusive entity known as international law. International law might conflict with domestic laws; it certainly restrained the conduct of nations. It could be very inconvenient, but she had on occasion stuck by it – at some cost.

The Americans, in particular, had already experienced the stickler's rebuke, when they invaded Grenada. Big countries, she said then, could not be permitted to send armies into a small one merely because they disliked the regime in power there. This was the principle Britain had upheld in the Falklands, and it could not now be dismantled.

At the beginning of 1986, she issued a similar caution against the use of illegal measures against international terrorism. Over Christmas there had been terrorist attacks at Rome and Vienna airports, which killed nineteen people, including five Americans. The Libyan Government of Colonel Muammar Gaddafi was widely held to be responsible, and both political and public opinion in the United States was demanding retaliation. Gaddafi, for his part, said in early January that the US might be preparing to launch a military attack on Libya, and he threatened his own retaliation against West European ports and cities harbouring an American presence.

In this atmosphere of heightened threat and counter-threat, the senior leader in the Western world gave her opinion. As it happened, she was already in the middle of a great deal of turbulence when she spoke to American correspondents; it was the day after Heseltine's resignation. But she declined to join the stampede to action. Reagan was now asking for a collective Nato stand on measures to be taken against the colonel, and the correspondents pressed the prime minister repeatedly to agree. She declined to do so. One suggestion was for economic sanctions, but she thought these 'don't work' as a tool of foreign policy. In any case, she said, there was no possibility of getting a consensus for them in Europe. Her strongest condemnation, however, was directed at the idea of a military strike against Libya. 'I do not believe in retaliatory strikes that are against international law,' she told the correspondents. They might produce 'much greater chaos' than terrorism itself. 'Once you start to go across borders,' she said, 'then I do not see an end to it. I uphold international law very firmly.'[7]

This looked like a principled and unequivocal rejection of the proposed American strategy. Three months later, no important fact had changed, but the Thatcher position was reversed. It was among the more arresting policy-switches of her time. It illustrated as well as any other episode the hold Reagan had on British policy when he really needed it – which over Grenada he didn't – and the impotence of collective cabinet government when faced with an unbreakable bond between president and prime minister.

In early April, Reagan notified his loyal friend that after another terrorist atrocity, this time in Berlin, he had decided to strike against Libya. He wasn't consulting but informing. The attack would go ahead anyway, but it would be rendered easier and also more precise in its targetry if F-111 bombers based in Britain could be deployed. Carrier-based aircraft, standing off the Libyan coast, could be used, but they would be at greater risk and would also cause more civilian damage. Reagan, in other words, wanted British permission to commit what the British prime minister already seemed to have described quite clearly as a breach of international law.

She was not unaware of the contradiction. And she didn't immediately acquiesce. What followed was a typical little setpiece in her approach to the trickier class of policy-making.

First she sought to expunge the contradiction and place herself in line with international law. Attorney-General Havers was summoned and asked to give an opinion about the legal propriety of bombing Libya. Might it not, after all, fall within the terms of Article 51 of the United Nations Charter, which allowed military action for the purpose of self-defence? Armed with enough positive indications on the point, and strengthened by the knowledge that Washington proposed to go ahead anyway, the prime minister gave her approval – but only on terms which, while she might be unable to enforce them, cleared her conscience and supplied her with a righteous apologia. The bombing could go ahead, but it had to be confined to very particular targets, all of them known to be linked with terrorism. Blanket bombing was not allowed, and there must be as few civilian casualties as the pilots could manage.

This was decided between the smallest possible group of ministers. So the second element of a classic Thatcher manoeuvre came into play: the presentation to the rest of the cabinet of a *fait accompli* – although it was one which, on this occasion, aroused more outspoken criticism than the leader was accustomed to.

The ministers involved from the start were Foreign Secretary Howe and the Defence Secretary, George Younger, together with Whitelaw. All had their reservations. Howe had already exposed his when, three weeks earlier, Reagan sent the Sixth Fleet to exercise close to the Libyan coast. As the Foreign Secretary began to list some predictable Foreign Office doubts about this initiative, Mrs Thatcher interrupted him, as one minister told me at the time, 'shrieking about the need to support the Americans and the need not to be fair-weather friends'. Younger went public with his anxieties, broadcast on a Scottish radio station. Whitelaw wanted to make a clear distinction between acceding to a request from an ally and enthusing about every action the ally proposed to take.

This was the opinion of most of the cabinet when it was informed of Reagan's request – on the night the bombing was actually conducted, 14/15 April. First in the oversea and defence committee, then in full cabinet, surprising voices expressed all kinds of reservation. A helpful minister ran down the list for me immediately after cabinet met. Chancellor Lawson and Norman Tebbit, now chairman of the party, were horrified at any idea of giving Reagan a blank cheque.

Douglas Hurd, John Biffen, Leader of the House, and Kenneth Baker, Environment Secretary, also voiced anxious criticism. Nobody thought Reagan's request could actually have been refused. But they looked for a seemly distancing of the British position from the American, as well as a clear indication to the Americans – also to British voters and Arab terrorists whose reprisals they feared in roughly equal measure – that any further request for use of the bases would put the British Government in an intolerable position.

This was precisely what the prime minister declined to supply, thus observing a third Thatcher norm, which required every decision, however agonised, to be defended as if no sane person could have contemplated any other. Indeed, the trickier a decision and the more evenly balanced the arguments for and against it, the more adamantine did the prime minister's tone necessarily become. It certainly did over the bombing of Libya. The cautious response to Washington, emphasised in lengthy interrogative telegrams from London, was supplanted, once a public defence was called for, by her assertion that it would have been 'inconceivable' to turn down the president's request. Not a single word could be said against the bombing. It was, she thought, utterly right and entirely in conformity with both legal obligations and political prudence.

Two days after the raid, she was prepared to be a little more circumspect. Yet another forensic device, also often deployed during the Falklands war, was put to work: first the fearless declaration, only then the signs of more muted deliberation. It had, after all, been a difficult decision. There were grave risks to this country, she said. 'I pondered them deeply with the ministers most closely involved.' And it was clearly understood, she added, that any further use of the bases would require a separate approach from Washington – which, she implied, might not necessarily be approved.

Such a tempering of language was prudent. The bombing was extraordinarily unpopular. Even the most faithful Conservative columnists withheld their support. Ferdinand Mount, who ran the prime minister's policy unit for two years bridging the 1983 election, ridiculed the notion that 'carefully selected targets', minimising civilian casualties, could include a target bang in the middle of Tripoli, the Libyan capital. Mount wrote that the episode might cost the Tories the next election, and his newspaper, the *Daily Telegraph*, usually a safe haven for Conservative prime ministers in trouble, also attacked the raid. When three British hostages were found murdered in the Lebanon two days later, the Opposition charge that they were 'sacrificial lambs' on the altar of a highly personal version of the special relationship was hard to rebut. Certainly, things had moved a long way since January, when the prime minister had given a seemingly unequivocal rejection of the idea that anyone should bomb Libya.

In the US, however, her change of mind signalled another personal triumph. One more proof of loyalty had been supplied, at a time when not one other European power was prepared to say, still less do, anything to align themselves with the American initiative. A resolution was introduced in Congress offering the British leader 'highest praise and thanks' for her co-operation. But her role in fact had wider effects, reaching beyond the Congress into two more potent zones of influence.

The first, it is fair to assume, was her own psyche. For the operation proved to be a success: or at any rate not a failure. Dire predictions were made about the safety of all Britons abroad, who were now reckoned to be at risk from uncounted waves of terrorists whom Gaddafi would unleash across Europe. But this did not happen. Although it was some time before it became apparent, the colonel behaved like a man who had been taught a lesson, and Libyan-inspired terrorism was much reduced in the months that followed.

Once again, therefore, Mrs Thatcher experienced the kind of vindi-cation which most singularly and decisively marked her prime minis-tership. Proof that she was right while almost all around her were wrong supplied repeated doses of oxygen just when the leader's assault on the mountain seemed to be failing. The important part of this was that the others were wrong. How often had they warned that unemployment levels were intolerable, that society would fall apart, that there would be blood on the streets, that the Falklands war might be lost, that the Conservative Party under her leadership was about to plunge into oblivion? How often had she rejected their analysis and forged ahead in pursuit of her instincts? And how often had their pessimism been set at nothing by her own inextinguishable capacity to do what was, above all, *right*?

The pattern, as she saw it, was consistent and it had, of course, an almost self-fulfilling capacity to repeat itself. The more the prophets of doom turned out to be in error, the less attention was she disposed to give to their advice. Over Libya, admittedly, she pre-empted rather than overrode it. She was also conveniently able to forget her emphatic opinion of three months earlier. But the point still stood; and even before the verdict was in, she was showing all the signs of a leader who, far from downcast by domestic unpopularity, was climbing to new heights of self-belief. At a world economic summit in Tokyo in early May, she carried a long record of undiplomatic conduct in the international arena to new levels of manifest arrogance. She drove the other leaders to accept a strong Reagan–Thatcher declaration on terrorism, tearing up the more cautious formulae of the Japanese. At the end, she announced with her inimitable crispness that she had secured all her objectives: 'In short, mission accomplished.' Reminded that she was now the senior member present, she modestly suggested that this might have happened 'because I am more right than my opponents'. Asked for the secret of her success, she replied: 'I would not care to reveal the magic formula. Others might cotton on to it.'

Never, perhaps, was a greater distance set between the manners of the old Conservatism, which tended towards the dry gentilities of British understatement, and the habits of the new. Margaret Thatcher rarely permitted even the inattentive observer to mistake the scale or brilliance of her contributions to history.

The second consequence of Libya was, however, still larger. Britain's support solidified British closeness to Washington at a time when this would soon need to be exploited. In October President Reagan, negotiating with General Secretary Gorbachev, came close to removing the cornerstone from the edifice on which the defence of Europe was based. In November, Mrs Thatcher, irresistibly inviting herself to Washington, was able, on behalf of Europe as a whole, to put it back in place.

Reagan's October vision occurred in Reykjavik, the capital of Iceland. He and Gorbachev got quite close to an agreement for the complete elimination of nuclear weapons. Or so Reagan thought. It was one of the more extraordinary encounters in the history of summit meetings, certainly the most extraordinary failure. Convened at short notice, it moved at headlong pace, with each leader capping the other's dramatic proposal for nuclear curtailment down to zero on either side. This would begin with the intermediate-range weapons, but would ultimately, in their shared vision, include all strategic missiles as well. It was an unscripted event, of which the White House chief of staff, Donald Regan, one of many Reagan people to leave the president's employment in abrasive circumstances, swiftly published a graphic account.

The summit had been prompted by a letter from Gorbachev. Regan takes up the story of the climactic Reykjavik conversation:

'What, Reagan asked Gorbachev, had he meant by the reference in his letter to "the elimination of all strategic forces"?

' "I meant I would favour eliminating all nuclear weapons," Gorbachev replied.

' "*All* nuclear weapons?" Reagan said. "Well, Mikhail, that's exactly what I've been talking about all along. That's what we have long wanted to do – get rid of all nuclear weapons. That's always been my goal."

'"Then why don't we agree on it?" Gorbachev asked.

'"We should," Reagan said. "That's what I've been trying to tell you."

'It was a historic moment. The two leaders had brought the world to one of its great turning points. Both understood this very clearly.'[8]

At this point, the summit broke down. Gorbachev would accept the vision only if Reagan agreed to a ban on all further development and testing of his vaunted SDI, or Star Wars, system outside the laboratory. Reagan would not have that at any price, so the summit concluded in some bitterness. The American public, in particular, were prone to believe that their president had blown the best chance ever created to abolish the nuclear threat.

That wasn't the way it seemed to most European leaders, the custodians of a defence system formally dependent on the theory and practice of nuclear deterrence. And although Reykjavik had finally collapsed, Reagan's non-nuclear dream had no such neat termination. In Washington confusion reigned. For although progress had foundered on the rock of SDI, it was still apparent that the president had been prepared to bargain away the entire presence of American nuclear weaponry in Europe and to push for a policy which would destroy Nato's nuclear strategy. Any strategic deal, moreover, would necessarily mean the end of Britain's independent nuclear weapon.

Plainly it was time for a European corrective, and the British leader supplied it. She was horrified by the dreams of Reykjavik. Europe was vulnerable to Soviet conventional and chemical as well as nuclear forces. Abolition of 'the nuclear', as she tended to call them, would leave Europe wide open. 'The fact is that nuclear weapons have prevented not only nuclear war but conventional war in Europe for forty years,' she told the Lord Mayor's banquet in mid-November. 'That is why we depend and will continue to depend on nuclear weapons for our defence.'

A few days later, she made the same case in Washington. It was one of her sharper encounters with Reagan, but was characterised by an adviser as a pivotal moment, hauling the president back from what would have been 'an utter disaster'. In fact she had both a general and a particular purpose. The general was encompassed in a joint statement which asserted that nothing had really changed. Nato's strategy was still based on 'forward defence and flexible response', including nuclear deterrence; and disarmament was now said to be a process that must include conventional as well as nuclear weapons. But the particular purpose, closer to home, was also met. Reagan confirmed that nothing would disturb arrangements for production and delivery of the promised Trident missiles for the new generation of the British deterrent. The threat to Trident was what really alarmed a leader who customarily staked everything on the British Bomb in her struggles with the Labour Party. She was desperate for reassurance.

Satisfaction was supplied at relatively small cost. The price was silence on the issue then preoccupying Washington, the opening phase of what became known as 'Irangate', a burgeoning scandal which involved several White House officials in trading arms for hostages with Iran and siphoning off some of the proceeds to aid Contra rebels in a civil war against the Nicaraguan Government. Questioned at the end of her visit, Mrs Thatcher went on record with a statement which hardly a single American politician of either party would at that moment have been prepared to sign. 'I believe implicitly in the president's total integrity on that subject,' she said.

It was his due reward, part of the exchange of political donations. Some thought, also, that on the main issue the Thatcher visit actually brought the president back to his senses. This was particularly so at the Pentagon, where they were equally disposed to regard the Reykjavik vision as a nightmare. Mrs Thatcher was always welcome, said Richard Perle, Assistant Secretary for Defence. But on this occasion especially so. She would counter Reagan's 'intemperate' views. 'So many of us regarded her as a voice of calm reason, and a much needed one, in particular on this issue of a world without nuclear weapons, which is dangerous nonsense.' The president talked about this often 'but never in close proximity with a visit from Mrs Thatcher'. She provided 'a brief respite from that rubbish'.[9]

So the closeness was not exclusively personal. Libya, and countless other moments of support, kept the entry-ticket to the White House in currency. From the White House, the frequent Thatcher presence radiated around Republican Washington. But what mattered to her in the end was Little England, and if the Pentagon were better allies in that cause, then Reagan's dreams could be painlessly dismissed.

*   *   *

The salvaging of Reykjavik was a bonus from Libya, but it took six months to accrue. Meanwhile, the bombing damaged still further a political position already much lowered by the Westland affair. In Downing Street, according to one of its oldest inhabitants, the night it happened, 14 April, was the nadir of Mrs Thatcher's second term. It coincided with a rare parliamentary defeat for the Government, when its majority of 140 spectacularly declined to muster in support of a second reading for the Shops Bill, to liberalise the Sunday trading laws. Beaten in the House, and a helpless if truculent spectator at the deployment of American military might, the prime minister was not happy.

In small part this was because she knew she was not popular. Prime ministers say they never read opinion polls, but even if they don't they employ advisers who do little else. This prime minister often rejoiced in unpopularity, as long as she knew she was right. Few other Conservatives would say the same. In early May 1986, two weeks after the bombing, both the Government and its leader sank close to the bottom of their ratings. Mori recorded the Conservatives at 32 per cent, Labour at 40, with the Liberal–SDP Alliance at 26. Mrs Thatcher's satisfaction rating, at only 30 per cent, was as low as it had been since before the Falklands war.

But the ratings as such were not, in her view, the problem. They were only a symptom of a crisis to which she responded with greater feeling. This was a crisis of control. All political leaders need to feel that they are in control of their own agenda and, which is even more necessary, that they are seen to be dominating whatever is the issue of the day. No political leader needed this more than Mrs Thatcher. Domination, whether of the Argentine or the miners or her dissident colleagues or her European enemies, was her special stock-in-trade. For many months – arguably, indeed, ever since the election – domination had persistently eluded her as one mess after another frustrated her desire for orderly government. She badly needed an issue of which she could be seen to be in charge.

For these purposes, it didn't matter much what the issue was. The crucial ingredient was not that it should be popular or attract an easy bipartisan consensus. Rather the opposite. It needed to show her as a fighter, preferably with her back to the wall and with enemies massing against her whom she would vanquish by the power of her argument and the righteousness of her cause. Naturally the emergence of such an issue was not something she could altogether control. But, when it happened, it filled the bill exactly.

It had been looming for a year, and the role it might play in the renewal of her self-projection had already been quite dramatically glimpsed. The 1985 Commonwealth conference, held in Nassau, capital of the Bahamas, was dominated by a single subject: what to do about South Africa. Most of the Commonwealth were thirsting for united action to impose a tough regime of economic sanctions, with a view to weakening and then, as they imagined, helping destroy the apartheid state. To this the British leader was adamantly opposed. She was not, she said, in favour of apartheid. But she preferred the constructive approach. She thought sanctions would only make things worse. Quite apart from the damage they would do to Britain's own economic self-interest, what was the point of a policy which would throw thousands of black South Africans out of work while hardening not softening the attitude of the Government led by P. W. Botha? She had received Botha at Chequers, impressed upon him the need for change, sent him on his way confident that he would take seriously the ministrations of a leader who, unlike the rest of the Western world, had not cast him into outer darkness.

At Nassau, she more or less sustained this position. As usual, she settled late and surrendered little. The Commonwealth majority had wanted a ban on fruit imports and an end to flights to and from South Africa. The final communiqué confined economic sanctions to a ban on the import of gold Krugerrands and an end to government assistance for trade delegations and exhibitions in South Africa. It also announced the setting-up of a group of 'eminent persons' to visit the Republic, meet its leaders and others, and report. The final act at Nassau afforded British voters one of their starkest direct experiences of the prime minister's approach to the international process. At a televised press conference, her entire concern was to emphasise not the measure of agreement secured but the utter insignificance of the concessions she had made to achieve it. Finger and thumb were dramatically offered to the cameras to demonstrate how she had moved only 'a tiny little bit'. The entire aspect of her face, with eyes blazing and lip faintly curling, was that of a leader devoid of magnanimity, concerned exclusively to deride the paucity of her opponents' success.

This performance in October 1985, however, was only a modest foretaste of things to come. While the Eminent Persons Group assembled and began touring round southern Africa, the issue disappeared from the top of the agenda, despite mounting chaos in South Africa which culminated, on 12 June 1986, with the imposition of a state of emergency. These developments, together with the EPG's urgent conclusion that there was no alternative to a concerted policy of economic sanctions, merely redoubled Mrs Thatcher's certainty that she was right and they were wrong. She had found, in her perversity, the elixir of political recovery.

Several elements contributed to the potion, a very personal prescription which the Foreign Office had little part in writing. That, from her point of view, was one of its merits. It took her back to territory on which her brute convictions could assert their mastery over the pettifogging anxieties of the diplomats. Howe, the Foreign Secretary, would later acknowledge that this was one subject on which he and the prime minister had not quite seen eye to eye, but he put this down to the fact that he, unlike her, had past experience of the place. Whatever the reason, he was assigned the fall-guy's part, anxious to make progress, sensitive to the feelings of black Africa, available to be insulted by its leaders when he journeyed to their countries to protest a British goodwill which hardly seemed to be proclaimed by the raucous certitudes of the lady who dominated his life.

One provocative element, for her, was the Commonwealth itself. Anything the Commonwealth as a whole preferred was likely, on her analysis, to demand British opposition. This far antedated South Africa. At the 1983 Commonwealth conference in New Delhi, the entire British effort was devoted to resisting declarations calling for greater justice between the countries of the rich north and the poor south. The defensive posture was habitual. It was the opinion of some Conservatives deeply steeped in foreign affairs that their leader's disdain for the European Community actually exceeded her dislike of the Commonwealth. Because the Commonwealth was originally British, they thought, and because English was the common language, it was to be preferred in her eyes to the collection of incomprehensible aliens across the Channel. But this was a minority view. Most people closest to the prime minister communicated her special impatience with the demands and hypocrisies of a multi-racial organisation excessively dominated by the representatives of the Third World.

Another ingredient South Africa offered was populist appeal. All that Mrs Thatcher felt about the Commonwealth was probably felt by a majority of the electorate. Opposing Commonwealth demands was a respectable way of aligning oneself with latent racialism at home, and recovering support for foreign policy which had been put in jeopardy by the Libyan event. Anti-Americanism, already apparently rising, increased after the bombing of Tripoli from British bases. Standing firm against moralising lectures from Robert Mugabe, even in a minority of one, would be a more than adequate counterpoise.

This was also, quite simply, pragmatic. Sanctions, to her, just did not add up. 'I do not believe apartheid will come to an end by creating unemployment,' she told Parliament after Nassau. Nor did she believe apartheid was the root of the problem. 'I do not accept that apartheid is the root of violence, and nor do most other people,' she said on the same occasion.[10] As for the desirability of an international consensus, this was a matter of almost triumphant irrelevance, as she explained to a television interviewer: 'If I were the odd one out and I were right, that would not matter, would it?'[11]

Part of this case for her own rightness was based on a claim to know what was really going on in South Africa. This was a common British supposition, not confined to the leader. 'We know more about the Afrikaner psychology than anyone in the world,' a Foreign Office minister confided at the time. This taught us, he went on, that Botha was now to be accounted a reformer, but one who would respond only to market forces not to threats from the Commonwealth.

Mrs Thatcher's own analysis was still more confident, when I interviewed her as she prepared for a resumed 'mini-summit' of Commonwealth leaders to consider the Eminent Persons' report. Apartheid, she said, was 'totally and utterly and particularly repugnant to us', but 'things are coming in the right direction'. 'It has to go and it is going,' she went on, and she instanced some of the evidence. The prohibition on mixed marriages had gone – 'as a matter of fact, I think it's the thing that signals the end of apartheid.' The pass laws were going. So was job reservation. So were enforced removals of unwanted communities. Even the Group Areas Act, she claimed, was 'starting to go'.[12]

Very little of this accorded with the truth. Two years later, the Group Areas Act remained effectively untouched. Under cover of the state of emergency, enforced removals were among the lesser violations visited on unwanted communities. For a leader who prided herself on her hard-headed realism and attention to facts, this was a suggestive venture into the realm of illusion. It showed how necessary to her anti-sanctions stance was a wild optimism about how much was already being achieved.

Another strand of feeling, however, was less vulnerable to demolition. This was the sheer fury she experienced at taunts about the immorality of British policy. Immorality, on the contrary, belonged entirely elsewhere. 'I find nothing *moral* about people sitting in comfortable circumstances,' she told me, 'with good salaries, inflation-proof pensions, good jobs, saying that we, as a matter of *morality*, will put x hundred thousand black people out of work, knowing that this could lead to starvation, poverty and unemployment, and even greater violence.' This theme was repeated in later years: the particular unpleasantness of sitting in luxury oneself and calling down destitution on others – as if the demand for sanctions did not come as strongly from the overcrowded slums of Soweto as from the well-padded salons of Hampstead or Georgetown. She was especially scornful of this contrast as presented in the European Community, which had just approved a sanctions package. 'I find it repugnant. We had it at the Community meeting. Nice conference centre. Nice hotels. Good jobs. And you really tell me you'll move people around as if they're pawns on a checkerboard, and say it's *moral?*'

She'd had some calculations done. A fruit boycott, for example, would cost 95,000 jobs. 'Blacks and their families out of work. *Moral?* Poof! *Moral?* No social security. *Moral?*'

Against this background, the summit opened in a mood of apprehension. She sought to distance herself from the consequences, by noting that it was no longer the British Commonwealth anyway. 'It's their club, their Commonwealth,' she told another interviewer. 'If they wish to break it up, I think that's absurd.'[13] She presented herself, all the same, as an ice-cold analyst. 'Emotions will be running high,' she told me beforehand. 'When that happens, you just have to let them run high and keep very calm yourself. It doesn't help if you let your own emotions run high, even though they feel as though they're running high.' Her objective would be calmly to present her interlocutors with some of the facts of life.

In the end, a cataclysm was avoided. Once again, after beating an intransigent drum for months, and spending the first two days of the meeting declining to concede an inch, she settled late for a small surrender. Britain was now prepared to support an EC ban on coal, iron and steel from South Africa, as well as Krugerrands. It would also encourage a voluntary ban on new investment there, and on the promotion of tourism. For the rest, the other participants, who included Canada and Australia as well as Zambia and Zimbabwe, agreed sullenly to differ.

This was one of Mrs Thatcher's most inept, yet characteristic, international performances. Having protested against concessions to the sanctions lobby, she then made them without forewarning and without winning any reward. The voluntary ban on new investment, being only voluntary, was not a major shift; in any case, outward investment from Britain had already almost ceased. But to announce it without seeking political credit for it, or offering it as a warning to Pretoria, was a measure of the extent to which the prime minister's prejudice and temperament were permitted to override elementary diplomatic prudence. Any student of foreign policy would have been obliged to note how, while preserving Britain from the need to impose the heaviest sanctions, it nevertheless offended the first rule of diplomatic conduct, which is to make the best not the worst of any action your country feels obliged to take.

In Downing Street, however, this is not the way the sanctions row was regarded. There the whole thing looked like a vindication. Kenneth Kaunda remarked that Mrs Thatcher had cut a pathetic figure. Mugabe said she was 'an ally of apartheid'. The Indian leader, Rajiv Gandhi, pronounced Britain to be 'losing its position as head of the Commonwealth, because it is compromising on basic values and principles'. But these were insults she could live with. They evoked her extraordinary capacity, so rare and yet so valuable in a politician, actually to draw strength from her attackers. The same effect was achieved soon after the summit, when she visited Norway, the acme of a social democratic society, where she was greeted with an acerbic lecture from Europe's other woman leader, Mrs Gro Harlem Brundtland, and the most ferocious demonstrations seen in Oslo for fifteen years. Their protests covered the spectrum of Thatcherism, from unemployment to sanctions, for which she repaid them with some heavy irony. 'So at home have you made me feel', she told the official dinner, 'that you have even got demonstrations outside. How very thoughtful of you! With the jungle drums I thought I might be nearer the equator than the Arctic.'

This announced, domestically, a leader who thought she had recovered her position. South Africa brought out the old nerveless incaution. Her colleagues noticed it in Parliament. 'She is an absolutely fearless politician,' said one of them, not a close admirer. 'You could see it the other day, when she went beyond her brief and indicated that she might go to South Africa herself. Just a moment's hesitation, before she plunged in. Whereas anyone else would hesitate, and want a clear idea what they'd get out of it, that wouldn't be her way.'

Among her entourage, the verdict was simpler. They thought that bashing the Commonwealth had restored her to a position of command which she would never have to relinquish.

It had, however, one discordant sub-text, rippling uncomfortably through the domestic scene. This was one of the oddest distractions of her time, but it was not unimportant. It had considerable symbolic resonance.

Two weeks before the Commonwealth summit, a story appeared in the press stating that the prime minister had a new political opponent, Her Majesty the Queen. According to the *Sunday Times*, the Queen was worried to the point of outrage by the possible effects which British policy towards South Africa would have on the unity of the Commonwealth.[14] While not necessarily in favour of sanctions, she was said to be determined to emphasise the need for compromise, to protect the institution of which she saw herself to be, in large measure, both inventor and guarantor.

Not only was this the Queen's opinion, said the newspaper, but she had authorised her senior officials to make it known to the world through the *Sunday Times*, and thus with malice aforethought intervened in the political process. Her catalogue of discontent with the Thatcher Government, furthermore, stretched well beyond South Africa and the Commonwealth. The newspaper reported that the Queen thought the Government lacked compassion for the underprivileged; that she had nurtured secret anxieties about the conduct of the miners' strike in 1984; that she had 'misgivings' about the Libyan bombing; and that altogether Mrs Thatcher was a menace to the consensus which, in the Queen's judgment, had served the country well ever since the war. All this, it was again emphasised, was something which the Queen, by conscious choice, now wanted to make public. For one brief weekend, the British public was invited to transport itself back to the eighteenth century or earlier, with a 'Royal' party apparently mobilising to overturn the coalition of forces now in charge.

This story turned out, on examination, to be almost entirely false. Such error might have been apparent from the beginning to a newspaper that had retained a better grasp on the workings of the constitution, or was more sensitive to the Queen's respect for the law. Whatever her opinions might be, it was not conceivable that so punctilious a constitutionalist would for a single moment have desired her servants to ventilate them through the pages of the *Sunday Times*. The interest of the episode, however, transcends that journalistic misconception. The telling point is that the story enjoyed, for a while, a certain credence. In its depiction of the two women's positions, it did not appear to be entirely outlandish. However improbable it might seem that the Queen should actually have wanted to see any of this in the public realm, the picture of herself as a traditional paternalist rendered increasingly anxious by the aggressive individualism of the prime minister was recognisable. And because there were these traces of credibility, which seemingly confirmed other rumours and assumptions, an image gained currency which depicted, on the one hand, a politician determined to include the monarchy on her aggressive march through British institutions, and, on the other, a sovereign determined to question and resist so importunate a challenge.

This picture, which at times entered the realm of caricature, was profoundly misleading.

Margaret Thatcher was from her earliest days, as one would expect from the daughter of an aldermanic household in middle England, a devoted monarchist. Hovering ambitiously on the threshold of public life, she always saw Queen Elizabeth's accession to the throne as supplying her with a significant role model. She wrote in the *Sunday Graphic* on 17 February 1952: 'If, as many earnestly pray, the accession of Elizabeth II can help to remove the last shreds of prejudice against women aspiring to the highest places, then a new era for women will indeed be at hand.' Since they were almost exact contemporaries, this royal event appeared to provide an especially telling basis for what followed: an attack by this newly married and thrusting young Tory politician on the common assumption that women could not raise families and occupy important positions at the same time.

Later, when the fulfilment of her ambition brought the alderman's daughter into regular contact with the monarch, all who observed their relationship noted only her elaborate humility in the presence of such an historic personage. One courtier found her 'excessively reverential'. Her curtsies before even the remoter royals reached lower than anyone else's, and this remained the case even when the passage of a decade might have made the habit more perfunctory. Always a punctual person, she invariably arrived fifteen minutes early for her weekly audience at the Palace. At a Christmas party for journalists in 1986, her instructions to the assembled company conveyed what appeared to be her own timeless habit: Get the Christmas lunch done nice and early, she said, so it's all finished before the Queen's broadcast.

The Queen, for her part, was, on all available evidence, just as loyal to the proprieties. There is no reason to suppose that she withheld from Mrs Thatcher what Harold Macmillan found to be her 'invariable graciousness and understanding'.[15] Naturally, there was some difference between entertaining prime ministers who engaged in the same country pursuits as the Royal Family and looking after one who neither fished nor shot. On her annual visit to the Queen's Scottish estate at Balmoral, courtiers spoke of the difficulty of finding 'something to do in the afternoon' – although this was mitigated by Mrs Thatcher's insatiable appetite for work on her boxes. The elderly gentlemen of the past, James Callaghan not least, experienced a quite different chemistry with the Queen than she was ever likely to enjoy with another woman. But by common repute the only one of the eight prime ministers of the present reign with whom the monarch never succeeded in developing an easy relationship was not Mrs Thatcher but Edward Heath: a failing which gave Her Majesty something in common with much of the human race.

So the proprieties were observed, almost to a fault. But it would be misleading to deny that there were some singular differences of outlook between the Queen and her eighth prime minister. The serious members of the Royal Family might best be described as a collection of Tory wets. They were worried paternalists who instinctively spoke for the kind of society that Mrs Thatcher felt it necessary to challenge. They did indeed believe in caring and compassion, and the Prince of Wales in particular was not afraid to say so. They thought that there was such a concept as the community, indeed that 'community' encompassed the very purpose to which citizens of every class and calling should bend their lives: whereas Mrs Thatcher once said, in one of her few unforgettable phrases, that 'There is no such thing as society.'[16] What she meant by that was that society had no meaning save as a grouping of individuals and families. These were the units that really mattered, whereas 'society' was some kind of abstraction and an alibi for individual responsibility. When the phrase became famous, official efforts were made to defuse its significance and insist that it didn't mean what it seemed to mean. But it did: and it expressed, among other things, a graphic contrast with anything which the Royal Family, with their interest in housing and the environment and inner cities and business ethics and a host of other essentially communal concerns, would ever have said.

The Commonwealth also presented a sharp contrast in attitudes. The prime minister's abrasive indifference coexisted with the Queen's constructive concern. This was perhaps the area where the sheer length of her experience had greatest effect. She had known the likes of Kaunda of Zambia and Nyerere of Tanzania for years before Mrs Thatcher could have been relied on accurately to locate their countries on a map. One-man leaders of one-party states enjoyed a special bond with this constitutional monarch, once their Queen as well as Britain's, who had been in office even longer than they had. At the 1979 Commonwealth Conference in Zambia, it was a royal intervention – not, as commonly reported, with Mrs Thatcher but with Kenneth Kaunda, persuading him to stop the local press denouncing the British leader and urging him to take a more optimistic view of the prospects – which was credited with assisting the preliminary agreement to settle the Rhodesian question. The Queen and Prince Charles, as was commonly observed by court and governments alike, had a more natural facility for unpatronising conversation with non-white people, whether leaders or faces in the crowd, than any British prime minister they had to deal with.

Thus there were differences of style and feel. These were two women who registered different vibrations. Moreover, as time wore on, the one was occasionally prone, for all her fawning deference, to take on some of the other's perquisites. The royal 'we' was a usage heard from royal lips only once a year, when the Queen read the speech from the throne at the beginning of the parliamentary session. The prime minister deployed it much more often. And although there were times when the plural could colourably be said to refer to the government collective, or even to herself and her husband travelling with her, there were others when 'we' did not appear on any construction to include anyone but this singular prime minister. By 1987 this habit had become almost inextinguishable. 'We are in the fortunate position, in Britain, of being, as it were, the senior person in power,' she told a BBC reporter on her way to visit Moscow.[17] 'We have learned so much and shall never forget the beauteous things that we have seen' was her message in the visitors' book at a Georgian museum. After visiting a Russian block of flats she declared, 'We have enjoyed ourselves immensely.'

Such *lèse-majesté* usually passed without comment. Indeed, it received a kind of vindication from the more sportive intellectuals in the lower reaches of her Government, who took to comparing her autocratic style with that of another domineering woman ruler, Queen

Elizabeth I. J. E. Neale's classic biography enjoyed a new circulation among the literate classes.[18] Some of Neale's descriptions rang an eerie modern chord. For the Queen, he wrote, 'work was the very breath of life, and she never seemed to lose her gusto for it': she was 'impossible to intimidate': 'it was in that financial sense of Elizabeth's, her resolute, irritating parsimony that the secret of greatness lay.' And, after the execution of treacherous Essex: 'She could only express her amazement that one who knew her spirit should have dared to think of dictating to her.'

Nor did the prime minister always permit personal deference to exclude political advantage. There were moments when she firmly asserted the ascendancy of political over royal considerations. One such was the military parade after the Falklands war, when the City of London was treated to the odd spectacle of fanfares and marching regiments with the prime minister instead of a prince on the saluting-base. She also went to some trouble, at times of natural disaster, to make sure not only that her visits to the scene did not clash with the royals, but that hers came first. When a British cross-Channel ferry sank outside Zeebrugge in spring 1987, she firmly instructed her staff to see to it that the Palace presence, in the persons of the Duke and Duchess of York, did not upstage her own.

Nonetheless, for all these personal foibles, the relationship between Mrs Thatcher and the House of Windsor was essentially conventional. Neither side, in truth, came anywhere near overstepping the line in a way which might give public scandal. Yet despite that, there were people who insisted at the time of the 1986 Commonwealth summit, when the matter came falsely to a head, that this wasn't so, and who were determined to maximise the constitutional damage which, they piously contended, was being done. And this itself makes an interesting commentary on the nature of Mrs Thatcher's enterprise as seen by some of its most committed supporters.

It was, we see from these reactions, a fragile and combustible project, surrounded, it would seem, by enemies on every side prepared to put a match to it. Among these enemies, according to the *Sunday Times*, were now to be numbered the entire leading cadre of the monarchy, who felt so strongly that they were able to break the constitutional conventions and say so. What the story encompassed, said *The Times*, now, admittedly, a paper far removed from its old eminence, was the escape from captivity of 'some monstrous caged beast', namely the political opinions of Her Majesty the Queen.[19] This was an intolerable occurrence. It unleashed against the elected

Government, the paper suggested, the only force which might conceivably command an equivalent popularity.

The editor of the *Sunday Telegraph*, Peregrine Worsthorne, was still more apocalyptic. A man who, despite being an intellectual mischief-maker, spoke for an important segment of Thatcherite High Tories, he thought that the Queen's displeasure had made 'an indelible impression on the public imagination', and that as a result 'the prime minister might actually have her spirit broken.'[20]

These were suggestive apprehensions, a reminder of the condition close to paranoia that Mrs Thatcher and her policies were capable of provoking. There had not been, as we see, any meaningful royal intervention. Cool inquiry at the time could have exorcised this terror, and in some other newspapers it did so. But the belief that it had occurred seemed sufficient, to her fiercer friends, to put her whole endeavour in mortal danger. As they saw it, she had been opposed by many other institutions – the Church, the BBC, the civil service, the universities – and brushed aside their resistance. Was the monarchy not now bringing out the biggest institutional gun, which on this occasion could not be so easily neutralised? Here, surely, was the establishment ranging against an anti-establishment politician the one figure whom she could not be certain of defeating. So, at any rate, thought Mr Worsthorne.

It was a dismal fantasy. But it was potent, because it said that everything was in peril. At the time, it seemed to these fevered minds as if a great populist leader and her great populist campaign for national recovery were about to be subverted by a kind of trick. Thus did they estimate the fragile growth on which they had lavished such devoted and loyal attention.

21

The Last Victory

FEAR OF LOSING was a common apprehension throughout the second term. It did not need the phantasm of a royal intervention to send a chilling shudder through the Conservative Party. Failure and eventual defeat were persistent spectres. But, starting with an especially futile first six months, the Government never seemed confident or purposeful. The spectre was only half exorcised by the defeat of the pit strike, a triumph for which Mrs Thatcher did not really receive the gratitude she deserved. With Westland, drift became something more like crisis, which was deepened by subsequent events.

Throughout this period, moreover, the position of the leader herself was less than fully secure. A consequence of being so dominant was that failures as well as successes were laid at only one door. This was something Whitelaw had always been particularly aware of and, from the earliest days, tried vainly to caution her against. If she insisted on assuming both power and responsibility to herself for every last detail of government, any setback was capable of having a devastating effect. My notebook records that, intermittently through the second term, as in the first, a feature of conversation in ministerial circles, at many particular moments when the fearful spectre hung over them all, was speculation about when and how the prime minister would have to depart. She was still in some people's eyes a contingent leader. This was not yet, bindingly and incontestably, her party.

One focal point of trouble was Francis Pym. Pym had been sacked, but he would not go quietly. On the contrary, the arbitrary and venomous circumstance of his removal only redoubled what he saw as his duty to save the party. Within a year he had written a book describing his personal vision of Conservatism which, extraordinarily, climbed high into the best-seller lists.[1] Buoyed up by this evidence of public demand, Pym began quietly to manoeuvre for position. He thought there was no doubt that the party would be better off without Mrs Thatcher, and became deeply fascinated with the timing of any move against her. In July 1984, when Downing Street put out erroneous reports that he was rounding up a group of dissident Tory leaders in the shire counties, he accused the prime minister's staff of getting rattled. Three months later, he was the first significant Conservative to break ranks over the pit strike when he charged the Government with neglecting 'the human side of the tragedy of this strike' and asserted that it was being prolonged by the absence of any visionary strategy to deal with unemployment.

He was not alone. In January 1985, a voice from the more distant past rose out of the darkness to denounce a great deal of what the Government stood for. The late Indian summer of Harold Macmillan was being spent in the House of Lords, whither he had belatedly gone as Earl of Stockton. Here, after years of silence, he rediscovered the joy of making shocking speeches, always delivered from memory and with the theatrical panache available only to a playful nonagenarian. 'Let us stop the purely theoretical, academic, economic arguments,' Macmillan said, dismissing monetarism at a stroke, 'and get back to the reality which is happening before our eyes.' This reality, he suggested, was that there was more industrial production in Taiwan and South Korea than in Britain, a deplorable state of affairs. In place of partisanship and division, Macmillan recommended the creation of a national government.[2]

In May 1985, building on a mood he thought to be pervasive, Pym made his move and announced the creation of a pressure group inside the parliamentary Conservative Party, called Centre Forward. It was the first attempt by anyone of any weight at the politics of the cabal, and it was almost immediately judged a pathetic failure. Although Pym himself accompanied the launch with a strong attack on the economic policy he had been supporting for four years in government, the enterprise backfired. Not enough MPs were willing to be publicly associated with it. Once again, Mrs Thatcher was preserved within the party by the congenital inability of Conservative politicians at any level, in or out of government, to organise a decent conspiracy against the leader.

Nevertheless, the mood continued to be bad. Embarrassing though Centre Forward turned out to be, Pym's diagnosis was not mistaken. There was a great deal of discontent on both the back benches and the front. The party seethed and incessantly whispered, as the Government lurched uncertainly. It was not being smoothly or even very effectively led. After Westland, followed by the bombing of Libya, the prime minister's weight in the cabinet balance of power was held by her colleagues to have been reduced, and her dominant style to have been forcibly tempered. As she fought to maintain both weight and style, some of them became more impertinent in their observations about her. In May 1986, John Biffen, speaking on television, advanced the case for the American concept of a 'balanced ticket' at the next election: a piece of public effrontery for which she never forgave him, and which was countered by Bernard Ingham with the equally irregular pronouncement that Biffen did not matter because he was only a 'semi-detached member of the cabinet'. But other members of the cabinet were scarcely less pointed in their critique of the prevailing style. At around the same time, Douglas Hurd made a public speech attacking the 'knuckle-headed view of politics' which downgraded the importance of 'community' values. There was an echo of 1981 in the coded interventions ministers were prepared to make in favour of more public spending. Kenneth Baker, the Environment Secretary, said that the electorate had suspended judgment and was waiting to see if the Government could recover 'our sense of direction'.

Another ingredient, meanwhile, had been added to the mix which in its own way did as much as anything to imperil public digestion of the Tory message. By appointing Norman Tebbit chairman of the party in September 1985, Mrs Thatcher took a risk which, in retrospect, she came bitterly to regret.

Tebbit had wanted the job for some time. And he certainly qualified as 'one of us'. He was a founder member of that club, from the time when it was exceedingly small. By origin and attitude, indeed, he was possibly the archetypal Thatcherite and certainly the emblematic new Conservative. His father was a jobbing builder, and after grammar school in north London Norman did not proceed to university but into the lower reaches of journalism before moving into the airline business and becoming a pilot. This formation made him very chippy. He conducted his political life with a permanent sneering prejudice against people with university degrees, not least because he was convinced that he was cleverer than any of them. But his origins also made him a Tory, and always kept him in touch, he delighted to think, with the unnumbered masses of people just like him, who wanted to make their way up the economic scale. From the age of fourteen, he once told an interviewer, 'I felt you should be able to make your own fortune. You should be master of your fate.'

The political skills he first developed were those of the street-fighter. He came to fame as a snarling backbencher, goad or scalpel at the ready for a well-prepared assault on prime ministers Wilson and Callaghan. He made the same weapons available to Margaret

Thatcher, when she was leader of the Opposition and in particular need of allies against an *ancien régime* that took an unconscionable time to recognise its own defeat. Of the many loathsome enemies with which Tebbit's life was surrounded, it would be hard to say which commanded his most unremitting scorn: the hard-left politicians like Tony Benn or Arthur Scargill, whom he considered to be the enemies of the working class; the well-heeled whigs personified by Roy Jenkins, whom he considered to have been the agents of national corruption through their paternity of the permissive society; or the old Conservative establishment, epitomised by Macmillan and Heath, whom he considered to be responsible for keeping the likes of himself out of power. By a narrow margin, the last group probably headed the catalogue of infamy. At any rate, it was as a fierce custodian of the Thatcherite revolution against the treacheries of these people that Tebbit recommended himself as chairman of the party in search of its third election victory.

Unfortunately, that was not the whole story about Tebbit, as the leader knew or would soon find out. Actually she knew most of it already, but she decided to take the gamble partly, it was said, because Norman deserved some reward for having been one of the worst casualties of the Brighton bomb and he saw the chairmanship as fitting this description. But he had not, she thought, been a particularly effective minister, latterly at the Department of Trade and Industry. Administration was not his forte. There were complaints about decisions not being made, and of great testiness with departmental officials, possibly induced by the pain he continued to suffer after Brighton but more likely the product of an insecure, suspicious disposition. She feared that Tebbit would bring more conspiratorial than administrative skills to the Conservative Central Office, and she was not mistaken.

Another odd aspect of the Tebbit appointment was that he was so obviously ambitious for himself, indeed had become by 1984 her most widely touted successor. Her previous chairmen had been too old or too young to pose any threat. To place Tebbit in this seat of party influence was to offer a kind of co-equality with her to a man not noted for his generosity of spirit. And it wasn't long before he began to stake out for himself the role of philosopher, delivering 'lectures' instead of speeches and ruminating from a great height upon the nature of Conservatism, while continuing at the same time to make trouble. A falling-out soon commenced between them. Tebbit was furious not to have been included in the group which decided to approve the bombing of Libya. He began to separate himself, or so she thought, from a number of her priorities and not to supply loyal support in cabinet. At the same time, he rejoiced in his part as the ugly and unacceptable face of Conservatism, when she thought this should be returned to the closet. He kept attacking the BBC, mainly for its coverage of Libya, long after she had earnestly and specifically told him to desist. It was because of his glowering presence, widely thought to be a menace to any Conservative MP defending a marginal seat, that Biffen felt it necessary to call, instead, for the balanced ticket.

Throughout these months of turbulence, which lasted roughly from the end of the miners' strike until the 1986 party conference, Mrs Thatcher reacted in the only way to which she was accustomed. It was hardly subtle, and it took little account of the facts at any given time. Her response, at all times and whatever the evidence to the contrary, was to assert that the momentum was unabated and the radical imperative as powerful as ever. Some people graced this with the tribute of great political cunning. The Thatcher style, they said, was always to talk radical and act conservative. And there remained a long agenda of unenacted radical ideas, especially in the social field. But in this period the rhetoric was so thoroughly at odds with what was going on as to suggest a leader thrashing about for the illusion of control.

To Pym's Centre Forward group she replied that the party could do without such 'fair-weather friends'. 'They would like to slow us down a bit,' she said in May 1985, 'to take stock, even to let a few sleeping dogs lie. "Consolidate," they say. "Forget about radical reform." No, there are still too many tasks to be done.' The party had 'the most constructive collection of long-term policies that I have known in my twenty-five years in Parliament'.[3] Talking to the 1922 Committee a few weeks later, she insisted that 'we will continue to be radical', and asserted: 'I am a more passionate Conservative now than on the day I stepped into No. 10 – and I was pretty passionate then.'[4] She also remained willing to answer expressions of dismay with her own offensive bursts of outrage. 'Stop being moaning minnies,' she instructed voters in North-east England who complained about high unemployment in their part of the world. 'If you want more jobs, you must go out and get more business.'[5]

In March 1986, with the afterglow of Westland still burning, she again showed that attack was the only form of defence she understood. Surveying her Government's past and future, she told an interviewer

that popular capitalism 'has only just got started', and promised that
it would be broadened with far more privatisation of state businesses.
Radical assaults were also promised on housing and education.
Another line reflected a national preoccupation of the moment, which
was not with the third Thatcher term but with something far more
messy on which her view was the opposite of Harold Macmillan's. 'I
do not like coalition governments,' she said, 'and I myself would be
unlikely ever to go into one.'[6] Did she have the 'guts' to sort out the
nation's problems? she inquired of herself when addressing the Scottish Conservatives in May 1986. 'There is only one answer to that:
yes, yes and yes.'

But this sort of bravado was at odds with the legislative performance
of the second term, in which the largest portion of parliamentary time
was devoted to abolishing the Greater London Council and other
metropolitan authorities, and immense reserves of political energy
were expended on the politically unrewarding task of restraining the
expenditure of all the agencies of local government. Privatisation
gathered pace, with the sale of British Telecom in 1984 and British
Gas in 1986. The way had been paved for deregulation in the City of
London, with the so-called Big Bang scheduled for October 1986.
But in this central phase, following the miners' strike, the signs of
palsy extended well beyond the Westland affair.

The most prominent events in the public realm were all essentially
negative. Having promised to refashion university finance, the
Government decided that not even its 140 majority was sufficient to
secure passage of a partial switch from student grants to loans. After
the first murmurings of displeasure from the middle-class heartland
of the Tory Party, which saw one of its perquisites in danger, the policy
was shelved. Elsewhere in education, schools policy was effectively
stultified by two years of militant industrial action by teachers, one
of whose victims was the Secretary of State himself, Sir Keith
Joseph.

In May 1986, Sir Keith departed from the Government, a paradoxical symbol of its highly conditional success. Mrs Thatcher gave him
a warm send-off, correctly observing in their exchange of letters that
'you more than anyone else . . . were the architect who shaped
the policies.' It was a suitably elegiac message. But Joseph went
unlamented by the nation, least of all by the constituency for which he
had been, in a sense, intellectually as well as ministerially responsible –
the world of the intellectuals themselves. If, as we have seen,[7] the
universities and their leading minds were left remarkably untouched

by the revolution that was supposed to have driven from the field every idea which wasn't consistent with Thatcherism, this was Joseph's failure as much as anyone's: a fact which, in his doleful way, he would readily confess, while girding himself to undertake, as a backbencher and later a peer, yet one more journey round the campuses to try and instil into stubborn minds the virtues – no, the axiomatic and irrefutable truths – of free-market capitalism.

Another negative signal came in a social security white paper in December 1985, in which the Government again retreated, this time from its original plan to abolish the state earnings-related pension scheme, or Serps. Under pressure from the Treasury, but also from the obvious losers among future pensioners, Mrs Thatcher abandoned the enthusiasm she had originally showed for abolition. Serps was simply scaled down. Although politically this was another sop to Tory opinion, it added to the impression of a government which lacked direction.[8]

This became still more publicly visible in the least likely territory, which the new Conservatism was thought to have made its own. Two exercises in privatisation were killed off in humiliating circumstances. First, the projected sale of parts of the state motor corporation, BL, to the American company General Motors did not survive its first airing among Conservative MPs. Land-rover, which was on offer alongside BL's trucks division, turned out to be so heavily associated with the Union Jack that its transfer to American ownership became unthinkable. For thirty Tory MPs who voted with Labour on the point, nationalism proved a more potent ideology than privatisation, and so it did for the leader herself. BL remained, for the moment, on the public balance-sheet. So, secondly, did the water supply, which at £7,000 million was one of the richest of all potential offerings to the market, but which also attracted a massive lobby that could see no good reason to remove it from public ownership. On 3 July 1986, Nicholas Ridley, a major theorist of privatisation in the earliest Opposition days, was obliged to announce that water would have to be indefinitely postponed.

This was, in short, an unimpressive and unhappy government. A huge parliamentary majority had not protected it against being driven, time and again, away from its stated objectives. Although Mrs Thatcher was to find personal therapy in the unlikely field of South Africa and the righteous struggle against sanctions, at the time this did not look like enough to restore credibility. The commonest expectation in the autumn of 1986 was that there would not in fact be a third term: that at best the Conservative Party would be faced with what the leader had already ruled out, some form of coalition. That, for example, was the underlying presumption of a conference of well-informed academics which was held at the London School of Economics at that time, whose deliberations were helpfully preserved in a book.[9]

Many of those who took part sympathised with the Thatcher Government. But the context of their discussion was one in which it seemed quite realistic to be contemplating the return of Labour, even if only as a minority government. A theme of the conference was how long Thatcherism would survive Mrs Thatcher. Professor S. E. Finer, for example, a learned political scientist by now almost besotted with admiration for the lady and all she stood for, repeatedly rooted his analysis 'in the event of a Labour victory', or 'if a Labour government is returned'. He comfortingly decided that, even in such an eventuality, Thatcherism would never die. A Labour intermission would be at worst brief, and would be unable to dismantle the pillars of the new orthodoxy. But the question Finer posed reflected an uncertainty which only later came to seem absurd.

This unimposing record, so powerfully at odds with both the size of the Government's majority and the scale of its pretensions, was not, however, what determined Mrs Thatcher's continuing life as prime minister. There were mitigating circumstances, which turned out conclusively to decide the case. Beneath the surface events, an unhappy combination of turbulence and inanition, other more profound realities were steadily at work, which more than made up for the phases of incompetence and petty chicanery. Two, in particular, made progress towards a third term irresistible, and would probably have done so even if the prime minister had been forced to sack half her staff after the Westland peccadilloes, and six other measures had suffered the indignity visited on the Shops Bill.

One was the state of the economy, particularly as felt and perceived by Conservative voters. Slow but steady growth had been registered each year since 1981. Inflation did not rise above 5 per cent at any point during this Parliament. In the four years after the 1983 election, average weekly earnings rose by 14 per cent in real terms. This was an achievement which, by any political standard, would be hard to answer. No government had ever been defeated after presiding over real increases in personal disposable income for two years before an election, and this one had done so for longer. North Sea oil, coming on stream in 1979, had protected the slow expansion, when it at last began, against normal balance of payments problems. One promise the Government delivered as its highest priority was the steady cutting of personal taxation; by 1987 it was three-quarters of the way towards its stated target of a 25 per cent standard rate (from 33 per cent when it came in).

All employed people, therefore, felt better off, even if ministers had made a mess of the rest of their programme. To this beneficence, a triumph any government would be pleased with, were added other material successes. The second Thatcher term coincided with a stock-market boom of unprecedented length. The *Financial Times* index quintupled in value between June 1983 and May 1987.[10] To those that had, much was given. If successful politics consists of furthering the interests of your own supporters, the privatisation programme was another consummate exercise in Conservative vote-winning. 'Overwhelmingly the most important element in making privatisation a positive political success', writes one of its keenest supporters, who also worked in the prime minister's policy unit, 'has been the fundamental step of creating a great interest group in its favour.'[11] Large parts of the programme – all of Gas, most of Telecom – consisted of handing over private monopolies at a favourable price to people who felt in consequence a consuming interest in preserving what they had got. There have been few more obviously potent seductions in the annals of electoral politics.

The material advance of the individual, in fact, had begun to supplant more traditional factors in determining the political verdict. Unemployment did not fall below 3.1 million for the whole of the four years; nor did it fail to be placed at the head of most respondents' list of concerns whenever these were polled in surveys of opinion. But this became an almost meaningless piece of evidence. One of the successes of the Thatcherite enterprise consisted in re-educating the electorate not seriously to care about unemployment. The longer it lasted, the more it was accepted as a seemingly unalterable fact of life. Slowly, and not incorrectly, burgeoning economic success became the headline story, and regions where this was manifest, like South-east England, began to efface from the national mind regions like the North-east where things got much worse. By the time of the election, optimism had replaced pessimism in sample surveys of popular opinion. In spring 1985, according to the Mori poll, pessimists about the economy exceeded optimists by 21 per cent; two years later, the optimists were ahead by 17 per cent.[12]

This was in one way an ambiguous performance. The steady improvement marched in parallel with a steady desertion of old economic nostrums. Thatcherism became, increasingly, pragmatism by another name. Technical monetarism proved to be as elusive and ineffective a tool as most of its critics had argued it was from the beginning. During the second term, the targetry which said that every important index of economic performance should submit to M3, the measure of money supply first made fashionable, was abandoned, its unreality having been exposed well before 1983. Chancellor Lawson formally announced this in October 1985, and despite efforts to isolate new and more reliable monetary measures, the old dogma had lost its power. Fiscal tightness and exchange-rate manipulation became the main weapons, but Tory politicians now looked more like any other politicians, dodging and weaving through the economic thickets rather than handing down prophetic truths from the mountain-top.

This transformation reached its climax in the autumn of 1986, with a sudden shift in the element of policy to which the Government had been most firmly attached, maintaining a curb on public spending. More than £5,000 million of new money was made available above the allotted sums for 1987–8, with the largest share going to education, health and housing. Lawson announced with a straight face that this constituted no change in policy. Since the economy was expanding, the extra money could be spent without imperilling the overall objective, which was to keep the public sector's share of gross domestic product level or lower than before. Originally, the aim had been more ambitious: to cut public spending in real terms. It then evolved more modestly, towards the still-stringent ambition of holding it level in real terms. Growth had certainly supplied the means through which the target could be softened further, satisfying the electoral requirements without palpably abandoning all restraint. All the same, the City was amazed. The chief economist at stockbrokers Phillips & Drew described Lawson's autumn statement as 'incredible, just incredible'.

Nor was the leader herself entirely free of embarrassment. She welcomed the political respite, but still marked the cards of those ministers who had applied the pressure. A new term of abuse entered her vocabulary, 'wet' having passed gently into oblivion. 'He's a spender,' she noted ferociously, running down the list of culprits with one of her intimates. Vengeance was vowed for the third term. She would, she said rather unconvincingly, be determined to get the money back.

Such developments were testimony to a government recovering its political instincts at the moment when these were most needed. What matter that they should depart from the original script? They touched voters where voters have always been most sensitive, and appeared to offer what the propaganda had so long insisted was not available: tax cuts *and* significant increases in spending on the social programmes. And yet it must be doubted whether even this achievement equalled in importance the second subterranean development which, at this crucial juncture, when the professors were preparing for a different result, rendered virtually irrelevant the Government's visible defects.

The reason why, in and out of the Tory Party, there was so little confident belief in the probability of a third term was that the Government spent all of 1985 and most of 1986 out of favour with the voters. The Liberal–SDP Alliance, after first slumping, averaged between 25 and 30 per cent support in the opinion polls, and won significant by-elections. It took Portsmouth South from the Conservatives in June 1984, Brecon and Radnor in July 1985, and Ryedale in May 1986. It was, quite obviously, the gathering-ground for Tory malcontents. Its performance terrified Conservative MPs with seats across a broad swath of the south of England particularly.

Just as significantly, Labour appeared to have recovered some of its credibility. Its new leader was making a reputation as a hard and modern politician. Neil Kinnock personified a socialism released from the geriatric penumbra which surrounded the images of Callaghan and Foot. Although young and totally inexperienced in any context other than the Labour Party, he turned this limitation to advantage by devoting himself in the first place to ridding the party machine of the Militant Tendency and other hard-left elements, a process in which he was much assisted by the Government's own onslaught against the excesses of local authorities. Those whom Kinnock failed to discipline through the cumbersome tribunals of the party, the minister often managed to run out of politics by the imposition of surcharges and other personal penalties for failure to obey new laws that limited spending. To some extent, the Government was doing its bit to make Labour more electable. Despite Kinnock's dismal failure in the Westland debate, the one moment when he might have had his chief antagonist staring into the abyss, his personal standing in fact improved during 1986.

And so it came to pass that during the summer of that year Labour inched past the 40 per cent mark in the polls, and people began to talk more seriously about a return to power – even, if they were especially bold, about an outright Labour victory. A certain professionalism was imparted, for the first time in the party's history, to its handling of public relations and television. There were, it seemed, the makings of an alternative government on the Labour front bench. For a few fleeting summer months, as the Government suffered the consequences of its floundering indecision over BL and unpopular Reaganite sycophancy over Libya, it became slightly more than the sport of fantasists to imagine Chancellor Hattersley rotundly opening his first budget and Foreign Secretary Healey moving, as if to the manner born, through the chancelleries of Europe – although it was never quite so possible to summon prime minister Kinnock into the frame.

There was an inherent flaw in this picture, as any psephologist could explain. The fact that there were still two opposition groupings was always going to work to the Government's advantage. Given the British voting system, as had already been shown quite clearly in 1983, even a diminished popular vote for Conservatism could return a Conservative government with an impregnable majority. The disappearance of the old two-party politics, on which every important feature of the parliamentary and electoral systems was based, meant that all evidence of voting intention was far more suspect than it used to be.

Nonetheless, the very uncertainty which this created appeared to redound to the Government's disadvantage more than anyone else's. That was the political perception, which only goes to show how little politics has in common with logic, still less with mathematical probability. Once again the books on minority government and coalitions and every other permutation to delight a student of political science were taken off the shelves and dusted down. Learned disquisitions on the royal prerogative, and the rights and wrongs of dissolving a hung Parliament, appeared from the same academic hands in the same newspapers as they had in 1983. The country was being prepared for a period of post-electoral turmoil in which, were it to come about, the only fixed feature would in all probability be the departure of the prime minister into exile in Dulwich, in a large, charmless modern house which she and her husband had bought as a retirement home on a private estate. As the meaning was examined of each new decimal point in the opinion poll returns, especially of the volatile and alarming Alliance vote, the illusion gained ground that there was an anti-Thatcher majority in the country which only needed to calibrate its vote correctly as between the different opposition parties in the appropriate constituencies for the Government to be swept from power.

This illusion was destroyed quite slowly. In some minds, particularly those of the most prominent players on each side, it persisted in some form until the election took place in June 1987. Uncertainty makes desperadoes of political leaders, whether they stand to win or lose. But the fact is that the opposition parties themselves, after the briefly thrilling vistas of spring and summer 1986, became the principal agents of their own undoing. It did not require the stubborn equations of three-sided politics to destroy their chances. They did the job themselves, long before the computers needed to be pressed into service.

The more spectacular act of suicide was performed by the Alliance. The marriage between the Liberals and the Social Democrats had never been particularly easy, but on the whole convenience had triumphed over the absence of love. The seats had been fairly distributed between them, and the relationship between their prickly leaders, David Steel for the Liberals and David Owen for the SDP, evolved into something like pragmatic compromise. One issue, however, still divided them, and this was to expose the Alliance's weakness to catastrophic effect. They could not fully agree about defence policy. Owen, having left the Labour Party partly because of its opposition to the British nuclear weapon, could not countenance an Alliance policy which showed any sign of softness on this point. Steel, although more malleable than Owen, headed a party with a large unilateralist element and a still larger body of members who saw Owen's self-righteous nuclear attitudes as indistinguishable from those of Mrs Thatcher, and on that account if no other were determined not to be worsted by him. Although a compromise was stitched together which satisfied the leaders, a single disorganised vote at the Liberal Assembly in September was enough to pick it apart. It not only showed the parties to be inherently split, it showed the leaders to be incapable of effective leadership: a depressing and ultimately fatal combination which plunged the Alliance from just above the threshold of credibility into the chasm from which even a national vote as large as 25 per cent would not be able to rescue it.

Labour's slide from grace was less spectacular. But it was apparent well before Christmas that during the summer it had flattered only to deceive. Its conference did not go badly. Kinnock's control of the machine concentrated the collective mind. But Labour, too, was inherently divided, as everyone knew, and as ongoing skirmishes in the outposts of city militancy continued to remind the world. And Kinnock's iron hand did not extend to the control of his own best interests in the House of Commons. Rarely an effective obstacle to the juggernaut of fact and argument with which Mrs Thatcher protected herself at the despatch-box, he now committed a blunder which seemed to have an effect out of all proportion to its importance.

It was a small point, but government strategists, reflecting afterwards on how the transition was made from anticipated disaster to unchallengeable triumph, identified it as the moment when Mrs Thatcher re-established herself beyond doubt as the only person fit to lead the country. The issue dominating the headlines in late 1986 was already one which signally failed to strike terror into the prophets of Tory populism: the interminable story of the British Government's efforts to prevent the publication of *Spycatcher* in Australia.[13] Nobody, as ministers crowed, was interested in news from the Australian court-room, deeply though it fascinated the media and the Labour Party. Kinnock, for decent motives but perhaps to unwisely wasteful effect, gave the case much attention in Parliament, hoping to tar the prime minister as an authoritarian manipulator of the law and an enemy of free publication.

Whatever Kinnock's intentions, he became the most specific political victim of the *Spycatcher* affair. Mrs Thatcher remained immune: preserved by the traditional indifference of British voters to free-speech questions. But Kinnock was found to have been consorting with the enemy. It emerged that he had been collecting some of his parliamentary ammunition on the telephone line, from the Australian lawyer acting against the British Government. Could treason have gone further? Very probably. This offence was minor in scale. But it was substantial in its folly. It seemed to confirm the worst suspicions about this youthful leader, that he was naïve as well as inexperienced, a man who simply lacked the weight for the job for which he presumed to offer himself.

In its way it was a replica of what happened to the Liberal–SDP Alliance. Each grouping was revealed as somehow devoid of the necessary seriousness. No doubt these errors were symptoms of a deeper malaise, and would not have happened to parties that were inherently stronger. But they were enough to set at nothing the errors of the Government: errors for which, in a different conjunction of politics, it would have been made to pay a heavy price. The various oppositions were in disarray well before the election began. And besides, they were about to be exposed to most convincing proof of one truth about the modern Conservative Party: that although it might not always run the Government as well as it might wish, it had no equal in the business of running and winning general elections.

The 1987 election campaign, which was in preparation for more than a year, epitomised in a number of ways some of the salient characteristics to be seen at work in the Thatcher Government during its first and second terms. It was not a smooth campaign, but was marked throughout by destructive episodes of personal rivalry and disagreement. Nor was it the campaign of a prime minister who at any stage rested securely on her laurels. It paid, as she invariably did, close attention to the instructions of people other than politicians, notably the self-proclaimed wizards of marketing and advertising. It enlisted the unfailing support of newspapers which had spent more than a decade giving a higher priority to political commitment than to journalistic detachment. It demanded the acquiescence of television in many of the manipulations which politicians have become more successful at deploying than the broadcasters have at resisting. It used, to brilliant effect, every advantage a government has in manoeuvring economic indicators into the closest alignment with electoral requirements.

It will serve, in short, as a model of the political style – both the vices and the virtues of the ruthless crusading leader who knew she was right and had a supreme duty to remain in power – by which Margaret Thatcher lived and was sometimes wishfully expected to die.

The work began in April 1986, with a terrible row. On 13 April – as it happened the day before the Libyan bombing, when the leader's nerves were already fragile – chairman Tebbit wheeled into her drawing room at Chequers some researchers who worked for Saatchis, who had been assessing the Government's standing with the voters. As it happened, I had been invited for a private conversation with her a few days before and noted for the first time that I was in the presence of a tired and distracted woman. Upon this temporarily debilitated figure the Saatchi presentation was not calculated to have a therapeutic effect.

What the researchers had found, they said, was that while public attitudes to the issues had not changed much since the Tories were returned in 1983, the public's opinion of the Government was markedly lower. It was seen as having lost its sense of direction and, moreover, to be excessively 'harsh' and 'uncaring'. What this came down to, as the Saatchi people imprudently made clear, was not so much a problem for Conservatism as for the leader of the Conservative Party. It appeared that she had lost the advantage of being thought purposeful without gaining any new credit for compassion or understanding. Put brutally in a nutshell, while Thatcherism might not be a problem, Mrs Thatcher was.

This was an unappetising dish to set before the queen. But it had, as she saw it, a more sinister aspect. It came with the endorsement of the Conservative Central Office. It seemed to be Tebbit himself who was explaining to her that she might no longer be the political asset she thought she was. She was so enraged by this that not only was it added to an already growing charge-sheet against the chairman, but she decided to call in some rival research from a different advertising agency, Young & Rubicam. This, while also discovering reasons for anxiety, especially in respect of the Tory appeal to those who cared about the less privileged sections of society, restored the leader to a more acceptable place. Young & Rubicam, unlike Saatchi & Saatchi, found that Mrs Thatcher was an asset not a liability: with the strange result that, for the rest of the pre-election period, while the party retained one set of marketing advisers, the prime minister retained another. As a sub-plot to the campaign there ensued a battle between advertising agencies. For a time, indeed, the central burning issue of 1987 Conservatism appeared to revolve around which of these two was the superior. And there was a taint of something unseemly about this contest. A lot of it, in the end, was about who could claim the credit, and who, therefore, make a fortune for one agency or another on the back of the Conservative Party. A fine example of Thatcherite entrepreneurship, perhaps: but one which, as different ministers backing different agencies jostled for position in the last days before the victory, presented a bizarre and unsavoury spectacle.

The early process, however, did yield one result. A species of collective leadership was put in place, to pre-empt Tebbit's dark intrigues. The leader appointed six ministers to form a campaign committee and supervise an election manifesto. This bore its first fruit at the party conference, which was a highly successful fusing of political and marketing skills. It was, in fact, a turning-point. Ministers, Tebbit included, could look back on it as a little triumph of political creativity, which began to transform the public impression of undirected inertia into one of constructive renewal. Saatchis had delivered the original message, that the Government was perceived as backward looking. Saatchis staged the show. Saatchis helped write the ministers' speeches, ensuring that each contained sufficient new promises to make good the conference theme, which Saatchis had also thought up: The Next Move Forward. The Saatchi hand lay behind the publicity drive to ensure maximum attention to the good news with which the party was now coming forward. A Saatchi officer – the deputy chairman, no less – had been appointed, under an oddly military appellation, as chief of staff to the chairman of the party.[14]

Of these tasks, perhaps the most straightforward was publicity. Mrs Thatcher had always had a good press. It was a feature, interrupted only once, of her entire prime ministership, and a blessing which no other British leader in the era of modern communications had enjoyed to the same extent. The only time when the vultures looked as though they were beginning to circle was at the climax of the Westland affair. To the beleaguered inhabitants of 10 Downing Street it seemed at that time as though even the *Daily Mail* was positioning itself for the kill. But even they conceded that their great adventure was accompanied for the most part by reliable cheerleaders. Bernard Ingham would read the press occasional lectures for its inattention to what he regarded as the facts or its regrettable intrusion into the private lives of public people. But he knew as well as anyone that the Thatcher era coincided with a broad retreat from the days when newspapers considered it a primary duty to make life difficult for those in power. Too much was at stake, or so some editors and proprietors seemed to believe, for anyone to interfere with the heroic task Mrs Thatcher had set herself, the regeneration of Britain.

A minister who once drew her into a discussion of the press, and remarked how favourable it had been, told me of her reaction. She showed a guileless lack of surprise. 'That's because I've been so kind to them,' she remarked. And this was undoubtedly the case. In the first term she offered knighthoods to the editors of the *Sun*, the *Sunday Express* and the *Daily Mail*.[15] More to the point, they accepted the accolade, apparently seeing no conflict between their credibility as editors and their acceptance of honours from the government of the day. Nor, in a sense, was there such a conflict, since they had long ago pledged their loyalty to a prime minister whom two of them, at least, appeared to hold in positively idolatrous regard.

So the drive for the third term was unlikely to be impeded by the tabloid press. Television, on the face of it, was more of a problem. Television did not have owners who could be cultivated, or editors who resembled in any way the editor of the *Sunday Express*. All television stations, moreover, were under a statutory obligation to maintain fairness and balance in their output. They were debarred from editorialising.

From the Conservative point of view, this was only the beginning of the difficulty, especially as regards the BBC. The most prominent among Tory voices did not conceal their belief that, under cover of a theoretical impartiality, the producers and editors of the major BBC news and current affairs programmes were persons of left-wing inclination, and in some cases out-and-out Marxists. No serious research was known to have been done before these sweeping denunciations were levelled. They were simply a convenient smear, privately circulated by such influential figures as the prime minister's husband and publicly canvassed by the more raucous among Tory backbenchers, not to mention Norman Tebbit's personal staff.[16]

With television, therefore, the Conservative tactic was more belligerent than with the press. Television, too, received its carrots. The principal political interviewers on BBC Television and Independent Television News were offered, and accepted, knighthoods.[17] But sticks were more in evidence. Attacking television programmes that offended government sensibilities, while not the exclusive propensity of this Government, was one which it indulged with a growing ruthlessness. Mrs Thatcher's direct criticisms may have been relatively infrequent, but there was an undertow of impatience when television failed to see its role as being precisely concordant with government policy, or lapsed from its duties in the ideological struggle. 'If the television of the Western world uses its freedom continually to show all that is worst in our society,' she said after the inner-city riots of 1981, 'while the centrally controlled television of the communist world and the dictatorships show only what is judged advantageous to them and suppress everything else – how are the uncommitted to judge between us?'[18] Falklands coverage had produced some famous Tory denunciations. Over Ireland, there were similar episodes of interference after, or sometimes before, 'unhelpful' programmes were screened. Over the Libyan bombing, Tebbit even went so far as to compile a detailed dossier of the BBC's alleged journalistic shortcomings.

What this amounted to was a form of intimidation, of a kind to which broadcasters were quite well accustomed, but accompanied on this occasion by the kind of action at the BBC which would in previous eras have been unthinkable. A new chairman was appointed and, within months, he had sacked the director-general. Early in 1987, the most important television strategist in the Thatcher circle gave me his assessment of the different news organisations which the election managers were preparing to do business with. ITN, he reckoned, was entirely 'sound'. The right people were in the key positions and were known to be sympathetic to the Government's problems. Channel Four News was entirely unsound, but since it was watched by a minority audience this deficiency did not matter. The BBC was the problem, he went on. Nobody could be sure who exactly was in charge there: to whom the complaints should be made and the pressure applied.

Quite soon, however, this problem too was solved, with a reorganisation of BBC personnel. But that wasn't perhaps the crucial factor. The steady drip of the Conservative attack had worked its effect on the self-confidence of the broadcasters. The new priority, unspoken and often unacknowledged even privately, was the avoidance of rows of the kind that Tebbit, in particular, had shown himself cynically adept at orchestrating. By the time the campaign looked all but certain to culminate in a June election, and not to be delayed any further, most of the important television coverage could be accounted 'sound'.

Before the date was finally selected, two more events were slotted into their proper place. There had to be a budget, and it had to be calculated for its political effect. The Chancellor had got himself into the position of being able to deliver a popular yet not apparently reckless package, which he duly achieved. Income tax was cut by 2p, and the duty on cigarettes and alcohol, which would normally have gone up, was held level for a year: a classic, give-away budget, which he was able to combine with a miraculous congruence of good news about unemployment coming down and the public sector deficit being within sight of zero. 'Our prospects are better than they've been for a generation,' Lawson told the nation on budget night.

Just as important as this, to the total effect of a leader sweeping irresistibly towards a third term, was Mrs Thatcher's final foreign journey. It was replete with irony, but also with triumph. For the first time, a British general election was launched from the steppes of the Soviet Union. The Iron Lady had come to this. Instead of denouncing the bear, she would travel to embrace him, proving thereby that she was a figure of truly global import.

The visit to renew acquaintance with General Secretary Gorbachev had been long planned, and it began with some criticism if not denunciation. On her way to Moscow, on 29 March, she reiterated her sincerely felt line about human rights, which had been the emotional origin of the speech that led to the invention of the 'Iron Lady' more than a decade before. But she linked it to present priorities which, after the Reykjavik summit, were all for agreement not discord. 'If a country persists in putting people in prison for their religious and political views,' she said, 'that's something you've got to take into account when you are gauging whether they are going to keep any agreements you make on arms control.'

This was not received with enthusiasm by the Soviet press. And in their public speeches, Gorbachev and his visitor made clear their disagreements. Gorbachev expressed incomprehension at Mrs Thatcher's constant desire 'to heap praise on nuclear arms'. She insisted on nuclear security. But these public statements were not important. What mattered were the private encounters, from which the British prime minister emerged, according to one of her staff, with the considered opinion that she had become 'the West's greatest living expert on Mr Gorbachev'.

What had begun in London in December 1984 was now continued with greater intensity. Of all her foreign visits, she told the travelling press, it was the one for which she had made the most thorough preparation. She was ready for a long dialogue, and she got it. The two leaders spent more than eleven hours together, in the company only of a note-taker and interpreter each. Their sessions began with an eighty-minute monologue by Gorbachev, in which, without referring to any text or papers, he described the condition of the Soviet Union and the scale of the problem he was up against. She thought it an extraordinary *tour de force*, in which he showed absolute mastery of facts and figures without losing control of the wider thrust of what he was trying to convey. Dinners were missed and appointments delayed as these two politicians, basking together in a shared sense of their powerful forensic qualities and acknowledging – however uneven the comparison – that each was engaged in grappling with deeply conservative countries, pursued a private argument they both greatly enjoyed.

But this, in a sense, was the lesser part of the enterprise. For as well as treating with Gorbachev, Mrs Thatcher met the Russian

people – on television and every evening. She took advantage of the
new Soviet appetite for Western contact not only to say her piece
about the release of dissidents but to move among the populace, who
received her exultantly. She went to the monastery at Zagorsk and lit
a candle. She was mobbed by crowds in Georgia and kissed by
a handsome young fellow, a gesture never known to have been
undertaken by a British voter, impulsively or otherwise. She gave a
television interview to three star Soviet commentators and hammered
them into the ground with such style that, when I visited Moscow
nine months later, her performance was still the subject of pleasurable
comment. When a British radio reporter asked her if her visit was
political, her response was contemptuous. 'Broaden your view,' she
said. 'I am on an historic mission representing my country.'

All the same, the reporter was not wrong. The greater the aura of
history that could be wrapped around it, the more successful the visit
would be judged as a political event. Bernard Ingham judged it very
successful indeed: the most successful such happening he had been
associated with for many years, he told reporters on the plane home.

It could not have been more beautifully timed. When the election
was called, on 11 May, the barrenness and misfortune which largely
dominated both 1985 and 1986 had been almost erased from the
national mind. In their place were the facts of the budget and the
images of an international leader now equipped, or so it seemed,
with an almost regal presence. Nor were these advantages bogus or
undeserved. There could not have been a give-away budget if a
certain underlying economic strength had not been produced by eight
years of Conservative economic management. And the Soviet visit
could not have succeeded if the prime minister had not proved herself,
for a variety of reasons, a worthy interlocutor for Mr Gorbachev.
Both these electoral bonuses were available more because of good
management than good luck. Yet what was still worth remarking
was the sheer elan with which they were managed, and the power
they had to wipe out the recent past.

When the campaign proper began, the opinion polls showed the
Conservatives at 43 per cent, Labour at 29 per cent, the SDP–Liberal
Alliance at 26 per cent. When it was over, the Conservatives secured
42.3 per cent of the vote, Labour 30.8 per cent and the Alliance 22.6
per cent, with the remainder distributed among fringe parties. The
campaign, therefore, would appear to have changed almost nothing.
The Conservatives were firmly positioned to win by a handy margin
from start to finish. Their standing shifted extraordinarily little from

the first day to the last, and showed them at all times to be the certain beneficiaries from the three-party split. And yet, before the issue was finally settled, there remained one more contest to be played out: one more set of disputants for this leader to master. Having begun her years in a permanent state of struggle with the left of the party, she now had to deal with an unpalatable threat from the other flank. Seeing this election as her climactic vindication, she faced the bizarre possibility that others were trying somehow to take it away from her.

The problem went back to her dawning discovery a year earlier of what her former friend, Mr Tebbit, thought he was doing with the party chairmanship. She began to understand that he saw the position not simply as one which made him the leader's principal agent but as a power-base of his own from which, to some extent, the leader might be excluded. Although Tebbit was entirely interested in winning the election, he appeared to her and her people to be somewhat less thoroughly committed to the idea that she, and she above all, should be seen as the victor. In Cecil Parkinson's day, for example, the chairman took personal command of the leader's election schedule, working out in meticulous detail how to deploy the party's greatest asset. Tebbit was not involving himself in that work. In Cecil's day also, the leader had a chairman who would hold her hand and soothe her brow and generally reassure her of his utter dedication to her triumph. Cecil, along with Tim Bell and Gordon Reece, was part of the old familiar team she liked to have around her. But Bell had now left Saatchis, and Reece had not found favour with Tebbit, and Parkinson was in purgatorial exile: and in their place was a man whom Mrs Thatcher would not now have trusted to hold her hand, even had he shown an inclination to do so.

She dealt with this predicament by setting up another field of tension. Alongside Tebbit she inserted, as a personal aide-de-camp and general factotum for the campaign, another of her favourites. David Young was one of her most glittering discoveries. A property millionaire, originally without strong political commitment, he was that rare breed in British public life, a businessman who succeeded in politics without ever having had a political formation.

Under the Thatcher Government, his rise was fast and steady, and was based originally on the development of a wide range of personal contacts. He made himself useful to a variety of ministers: first to Joseph in the revisionist Centre for Policy Studies, then to Prior at the Department of Employment, to Joseph again at Industry, and to other middle-ranking ministers such as Lawson and Brittan. Young was a contact man, but also a man of action. He teemed with ideas, especially in the area of training and employment, which qualified him for appointment in 1982 as chairman of the Tories' main operating body in that field, the Manpower Services Commission, with a budget of £2,000 million a year. Here he proved to be, among other things, an unusually competent salesman for the massive schemes with which government sought to wipe away, sometimes at an administrative stroke, the futile miseries of unemployment. There was a kind of inevitability about his transfer, in 1984, from this quango to the supreme quango itself, the House of Lords, with a seat in the cabinet. There, as Employment Secretary, he often irritated his colleagues by the enthusiasm with which he, an unelected politician, took to manoeuvring and politicking against and around and behind those like themselves who had spent half a lifetime struggling to reach their present eminence. But the leader was pleased with him. She placed a motto on his escutcheon which nobody was allowed to forget. 'Other people bring me problems,' she once supposedly said, 'but David brings me solutions.'

Young never entirely lost the businessman's approach to politics, the tendency to surrender on all occasions to the logic of the bottom line. When, later, he was pressing hard to take over from Tebbit as chairman of the party while retaining his place as a departmental minister, he remarked that since the Conservative Party turned over only £5 million a year it was only worth one day a week of anyone's time, so why couldn't he have both jobs? But now the solution he was required to find was a way of filling the gaps left by Tebbit in the leader's arrangements, perhaps even in her psyche.

Aware that Tebbit was seeking to exclude her from the front line of campaigning, she took her own measures to finesse the opinion, which was not, it must be said, confined to Tebbit but reached even as far as the devoted Whitelaw, that she was a negative factor in the Conservative appeal. At an early stage she boldly announced that, far from seeking election for only a year or two more, she would 'go on and on' as leader: a vision which struck terror into the hearts of some Conservative candidates and was quite widely accounted a clumsy mistake, but which showed them and the world at large and not least herself that there would be no trace of ambiguity about the meaning of the voters' verdict. For her there was one ghost to exorcise: the apparition, which was present before, during and after the 1983 election, of the Falklands war. She was determined to prove once and for all that that election, and the permanence of her sort of

Conservatism which it seemed to establish, was not due to the adventitious circumstance of a battle bizarrely won. The way to do this was to win the 1987 election, and to do so with Britannia herself, now in civilian clothes, leading from the front.

For one brief moment, she seems to have thought this might not happen. The episode recalls the blind panic to which politicians are heir when the stakes are high, as they always are at an election. One week before polling day, the leadership experienced the crazy apprehension that everything was going wrong. She was finally obliged to wrench control of the last days out of the hands of Tebbit and Saatchis and the rest of the gang, and return it to those of her old familiars who were waiting in the wings. Tim Bell wrote some new advertisements, and the party spent £2 million in a week blanketing them through the press, and all concerned believed they had by this stratagem snatched victory from the jaws of disaster.[19]

What they did not believe, in other words, was that Britain had yet become incontestably Margaret Thatcher's country. Notwithstanding the divided opposition, and the congruence of the economic figures, and the message of the polls, and the sympathetic disposition of a hundred other omens, they – the leader included – were capable of behaving like all-time losers, who were not confident that they had really captured the kingdom. They had talked a thousand times about there being no alternative to the Conservative way of doing things. They detested Labour, scorned the Alliance, considered that no sane voter, and certainly no sane majority, could support them. But somewhere in their minds they were still uneasily conscious that theirs was still a contingent revolution, and their leader one who continued to be on probation. And they were not entirely mistaken. It was only when the votes were in and a parliamentary majority of 102 was counted that she could know she had changed the course of history.

22

An Era in Place

POLITICAL HISTORY HAS always been a prey to false dawns, and to eras artificially defined as having ended. It is as if the historian, still more the journalist, absorbs the politician's own inexhaustible supply of that kind of language. The politician needs to believe, or perhaps assumes the voters need to believe, that the events in which he is taking part belong to a sequence which is nearing its heroic and predestined completion; or, alternatively, that what he promises for the future will wipe away the present and the past before shaping something wholly new in the affairs of men. The language of blurred continuity, which of course describes the real life of the average citizen, is anathema to the political leader. But the chronicler, for his part, should struggle in the cause of truth to hang on to it, particularly when the eponymous figure from which the era in question draws its name has not departed the scene.

All the same, it would be a violation of the truth to deny that the 1987 election marked a decisive moment in British politics. It did not end the Thatcher era but did something rather more telling. It locked the Thatcher era into place, as a phase in Britain's political evolution of which the end was not in sight. Until the election, as we have seen, this wasn't the case. However unmenacing the other parties appeared to most disinterested spectators, the opposition which mattered, the one located inside her own party, bulked large in the leader's imagination, and in their own, and therefore in politics generally. The third victory transformed this utterly. It removed from the battlefield a force which the commander had had to take account of, in variable measure, throughout the previous eight years: the old pre-Thatcher paternalists and what they stood for and (which was the important point) what she feared they might still be able to articulate and mobilise in the parliamentary party.

Their careers reached different sorts of destination. The largest number shuffled off into the House of Lords. All former cabinet ministers save one, including those who had most tormented her, received a peerage on leaving the Commons. The exception, rather oddly, was Nott, the former defence minister and apostate monetarist, who evidently made such a particular fuss about which brand of knighthood, out of the cornucopia of titles available in the honours system, he would accept on leaving office in 1983 that further preferment was for the moment withheld. For the rest, Lord Prior, Lord Pym, Lord St John and the others had to content themselves with making occasional cautionary noises, of no political significance, from the museum of extinct volcanoes.

Others of their company essayed a more adventurous course, but came to look the more pitiable as a result. Sir Ian Gilmour, the earliest and most eloquent dissenter from monetarist economics, decided to stand again for Parliament in the hope that the Conservatives would not secure a majority. In that event, people like Gilmour would have had a lot to say. So would Edward Heath. Heath's calculation was less refined than Gilmour's. He would have felt it his duty to stand whatever the likely result, simply because it came to his attention that the Thatcher people were putting it about that he would not.

However, these turned out to be futile gestures, as the wry Gilmour would have been the first to understand. Heath was unabashed. He continued to erupt at unpredictable intervals, his scorn for every major policy the Government undertook reaching a new pitch of virulence. To these customary fulminations he now added abrupt public assessments, available to anyone with a microphone, of any minister who hove into the headlines. When the Department of Health and Social Security was judged to be too large for a single minister, and was therefore split in two in July 1988, the former leader remarked that it required 'a man of talent and decision-making capability' to run a great department, and 'they have all been sacked or they are not there.' When Leon Brittan was appointed Britain's senior European Commissioner in Brussels, Heath called him 'a discredited minister', and the circumstances of his appointment 'a disgrace and a public scandal'. But nobody any longer cared what Heath had to say. The fate he brought on himself was to be patronised and insulted from his own backbenches, by estate agents and car salesmen who were still at school when he was prime minister.

A different, and mildly more disturbing, voice was Biffen's. After 1987 Biffen played the identical role Pym had played after 1983. He was made the scapegoat for victory, his dismissal long anticipated by the Downing Street information machine for no better reason than that he took an independent, even though fundamentally supportive, line. Within a month of the election, Biffen impudently announced his intention of 'not making life easy' for the prime minister, and gave an indication of his state of mind by calling her views on education 'dotty' and attacking the 'Stalinist regime' which she imposed on cabinet discussion. He continued to make some well-judged interventions, which carried the more credence since they came from a genuine economic conservative and commanded the more space because of the amusing elegance with which they were often put. But Biffen had no troops. Nobody had any troops. Although Tebbit, too, lurked, having decided by mutual agreement to take lucrative retirement into the private sector, he became a man of no consequence. All the troops had deserted to the winning side, whose leader they could now be relied on obediently to follow.

A simultaneous effect of victory was the release of a lot of pent-up radical inhibitions. Just as the old and sometimes unreliable soldiers were pensioned off, the newer ones, also unreliable in their day, came to understand without equivocation that they must fall into line or perish. In the difficult months of 1986, men like Douglas Hurd and Kenneth Baker used to talk with great confidence about the resurgence of their kind of Conservatism. They were sure that one of the consequences of Westland and Libya and Tebbit's unlooked-for machinations, and the general deterioration of 'presidential' government, would be the ascendancy of consolidators like themselves, who would now exert a collective influence in the cabinet to draw the party back towards more traditional paths. But the election set that at nothing. It was a victory for the radical they had thought discredited. And they had no alternative but to become its vehicles. Being realists, they did not seek one, or imagine for a moment that there would now ensue anything resembling the struggles of the early 1980s.

The programme on which they fought was itself quite full of radical energy. The Saatchis had got the point. The danger which any third-term government faced was a loss of momentum, and the Next Move Forward had to be converted into plural Moves across many fields of policy. But this was no ordinary third term. It followed a second term which, as everyone knew, never had a coherent shape and in the course of time lost such distinctive features as it was supposed to have. Nobody knew this better than the leader. For her, therefore, the victory was the signal to re-ignite the radical machine. It released her personal psychic restraints. 'She had nothing left to prove,' one of her more reflective intimates told me a few months later. 'She now thinks about the future records she can break if she wants to, the longest-serving this and the most experienced that.' But it also meant that policies could be advanced, at last, with an often reckless disdain for the critics, wherever they were located.

The keynotes were energy, drive and the exertion of political will. A new charter for education was in preparation, under Baker's hand, before the election. The thrust of it was to revolutionise a schools system which had been in place for more than forty years, with the twin purposes of seizing central control over classroom curricula – a continental practice hitherto frowned on by the British – and giving schools the chance to remove themselves entirely from local government control. This was a massive reform, chaotically in embryo when the election was called and still far from worked out when the Bill was drafted. It was quite apparent that the leader and her Education Secretary had different ideas about how it should work, and electoral discussion did not clarify the mandate the voters were being asked to endorse. But the Bill would indisputably constitute action on a major scale, addressed to a branch of social policy widely seen to be defective. When it came to Parliament, Baker continued to make policy on the run. The universities were added to the reformer's list, and attended to with triumphant disregard for prissy objections to an assault on their domain. Hundreds of amendments, most of them the minister's own, were introduced during the parliamentary passage, and the universities, if not the schools, thought they had eventually secured important territory against the march of the Visigoths. But as a demonstration of the radical imperative – action before words, decision before debate, the presumption of guilt exceeding all possibility of innocence in the previous way of doing things – the Education Reform Act 1988 had few equals in the first Thatcher term and none in the second.

Similarly, the privatisation programme was now extended into the most sensitive areas. Earlier anxieties were banished and the monopoly utilities prepared for market. One of the reasons why the arch-privatiser Ridley had failed to sell off the water supply in 1986 was the volume of objection from customers, from the managers of regional water companies, and from environmental interests. He reorganised his plan to meet some of the objections of the last group. But what was more noticeable after 1987 was the collapse of resistance elsewhere. Although there was much reason to doubt the merit of creating a private monopoly in the most basic essential of life, a meek subservience characterised most of the public and industrial reaction. Electricity was open to similar anxieties. Cecil Parkinson, rehabilitated at last as Secretary of State for Energy, was put in charge of selling it off and spent a long time devising a scheme designed not to be monopolistic. But this scheme seemed far from fool-proof, and the first experience of all consumers was a whacking increase in charges. Again, however, a kind of dispirited acquiescence, enlivened by the prospect of buying some under-priced shares in a business that couldn't fail, was the commonest response. There was now nothing in the productive part of the public sector which it was impossible to imagine being sold off.

Next, a new form of local taxation, the community charge, was brought forward for enactment. Otherwise known as the poll tax, this was stripped of most of its defences when first canvassed in a green paper. Critics in and out of the Conservative Party found it to be regressive, unjust, administratively expensive, hard to collect and menacing in its implications for civil liberty; and on most of these counts inferior to the existing property tax, the rates. But the rates had their disadvantages, as had long been agreed by all parties. As long ago as 1974, Margaret Thatcher had personally pledged herself and her party to abolish them. What was different, thirteen years later, was the presence in power of a leader whose will to override difficulties was more potent than the logic which made those difficulties real. This was one issue on which the Conservative backbenches, sensitive to intense local feeling in their constituencies, did produce a small rebellion. It was seen off with contemptuous ease, many of its early supporters scuttling for cover when they contemplated the trade-off between pleasing marginal constituents and not displeasing the person who exerted absolute control over their political careers.

The Shops Act, which foundered on massive Tory opposition in April 1986, was prepared for another run. Housing reforms which would further fragment the power of local authorities were readied for passage. The review of social security, which had eventually concluded without the abolition of the state earnings-related pension scheme, made itself felt in the lives of many more people at the lower end of society than had previously experienced the bite of Thatcherism. In April 1988, a million people who had until then received housing benefit were deprived of it on account of the fact that their lifetime's savings amounted to £8,000 or more. Grants to the very poor for one-off necessities they couldn't afford were replaced by a Social Fund oriented towards loans rather than grants. At the furthest perimeter of society, the squeeze was now discernibly applied against a disease long identified in Thatcherite rhetoric as the 'dependency culture', but hitherto thought too dangerous to try and cure by deprivation. Fear and dislike of the dependency culture jockeyed, until 1988, with remnants of a belief in post-war notions of social justice and progressive taxation. The 1988 budget supplied a definitive resolution of this contest, when the top rate of tax was cut to 40 per cent, with the Chancellor arguing (plausibly) that a lower top rate would produce a larger haul from the highest earners but overriding (symptomatically) the view which said, and had said for so long, that perceived fairness as between citizens was a no less important consideration. This view was now described not as the politics of justice but as the politics of envy. It thereby conveniently attached to itself the moral obloquy, not merely the practical weakness, in which Thatcherism usually liked to vest the targets of its attack.

To this record of rampant triumphalism there were one or two exceptions. The most notable concerned the National Health Service. Thatcherite ultras had long been examining methods of applying market economics to this element of the welfare state, or at least reducing the range of health services which remained free to all at the point of use. It was probably the subject of more studies in the think tanks of Conservatism in the later 1980s than any other issue. The prime minister and her colleagues had already pressed hard on hospitals to enter the market-place at least to the extent of contracting out the non-medical services. But the transition from a free health service to an insurance-based alternative, although contemplated in DHSS studies as early as 1980, was no nearer acceptance in 1988. The NHS was one pillar of post-war creation which proved unamenable to the grand assumption that almost any of the constructs of that era could be dismantled with impunity. By autumn 1988, indeed, the Government's proudest boast, based upon its sensitive apprehension of public opinion, was that it was now in a position to pour more than £2,000 million of new money into the public health service.

Nor did the beginning of this term show that it would necessarily be free of the wrangles and highly personal public rows which were already an established consequence of the prime minister's style of doing business. One which came to the surface within a year of the election had a claim to be listed among the most unusual in a nine-year catalogue.

In March 1988, Mrs Thatcher fell out publicly with the Chancellor of the Exchequer in a way for which there was no precedent, unless it was the row between Macmillan and Peter Thorneycroft thirty years before. But Thorneycroft ended that one by resigning, over public expenditure. In the present case, Chancellor Lawson was operating an exchange-rate policy according to one strategy when it was casually knocked aside by the prime minister's personal insistence on another. For months, sterling was informally pegged to the Deutschmark; in this way Britain was able to adopt an exchange-rate target without the need to admit it, and without the political inconvenience of joining the exchange-rate mechanism of the European Monetary System. For reasons essentially rooted in her attitude to national sovereignty, Mrs Thatcher always resisted pressure to join the EMS. It was one of her more completely personal contributions to British foreign policy. But Lawson had come round to believing in managed exchange-rates and was, in practice, managing sterling. With evident insouciance, and giving some people the incorrect impression that she didn't know what she was doing, the prime minister repudiated this in a single parliamentary answer one day in March 1988. The ensuing relations between the two of them were for a time as frosty as any between the early Thatcher and the early Prior, the temperature cooled rather than warmed by the fact that these people were meant to be friends: joint architects, indeed, of the economic miracle which had returned the Tories for the third time.

In normal times – times, that is, of some political uncertainty, with government experiencing the odd fugitive breeze of trepidation about the future – this epic argument would have shaken Westminster as much as it bewildered all whose business depended on the future of sterling. But it did not. To that extent, the political system had reached a kind of impasse; or perhaps, depending on your point of view, a state of perfect equilibrium, in which the elected government could be sure of being left alone to carry on its business, undeflected by public opinion without or major disturbances within. The way was clear for the pursuit of a brand of Conservatism which no longer had quite the same need to answer to the customary hazards of democratic existence. It was in place, as it seemed, unchallengeably. And so, without question, was its leader: confirmed in her luxuriant conviction that she had carried Britain, by the only honest policies available, towards the destiny her people desired and the world would strive to emulate.

Three election victories make their own case for a political transformation. They are a verdict which, in an important sense, allows of no rebuttal. They happened; and in the democratic system a third strong mandate, with no reason to doubt the possibility of a fourth, is such a mighty force that the claims of those who secured it have a certain irresistible power. The Conservatives' claim to have assembled a new majority, and positioned themselves favourably in the moving currents of politics and society, had a fair amount of evidence on its side.

Analysis of the voting in 1987 showed how a new, more Thatcherite nation had been made. Some of its lineaments were particularly striking. The most telling of them, both socially and electorally, was the predominance of the working class.[1] The Tory share of the manual workers' vote, at 36 per cent, was larger than at any post-war election. Throughout the South of England, far beyond the Home Counties, manual workers alone went more heavily for the Conservatives (46 per cent to 28 per cent) than the electorate as a whole. Higher up the scale, among skilled workers, the Tory encroachment on traditional Labour territory reached even further. These proved to be the shock-troops in the Conservatives' electoral advance, the most specific beneficiaries of much that the Government had done and now cemented into place as a massively important segment of the Tory vote. In 1979, Labour was still securing 45 per cent of the skilled-worker vote, not much less than in 1974. After eight years of Thatcherism, the figure was down to 34 per cent, with the Tories now 9 per cent ahead.

All the polling showed that this was connected – specifically and predictably and not at all disreputably – to certain government actions. Over a million tenants had bought their own council houses, and were substantially more likely to vote Tory as a result. Among first-time buyers of shares in British Telecom, British Gas and the rest of the privatised portfolio, well over half of whom were skilled or unskilled workers, Conservative support ran at 54 per cent. With Labour still ambivalent in its attitude to these shares, and some Labour councils still holding out against easy purchase of council houses, the politics of property seemed to ensure the creation of a client Tory vote closely resembling the client Labour vote of old, and in many cases consisting of the same people. Whereas council tenants would vote for the party which looked after them, first-time house- and share-owners would keep in power the party pledged to maintain them in their new-found prosperity.

A similar shift was discernible in the middle-class vote. For the third consecutive election the Tory share of the total non-manual vote fell. Although the Conservatives still had a majority of the middle classes, at 55 per cent this was the lowest since 1974. The slide spoke eloquently for the nature of Thatcherism's populist appeal. Among the public sector middle class, support dropped by 4 per cent, mainly to the benefit of the Alliance. Among university graduates the fall in the Tory vote was as much as 9 per cent. Since the intelligentsia and the government salariat featured high among the enemies identified by the new Conservatism, this was suitably predictable. One of the most reliable of all Tory majorities was among the self-made middle class who had had no further education of any kind. These, the people whom Norman Tebbit was proud to speak for, registered 74 per cent Conservative.

Along with the upwardly mobile working-class Tories, they personified a development, ethical as much as economic, which Kenneth Baker identified in April 1988. As one of the younger representatives of what used to be described as the wet wing of the party, Baker still permitted a trace of embarrassed restraint to enter his phraseology. But actually it was his way of aligning himself with an orthodoxy he once rather despised. Tories did not need to apologise, he assured the Bow Group, 'for the increased scope we have given to what might be called acquisitive individualism'.

That was what enough of the British thought to give Mrs Thatcher her third victory. She had, after all, delivered its fruits. She cast aside British guilt about material advance, which infected alike egalitarian socialists who had no money and paternalist Conservatives born with plenty of it. She regarded this as elitist and destructive nonsense, and found an answering chord, across the South of England especially, which resounded through the ballot boxes and would probably continue to do so.

Her economic policy was also congruent with developments on a much wider plane. When she came to power, governments all over the industrialised world were becoming more conservative, starting with the Labour Government which she routed from office. By the middle 1970s, partly as a result of the first leap in the oil price, inflation was becoming the greatest enemy of stability, and anti-inflationary strategy dominated the thinking of all governments in a way it had not previously done. This led to the monetary control and fiscal stringency first seriously imported into the British economy by prime minister Callaghan and his principal lieutenant, Denis Healey. But it could be seen in the tendency of many electorates during the eighties to elect conservative governments, and that of such socialist governments as were elected – in France, Australia and New Zealand, for example – to adopt highly conservative economic policies. By 1988, with the large exception of the United States, the anti-Keynesian posture of British Conservatism towards budget deficits had been the global norm for most of a decade.

As time passed, Mrs Thatcher and her more exuberant ministers claimed for themselves a leading creative role in this process. They wanted to be depicted not merely as sympathetic local agents of a worldwide trend, but as first begetters of a set of policies which other people imitated. 'Many other governments are now Thatcherite,' the prime minister told an interviewer in January 1984. 'They are following me in trying to hold public expenditure, and following me in trying not to borrow too much. My performance against that of other countries in the real world is such that the majority of them are following us and not us following them.'² This hugely overstated the propensity of any government to 'follow' any other, rather than respond in a common way to forces commonly insinuating themselves into the lives of all countries and all governments. The political strength and sheer longevity of Mrs Thatcher often persuaded her to exaggerate the instructive role she played round the world. All the same, it was true enough that she stood earlier than some, notably the French, for positions that later became enforced on all countries. At the very least it could be said that she did nothing, as another sort of Tory leader might have, to resist the *zeitgeist*.

Her other major point of contact with an underlying trend which reached beyond Britain was more positive. She arrived in power at a time when the role of the state and the frontiers of its power, and particularly its relationship to the forces of the market, were beginning to be questioned. This was probably more pronounced in Britain than elsewhere, but came to have a distinct analogy in the Antipodes, where even left-wing governments began to challenge statist assumptions. A prime Thatcherite assumption was that, in the social and economic realms, the state was too big and hopelessly inefficient. She took an almost American view of the state and its proper place. Since many state institutions palpably *were* inefficient and did deliver a very poor service, the cautious release of market forces into parts of the public sector responded to deep dissatisfaction among the customers. The reinvestigation of market liberalism, to put it no higher, was a tendency which went hand in hand with global economic conservatism; and of this Mrs Thatcher was an enthusiastic exponent.

Did she, however, preside over the development of a wholly new consensus? Did these trends, both global and national, produce after a decade of Thatcherism a true and incontestable concordance between the people and their leader? Did the three election victories, while their political reality was not open to dispute, also deliver a nation which was spiritually integrated into a new way of thinking? Here the evidence was more problematic.

First, it was quite palpably not one nation. Regional differences were great, and getting greater. In late 1986, the Department of Trade and Industry delivered to the European Commission the official assumptions about employment and industry until 1990. These identified the North-east, the South-west, Wales and Northern Ireland, along with cities like Liverpool and Manchester, as places where the economic recovery had not arrived and unemployment would continue to go up. 'Decay and obsolescence' was the commonest official description of the state of the social infrastructure in these places. This was reflected in the 1987 voting, which produced a swing to Labour in Scotland, Wales and the North of England, and left Manchester, Liverpool, Bradford, Leicester and Newcastle upon Tyne among the places without a single Conservative MP. Plainly there were large parts of the country into which neither the benefits of Thatcherism nor respect for its leader could be seen to reach.

The extreme example was Scotland. While the Thatcherite majority dug deeper into the soil of Britain as a whole, in Scotland the Tories' position weakened inexorably. In 1987 they lost half their remaining seats, and six of every seven constituencies returned an anti-Conservative MP. Mrs Thatcher appeared to find this incomprehensible. 'The Scots invented Thatcherism, long before I was thought of,' she once said, in what was believed to be a reference to Adam Smith, the economist, and possibly the philosopher David Hume. In June 1988 she also said: 'Tory values are in tune with everything that is finest in the Scottish character. Scottish values are Tory values – and vice versa.'[3] These assertions remained stubbornly unsupported by the political behaviour of Scottish voters. Although it was probable that some of the leader's personal emanations – bossiness, smugness, righteousness and inextinguishably English gentility – made her peculiarly rebarbative to a nation with a powerful sense of its own identity, deeper attitudes were also important. Quite obviously, Scotland had to be excluded from any claim that Britain was unified around a Thatcherite consensus.

There were other bits of evidence which cast some doubt on the nature of the consensus itself. The Government was returned for three terms. But in 1987 still only 32 per cent of the whole electorate voted for it. How thorough was the conversion of Britain? The more triumphalist prophets had cause for disappointment.

Opinion polling in the later 1980s tended to reveal a nation somewhat to the left of the Government it had elected. The 1986 report, *British Social Attitudes*, showed a decline in support for Conservative values. Strength of feeling about unemployment, for example, remained unmoderated, with 74 per cent of the sample deeming it a more important priority than inflation, despite a seven-year Tory campaign urging the opposite proposition. There was continued heavy support for higher spending on health and education, two areas where spending had already gone up but where government had spent a lot of effort trying to persuade the country that money was not the problem. The 1987 edition of the same survey revealed a similar picture. Thatcherite values appeared far from dominant in the national mind. What had changed, which helped explain the election result, was public evaluation of the economic position. People revealed a suddenly greater optimism about inflation and their personal prospects, which, at the moment of truth, masked some of their underlying opinions about society.

This trend was vividly confirmed a year after the election. A Mori poll found significant majority opinion ranged against some of the Government's main third-term initiatives.[4] More than two-thirds of the sample opposed the privatisation of water, and almost as many were against selling off electricity supply. There was heavy opposition to the poll tax. Preserving health care as an entirely public service was supported by six voters in ten, a fact which sharply narrowed the reformers' options. The total state funding of schools, without ambiguity or qualification, was backed by more than seven to one. There was virtually no encouragement anywhere in the survey, in fact, for another Thatcherite leap forward.

Even more suggestive than the inquiry into policy attitudes was Mori's testing of what it termed the core values of society. Nine years after the arrival in power of one of the most fearlessly ideological governments of modern times, remarkably few of its injunctions about the good and proper life appeared to have impinged on the British mind. Respondents were asked about how they saw Britain today, but also how they would like Britain to be. They saw it, with a fine perception, as more 'Thatcherist' than socialist. It was, they considered, a mainly capitalist society in which private interests were most important; a society where the individual was encouraged to be self-sufficient, where people were allowed to make and keep as much as they could, and which emphasised efficiency rather than employment.

What was striking was the overwhelming judgment that this society, although real enough, was very much a second best. Asked to define the ideal society, 49 per cent preferred one in which socialism and a more controlled economy predominated, as against only 43 per cent for capitalism; 55 per cent preferred collectivism to self-sufficiency in welfare; 79 per cent opted for a society which valued caring more highly than wealth-creation. A later poll by Marplan seemed to confirm this stubborn reluctance on the part of the majority to revise long-cherished assumptions. In September 1988 Marplan found, for example, that 53 per cent of people disagreed with the proposition that profitable state industries should be sold off, while 59 per cent (including 60 per cent of Conservative voters) still thought it would be better to pay higher taxes and have better public services than pay lower taxes and see services deteriorate.[5]

This, on the face of it, was a startling measure of Thatcherism's failure in its didactic task. The many years' ascendancy of the business culture and the economic imperative had evidently failed to instil a true popular understanding of their proper supremacy as the guiding light of all modern policy-makers. This must qualify such confident assertions as were made about British attitudes having been transformed in a decade. At the same time it compels attention to another aspect of the Thatcher phenomenon, which cannot be excluded from the reckoning.

The absence of an effective parliamentary opposition was central to a great deal of what happened throughout the decade from 1979. What most prime ministers normally have to be concerned about at all times, Mrs Thatcher rarely had even to consider. She was always attentive to the House of Commons, but strictly to her own side of it. The Labour Party could be discounted, and successive Labour leaders regarded with a justified contempt. This certainty that no problem would be posed by the other side provided massive reassurance at each critical moment of the three terms. It fortified government throughout the dark days of 1981, enabling the passage of that year's key budget to proceed with impunity. It underpinned the Falklands war to such an extent that, even if the task force had returned defeated, the Labour Party was never likely to collect the political spoils. It was government's great accomplice during the coal dispute, when any political difficulties which ministers faced were as nothing compared with Labour's cruel embarrassment at having to defend Arthur Scargill's strike. When the Westland affair seriously imperilled Mrs Thatcher's position, the incompetence of Neil Kinnock compounded the weakness of his party in assuring her survival. For the whole of the decade, the Government enjoyed immunity from at least half the customary pressures of political life. It seemed at times as if parliamentary democracy had gone into suspension.

Among Thatcherites, this was always seen – and with greater intensity as time passed – not as a happy accident but as further proof of their irresistible political virtue. The failure of Labour, they thought, was essentially brought about by the power of Conservative ideas. Thatcherism in action had relentlessly proved that there existed no conceivable basis for another sort of politics. According to them, the collapse of the left as a political force was due to factors much more profound than the inability of the Labour Party to organise and reform itself. The Labour split, the formation of the SDP, the continuing internecine warfare between the leadership and the hard left: all these were symptoms of deep social and political change which Conservatism recognised and articulated but which socialism, under labels new or old, was simply unable to accommodate. In face of these changes, it was argued, Labour and the Liberals and the SDP were destined to thrash about in a state of abject confusion. Thus, the British people in the 1980s were quite widely thought to have found in Thatcherism a synthesis, and in Mrs Thatcher a leader, that no party of the left could have hoped to challenge.

There was something in this, but less than was often claimed. It was certainly the case that the electorate rejected the socialism of Michael Foot's and Neil Kinnock's Labour Party. There was never any sign of majority support for Labour's unilateralist defence policy, unchanged through the 1980s, nor of any confidence that a party dominated by the unions could deliver sounder economic promises than the Thatcher Government, at least by the middle of its second term, could begin to point to. Through the murk of a voting system which continuously returned the Conservatives with minority national support, it was easy to discern that the anti-socialist majority was a more committed entity than the anti-Thatcher majority. The voting figures at all the elections, with large third-party support, were arithmetically open to either interpretation. Only the deluded left could persuade itself that the non-Tory vote, 58 per cent in 1987, was politically more significant than the non-Labour vote of 69 per cent.

Did this mean, however, that there was an acquiescent, if not active, pro-Thatcher majority? No evidence really supports the idea. The voters submitted to a result. British stoicism guaranteed the peace, and respect for democratic election results is a tradition maintained with iron discipline since the introduction of universal suffrage. But, as the Mori and Marplan polls showed, a deep well of sympathy for collectivist ideas still existed after the decade's battering these took from the prophets and practitioners of individualism. The majority recognised the power of a seemingly invincible party. Many of them also enjoyed increases in personal prosperity, the promise all democratic parties always make. Their conversion to the uniquely seductive package of nostrums and prejudices called Thatcherism was far less evident.

It follows from this that the Thatcherite analysis looks too simplistic. It is perfectly true that in the event there was, to recall a famous phrase, no alternative. It is not so obvious that no alternative could ever have been available. It was the failure of non-Conservative opinion to modernise and organise itself, rather than the impossibility of such opinion ever speaking for a British majority, which enabled the Thatcherite experiment to turn, in the course of three terms, into the new orthodoxy. The reasons for that failure lay in histories and institutions and personalities which are another story for another day. As far as the history of prime minister Thatcher is concerned, one need note only that it was integral to her existence and survival: an adventitious blessing, which need not have happened but which, if you were seized as she was of the need to save Britain by a revolutionary offensive against old ideas, could not have been more helpful.

In any case, it happened. The left was excluded for a decade, the right installed with an unchallenged opportunity to put its new ideas into practice. That was the fact. It left its mark: on the economy, on society, on government, on the world, on the whole quality of life in late-twentieth-century Britain. In ten years it could hardly do otherwise. Any government lasting that long would leave a deposit. This one, so keenly bent on change, left a larger one than any government since Attlee's. But in each sphere, if one tried to consider it in the round, the effect was ambiguous. Britain enjoyed a considerable economic recovery. By mid-1988, still growing at 4 per cent after seven years' continuous expansion, the economy had unquestionably ceased to look like the sick man of Europe. Inflation had been driven down and, until the acceleration of 1988, held down, and anyone in employment or living off the stock market had done well out of it. In the estimation of the world, which mattered a lot, Britain was now among the strong economies. Productivity, in particular, was dramatically higher than a decade before: an average annual improvement of 4.5 per cent. The overmanning of the 1970s was a thing of the past. The Thatcherite economy was a slimmed-down, more efficient unit in some respects than the economy immediately preceding it.

Some of the policies which contributed to this were distinctive Thatcherite policies, and were remarkably successful. Prime place among them was almost universally accorded to the remorseless shrinking of trade union power. By the late 1980s, British unions would have been incapable of launching a winter of discontent of the kind that ushered Mrs Thatcher into power even if they had wanted to. They occupied a position in the country which accorded more with the one they enjoyed in competitor nations, and a direct line could be drawn from the intentions announced by the Tories when they came in and the outcome they achieved – although continuously high unemployment also played its part. But there were other effective economic initiatives too. British Steel, which was once losing over £600 million a year, was acclaimed in 1988 as the most efficient steel producer in the world. Some of the privatised corporations, notably British Telecom, became better geared to satisfying customers. Having a politician at the top who believed in business, in profits, in the absolute primacy of the balance-sheet and the bottom line, not to mention the opposite necessity for lame ducks to go to the wall, had an inspiring impact on some segments of the business community.

Some of the economy's performance, admittedly, stemmed not from government policy but from a reversal of government policy. The most conspicuous concerned the core doctrine of monetarism itself. In 1981, the key year around which most of the economic argument raged, the money supply began to rise far faster than monetarist dogma indicated or than the Treasury laid down as a target. Between 1981 and 1984 it rose by 50 per cent, as against a target range of 16–30 per cent, and it went on rising at around 20 per cent a year. That part of monetarism was plainly abandoned, which left a substantial unresolved dispute between government supporters, who contended that the rigour of the 1981 budget was the source of all future growth, and government critics who said the 1981 policy wouldn't work. It remained the critics' fierce belief that a change of policy, signified by the money supply figures, was what lay behind the eventual start of the recovery.

Even on the issue of inflation, it was possible to detract from the Government's achievement by noting how much of it was due to the sharp decline in world commodity prices in the early 1980s, rather than to the brilliance of Sir Geoffrey Howe's stewardship of the Treasury. And such matters were of great interest to all who had been bruised by the certitudes of early Thatcherism, including especially the wet wing of the Conservative Party. But in a sense they were secondary to the assessment. If there had been a recovery, did it matter enormously by what pragmatic contrivances and unadmitted compromises this had been accomplished? If a government is in power for ten years, such convolutions are bound to play their part. More relevant was the question of whether the recovery was great, and how long it would last.

Integral to this was how you measured it. Between 1979 and 1981, output from manufacturing industry fell by more than 15 per cent and nearly 1.5 million jobs disappeared. Measured from 1979, therefore, output-growth had barely recovered to its old level by 1987. Over the lifetime of the Thatcher Government, the record was poor. Only by discounting the first colossal industrial shock could the recovery graph be shown moving smoothly upwards. Compared with Japanese manufacturing, which rose by 31 per cent during the first two Thatcher terms, or American which rose by 17 per cent, or West German which rose by 11 per cent, Britain declined a very long way before starting to make ground again. It was often said later that the extremity of this shock was not intended by the ministers in question, who never properly foresaw the impact of a steep appreciation in sterling, and always claimed that the decimation of manufacturing industry was an unfortunate accident – although one with therapeutic side-effects. As the country contemplated drowning in a rising tide of imports during the later recovery years, this seemed an inadequate apologia: one for which, in other circumstances, ministers would have been made to pay a high political price.

Unemployment, furthermore, was a problem which the Thatcher Government did not solve in ten years. It declined in political importance. How to stop worrying and live with unemployment was one of the principal lessons Thatcherism administered to the country, and it achieved a permanent social shift in the process. After the 1987 election, unemployment finally started to come down quite fast from its plateau above 3 million. But no judgment on the record can ignore the fact that for most of the Thatcher years the economy was being run at about 80 per cent of capacity. A great deal of production was lost in UK Limited, and a lot of national wealth therefore went missing for ever. If the task of economic policy is to put every resource to use in order to maximise the national product, and thereby universally to enhance the quality of national life, Mrs Thatcher's record was a disappointment. That large failure, for which there were myriad explanations, not all of them creditable, loomed over the successes: the control of inflation, the spread of wealth, the improved efficiency, the expanding financial markets, the growth of small businesses. After ten years, the question was not 'Would an alternative have worked better?' but 'Was this policy a triumph?' As the decade closed, with inflation edging upwards again, the Tory answer was usually more ecstatic than it had any right to be. It depended heavily on comparisons. At 2.9 per cent a year between 1981 and 1987, the growth in gross domestic product per head put Britain second only to Japan in the international league. Along with the greater productivity, this helped create the impression of a new Britain. But 2.9 per cent was also the growth figure between 1968 and 1973, when it left Britain close to the bottom of the league, and was regarded as a dismal performance. If there was a miracle in the 1980s, it was of relatively mundane dimension.

Less ambiguity attached to another shift. Inequality increased, as it was always intended to. The Thatcher Government believed more clearly than any of its post-war predecessors in the virtue of inequality, both as a motor for getting the economy moving and as a measure by which its fruits should be distributed. Ten years' commitment to this cause etched itself deep into the social fabric.

There was, true enough, a general increase in earnings which spread through the nation. Average earnings rose by nearly 25 per cent after inflation. But in terms of social change, other trends had more historic significance. For the first time since the Second World War, a forty-year pattern whereby incomes were becoming more equal was reversed. The share of total income earned by the top 1 per cent of earners grew by around a quarter, and in 1988 the best-off tenth of the population enjoyed nearly nine times more income than the worst-off tenth: in 1979 they were only six and a half times better off.[6] This was the result of escalating earnings, but, to a much greater extent, of income tax cuts. These were massively weighted towards the already prosperous. No less than half went to the richest 10 per cent, and one-third to the richest 5 per cent.

Although this reversal of an historic trend was justified by Mrs Thatcher and her allies in economic terms, its social consequences left a more distinctive mark, for better or for worse. With inequality now made respectable by the politicians, social guilt became as unfashionable as a belief in what used to be called social justice. Even though the opinion polls continued to identify large swaths of public opinion that disapproved of this, and wanted policies which better reflected traditional British norms, private money became legitimised as the most valuable and worthwhile proof of success.

This had consequences which even some Conservatives did not like. They were epitomised just before the 1987 election by an apt formulation in the *Sunday Telegraph*, the last High Tory newspaper. Peregrine Worsthorne, its editor, cautioned the party against the dangers of 'bourgeois triumphalism'. Worsthorne saw this dread condition in the ascendancy of finance over industry in the economic order, and the conspicuous consumption shamelessly favoured by the *parvenus* who had made their fortune in the City of London. 'Vulgarity rules OK,' the fastidious editor wrote, 'and the yuppies feel confident enough to shed all inhibitions about enjoying the spoils of the class war which they think Mrs Thatcher has fought on their behalf.' These people, he thought, were a serious threat to the reputation of the only party capable of governing Britain, and he remarked unfavourably on the leader's refusal to utter a word of criticism.[7]

Politically, the party survived this ugly association, as it did the parallel emergence of a larger under-class, more visibly deprived, than had generally been permitted by the policies of the despised post-war consensus. The wider gulf between rich and poor, hitherto regarded as a suitable object of community concern, its consequences to be softened as far as possible by the ministrations of the state, received instead a new ideological justification. Mrs Thatcher's statement that 'There is no such thing as society' became one of her most famous utterances, seized on by opponents but never, significantly, either denied or glossed by her supporters. It supplied the text for an individualist age, in which the family became the largest unit of mutual assistance and the role of government as agent of a wider social collective, providing help to each according to their need, was decisively challenged. When this in turn came under attack, from churchmen and others, the prime minister's characteristic response was not to qualify but to embellish what she had said. In May 1988, she devoted an entire speech, to the General Assembly of the Church of Scotland, to asserting the link between Thatcherite individualism and Christianity. Religious faith ordained the making and keeping of money, she said.[8] This caused a row, but it wasn't greeted with incredulity. Repetition of the thought helped to establish a new social norm, if not universal approval for it. It was now fashionable to be rich not poor, to consume rather than to 'care'.

This was the territory on which the Thatcher years came closest to delivering what had been promised in their early stages. They somewhat changed the hierarchy of social and economic values observed at the upper end of society, especially among the political and business elite and those who aspired to that station in life. The prosperity principle no longer needed to justify itself in the court of public opinion. The equality principle, although evidently still approved by at least half the country, receded apologetically from mainstream political life.

That shift was in vivid contrast to another, in which the Conservatives' stated intentions proved to be the reverse of what they did.

One of the prime objectives of the Thatcher Government, repeated from a thousand platforms and rehearsed in scores of policy documents, was to reduce the role of government itself in the life of the nation. This was seen as a matter of economic efficiency: believers in market liberalism held as an axiomatic principle that state intervention in what markets did to the economy should be held to a minimum. But it was also a matter of philosophy. Big government was a socialist aberration, small government a Conservative promise reflecting what the party saw as its classic commitment – often neglected, not least by the hated Heath – to individual liberty.

In one major area, this quest for smaller government was made good. Each time a nationalised industry was sold into private hands, the role of government did indubitably diminish. Whatever might be said about the way this was done, and the indifference which the process often showed to the market principle of competition, the gentlemen in Whitehall no longer ran the gas industry or the telephone service. It was open to question whether the tyranny of the bureaucrat had been any more oppressive, from the consumer's point of view, than that of the accountant, whose job was to ensure that the privatised industry made a profit. It was also obvious that the thrust to privatise more and yet more public sector activities had a great deal to do with economics, not freedom: the need to bring in the funds which would assist the major objective of tax cuts, not the incontrovertible evidence that this species of freedom would cause them to be run better. All the same, government did get off these corporations' backs. The reach of ministers into the running of great industries was much reduced.

Such expansion of business freedom, however, was not matched by a growth in political freedom – of the individual, or anyone else below the level of central government itself. Despite its protestations, the Thatcher Government was no more immune than any other from the tendency to amass all the power it could. Because of its unchallenged strength, it exercised this power with more confidence than any of its predecessors. This was an alarming combination. The pieties of modern Conservatism permitted ministers, above all the prime minister, to lay claim to a withdrawal of government from the business of governing. But their certainty that they were right, unmoderated by the normal constraints of adversarial politics, drove them in practice to intervene in many quarters hitherto regarded as independent. Far from reducing the role of government, Mrs Thatcher made it felt wherever she regarded its superior wisdom as a blessing of which no one should be deprived.

Institutionally, the key target was local government. The validity of local government as a function relevant to British democracy ceased to be taken for granted. Wave upon wave of assaults on the financial independence of local authorities weakened their power and cast doubt on their point. This was in part provoked by the disintegration of the Labour Party, and the reckless financial irresponsibility of Labour outposts in the big cities. But the measure to curb them affected all authorities, and culminated in the poll tax, which ensured that 75 per cent of local spending would henceforth be determined from Whitehall.

Along with money, local government also lost powers. Education and housing, its core activities, were both reorganised in ways calculated to reduce or even exclude the concept of local democracy. In each case, ministers were sensitive to this. They repelled the charge of centralisation by arguing that what they were doing was to replace the dead hand of local bureaucracy with a more genuine form of local control. Power would drip down to the people, as tenants' co-operatives took over their own council flats and parent-governors replaced local politicians in deciding the fate of their children's schools. With housing, the later of the two to be reformed, this stood some chance of not being a fiction, although its first effect, as with some other Thatcherite reforms, was to raise the market price of an essential commodity. In the case of schools, the new arrangements constituted a massive shift of power away from the locality and into the Department of Education. This the relevant ministers hardly bothered to conceal. It was also true of universities. Education in all its forms became the focus of Thatcherite centralism, the arena in which the crusading conviction of the leader and her party effaced all conservative instincts concerning the natural fallibility of government. The content of curricula, the priorities in university courses, the administrative arrangements under which these were delivered to the customers: all were made to submit to the will of the politicians.

Whatever else this might be, it was not an exercise in reducing the power of the central state. Rather, bodies that might rival the central state were emasculated or dismantled. The idea of genuine independence, even of competing sources of wisdom and advice, became increasingly uncongenial to a government which was so little obliged to attend to them in Parliament itself. The absence of a powerful Opposition bred the habit of disrespect for opposition. A laboratory test was performed on the truth of Lord Acton's famous dictum that power tends to corrupt. For the Government did have great, untrammelled power. And the test proved positive. The corruption did set in, if not absolutely.

Alongside the formal Acts by which power was centralised went an informal attitude which narrowed the limits of liberty. As the Government felt its strength, its interferences grew more extensive. It placed no high value on the freedom of the press, for example. Its relentless pursuit of the publishers of *Spycatcher*, long after the book was out, revealed an unusual willingness to use the bottomless public purse in an effort to establish that the official definition of national security must on all occasions transcend the right to publish. A succession of cases involving Northern Ireland showed ministers utterly hostile to the possibility that, where security was concerned, the media should be left free to decide what they had a right or a duty to publish. Leaning on television editors became, to an extent not known before, the natural instinct of ministers who suspected they might not like what they saw. Again, perhaps, this was a consequence of what they had become used to. Just as the state of politics drained them of the need to account to an opposition, so the state of the press accustomed them to almost universal admiration. When a television programme broke ranks, its efforts were thus more likely to be treated as an affront to propriety than as a legitimate journalistic enterprise.

So this was a government which enjoyed the power it possessed, and showed no less inclination than any other to exercise it. But, because it had more power, such an unresisted inclination became more than usually prominent. As the third term advanced, nobody could deny that it was in command: a fact which may have been more widely appreciated abroad than at home.

There, the perception of Britain undoubtedly changed. It is a universal law of international politics that foreigners prefer to deal with strong governments than with weak ones. Diplomacy is rendered somewhat simpler if the government is in charge of the country, and the leader in charge of the government. For all the perils which put Mrs Thatcher's position at risk from time to time, this situation was widely seen to obtain in Britain for most of the 1980s, and it brought forth a certain respect.

Three components were important. The first, in all probability, was the Falklands war. Here, as into so much of the political life of this leader, the war reached deep. Although foreigners were often disposed to see the operation as a piece of British eccentricity, which they thought led nowhere, its very improbability enhanced the reputation of the country that won it. This is an age when few industrialised countries have known war, and all their leaders look forward only to maintaining the peace. But the fact of a clean victory in war appeals to the atavistic instincts of many who are placed in charge of their nation's destiny. It is the task which, were their country faced with it, they would have the awful responsibility of undertaking. That Britain should have stood up for a principle so far from home, and returned victorious, gave her a special standing in the club of nations, which the years did not erase.

Second, economic recovery, with all its limitations, caused an important revision in the way Britain was seen. This was now a country rising in the recovery league, and even though it now stood sixth in the free world's order of prosperity, having been overtaken by Italy under Mrs Thatcher's leadership, it was a sounder economy, and London survived deregulation to remain one of the three leading financial capitals. With less debt and more growth, and with the curse of trade union power apparently exorcised, Britain was no longer a supplicant for the world's attention. It was seen to have entered the concert of modern nations.

A third positive element was supplied by the leader of this nation herself. Again her very strength and long political life excited the admiration of the club, where all the members had a special appreciation of what these qualities entailed. In her person, she became unmistakable. Amazement at her sex evolved into astonishment at her survival. In many of the countries she visited, she fascinated the people as much as she mesmerised the politicians. She acquired, therefore, a reputation which any other British leader would find hard to replicate. In 1984, Yasser Arafat, chairman of the Palestine Liberation Organisation, called her the 'Iron Man' of British politics. In 1986, the Singapore leader, Lee Kuan Yew, said, 'She has guts and stands up for what she believes in,' and added that she deserved the thanks of the British people 'for teaching Mr Scargill a lesson'. In 1988, the Polish leader, General Jaruzelski, on the eve of a visit she was making to his country, presumed to judge her 'one of the outstanding figures in British history'. Even in Western Europe, which most often felt the sharpness of her tongue, initial detestation grew into watchful respect.

Having such a visible leader achieved, of itself, some improvement in Britain's standing. Coupled with economic growth, it added quite a lot to the balance-sheet. A big question remained, however, about how this credit was put to work. Did Britain deploy its new and burgeoning assets to best advantage? Here the record was flawed by the narrowness of vision at the top, and the tendency, not diminished as time passed, to apply to all international questions an overriding test of the British national interest – and almost always in the short term.

Thus, the Falklands war was fought and won, but seven years later no hint of an initiative to make a settlement with Argentina had appeared on the Foreign Office agenda. The Foreign Office, indeed, was a somewhat emaciated force, its instincts for diplomacy continually whittled down from the other side of Downing Street. The Falklands garrison continued to eat into the defence budget: an untouchable element, and likely to remain so for as long as Mrs Thatcher was prime minister.

In Europe, this narrow determination was still more public and much more important. Winning the battle over Britain's contribution to the Community budget did not herald a new era of Euro-minded leadership. The country remained hooked on its special relationship with the United States, and a combative relationship all points east of Dover. In June 1988, President Reagan paid his last visit to Britain, and the occasion was dominated not by the future but by the past, with president and prime minister drenching each other in sentiment about the Second World War. At no point did Britain position itself in concerted fashion to intervene as West Germany continued to grow closer to France. Britain, instead, appeared not to want to lead. With the single European market beckoning in 1992, Britain's role was to spoil the party and set a firm limit to the measure of unification it would tolerate.

Into the changing scenery of the later eighties, in short, Britain did not easily fit. As Washington looked west, and the signs multiplied of a remorseless shift in the shape of the continents, a stronger Britain nonetheless fought to resist the inescapable consequence: that Europe must draw closer.

How much leaders matter, as compared with such shifts in the structure, whether on the world plane or the national, is a matter of perennial discussion. In the case of Mrs Thatcher's leadership of a decade of Conservative government in Britain, there are those who have contended that the leader was more an accident than an instrument of the political environment in which she found herself. Others, not far distant from this, have depicted her as the agent of a force so much larger than she was as to render her personal contribution little more than incidental to the project that came to bear her name. This was an opinion favoured throughout the decade, and with increasing fervour, on the far left. Although the left reviled Mrs Thatcher personally, deploying her as a totemic hate-object to rally their devotees, they also allowed a sneaking admiration for one whom they perceived as being engaged on as massive a revolutionary task as they set themselves. They tended to represent Thatcherism as a bold, organised, sometimes 'hegemonic' initiative in the class war, to which the personality of its eponymous heroine did not greatly matter.[9]

This was not the view generally transmitted to the British people. Nor was it correct. Whatever qualities she lacked, dominance was not one of them. One had only to cast an eye over the newspapers any day of any week of any year to understand the measure of her domination, as perceived not only by editors but by the politicians, the information men, the lobbyists and the image-makers who supplied the material for their headlines. There was no corner of British society to which 'Maggie' could not sooner or later turn her hand; no problem which she could not solve, no governmental triumph that failed to be peculiarly hers. On the upper scale, Maggie would order Europe, instruct Reagan, see off the Russians, direct the Commonwealth. On the lower she took charge of problems large and small, from football hooliganism to the drugs crisis, from a detailed sub-clause in the Law of the Sea treaty to the precise configuration of the customs hall at the British end of the Channel Tunnel. She was portrayed as the person without whom nothing could be decided, and nothing *was* decided. More often than with any of her predecessors, this was true. She wanted to take charge. She did take charge.

Nor was she modest about it. She became ever more aware of her own importance. After three elections, she spoke of herself as a venerable part of the furniture of British life and, more optimistically, as one who would be missed if she went. 'I think I have become a bit of an institution,' she told an interviewer. 'And the place wouldn't be quite the same without this old institution. People seem to think, "She isn't so bad is she, this Maggie?" They wanted their children to meet you. Americans, of course, are absolutely amazed. They say, "We've never had a chance to meet a person like this." '[10]

This was not a false estimation. Her presence came to overshadow the whole of public life, and a fair amount of private conversation. Along with dominance went the same extinction of rival forces in the cabinet as was applied to rival centres of influence outside it. It was one of her shortcomings as a prime minister that all around her were close to being pygmies. Over nine years she kept only three cabinet members who were there from the start, and none who might constitute a source of countervailing advice, let alone power, to her own. In terms of broad quality among its members, her ministry was not distinguished. It wasn't the equal of Attlee's, with whose impact on Britain Mrs Thatcher's was often compared. After the first two years, it was a case of Maggie first and the rest nowhere. Add to this a power of patronage exercised with more meticulous personal attention from Downing Street than ever happened before, reaching out from the civil service into the entire public world up and down the country, and it becomes difficult to withhold from her the greatest share of responsibility for what happened.

How, in sum, did she exercise it? What was her personal contribution? What was the peculiar quality she brought, and what, if anything, was the dark side of that quality? Two particular characteristics, which infused most of what she did, suggest themselves.

The first quality was a sense of moral rectitude, which accounted for the single main achievement that would not have happened without her. This was the attachment to fiscal rigour in the early years, which, whatever analysis is made of its consequences, was an extraordinary exercise in political will. As the famous cabinet of 23 July 1981 showed, the pressure for retreat was almost universal among her colleagues. And a retreat of sorts was performed. But the determination to pursue the economics of sound housekeeping, preached at the knee of the father she constantly invoked, and elevated above the merely political to the moral level, came from within her more than anybody else. It was her special contribution. All leaders lay claim to higher purposes, but most of them experience at least a portion of private cynicism. She was not burdened with such a feeling, at least about herself or what she was doing.

The appeal to righteousness stretched much further than economic management. It could be said without exaggeration to have been what, in her own mind, drove her on. It fed the sheer energy and enthusiasm which she continued to bring to political leadership in the tenth year of the decade just as plentifully as in the first. Some said her zeal now was even greater, as her ambitions at last looked unlikely to be frustrated by any other politician. The grey men who preceded her surrendered to despair after less than half the span of her time in office. But among the advantages they lacked was the kind of inspirational certainty which was the political equivalent of hormone replacement therapy.

This was not, however, a trait without faults and shadows. It carried its own risks, which emerged at moments that can hardly be forgotten. Such a pious belief in the higher rightness of what a leader is about, not to mention the infamy of what her opponents propose, may induce in her the belief that she can do no wrong. Because it was simply inconceivable, to a politician with Mrs Thatcher's image of herself, that she could have behaved basely during the Westland affair or at any other time, she felt entirely justified in conspiring with her staff to prevent the whole truth coming out. Equally, this driving sense of mission induced in her a greater willingness to learn from her successes than her failures. The defeats of Galtieri and Scargill were for her the instructive events, not the mishandling of affairs in Europe, or the futile chaos produced by public sector strikes from the civil servants in 1981 to the teachers in 1986, or the repeated farces produced by her attitude to security matters. The moral dimension, while a key to her dynamism, also made her blind.

Beside this need for rectitude was her pragmatism. That was the second all-pervasive quality. She had to a fine degree the political leader's sense of what would play well with the voters, and, very often, where to compromise with her own instincts in order to secure the greater political good. She was a consummate populist. Whether on union reform, or the nuclear bomb, or South Africa, or hanging, or censorship, or selling council houses, or attitudes to money, she invariably touched the majority nerve. Furthermore, where, as was sometimes the case, prudence dictated a more cautious approach than she would personally have preferred, she developed a rare capacity to disclaim responsibility for what had occurred. This was not really her government, she managed to imply when it suited her: for example, when Jim Prior was running policies she did not approve of, first over the unions and then in Ulster. More extraordinarily, this was a facility she continued to deploy after many years in power. In this way, she could retain populist support without taking unnecessary risks to gratify it. Equally, as in her attitude to the National Health Service, she could identify an issue on which not even she would have been prepared to affront entrenched opinion.

However, this populism, too, was marked by a disabling paradox. It hung ambiguously over her relations with the nation she led for ten years. She might be a populist, but at another level she had a narrow understanding of the people.

It was an abrasive not a smooth relationship. Little evidence could ever be produced that many people liked her, still less loved her. For her part, she did not seem to like them. She was not perceived as understanding them. Did not the polls continuously find, from the beginning to the end, that she was held to be out of touch with how ordinary people lived? In particular, she omitted to understand those who were not like her, or who neglected to play their part in the historic mission which she reckoned she had set under way. She understood successes, but not failures: the leaders not the followers, the elite and not the masses. Although a populist, she was the ultimate argument against the contention that a political leader needs, in her person, to be popular.

For a leader who lasted so long, this was an odd state of affairs. She was one of us. By now, indeed, she was arguably our supreme representative: the complete personification of what we were. And yet, after ten years, she remained different. In an important sense, she wasn't one of us at all. She was altogether too superior.

But she intended to remain. 'I hang on', she told an interviewer after nine years as prime minister, 'until I believe there are people who can take the banner forward with the same commitment, belief, vision, strength and singleness of purpose.'[11] Since the men who might meet these modest specifications were nowhere to be seen, Margaret Thatcher promised to stay where she was, into an indefinite future.

Notes and References

Bibliography

Index

Notes and References

Chapter 1: The Alderman's Daughter

1 Yorkshire Television, 18, Woman to Woman, November 1985.
2 Charles Loch Mowat, *Britain between the Wars 1918–1940* (London, 1955), p. 480.
3 For a fuller discussion of this religious odyssey, see Chapter 18.
4 Tricia Murray, *Margaret Thatcher* (London, 1978), p. 17.
5 Mowat, *Britain between the Wars*, p. 490.
6 Nicholas Wapshott and George Brock, *Thatcher* (London, 1979), p. 200.
7 Hugo Young and Anne Sloman, *The Thatcher Phenomenon* (London, 1986), p. 19.

Chapter 2: Into the Network

1 Young and Sloman, *The Thatcher Phenomenon*, p. 17.
2 Ibid.
3 Paul Addison, *The Road to 1945* (London, 1975), p. 23.
4 Hartmut Kopsch, The Approach of the Conservative Party to Social Policy during World War II, unpublished, University of London PhD thesis, 1974.
5 See Murray, *Margaret Thatcher*, p. 42.
6 Conversation with the author, April 1986.
7 Harold Macmillan, *Tides of Fortune* (London, 1969).
8 Young and Sloman, *The Thatcher Phenomenon*, p. 17.
9 Ibid.
10 Ibid., p. 23.

Chapter 3: Finchley Decides

1 Yorkshire Television, 18 November 1985.
2 Quoted in Penny Junor, *Margaret Thatcher: Wife, mother, politician* (London, 1983), p. 32.
3 See ibid.; also Wapshott and Brock, *Thatcher*.
4 BBC Radio Four, 31 July 1974.
5 George Gardiner, *Margaret Thatcher: From Childhood to Leadership* (London, 1975), p. 46.

6 Malcolm Rutherford, *Financial Times*, 8 March 1986.
7 Quoted in Gardiner, *Margaret Thatcher*.
8 For fuller discussion of the Jewish connection, see Chapter 18.

Chapter 4: Years of Misrule

1 Young and Sloman, *The Thatcher Phenomenon*, p. 23.
2 Wapshott and Brock, *Thatcher*, p. 81.

Chapter 5: Heath's Woman

1 Jim Prior, *A Balance of Power* (London, 1986), p. 42.
2 Timothy Raison, *Conflict and Conservatism* (London, 1965). Quoted in Andrew Gamble, *The Conservative Nation* (London, 1974). I'm indebted to Gamble's notably percipient analysis of post-war Conservative ideology.
3 See Nigel Lawson, *Conservatism Today* (London, 1966).
4 Robert Blake, *The Conservative Party from Peel to Thatcher* (London, 1985), p. 307.
5 Quoted in Gamble, *The Conservative Nation*, p. 104.
6 Enoch Powell, *Freedom and Reality* (London, 1969).

Chapter 6: Public Spender

1 Interview with the author, September 1984.
2 Young and Sloman, *The Thatcher Phenomenon*, p. 24.
3 House of Commons, 20 July 1976.
4 Young and Sloman, *The Thatcher Phenomenon*, p. 59.
5 Ibid., p. 27.
6 Keith Joseph, *Reversing the Trend* (London, 1975), p. 4.

Chapter 7: Heroine of the Peasants

1 See, for example, Gardiner, *Margaret Thatcher*, p. 142.
2 Young and Sloman, *The Thatcher Phenomenon*, p. 28.
3 Alan Walters became personal economic adviser to Mrs Thatcher, 1981–3. See below, p. 212. He has documented his rejection of the Heath policies. See *Britain's Economic Renaissance* (London, 1986), p. 118: 'I had accurately predicted the 15 per cent inflation of 1974 by using M3 statistics in 1971–2.'
4 Young and Sloman, *The Thatcher Phenomenon*, p. 30.

5 Ibid., p. 29.
6 Heath seemingly did not intend to use this phrase. The original text
   from which he spoke, of which Lonrho secured a copy, referred to 'an
   unacceptable *facet* of capitalism'. The phrase was nonetheless spoken,
   and passed inextinguishably into political lore, as perhaps the only
   memorable utterance of a prime minister never noted for his compelling
   use of words.
7 Young and Sloman, *The Thatcher Phenomenon*, p. 32.
8 Ibid., p. 33.

Chapter 8: The Stepping Stone

1 *Reversing the Trend* (London, 1975) and *Stranded on the Middle Ground*
   (London, 1976) collect Joseph's key speeches and writings of the period,
   although they omit the Birmingham speech of October 1974, which
   compelled him to quit his campaign for the leadership.
2 Quoted in Allan J. Mayer, *Madam Prime Minister* (New York, 1979).
3 Granada Television, 30 January 1978.
4 Quoted in Murray, *Margaret Thatcher*, p. 127.
5 Young and Sloman, *The Thatcher Phenomenon*, p. 97.
6 *The Castle Diaries 1974–76* (London, 1980), p. 309.
7 According to Mayer, *Madam Prime Minister*.

Chapter 9: Not Dogma but Reason

1   Prior, *A Balance of Power*, p. 138.
2   *Sunday Times*, 3 August 1980.
3   See David Howell, *Blind Victory* (London, 1986), for a full discussion
    of the author's disenchantment with Thatcherite economics.
4   Young and Sloman, *The Thatcher Phenomenon*, p. 61.
5   Quoted in William Keegan, *Mrs Thatcher's Economic Experiment*
    (London, 1984), p. 120. I acknowledge a debt to Keegan's valuable book,
    and to another which is equally indispensable to any student of economic
    Thatcherism: Peter Riddell, *The Thatcher Government* (London, 1983).
6   *Observer*, 25 February 1979.
7   Prior, *A Balance of Power*, p. 119.
8   Ibid., p. 122.
9   Young and Sloman, *The Thatcher Phenomenon*, p. 48.
10 Quoted in Ian Gilmour, *Britain Can Work* (London, 1983), p. 137.
11 See above, pp. 115–8.
12 See Prior, *A Balance of Power*, p. 136.
13 House of Commons, 24 May 1979.

Chapter 10: La Fille d'Epicier

1   Young and Sloman, *The Thatcher Phenomenon*, p. 99.
2   Patrick Cosgrave, *Thatcher: The First Term* (London, 1985), p. 78. Cosgrave, a speech-writer and confidant during Mrs Thatcher's leadership of the Opposition, faded out soon after she got into power. But he remained a perceptive observer. Having been sent on a private mission to President Kaunda, he became a first-hand witness at the Lusaka conference, although I believe he is too dismissive of the Foreign Office's role as instigator of the settlement.
3   Anthony Verrier, *The Road to Zimbabwe* (London, 1986).
4   *Daily Telegraph*, 19 February 1986.
5   Christopher Tugendhat, *Making Sense of Europe* (London, 1986), p. 121.
6   Young and Sloman, *The Thatcher Phenomenon*, p. 113.

Chapter 11: The Capture of the Cabinet

1   Prior, *A Balance of Power*, p. 157.
2   Ibid., p. 165.
3   'Panorama', BBC Television, 25 February 1980.
4   Francis Pym, *The Politics of Consent* (London, 1984). This book, the honest and painstaking credo of a committed wet, enjoyed unexpected success as a best-seller when it first appeared. Of 'wet', the author writes: 'I did not care for this epithet originally, but I am now resigned to it.'
5   Keegan, *Mrs Thatcher's Economic Experiment*, p. 145.
6   Prior, *A Balance of Power*, p. 140.
7   *Sunday Times*, 3 August 1980.
8   Norman St John Stevas, *The Two Cities* (London, 1984), p. 19. Stevas' book, although thin on historical detail, and as much concerned with religion as with politics, is a witty and reflective expression of its author's spacious personality.
9   Young and Sloman, *The Thatcher Phenomenon*, p. 65.
10 *Sebag Gilt-Edged Review*, July 1972.
11 For a good account of the intricacies of the technical arguments preceding the 1981 budget, see Keegan, *Mrs Thatcher's Economic Experiment*, pp. 152–69.
12 Young and Sloman, *The Thatcher Phenomenon*, p. 65.
13 On 30 March 1981, 364 economists issued a collective statement urging a change of direction in economic policy, and asserting that recovery was impossible without it.
14 Prior, *A Balance of Power*, p. 140.

Notes and References

Chapter 12: Those Poor Shopkeepers

1 Young and Sloman, *The Thatcher Phenomenon*, p. 45.
2 House of Commons, 31 March 1981.
3 House of Commons, 14 April 1981.
4 On 8 July 1981.
5 St John Stevas, *The Two Cities*, p. 83.
6 Young and Sloman, *The Thatcher Phenomenon*, p. 44.
7 Ibid., p. 57.

Chapter 13: The Falklands Guarantee

1 Young and Sloman, *The Thatcher Phenomenon*, p. 35.
2 *Time*, 8 December 1986.
3 *New York Times* magazine, 6 October 1985.
4 Alexander M. Haig, Jr, *Caveat: Realism, Reagan and Foreign Policy* (London, 1984). Haig's book, a prolonged diatribe against intriguers and manipulators in the White House and elsewhere who, he contends, made his job impossible, is a mine of information on American foreign policy during the first eighteen months of Reagan's first presidency.
5 Ibid., pp. 255–6.
6 Young and Sloman, *The Thatcher Phenomenon*, p. 108.
7 Quoted Max Hastings and Simon Jenkins, *The Battle for the Falklands* (London, 1983). This book although written at speed, remains the most thorough and best-informed account of the military and diplomatic history of the war.
8 See above, p. 210.
9 Keith Speed, *Sea Change* (London, 1982), p. 102. This book survives the self-conscious discretion with which it is written, and throws useful light on military, especially naval, thinking in the early 1980s.
10 Published in January 1983, the Franks Report supplied an unusual wealth of detail about defence, diplomatic and intelligence decision-making. But see below, pp. 283ff.
11 See ibid., para. 287.
12 Haig, *Caveat*, pp. 261–302.
13 Arthur Gavshon and Desmond Rice, *The Sinking of the Belgrano* (London, 1984).
14 Lecture, Royal United Services Institute, 20 October 1982.
15 *Woman's Own*, 28 August 1982.
16 See below, pp. 416ff.
17 'The Falklands War – the untold story', Yorkshire Television, 1 April 1987.
18 There is an extensive *Belgrano* literature. Apart from Gavshon and Rice, already cited, the texts most worth consulting include: Clive Ponting, *The Right to Know* (London, 1985); *Granta* 15, Spring 1985 (Cambridge); Tam Dalyell, *Misrule* (London, 1987); and, perhaps most

valuably, *The Events of 1–2 May 1982*, a draft report by the Opposition members of the House of Commons Select Committee on Foreign Affairs.

19   'Nationwide', BBC Television, 24 May 1983.
20   See above, p. 276.
21   See Ponting, *The Right to Know*, chs 4 and 5, for a graphic account of the culture of misinformation in action.
22   This had been shown most notably in 1980, when a small cabinet committee was formed under her chairmanship to consider the implications of the Prince of Wales marrying a Catholic, which at one time appeared to be a possibility. In the event, its deliberations proved academic. But one member of the committee was struck by the 'extreme anti-Catholicism' which emerged from the prime minister's approach.
23   Nicholas Henderson, *Channels and Tunnels* (London, 1987), p. 108.
24   Young and Sloman, *The Thatcher Phenomenon*, p. 116.

Chapter 14: Elected Unopposed

 1   Notably, David Butler, *Governing without a Majority* (London, 1983), and Vernon Bogdanor, *Multi-Party Politics and the Constitution* (Cambridge, 1983).
 2   Beatrix Campbell, *The Iron Ladies* (London, 1987). Subtitled 'Why Do Women Vote Tory?', this is a study, not seriously deformed by its Marxist perspective, of women and their role in the Conservative Party as well as of the female Tory voter.
 3   Young and Sloman, *The Thatcher Phenomenon*, p. 36.
 4   Marina Warner, *Monuments and Maidens* (London, 1985), pp. 51ff.
 5   Cosgrave, *Thatcher*.
 6   The first Dame Margery Ashby memorial lecture, 26 July 1982, quoted in Campbell, *The Iron Ladies*.
 7   Young and Sloman, *The Thatcher Phenomenon*, p. 132.
 8   Ibid., p. 38.
 9   'The Englishwoman's Wardrobe', BBC Television, 20 November 1986.
10   *The Times*, 29 July 1986.
11   See Junor, *Margaret Thatcher*. This remains the best account available of Mrs Thatcher's personal life.
12   Interview with Miriam Stoppard, Yorkshire Television, 18 November 1985.
13   Tugendhat, *Making Sense of Europe*, p. 122.
14   Young and Sloman, *The Thatcher Phenomenon*, p. 39.
15   Ibid., p. 41.
16   Prior, *A Balance of Power*, p. 138.
17   Ibid., p. 139.
18   Christopher Lawson, director of Mars Ltd and Mars Inc.: knighted 1984.
19   Keegan, *Mrs Thatcher's Economic Experiment*, p. 195.

20 *Contemporary Record*, Spring 1987. This journal, published by the Institute of Contemporary British History, makes an important contribution to the understanding of government, notably by interviews with recent ministers.
21 Quoted in Gilmour, *Britain Can Work*, p.153.
22 See above, p. 144.
23 *Contemporary Record*, Spring 1987.
24 *Sunday Times*, 27 February 1983, Hugo Young talks fundamentalism with Mrs Thatcher.
25 *The Economist*, 21 May, 4 June 1983.
26 See Dennis Kavanagh, *Thatcherism and British Politics* (London, 1987), pp. 304–9, for a useful survey of international trends.
27 Blake, *The Conservative Party from Peel to Thatcher*, p. 216.

Chapter 15: Trouble with Friends

1 Quoted in David Butler and Dennis Kavanagh, *The British General Election, 1983* (London, 1984), p. 41.
2 Pym, *The Politics of Consent*, p. ix.
3 *Sunday Telegraph*, 11 March 1962.
4 Central Television, 29 March 1983.
5 'Panorama', BBC Television, 16 May 1983.
6 See above, pp. 185–6.
7 12 October 1982.
8 Lecture, 'The Establishment, the Constitution and Reform', 19 January 1984, Macfarlanes Conferences Pan-European Symposium.
9 *The Times*, 1 September 1984.
10 Lecture, 'The Public Service in Modern Society', 2 December 1982, Royal Institute of Public Administration.
11 *Daily Telegraph*, 6 September 1983.
12 *Man of the House: The Life and Political Memoirs of Speaker Tip O'Neill* (London, 1988).
13 Young and Sloman, *The Thatcher Phenomenon*, p. 109.
14 *Daily Mirror*, 24 November 1983, quoting the *Melbourne Age*.
15 *Daily Mail*, 1 May 1982.
16 *Observer*, 20 November 1983.

Chapter 16: Vanquishing Lucifer

1 *Daily Telegraph*, 18 September 1984.
2 See above, p. 000.
3 Leaked to *The Economist*, 27 May 1978.
4 Quoted in Riddell, *The Thatcher Government*, p. 174.
5 Young and Sloman, *The Thatcher Phenomenon*, p. 75.

6   Michael Edwardes, *Back from the Brink* (London, 1983), p. 233.
7   House of Lords Select Committee Report on Overseas Trade, October
     1985.
8   *Financial Times*, 7 May 1983.
9   Anglia Television, 8 April 1986.
10   Ian MacGregor, *The Enemies Within* (London, 1986), is the source for
     these career details.
11   Ibid., p. 58.
12   Ibid., p. 94.
13   Prior, *A Balance of Power*, p. 130.
14   *Trust the People: The Selected Essays and Speeches of Peter Walker*
     (London, 1987), p. 92.
15   MacGregor, *The Enemies Within*, p. 111.
16   *Daily Mirror*, 6 June 1984.
17   House of Commons, 7 June 1984.
18   The Second Carlton Lecture, 26 November 1984.
19   MacGregor, *The Enemies Within*, p. 281.
20   *Sunday Times*, 28 September 1986.
21   *Sunday Telegraph*, 28 July 1985.

Chapter 17: Small World

1   Young and Sloman, *The Thatcher Phenomenon*, p. 102.
2   *Guardian*, 29 October 1984.
3   Young and Sloman, *The Thatcher Phenomenon*, p. 113.
4   See above, p. 189.
5   According to John Newhouse, 'One Against Nine', *New Yorker*, 22
     October 1984.
6   *Daily Express*, 4 June 1984.
7   Newhouse, 'One Against Nine'.
8   Tugendhat, *Making Sense of Europe*, p. 123.
9   Young and Sloman, *The Thatcher Phenomenon*, p. 113.
10   Avignon, 30 November 1984.
11   Speech to Les Grandes Conférences Catholiques, Brussels, 23 June
     1978.
12   Interview in the *New York Times*, 22 January 1984.
13   Ibid.
14   Ibid.
15   *Fortune*, 16 May 1983.
16   *New York Times*, 22 January 1984.
17   *New Yorker*, 10 February 1986.
18   Quoted in the *New Yorker*, 22 July 1985.
19   15 March 1985.
20   *Observer*, 29 July 1985.

Chapter 18: Treason of the Intellectuals

1 Richard Gombrich and Steven Lukes, *Guardian*, 21 January 1985.
2 Blake, *The Conservative Party from Peel to Thatcher*, p. 186.
3 Marina Warner.
4 Published in London in 1943.
5 See above, p. 212.
6 Anthony Quinton, *Political Philosophy* (Oxford, 1967), p. 2.
7 Lord Thomas, Lord Quinton, Lord Bauer, Lord Blake, Lord Sieff and Lord Weinstock. Although the last two were 'industrialist' peers, Mrs Thatcher met them for the first time at the CPG: as she did the banker Robin Leigh-Pemberton, who was appointed Governor of the Bank of England in 1983.
8 *New Yorker*, 10 February 1986.
9 *Sunday Telegraph*, 28 June 1987.
10 Russell Harty, BBC Television, 23 July 1987.
11 Young and Sloman, *The Thatcher Phenomenon*, p. 62.
12 *Spectator*, 4 June 1983.
13 *New Statesman*, 3 June 1983.
14 *Sunday Telegraph*, 10 January 1988, in an interview with Graham Turner. Turner's piece, from which subsequent quotations are also taken, remains a *locus classicus* on the political and social attitudes of the British cultural establishment.
15 See, for example, 'The Woman at No. 10', Central Television, 29 March 1983.
16 Cmnd 9524, May 1985.
17 *Daily Telegraph*, 18 September 1984.
18 London Conference on Communism and Liberal Democracy, reported in the *Spectator*, 30 March 1985.
19 BBC Radio Three, 17 December 1985.
20 See above, p. 281.
21 For an interesting discussion of this theme, see Raphael Samuel, 'The Tory Party at Prayer', *New Statesman*, 28 January 1983.
22 Central Television, 29 March 1983.
23 Ibid.
24 *Sunday Times*, 27 February 1983.
25 *Sunday Telegraph*, 28 June 1987.
26 *Woman's Own*, 31 October 1987.
27 Reported in David Butler and Richard Rose, *The British General Election, 1959* (London, 1960).
28 Edinburgh, 21 May 1988.

Chapter 19: Economy with the Truth

1 Max Atkinson, *Our Masters' Voices* (London, 1984), p. 113.
2 Figures taken from Peter Hennessy, *Cabinet* (Oxford, 1986), p.101.

3 Ibid., p. 99.
4 'MI5's Official Secrets', Channel Four Television, 8 March 1985.
5 House of Commons, 18 February 1985.
6 Prior, *A Balance of Power*, p. 150.
7 Magnus Linklater and David Leigh, *Not with Honour* (London, 1986), provides a thorough if hasty account of the Westland affair. But the best record of it appears, unusually, in a House of Commons paper: *The Fourth Report from the Defence Committee*, 23 July 1986. This, although produced against a background of determined government obstruction, is one of the most revealing inquiries into misconduct ever produced by an all-party select committee.
8 In 'Real Lives: At the Edge of the Union', a programme withdrawn by the BBC governors under Home Office pressure, but sebsequently shown on 16 October 1985.
9 'Panorama', BBC Television, 13 January 1986.
10 *Observer*, 12 January 1986.
11 House of Commons, 15 January 1986.
12 Face the Press, Tyne-Tees Television, 26 January 1986.
13 House of Commons, 27 January 1986.
14 See Defence Committee report, paras 146–7.
15 Ibid., para. 151.
16 House of Commons, 23 January 1986.
17 Lecture to the Guild of British Newspaper Editors, Cardiff, May 1983.
18 House of Commons, 7 February 1983.
19 Defence Committee report, para. 142.
20 Ibid., para. 151.
21 Quoted in Linklater and Leigh, *Not with Honour*, p. 160.
22 Reported at the time, and confirmed by Mrs Thatcher in interview with David Frost, TVam, 7 June 1987.
23 See Richard Deacon, *'C': A Biography of Sir Maurice Oldfield* (London, 1985).
24 House of Commons, 21 November 1979.
25 Andrew Boyle, *The Climate of Treason* (London, 1979).
26 Chapman Pincher, *Their Trade Is Treachery* (London, 1981). See House of Commons Hansard, 25 March 1981.
27 For example, an account of British deception operations during the Second World War, written by Sir Michael Howard.

Chapter 20: The New Diplomacy

1 See Joe Joyce and Peter Murtagh, *The Boss: Charles J. Haughey in Government* (Dublin, 1983), pp. 148 ff.
2 See above, p. 221.
3 Prior, *A Balance of Power*, pp. 177 ff.
4 *Tablet*, 15 March 1986.
5 Speech at Carrickfergus, 9 January 1987.

6   BBC Radio Three, 17 December 1985.
7   *New York Times*, 11 January 1986.
8   Donald T. Regan, *For the Record* (London, 1988), p. 350.
9   Quoted in David Dimbleby and David Reynolds, *An Ocean Apart* (London, 1988), p. 328.
10 House of Commons, 29 October 1985.
11 Channel Four News, 13 June 1986.
12 *Guardian*, 9 July 1986.
13 *Sunday Telegraph*, 27 July 1986.
14 *Sunday Times*, 20 July 1986.
15 Harold Macmillan, *Pointing the Way* (London, 1972), p. 30.
16 *Woman's Own*, 31 October 1987.
17 BBC Radio Four, 28 March 1987.
18 J. E. Neale, *Queen Elizabeth* (London, 1934).
19 *The Times*, 29 July 1986.
20 *Sunday Telegraph*, 27 July 1986.

Chapter 21: The Last Victory

1   *The Politics of Consent.*
2   House of Lords, 23 January 1985
3   Conservative Women's conference, 22 May 1985.
4   On 18 July 1985.
5   Wallsend, 11 September 1985.
6   *The Times*, 28 March 1986.
7   See above, Chapter 18.
8   Nicholas Deakin, *The Politics of Welfare* (London, 1987), supplies a thorough and well-informed account of the evolution of social policy under the Thatcher Government.
9   Kenneth Minogue and Michael Biddiss (eds), *Thatcherism: Personality and Politics* (London, 1987).
10 Noted in David Butler and Dennis Kavanagh, *The British General Election of 1987* (London, 1988), p. 19.
11 Oliver Letwin, *Privatising the World* (London, 1988), p. 72.
12 Quoted in Butler and Kavanagh, *The British General Election of 1987*, p. 19.
13 See above, p. 461.
14 Michael Dobbs.
15 Larry Lamb, knighted 1980; John Junor, knighted 1980; David English, knighted 1982.
16 The party newspaper, *Newsline*, carried a letter in June 1986 attacking 'those Reds at the BBC and ITV', and another urging readers to complain about 'the biased and distorted views of the Left' which allegedly dominated political television. The writer, Beryl Goldsmith, was not identified as Tebbit's secretary. See Michael Cockerell, *Live from Number 10* (London, 1988).

17 Robin Day, knighted 1981; Alastair Burnet, knighted 1984.
18 Speech to Parliamentary Press Gallery, 11 July 1981, quoted in Cockerell, *Live from Number 10*, p. 267.
19 See Rodney Tyler, *Campaign* (London, 1987), for the fullest account of this improbable analysis. Also Butler and Kavanagh, *The British General Election of 1987*.

Chapter 22: An Era in Place

1 For helpful discussion of these matters, see Ivor Crewe, *Guardian*, 15 June 1987; Butler and Kavanagh, *The British General Election of 1987*.
2 London Weekend Television, 15 January 1984.
3 Quoted by Neal Ascherson, *Observer*, 26 June 1988.
4 *Sunday Times*, 12 June 1988.
5 *Guardian*, 17 September 1988.
6 Figures taken from John Rentoul, *New Statesman*, 25 March 1988. Rentoul's book, *The Rich Get Richer* (London, 1987), is a dependable source of data on this theme.
7 *Sunday Telegraph*, 7 June 1987.
8 Edinburgh, 23 May 1988.
9 For an intelligent exposition, with strong traces of this analysis, see Andrew Gamble, *The Free Economy and the Strong State: The Politics of Thatcherism* (London, 1988).
10 Tyler, *Campaign*, p. 247.
11 *Sunday Times*, 8 May 1988.

Bibliography

Books of relevance to the political lifetime of Margaret Thatcher are numerous, and of varied quality. This is a list of the ones I have drawn on, or found in some way useful.

Addison, P., *The Road to 1945* (London, 1975).
Adeney, M. and Lloyd, J., *The Miners' Strike 1984–85* (London, 1986).
Agar, H., *A Time for Greatness* (London, 1943).
Arthur, P. and Jeffrey, K., *Northern Ireland since 1968* (London, 1988).
Atkinson, M., *Our Masters' Voices* (London, 1984).
Blake, R., *The Conservative Party from Peel to Thatcher* (London, 1985).
Boyle, A., *The Climate of Treason* (London, 1979).
Brittan, S., *A Restatement of Economic Liberalism*, (London, 1988).
Bruce-Gardyne, J., *Mrs Thatcher's First Administration* (London, 1984).
Butler, D., *Governing without a Majority* (London, 1983).
Butler, D. and Kavanagh, D., *The British General Election of 1979* (London, 1980).
Butler, D. and Kavanagh, D., *The British General Election of 1983* (London, 1984).
Butler, D. and Kavanagh, D., *The British General Election of 1987* (London, 1988).
Butler, D. and Rose, R., *The British General Election, 1959* (London, 1960)
Campbell, B., *The Iron Ladies* (London, 1987).
Castle, B., *The Castle Diaries 1974–76* (London, 1980).
Cockerell, M., *Live from Number 10* (London, 1988).
Cosgrave, P., *Thatcher: The First Term* (London, 1985).
Dalyell, T., *Misrule* (London, 1987).
Deakin, N., *The Politics of the Welfare State* (London, 1987).
Dimbleby, D. and Reynolds, D., *An Ocean Apart* (London, 1988).
Edwardes, M., *Back from the Brink* (London, 1981).
Gamble, A., *The Conservative Nation* (London, 1974).
Gamble, A., *The Free Economy and the Strong State* (London, 1988).
Gardiner, G., *Margaret Thatcher: From Childhood to Leadership* (London, 1975).
Gavshon, A. and Rice, D., *The Sinking of the Belgrano* (London, 1984).
Gilmour, I., *Britain Can Work* (Oxford, 1983).
Gilmour, I., *Inside Right: A Study of Conservatism* (London, 1977).
Jenkins, P., *Mrs Thatcher's Revolution* (London, 1987).

Joseph, K., *Reversing the Trend* (London, 1975).
Joseph, K., *Stranded on the Middle Ground* (London, 1976).
Joyce, J. and Murtagh, P., *The Boss: Charles J. Haughey in Government* (Dublin, 1983).
Junor, P., *Margaret Thatcher* (London, 1983).
Haig, A., *Caveat: Realism, Reagan and Foreign Policy* (London, 1984).
Hastings, M. and Jenkins, S., *The Battle for the Falklands* (London, 1983).
Henderson, N., *Channels and Tunnels* (London, 1987).
Hennessy, P., *Cabinet* (Oxford, 1986).
Hurd, D., *An End to Promises* (London, 1977).
Kavanagh, D., *Thatcherism and British Politics* (London, 1987).
Keegan, W., *Mrs Thatcher's Economic Experiment* (London, 1984).
Laing, M., *Edward Heath: Prime Minister* (London, 1972).
Letwin, O., *Privatising the World* (London, 1988).
Linklater, M. and Leigh, D., *Not with Honour* (London, 1986).
MacGregor, I., *The Enemies Within* (London, 1986).
Macmillan, H., *Tides of Fortune* (London, 1969).
Macmillan, H., *Pointing the Way* (London, 1972).
Mayer, A., *Madam Prime Minister* (New York, 1979).
Minogue, K. and Biddiss, M. (eds), *Thatcherism: Personality and Politics* (London, 1987).
Mowat, C. L., *Britain between the Wars, 1918–1940* (London, 1955).
Murray, T., *Margaret Thatcher* (London, 1978).
Neale, J. E., *Queen Elizabeth* (London, 1934).
Norton, P. and Aughey, A., *Conservatives and Conservatism* (London, 1981).
O'Neill, T., *Man of the House* (London, 1988).
Pincher, C., *Their Trade Is Treachery* (London, 1981).
Ponting, C., *The Right to Know* (London, 1985).
Powell, E., *Freedom and Reality* (London, 1969).
Prior, J., *A Balance of Power* (London, 1986).
Pym, F., *The Politics of Consent* (London, 1984).
Regan, D. T., *For the Record* (London, 1988).
Rentoul, J., *The Rich Get Richer* (London, 1987).
Riddell, P., *The Thatcher Government* (London, 1983).
St John Stevas, N., *The Two Cities* (London, 1984).
Speed, K., *Sea Change* (London, 1982).
Tugendhat, C., *Making Sense of Europe* (London, 1986).
Tyler, R., *Campaign* (London, 1987).
Verrier, A., *The Road to Zimbabwe* (London, 1986).
Walker, P., *Trust the People* (London, 1987).
Walters, A., *Britain's Economic Renaissance* (London, 1986).
Wapshott, N. and Brock, G., *Thatcher* (London, 1979).
Warner, M., *Monuments and Maidens* (London, 1985).
Young, H. and Sloman, A., *The Thatcher Phenomenon* (London, 1986).

Index